Tudor Sea Power

The Foundation of Greatness

DAVID CHILDS

Tudor Sea Power

The Foundation of Greatness

DAVID CHILDS

Seaforth
PUBLISHING

FRONTISPIECE: *A galleon ramming a galley. During the Tudor era the English fleet progressed from a fear of the fighting qualities of the oared galley to complete confidence in the superiority of their own chosen weapon – the 'race-built' galleon, armed with a broadside of heavy guns and the sailing qualities to use them effectively.* (Royal Naval Museum, Portsmouth)

Copyright © David Childs 2009

First published in Great Britain in 2009 by
Seaforth Publishing
An imprint of Pen & Sword Books Ltd
47 Church Street, Barnsley
S Yorkshire S70 2AS

www.seaforthpublishing.com
Email info@seaforthpublishing.com

British Library Cataloguing in Publication Data
A CIP data record for this book is available from the British Library

ISBN 978-1-84832-031-4

Typeset and designed by Tim Foster
Printed and bound in Thailand

Contents

Acknowledgements 7

Introduction: The Birth of Greatness 9

Chapter 1   Background: Father to the Man 10

Chapter 2   Ship Types 18

Chapter 3   Building the Fleet 34

Chapter 4   Arming the Fleet 56

Chapter 5   Feeding the Fleet 84

Chapter 6   Command and Control and the Company 100

Chapter 7   A Sailor's Life 118

Chapter 8   Pilotage, Navigation and Seamanship 136

Chapter 9   Havens and Harbours 166

Chapter 10   Plunder, Piracy and Professionalism 180

Chapter 11   The Fighting Fleet 200

Chapter 12   Shore Support 248

Chapter 13   The Legacy 272

References 275
Bibliography 280
Appendices:
1   Chronology 283
2   The Ships of the Tudor Navy 286
3   A Ship's Company 294
4   Gun Drills for Breech-Loading and Muzzle-Loading Guns 295
5   Keeping it in the Family: The Tudor and Howard Lord Admirals 296
6   Officials of the Navy Royal 298
7   Visiting the Tudor Navy 298
Index 300

TO JANE
for her feel for History

Acknowledgements

First of all I must express my appreciation to Rob Gardiner for commissioning this work, which has given me many months of pleasure, and to Fiona Little, who has spent, I am sure, a less pleasurable time as my copy-editor, examining my text in great detail and pointing out and correcting my many editorial errors, thereby creating what is, I believe, a better read. After such scrutiny any errors that remain are very much of my own making.

In the course of my research the assistance of the Mary Rose Trust has been invaluable. In particular I would like to express my thanks to Rear Admiral John Lippiett, the Chief Executive, for freeing up his staff; Dr Mark Jones and Andy Elkerton, for their technical advice; Christopher Dobbs and Alexzandra Hildred, for their archaeological guidance; Peter Crossman for the provision of illustrations and drawings; and to Sue Judge, Sally Tyrrell and Helen Twiss for their easing of my path. Jenny Wraight provided much support from the Royal Naval Library, while the Chart Depot, also at Portsmouth Dockyard, gave much technical help. The charts in the text were drafted by Simon Williams, who is just starting out on what I hope will be an enjoyable academic career.

Above all, I am indebted to my wife, Jane, for her encouragement and indulgence and in letting me off the many domestic chores that I should have been undertaking rather than sitting in front of my PC.

Introduction

The Birth of Greatness

It takes three years to build a ship: it takes three hundred to create a tradition. The evacuation goes on.

Admiral A B C Cunningham, 1942, talking about the evacuation of Crete

Fighting to lift the remains of the Allied army from the beaches of Crete, while all the time haemorrhaging warships through persistent German air attack, those who heard the stirring words of Admiral Cunningham, the Commander-in-Chief, Mediterranean, would have cast their minds back to another time when England was fighting for her dear life, smiled grimly, gritted their teeth and willingly turned their faces once more to meet the foe. The names that their admiral's words would have brought to mind would have been Effingham, Grenville, Ralegh and Drake, and the incident, above all others, that would have sprung to their minds would have been the defeat of the Spanish Armada.

It could be argued that the tradition of which they were a part, and to which, by their efforts, they were adding, was not born in the sixteenth century, but was itself created 300 years later by adoring writers such as Corbett, and poets of the likes of Noyes, Kipling, Tennyson and Newbold, who made saints out of England's sea dogs and in doing so gave rise to legend. A legend based on the fact that a small nation summoned up the spirit to defend itself against enemies far larger, stronger, wealthier and advanced than it was itself. A legend that cast a lighthouse ray on what lay at the heart of the tradition which was the defence against invasion provided by England's wooden walls. Spain launched three armadas against England, in 1588, 1596 and 1597; their failure created a sense of English inviolability that served her well for centuries and made many think that even the winds and waves obeyed her. Elizabeth's speech at Tilbury in 1588 would have been very much at the forefront of Churchill's thinking when he penned his 'fight them on the beaches' speech in 1940.

The sea hides its history. The waves that roll along the route on which the Spanish Armada sailed offer no clues as to what has passed before or lies beneath. There are no Tudor seascapes that inform of that time as well as a Fountains Abbey, a Hampton Court or Hardwick Hall; no ambassador's acerbic wit, courier's clever comment or poet's pen informs of the goings-on at sea, on whose surface no royal adulterers or favourites achieved a scandalous longevity or a brutal brevity; the sea was governed by no contentious Bible or prayer book, for it kept its own unwritten laws and obeyed them without needing to gibe when the political or spiritual wind changed direction. Its laws largely unwritten and its codes of conduct unscripted, it became a power the mastering of which was passed on to subsequent generations by lore, example and achievement and the myths that arose from them. These tended to be strongest among those who followed the life afloat, and so the contribution of her seamen to her survival registers but little space in most general histories of Tudor England. Yet without the infant navy the nation would have become insignificantly, not triumphantly, Protestant, another Denmark or Sweden, not a global empire. It was the creation of naval, not royal, supremacy that was to make England the nation it became, with its fighting fleet the greatest jewel in its imperial crown and the foundations of its greatness.

This all began in an age of massive change, during which the nation endeavoured not to tear itself apart. During this time the naval tapestry grew continually, without much change to the pattern whoever the master weaver was and whatever spiritual influence distracted attention from the task. Its warp was made from the following skeins:

1. The creation of a full-time navy;
2. The development of ship design to counter the threat of both galleys and galleons;
3. The move from a coastal to an ocean-capable fleet;
4. The provision of specialised ship weaponry;
5. The recognition of naval warfare as a separate skill from land fighting;
6. The acknowledgement of sea experience as a qualification for high command;
7. The command of the Channel;
8. The legitimisation of plunder as a weapon of war.

Its weft was the work of those who imposed their will upon the world in which they voyaged. The motifs thus created can be identified clearly at any position along that century-sized canvas, even when it became frayed or faded through neglect or incompetence. When displayed it showed that the Tudors had created a dazzling and lasting work of art on which to lay their lusty infant Navy Royal – a navy which, after a long century of growth, commanded an international admiration, envy and respect which no other part of English life could equal. Yet the English spared scarce a glance at this fine tapestry in which they were wrapped, warm, safe and secure.

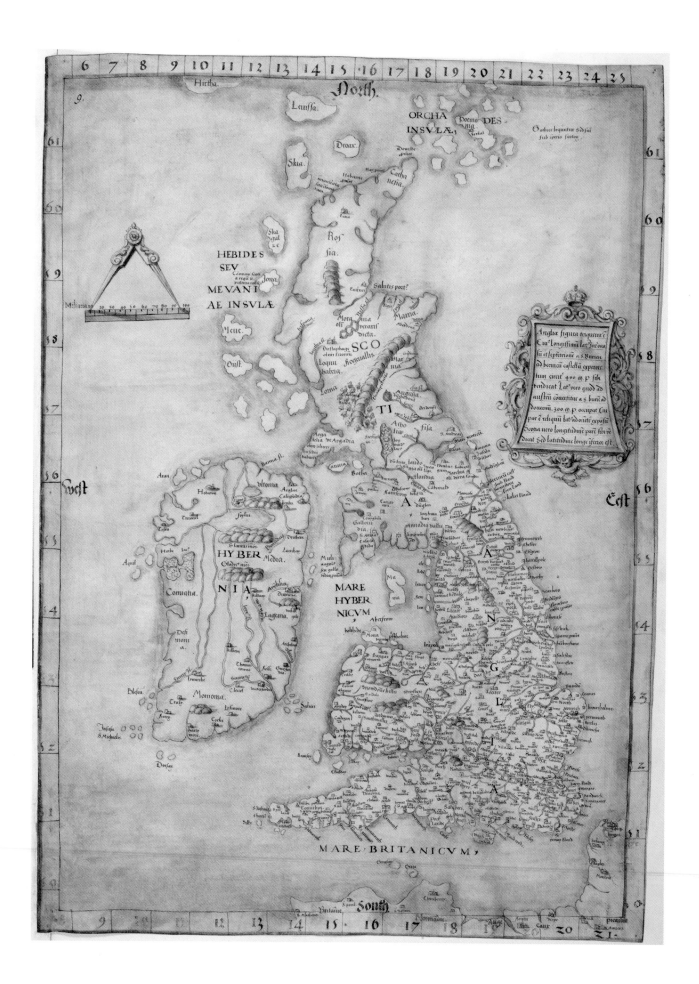

Chapter One

Background: Father to the Man

... Suppose that you have seen
The well-appointed king at Dover pier
Embark his royalty, and his brave fleet
With silken streamers the young Phoebus fanning.
Play with your fancies, and in them behold
Upon the hempen tackle ship-boys climbing;
Hear the shrill whistle, which doth order give
To sounds confused; behold the threaden sails,
Borne with th'invisible and creeping wind,
Draw the huge bottoms through the furrowed sea,
Breasting the lofty surge. O do but think
You stand upon the ravage and behold
A city on th'inconstant billows dancing –
For so appears this fleet majestical ...
Shakespeare, Henry V

To deny the Tudor infancy of the Royal Navy is not to see the father in the child. Of course, the Tudor navy did not rise up from its cradle and, like the infant Hercules, reach out and strangle the twin serpents of France and Spain. Like any infant, it could not venture too far or for too long from its mother's breast; like every child, it did not understand the sophistication of tactics and strategy; it felt safest in its own front yard, but it was here that it learned the skills that would one day mean it could cross oceans without fear. It was a prolonged period of growth, but it was a continuous one, bar a few setbacks such as any child might suffer. It is true that its behaviour was sometimes delinquent, but frequently it was that loutish behaviour that won it, albeit secretly, the admiration of its parent monarch whose proud creation it was. Generally, it put its infancy to good use: it learned its capabilities and limitations and how to improve them; it became aware of its enemies and learned to best them; it suffered hunger and thirst and learned how to overcome them; it went short of money and learned how to fund itself; it got to know

of a world beyond its horizons and learned how to master it. It passed into Stuart adolescence a healthy and likely lad. Those who study its early days of growth are witness to the birth of greatness.

The medieval English were not a seafaring people. This is surprising given the nation's setting, bounded on three sides by rich and variable seas. However, the land was not too desolate, nor the governance too despotic, to drive people to seek their sustenance far from its shores. More rugged or harsher terrains, such as that of Spain or Scotland, gave rise to fishermen with ploughs, but England's bounteous earth kept the two occupations separate so that, one league inshore, the scent of the sea was seldom apparent except on market day. The seafaring life was also a southern one. A shipping survey of 1582 showed that East Anglia had 27 per cent of all the English vessels, and that a further 18 per cent were based in London, 16 per cent in the south-east and 20 per cent in the south-west, while only 2 per cent could be found between Aberystwyth and the Scottish borders.

The coastal fringe kept itself apart from the political and cultural developments that shaped the nation, and, in return, its merchant and fishing communities were left alone. The result was a breed of professional seamen whose activities were little seen or known about except

Map of the British Isles presented to Henry VIII in 1537: its limitations show well why each ship's master preferred to sail with charts they had drawn themselves from their own observations. (British Library)

11

on the ferry crossing between Dover and Calais. Yet the sovereign knew that these were the men upon whom the security of his throne depended. In order to keep them available to render the crown some service, theirs was the first major industry to receive active government support, including an insistence that the nation ate fish at least twice a week, a requirement that was even raised, briefly, to three times a week in Elizabeth's time.

Both Tudor Henrys issued Navigation Acts aimed at ensuring that English trade goods were transported in English ships, if possible in the king's own vessels, such as *Sovereign* and *Regent*: the latter was despatched in 1509 to the Mediterranean on a trading voyage which linked the Bolognese merchant who hired the vessel with several of the king's senior administrators, most of whom, especially the Howards, were traders in their own right. The coterie at court could do exceedingly well from such ventures, and the arrangements illustrate clearly the Tudor concept of retaining wealth within a small blessed band

while the rest of the population enjoyed short rations.

In 1511, while preparing to disrupt this trade through war with France, Henry VIII issued a 'remembrance for the advancing and setting forward of the King's ships in voyages'. In it he stated:

> The chief commodity in this realm for their lading is wool, which is conveyed out by Venetians, Florentines and other strangers in galleys and other ships, to the decay of the King's navy. If it please the King to call in licence granted to strangers and to licence only English merchants, his subjects, to convey wool beyond the Straits of Moroc, four ships of 200 or 300 tons would be set forth every year.[1]

Apart from the trading advantage, the sovereign needed a pool of seamen whose services could be called upon when the kingdom was under threat from piracy or foreign foes. This was made clear in laws, such as the Act of Maintenance of the Navy of 1540, which stated that:

A twentieth-century visualisation of Henry VII's Regent *and* Sovereign. *Although he had them built along traditional lines, his laying down of two purpose-built warships establishes his right to be considered the true founder of the Royal Navy.*

The maintenance of my master mariners making them expert and cunning in the art and science of shipmen and sailing, and they, their wives and children have had their living of and by the same ... and have also been the chief maintenance and support of the cities, towns, villages, havens, and creeks, near adjoining the sea coast; and the king's subjects, bakers, brewers, butchers, smiths, ropers, shipwright, tailors, shoemakers, and other victuallers and handicraftsmen inhabiting and dwelling near the said coasts have also had by the same a great part of the living.[2]

While the majority of seafarers were fisherman, most of those qualified to act as masters of the king's ships were involved in short-haul cross-Channel trade taking wool and cloth to Calais or Flanders, voyages which, being prone to storm, tidal streams and coastal currents, required a certain level of skill if ships were to be kept off shoals. On other traditional routes coal was brought from Newcastle to London or from Neath to Plymouth, both inshore voyages.

There were two established trade routes of greater duration: one involving the importation of wine from Bordeaux and the other the delivery of spices and other exotics from Venice, whose ambassadors to England wrote extensively of what they witnessed. In 1497 one reported that 'The riches of England are greater than of any other country in Europe ... This is mainly due, in the first place, to the great fertility of the soil, which is such that, with the exception of wine, they import nothing from abroad for their subsistence.'

Fifty-seven years later little had changed. August 1554 saw the Venetian ambassador, Soranzo, writing in his report on England:

The soil, especially in England, proper produces wheat, oats and barley, in such plenty that they have usually enough for their own consumption, but were they to work more diligently, and with greater skill, and bring the soil into higher cultivation, England might supply grain for export ... they also consume a great quantity of wine, which is brought from Candia, Spain, the Rhine and France [and] as they have no olive trees ... they import oil from Spain, and the Venetian possessions, but the consumption is small, as for food they use mainly butter.[3]

The main export, Soranzo continued, remained 'wool which is in such universal repute [with] a great part of this wool manufactured in England ... the rest being exported, and taken usually to Calais on account of the staplers, who sell it on the spot, and have the monopoly of the wool exports'.

Wool and wine: the fact that the nation exported the produce of peasant shepherds and impoverished weavers and imported wine for the pleasure of the wealthy few casts a bright beam on the social arrangements of England under the Tudors. The trade itself was a risky business because of the presence of pirates, which meant that the ships had to be banded together into fleets and be 'wafted', or convoyed, by armed escorts. However, the Venetian galleys – for it was in their own ships that they came each year to Southampton – sailed

England may well have remained a bucolic island exporting mainly woollen goods had not Henry VIII's ego demanded that she play a part in European politics. (British Library)

The annual visit of the Venetian fleet to London and Southampton kept the isolated English in touch not only with the latest exotic goods but also showed them developments in naval ship and artillery design. For this northern European trade the Venetians built a particular type they called a 'Flanders galley', and this drawing of one is from a fifteenth-century naval architectural treatise. As the drawing suggest, they made much of the voyage under sail rather than oars.

without escorts, relying on their own armament, manpower and organisation to deter any pirates.

Given the necessary protection, the trade flourished, and with such peaceful pursuits England could have continued to be a bucolic backwater at peace with her more adventurous and quarrelsome neighbours. Henry VII invested twenty-four years to achieve this quiet state. In two years his son Henry VIII began its destruction through ambition, adultery, apostasy and avarice, the first three necessitating a stronger navy while the last was needed to pay for it.

The realm of which Henry VIII was to make Europe aware formed just a part of a small island, cast adrift from mainland Europe both geographically and politically. Indeed, after the loss of Calais in Mary's reign, and excluding the ungovernable bog of Ireland, no English monarch since Edward the Confessor held sway over so small a territory as did the Tudors. In such circumstances there seemed to be no need for anything other than a small royal fleet, augmented for expeditions to France or Scotland by merchant ships taken up from trade. This all changed when a king who had no wish for foreign adventures was succeeded by one whose European policy meant that in future the survival of the dynasty would depend on command of the seas.

A monumental brass of a wealthy but anonymous 'Woolman' standing on a woolsack, from the church of Northleach, Gloucestershire. The village was a centre of the Cotswold wool trade, and many of its merchants left such brasses as indicators of their local importance. (Author)

Although the value to this small nation of a professional navy was soon apparent, its cost-effectiveness as an arm of state over an unprofessional army took years to be appreciated, despite the fact that the exploits of Tudor soldiering in continental Europe were characterised by seldom-relieved disasters brought about by two main factors, leadership and liquor: too little of the former, too much of the latter.

Lord Darcy's expedition to Cadiz in 1511 set the precedent: it ran out of money and the troops got roaring drunk ashore before returning home having accomplished nothing. The Earl of Dorset's expedition to Spain in 1512 in support of Ferdinand of Aragon's Navarre campaign ended in much the same way, with that noble returning in disgrace with a much reduced force, having lost hundreds of soldiers to dysentery brought about by imbibing too much wine. Henry VIII's own expeditions into France achieved far less than had been anticipated. Henry Brandon, the Earl of Suffolk, one of a small coterie of nobles from whom the king selected campaign leaders, had

his shortcomings amply demonstrated during his march on Paris in 1523. Henry Howard, scion of another noble family, failed spectacularly at Boulogne; Elizabeth's favourites, Essex and Leicester, came to grief in Ireland and the Netherlands, and generally, when the navy landed amphibious forces of any strength in either Iberia or the Low Countries the troops failed to achieve their aim. In nearly every instance of failure the commander was a member of the nobility, chosen because of his rank and courage at the jousts. Indeed, if one leaves out Scotland, a home international with an almost guaranteed victory, either home or away, the escutcheon of the great lords who led the troops is invariably blotted by their failure in leadership. Norfolk, Suffolk, Essex, Leicester, Surrey, Derby, Somerset: these are illustrious names which glow but dimly when compared with those of the men who really earned respect for their small nation's name: Drake, Hawkins, Frobisher, Gonson, Winter, Leveson, in whose company just one noble name, Howard of Effingham, can be included. Yet England persisted with the myth that the right to command was a noble's christening gift and that war on land represented good value for money. Wiser, but quieter, men thought otherwise. As Lord Russell, who had been Lord Admiral, wrote to Sir Anthony Browne, the Captain of the King's Horse, on 1 July 1544, he had seen the king make 'four sundry voyages to France, and yet he hath there not one foot more than he had forty years past'.[4]

And, unless it be thought that military extravagance was a feature solely of Henry's reign, Protector Somerset spent, in Edward's short sojourn, £580,393 on his futile Scottish campaign, double the amount that Henry consumed in the wars of his later years, and in half the time,[5] Elizabeth's support of the Huguenot French and rebellious Dutch similarly poured money on to barren foreign soil.

Only at sea, where a professional knowledge that could not be imparted on the chase, tournament, butts or tennis court ensured that the selection of commanders was based on merit and experience, was England to enhance her reputation and win respect. Paradoxically, she was to do so by methods that were disreputable but in keeping with the nation's overarching philosophy – greed. It was an age of avarice when nothing became a man more than the acquisition of wealth or property, by whatever means this could be achieved. Those with access

The Wool Store at West Quay, Southampton (now the maritime museum). Wool and woollen goods were stored here to be loaded on to merchant ships and the Venetian galleys who relied on its supply to keep thousands of weavers and cloth workers employed in Venice. (Author)

John Hawkins proudly and unashamedly displayed a slave in shackles on his coat of arms – one of the clearest indicators that Tudor social mores were far removed form those of the modern age.

This scene of soldiers disembarking during the siege of Boulogne in 1544 demonstrates what was traditionally the main role of the sovereign's ships – the ferrying of troops across the Channel.

having earlier assaulted a traveller and stolen 21s 7d from him.[6] Perhaps it was the notoriety or the threat of prosecution that led this farmer to flee to Kent, where he became a peripatetic preacher among the warships lying on the Medway mud. It was from him that Drake absorbed his fierce Protestant faith but, presumably, with little emphasis on the need to obey the eighth commandment.

Given this overarching desire for personal gratification, especially in the second Henry, it is difficult to see in the split from Rome and the dissolution of the monasteries any motive more dominant than the king's concern with sex, supremacy and the succession, and his lust for the wealth of others. This avaricious and cynical approach to government influenced the development of the navy, firstly, because the nation's behaviour provoked antagonism that could best be fended off at sea; secondly, without the appropriation of such wealth, including that afloat on the high seas, the money to build a fleet and the willingness to keep it in being would not have been found, and finally, those in command of this navy used their positions, whether on active service at sea or directing operations from shore, to increase their own material well-being. Thus avarice affected the way in which naval operations were planned and conducted, and the lack of scruples in the affairs of state legitimised many a deed at sea, the legality of which was dubious and the immorality of which was never in doubt. It was also important in that gain through greed was considered a legitimate reward for the rich, and the captains of naval ships at sea had plenty of opportunity to grab great, and often illegal, wealth, not only for themselves but for their sovereign and superiors ashore. Although the 'trickle-down' effect, as far as the crews were concerned, was never that evident, seamen still willingly risked their lives to attack and seize booty, most of which would be poured into their commanders' commodious pockets and not their own. This reflected the general condition of the poor, which was so close to subsistence level that any addition, however meagre, brought benefit – even if only one candle to light one night in the otherwise stygian gloom in which the majority of the English existed. Just two examples selected at random will suffice. In Great Yarmouth, a fishing and trading port from where naval crews were pressed, in 1522 five people between them owned one-quarter of the wealth while twenty-three owned over half. At the other end of the country, in Morebath on the southern flanks of Exmoor, a parishioner who had lost 17d of the church's money was forgiven his debt after fourteen years during which, despite all his efforts, he had been unable to repay it. The indicators are of a life beset by poverty, liable to devastating epidemics, seasonal and annual plague, famine and hunger. If one was not a member of the acquiring classes, a life at sea might be the only way to rise above subsistence level and better one's day-to-day existence.

Erasmus considered domestic life even in the dwellings of the rich to be sordid, writing home that there was nothing so unclean as an Englishman's home, it being full of, 'the vomitings, the leakages of dogs and men, ale-droppings and abominations not fit to be mentioned'. Given that opinion, criticism of conditions on board ship would seem to be unfair.

With such indicators the state could have imploded into continuous civil unrest and growing poverty. The nation had little trade, with only about a twentieth of its goods being exported, and of these there

to the means held true to the concept of 'fleece thy neighbour' and would have read the story of King David's coveting of Naboth's vineyard and the action he took to get hold of it as an exemplar to be applauded by all excepting Mary among England's God-fearing monarchs.

It was an age when criminality and opportunism shared the same track, with little ill being thought of those who robbed those beneath them, although stealing from one's superior was a dangerous occupation. Given the chance the least likely people robbed. Thus the patent rolls of 1548 record that Drake's father, Edmund, whom one might consider a poor but upright yeoman farmer, stole a horse worth £3

was over-reliance on wool and woven cloth. No nation grows wealthy on just one such commonplace primary product. Imports reflected the social divide, with wine from Gascony dominating this trade (over 10,000 tunnes a year for each year of Henry VII's reign) and often being carried in foreign hulls. Change was overdue.

Henry Tudor began the turn-around in a quietly efficacious manner which, although it allowed the malaise that was English society to remain, quietened the factions of the nobility and avoided major foreign adventures. Indeed, his one foray into France was both short, lasting from 2 to 18 October 1492, and financially rewarding, with Parliament funding him to fight and the French bribing him not to. Such canniness gained admiration and respect and created a treasury which would enable his son to demand that other nations pay England the respect that he considered her due. In 1524 the population of England and Wales was about 2,360,000; at the end of the century it had risen to 4.5 million, but this still did not make it a populous nation. For comparison, the populations of other European states by then were:

Scotland	1.5 million
France	16 million
Spain and Portugal	9 million
Netherlands	3 million

In view of these figures, Henry VII's twenty-four years of sailing in calm waters and weathering squalls with a well-trained loyal crew

made good sense. Given the disparity in numbers, such a policy could be overturned successfully only by seamen, not soldiers.

The ambassadors, spending most of their time in London and at the court, tended to paint a rosier picture of the realm than did those who travelled around it and reflected on what they saw. Edward VI, who one might have thought would have been proud of the land he had inherited, wrote a very telling 'state of the nation' entry in his diary:

> ... slack execution of the law have been the chiefest sore of all. The laws have been manifestly broken, the offenders punished, and either by bribery or foolish pity escaped punishment. The dissention and disagreement, both for private matters and also in matters of religion, has been no little cause, but the principal has been the disobedient and continuous talking and doing of foolish and fond people, which for lack of teaching have wandered and broken, wilfully and disobediently, the laws of this realm. The lawyers also, and judges, have much offended in corruption and bribery ... What shall I say of those that buy and sell offices of trust, that impropriate benefices, that destroy timber, that – not considering the sustaining of men ... turn till-ground to pasture, that use excesses in apparel, in diet, and in building; of enclosures of wastes and commons; of those that cast false and seditious bills – but that thing is so tedious, long and lamentable to entreat of the particular that I am weary to go any further in the particulars.[7]

Such disillusion and disgust, covering town and country, do indicate that the seafarer was well out of it. Yet every malfeasance that Edward mentions could be laid upon those who administered the navy. Whether it be; Judge Julius Caesar's amendments to sentences passed at the Admiralty Court at the behest of the Lord Admiral; Thomas Seymour's haven of pirates in the Scillies: the breaking-out of prize cargo or the provisioning of fewer victuals than listed on the manifest, the Navy Royal was afloat on a sea of corrupt practice. In this respect it was a child growing up in a society whose mores it adopted and reflected and which, given ample opportunity, found its own sorts of what these days might be called 'inappropriate behaviour'.

This was an age in which England set her course contrary to that being steered by Europe's one universal spititual leader and three most powerful rulers. However, whatever winds buffeted it, the bark of England rode out the fierce waves and headed over a horizon not knowing what might lie beyond, except that it would be a destination of her choosing. In the end it was those in the Catholic convoy who found the winds to be adverse. This gleeful comment made by John Jewel, Bishop of Salisbury, about the shipwreck of a Catholic bishop on passage towards Scotland, may serve as a metaphor for the fate of Europe south of Calais: 'In the meantime this ship of king Philip, tossed about by the winds and tempests, shattered and broken by the waves, with its mast sprung, its timbers stove in, the pilots lost, bereft

The dull, efficient and peaceful Henry Tudor might have been eclipsed by his more charismatic and outgoing son and younger grand-daughter, but it was through his firm foundations that the Tudor dynasty was able to withstand its many shockwaves protected by a fleet that he had begun. (National Maritime Museum BHC2762)

of crew and cargo, is driven, a mere wreck, and filled with water, upon the coast of England.'[8]

Throughout this period of conflict England used its non-naval seamen as instruments of state, providing them with clandestine support. Drake's circumnavigation, as he claimed, developed from his being summoned to discuss, with Secretary Walsingham, how the nation might recoup the losses that Spain had inflicted on it in the Netherlands, by seizing Spanish assets in the Pacific while at the same time seeking a north-west passage to the riches of Cathay free of Spanish interference. Proof that the queen herself approved of this scheme is hard to come by, for it was kept secret from the peace-loving Burghley, who would have advised caution, but it can nevertheless be assumed, not just from the voyage itself but from the first words uttered by Drake on his return, 'Does the Queen still live?' He need not have asked if she was still desperate for gold; with no Midas touch of her own she craved the assurance that only gold arriving in her treasury could bring. If that gold and silver had been destined to be placed in the empty coffers of bankrupt Spain, so much the better. If it paid for her expensive campaign to crush the Irish rebels and support the Dutch ones, she was not going to trouble herself with diplomatic niceties for Drake, not yet an officer in her nascent fighting navy, could be disowned once he had delivered.

It suited England's rulers to encourage the idea that their country was waging a crusade against the Anti-Christ, but in fact it was gold, not God, and temporal, not spiritual, power that drove the combatants. Catholicism was a convenience, Protestantism a ploy: whoever they acknowledged as their supreme spiritual authority on earth, the nations of Europe would have fought like fiends to corner commerce, whatever their creed and confession.

England was able to grow in her exotic way because of the existence of the Channel and her ability to defend it against all comers. It became her curtilage and, although she did not claim it, she controlled it. Elizabeth's Tilbury speech has some of the pride and conviction that twenty miles of sea gave the nation, but its true worth is better summarised by Secretary Walsingham in a friendly letter warning the young King James VI of Scotland not to come embroiled in England's quarrels now that his mother, Mary had been executed, for, he informs James, England need not fear 'what all the potentates of Europe, being banded together against us can do' because the state is 'so prepared ... to defend itself ... by sea'.[9] Walsingham had no doubt that Tudor England was a nation established through domination of the sea. Given the incompetence of its land commanders this was just as well, but what enabled the nation's seamen to achieve immortality was the creation from the nation's second greatest natural asset, trees, a fighting fleet that would challenge and overcome all who sailed against the realm.

The English Channel. (Map by Peter Wilkinson)

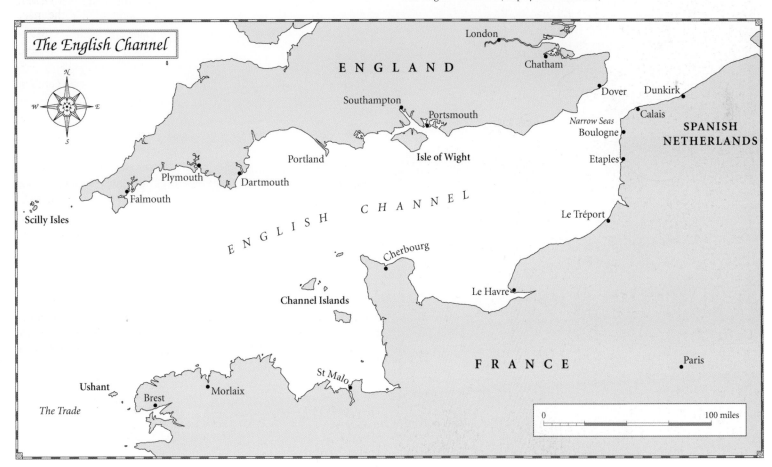

17

Chapter Two

Ship Types

*Make an arcke of pyne tree and make chambbers in the arcke and pytch it
wythin and wythout with pytch. And of this faction shalt thou make it. The
length of the arcke shall be three hundred cubytes, the breadth of it fifty
cubytes, and the heyth of it thirty cubits. A wyndow shalt thou make above in
the arcke. And wythin a cubyte compasse shalt thou finysh it. And the door
of the arcke shalt thou sette in ye syde of it: and thou shalt make it with three
loftes one above an other.*

Book of Genesis, Chapter 6, verses 14–15, Tyndale's translation, 1530

In our age of specialisation by function it is easy to identify the
purpose for which a ship has been designed and built: super-tanker,
freighter, trawler, aircraft carrier, ferry, minesweeper – each has its
own characteristics and could not be adapted for a very different role.
With early Tudor vessels this was not so, and the function was often
dictated not only by the voyage being undertaken but by circumstances experienced on passage. Thus one ship and the same crew
could sail on a legitimate trading voyage and then undertake some
privateering and a little piracy. There was little to show a craft passing
upon the sea upon its lawful occasion that the ship closing it was
about to exchange pleasantries or shot: an advantage that Drake was
to exploit well in the Pacific. Iberia might have its stately Spanish
galleons bringing silver from Potosi or spices from Sumatra with no
other purpose than that, but the English were different.

During the century the ability to deploy a naval ship on a trading
voyage decreased, as marine design moved away from being multi-
purpose. It is true that the shingle ballast in the hold could be
jettisoned and replaced with weightier gold and silver bars, but
general-purpose cargo was too bulky and too valueless to 'make' a
voyage, so, by the 1550s, vessels such as galleys, rowbarges, galleasses
and then, later, galleons appeared with the sole purpose of acting as
men-of-war.

The crown needed naval vessels for seven traditional purposes:

1. To ferry the army abroad;
2. To discourage piracy;
3. To raid enemy ports and coasts;
4. To defend against invasion;
5. To display royal prestige;
6. To convoy, or 'waft' the wine and fisheries fleets;
7. To transport crown goods.

To which was added in due course:

8. To plunder enemy ships and ports.

For most of these purposes an occasional navy was best, allowing the
ruler both to hire ships as required and to hire out those that he did
possess to merchants for trading voyages. The greater number of ships
was always needed for transportation. On these occasions it was
highly unlikely that the fleet would come across enemy vessels except
inshore at or off the port of disembarkation. Sea-keeping qualities, the
effects of wind and tide and the lack of communications meant that

This replica of the 50-ton Matthew *in which John Cabot sailed to America gives
us an idea of how small were the first ships to cross the Atlantic from England.*
(Matthew of Bristol)

meeting other than by chance was highly unlikely, as was a protracted engagement at sea. If contact was made, then any struggle was the equivalent of a land battle at sea, with the master laying his ship alongside the enemy so that the soldiers could discharge arrows and ordnance at their opponents before the vessels were grappled together, when a successful boarding would result in the surrender of the other ship. Any guns, and a large number were carried, were mainly for anti-personnel use, and the idea of sinking the enemy did not exist, nor did the heavy weapons necessary for such a conclusion. Embarked soldiery could thus be used to protect the vessels on which they were being transported before they disembarked, because the weaponry and the tactics afloat were similar to those ashore. What soldiers did need was the advantage of height so that they could sweep an enemy's deck clear of personnel before leaping on board. This was bestowed by lofty castles both fore and aft, which gave the sixteenth-century carrack its distinctive lines. Yet even castles did not have to be permanent. A number of prefabricated ones, made of light fir planking, existed and could be secured on to the bow and stern of a merchant ship to convert it for war.

The Carrack

In the fifteenth century the tub-like vessels that had carried most northern European trade, with a single mast carrying a large square sail, were replaced by longer, larger, leaner, multi-masted vessels with several decks and well-raised fore- and after-castles. The new ships were also built with the stern squared off whereas previously it had been rounded, an alteration that, although it improved the speed, adversely affected steering because it involved the replacement of a side-rudder with one centrally aligned on the stern, where water turbulence affected performance.[1] To an extent this setback was offset by the introduction of more masts, which not only gave more sail area, and thus better speeds, but also, with the introduction of lateen sails on the after mizzen and bonaventure masts, enabled a ship to sail closer to the wind. More than one sail per mast and the securing of extra sails, or bonnets, to the lower edge of the main sails also increased sailing potential. These new vessels were generically referred to as carracks. Of the contemporary records that depict such ships, the earliest is an engraving by the Flemish artist William à Crucis, dated to 1468. Another, believed to date from 1520, is a painting at the National Maritime Museum in Greenwich that possibly represents the enormous Portuguese warship *Santa Catarina do Monte Sinai*, a vessel with a vast main sail, a newly introduced fore topsail, six decks and some 150 guns. As far as English ships are concerned, there is a painting of around 1540 in the royal collection in Hampton Court, which is thought to depict Henry departing from Dover to meet Francis at the Field of the Cloth of Gold. The king is embarked in *Henry Grace à Dieu,* around which are assembled five other large carracks, assumed to include *Mary Rose, Peter Pomegranate* and *Katherine Fortileza.* They represent a powerful fleet and a clear indication of the king's might at sea. Towards the end of Henry's reign, Sir Anthony Browne commissioned a painting of the 1545 battle of the Solent which, although its purpose was to show its patron riding close to the king on Southsea Common, does also show the opposing fleets and two masts of the sunken *Mary Rose.*[2] Finally, one year after that

This modern painting of the Mary Rose *by Bill Bishop captures the grace of a great ship under sail with a favourable wind.* (Mary Rose Trust)

incident, in 1546 the king's armourer, Anthony Anthony, produced what was to all intents and purposes the first *Jane's Fighting Ships*, being a complete record of all the Navy Royal, including a drawing of each vessel and a list of her armament and complement. For many years the painting and the drawing were the best available information as to what these vessels looked like, and then *Mary Rose* was raised, and the Anthony drawings had to be looked at as indicative rather than accurate: for one thing, in the case of *Mary Rose* they showed one extra gun-deck which may have been good for propaganda but is less useful for research.

The better sea-handling qualities of the carrack were, to a certain extent, offset by the adding of castles, which made the ships very liable to being pushed sideways in any wind that was not blowing directly astern. However, for the soldiery, these fittings had the added advantage in combat that if the enemy had been approached from the windward side (with the weather gage) then the wind would hold the two ships fast against each other whether they remained grappled together or not.

If merchant ships, fitted with castles, could serve a king's desires for his fighting navy, it was logical that any such ships that were permanently on his books need be nothing more than converted merchantmen, which is how Henry Tudor began his reign. However, his additions to the fleet were purpose-built warships, with the larger ones remaining carrack-like in their construction, for their efficient sailing rig enabled them to sail with a crew ratio of one seaman per ten tonnes burden, which gave plenty of room for additional soldiers and sufficient hold space for stores on the short voyages undertaken around the coast.

Carrack design continued to dominate the great shipbuilding programme well into the sixteenth century, but with a major modification. Although the design remained traditional, Henry Tudor's first ships had been built in clinker fashion, their sides formed with overlapping planks, rather like garden fencing; with his later ones, the shipwrights used carvel techniques whereby each plank was butted, edge to edge, with the one below. This gave both a stronger hull, built

Large Spanish carracks from a seventeenth-century work on naval architecture but based on an engraving done by Peter Breughel, probably in the 1550s. The ships on the right seem to represent a step towards the galleon, with a narrower stern and a lower forecastle and a protruding beakhead.

as it was around a rigid skeleton of ribs, and smooth sides, which not only gave the ship superior hydrodynamic qualities, but enabled gunports to be cut into the ship's sides and thus heavier weapons to be carried lower down, where their presence had less effect on the ship's stability. So when Henry VIII wanted to get modern, prestigious, heavy bronze muzzle loaders to sea he could do so by placing them along the main deck, thus retaining the ship's stability and counter-balancing the many light 'murderers' and other weapons mounted in the castles.

The building of great carracks was superseded in England by the introduction of the galleon, but the Iberian nations continued to build such vessels for their great trading voyages. A comparison between the known dimensions of a warship, *Mary Rose,* and the estimated ones of the rich prize Portuguese merchant ship *Madre de Dios,* captured in 1592, reveals the differences (see the table below).

Comparison of Carrack Sizes

Measurement	*Mary Rose*	*Madre de Dios*
Tonnes burden	700	1,600
Length	140	165
Beam	38ft 4in	46ft 10in
Draught	14ft 7in	31ft laden
Decks	Orlop, main, upper, two castles	Orlop, three closed decks, main, two castles
Main mast		121ft
Main yard		106ft
Keel	96ft	100ft
Crew	500 (wartime)	700

The Galleasse

In support of his carracks, Henry Tudor ordered two lighter vessels, *Sweepstake* and *Mary Fortune,* to be built. Although little-known, they deserve their place in history, not only because the former was the first naval vessel to be built at Portsmouth and the latter the last to be constructed on the banks of the rapidly silting-up River Rother in Kent, but, more importantly, because these eighty-tonne ships, powered by both oars and sails, had in their hull design the genesis of the galleon, the ship with which the age would achieve its greatest triumph at sea and the design which it would bequeath to the next century. As built they were fitted with sixty oars and a crew of just sixty-six seamen. This meant that they could only have been rowed in and out of harbour, because with sails set on their three masts more than six seamen would have been required on deck. At the time they were known as rowbarges; later similar hybrids would be referred to as galleasses. Whatever their name, the challenge remained to produce an oared vessel which would be more seaworthy in the tidal and stormy conditions around the coast of Britain than would be traditional low freeboard galleys. It was a challenge which Henry and his designers took up. Five classes of galleasse were built between 1536 and 1546, ranging from the eighty-ton *George* to the 450-tonne *Grand Mistress* and *Anne Gallant.* Most had four masts and lay low in the water.

Galleasses and their supporting oared vessels were to perform a major role in the Channel war of 1545–6, especially when out of sight of the cautious king, their proud creator. On the day *Mary Rose* sank, the French eye-witness Du Bellay mentioned that as the French galleys retired slowly from the Spithead anchorage, where they had been able to assault the English carracks with impunity in the flat calm, they were surprised to find themselves being chased by:

> special ships, which they call Ramberges. In shape they were long for their breadth and much narrower than the galleys so as to be better steered and controlled in the currents that are common in that sea; and the crews are so skilled that in these ships they can rival the speed of a galley. A few of them followed astern of our galleys at an incredible speed and badly harassed them with their artillery, against which the galleys had no defence, having no artillery astern.[3]

Annoyed at being pursued by such parvenus, the experienced galley commander Leo Strozzi turned to face his foe, at which manoeuvre the English in their turn retired with alacrity. Although Du Bellay's term 'ramberge' is very similar to the English descriptive term 'rowbarge', to judge from events over the next twelve months the vessels to which he refers were probably galleasses.[4]

The English admiral John Dudley, Viscount Lisle, was also favourably impressed by these vessels, and several days later, when he met the French for another inconclusive scuffle on 15 August, he stated in a letter to Henry that '*The Mistress,* the *Ann Gallant* and the *Greyhound* with all your Highness's shallops and rowing pieces did their parts well, but especially the *Mistress* and the *Ann Gallant* did so handle the galleys as well with their sides as with their prows, that your great-ships in a manner had little to do.'[5]

This colourful and imaginative, although contemporary, representation of Henry VIII's embarkation at Dover for the Field of the Cloth of Gold meeting with Francis I shows the major ships of his navy in great detail. The number of stern-facing guns is surprising, as is the small number of gunports on the beam. Henry himself can be seen in the waist of the second ship from the right, presumably Henry Grace à Dieu.

By this time, the larger, and earlier commissioned, of these hybrid vessels were between 140 and 450 tonnes, and were armed with a greater weight of ordnance than a galley possessed, including both forward-facing and broadside weapons. They entered the fleet before a new class of rowbarges which, although intended to counter a French invasion, had not been completed by the time the enemy armada appeared off Portsmouth. Yet even without the rowbarges, Lisle had over forty oared vessels to form the wing he ordered in his fighting instructions of 3 August 1545, and felt that they had sufficient prestige to be commanded by Captain William Tyrell, the vice-admiral, on board the 450-tonne galleasse *Grand Mistress*, which had been completed earlier that year along with *Anne Gallant* and *Greyhound*.

Unlike galleys, these galleasses had a full set of masts, three in the first pre-1540 group and from then on four, with square rigs on their fore and main masts and lateen sails on their mizzen and bonaventure masts. As forerunners of the galleons, they show that the problem of carrying a respectable weight of shot facing forward was in the process of being solved, for they had guns ahead of the foremast and below the bowsprit. Of Henry's fourteen galleasses, three were built before 1540, two in 1544, three in 1545 and four in 1546, indicating the seriousness with which the invasion crisis of those years was taken. The other two galleasses were *Salamander* and *Unicorn*, captured from the Scots in 1544.

However, none of the galleasses depicted in the Anthony Roll of 1546 are shown with oars, so one can assume that rowing was very much an auxiliary method of propulsion. In the earlier vessels the oars,

when deployed, would have had to protrude from the lower gun-deck, and the picture of *Grand Mistress* seems to show small oar-ports between the guns, making for a very crowded lower deck. By 1546 Henry may have moved on in his thinking, sacrificing manoeuvrability for a greater weight of armour, for *Grand Mistress*, *Anne Gallant* and *Greyhound* carried, respectively, twenty-eight, fifty and forty-five guns, with the heaviest armaments being, in order, two demi-cannon, four culverins and one culverin – the weight of which would have made them exceedingly top-heavy if just carried on the upper deck. The four ships built in 1546, *Hart*, *Antelope*, *Tiger* and *Bull*, were flush-decked, with between six and nine guns on their main deck, below which, the drawings show between twenty and twenty-eight oar-ports on either side.

The Pinnace

The most famous anonymous vessel in English naval history is the pinnace, which 'like a fluttering bird came flying from far away' to warn Thomas Howard and Grenville of 'Spanish ships of war at sea'. The great ships of Henry and the galleons that succeeded them did not fly across the waves. For scouting and message despatch, lighter vessels were needed which could also join in support of those ships which were being heavily pressed in any sea fight. Pinnaces were suited to this role. They were light, indeed so light that they could be carried on deck in prefabricated form during Atlantic crossings, to be used to scout up tropical rivers or intercept unsuspecting unarmed craft. For his 1595 expedition Drake took fourteen pinnaces in kit form, paying £837 for them and an additional £13 15s 4d for their masts; they were

This painting from the school of Joachim Patinir is believed to show the Portuguese carrack Santa Caterina de Monte Sinai *arriving off Villefranche in 1521. The fine detail of the ship and the welcoming galley indicate the accuracy of the portrayal.* (National Maritime Museum BHC0705)

Originally French, Unicorn *was captured from the Scots in 1544 only to be sold in 1552 for £10. She was one of only two ships in Henry's fleet (and both captured) to carry what is obviously a figurehead.* (British Library)

23

to be the workhorses of his expedition. Most could be powered by both oars and sails and were thus ideal for inshore work. Although the ten drawn by Anthony Anthony do not have oars he clearly indicates lines of oar-ports below the guns, ranging from twenty-two in the case of the eighty-tonne *Roo* to seventeen for the fifteen-tonne *Hare*. Crew numbers varied from sixty in the larger pinnaces to just thirty in little *Hare,* which was armed with one saker, twelve iron bases, four hail-shot pieces and six handguns, indicating that her task was to support a larger ship by enfilade fire against the decks of an opponent. The larger *Roo* had a culverin perrier, two demi-culverins, two brass chamber pieces and twelve bases, six hailshot pieces and also six hand-guns. Yet without Anthony's details of manning, tonnage and armament alongside his drawings it would be difficult to tell from them which was the greater pinnace and which the lesser. Each lies low, its waist covered with anti-boarding nets, and with three masts, one fighting top and four sails, excluding a spritsail. There was probably little difference in the design and usage of such vessels in the years following Anthony's drawings, for the pinnace *Sun* of 1586, the first naval warship built at Chatham, was a similar vessel, being of thirty-nine tonnes and fitted with nine guns.

On 13 November 1595 Drake led twenty-five pinnaces and long-boats on a night attack against San Juan in Puerto Rico. He succeeded in firing four frigates, but the flames exposed his lightly defended force and they were driven off. It was to be his last serious action before his death two months later off Nombre de Dios, which, at the start of his career in 1572, he had seized with just three pinnaces. He might have gained his reputation in *Golden Hind, Elizabeth Bonaventure* and *Revenge*, but the lowly unnamed pinnace was his constant companion on his way to wealth and remained faithful until death.

A sophisticated prefabricated pinnace also featured in James Lancaster's privateering raid on Brazil in 1594. He referred to her as a 'galley frigate', and she does seem to have been a hybrid, powered by fourteen banks of oars and carrying a single sail.[6] She was sacrificed, along with another boat, to put spirit into his men, for, on landing on the beach at Pernambuco, he ordered his skippers to drive the boats so hard on to the beach that their backs would break, thereby destroying the English attackers' means of retreat.

The Frigate

In 1575 the Earl of Essex, keen to prevent Scottish reinforcements from reaching Ireland, told the Privy Council that he wished:

... to buy certain frigates which one Drake brought out of the Indies, whereof one is in possession of Mr. Hawkins, one of Sir Arthur Champernowne. The third is yet to be had, as I hearsay in Dartmouth.
They were bought at easy price. If two of these might be sent they might be kept with less cost than one ship and do much more service than any other vessel. They will brook sea well and carry 200 soldiers, as I am informed, and yet they draw so little water, as they may pass into every river, island or creek, where the Scottish galleys may flee, and are of better strength and stowage than other, for the galleys are made more slight and thin than the wherries upon the Thames. No shipping therefore is so good for

this purpose in my opinion as the frigates. I have slight ordnance for them, but I lack oars and such necessaries ...

And, showing that he did know something about his men, he added: 'Good choice must be made of mariners for these boats, for ordinary sailors love not to pull an oar.'[7]

This appears to be the first use of the term 'frigate' in a naval context, and, to judge from Essex's description, it was being applied to small vessels propelled by both oars and sails. Drake employed himself as master in *Falcon* and drew pay for another twenty-two men, which would suggest that these 'frigates' were of about twenty-five tonnes. Their use would suggest that they were the 'gofers' of the navy, adaptable and utilitarian, the characteristics that would for ever define them as a class.

The galleasse Greyhound *based on the depiction in the Anthony Anthony Roll. These sail-and-oar hybrids prefigured the hull-form of later galleons.* (Veres László)

Pinnaces were the inshore workhorses of the fleet, ferrying men ashore and water and supplies out to the ships. They also acted as scouts and messenger carriers; it was a pinnace that warned Lord Howard of the approach of the Spanish fleet off Flores in the Azores in 1591. This drawing is based on a contemporary depiction of the Black Pynnes *that brought back the body of Sir Philip Sydney after the battle of Zutphen in 1586. The ship's topsides are obscured by the funereal arming cloths.* (Veres László)

The Galley and Other Oared Vessels

The sixteenth century saw both the apotheosis and the decline of the oared fighting galley as a principal weapon of sea warfare in the fleets of European powers. The apotheosis was the battle of Lepanto in October 1571, when a Christian coalition comprising 207 galleys and six galleasses crushed the Ottoman fleet of 230 galleys and seventy galliots, killing some thirty thousand of their crew in the process, including many of the skilled specialists essential to maintain Muslim hegemony over the eastern Mediterranean and the north African littoral. The nadir was delivered, piecemeal but effectively, by the English navy, who, after years of fearing well-armed galleys, had developed a warship, the race-built galleon, that brushed the rowing fleets aside in waters that the galleys would have considered their own: at Cadiz in 1587 and 1596, at Cezimbra near Lisbon in 1602 and, finally, off Calais later that same year. In the seventy years between the loss of Edward Howard, fighting French galleys in Brittany in 1513, and Drake's burning the King of Spain's galleys in Cadiz, the English had thought of many ways to gain the upper hand over these irritating craft, short of building a similar fleet of galleys for themselves. Their experiments, trials and, it has to be said, failures, until the unanticipated metamorphosis of the oared galleasse into the sailing galleon, show that shipbuilding was also subject to the law of the survival of the fittest and, in this case, the fleetest. Blessed with a king who considered himself a naval architect of some merit, Henry's shipwrights spent many years building vessels designed in the king's mind, often aided by the advice of foreign experts of dubious national loyalty.

The Tudors were familiar with galleys but mainly those used as trading vessels, for both Venetian and Genoese merchants made annual voyages to Southampton in these craft. They were also aware that galleys made useful troop carriers, and within a few days of Henry's accession the doge was informed not only that Henry intended to go to war against France but, falsely, that he was retaining their trading galleys to load troops for his invasion. In 1512 Queen Katherine enquired of the Venetian ambassador the cost of hiring four galleasses and two galleys from the Republic. The hire charge of £200 per ship per month was prohibitive and preposterous, probably being quoted as a diplomatic way of refusing the request.[8]

The English decision not to have its own galleys was based on sound geographic sense, summed up by the Venetian legate, Daniel Barbaro, in a lengthy and detailed report to his Senate in 1551:

> They do not use galleys by reason of the very great strength of the tide in the ocean so that as the reporter was told by the Prior of Capua [Leo Strozzi] when he went with six galleys to fetch the Queen of Scotland [July 1550] the navigation of those seas differs from that of all others, so unless the tide be favourable the wind is of very little use[9]

– although he does go on to say that two galleys were kept at standby

A carving in the town church in Lannion, Brittany of a vessel with hybrid sail and oar propulsion. It may have been described at the time as a galleasse or possibly a frigate. (Author)

for use if ships got into difficulties because of high tides and currents in the estuaries.

Henry did build the occasional galley. In 1515 *Great Galley*, not exactly true to type, was reported to have been fitted out with '207 pieces of artillery, 70 of them brass, the rest of iron, 4,000 or 5,000 bullets, and 400 or 500 barrels of powder. She has 120 oars and will hold 800 or 1000 fighting men'.[10] This might have been a one-off, but the king's interest in galleys remained, and in June 1518 he arranged to have a tour of the visiting Venetian galleys. In a letter that casts an interesting light on Henry's hypochondria and paranoia, it was reported that the king desired that none of the crew of the flag-galley be on board for his visit, as he had heard that the galleys were infected by plague, and that also all their gunpowder should be disembarked for the period, while no gun salutes should be fired during his time on board.[11] Given these restrictions, the Venetians did the king proud. The flag-galley was decked with silks and tapestries, and four rows of tables were laid to feed 500 guests with a most sumptuous meal. After dinner the crews must have returned on board, for they staged a performance of aerial gymnastics in the rigging.

Despite his caveats on gun salutes, the next day the king ordered the galleys to carry out lengthy gun drills so that he could mark their range, as he was 'very curious about such matters'. To keep him informed the Venetian ambassador, Carlo Capello, was told by the doge to tell the king of the warlike preparations of the sultan, which included arming his new galleys with 'nine guns at the prow, namely, three very handsome great guns, and falconets', and an abundance of cannon elsewhere.[12] This was standard for the sixteenth-century Western fighting galleys, which had moved from being troop carriers to gun-boats. A typical fighting galley was long and narrow, with twenty-four banks of oars and 144 oarsmen and up to three masts carrying lateen sails. In 1536 the Spanish galley flagship carried up forward a large cannon, two demi-culverins, three sakers and a perrier augmented by a number of swivel guns on the beam. This, in a vessel 140 feet long and 16½ feet wide and drawing just over four feet, meant that her 186-tonne displacement included over 9¾ tonnes of ordnance.[13] On a calm day she would have been capable of attaining seven and a half knots flat out for twenty minutes or cruising at three and a half knots under oars and at up to eight knots under sail: sufficient speed to keep company with larger sailing vessels while the weather held.[14] As soon as the wind arose the galleys were in trouble, a fact best illustrated by the fact that none of those that sailed with the Armada in 1588 made it as far as Ushant. Yet on the occasions they passed north of that point they caused consternation, because the English had no similar weapon with which to counter them, although Henry's Venetian friends did. So in May 1522, with war in the offing, the subtlety of diplomacy was cast aside as the Venetian galley fleet loading at Southampton was commandeered to escort the visiting Emperor Charles back to Spain. While the king and emperor were celebrating Mass at Canterbury Cathedral, Wolsey and Lord Admiral

Surrey called the Venetian ambassadors to one side and told them that as the king was anxious to ensure that the emperor had a safe passage that they were to unload the galleys, hand over their cannon, and reduce the crews to a hundred per vessel to enable the emperor's entourage to embark. The captains obeyed with understandable ill-grace. Henry and Wolsey's behaviour was glossed over by the doge who saw some diplomatic advantages in its toleration for, although it was a flagrant breach of international mores, the Venetians, made impotent by reason of distance and by their need for wool, had no option other than to comply with teeth-grinding grace.[15]

The fear of galleys continued throughout Henry's reign although several squadrons were bested in action. Their final defeat came when the galleon, developed by John Hawkins, proved that they did not need to be met oar against oar, as would happen at Lepanto in 1571, but would fail against sailing warships that could approach them not as equals but as superiors. Until then the experimentation continued.

The English Galley

The description of English oared vessels adds to the difficulty of defining which royal ships were galleys. Henry VIII had four ships that were referred to as galleys, *Rose*, *Katherine*, *Great* and *Galley Subtile*, but only the latter was true to form, her name, in fact, echoing the French generic term for a 'narrow galley'. As with so many of the English military developments her building was influenced by the co-ordination of the king and foreign experts.

In July 1541 the imperial ambassador Chapuys reported to Charles V that 'The King has also sent to Italy for three shipwrights expert at making galleys', but Chapuys added that he thought that they would not be set to work as Henry had begun to make ships with oars, of which he was the architect.

However, in November 1542 the English captured the French ship *Ferronière* off Dartmouth and found on board Pierre de Bidoux, nephew of Prégent de Bidoux, who, as galley commander, had driven the English from Brest in 1513. Interned for several months, Pierre offered to buy his freedom in exchange for instructing the English in the art of galley construction. This offer was gratefully accepted by the

king, and de Bidoux received a generous grant of £50 a year in 1543, which two years later was raised to £75. For this sum the traitor seems only to have overseen the construction of the king's one true galley, *Galley Subtile*, a flush-deck 200-tonne vessel with twenty-four banks of oars on each side and a crew of 242 mariners and eight gunners. She had a single mast carrying a large lateen sail, the yard for which was made from two spars fished together for about a third of the total length and bound sturdily. Above the yard a deep crow's nest is shown in the Anthony Roll drawing, along with a great number of flags and pendants and a massive brocade bearing the royal arms stretched over the cabin right aft. The galley carried a large cannon and two sakers facing forward at the bow and three other brass guns and numerous smaller iron pieces. For close-quarters confrontations she also had a hundred bows and a variety of boarding weapons. Anthony Anthony shows her beak ending in an iron-tipped spike, indicating that ramming was still considered an effective technique, although the beak was generally used as a method of boarding an enemy vessel.

Galley Subtile was deployed as an escort for the invasion of Scotland in 1544 and led the attack and seizure of the fort of Inchgarvie in the Firth of Forth. She remained 'on the books' until she was condemned and disposed of in 1560.

Henry was not content with just one galley in his fleet, and in December 1544 he asked Charles V to loan or sell him a further ten complete with mariners, slaves and ordnance.[16] His plea was unsuccessful because the emperor wished to use all his galleys in an attack on the Turks. Nevertheless, in May 1545 the Mayor and Sheriffs of London were instructed that the king, aware of the numerous 'ruffians and vagabonds' who scorned work and chose to live through theft and falsehood, hanging around the Bank and 'such like naughty places' which they haunted nightly for the 'accomplishment and satisfying of their vile, wretched and filthy purposes', intended to use all such 'ruffians, vagabonds, masterless men, common players and evil disposed persons to serve him in these wars in certain galleys to be armed before 1 June next'.[17] If this order was obeyed then there is a chance that these men formed part of the successful rowing squadron that acquitted itself so well on 15 August 1545 in the short sharp exchange with the French fleet.

This fight had resulted in four rowed vessels, *Grand Mistress*, *Galley Subtile*, *Foyst* and *Brigantine*, having to return to harbour for repairs. Nevertheless, on 21 May the following year *Grand Mistress* was in the fleet with which Lord William Howard, after a day-long engagement, drove off a French force of ten galleys and which, together with *Anne Gallant*, *Greyhound* and the small pinnace *Phoenix*, shared in the capture of the *Galley Blanchard*, an event that thrilled the people of London when the prize was brought up the Thames. On board the French ship was a Portuguese pilot, Fernando Oliviera, whose expertise, like that of de Bidoux before him, Henry appreciated and rewarded with employment. Years later Oliviera was to write in his learned work on sea warfare, *Arte da guerr do mar:*

In the war of Boulogne, the English King ordered some galleys to

A Mediterranean galley at sea, from an early sixteenth-century painting. The main armament was usually large forward-firing guns in the bow, but this example seems to have a gun amidships. (Detail from National Maritime Museum BHC0705)

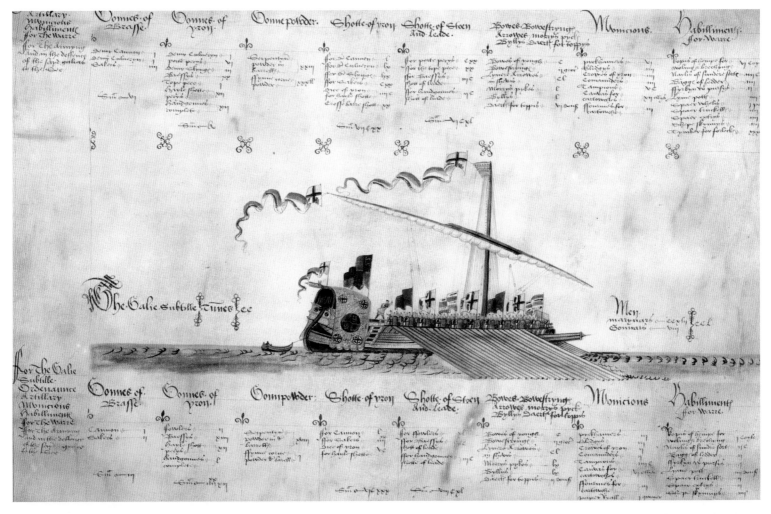

be built in his kingdom, to remove the fear [of French Galleys] from his men, solely so that his men should see what the thing was, and not be astonished by those of France; which galleys would serve him there for no other thing, and he knew well that they would be able to serve him, and therefore did not make more than a few for show. With which strategy he so emboldened his men that they had no esteem for the galleys of France.[18]

The concept of building training vessels based on enemy weapon platforms seems very modern, and in this case can be linked to the few fast patrol boats that the Royal Navy built in the 1960s to simulate enemy missile-launching vessels, a craft for which the navy itself had no use. It also clears Henry of the charge that his galleys or rowbarges, completed by April 1546, were built solely to counter the French invasion of 1545.

Van der Delft, in his report to the emperor on 29 April 1546, wrote that 'During the last three days 18 pinnaces, newly built in the form of foysts, have sailed from her [London]. They have on each side fifteen or sixteen oars, and are all well and similarly equipped both with regard to the size of their artillery and to their crews.'[19]

The thirteen, rather than eighteen, twenty-tonne rowbarges to which this intelligence refers were long, low vessels, miniature galleasses, built with three masts with a single yard on each. They had a crew of around thirty-five seamen and four gunners to service their forward-facing demi-culverin or saker, and the six iron guns, including

For all his interest in them, Galley Subtile *was Henry VIII's only true galley and her handling had to be entrusted to a Venetian captain acting through an interpreter.* (British Library)

One of Henry's answers to the French galley threat was a class of thirteen row barges such as Rose in the Sun *shown here. Of 20 tons burden and powered by both oars and sails, they were not a success and lasted from between two and six years.* (Magdalene College, Cambridge)

one or two pairs, mounted aft. Where, as in the case of *Maidenhead, Roseslip, Gillyflower* and *Sun*, only a single pair of guns was mounted aft, a pair of stern-chasers was also fitted. Like the galleasses they also seem to have had a spiked ram forward and to have been equipped with plenty of bows and weapons for boarding operations. They were both the first class of ship to be produced to a single design, and the first whose names were linked together, in this case being named after parts of the royal coat of arms. Like many small ships in the Royal Navy, they may well have been great fun to serve in and have given many a young inexperienced seaman a grounding in his profession. In later years they might have been ideal support vessels for the Virginia colonists, but with the end of Henry's French wars the purpose for which they were intended disappeared, and by 1549 ten had been sold, the final three being disposed of by 1555.

Although much of the action in the succeeding wars with Spain was fought in more distant waters and no galleys reached the Channel with the Armada in 1588, the fear of their potency remained and the idea of having a counterforce in the English fighting fleet was retained, as for example when, in August 1592, two counterfeiters were sentenced to serve chained in 'the new galleys',[20] but there is little other reference to the existence of such vessels, although the five-gun, 140-tonne *Seven Stars* was built as such in 1586, as was the six-gun, eighty-tonne ill-built galley *Mercury*, launched at Deptford in 1592; it was therefore probably the latter, converted to a pinnace in 1604, that was the destination of the two miscreants. The only attempt at forming an English galley squadron was made in 1601, when four galleys were built on the Thames in response to the stationing of a Spanish squadron at Gravelines.

In the end Henry's navy had for a brief period been served by four types of oared vessels: galleys, rowboats (or rowbarges), pinnaces and galleasses. Of these only the latter had the potential for further development, for its successor was to be the next revolutionary English vessel, the galleon.

The Galleon

John Hawkins is credited with introducing into naval design a new class of ship that would dominate the waters around Britain and bring fear to the coasts of Spain, where it scorned the threat of the galleys. Like many revolutionary ideas his concept of the 'race-built' galleon did not spring forth unheralded and with no antecedent, but it took his genius to make an evolutionary breakthrough of a significance that has justly been compared to Fisher's 1906 *Dreadnought*.

The development of the English galleon began with the much deprecated Mary, whose three major new ships could all be classed as such. The main difference between the galleons and carracks was that the newer ships lay lower in the water and no longer had extravagant fore- and after-castles. Indeed the forecastle was a much reduced 'coach house' with a low, long beak-head forward of it which would cleave its way through the water. The tonnage of these ships varied greatly although none were large: *Triumph* was 740 tonnes, the 'little' *Revenge* 465 tonnes, Drake's *Elizabeth Bonaventure* 600 tonnes, and Seymour's flagship *Rainbow* a mere 384 tonnes, while *Advantage* was classified as a galleon although of a mere 170 tonnes burden. By comparison, the ships captured by the English in 1588 and 1596

included *Rosario* of 1,150 tonnes, *St Andrew* of 900 tonnes and *St Matthew*, another galleon, of 1,000 tonnes. This weight discrepancy does not signify disadvantage. *Revenge* punched with 185 pounds of shot from her twenty-eight muzzle-loaders, an effective broadside from a ship of her size. Also, when closed to point-blank range, her low lines, as with most other English galleons, placed her hull below the angle of depression achievable by Spanish gunners working from higher decks. Drake, given a free hand to arm *Elizabeth Bonaventure* in 1585, achieved a shot weight of 522lb. By the end of the century the 522-tonne *Warspite* was fitted with guns giving her a weight of shot of just 444lb, but this had been achieved as part of the move towards lighter guns with, theoretically, greater range.

As far as their masts and sails were concerned, most galleons retained the four masts but were able to lower the upper sections in bad weather. Proof of their excellent sea-keeping qualities is evident in the fact that they kept the seas and, by now the oceans, without suffering loss in storms. This must reflect well on Hawkins, who, combining his knowledge of shipbuilding, sea-going, finance and business contacts, produced a new design that incorporated the following features:[21]

> A new keel length-to-beam ratio of 3:1, giving a slimmer, better hydrodynamic shape;
> An underwater hull form based on the successful galleasse lines;
> A stepped gun-deck running through the ship to provide more freeboard for the heavy weapons;
> A dedicated cargo deck below the gun-deck;
> Greater draught to reduce leeway and improve stability;
> Enclosing the waist to create a second gun-deck for lighter weapons;
> Reducing the upper works to half-deck, quarter-deck with small poop and a low forecastle, thus reducing windage;
> A long beak-head and raked stem to cut through head-on seas and provide a drier upper deck;
> A steep angled bowsprit carrying a greater sail more effectively, thus improving ship-handling.

Another feature of Hawkins's design was that it could be adapted to convert older vessels to the new fighting form. Thus in 1570, the year in which *Foresight*, the prototype of the race-built galleons, was built from first principles, both *Bull* and *Tiger*, 160-tonne galleasses, were rebuilt on galleon lines although in a smaller size. Hawkins was also building to last. *Rainbow*, built at Deptford in 1586 in time to serve as Lord Henry Seymour's flagship in command of the eastern Channel squadron against the Armada, was sunk as a breakwater at Sheerness in 1680, while Vice-Admiral William Winter's Armada campaign flagship, *Vanguard*, having been built at Woolwich in 1586, was also sunk as a Medway blockship, only to be raised and sold in 1667. By 1588 the navy had sixteen of this class to sail against the Armada: of these, eight had been built to Hawkins's design, one, *Ark Royal*, had been purchased from Ralegh, and seven were converted older vessels.

Boats

A cursory glance at the Anthony Roll will show that all the major vessels are towing a boat astern. Boats were vital and integral units for, once at sea, there were few places where a ship of any size might lie

Ark Ralegh, *named after her owner, and designed for piratical ventures, was the most powerful English warship. Self-interest led to Ralegh presenting her to the queen at which time she was renamed* Ark Royal, *becoming the first vessel to carry one of the most illustrious of British warship names, and acting as Howard's flagship during the Armada campaign. This engraving by Visscher was done some time later, and experts have cast doubt on some details of the depiction.* (National Maritime Museum neg 2246)

Another of Visscher's engravings of Armada ships, this purports to be the Tiger, *one of the first race-built galleons. The low topsides shown accord well with a ship that was a rebuilt galleasse, a feature also shown in the Smerwick illustration reproduced overleaf.* (National Maritime Museum neg 1293)

alongside securely to land men or replenish stores. Boats were essential for ferrying captains over to the admiral for conferences, while they sometimes saw service as an open cell for those who needed to cool off for some hours or days. Most importantly, boats were sometimes needed to assist in raising the anchor and, when the winds were still or contrary, to lay out kedge anchors to which the ships could haul themselves and thus, often by many repetitions, leave harbour. This exhausting evolution was most famously necessary when the Spanish Armada arrived off Devon, catching the English fleet embarrassed by tide and wind, and needing to be warped out of the Cattewater and then towed into the Sound until the breeze stirred their sails. The use of boats when the wind died with an enemy at close quarters also saved many a ship from capture or destruction. The absence of boats in similar circumstances could create fear or, occasionally, farce.

In 1585 Richard Grenville, returning on board the queen's elderly converted galleon, *Tiger*, from landing the first settlers in Virginia 'Descried a tall ship ... unto whom he gave chase, and in a few hours by goodness of sail overtook, and by violence won'.[22] However, having had the *Santa Maria* surrender after holing her just above the water-line, Grenville appears not to have had a means to board her. He therefore caused a jury-rigged boat to be cobbled together from 'boards of chests', with which he barely made the crossing before it fell apart and sank. A few weeks earlier Grenville had led an expedition up the Pamlico river, opposite Roanoke island, using his ship's boats, so they were obviously serviceable at that time; perhaps he left them behind for Governor Lane's use when he himself returned to England.

Boats were not always towed astern. Many ships had up to three boats: a great boat, almost pinnace-like in size; a cock-boat and a jolly-boat, some of which could be hoisted on board, where they would have been secured amidships on top of the grating that covered the main hatch. In some cases large boats or pinnaces were carried in kit form for launching when they were needed; often on the western Atlantic and Pacific seaboards they were relaunched to enter and explore the waterways of the Caribbean and other likely sources of plunder.

Boats were also needed for amphibious operations, to ferry the army or armed sailors ashore, although galleys were ideal for this work, for their forward-firing guns and shallow draught meant that they could keep an opposing force at bay while the troops established a beachhead. Contemporary paintings show them being used in this role by the French off Brighton, but the English, without such vessels, had to rely on the fleet working its way inshore to provide covering fire. This was not always possible. Edward Howard, unable to close the French galleys beached in White Sands Bay in 1513, was forced to put his men into inadequate and inappropriate boats for his fatal assault. On other occasions, the army had to be landed far further from its objective than was sensible, and it struggled. Norris had to march forty miles from Peniche to Lisbon in 1587 and on arrival had only just enough force to knock on the gates and depart, while Baskerville found it impossible to fight his way through the saturated American undergrowth to reach Panama in 1595. Worse still could be an absence of sufficient boats or boats of the right sort. In 1544 Thomas Seymour wrote to the Privy Council that he trusted that his service would be only at sea, as he had just six boats 'which will not carry 200 men besides they that must keep the boats'.[23]

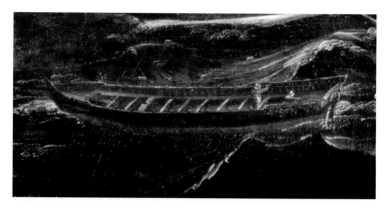

Although little attention has been paid to them, boats were an essential part of naval power in the age of sail. With few alongside berths available, once launched most ships had to rely on boats to ferry both men and victuals to them and also to transfer personnel and messages while at sea. Contrary winds meant boats were also needed to raise anchors and warp or tow ships out to sea or away from danger. The main ship's boat – the longboat – was so large it had to be towed at sea, and this detail from a painting by Vroom shows the boat keepers whose job was to ensure the safety of the craft when under tow.

The naval attack by Sir William Winter's squadron on the Spanish force besieged in Smerwick in Ireland in 1580 was recorded by the admiral's son in great detail. It shows the heavy guns, both bow and stern chasers, being used (from the top of the map) by Swiftsure, Ayd, Marlyon, Revenge, Achates *and* Tiger, *all of which are at anchor to help the gunners aim with accuracy.* (National Archives, Kew)

What the successful navy needed, then, was a mixture of craft: great ships or galleons to lead the fight, frigates to work in support, pinnaces to reconnoitre, espy and carry messages, and oared vessels to land men and bring out stores. In addition there remained the need to employ merchant ships as victuallers or to add investment and strength to joint ventures. Through constant usage the right mix emerged to form a truly formidable and flexible fighting fleet.

The Fleet in Being

When Henry VII proclaimed himself king, the day before his decisive victory at Bosworth Field in 1485, he inherited a navy consisting of seven carracks and a ship, all of which were ex-merchant vessels. In a very short time the majority of these were disposed of and new ships ordered to be built specifically as warships. The first two were prestigious vessels, *Regent* and *Sovereign,* but their design and armament, consisting of hundreds of small breech-loaders, reflected an age that was moving to its close. The first indication of change took place with the two galleasses, *Sweepstake* and *Mary Fortune,* whose lines made them the ancestors of the galleon. Like many evolutionary forebears they bore little resemblance to their illustrious successors, being small and powered by oars as well as sail. But their hull design made them far more logical predecessors than *Mary Rose* and *Peter Pomegranate,* which, far from being revolutionary warships, marked the last flourish of those great ship dinosaurs, the carracks.

There is some debate as to why Henry Tudor, a monarch desiring peace, should have ordered the 800-tonne *Sovereign* and the 1,000-tonne *Regent.* Perhaps it reflected on his long period of exile in Brittany, when he would have been very aware not only of his own

With great attention to the archaeological record Bill Bishop recreated this picture of Mary Rose *at anchor before the fortifications at Portsmouth.* (Mary Rose Trust)

inability to raid England but also, more importantly, the ease with which a malcontent abroad could land on the English coast unchallenged unless the monarch had a fleet at sea on patrol. Perhaps the expansion of the French state along the whole southern littoral of the Channel alarmed him. Perhaps the two strange uprisings that brought Perkin Warbeck and Lambert Simnel safely across the sea, as well as his own unopposed landing, influenced his thinking. Whatever the reason, these two ships marked the first step towards the creation of a standing navy. What they did not do is advance the design of such vessels beyond the medieval. For example, *Regent* carried 225 guns, all serpentines designed to clear decks, while *Sovereign* was fitted for 110 serpentines and 31 stone guns. All of these would have been carried on the upper deck or castles, and even when converted to carvel hulls, neither ship appears to have been fitted with gunports.[24]

Henry VII's last pair of vessels were built at Portsmouth. He died before they were completed and their naming was left to his son, who called the larger, 500-tonne vessel *Mary Rose,* and the 450-tonne one *Peter Pomegranate*; the first name was chosen by combining the 'Mystic Rose', his favourite saint, the Virgin Mary, with his dynastic emblem, the second by linking Saint Peter with the symbol of the House of Aragon. There is no evidence to suggest that *Mary Rose* was named after the new king's younger sister to counter the Scottish King James's naming of his new vessel *Margaret* after his wife and Henry's elder sister.[25]

The fleet afloat that Henry Tudor bequeathed to his son was just six ships strong, but these were all either new or recently refitted. A further two were under construction, so for the first time the sovereign had a navy designed to fight – and Henry VIII was determined that it would do just that. He also realised that a force of eight ships was not enough for attacking France, especially as his plan involved sending troops to northern Spain, a voyage that would necessitate them sailing past Brest, France's premier naval port. To do this successfully would require both escorts and, if practicable, the blockading of the enemy fleet in its harbour. Although war with France did not break out until 1512, there was little time and few resources to build a suitable fleet, and so between 1510 and 1513 Henry bought himself a navy, although his first acquisitions were the two Scottish pirate ships, *Lion* and *Jennet Prywin,* captured by the Howard brothers, Edward and Thomas, who were to be appointed his first two Lord Admirals. A programme of building smaller ships was begun but, apart from *Great Bark* (250 tonnes), those over 200 tonnes, *Christ, Maria de Larreto,*

Where galleys were not available, ships used their boats to land troops for raids ashore. Morlaix was taken in 1522 by just such an attack, as were many small towns in the West Indies. This engraving is slightly outside the period of this book, showing the English expedition to the Île de Rhé in 1627, but the troop-laden boats are very similar to those of the previous century.

Henry Grace á Dieu was the most prestigious vessel built by Henry VIII but designed to fight as well as show the flag. Note for example, the sheer hooks attached at the end of her yards to cut through an enemy's rigging at close quarters and the grapnel on the end of the bowsprit designed to drop onto an opponents deck to hold the two ships together so that boarding could take place. (Veres László)

Katherine Fortileza, Gabriel Royal, John Baptist, Mary James, Great Nicholas and *Great Barbara*, were all purchased. During the course of the two-year war the navy was, theoretically, able to put thirty of the king's ships to sea, supported by many more merchant ships taken up from trade and used as transports or victuallers. In April 1513 Edward Howard arrived off Brest with twenty-three royal ships and twenty-two chartered English ships over seventy tonnes, a clear indication of the high state of maintenance of the Navy Royal.

As so often happens, the royal building programme fell behind political developments, and the king's pride and joy, the 1,500-tonne, modestly named *Henry Grace à Dieu* was launched too late for active service, as was *Great Galley*, which was renamed, more appropriately, *Great Bark* in 1543, by which time she had been converted to become an efficient sailing vessel which was later reconstructed to become the galleon *White Bear*.

When the second French war broke out in 1522, Henry had some

twenty-three royal vessels fit for service. Over the next few years this number increased slightly, but there was a major falling-away by 1533, when the numbers of ships listed shrank to just ten. After that low point, the response to England's isolation and threat of invasion from 1534 onwards was a new building programme, with the emphasis firstly on galleasses and then on the thirteen beautifully-named but inefficient rowbarges that were launched in 1546.

If the loss of *Mary Rose* in 1545 represents the last tragic act of Henry's navy, then the Anthony Roll of 1546 was the fleet's curtain call, for which quite rightly the tragic heroine was revived to take her bow. The next half-century was to produce very different characters for a very different play.

Converted galleasses and rowbarges made up the majority of the fifty-seven ships that Henry passed on to Edward in 1547. Yet with eighteen major fighting ships in the fleet, the young king inherited a most formidable force, to which he added seventeen more vessels, of which only four smaller ships and four pinnaces were built, the remainder being prizes and purchases. However, a number of the ships, including the rowbarges, were condemned, meaning that at the end of his reign the size of the fleet had been reduced to just thirty-nine, although as the number of vessels classified as ships had increased to twenty-five, this is no indication that the fighting strength had in any meaningful way diminished.

There were only four fewer ships on the establishment at the end of Mary's reign. In fact, she who is so often condemned for her handling of the nation's defences began a revolution in design that was to have them appropriately strengthened at her sister's greatest hour of need. For it was with Mary that the concept of the galleon as the successor to the by now antiquated great ship or carrack came about. What is more, she was able to get a great number of her ships to sea when the need arose, an indication of a first-class maintenance programme. In part this was due to the influence of her husband, Philip of Spain, who wished to use the Navy Royal to support his fight in the Netherlands, but as the English court had little time for this foreign prince, Mary's influence has to be seen in this positive response to crisis. Back in the Thames, slack ship-keepers allowed *Henry Grace à Dieu* to burn down to the water-line at her moorings. Perhaps the loss of the most prestigious great ship was a portent of change, for no more such vessels were to be built.

Instead Mary built three galleons, *Philip and Mary*, the second *Mary Rose* and *Golden Lion*. These were longer, narrower and lower than their predecessors and were built to the highest of specifications: they lasted a long time, although they were extensively refitted as race-built galleons. *Philip and Mary*, her name changed twice, to *Nonpareil* and then *Nonsuch*, was last recorded in 1645. *Mary Rose* ended up as a wharf at Chatham in 1618, while *Lion*, which was to be Lord Thomas Howard's command against the Armada, was sold off in 1698, after 141 years of service!

In addition to her new builds, Mary had three large pinnaces converted to ships, four rowbarges reclassified as pinnaces, and ordered six of her father's galleasses to be converted to galleons. Thus, despite losing the expensive appendage of Calais, Mary bequeathed to her sister a fleet that could defend the realm with a number of ships whose design and potential formed a good base on which to build to meet the fresh challenges of the new reign. Of the thirty-five ships in the Navy Royal at her succession, twenty-seven were well-equipped fighting vessels.

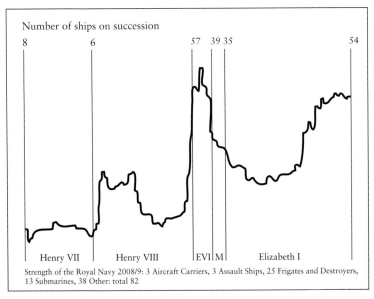

The strength of the fleet during the Tudor era. (Author)

Elizabeth started slowly, with twelve ships being taken off the establishment following surveys at the start of her reign. Other amendments meant that by 1560 her fleet had been reduced to twenty-two vessels, but these were good ships, fifteen of them being less than five years old. There then came about the modifications and introductions that made her fleet almost reborn as a fighting force, aided by the fact that Hawkins's concept of the galleon was so skilfully concocted that old as well as new-build vessels could be produced to the new specifications. From 1570 onwards the story of the Royal Navy is very much the story of the galleon and its triumph over both the sailing and oared ships of England's enemies.

Thus Henry Tudor's son and grandchildren each developed and improved the fighting capability of the fleet so that, at the last, Elizabeth was able to leave fifty-four ships to James I, of which forty-two could be considered serviceable and thirty were of the galleon construction. As a throwback to a bygone age, Elizabeth's final fleet also included five exotically-named galleys, four of which were built in the Thames in 1601 and 1602 in response to the presence of a Spanish squadron stationed in the Netherlands; however, these galleys were to play no part in their neutralisation, for it was to be the galleons that would drive the last galleys from the seas around England and usher in a new age of naval warfare.

Chapter Three

Building the Fleet

I'll give the tackling made of rivell'd gold,

Wound on the barks of odoriferous trees;

Oars of massy ivory, full of holes,

Through which the water shall delight to play;

Thy anchors shall be hew'd from crystal rocks,

Which, if thou lose, shall shine above the waves;

The masts, whereon thy swelling sails shall hang,

Hollow pyramids of silver plate;

The sails of folded lawn, ...

For ballast, empty Dido's treasury ...

Christopher Marlowe, Dido, Queen of Carthage

The ships that were to form the Tudor fleet were the most complex machines that had been created by the ingenuity of the human mind, the vision of the human eye and the skill of the human hand. Their design was for the most part carried around in the portfolio of the shipwright's brain, and the blueprint was his spoken word. The result was that each ship tended to be a unique creation with her own particular measurements and peculiar characteristics. Later, designs and directions were committed to paper, allowing standardisation, rationalisation and savings to be made as well as leaving a record from which later generations were able to get an idea as to how these ships were built.

That recorded knowledge has been long known. In the Pepys Library at Magdalene College, Cambridge, a copy of *Fragments of Ancient English Shipwrightry*, written in 1582 by Matthew Baker, the royal master shipwright, contains not only formulae but the first scale drawings of contemporary warships. A 'Table of General Details' of 1602 gives further and comprehensive details of the fleet in the last year of Elizabeth's reign.[1] Such information proved to be both useful and adequate when replicas of ships such as *Golden Hind, Matthew* and *Mayflower* were constructed. Then, on 11 October 1982, supposition was banished as the hull of *Mary Rose* resurfaced following a painstaking epic of searching, discovery, excavation and recovery. For the first time in over 400 years the evidence as to how the Tudors built their ships could be witnessed, recorded and researched. It was the maritime equivalent of the unearthing of Pompeii, the like of which is

unlikely ever to be seen again. And it was not just any ship, for this vessel, which had been Henry VIII's flagship, was long in years when a tragic accident in 1545 meant that she was both lost and preserved. Laid down in 1509, her timbers represent almost half a century of ship-building and refitting techniques. Her survival is a maritime miracle, her display a marine marvel, and a visit a maritime must. She is a tribute to the untiring search for her remains by Alexander McKee, her ground-breaking recovery by Margaret Rule and her conservation, along with thousands of unique and priceless artefacts, by Mark Jones.

This illustration from the Nuremburg Chronicle, *first published in 1493, purports to show the building of Noah's Ark, but demonstrates how shipwrights of the time plied their trade. Many of the basic carpentry techniques remained virtually unchanged during the whole era of wooden shipbuilding.* (National Maritime Museum PU8304)

Elsewhere in England a *Golden Hind* exists at both St Mary Overie's Dock, London, and Brixham, Devon, because two reconstructions were built on the basis of research, giving a double opportunity to wander over a ship that closely resembles that in which Drake made his epic voyage around the world. One can be amazed at her small size, her rigging and stowage and Drake's cabin, which was so central to the way in which he commanded. A similar understanding of the challenges facing those who crossed the oceans in small ships is gained by a tour of the replica of John Cabot's ship *Matthew*, which lies appropriately in the docks at Bristol, dwarfed by the neighbouring *SS Great Britain*.

In the Middle Ages the techniques of ship-making in northern and southern Europe diverged. In the north, where axe and adze were the main tools for creating planks, logs were split and re-split until wedge-shaped lengths of a usable thickness were produced, ideal for laying as overlapping timbers but with rough edges that did not permit them to be laid edge to edge. These timbers were joined one to the other by nails that were bent back on the inside of the hull to secure them firmly. In this system the stepped hull was formed first, and then into this skin was inserted a frame that held the structure together but allowed it to flex with the movement and pressure of the sea. However, beyond a certain size the flexing was unmanageable and the ship unseaworthy. In the case of Henry V's vast vessel, the 1,500-tonne

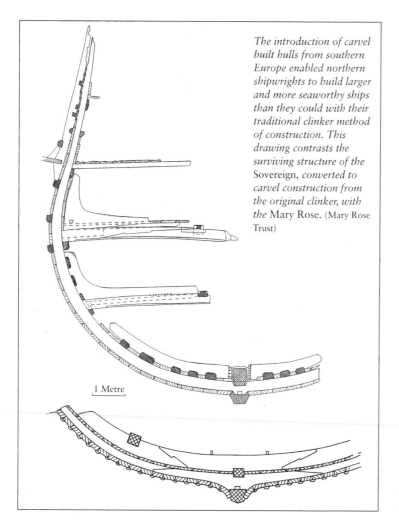

The introduction of carvel built hulls from southern Europe enabled northern shipwrights to build larger and more seaworthy ships than they could with their traditional clinker method of construction. This drawing contrasts the surviving structure of the Sovereign, *converted to carvel construction from the original clinker, with the* Mary Rose. (Mary Rose Trust)

1 Metre

Grace Dieu, an attempt was made to make her hull more rigid by over-lapping timbers three times, an enormously challenging method and certainly one that was too expensive to apply to any other than the most prestigious of vessels, for *Grace Dieu* required over seventeen tons of nails to hold her multi-skinned hull in place. These 'clinker-built' ships also needed their hull planking to be made from radially split oak, which required large, straight-boled trees. This produced excellent laminar flow but was expensive on timber while, at the same time, not efficient in making use of the standard, stubby English oak.

In the Mediterranean, larger vessels were built with a frame-first system whereby the ribs of a ship were attached to her keel, followed by the timber 'skin' bent to shape, with the individual timbers butted on top of each other in 'carvel' fashion and the gaps in between sealed with oakum and pitchblende. This building method needed smooth-edged planks cut from sawn timber but was a cheaper way to produce a sturdier vessel with far fewer specialist skills involved. Yet it was a new technique and, as such, was not entirely trusted when it was introduced into England. In 1912 the remains of a ship, thought to be Henry Tudor's *Sovereign*, was discovered in the mud at Woolwich. The evidence indicated that she had been built (in 1488) in clinker fashion but later converted, in 1509, to have carvel sides. However, the presence of wooden battens secured along the external plank seams indicates that the seamen did not place total faith in their safety on the caulking alone.[2]

Clinker ships had also developed in an age when they were powered by one large square sail, which made them speedy in a following wind but difficult to handle with any wind forward of the beam. The improvement in sailing qualities also came from the south, where multi-masted vessels, some with the quintessentially Mediterranean triangular lateen sail, a great aid to steering and sailing, were able to sail closer to the wind.

When Henry Tudor came to the throne the southern ideas of ship construction were known but not widely used in English shipyards. There is evidence to suggest that Sir John Howard had a three-masted carvel built for his own use at Dunwich between 1463 and 1466, and that although both of Henry Tudor's great ships, *Regent* and *Sovereign*, may have been built in clinker fashion, they were refitted in the carvel manner. Their accounts show only small payments to the specialist craftsmen, clenchers, berders and holders, who drove the thousands of nails into the planks and bent over the ends from inboard.[3] Henry's lesser vessels, such as *Sweepstake*, were still clinker-built, but then this method of construction fell out of favour until only small ships' boats, such as whalers and cutters, remained to preserve this ancient skill and remind the observer of the great Viking longships which were the apotheosis of this form.

Payment and Ordering

The simplest method of paying for a ship to be built was for the sovereign to order the Treasurer to pay the money over to the builder, as happened when Sir Reginald Bray made several payments to Robert Brygandyne for the building of the Portsmouth dry dock and the refitting of *Sovereign*.[4] Another method was to divert income. Henry VIII, for example, ordered that the customs receipts from Southampton be put towards the new building of *Mary Rose* and *Peter Pomegranate*. In some instances payment for ship-building came almost in the form of barter. The grants of April 1532 include one to a yeoman of the guard, Adam Sampson, to export 300 quarters of wheat free of duty, in consideration of his 'causing to be made a ship for the King's navy, called the *Trinity Guildford*'.[5]

Even the king's most senior servant, Thomas Cromwell, seems to have been involved in ship-building on the side. In December 1535 he received a letter from Nicholas Thorne, telling him that he had contracted with a shipwright of Dartmouth to new-make *Saviour* and inviting his master to direct certain abbots near Bristol to provide thirty to forty pieces of timber each for the work. Thorne also makes the point that 'there are divers woods in Wales and the forest of Dean, near the water-side, belonging to the King ... very necessary for your business'.[6]

Cromwell knew by this stage that he needed to justify his own position, and in the autumn of 1536 he set down what his administration had achieved. A great deal of this involved the Navy Royal, for which he claimed he had refitted *Mary Rose*, *Peter Pomegranate*, *Lyon*, *Katheryn Galley*, *Barke* (meaning *Less Barke*), *Minion* and *Sweepstake* as well as purchasing woods near to Portsmouth which would provide sufficient timber to new-make both *Henry Grace à Dieu* (also known as *Great Harry*) and *Great Galley*. Such a refitting programme, clearly indicated by the dendrochronology of *Mary Rose*'s surviving timbers, shows that there was no shortage of timbers of the right quality.

Work in the dockyards could be disrupted for the same reasons as elsewhere. In September 1537 Lord Admiral Fitzwilliam had to inform Cromwell that a severe outbreak of plague had been rampant in Portsmouth for the past six weeks and had killed one of the workmen on the king's new ship (presumably *Jennet*) and made two others sick, and that, as the workmen were all housed together, the rest were threatening to leave. The result caused a delay in the launch date.[7]

The use of ships for prestige lasted throughout the century, often as an indication to a foreign ruler or his representatives that the kingdom of England was not to be trifled with. Such posturing began with the launch. Thus in 1514 Sebastian Giustinian of Venice reported to the doge that Henry had launched 'a galleass of unusual magnitude ... with such a number of heavy guns that we doubt whether any fortress however strong could resist their fire', adding, gleefully, that neither the French nor the Spanish ambassadors had been invited to the launch, much to the former's resentment.[8] However, in the spring of 1538, when tensions were building up between England and France, Henry took another French ambassador, Castillon, to Greenwich and wined and dined him to the accompaniment of 'marvellous' music on board one of his great ships anchored in mid-river with two of her

Reconstructive archaeologists working timber with traditional shipwights' tools. (Author)

consorts. Castillon reported his distrust of Henry but it is also clear that he was impressed by the display of naval might.[9]

By Elizabeth's reign the funding of the building programme had been placed on a surer footing with professional shipwrights and their overseers being given a budget with which to build and repair the Navy Royal. This smooth arrangement would function well, until the question of inland counties being charged 'ship tax' led to revolution and regicide.

The Building of *Mary Rose*

Mary Rose has been studied more thoroughly than any other Tudor warship, both archaeologically and in her historical context.[10] For many years the order to build her has been ascribed to Henry VIII. However, the first reference to her occurs in a letter bearing the privy seal dated 29 January 1510 which orders the reimbursement of monies to John Dawtrey, the chief customs officer of Southampton, which he had paid out to Robert Brygandyne for the 'timber, ironwork, and workmanship of two new ships [*Mary Rose* and *Peter Pomegranate*]' plus:

> ... three hundred and sixteen pounds thirteen shillings and four pence for all manner of implements and necessaries to the same two ships belonging as particularly hereafter ensueth, first for sails, twine, marline, ropes, cables, cablets, shrouds, hawsers, buoy ropes, stays, sheets, buoy lines, tacks, lifts, top armours, streamers, standards, compasses, running glasses, tankards, bowls, dishes, lanterns, shivers of brass and pulleys ... victuals and wages of men for setting up of the masts, shrouds and all other tacklings ... which aid several sums will extend in the whole to the sum of two thousand three hundred threescore and twelve pounds eleven shillings and eleven pence.[11]

Although the statements in this document are in the future tense and talk of the ships 'to be made for us', the details of the costs involved are certainly not a speculative estimate, besides which all the previous records submitted by Brygandyne relate to work completed. It was a general Tudor rule that if you worked for the government you were paid once the job was done. For example, the smaller *Sweepstake* cost £120 3s 2d to build, while *Sovereign*'s refit in 1495 cost £595 6s 5d, and her later remaking £1,175 14s 2d. Every single penny of expenditure for these ships was accounted for ahead of payment, and it must be assumed that this was true for *Mary Rose* and *Peter Pomegranate*, which were also built by Brygandyne. If so, then it would be appropriate to think that they were the last ships ordered by Henry Tudor and not the first put down for the new king. The claim that the above warrant indicates that they were laid down in January 1510 does not therefore hold up to scrutiny, and the belief that Henry

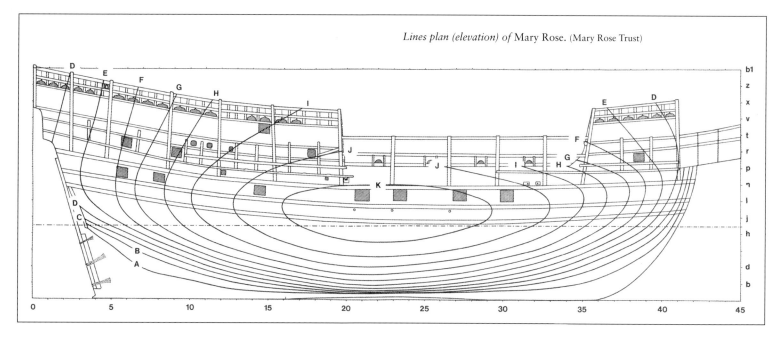

Lines plan (elevation) of Mary Rose. *(Mary Rose Trust)*

VIII founded the navy with these two new vessels is yet another myth. There are other indicators to support this idea. Firstly, in Scotland, James IV had built the 700-tonne *Margaret*, named after his wife and Henry Tudor's daughter, between 1504 and 1507, and the 1,000-tonne *Michael*, on which work began in 1506 and lasted until 1512. Admiring reports of both these great vessels filtering back to the English court would have given the young monarch pause for thought. Henry VIII was nothing if not competitive, and big ships were as great an indicator of a sovereign's virility as could be imagined. He would not have responded with two ships a third of the size of those built for his brother-in-law. It is far more likely that he would show his pride in ordering his own great ship, the flamboyant, and not too useful, 1,400-tonne *Henry Grace à Dieu*, named after himself rather than a feeble woman or guardian angel. Further support for this idea comes from the fact that, after *Mary Rose* and *Peter Pomegranate*, both well-built vessels, were completed at Portsmouth, Brygandyne was effectively demoted and further orders were not given to that yard. Instead Henry concentrated his shipbuilding on the Thames, where he could keep an eye on progress. If that is what he wished to do, he had no reason to order his first two ships from the yard favoured by his father.

Mary Rose, begun in the first decade of the new century, may well have been a carvel-sided ship from the start. Thus a revolution in ship-building techniques came about in the period of one reign. The next stage in the modernisation process was to involve changes in warship design itself.

Changes arose for a number of reasons. One was undoubtedly prestige. To own a great warship demonstrated royal affluence, just as a great park in later years would demonstrate wealth, not through what it was used for but rather rather in the sense that it did not need

to be made to provide an income for the owner. After prestige came belligerence. Henry wanted war, and the occasional skirmish against the Scots was not going to satisfy his ego, for he wanted to be seen to be able to punch above his weight. This meant European fixtures, and to play away he needed to secure his routes while denying them to an enemy – which required ships. If one can attach a certain amount of prescience to the royal mind, another reason for royal ships to be built would have been the move towards the fitting of more and heavier guns into warships, which would greatly alter the way in which a battle was conducted at sea. Such weapons could easily overpower England's small merchant ships and needed to be resisted by heavier, stouter vessels. This requirement lasted the century, and to meet it the nation was blessed with an abundance of the resource it needed to sustain a shipbuilding programme – wood.

The availability of timber does not appear to have been a major source of concern during the century. Not only the king's own estates

Smallhythe Place, a Tudor house near Tenterden, now owned by the National Trust but believed to have been built for a local shipwright. The River Rother which flowed at the bottom of the garden used to be wide and deep enough to allow ships as large as the 80-ton Mary Fortune *to be built here in Brygandyne's back yard, while the 1000-ton* Regent *was built just a little further downstream. (Author)*

but those of the wealthy landowners seemed to have it available in sufficiency. There were, however, exceptions. In April 1535 Thomas Cromwell was informed that the keeper of Woodstock Park considered that the 'marking out' of 1,100 oaks in Horam Wood designated too many from one place:[12] yet this was the measure of timber that had often to be cut to keep the new builds and refits in progress. For the building of the dry dock at Portsmouth in 1495, Robert Brygandyne paid Thomas Stutler and John Keyte a shilling a load at the start of the work for forty-nine loads of timber to be taken out of the royal forest at Hurst, just north of Portsdown Hill; they were paid a further 32s 6d the following week for another thirty-two loads of cut timber from the same source. Royal forests, of which the New Forest was the most extensive in the area, were good sources of timber for shipbuilding, not only because they were protected and managed but because large areas of them were very open, encouraging trees, especially oaks, to grow the massive angled branches that were so vital in providing strong but shaped pieces. Trees growing closely together in woodland tended to rise tall as they competed for light and, although good for planking, lacked the many shapes needed by the shipwright's team. The estates of the nobility were also good sources of supply for similar reasons. In August 1535 James Hawksworth informed Lord Lisle that he had received 3,000 pieces of timber owed to him, and that he had a further 10,000 close to the seaside and could produce 30,000 more.[13] However, a bill was presented to Parliament in 1523 to 'restrain waste of the King's woods'. It spelled out the causes of decay and destruction and ordered remedial action, such as the banning of cattle from grazing on saplings, to be taken. It also listed the many abuses practised by the keepers 'for

Above *An ancient oak tree showing the curved timbers ideal for shipbuilding.* (Author)
Below *The introduction of planks sawn (rather than split along the grain) enabled ships to be built in carvel rather than clinker form.* (Mary Rose Trust)

their own profits' and stated that as all the officials were in each other's pockets and sessions only held every twenty years 'offences were going unpunished'.[14]

The size of the major vessels of the Navy Royal soon outdid anything that was being built for the merchant fleet. By 1626, after years of trade expansion, only four of the ships operating out of Bristol were as large as 200 to 250 tonnes, and the majority were much smaller, reflecting the still limited horizons of English trade. The great ships were thus justly referred to as such, floating cathedrals among a host of parish chapels. They would have impressed and were employed frequently to do just that. Yet largeness carried with it the

problem of manning. Before 1578 the norm was viewed as one man for every one and a half tonnes; after that date a healthier and more economical ratio of one man per two tonnes appears to have been adopted. Thus in 1546 the Anthony Roll, recording *Great Harry* as being of 1,000 tonnes, lists her crew as numbering 700, implying that when the fleet was on a war footing it had to be manned by many thousands. Given the costs in wages and victuals it is not surprising that the policy of paying the men off as soon as possible, leaving a much smaller permanent staff of ship-keepers on board, was never breached. The principle also meant that the larger vessels were only manned when dire necessity dictated. *Great Harry* and *Mary Rose* spent most of their careers laid up: it was ships such as *Minion* (300 tonnes, crew without soldiers 120) and the 160-tonne *Mary Guildford* that were used as the royal workhorses in time of peace.

The stout, many-branched English oaks *Quercus petrea* and *Quercus robur* grew ideally for the shipwright's purpose, for his practised eye needed to see the frame and timbers of his vessel in every straight trunk and angled branch in just the same way as a Renaissance sculptor could see his finished work in a block of Carrera marble. The five types of timber needed were:

1 Great timbers: these were over twenty feet long and almost two feet across and were needed for the keelson and the stern post;
2 Compass (or crooked) timber: the large curved logs used for frames and the stem;
3 Straight timber: large straight logs used for the deck beams, wales and stringers;
4 Planks and boards: thinner pieces of straight wood cut to about one to six inches thick;
5 Knee timber: angular logs used for knees and similar positions.

The master shipwright or his agent would identify the trees that were to be felled to provide these timbers, and payment was agreed before felling began. This involved a laborious process of sawing and axing before loads could be made suitable for hauling out of the woods on carts or tugs drawn by two or three horses. Brygandyne was regularly recording such entries as 'Also paid in likewise for the hire and wages of five cartmen each of them with his eleven horses carrying stuff to the said dock ...' and 'Also paid to William Purcer and his company by covenant in great made at Hampton as well for carriage of certain masts to the waterside and there to be made in a raft and so to be conveyed to Portsmouth – 14s.'[15]

How the calculations as to what timbers were needed is made clear in a document of 1514 on the building of the *Great Galley,* where we find laid down much detail on the measurements of the ship and her timbers and lists of the materials used in her construction.[16]

It did not always suit Henry to demonstrate his bellicose plans for his fleet. In 1515 the French ambassador, De Bapaume, wrote to the Regent of France that Henry had ignored suggestions that he should take advantage of Francis's absence on campaign to invade France himself. Far from building his great ships for war, Henry explained, he had built them merely to 'please his Queen and his sister Mary', for they 'were not built to make war on either France or Scotland, but merely to be in readiness for anything that might happen'. De Bapaume went on to describe how Henry delighted in his new ship, for he had:

> ... acted a pilot, and wore a sailor's coat and trousers made of cloth of gold, and a gold chain with the inscription *'Dieu est mon Droit',* to which was suspended a whistle, which he blew nearly as loud as a trumpet. Mass was performed on board by the Bishop of Durham, and the Queen named the galley *'The Princess Mary'.*[17]

With the timber arriving at the yard the work on the building could begin. In the early years it would appear that the vision of the ship existed solely in the master shipwright's mind, where he guarded it jealously, but with the development of printing and the spread of reading skills ideas were gradually, and with some trepidation, committed to paper. This was a major breakthrough for construction. Whereas previously a shipwright had to be present to ensure that his plans were executed, now, with a plan and a drawing, a set of instructions could be despatched to a yard with orders to make good the design.

The sails for all these vessels began life in fields of flax and hemp such as those around Bridport in Dorset, where production was supported by state decree. Sailcloth itself was produced in East Anglia, but eventually the majority was imported from Brittany; evidence of how lucrative a trade it was can be seen today in the fine merchants' houses in the village of Locronan, which produced a wider cloth, allowing the sails to have fewer seams and therefore more strength. Much of this sailcloth was exported through the port of Pouldavid, which gave the material its name 'Poldavys'.

So important was the trade in sailcloth to both England and the Breton merchants that ways were sought to keep the supply flowing even in periods of tension or open warfare. Thus in January 1539, the French ambassador, Castillon, wrote to Montmorency, the Constable of France, explaining that Henry had sent a deputation to him requesting not only that the Frenchman use his influence to secure the release of a delivery of sailcloth, already paid for, that was impounded in France but that the English be permitted to purchase a further 3,000 pieces of sailcloth from France. Since most ships required only between twenty and twenty-five pieces, Castillon saw this as a clear indication of preparations for war. He advised that not a single piece should be exported without licence, and also recommended additional caution, for he realised that the Breton merchants would trade with or without such authority.[18] Castillon was in no doubt that should his intervention be discovered he would be in danger, for in the next paragraph he begged to be recalled because Henry, 'the most dangerous and cruel man in the world ... is in a fury and has neither reason nor understanding left'.

Although Henry was building his own fleet, at times of crisis there was still a need for the state to take ships up from trade. London and Bristol were the obvious ports from which ships could be hired and then fitted out for their operational role. In 1513 men were employed for most of February at 15d per week to rig both *Mary Craddock* and *Anthony Craddock,* while conduct money of 6d per man for every twelve miles was paid to bring sixty mariners from Pembroke to Bristol to man them. Additional money, some £251, was paid for retaining other Bristol ships to serve the 'King's army royal by sea'.[19] A manuscript of 1513 lists twenty-four ships hired to support Edward Howard's fleet, including ones from Bristol, Newcastle, Topsham, Dartmouth, Hull, Harwich, Brixham and Calais as well as five Spanish vessels, whose owners did rather better on the deal, being paid 1s 3¾d

Above The imposing merchants' houses of Locronan in Brittany give a good indication as to the wealth generated by the manufacture of sailcloth. (Author)
Below Locronan's top-quality sailcloth was produced on looms like the one shown here in a museum in the town. (Author)

per tonne as against the 1s per tonne paid to the English.[20] One of the English ships, *Nicholas of Hampton*, was lost when Arthur Plantagenet sailed her on to the rocks off Brest, and another was sunk by the French galleys. [21]

Other ships were purchased by the speculatively ambitious such as Thomas Seymour, who as Lord Admiral established his own regular pirate 'car-boot sale' in the Scillies, wrote in November 1544 to the Privy Council enquiring whether the king wished to buy *Mary of Hamborrow* for £350. If not, Seymour indicated, he was prepared to fund her purchase himself.[22] The crown did conclude the deal, only to sell her for £20 in 1558.

The age also saw a change in the names given to royal ships. The old tradition was to use, literally, Christian names, often linking them to the sovereign. Thus Henry VIII held a nap hand of *Henry Grace à Dieu*, *Christ*, *Jesus of Lubeck*, *Trinity Henry*, *Gabriel Royal*, *John Baptist*, *Mary Rose* and *Peter Pomegranate*.[23] None of Edward's new ships had such names, nor surprisingly had Mary's additions. By the sixth decade the tradition had faded away, and the new names continued to be held by ships of the Royal Navy up to and including the twentieth and twenty-first centuries. Thus there have been seven ships named *Mary Rose*, thirteen called *Revenge*, ten named *Dreadnought* and five named *Ark Royal*, all but the first entering the records as race-built galleons of Elizabeth's reign.

Whatever the name, in general sea-going commanders were pleased with their vessels. Sir Edward Howard's great delight leaps from the pages of his correspondence. John Hawkins was to write to Burghley that 'The four great ships, *Trinity*, *Elizabeth Jonas*, *Bear* and *Victory* are in the most royal and perfect state: you could not tell them that they had been at sea more if they had ridden at Chatham.' His brother William considered the Plymouth ships to 'sit aground so strongly and are so staunch as if they were made of a whole tree'. The shipwrights' skill was to convince those on board that what the Hawkins brothers mused about was, to all intents, true, but it was a difficult task.

The Keel

It was upon the keel that the strength of the ship depended. So important was this great timber that often a false keel was secured beneath it to protect the main keel from damage that might be inflicted by the ship running aground, which in a time of limited charted information and constant struggles with the elements was a frequent danger. Drake's epic circumnavigation might have ended in disaster, even though he had accomplished all that he had set out to do, when *Golden Hind* drove herself firmly on to a coral reef. That she did not founder there and then was due to the double sheathing, including a false keel, with which she had been fitted. The ship's preacher, Fletcher, might have considered the peril just reward for the crew's past sins, but their salvation came from having a good sound hull and a good sound seaman in command. Nevertheless the ship's survival was very much in doubt, as was made clear:

As touching the ship ... lying there confined already upon the hard and pinching rocks, did tell us plain, that she continually expected her speedy dispatch, as soon as winds should come, to be the

A contemporary illustration of the building of the Ark shows the initial stages of ship construction: the keel has been laid, and stem piece set up. The main frames are temporarily shored up and a shipwright is shaping them with an adze. In the background a raft of timber is being poled down the river. (National Maritime Museum PW8304)

severe executioners of that heavy judgement, by the appointment of the eternal judge already given upon her, who had committed her there to Adamantine bonds in a most narrow prison.[24]

The timber of choice for a keel was elm, which was long and straight and defied rot when immersed in water. The alternative was oak, which was not as long-lasting, especially if used when green. The length of most warships meant that no one timber could be produced long, straight and sturdy enough to serve as the keel, so sections had to be joined together. *Mary Rose*'s thirty-two-metre keel, roughly 0.35m square, consists of both oak and elm, which might indicate that pressure was being placed on completing her construction within a given time. The joints by which the keel timbers were held together, along with the stem and stern posts at either end, were the most important in the entire ship, for this was the backbone of the vessel and it could not afford to have any weaknesses. The timbers were thus secured using long vertical angled joints, known as scarphs, held together by long bolts. A contract of 1583 for a 200-tonne ship stated that the fifty-eight-foot keel was to be made from two fourteen-inch square timbers bolted together through a six-foot scarph. With such joinery the keel would endure.

The keel would have been laid upon blocks raised above the slipway to enable work to take place easily underneath the vessel when the frames and planking were fitted. It would have been necessary to place these blocks accurately to prevent the keel from hogging or sagging as the weight of the ship increased above it. In spite of this, measurements of *Mary Rose*'s keel show that it was distorted in both the horizontal and the vertical planes, an indication, unless caused by centuries on the sea bed, that construction still relied on the craftsman's eye and experience in handling natural materials such as wood. On top of the keel another long scarphed timber was bolted – the keelson – to which the frame of the ship could be attached.

The Stem

In 2005 a dive sponsored by the Ministry of Defence led to the raising of the stem of the *Mary Rose*, enabling another piece of the jigsaw of naval ship construction to be confirmed by solid evidence. The stem post, a curved structure, was scarphed both along its length and on to the forward end of the keel. Its forward 'rake', together with the lesser outward angle of the stem post, created an increase in the ship's length overall compared with that of just the keel itself. There is no reason to suppose that throughout the long Tudor century stems varied in any significant detail from that raised from the Solent in 2005.

The Stern

The concept of a flat wide stern, as opposed to a narrow rounded one, had been introduced some while earlier, although there remained merchant ships whose sterns resembled their bows. The flat transom stern was not only believed to improve steering but also created a deck upon which heavy 'stern-chaser' guns could be mounted. Philip of Cleves, an early producer of fighting instructions, stated that 'On each side of the rudder there should be a ... cannon mounted suitably for this position. They should have port [lids] which can be hoisted with lines at will, so that they can be fired whenever the weather permits.'[25]

The Anthony Roll shows how widespread the practice had become by mid-century, with each major vessel fitted with at least two stern-chasers low down, supported by lighter guns above them: eight in the case of *Henry Grace à Dieu* and six on board *Mary Rose*.

Below the water-line the stern remained narrow, with the frames and planking rising significantly to form a narrow open triangle between stern post and ship's side. This gap had caused the turbulence that degraded the rudder's performance once it was moved from the side to the stern of the vessel. The answer was to fill the space with 'deadwood', shaped to increase the laminar flow of water at the stern and therefore to give the rudder, suspended from the stern post, more bite and thus improve the steering of the vessel, especially at slow speed. The stern itself derived its shape from the aftermost frames of the ship's side, which were more solid than the others and were curved to form 'fashion-pieces' which gave form to the sides of the stern and a secure frame, on to which the sternmost hull planking was attached by the use of a rabbet (or rebate). The stem post itself had to be solid and secure enough to take the massive weight of the ship's rudder, which was attached to it by several large iron rings swivelling on great pins. Solid though this area was planned to be, it does seem to have had a structural weakness. In 1589 the leaky great carrack *Sâo Thomé*, built in a similar way to English vessels,

> ... began to ship water in a greater quantity than before and by another and more dangerous place, which was at the stem, below the sleepers by the aftermost fashion-pieces, where it is most difficult to get at them than in any other part ... the water which was very violent, as it was expelling oakum from the seams and the lead plates which were nailed on top.[26]

The Rudder and Tiller

The rudder was a truly enormous barn-door-like structure whose great unbalanced weight had to move readily in response to the muscle

The transom stern of the London replica of Golden Hind *demonstrates how the rudder was hung and the low position that the tiller entered the hull.* (Author)

power of a single steersman at the end of a whipstaff attached to the tiller. To achieve this, the rudder was mounted to the stern with two or more hinge-like fittings. On the rudder itself long bands ended in downward-facing pins, called pintles, which were placed in strong sockets, called gudgeons, mounted on the hull. Being made of iron, these hinges rusted readily in salt water and would need constant maintenance and replacement if they were not to snap off under the great weight which they had to bear. Similarly, large seas, especially from the stern, could shift the rudder bodily off its mountings. All ships' carpenters would have had to be prepared to rig jury rudders to avoid disaster. The engraving of a carrack made by William à Crucis in 1468 seems to show a line and purchase being secured to the ship's rudder, which, although an eminently sensible precaution, features in none of the Anthony Roll drawings.

The Whipstaff

The sixteenth century saw little advance in the methods by which a ship was steered. It is most likely, although the evidence is not present, for example in the recovered hull of *Mary Rose*, that Tudor warships were steered by means of a whipstaff, as the first ship's wheel does not appear to have been fitted until at least 1704. This extraordinarily late development, given the great force over which the steersmen had to exercise his authority, might appear inexplicable, but the absence of such a logical and efficient apparatus illustrates how good the response of the crew was, and had to be, to the shouted command.

Steering by whipstaff was simple but manpower-intensive. At the top forward end of the rudder a short tiller entered the ship at main deck level, and to this, at its forward end, was attached a post rising vertically to the upper deck. By pushing this pole to larboard or starboard the rudder could be moved a few degrees in either direction. In front of the whipstaff, and lit by a shielded candle, would have been a compass rose so that the helmsman could steer the ordered course. What he could not do from his position was to see where the ship needed to go and to steer her accordingly, as when entering or leaving harbour or when keeping station on a ship ahead, although in some vessels he could see the sails and adjust his course to keep the wind at the desired angle for the set of the sails. Manoeuvring orders would have had to be relayed from the master or officer of the watch. It was an awkward arrangement, with the potential for both error and erratic steering, but it seemed to work, and there are few examples of naval ships being grounded or lost through poor steering. Although such disasters did occur, the general report is of ships that responded well when handled well.

The Frame

The move to carvel construction meant that the frames were fitted next over the top of the keel to give the ship the ribs of its skeleton. Yet again, no oak timber was large enough for a ship's frame to be made from one shaped piece, so numerous lengths, or futtocks, were used, and these too were scarphed together. The frames closest to the keel were called 'floor-timbers' and were bolted at right angles to the keel. They were fitted closely together but with gaps between them and with limber holes cut to allow waste water and filth to drain down to the lowermost point of the vessel, from which a bilge pump could extract them. The frames, of course, gave the ship its symmetrical shape. The timbers had thus to be shaped in pairs and then raised together to ensure that they matched in distance from the centre-line throughout their entire length. They would have been assembled alongside the vessel and then raised together by sheer-legs. In all probability the midships and widest frame would have been positioned first, followed by a forward and an after frame so that the lines of the ship could be easily seen and adjustments made to subsequent frames. At this stage the frames were insecure and liable to move from the vertical: they

The ergonomic inefficiency of whipstaff steering is clearly indicated in this drawing: in heavy seas the steersman would require assistance from other crew members and the use of a block and tackle to keep the ship on a reasonably steady course.

were therefore joined together by thin long strips of wood, known as ribbands (ribbands), that would be removed once the planking was in place. The ribbands would also emphasise any irregularity in the potential curve of the planking caused by inexact fitting of the frames; as these were not fully secured, adjustments could be made to ensure that the ribs were true before the planking was secured to the frames by wooden dowels up to a metre long, known as treenails, or trenalls.

The Planking

Oak was once again the wood from which the ship's planks were made. These timbers, ranging from two to four inches thick depending on their location and the size of vessel being built, were fitted horizontally, and care was taken that no two joints lay above each other causing a potential line of weakness in the hull. At the stem and stern the planks would have fitted into a rabbet cut into the appropriate post. With clinker-built ships the planks overlapped and were held together by long nails. In carvel construction, rather than the planks being laid immediately upon each other in the horizontal plane, a gap was left between each line of planks which would later be filled with tarred fibre to make a watertight seam, its integrity increasing as the timber either side of it swelled when wet. This created a problem in marrying a long plank to the side, as it had nothing horizontal to rest against. Nails would have been used at the extremities to hold the plank in place, and then a carpenter would use a long auger to bore a hole through the plank and into the frame behind. Into this hole, sometimes tarred first, a trenall would be driven and hammered home, and then, occasionally, a wedge would be driven into the end to tighten the joint further.

Occasionally the shipwrights got it wrong and leakages or even flooding could ensue. In the Scottish war of 1497 a store ship, *Marie Orford*, leaked so badly that 'bowstrings 3 barrels; 3 bills, 10 marlin

The starboard side of Mary Rose, *the largest surviving section of a sixteenth-century warship in the world.* (Mary Rose Trust)

spikes; 1 hackebush; 1 barrel of gunpowder; i barrel of charging ladles; 16 spade and shovels; and a cresset and cresset stave' had to be written off.[27]

On other occasions the leakage could be more alarming. In 1513 Edward Howard voiced his concerns in a letter to Wolsey, stating: 'Sir, the *Katherine Fortileza* has so many leaks by reason of Bedell the carpenter that worked in her at Woolwich that we have had much to do to keep her above water. He hath bored an 100 auger holes in her and left it unstopped that the water came in as it were a sieve.'[28]

Howard was forced to send a maintenance party of caulkers over to the leaking vessel to keep her afloat. Crew morale would not have been improved by the fact that she was also a badly victualled ship, with the admiral himself having to replenish her with his own beer and food. Ships such as this gained a reputation for being unlucky, and it is no surprise that *Katherine Fortileza* ended her career early after suffering storm damage in 1521.

Trenalls were never placed in line either vertically or horizontally: to do so might have encouraged the planks or frames to split along a weak grain. To secure the 'skin' further to the 'skeleton', the lowermost planks were fitted into a rabbet on the keel, and they were sometimes also made of elm to delay the onset of rot.

The Wales

The first planking timbers to be fitted, known as 'wales', were much thicker than the others and served to both strengthen and protect the thinner planks above the water-line; being larger and stronger, they ensured that the frame shape remained true while the remainder of the planking was being attached. Once the wales were fitted the ribbands could be removed. After gun-ports became common the wales ran above and below the openings, thus adding strength to this potentially weaker area of the ship's side. The wales were also used for the attachment of standing rigging and were a useful handhold and foothold for anyone trying to climb up the ship's side from a boat. On the topmost wale, or 'gunwale', it was possible to fix spigots on which swivel guns could be mounted.

The Castles

The distinguishing feature of fighting carracks was their towering fore- and after- castles. Had these been built, like the rest of the hull, from stout timbers, the vessels would have been far too top-heavy not to overturn in even a moderate sea. To avoid this, they were constructed from a frame made from light lengths of fir, to which equally light boards of poplar, or fir, were attached. This provided adequate cover against the weapons that the soldiery gathered here would face, while not producing too much top-weight, especially when they were manned for action. Another advantage of having a light frame was that castles could be prefabricated and left ashore, to be raised on to the decks of merchant ships only when the monarch required them for military purposes. The introduction of heavier weaponry and different tactics made these tall structures redundant.

Inboard Planking

The inner frames of the ship were also joined longitudinally by oak planks, which further increased the ship's strength and its resilience to battle damage. At the level of the hold, extra-thick planks, known as stringers, were fastened to the frame to provide even greater strength. Over the keel itself, to which it was attached by iron bolts, a bulky timber, known as the keelson, ran the whole length of the ship. This not only increased the strength of the ship's bottom but provided additional bulk to absorb and distribute both the weight and the flexing of the main mast, which was secured here in a box-like structure called the mast step. Up forward a smaller step housed the fore mast, which was probably built on to the stem. To reinforce the ship's bottom a number of short and bulky internal frames, known as riders, were fitted across the keel. Finally, timber braces, both vertical and diagonal, were fitted to the hull internally to complete the reinforcement.

The completed hull represented the most complicated dynamic structure of its age, well

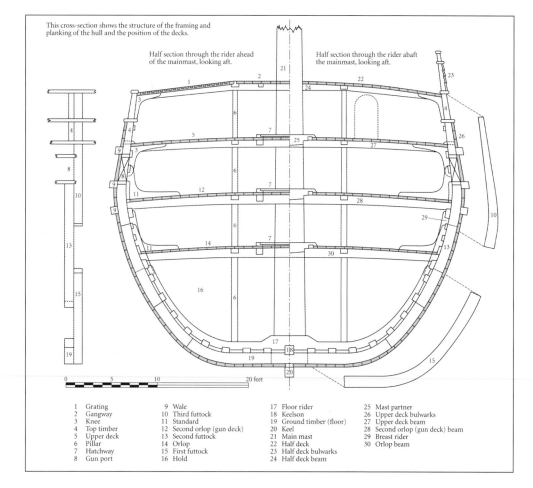

This cross-section shows the structure of the framing and planking of the hull and the position of the decks.

Half section through the rider ahead of the mainmast, looking aft.

Half section through the rider abaft the mainmast, looking aft.

0   5   10   20 feet

1	Grating	9	Wale	17	Floor rider	25	Mast partner
2	Gangway	10	Third futtock	18	Keelson	26	Upper deck bulwarks
3	Knee	11	Standard	19	Ground timber (floor)	27	Upper deck beam
4	Top timber	12	Second orlop (gun deck)	20	Keel	28	Second orlop (gun deck) beam
5	Upper deck	13	Second futtock	21	Main mast	29	Breast rider
6	Pillar	14	Orlop	22	Half deck	30	Orlop beam
7	Hatchway	15	First futtock	23	Half deck bulwarks		
8	Gun port	16	Hold	24	Half deck beam		

A reconstruction of the probable structure of one of Hawkins's 'race-built' galleons. By later standards the framing was not massive and the hull form was relatively fine. (Drawing by Peter Wilkinson)

able to handle the buffeting of wind and water and the occasional grounding. Like any skeleton it became invisible when the outer skin and inner fittings were in place. This is one reason why *Mary Rose* is such a delight; she is the one ship's skeleton we have from an age when ship construction was developing rapidly throughout Western Europe. If close observation is not possible, however, there is one other place where the complexity and skill of the shipbuilder can be imagined. Walk into any tithe barn, such as that at Bradford-upon-Avon, near Bath, and gaze upwards: here, in a more limited form is presented the marvel of the work of a master craftsman in wood. The Tudor ship's hull was similar, but its construction required a greater understanding of the complexity of spherical geometry than for any static structure erected upon shore.

At this stage the ship, with its empty cavernous interior, did resemble an upturned barn. Now was the time for the carpenters to go inside to convert the hulk into a habitable and usable fighting ship with decks for guns, accommodation and stores. This involved the fitting of beams to support a number of decks within the hull and the raising of castles both fore and aft.

The Hold

Below any deck, at the bottom of the ship, lay the hold. Here, below the water-line, space had to be available for sufficient ballast to create stability as well as room enough for bulky stores such as spare hawsers, barrels of tar and victuals, and beer and water, also contained in barrels.

The Masts

A ship would be launched before her masts or ballast had been fitted. This gave the shipwrights the opportunity to survey the empty vessel for any weaknesses or signs of leakage before these were hidden by fittings or ballast. The hull, afloat for the first time, was thus temporarily unstable, and so great care was taken to secure her in a way that would not lead to her swaying to the effects of wind and tide.

The masts were vast trunks of wood, as many as three of them rising above each other to form the main mast and fore mast. A great ship like *Mary Rose* had nine masts situated in five positions: the bowsprit, fore mast, fore topmast, main mast, main topmast, main topgallant mast, mizzen mast, mizzen topmast and, furthest aft, the bonaventure mizzen mast. This arrangement provided a far more sophisticated and efficient way of handling the ship than did the single masts and huge square sails of the previous century.

The requirement for large, lengthy and straight timber for masts placed a great strain on the woodlands of England, where such trees were rare. Ideally, for the sake of strength a mast would have been shaped from a single tree, but composite masts, with timbers being bound around a central spindle, were not uncommon; indeed, such an arrangement could give the mast a flexibility that would make it less likely to break when under great strain. A study of the wreck of *Mary Rose* indicates that her main mast had a diameter of about four feet and her fore mast was two feet thick, while both masts would have exceeded a hundred feet in height.[29]

Raising such a mast vertically and swinging it over to be lowered into a ship would have required sizeable blocks and tackle; among the items that Brygandyne ordered for the dock at Portsmouth were eight

This replica top in Golden Hind *has sufficient space for a number of suitably armed men to take station.* (Author)

'great block pulleys for raising up of masts'. These would have been supported either on sheer-legs built at the dock side for ships in refit or on rafts for vessels being new-built.

Rather like a sapling being planted but on a much larger scale, a mast needed to be heeled in at the base and secured along its length to prevent movement and to distribute the forces that would act upon it at sea. At the lowest end of the mast a tenon was shaped to fit neatly into a mortised socket in the mast step, a rectangular bulk of wood placed upon the keelson. The mast step was further held tight by short timbers buttressing it against the first stringer on either side of the keelson and by being trenalled to the timbers beneath. Protection against rot was provided by tarring the heel and drilling holes in the mast step to allow water to drain into the bilge. Where the mast passed through a deck it was clamped in position by two semi-circular timbers, or mast partners, which because they were secured to the deck timber in turn transmitted the strain to the hull as well as checking any sideways movement.

The fore masts of these ships were too far forward to be attached to the keelson and so had to be stepped to the stem, while the smaller mizzen mast generally ended on the orlop deck. The requirement for space in which to move the tiller or whipstaff through its whole arc meant that the bonaventure mast would have to be heeled in even higher in the ship.

Masts were purchased from wherever they might be available, but, they were also taken from ships being broken up and transferred to those being refitted. Thus Robert Brygandyne paid Adrian Lockyer of Southampton to provide *Regent*'s fore mast, bonaventure and main topmast but bought her bowsprit from Brankyn, a Dutchman. Lockyer was also paid to repair the *Regent*'s main mast by 'fishing', that is, for replacing rotten sections with sound timber and then binding them together.

Moving such great lengths of timber to the yards must have been tricky, and using water transport the only feasible way to do this. It would, therefore, be interesting to know how and where *Regent* was fitted with her original suite of masts, built as she was upstream on the banks of the narrow river Rother.

The Yards

The great timbers to which the sails were attached were themselves the size of small masts and so sometimes could not be made from a single length of wood. Thus one-half of *Regent*'s main yard was delivered by Adrian Lockyer while the other half was provided by John Dawtrey. However, the Anthony Roll records just two two-piece yards, the main yard of *Henry Grace à Dieu* and the long single lateen yard of *Galley Subtile*; it must be assumed that other great ships had similar composite yards.

The choice of spruce indicates that shipwrights knew their timbers: unlike fir, although equally light and long, a spruce timber has its strength concentrated on its surface rather than in the heart wood. English shipbuilders were trading with the Baltic from an early date for mast and spar timbers, and Prussia was the major source of supply, a fact reflected in the derivation of the English word 'spruce' from that nation's name.

To haul such a large timber as a yard up a mast required a great deal of manpower. In order to overcome the friction, the yard was secured to the mast with a set of rollers known as parrels. This allowed the yard to be rolled up the mast, reducing the resistance and making the task easier for the many seamen straining at the ropes. The roller balls themselves, each set grouped in a line of ribs, were fashioned from walnut, a tree whose wood exudes natural oils and is thus self-lubricating.

The Rigging

Rigging had two main functions: to support the masts and to control the sails. In the first instance it was termed 'standing' rigging as it needed to be tensioned and unmoving to restrict as far as possible the tendency of the masts to sway both laterally and fore and aft as they responded to the immense pressures being imposed upon them by wind and weather.

Standing rigging was generally tarred to preserve it; most of that which was recovered from *Mary Rose* was of this type, the smell still apparent after centuries of immersion. Fore and aft movement of the masts was restricted by a line of standing rigging stays running from the bow to the stern, bracing the masts against the enormous force of the wind. The snapping of a stay through either wind or battle damage could result in the catastrophic collapse of a mast. Firing chain shot into the rigging was thus an excellent tactic with which not only to slow an enemy vessel but to cause mayhem on board as mast and sail crashed down on to the deck. There is little evidence, however, of the English firing high during the Armada campaign.

Along the hull, standing rigging shrouds were secured to the hull by means of chains and dead-eyes, forming a tackle that could be tensioned to take up the effects of the rope stretching through wet and

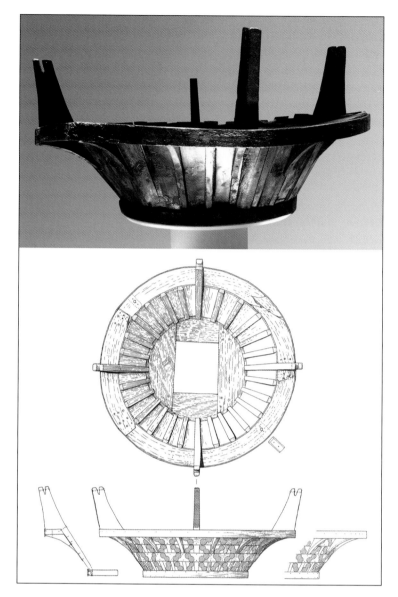

This much smaller top recovered from Mary Rose *shows a structure that could only have provided space for a lookout or a refuge for a sailor working aloft.* (Mary Rose Trust)

wear. To prevent chafing and to give the rigging a clear run to the mast head, the lower dead-eyes of the chain purchases were secured to a chain-wale or wide plank channel that also helped to spread the load along the length of the hull. As it rose upwards above the upper deck, the standing rigging had cord tied across it to form rat-lines, making a rope ladder to help seamen clamber aloft. The first set of rigging met the mast at the junction between main mast and top mast, where a refuge provided a lookout, a resting place and a fighting-top from which to fire down upon an enemy's deck. A complete top was recovered from *Mary Rose* which has scarcely room for two men to secure themselves, a far cry from the many manned fighting-tops that can be seen in the much later *Victory*.

Running rigging for handling the sails formed the most complicated part of the sailing tackle. Numerous sheets and lines led to each sail and yard, and it was in the management of the handling of these by the crew that a master gained his reputation. Some lines were straightforward lengths of rope; others led through blocks or tackle to form purchases so as to increase the advantage for those hauling on them. Each line leading to a yard or sail had its own place on the ship's side or by the mast where it and only it was secured; 'learning the ropes' was what turned a landsman into a seaman. In a ship such as *Mary Rose* or *Revenge*, the total length amount of rope in use measured several miles.

In the fourteenth century Bridport in Dorset gained a reputation for making both good rope and canvas. Gradually it lost its preeminence, and even ships being fitted out in Portsmouth had much of their cordage delivered from (King's) Lynn on the Wash or, when international relations allowed, from Brittany and Normandy. Action was occasionally taken to support cable making at Bridport, such as the Act of Parliament in 1529, but economic reality meant that production from there was bound to decline.

By 1536 Richard Cavendish was writing to Cromwell that he had:

> ... received £400 to expend on ropes and cables for the King's ships; but, finding no provision of such in Hamburg, has expended part of the money in pitch and tar, which are dear in England [and that he had] sent home by the Minion 4 last of pitch and 18 last of tar, and still has 24 last of tar which has been paid for.

Soon after this he reported that Gonson had written to him 'desiring him to procure cable, yarn, or hemp which cannot be got in Flanders or France'. Having considered foreign markets, he eventually procured this from a merchant of Rye for £600.[30]

By 1557 the English had established rope walks at Kholmogory and Vologda in Russia, and in 1588 Hawkins placed an urgent order for 'great cables to be made in Muscovey' to the value of £3,000, a staggering contract which by the end of the century had increased to £10,000 per annum, thus writing off the future for the Bridport workers: then as now, international trade had local repercussions.

The Hawsers

Thicker rope was required for such tasks as berthing and for the anchor cables. The latter required great cables, which were provided according to a formula for each anchor. The best sheet anchor required cable of a circumference of half an inch for every foot of breadth of the ship at her midship point; thus a 32ft beam vessel needed a sixteen-inch cable. The cable circumference was then reduced by an inch for each of the lesser anchors in turn. The size of the anchor to be attached was worked out by squaring the cable circumference and dividing the answer by sixteen to give the weight of the anchor in hundredweight. Thus in the example above a sixteen-inch cable held a sixteen-hundredweight anchor, while a twelve-inch cable was sufficient for a nine-hundredweight anchor. The formula was used all the way down to the ship's boats, so that one with a six-foot beam was provided with a three-inch hawser, to which was attached an anchor weighing 2qtr 7lb.

The rope walks of Lynn outlasted those of Bridport although, unsure of their quality, Brygandyne sent John Easton of Portsmouth to Lynn to examine the product there. His report was obviously favourable, for a crayer (small cargo ship) was hired to bring hawsers for *Regent* from Lynn to Portsmouth. But Brygandyne also had a

Deadeyes could be made on board by the ship's carpenter as they did not need to be as well crafted as blocks with pulleys. (Mary Rose Trust)

The heart-shaped deadeyes on the Golden Hind replica show how the standing rigging was secured to the ship's side. (Author)

Parrels provided a roller mechanism to ease the raising and lowering of yards and to help to swing the yard around the mast to trim the sail to the prevailing wind. (Mary Rose Trust)

A ship required hundreds of blocks and pulleys to work the rigging and raise the anchors. A selection of types and sizes from the Mary Rose. *(Mary Rose Trust)*

A selection of sheaves from the Mary Rose *indicates the variation in design necessary to suit the task of each item. They are generally made of a single piece of ash or elm. (Mary Rose Trust)*

Tudor vessels required miles of rope of varying circumference, requiring acres of fields in which to grow hemp and hundreds of men to work in ropewalks to keep the fleet supplied. These examples were recovered from the Mary Rose. *(Mary Rose Trust)*

A detail from a contemporary map showing a ship riding to double anchors; this not only provided a firmer hold but also reduced the swinging circle in confined waters.

favourite more local supplier, and 'my lady Astrye Saylyng', also known as 'Dame Margery Astrie, widow, of Southampton', features in many of his accounts as a provider of cordage.

Rigging was also held in the great storehouses at Portsmouth, Chatham and the Thames, for this, the vital thread for any sailing ship, frayed easily, aged quickly and soon lost its tensile strength. All ships carried spare lengths, from anchor hawser to sail-making twine, and much time on board would have been spent splicing, sewing and replacing worn cordage.

The Sails

The actual making of the sails was from the earliest times a dockyard activity. Bolts of canvas, one yard broad and twenty-eight yards long, would be delivered sufficient for each ship, and a sail-maker would stitch them together. In 1602, according to the records, *Triumph* required ninety-five bolts of canvas for her sails, *Ark Royal* some eighty-five and the smallest galleon, *Advantage*, thirty-six, while the pinnace *Spy*, of forty-two tonnes, needed just fifteen bolts.

Sewing the canvas strips together was a specialist task, for seams needed to be sturdy enough not to split when under full sail. Along the sail edge bolt-rope was sewn in to prevent fraying and to give both tautness to the sails when spread and a position to which eyes could be

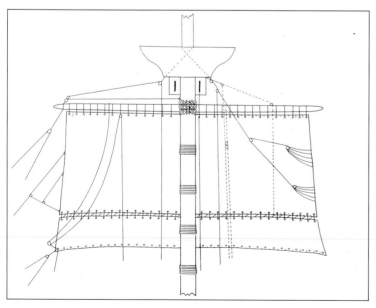

The rigging of the Mary Rose's *main sail shows how complex a machine the Tudor warship could be.* (Mary Rose Trust)

fitted for lines to be attached, such as those required to secure a 'bonnet' to increase the sail area when the wind was favourable. Although the early records show sail-making taking place at the dockyards, two Breton craftsmen were brought to Deptford in 1552 for the purpose of training local sail-makers in the 'manufacture' of the heavy durable Poldavys sail cloth, made from good-quality hemp cloth.[31]

Painting and Bunting

Royal ships by their very title were required to cut a dash, and a coat of paint and some flags blowing in the breeze quickly added a grandeur to their presence and a sight of which their sovereign could be proud. Robert Dewke, a painter with a team of four, worked on *Regent* from March until May 1495 to coat the ship with 'diverse colour and other stuff'. For the nine weeks' work the men received £13 plus victualling, while when *Mary Rose* and *Peter Pomegranate* arrived in London on their maiden voyage, a John Browne was paid £142 4s 6d to paint and stain banners and streamers for them which had already cost over £50 to purchase. *Mary of the Tower* was decorated by another Londoner, Thomas Haden, using say cloth painted red, yellow, green and white.

The ships of the Anthony Roll are magnificent in their finery: great long pennants, with the red cross of St. George at the halyard, and yards of Tudor green and white bunting streaming well aft from every mast; massive square banners, thirteen in the case of the flagship *Henry Grace à Dieu*, fly the length of the ships at upper deck level. That this pageantry is not exaggerated can be confirmed by a swift glance at the 1514 inventory,[32] in which the flagship is recorded as carrying sixty large and one hundred little flags, eight streamers and forty-nine standard staves. For *Katherine Fortileza* these are listed in greater detail as:

Streamers	2
Pendants	24
Spanish paveses	2 dozen
Banners of Saint George the field silver	6
Banners of the arms of England in metal	3
Banners of Saint Edward's arms in metal	3
Banners of the arms of England and Castile	4
Banners of the same sort in colours	4
Banners of Castile in metal	4
Banners of the rose crowned in metal	4
Of the same sort in colours	1
Banners of the rose and pomegranate crowned in metal	3
Of the same sort in colours	2
Banners of the portcullis crowned in metal	3
Banners of Saint Anne in metal	1
Streamers of the dragon and greyhound in colours	2

These were magnificent habiliments, and yet the painting of the ships mentioned above, supposedly showing Henry embarking at Dover for the Field of the Cloth of Gold, an occasion for pageantry if ever there was one, shows the great ships soberly flying just short St George's ensigns from their mast heads, with only *Great Harry* indicating the king's presence on board with three royal standards. The pomp continued, and at the end of the century Hawkins and Drake sailed to

The Navy Royal was built to impress and each ship carried standards, flags and streamers to impress foreign dignitaries and ambassadors. This detail from the famous Cowdray print shows the English fleet arrayed for battle.

shifted from side to side, inducing a state of loll. For another, it did not breathe, allowing noxious effluents to gather in a noisome manner, a perfect stew in which both rats and disease could breed. The problem was summed up in graphic detail by Sir William Winter when he wrote on 21 October 1578 to Lord Admiral Clinton about the reason why ships' timbers were decaying, a problem that he placed squarely on the use of gravel or shingle ballast:

> I do find that it is the ballast being gravel which could not be trenched by reason of the Cook rooms that were made upon the same, and of the often leakage of beer with the shedding of water upon the said ballast which did breed such a damp therein as it did taint both timber, plank, trennel, and the iron work that lay near unto it: for remedy whereof ... it is thought good that there be cooks' rooms devised upon the orlop in the best wise that may be for safety, and that the ships be ballasted with stones which will suffer air to go through: The quality of stones that most serve for the Navy would grow to a round charge if it should altogether be had from the quarries near Maidstone.[33]

Winter believed that not much stone would be necessary from this source, as he wanted the Treasurer also to authorise the digging up

the Indies with four royal standards, thirty flags displaying the cross of St George, eighty-three streamers and twenty-six ensigns.

The Ballast

Ships built in Portsmouth had no problem with ballasting. As anyone who has strolled along the city's foreshore knows full well, the whole seafront is a long stretch of shingle, which is easy and free to load up by boat and carry into the harbour. Shingle was thus often the ballast of choice, but it had disadvantages. For one thing, if it became water-logged it could flow like a liquid and make the ship unstable as it

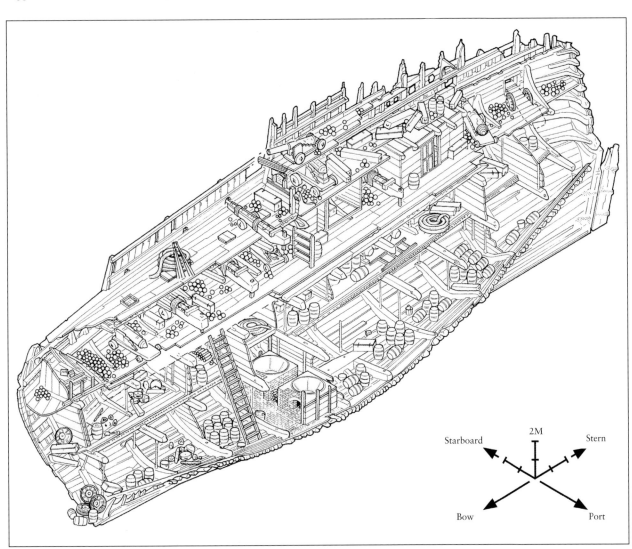

Starboard 2M Stern

Bow Port

An isometric projection of the Mary Rose *showing the internal arrangements and the positions within the hull from which the various objects were recovered.*
(Mary Rose Trust)

and removal of the stones that formed the foundation to Rochester Castle! The Maidstone quarries that he mentioned had produced the Kentish ragstone, which was chipped to form the stone shot supplied to vessels such as *Mary Rose*. If Winter had had his way, rather than run short of shot during the Armada campaign Howard's fleet could have loaded their guns with ballast! A brilliant reserve armoury which did not materialise.

Neither was shingle as easy to remove or clean as rock when it was considered necessary for reasons of health to replace it and inspect, scrub and disinfect the timber beneath. This required either the ship being taken into dock or, if no dock was available, careening her over on her side, never an evolution without inherent dangers. Drake did this in the Spice Islands, but by then much of his original ballast had been replaced by ingots of gold and silver. More prosaically, many a captain, uncertain of the effect on his ship's stability of the weight of weaponry on his higher decks, placed some guns in the hold to serve as ballast until they needed to be hauled up when action was imminent. It was the need to rummage (clean out) his ballast that brought Thomas Howard and his fleet into a bay in Flores, where, but for the timely delivery of a warning from Cumberland, they might have been trapped along with *Revenge* by the Spanish navy in 1591.

Because ballast was bulky and expensive to transport, it was brought to ships from the nearest source of supply. *Sovereign*, while berthed at Erith in the Thames prior to her voyage to Portsmouth for refitting, was ballasted with 110 tons of ballast brought to her by local tradesmen. This provisioning provided a useful source of income, and it was the handing-over of the sales rights for such ballast in the Thames that guaranteed the future of Trinity House.

Above the ballast the hold could also be used literally as a 'hold' into which prisoners could be placed, secure but uncomfortable in conditions as miserable and morale-sapping as those in any oubliette ashore, although those for whom a ransom might be anticipated would have been accommodated in more pleasant surroundings.

The hold also held one of the most important fittings of the ship – the galley. Placed here, the weight of its ovens added to that of the ballast, and their heat could rise up through the decks of the ship, providing the only source of warmth. This did have its down side, not only as indicated by Winter; it was also thought by some that the heat of the ovens, placed directly on top of the ballast, dried and shrank the bottom timbers, causing the seams to open and the ship to leak – a good excuse for poor husbandry.

The Pumps

A visitor to *Mary Rose* today cannot but be impressed by how snug her bottom timbers fit even after hundreds of year on the sea bed, but however well built they are, wooden ships inevitably leak, and it is the reduction and management of these leaks that indicate the most skilful shipwright and the most cunning carpenter. As long as planking did not spring or split, and as long as battle damage, grounding or poor handling did not create potential disaster, day-to-day leaks, along with the draining of rainwater and other of liquids, could be controlled and discharged by use of a pump.

Ships pumps' were marvels of technical skill. Many consisted of a single length of timber – alder would have been a good wood to use –

out of which the core was drilled using an auger many feet in length. Judging, by eye, the line of the bit so that it kept true to the centre was a skill that almost defies belief. Down through this tube ran an endless rope or chain to which were fitted shallow cups that were drawn up through a series of waterproof leather seals, and these, once at the top, discharged their content into a drain or 'dale' leading to the scuppers from which the water flowed overboard. The pump was positioned next to the main mast, for not only was the main mast step the lowest part of the ship, to which all waste water would naturally flow, but it was also imperative to keep the mast's base as dry as possible to delay the onset of rot.

It was an arduous, continuous and necessary process, for pumps were ship savers. They had saved Drake in *Revenge*, and at the start of the Azores voyage in 1597 Essex reported that *Mer Honour*, which had been launched only in 1595, was '... falling asunder, having a leak that we pumped eighty tons of water a day out of her ... most of her beams broken and rent, besides the opening of all her seams'.[34] On other vessels whose documents of despair have not survived, the crew would have had to pump even harder.

The Orlop Deck

Above the hold, deck beams, about a foot wide and slightly less thick, stretched across the hull to form the orlop or overlap deck. At their ends they rested upon a 'clamp' of timbers which ran along and were secured to the ship's side through the frames. Further security was provided by shaped rising knees bolted to each deck beam and also to the ship's side. The knees were each cut from a single piece of timber, their angular shape proof of the importance of crooked as well as straight timber in ship construction. Longitudinally on top of the beams were placed the deck planks. Further reinforcement and allowance for hatches and the ventilation of the galley were created by the use of half-beams and sturdy square-cut 'carlines' that ran fore and aft. There are indications that the thin planking of the orlop deck was subject to wear and rot. When Brygandyne refitted *Regent* in 1495 he paid thirty shillings for a hundred fir planks to repair her orlop and poop decks. Fir would not have been very durable; at the time when *Mary Rose* sank, her orlop deck planks were mostly made from thinly-sawn elm which appears to have been recently fitted, suggesting that a more durable planking had been selected to cure the problem of rot.

The Hatches and Companionways

Access between decks was through hatches, most of which, especially those on the upper deck, had covers made from a number of oak planks nailed together. Through the hatches, removable ladders or stairs linked the decks. As these were not load-bearing and often needed to be removed so that the hatches could be closed, they were made from lighter timbers such as pine. All around the hatches a combing of raised timber was built to prevent any water sloshing about on the deck from flowing down to the deck below.

The Bulkheads

Each deck was divided into compartments by a number of transverse bulkheads, which were made from thin planks taken from lighter wood. These served to divide areas of storage one from another and,

to scuppers and thence overboard. Where the masts passed through the deck, half-beams and carlings would have provided a strongly edged opening sufficient to minimise structural damage should a mast shift or be sprung. The mizzen mast and bowsprit step were housed in mast steps at this level, adding their great weight and pressure to the load-bearing requirement and stress that this deck had to withstand.

Although the main deck was the crew's living space, it made for a troglodyte existence. If the hatches were open then a rectangle of light would exist around the companionway, but the gun-ports would have been kept closed while at sea until action was imminent, for, as *Mary Rose* demonstrated all too tragically, open ports invited the sea to enter whenever the ship heeled. Lanterns provided some relief from the gloom before 'lights out', when only those in cabins were allowed to retain lit candles and then only if these were enclosed. In *Mary Rose* a small rectangular ventilation shaft was cut in the deck head above the guns to allow the egress of gun-smoke, but this would have allowed very little light below decks. Stygian gloom it might have been, but with so many bodies crammed so tightly together it was warm, companionable and, as long as a breeze blew through, not too smelly.

The Gun-Ports

The breakthrough in warship development came when the main deck was converted into a gun-deck. This innovation appears to have been introduced in France around 1490 by a Breton shipwright, Descharges, who cut square holes into a ship's side and made them watertight by fitting closely sealing lids made from thick oak, which could be raised by a purchase and closed snug by bolts. Ports themselves were not so new, for a 1468 picture of a carrack at anchor shows a large cargo port cut below the upper deck. Interestingly, she appears to be of carvel construction, for to add such a feature on a clinker-built ship would not only weaken the integrity of the hull but also render it most difficult to make watertight, given the overlapping form of the surrounding timbers. The difference that gun-ports made can be best seen by comparing a picture of the (reconstructed) fifty-tonne *Matthew*, John Cabot's flagship, built originally in the 1490s with her small circular upper-deck gun-ports, with the similarly sized and rigged *Falcon* of 1544, whose guns are clearly one deck lower. A picture of the French flagship of 1512, *Grand Louise*, also shows circular gun-ports, but these have been cut into the main deck. The design, and the method of fighting that these ports engendered, would last until HMS *Warrior* joined the reserve fleet in 1896, its demise coming about only with the introduction of the traversing turret gun. Just as importantly, the introduction of the gun-port signified the breakaway of warships from merchant ships. While both continued to carry guns, the arming of the main deck of warships rendered them of little use for carrying bulk cargo. Of course, room could always be found for small, highly valuable items, such as ingots, jewels and spices, but because these were normally acquired by force their transportation did not conflict with, and indeed was made more likely by, the possession of a well-armed vessel.

The Castles

With the main frames of the ship and thus its planking ending just above the upper deck, the two castles could be built lighter because

An overhead view of the decks of Mary Rose. (Mary Rose Trust)

on higher decks, the cabin accommodation for the officers. None were watertight

The Main Deck

Once the main deck became the deck upon which the main armament of the ship was placed, it had a heavy load to bear. This was reflected in its construction, in which every feature was substantial and well secured.

The deck clamp for the main deck beams would have consisted of as many as seven or eight sections of timber, secured to the hull by trenalls. At this height above the keel the distance across would have been wide enough to require the midship deck beams to be made from at least two sections of timber scarphed together. Their own weight and the load they had to bear meant that as well as using rising knees they would have been secured to the hull with horizontal 'lodging' knees. It was also considered necessary for the ship's watertight integrity to waterproof the main deck, so the seams between the deck planks were caulked and drainage courses were cut to channel water

One of the large bronze guns recovered from the Mary Rose displayed in the ship's museum, in front of a reconstructed section of the hull showing the gunports. The weight of guns that could be taken to sea had been limited by stability considerations, but the introduction of the gunport allowed the biggest guns to be carried low down in the hull, eventually leading to the creation of ships able to sink their enemy by weight of fire. (Mary Rose Trust)

they were not integral to the strength of the vessel. Thus they could provide height for offensive close-quarters action and protection to those gathered there without too much effect on the ship's stability. Concerns about the latter were also alleviated by curving the sides inward from above the main deck; the resultant tumble-home was thought to add to stability by keeping upper-deck weapons closer to the centre-line. However, the lightness with which castles could be built encouraged the early builders to elevate them so far that the vessel crabbed sideways in the wind; an effect that the false keel mitigated but by no means cured. The main change in design in the move from carrack to galleon was the removal of the towering castles in favour of vessels with lower lines.

The Cabins

Apart from the captain, whose cabin was aft, those officers who had their own cabins lived in cramped conditions, their main and obvious luxury being a bunk. Those who had a working trade – the pilot, carpenter, barber-surgeon – kept their tools with them and in the case of the barber-surgeon would have used their cabin for their business.

Also to enhance their dignity, they probably kept a 'piss-pot' by their bunk. For those who were not seamen, such as embarked army officers, a cabin also gave them somewhere in which to retire to when the misery of seasickness took hold. In his poem written during the 'Island Voyage' of 1596, John Donne illustrated the misery of the cabined landlubber:

> Some coffin'd in their cabins lie, equally
> Griev'd that they are not dead, and yet must die;
> And as sin-burd'ned souls from grave will creep,
> At the last day, some forth their cabins peep:
> And tremblingly ask what news, and do hear so,
> Like jealous husbands, what they would not know.

Drake's cabin in *Golden Hind*, of which we have several good descriptions emphasising the high standard of living and entertainment that he maintained, even during the protracted circumnavigation, was very small, measuring just 5m by 2.25m at its widest point and narrowing to just 1.45m at the stern, with a height of 1.75m. The admiral and captains may have lived apart, but they shared, in a much more immediate way than did their land army equivalents, the discomfort, deprivation and danger of their men.

Mess-decks were a much later introduction into warships; the Tudor seamen lay down where space was available. For most of the men, 'bed' consisted of a lozenge of the main deck where one could avoid being trampled on by those on watch doing their rounds. Naturally members of a gun crew would gather around their weapon, but for most any place where they laid their heads was home.

The external hull of the Mary Rose with the castles and other superstructure reconstructed.
(Mary Rose Trust)

From his small cabin in Golden Hind *Drake was able to plan his voyage round the world and to entertain with panache his officers and impress many a reluctant guest with his lifestyle. This reconstruction aboard the* London *replica is based on the many surviving descriptions.* (Author)

The Upper Deck

Stability, as well as a lighter load, dictated that the upper deck could be of a lighter construction than the main deck beneath. It was also a more complex structure, consisting of an open central waist and a fore and after-castle. The natural curvature of the decks at this level also meant that it was often stepped at its ends to maintain sufficient headroom within the castles.

This was the working area of the ship, exposed to both wind and sea, but access as well as protection was needed. To retain an uncluttered, obstruction-free deck, instead of using rising knees the upper deck beams were attached to the hull by 'hanging knees', i.e. secured from below. The main timber along the ship's side was the gunwale, whose position marked the top of the main frames. At right angles to this were placed oak 'standards', and between these were fitted light wooden flats or pavises, some of which were removable to allow archers to fire at an enemy while they themselves were protected by the blind in place. The flats were made of lighter wood, poplar in the case of *Regent*, for which two sawyers were paid 4d a day for making

one hundred of them. The watertight integrity of the vessel was aided by the deck planking being well caulked and by care being taken to ensure snug fits at the butt ends. As with the main deck, water was encouraged to drain overboard through scuppers, which were sealed with scupper leathers to prevent seawater from flowing back through them. Robert Brygandyne paid 3s for eleven scupper leathers when building *Mary Fortune*.

The work of construction and the skills and techniques involved in building a royal ship were just a part of the story of creating a fleet. Funding had to be found, orders placed and paid for and, most importantly costs recorded, justified and audited. Thus while work got under way out in the yard, the shipwright and his team had to rely on a man working in a cramped office to ensure that materials of the right quantity and quality were delivered in a timely fashion. This was the task for a project manager; pre-eminent among those in the early Tudor period was Robert Brygandyne, appointed Clerk of Ships by Henry Tudor in 1495 and remaining in post until some time after 1523. The two Henrys may have shared and funded a vision; it was to be Brygandyne who made it a reality, for the creation of a viable standing navy relied on his officialdom and orderliness for its survival just as, two centuries later, similar dedication was to earn Pepys the epithet of 'Saviour of the Navy'.

Caulking and Sheathing

However well built a ship was, and however watertight her seams were, she was destined to spend her life with her hull in water, which of itself and with the creatures it supported would attack her timbers until, without due care, they perished. Before she had been long at sea, weed would attach to a ship's side, and this in turn attracted barnacles and other creatures, many of which – such as the infamous and aptly named ship-worm *Teredo navalis* and the isopod *Limnoria* – had a voracious appetite for wood. The inevitability and speed with which exposed wood failed increased when vessels entered the warmer waters of the south. But even in the north, salt sea worms, crustaceans and rot reduced stout timbers to sponge and then nothingness. Not a single timber of *Mary Rose* that was not covered up by conserving silt survived to be brought to the surface. In contrast, a ship such as the Swedish warship *Vasa*, which sank in icy, almost fresh, water was recovered with her timbers intact.

To prevent and deter rot, the exposed underwater timbers of a ship were coated with a mix of tallow and pitch, spread on with sheep skins. Brygandyne required four dozen fleeces, for which he paid 12s, to make 'mappes for laying on of piche rosyn and tallow' on the hull of *Sovereign* in 1495. The smaller *Sweepstake* required just one dozen for the same job.

However well the initial work was carried out, a standing navy needed to ensure that at relatively short intervals, a ship was brought into dry dock or up slips so that its bottom could be cleaned and re-treated. This usually involved burning off the growth and scorching the surface until it was bare wood once more. With no blow-torches in their chests, shipwrights set light to large bunches of broom, which created a good but controllable blaze. Before the re-caulking described above, *Brygandyne* burned or 'bremed' *Sovereign*'s hull with eight loads of broom bought for 10s 8d from Stoke, near the dockyard.

Wooden vessels needed to be hauled out of the water periodically and the sides cleaned and recaulked and tarred. Furthermore, the weed and other encrustation clinging to the hull, which severely reduced the vessel's speed, needed to be burnt off with twigs of broom in a process known as breaming – as shown in this contemporary Dutch engraving.

Such treatment was needed not only to prevent rot, but also to clear away the weed, whose presence had a noticeable effect on the ship's speed. Keeping the underside streamlined was important not only for vessels, especially pirates' ships, that needed to catch an escaping vessel, but also for merchant ships wishing to escape. Yet to be effective this time-consuming and labour-intensive activity needed to be repeated often. In an effort to reduce its frequency John Hawkins introduced the concept of sacrificial sheathing, whereby an outer skin of timber was placed over the ship's main planking with a sandwich of tar and horsehair in between, which in Richard Hawkins's opinion either was poisonous for the worms or, more likely, choked them.

Away from dockyards, ships' captains had to find suitable beaches on which to drag their ships, relying on the local tidal range to expose sufficient timber, when the ship was careened, for the hull to be scraped and treated. This Drake felt obliged to do, for both the reasons described above, on the coast of California, at a site whose whereabouts are still the subject of controversy. The laying of a ship almost on its beam ends could be dangerous both at the time, if water-tight integrity was compromised, and in the longer term, because the strains imposed might inflict permanent damage. The following report, although referring specifically to a Portuguese experience, the loss of *Santo Alberto* in 1593, illustrates the point well, for her foundering was blamed not on storms but on:

> ... careening ... because it costs much less to careen a ship than to lay her aground ... for besides the rotting of the timber caused by being so long in the sea, it is unduly strained when the hull is heeled over for careening, with the great weight of such huge carracks. When they are caulked this way they do not take the oakum properly, being damp and badly dried. And afterwards during a voyage, when they are tossed by heavy seas and buffeted by strong winds, the caulking comes away and the open seams let the water in.[35]

The Anchors

Before a ship could sail away she needed to have her anchors delivered and secured. These not only fulfilled the obvious function of keeping her at rest in a harbour, where she could swing around her anchor with the tide, but, much more importantly, held her off the rocks when stormy seas tried to drive her ashore. They were her first and last resort, and it is no wonder that ships carried several of these great iron works. The 1514 inventory records *Henry Grace à Dieu* as having

The recovery of one of the Mary Rose's *anchors. Up to eight were carried by the largest warships to provide some security when anchored in strong winds.*
(Mary Rose Trust)

'two sterbord, two ladbord, two destrelles to sterbord, two destrelles to ladbord, one shot [sheet] anchor, one cagger [kedging], and ten spare'.

The largest anchor recovered from *Mary Rose* is almost 5m long with each arm 2.4m in length, and with flukes 0.6m wide. In 1495 Brygandyne paid £12 for a second-hand anchor to use as the starboard bower for *Regent* and £25 for two others, 'one of them serving for a laterborde Bower the other for a laterborde destrell'.[36] For the much smaller *Mary Fortune*, he paid out £3 15s 4d for three of her anchors, while that ship's boat anchor and a hook cost 21d for 14lb of iron. The stock cost an additional 8d.

Prizes, Purchases and Impressments

As with many a navy, a building programme was not the only way to increase the size of the fleet. The Scottish pirate Andrew Barton's two ships, *Lion* and *Andrew Barton* (renamed *Jennet Prywin*), captured by the Howard brothers in 1511, entered the fleet for a brief period, disappearing from the record by 1513. Thomas Howard's French prizes, captured in Morlaix in 1522, lasted only a little longer, nothing more being heard of them after 1525. The Scottish prize galleasses *Unicorn* and *Salamander* lasted from 1544 to 1552 and 1559 respectively, with the former being sold for £10, while the two French prizes captured in the Forth in 1560, *Speedwell* and *Trywright*, were not broken up until 1579. Ralegh was to add the large Spanish galleons *St Andrew* and *St Matthew* to the royal collection following the raid on Cadiz in 1596 but they were given away in 1604, confirming the view that English seamen had an obvious preference for English hulls.

It was not all one-sided, however: *Mary Willoughby* was taken by the Scots in 1536 and not recaptured until 1547. The French also captured the pinnaces *Roo* and *Brigantine* and the rowbarge *Flower de Luce*.

A temporary need to increase numbers, especially for such auxiliaries as victuallers, was always catered for by hire or impressment – which only meant being hired without the option to refuse. In 1513, for example, thirty-nine ships totalling some 2,039 tonnes were pressed from eighteen south coast ports, and the owners were paid £306 11s 6d.

More permanent planned additions came about through the purchase of merchant ships. On 5 September 1539, during the invasion crisis, Thomas Spert wrote to Gonson that he had viewed *Great Nicholas* of Bristol and could find no fault with her except that she drew three fathoms of water in ballast and three and a half when laden. She also carried a number of guns, and anchors and hawsers, and he considered her to be worth £700 except for her deep draught.[37] Within the household expenses of the king for that year is a record showing that on 15 November, William Spratt was paid £600 for the ship,[38] so her draft clearly cost him dear. For comparison, the draft of *Mary Rose* was 4.6 metres.

It was Sir Thomas Seymour who realised, in 1544, that *Jesus of Lubeck*, with her owner drowned, might be sold by the hapless man's brother for a bargain £400,[39] thus adding a name to the fleet that would achieve notoriety when her elderly timbers were smashed to pieces by the Spanish at San Juan de Ulua in 1567. At least she lived to be elderly: Henry's other great Lubecker, *Great Elizabeth*, was wrecked off Calais in 1514, only months after being purchased and fitted out, writing off a £2,333 6s 4d investment. Only a marginally better investment was the leaky Genoese *Katherine Fortileza*, which served from 1512 until being damaged by storms in 1521, her crankiness possibly due to her being built for kinder climes.

With so many senior naval men running their own private navies, it is no surprise that a two-way trade between them and the state sprang up for either the hire or the purchase of hulls. Thomas Seymour was gifted *Minion* for his piratical purposes in 1549, and, most famously of all, Walter Ralegh's *Ark Ralegh* (renamed *Ark Royal*) travelled the opposite way to legitimacy in 1587.

Summary

It is probably best to leave the summary of what had been achieved in a century of development to the views of a contemporary. Admiral Sir William Monson, writing once the eighteen-year-long war against Spain was over, eulogised the royal ships which had been:

> ... continually employed on the Spanish coast, in the Indies , and other places, continually abiding and enduring the fury of all winds and weather, never out of motion and working in troublesome waters, never for the space of three, four, five or six months so much as putting into harbour or anchoring, and having any other refreshment from shore, but tossing on the waves of mountainous seas that never break, in comparison of ours that seem but little hills to them ... yet, not one of her Majesty's ships ever miscarried, but of *Revenge* ... by the unadvised, negligent and wilful obstinacy of the captain.[40]

And even *Revenge* was to earn a positive place in naval history.

Chapter Four

Arming the Fleet

These iron-hearted navies ...

Hasting to meet each other in the face;

At last conjoined, and by their admiral

Our admiral encountered many a shot.

By this, the other, that beheld the twain

Give earnest-penny of a further wreck,

Like fiery dragons took their haughty flight;

And likewise meeting, from their smoky wombs

Sent many grim ambassadors of death.

Then 'gan the day to turn to gloomy night,

And darkness did well enclose the quick

As those that were but newly reft of life.

No leisure served for friends to bid farewell,

And if it had, the hideous noise was such

As each to other seemed deaf and dumb.

Purple the sea whose channel filled as fast

With streaming gore that from the maimed fell.

Shakespeare, Edward III

By the end of the fifteenth century England's industrial development still lagged behind that of mainland Europe in many areas, including the manufacture of weaponry, especially artillery. By the end of the sixteenth century she was an arms exporter and, in the area of naval weaponry, had achieved a pre-eminence that was to last for over 400 years. The first decades of those hundred years saw a marked change in ordnance, as a result of which the most modern of the heavy guns that went to sea in *Mary Rose* resembled those that were used by both Nelson's gun crews and the men on board HMS *Warrior* in the middle of the nineteenth century. While the world changed, however, a seaman gunner's life both above and below decks stubbornly stayed the same; Robins's statement of 1742, 'The formation of artillery hath been very little improved in the last two hundred years; the best pieces now cast not differing greatly from those made in the time of the Emperor Charles V', could have been written a hundred years later with equal validity.

So the developments that took place in Tudor times, although not simple, straightforward, or entirely progressive, ushered in a new age of warfare at sea, based on the heavy gun fired by a professional naval gun's crew, rather than on lighter shot fired by an individual who was often a soldier embarked for just one voyage.

Given a free hand to produce the ideal heavy weapon for the gun-deck of a Tudor ship, the designer would have wanted a quick-firing, breech-loaded, short-barrelled weapon that was cheap to produce and fired a standard shot. Instead, ships were fitted with long-barrelled muzzle-loaders which were slow to reload and whose expensive barrels were all of slightly differing bore sizes. The reasons for this paradox were linked to metallurgy, manufacture, safety and the quality of gunpowder. It was not, essentially, an issue of tactics or range, but it led to the demise of the intrinsically useful quick-firing breech-loaded iron gun until it could be revived in the age of steel.

As might be expected at a time when both new methods of manufacture and new materials were being introduced into warfare, a large variety of weapons was produced with a plethora of names until the stable solution of the cast-iron cannon overcame all competition. Tables of armament, either contemporaneous or modern, tend to contradict each other, for the boundaries between the names and descriptions of various types of weapon, measured by shot diameter (calibre), shot weight, shot type (iron, stone, lead, etc) or barrel length (in calibres), were never exact. There are, however, some categories which define a weapon according to whether it was made of brass or of wrought or cast iron, and whether it was breech or muzzle-loaded.

The few fixed points include the fact that most bronze weapons were muzzle-loaded and fired iron shot while most wrought-iron weapons were breech-loaded and fired stone shot, but in the period of transition during the early Tudor years even this definition did not hold true in all cases.[1]

In addition to the fluidity of nomenclature there were subdivisions to be considered, depending on either the thickness of metal in relation to the calibre at the touch-hole, trunnions and muzzle or, more identifiably, the relationship of the bore to the weapon's length. In the latter instance the following definitions applied:

Legitimate pieces: guns of a standard bore-to-length ratio;
Bastard pieces: guns with a larger bore and shorter length than standard;
Extraordinary pieces: guns with a smaller bore and a longer length than standard.

Thus the best-crafted weapon recovered from *Mary Rose* is defined as a bastard demi-culverin – much to the delight of visiting schoolchildren.

The confusion caused by the multiplicity of names and size was recognised at the time. Lucar, the great authority on all gunnery matters, wrote:

Through an intolerable fault of careless or unskilful gun-founders all our great pieces of one name are not of one length, nor of one-weight nor of one height [calibre] in their mouths, and therefore the gunner's books, which do show that all our great pieces of one name are of an equal length and of an equal weight and of an equal height in their mouths are erroneous.

Given the view of the experts, who, after all, had to ensure that the ordnance worked to best advantage in battle, those with just an academic interest may have spent too long discussing the perceived variations. Any list must thus be a compromise between clarity and diffuseness.

Weapons of Wrought Iron

Listing weapons of iron is even less straightforward than listing those of brass, which itself is not easy. Being of greater antiquity, the former retained their medieval nomenclature, which related more to the fact that they spewed out fire and smoke than to their length or size of shot.

Before the age of mass production almost every gun cast was unique in bore, length and shape. These examples were raised from the Mary Rose *site and are now displayed in the museum.* (Mary Rose Trust)

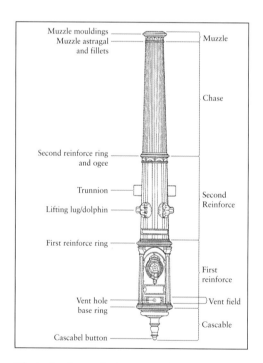

Muzzle mouldings
Muzzle astragal and fillets
Muzzle

Chase

Second reinforce ring and ogee

Trunnion
Lifting lug/dolphin

Second Reinforce

First reinforce ring

First reinforce

Vent hole base ring
Vent field

Cascable

Cascabel button

The parts of a standard cast gun. (Mary Rose Trust)

Thus the heavy bow-mounted galley gun was a *basilisk* (the mythical dragon that could kill with its breath), and the *serpentine* was named for similar reasons, while the rather confusing *sling* was not named from the way it was mounted but from the German word *Schlange*, a snake. The concept lasted into the Bronze Gun Age, with the word *culverin* being derived from the Latin *coluber*, also meaning a snake. The aptly named *murderer* defines its own purpose, while *hail-shot pieces* are also self-explanatory. *Port pieces* acquired their name more understandably, being weapons that protruded through gun-ports in the ship's side rather than being mounted on the upper or castle decks.

The term *serpentine* was so widely used that it must have been a generic name for a mounted gun, in the way that 'cannon' was to be. It was one of the few terms used for both brass and iron chambered ordnance, with *Regent* being listed as carrying twenty-nine brass serpentines and 141 iron ones. This listing gives an idea of the reliability of the various types of material, for on returning from the Scottish campaign of 1497 *Regent* landed twenty broken iron serpentines and only one damaged brass one.[2] However, the record does not give an idea of the individual sizes. Given that neither *Regent* nor *Sovereign* had gun-ports, they would have had to confine their heavy ordnance in the waist, with lighter weaponry being placed in the castles, so the 225 serpentines in the former and the 141 in the latter must have varied considerably in size. L G C Laughton considered the serpentines carried on *Katherine Fortileza* in 1513 to be 30-calibre guns firing a 1½lb shot and weighing 1,176lb,[3] but Corbett considered an Elizabethan serpentine to be a 400lb gun, firing a 5⅓ ounce ball charged with ⅓lb of powder. Whatever their size and distribution, their function was to be used at close quarters in the anti-personnel role.

The serpentine thus became a weapon of transition, being finally made of brass while still employing the tried and tested method, used in iron guns, of breech-loading with spare chambers, until sufficient confidence and experience was gained with the new material to complete the transition to muzzle-loading. This concern may have lain behind Henry's determined but cautious reform and development of his royal arsenal. His first order to the Malines gun-founder Hans Poppenreuter included a dozen brass serpentines as well as muzzle-loading curtows.[4] This movement towards brass muzzle-loaders can be

Port pieces had a distinctively medieval look about them, with a barrel made up of welded staves, and a separate breech chamber. They were the first type of gun to go to sea, but were eventually replaced by cast bronze and iron guns. (Mary Rose Trust)

seen in the reduction of serpentines and other iron guns recorded in various inventories as the century progressed, although the smaller iron weaponry remained.

Port Pieces

The first major weapons that the navy took to sea were breech-loaders. These were made from wrought-iron staves, about two inches wide and half an inch thick, welded together around a wooden core or mandrel and secured in place by white-hot hoops of iron slid over them and hammered into place as they shrank. The barrel thus produced was an open-ended tube to which, at the breech end, a 'chamber' of similar diameter, fitted with a handle, could be lifted into place when required for firing. Shot was placed in the barrel, jammed in by a wad, and the chamber, loaded with gunpowder, placed behind the barrel and firmly secured in place by both a soft wooden wedge and a hard iron disc. The gunner then poured some gunpowder from the powder horn slung around his neck through the 'vent' hole and, once the target was lined up, blew on his fuze of slow-burning cord, wrapped around a yard-long wooden rod called a *linstock*, and lit the powder train. There would have been a noticeable delay while the powder burned down before the gun itself fired, but then the chamber could be quickly removed and a new shot inserted, behind which could be placed another loaded chamber already prepared.

The most sophisticated powder horns had a spring mechanism behind the pourer that would shut it off as soon as the gunner removed his finger. This not only prevented powder from spilling out but meant that, by the use of a simple count while the horn was in use, the gunner could fill the vent with an identical charge of powder each time. A linstock was carved in the form of an open dragon's mouth, through which the fuze was led after being wrapped around the stock. These personal possessions gave an opportunity for creativity, and some are beautifully carved, displaying the gunners' pride in their work.

Whereas the expert Lucar considered that, 'every chamber piece ought to have three chambers', the Tudor inventories show that each weapon usually came with two chambers, another example of their parsimony at work. Thus the 1514 inventory of *Mary Rose* records

weapons as listed in the table below. It also lists a number of forelocks (wedges) for the various types of guns and the hammers to drive them home.

Weapons Recorded in the Inventory of *Mary Rose*

Murderers of iron	1	Chambers to the same	2
Cast pieces of iron	2	Chambers to the same	4
Murderers of iron of another sort	1	Chambers to the same	2
Slings of iron called demi-slings	2	Chambers to the same	4
Serpentines of iron	28	Chambers to the same	107

To aid the movement of the larger guns the barrels were mounted on 'stocks', some of which had a pair of wheels fixed to them, while others simply lay on the deck. Eight were recovered from *Mary Rose*, along with the remains of some of the stocks on which they were mounted. This could mean that the heavy guns facing aft, the stern-chasers, were also port pieces. The very heaviness of the larger guns was one of their drawbacks, for the chamber, which had to be lifted and wedged into place each time the gun fired and then removed, required four men to lift and shift, and even then the men needed the barrel at the breech end to be low enough for them to achieve this. As a result, the trunionless guns slumped on low beds of elm were hard to train and elevate whether a pair of wheels were fitted or not.

Not all wrought-iron guns were mighty port pieces. The quick-firing nature of the weapons meant that they were ideal for use close in to an enemy ship, either to clear her decks prior to boarding or to discourage her boarders from entering one's own vessel. The lighter guns, known as fowlers, slings, bases and murderers, could be placed higher in the ship and mounted on the side by a spigot and fitted with an iron rod protruding behind the chamber holder, thus enabling the gun to be

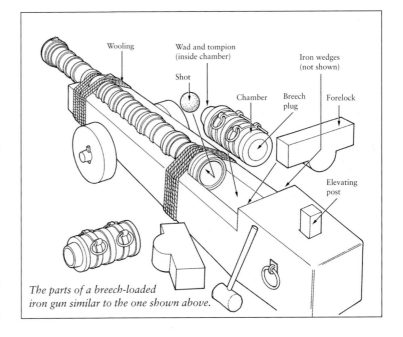

The parts of a breech-loaded iron gun similar to the one shown above.

trained with one hand for close-range use while the other hand held the fuze. Richard Hawkins admired them greatly, 'for that their execution and speedy charging and discharging is of great moment'.[5]

The most famous reference to these weapons comes in Thomas Audley's fighting instructions, where he wrote about boarding:

> In case you board your enemy enter not till you see the smoke gone and then shoot off all your pieces, your port-pieces, the pieces of hail-shot, crossbow shot, to beat his cage deck, and if you see his deck well ridden then enter with your best men, but first win his tops in any wise possible. In case you see rescue, scuttle the enemy ship but first take the captain with certain of the best with him, the rest be committed to the sea, for else they will turn upon you to your confusion.[6]

Because of their man-maiming role, the bases and murderers were given a wide range of shot to discharge. This included lead, which was formed around an off-centre iron wedge to produce a spin, and cannister shot, sharp shards of flint or iron held loosely together in a wooden tube which would scatter on firing.

In theory this made for a weapon that could keep up a reasonable rate of fire provided that both barrel and chamber did not overheat and cause a premature explosion. The problem lay in the wedge. Firstly, it was almost impossible to get a perfect seal around the chamber. This led to the escape of gases and hence a diminution in muzzle velocity and thus range. The second problem at the back end was that a badly inserted wedge or too much powder could result in the wedge being expelled with great force to injure the gun's crew. Lucar, writing in 1588, stated:

> How you may duely charge any Chamberpeece of Artillery ... Put into every chamber so much powder as his peece requireth for a due charge, and with a rammer beate a tompion of softe wood down upon the gunpowder. Moreover, put a bigge wadde into the peece at that end where the mouth of the chamber must goe in, and after that wadde thrust into the peece at the sayde end a fitte pellet, & when you have done all this, put the chamber into the lowest end of the peece, lock them fast together an cause the saide tompion to lie hard upon the powder in the sayde chamber, and the pellet to tooch the tompion, and the wadde to lie close by the pellet ... and when a Gunner will give fire to a chamber peece, he ought not to stand upon that side of the peece where a wedge of yron is put to

locke the chamber in the peece, because the sayde wedge may through the discharge of the peece flie out and kill the Gunner.7

The evidence indicates that this latter warning was not of just a theoretical danger. In 1515 a Venetian wrote from Palermo to his brothers in Venice about an English merchant vessel that, being attacked by a galley and a bark, had fired an iron mortar piece at his assailants, causing much damage to the galley with his first shot. However, with his second shot the mortar burst, allowing the corsairs to board with their handguns and kill and wound all but a handful on board.[8] Thirty years later, weapon unreliability was still causing problems. In June 1545, when the English endeavoured to attack the French fleet, preparing for invasion in Le Havre, with fireships provided by impressed merchant vessels, these latter took advantage of a sudden wind to escape. The pursuing Sir John Berkely in *Less Galley* fired a warning shot after them from one of his sakers, only for the weapon to explode, wounding him.[9] A close study of the Cowdray print showing the battle of the Solent might perhaps indicate a man with his arm in a sling standing on the deck of *Less Galley*. A short while later, his wound proving fatal, Sir John died.

Many years on, after a most rewarding and incident-packed voyage to Brazil that must have involved a great deal of gunnery, James Lancaster brought his fleet to anchor in the Downs in July 1595 and ordered a royal salute to be fired. Hakluyt recorded what happened:

> The gunner being careless, as they are many time of their powder in discharging certain pieces in the gunroom, set a barrel of powder on fire, which blew up the admiral's cabin, slew the gunner with 2 others outright, and hurt 20 more, of which 4 or 5 died. This powder made such a smoke in the ship with the fire that burnt in the gunroom, that no man at first wrist what to do: but recalling back their fear (for the Queen's ships now and also the other ships that were in our company came presently to help) that, God be praised, we put out the fire and saved all.[10]

Occasionally a scapegoat could be found to blame, often an inexperienced gunner who had overcharged his weapon. In 1512 a Flemish subject, Jacques Berenghier, was pressed into service in *Mary John* as a gunner. During a fight with the French several of *Mary John*'s guns malfunctioned; an inquiry suggested that Berenghier had double-loaded the guns placed in his care with two stones so that they failed to fire properly, and also that he had kept some gunpowder in his shoe ready for an act of sabotage – which, as he was entrusted with the usual powder horn around his neck, sounds unlikely. More probably, Berenghier was picked upon because he was a foreigner. He was then dealt with most harshly, losing a leg from torture as well as having his ears slit during a long imprisonment. After he limped home, Margaret of Savoy left Henry in no doubt of the opinion she had of those who treated her subjects in this manner.[11]

Wrought-iron guns had another unnerving characteristic: when they burst, as well they might if overloaded with powder and shot, they did so without warning. The concern with the safe discharge of the weapon meant that a good gunner was judged by his crew not so much on whether or not he could hit his target at range, or even reload with

Some port pieces were placed directly on the deck others were mounted on carriages with a single pair of wheels. This shows one of the latter superimposed on to a picture of the Mary Rose's *surviving deck.* (Mary Rose Trust)

rapidity, but on whether he loaded his weapon and discharged it safely.

Despite the inherent problems of the breech-loaded wrought-iron guns they were not withdrawn from service when newer weapons became available. In 1545 *Mary Rose* had twelve port pieces placed side by side with her bronze cannons and culverins. They look decidedly medieval, which indeed they are, but their presence illustrates another aspect of Tudor naval administration: if it works, don't replace it.

Weapons of Bronze

With the introduction of brass muzzle-loaders the fleet received a weapon that did not suffer from the escape of gases around a chamber and thus could discharge shot at greater velocity than could the breech-loaded iron guns with which Henry Tudor's great ships *Regent* and *Sovereign* had almost exclusively been fitted. Yet because the weapons were new, it took some time before there was general agreement on the most cost-effective combination of bore and barrel length. Before that, the variety and possible combinations produced what Corbett described as a violation of every system of nomenclature.[12] The table below is thus a compromise for the sake of clarity.

The main division among the heavier weapons was that between culverin and cannon. The culverin class included falconets, falcons, sakers and the culverin itself, all with their sub-divisions. They were smooth-bored brass guns with long barrels (usually more than twenty-six calibres long) that supposedly threw a shot further than would a cannon. The latter had shorter bores and often thinner barrels and required less powder to fire their shot, so although the method of manufacture made the culverin the gunners' weapon of choice as it was less likely to explode in use, economic factors, coupled with better reliability as casting method improved, meant that by the century's end the cannon was succeeding the culverin, with the added advantage that its shorter barrel eased loading and recoil management on board.[13] Once cast-iron heavy guns had come to be mass-produced, they were all referred to as cannon – the specific triumphing as the generic. So although by the first decade of the sixteenth century, bronze had become the metal of choice for gun-making (signifying a change from

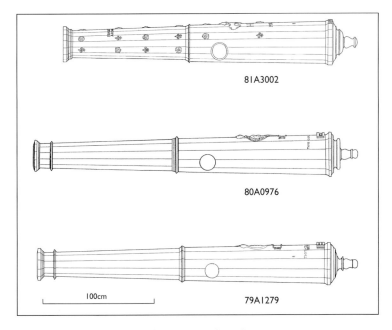

Scale drawings of a selection of bronze guns from the Mary Rose. (Mary Rose Trust)

forges to foundries as iron strips yielded to cast bronze), their time on centre stage was short and ended when they were themselves replaced by the cheaper cast iron once demand increased substantially after 1650, by which time the problems of reliability had been overcome. Thus the age of bronze was short, but while it lasted England produced some of the most beautiful weapons ever made for use at sea. Their grandeur both flattered and deceived. On 26 February 1593 Sir John Fortescue rose in the House of Commons to proclaim that Her Majesty 'hath with her ships encompassed the whole world whereby this land is famous throughout all places. She did find in her Navy all iron pieces, but she hath furnished it with artillery of brass, so that one of her ships is not a subject's but a petty King's.'[14]

The change to brass cannons was one of Henry VIII's earliest interventions in the modernisation of his navy. He came to the throne

The Outfits of Guns for Certain Ships

Name	Calibre (in)	Weight of shot (lb)	Length (ft)	Weight of gun (lb)
Cannon-royal	8	63	12	8,000
Cannon	7	39	11	7,000
Demi-cannon	6.5	30	10	6,000
Culverin	5	15	9	4,300
Demi-culverin	4.5	10.5	8	2,400
Saker	3.5	5	9	1,550
Minion	3	3	7.5	1,200
Falcon	2.75	2	7	700
Falconet	2.25	1.2	6	500
Base	1.25	5	3	200

This bronze bastard demi-culverin, cast by the Owen brothers for the Mary Rose, *is one of the most beautiful guns that survives from the sixteenth century, reflecting its makers' pride in creating such improved weaponry for ships. It is displayed on a reconstruction of its carriage. Note the gunport behind which shows what a limited view the gunners had of their target once their gun was run out.* (Mary Rose Trust)

knowing that hooped iron guns were old-fashioned and that no Englishman could make the newer brass weapons that he craved. His first move was to seek a supply of the new muzzle-loaders from Flanders; his second was to establish a more modern gun-foundry of his own. Gun-founders did practise their trade in London – one such artisan, Humphrey Walker, was appointed a gunner for life in the Tower in 1509 – but their skills did not match those of the Europeans, especially those from the region of Malines, where a history of bell-making (the bell from *Mary Rose* was cast here) had established the tradition of casting in bronze. The result was very soon apparent in the economy. As early as October 1509 a John Heron was paid £1,000 for the provision of metal for 'making of certain our artilleries and ordnances',[15] and by December of the same year the ever-vigilant Venetians were being informed that the price of tin in England had risen because Henry had bought sufficient to make a hundred pieces of artillery, with which he wished to arm four ships that he was 'making in Hampton'.[16]

Bronze cast guns also brought the craftsman's pride to the fore. Whereas when one looks at an iron port piece, one can almost see the blacksmith's arm being raised and lowered as his mighty muscles beat an iron gun into shape in his Vulcan's forge, when one turns to a bronze cannon or culverin, one sees the bronze-founder's joy in perfecting his work. The lion heads on the trunnions, the patterns of shells, fleur-de-lys or acanthus columns, the coats of arm on the barrel, indicate a craftsman's pride, which can be summed up in the words inscribed on one of *Mary Rose's* bastard culverins:

ROBERT AND JOHN OWYN BRETHERYN BORNE IN THE CYTE OF LONDON THE SOMNNES OF AN INGLISH MADE THYS BASTARD ANNO DNI 1537

Casting in bronze gave ample opportunity for Tudor pride of ownership and love of power to be recorded in careful detail on each gun. This is the Owen (or Owyn) brothers' gun. (Mary Rose Trust)

Henry took pride in this creation as well, and was a frequent visitor to the Houndsditch foundry, where on one occasion a demonstration firing that he requested resulted in a row of houses being knocked down. More soberly, the whole false bubble of his foreign policy is written pompously large on the same gun barrel:

HENRY EIGHT BY THE GRACE KING OF ENGLAND AND FRANCE, DEFENDER OF THE FAITH, LORD OF IRELAND AND ON EARTH SUPREME HEAD OF THE ENGLISH CHURCH

By the year in which this gun was cast Henry held Calais as his sole foothold in France, had little sway in Ireland and was an outcast and an enemy of the church whose faith he claimed to defend.

The use of bronze heralded the change from forge to foundry that would eventually, with the successful casting of iron, spark the English industrial revolution. It began in 1511 when a London blacksmith was paid to provide bellows and other necessaries for the construction of a new forge at Greenwich for the use of 'armourers of Brussels', who had come over not only to cast their own weapons but also to teach the English how to do this very skilled work. And skilled it was, from the selection of metal suitable for the alloy of 90 per cent copper and 10 per cent tin to the casting itself. The initial shape of the gun barrel was formed of wax, into which the mould of clay, mixed with wood shavings and horse manure to absorb moisture, was shaped. The mould was then placed in a pit and packed around with earth to ensure that the metal set slowly and under pressure. Alongside this, molten metal was stirred and added to until the temperature and mix were judged by eye and by the heat given off to be just right. It was then poured into the mould, which was capped to retain the pressure.

The result was a weapon of reliability, with its greatest material strength being at the breech end, where the explosive pressures on firing would be at their maximum. In later years the core of the gun would be bored out after casting, but in the fifteenth century a solid core was placed inside the outer mould and centred with iron pins. This produced guns whose calibres varied slightly, with the result that each weapon had to have its shot carefully checked before loading to ensure that it did not jam and, conversely, that windage around the shot, coupled with its erratic travel down the barrel, did not reduce the weapon's range and accuracy more than was anticipated.

The high cost of metal for gun-founding carried with it the usual temptation in this age of plunder. In 1531 Henry Johnson, the king's gunsmith, made an investigation into the claims that were being made for wastage. The gun-founders were asking for 12lb in every hundredweight delivered (roughly 3 per cent) to be written off as waste, and as they had received almost 4,000cwt of metal valued at 22s per hundredweight, the wastage amounted to £422; a further loss was reported in breaking the moulds.

The investigation was simple. The Owen brothers, gun-founders, had received from Johnson 429cwt 24lb of metal from Johnson and had converted it into four falcons, nine sakers, four demi-culverins, three culverins and a cannon with a total weight of 277cwt 3qtr 3lb, which represented a wastage of almost one quarter by weight! Walking around their Houndsditch yard, Johnson then came across a 43cwt great cannon, which the brothers stated was their own but then confessed to have been made from the excess waste. Johnson immediately reduced the amount to be claimed as waste to 2½ to 3lb per hundredweight and made plans to pay similar investigatory visits to the other contractors.[17]

By mid-century the production of heavy weaponry was firmly established in England, but it was still not enough to handle a major crisis. In June 1545 Lord Admiral Lisle commandeered some thirty Flemish hulks (capacious merchant ships) off the Downs and removed their 'bases and other ordnance' for collection by Sir George Carew's squadron, which was on its way to join him at Portsmouth, because he knew that Carew's ships would be short of such weapons.[18]

Cast-Iron Guns

Henry had encouraged the development in iron weaponry through the establishment of eight foundries in the Kent and Sussex Weald, beginning with that of the Levett brothers in Buxted in 1541. Here, with the help of foreign expertise, the problems with impurities such as sulphur and phosphorous, and the weakening honeycombing of iron with air bubbles, were overcome so that iron strong enough to be used for casting heavy ordnance could be guaranteed. By 1549 there were fifty-three forges and furnaces in the Weald, and by 1574 there were 110, many of which were producing ordnance. True, pound for pound iron guns were still weaker than bronze ones, and so the casting had to be thicker and the barrel thus heavier, but the metal had one major advantage – it was cheaper. An iron culverin cost £10 a ton, a bronze one about four times as much. Word spread, and soon the English were exporting, under strict controls, their 'jewels of great value'.

However, cannon foundries and shipbuilding both required wood as a major raw material, in the former case as charcoal for the furnaces. In the Weald this produced a conflict of interest and a chorus of complaints from ports and public about the forges, ranging from the destruction of the roads to the lack of firewood and ships' timber. Somerset, as Lord Protector, ordered an inquiry in 1548, which heard much evidence and achieved nothing. In 1558 Elizabeth's government passed a law forbidding the felling of trees for charcoal making, but then had to make an exception for the Wealden iron-masters. Faced with the obvious pressures from above, the latter started to coppice wood, and so by the time a firmer ban on felling came into being in 1581 the forges were using 'copse wood' rather than 'log wood' and therefore once again gained exemption. What

The recovery of guns from the Elizabethan wreck off Alderney indicates that by the end of the century there was a trend towards the standardisation of the main armament onboard warships.
(Alderney Maritime Trust)

the iron-masters could not so easily avoid was the accusation of trading with the enemy, a particular concern of Secretary Walsingham. In 1574 they were summoned to explain their behaviour and face questioning; it was the implicit threat rather than the inquiry that succeeded in curtailing their business.

A further advance in iron ordnance came when the Master of Naval Ordnance, William Winter, introduced a shorter-barrelled culverin (about nine feet long) which was thus significantly lighter and easier to manhandle than its bronze predecessor. Winter also produced a list detailing the armaments that should be carried by each of the queen's ships, but a comparison with the list of guns that Drake actually took from the Tower in 1585 for *Elizabeth Bonaventure* indicates some differences from the official fit.

As Nelson, from whom this list is taken, points out, Drake's fit was a far more aggressive one, raising his weight of shot from 406lb to 522lb.[19] Yet they were all bronze guns; the cast-iron revolution was by no means complete by the time when the Armada hove into view three years later. What was new was a greater reliance on lighter guns on the broadside, with heavy weapons in the gunroom and the longer-barrelled culverins being utilised as bow-chasers, where their station, roughly parallel to the ship's side, eased the loading difficulties posed by their length.

The gun establishment audit of 1585 showed the the twenty-one ships in service were fitted with:

Demi-cannons	44
Cannons perrier	44
Culverins	103
Demi-culverins	126
Sakers	142
Minions	33
Falcons	79
Falconets	5
Port pieces	56
Fowlers	122
Bases	178

The Guns of *Elizabeth Bonaventure*

Gun	Demi-cannon	Cannon perrier	Culverin	Demi-culverin	Saker	Minion	Falcon	Port piece	Fowler	Base
Official fit	4	2	6	8	6	2	2	2	6	12
Drake's fit	4	4	8	12	6	1	3			

By way of comparison, a 1603 list of naval ordnance showed that the thirty-three ships listed as being on establishment were armed as shown in the table below.[20]

Gun Establishments

Gun	Brass	Iron
Demi-cannon	55	
Cannon perrier	29	
Culverin	241	5
Demi-culverin	248	44
Saker	166	26
Minion	44	11
Falcon	30	
Fowler	65	
Port piece	28	
Total	**876**	**116**

This suggests that cast-iron guns were still a long way from replacing those of bronze.

Bombards, Cannons Perrier and Mortars

An additional type of gun was that used as a mortar to throw a heavy stone shot at a plunging angle on to the deck of an enemy ship. This too was referred to by several names, including 'cannon perrier' and 'curtal'. These six- to eight-calibre weapons were unwieldy and were dismissed in Boteler's dialogues as 'both troublesome and dangerous, and in regard to their overshortness are of little use or no execution beyond the common mortar piece'. They had no future in a navy dedicated to withering broadside fire.

Gun-Ports

The introduction of gun-ports solved the problem of taking heavy, and thus destabilising, weapons to sea. There were other advantages too, in that they allowed such weapons to be distributed further along the ship's side than just the waist, which meant that the ship could be armed along the length of her broadside. In addition, the development of the flat (transom) stern meant that heavy guns could be fitted facing aft in the sternmost compartment, which from then on was referred to as the gunroom. Although having stern-chasers facing aft might seem incongruous in a warship devoted to attack, their position increased

Most stone shot was cut from Kentish ragstone, but the discovery in the wreck of Mary Rose of this one shot quarried from the West Country or Brittany has given support to the theory that the ship was sunk by French gunfire. (Mary Rose Trust)

Gunports, introduced at the beginning of the sixteenth century, enabled heavy guns to be mounted at sea. This one is on the broadside of the Mary Rose. (Mary Rose Trust)

the firing options available to the captain, who could bring them to bear while turning away from a vessel at which he had already fired his broadside guns. He could also fire them at a ship overhauling him and defend himself against a stern boarding, or use them against shore fortifications while anchored stern-to and thus offering the smallest target at the same time.[21] Reducing his target profile was also an important consideration if engaging galleys, which previously had to be fought beam-on, a most exposed position. This tactic was well reported in the engagement in 1628 between *Mary Sampson* and the Knights of Malta:

> Captain William Rainsborrow (who behaved himself with brave courage and temper) finding a breath of wind to give the ship motion; considering that he was a great mark on the broad-side, and the galleys very narrow, keeping their prows sharp toward him, and that he could bear little upon them, trimmed his sails before the wind, and brought them to a stern fight ... the *Sampson* could then bear upon them two whole culverin in her stern-chase, and two transom culverins in the gunroom and two sakers in the great cabin.[22]

The other major advantage of gunports was that the crews manning the guns were protected and hidden from enemy fire by their own ship's side, unlike those on the upper deck, who could rely only on thin pavises behind which, when the vessels were close, they could be spotted and shot at. A gun-deck crew could keep firing even with ships

It was essential for the watertight integrity of ships that the large gunports were tightly secured both in foul weather and when making major alterations of course, such as while entering harbour. This required a substantial port lid, like this example from the Mary Rose. Open ports led to the sinking of that ship and were to put several other warships in dangerous situations, which suggests that the port lids could not always be closed quickly enough. (Mary Rose Trust)

fighting alongside each other, which is precisely what *Revenge*'s crew had to do in 1591.

The lowness of the main deck in relation to the water-line meant that open gunports were positioned dangerously close to the sea, although it had advantages, especially when fighting galleys, where guns that were mounted higher up, however depressed they were on their carriages, might fire over the approaching enemy. Conversely, it was noted in the last fight of *Revenge* that many of the attacking ships' guns could fire only into her upper works, leaving her hull intact. Yet gunports, left open and unattended when not in action, caused a risk from flooding to the whole ship, so 'yeomen of the ports' were tasked on each vessel with the express purpose of ensuring the lids were closed and sealed when the ship was at sea. Hawkins was emphatic in his advice that ports must be shut when entering or leaving harbour, as any manoeuvring by the ship could bring these openings perilously close to the water. He was obviously influenced by the loss of *Mary Rose* on a breezy summer afternoon in 1545 as she endeavoured to turn stern towards the galleys, which lay between her and the main French fleet, and heeled over so far that she flooded through her open gunports and foundered.[23]

Ship Fit

The weapon fit of Henry Tudor's great ships has already been mentioned. With the introduction of muzzle-loaders and gunports, the ordnance carried in Henry VIII's fleet changed radically, as shown in the table overleaf.

It also changed uniformly. A glance through the Anthony Roll shows ships, size for size, armed in an identical fashion, but looking like vessels that could give an account of themselves firing at a short distance from their enemy rather than grappled together. Not that grappling disappeared: the drawings of *Henry Grace à Dieu*, *Mary Rose*, *Peter Pomegranate*, *Jesus*, *Matthew* and *Pawncey* all show shear hooks fitted at the end of the main yard and designed to cut an enemy's rigging and hold her in a tight embrace so that boarding could take place; at the end of the bowsprit a grapnel is shown secured by a length of iron chain, so that once dropped upon an enemy deck it could not be cut free, as had happened to the grappling-line thrown on board the French galley by Sir Edward Howard's crew at the start of his fatal boarding in 1513. Even the navy that sailed against the Armada had shear hooks, so if a contemporary drawing of the then-modern galleon *White Bear* can be taken as an indicator, battering and boarding remained bedfellows throughout the century.

What the table overleaf does not indicate is the increase in the weight of ordnance, and hence the weight of shot, that was now being fitted on board warships, making them far more efficient weapon carriers and, incidentally, less useful as alternative merchant ship hulls during times of peace. This progression can be traced from ordnance amounting to about 3 per cent of tonnage at the middle of the century

This engraving by Visscher of the White Bear *clearly shows sheer hooks on her yards, so the concept of close quarters fighting may not have been entirely abandoned by the time of the Spanish Armada.* (National Maritime Museum neg 1053)

Ship Gun Outfits

Ship	Regent	Mary Rose	Mary Rose	Mary Rose	Great Harry	Revenge
Date recorded	1487	1514	1541	1545	1546	1588
Guns of brass						
Curtows		5				
Cannons				2	4	
Demi-cannons			4	2	3	2
Cannons perrier					2	3
Culverins			2	2	4	10
Demi-culverins			2	6	2	6
Sakers			5	2	4	10
Falcons		2	2	1	2	2
Falconets		3				
Murderers		2				
Guns of iron						
Port pieces			9	12	14	2
Slings			6	2	4	
Demi-slings			2	3	2	
Quarter-slings			6	1		
Fowlers				6	8	3
Bases			60	30	60	6
Top pieces			3	2	2	
Hail-shot pieces				20	40	
Serpentines	225	28				
Murderers		3				
Stone guns		26				
Hand-guns		20		1	100	
Bows		123		250		

to 4.5 per cent in the 1570s with *Dreadnought*, and over 10 per cent in the newer ships that sailed to meet the Armada in 1588. There were practical limits, in that the galleon had a single gun-deck, which meant that it was possible to increase the weight of individual weapons but not the number carried. The English design, moreover, produced a ship whose very strength in ordnance restricted both stowage and sea-keeping qualities. Spanish and Portuguese galleons, on the other hand, were built to undertake lengthy ocean voyages, which required them to be both stout and well-victualled, and as a result they were less heavily armed. In the coastal waters of the Channel in 1588, this difference was significant.

It had also been significant in the Pacific in 1578, when Drake's *Golden Hind*, admittedly privately armed, was described by Nuño da Silva as having '… seven armed port-holes on each side, and inside she carries eighteen pieces of artillery, thirteen being of bronze, the rest of cast-iron …'; most of these heavy weapons were demi-culverins carried to scare with warning shots and bring down the rigging of lightly armed bullion carriers.[24] For close-quarters work there were many swivel pieces, which would have been brought up and mounted on the ship's side when needed. Drake, who took great pride in his vessel, used to give those he captured a tour of the ship so that they could also see the fine armoury of arquebuses, pistols, pikes, fire-bombs and bows and arrows which he carried within the ship's hundred-tonne hull. By contrast, the queen's *Scout*, a bark of slightly greater tonnage built in 1577, carried no culverins, eight sakers, two minions, eight falcons and falconets, two fowlers and four bases. Those going a-pirating could be guaranteed to carry more armaments, but after the pirates became respectable state employees, they brought with them their delight in heavier weapon fits and their experience in how best to use them, all to the state's advantage. The only other nation to have such expertise available was the emergent Netherlands, whose 'Sea-Beggars' were voracious patriotic pirates, so it is not surprising that when the two nations clashed at sea in the seventeenth century, the fight was bloody and bruising.

In addition to increasing the weight of ordnance, the new designs altered where the heaviest guns were sited. In carracks the heaviest guns were fitted in the waist, and, latterly the stern, with lighter weapons being placed on the castle decks. Many of the latter were swivel-mounted to command the decks of an enemy ship and drive those gathered to repel boarders under cover.

In 1495 *Sovereign* was inventoried as having the guns shown in the table overleaf.[25]

By the time Henry VIII's navy was operational, the number of chambers per gun had been reduced to an average of two, reflecting either a way of saving money or weight, or the greater reliance on muzzle-loaded weaponry. The distribution of these guns, high up in the castles in many cases, also indicates that they had to be light, for otherwise the ship would have been unstable when they were carried.[26] The fact that they were mounted on swivels would have helped, for they would have been unshipped and stowed below until needed, thereby improving the ship's sea-keeping qualities. Their light weight also indicates that they were carried for use close to an enemy, with the object of ripping apart her sails and seamen so that she could be stopped, grappled and boarded.

Just as importantly, in case an enemy tried to board one's vessel, some guns in the castles faced fore and aft to cover the waist and to convert both castles into defensible strongholds. The area that they could not cover lay dead ahead, and this was the preferred place for an enemy to place his ship if he wished to board. The lack of forward-firing guns also placed ships at a disadvantage when closing an enemy or while engaging a galley. *Mary Rose* and others of her type had long-range culverins placed facing forward on the stern castle, which needed both the main sail and foresail to be furled to give them good sight of their target.

The debate as to what mix of gun types was ideal does not appear to have been solved by consensus. So often personal experience influenced belief, as in the case of the defeated but defiant Richard Hawkins, who when recalling his fight in *Dainty* against three Spanish ships in 1594 wrote:

> although their artillery was longer, weightier and many more than ours, and in truth did pierce with greater violence; yet our being of greater bore and carrying weightier and greater shot, was of more importance and of greater effect for sinking and spoiling, for the smaller shot passeth through and maketh but his hole and harmeth that which lieth in the way; but the greater shaketh and shivereth all it meeteth, and with the splinters, or that which it encountereth, many times doth hurt more with his proper circumference[27]

– which was really the lesson that should have been learned during the

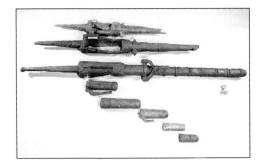

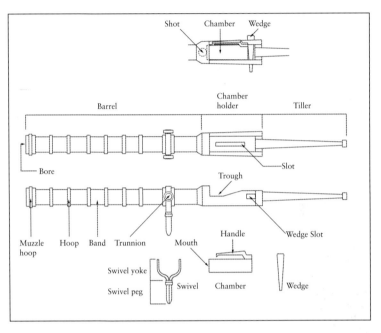

Drawing of the parts of a swivel gun. (Mary Rose Trust)

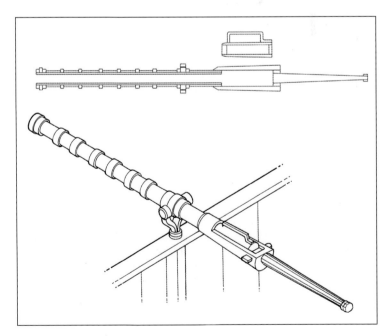

Drawing of a swivel gun mounted on a gunwale. Similar weapons, known as petereroes, survived until the end of the seventeenth century, becoming the last of this style of breech-loaders in naval use. (Mary Rose Trust)

The Inventory of *Sovereign*, 1495

Iron guns

	Location		Chambers		
Serpentines	Forecastle	16	48	with swivels	
	Lower forecastle	24	72	with swivels	
	Lower summer castle	24	72	with swivels	
	Summer castle	20	60	with swivels	
	Upper summer castle	25	75		
	Stern	4	12		
	Poop	20	60		
Stone guns					
	Waist	20	60		
	Summer castle	11			
Brass guns					
Serpentines		1			

Armada campaign, where the weight of shot discharged at range by the English created far less damage to the enemy than its volume might have suggested was possible.

The breakthrough that allowed ships to be fitted with powerful forward-facing guns mounted in the bow came with the introduction of the galleon, and especially the race-built galleon developed by Hawkins. These vessels were designed with a low forecastle and with underwater lines that gave extra buoyancy up forward, where two heavy bow-chasers were mounted under the forecastle and two smaller guns on the forecastle itself. This put muscle into the straight left or right punch of the galleon, turning a jab into a knock-out blow and giving those entering a fray added confidence.

Howard, after one morning engagement with the Armada's galleasses, reported that they had '... fought for a long time and much damaged them, that one of them was fain to be carried away upon the careen [listing] and another, by a shot from the *Ark*, lost her lantern which came swimmingly by, and a third his nose [beak-head]', which seems precious little return from the expenditure, although he did go on to say that after this exchange the Spanish galleasses were never 'seen in fight any more, so bad was their entertainment in this encounter'.

When the last of the Elizabethan galleons, the 500-tonne *Warspite*, was launched in 1595, her suite of heavy guns was as follows:

Orlop deck	12 culverins
Stern and prow at orlop deck level	4 culverins
Capstan deck	8 demi-culverins
Stern and prow gun-deck	4 demi-culverins
Waist	6 sakers
Half-deck	2 sakers

– indicating that some degree of standardisation was at last taking place. Yet with this came a renewed emphasis on heavy weapons, which created instability in the new galleons. The response was two-fold: firstly, the ships were refitted to improve their buoyancy; and secondly, the heaviest gun, full cannons, were removed from the establishment and replaced with lighter cannons perrier. Investigations of the Alderney wreck which sank in 1592 have suggested that by the end of the century a degree of standardisation was taking place, as all this ship's main armament is of a similar design and calibre.

Eventually, and in quick time, the galleon design no longer delivered what gunnery demanded. The end came with James I and the building in 1610 of *Royal Prince*, a 1,900-tonne vessel carrying fifty-five heavy guns mounted – and here was the breakthrough – on two gun-decks. *Sovereign of the Seas*, launched in 1637, had three full-length gun-decks and in layout looked identical to many an early nineteenth-century warship. Thus within a few years of the apotheosis of the Tudor naval galleon, the navy moved on to create the ship-of-the-line. Still, with the introduction of the gunport and the galleon, the Tudors could claim to have advanced warship design most significantly.

Fighting-Tops

The fighting-top began life as a refuge and resting place for seamen working the mast and a station for a lookout. It was to the top that Peter Carew climbed to sight the French fleet approaching Portsmouth in 1545, and it was from the top that John Drake was the first to sight Drake's rich prize *Cacafuego* during his circumnavigation. Yet it cannot have been long before the idea of placing archers or gunmen in the tops occurred to those wishing to gain advantage at close quarters. A drawing of the battle of Zonchio in 1499 shows the opposing ships' fighting-tops crammed with archers and spearmen; in the sixteenth century musketeers would join them. It is recorded that *Katherine*

A diver uncovering one of the guns from the Alderney wreck. The most important discovery since the Mary Rose, *this end-of-century Tudor ship has produced important new finds of ordnance and weaponry.* (Alderney Maritime Trust)

Fortileza had a stone gun in her main top with four chambers, weighing over a hundredweight, and several more but lighter guns in the fore and mizzen-tops. However, Edward Howard in his report to the king about the state of his fleet in 1513 complained that the 550-tonne *Katherine* was 'overladen with ordnance, beside her heavy tops, which are big enough for a ship of 8 or 900 tons', which would indicate that she was unstable because of excessive top-weight.[28] *Great Elizabeth* in her short career of 1514 was fitted with six serpentines and two stone guns with thirty chambers in her main top and more guns in the tops of her other masts. Whether these were meant to be hauled up for action and then lowered is not known, for the few months in which *Great Elizabeth* was in service were peaceful ones. Since *Great Elizabeth* foundered off Calais just after she had been converted from a Lubeck trader to a fighting ship, and had guns mounted in her tops, her loss may also be attributed to increased instability.

Incendiaries

Incendiaries played only a minor role in battle, but there was great interest in them. Oxenham, Drake's one-time companion, and his men were questioned after their capture by the Spanish in Panama specifically about how to make 'fire-wings' with nails. They explained that one needed to begin with a mixture of powder, oil, pitch, sulphur, camphor and spirits ground into a paste and firmed around an arrow head or made into pitch-coated 'grenades'. When needed, a touch-hole was pushed into the mix, powder poured in and lit, and the grenade thrown with rapidity. The Spaniards also recorded that their prisoners stated that they had seen incendiaries 'more than a thousand times' on ships and that they were much used in England 'to defend ships and burn others'.[29] One has the distinct impression that the Englishmen were indulging in one of the few luxuries granted a prisoner-of-war, pulling their captors' legs, for there is little evidence of widespread use. Fire was after all an indiscriminate weapon, and Sir Richard Hawkins

even warned against using heavy weapons close to an enemy for fear of setting off a mutually-destructive blaze.

However, when the Indies fleet returned in 1596, the ships had expended all their stores of incendiaries as well as the 'stuff for fireworks', a list of over a dozen chemical compounds, including saltpetre, sulphur, camphor, rosin turpentine and pitch, none of which was returned to the stores.

Shot

Most guns fired either stone or iron shot, with the former disappearing as the century progressed. This was not because cast-iron balls were superior as projectiles but because they were so much cheaper to manufacture. Cutting a stone ball from Kentish ragstone (the preferred material) took a craftsman many hours at a cost which was equivalent to that of at least ten similar moulded iron ones, but it would be wrong to assume that it was any less efficacious, pound for pound, than its iron counterpart. It certainly did not shatter on impact. Captain Rainsborrow, in *Sampson* in 1628, is quoted as stating that a twenty-five-pound stone shot, unlike the smaller iron projectiles that did less damage, 'staved on our lower deck two barrels of beef, two of pease, a Butt of Wine; some of the shot passing through nineteen inches of planke and timber and made us leakie'.[30]

The weight of shot for each type of gun again varied with the irregularities of bore size, but can be taken to have been approximately as shown on page 61. Apart from the straightforward shot, variants were produced, such as a pair of balls linked with chain, a projectile that would rip sail or rigging apart or bring down masts or yards. At closer range anti-personnel shrapnel was broadcast around the decks, especially when fired from hail-shot pieces, whose muzzles were shaped like letter-boxes to scatter their shot. These were the guns most suited for purpose at the start of the century, when boarding was the main aim and the gun used to soften resistance. As Monson stated: 'after a ship is boarded and entered or lieth board and board ... a murderer or a fowler being shot out of their own ship, laden with dice-shot, will scour the deck of the enemy and not suffer a man to appear'.[31]

This view is reinforced by Sir Richard Hawkins, among others, who held 'nothing more convenient in ships of war than fowlers and

An incendiary grenade from the Alderney wreck. These were made from glass or pottery, with tubes to hold lighted fuzes. On impact they shattered causing the gunpowder within to ignite. (Alderney Maritime Trust)

great-bases in the cage-works and murderers in cobridge-heads [fore-castle bulkhead], for that their execution and speedy charging and discharging is of great moment'.

They were equally useful in defence, and William Bourne strongly recommended that fowlers, slings, bases and port pieces be charged and shot 'at the first boarding'.[32] That these fighting instructions appeared late in the century is an sign that, far from moving away from boarding in favour of ship-killing stand-off tactics, the English still saw a need to leap on board an enemy vessel. This will be discussed later, but Corbett indicates caution, quoting Richard Hawkins as writing after 1593: 'Many I know have left the use of shere-hooks, stones in the tops, and arming them ... but upon what inducement I cannot relate, unless it be because they never knew their effect and benefits.'[33]

Hawkins's view is supported by the fact that between 1567 and 1570 Winter returned over 600 short-range iron guns to the Tower as either unserviceable or obsolete. Clearly there were two schools of thought as to the efficacy of boarding.

Hawkins's concern that big guns might cause fire to spread if discharged 'board to board' reflects the quality of the gunpowder then in use, and a change in the appreciation of its benefit and disadvantages. In carrack days, heavy guns that were discharged at close range delivered the shock and awe of flame, smoke and concussion as well as the shot itself, making an enemy in close proximity as likely to be disorientated as disembowelled. Firing at range reduced all but one of these effects: greater accuracy and better penetration were thus necessary as compensations, while at the same time the smoke and flame caused by inefficient gunpowder became a nuisance, not an advantage, to the firing ship.

Recent discoveries from the Alderney wreck, which sank in 1592, have brought to light examples of both cross-bar and expanding (or langrell) shot.[34] The former was an incendiary device best described by John Smith in his *Sea Grammar*: 'Cross-bar shot is also a round shot, but it hath a long spike of iron cast with it as if it did go through the midst of it, its ends whereof are commonly armed for fear of bursting the Piece, which is to bind a little oakum in a little canvas at the end of each spike.'

Expanding shot is first mentioned in a 1620 inventory of the Royal Armouries, although John Smith also describes it:

> Langrell shot runs loose with a shackle, to be shortened when you put it into the piece, and when it flies out it doth spread itself, it hath at the end of either bar a half bullet either of lead or iron ... these are used when you near a ship to shoot down masts, yards, shrouds, tear the sails, spoil the men, or anything that is above the decks.

As so often, archaeological discoveries are pushing back the dates at which we now know many objects were first used, or invented.

Of course, the greatest practical difficulty of having guns of such varying calibre on board ship was that each weapon required its own ammunition supply. The 1514 inventory of *Mary Rose* records her as having 500 stone shot, great and small, 457 shot of iron of diverse sorts, 120 cross-bar shot, 1,000 lead pellets for swivel guns and a further 900 for arquebuses. The Anthony Roll is more specific, breaking down the ordnance per type of gun as shown in the table below.

Comparison of Gun Outfits

Ship	Great Harry		Mary Rose	
	Number of guns	Shot	Number of guns	Shot
Brass guns				
Cannon	4	100	2	50
Demi-cannon	3	60	2	60
Culverin	4	120	2	60
Demi-culverin	2	70	6	140
Saker	4	120	2	80
Cannon perrier	2	60		
Falcon	2	100	1	40
Iron guns				
Port piece	14	300 stone	12	100 stone
Sling	4	100	2	40
Demi-sling	2	50	3	40
Quarter-sling			1	50
Fowler	8	100	6	170
Base	60	2,000 lead	30	400 lead
Top piece	2	40	2	20
Hail-shot piece	40	4,000	20	1,500
Handgun	100	2,000 lead	1	2,000 lead

Such a variety (bearing in mind that each class also had a variety of calibres) meant that in a major engagement, or a series of fights, gun after gun could fall silent as its particular size of ammunition ran out. The one kind of ammunition which could be re-supplied on board was lead shot, by using the ship's galley range as a furnace to heat the lead before pouring it into moulds. In 1514 *Mary Rose* was supplied with:

2 sowes of lead, 1 quarter and certain casts
2 charging ladles of copper
2 ladles of iron for casting of pellets

Nevertheless, Henry's larger ships had more than sufficient shot for several major engagements before they would need to return to harbour to replenish. The Anthony Roll also indicates that smaller vessels, like *Greyhound*, which gave a good account of herself against the French after the battle of the Solent, had sixty shot for her one culverin and a hundred for her two sakers. Master gunners probably took no chances, stocking their ships with more shot than the official allowance. Divers on *Mary Rose*, for example, recovered nearly twice the number of iron shot inventoried and over twenty more stone shot, and that is just what was found on the sea bed – where much more probably still lies scattered.

Until the standardisation of weapon production, almost every gun onboard required its own ammunition – as vividly demonstrated by this selection from the Mary Rose. (Mary Rose Trust)

A hail-shot piece. At close-quarters hail-shot could inflict death or serious injury, and was much used to clear decks before or during boarding. (Mary Rose Trust)

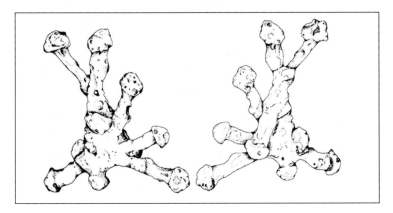

Various forms of expanding, or langrell, shot were ideal for cutting through rigging, thus causing masts to fall, ripping sails apart, or slicing off human limbs or heads. This concreted example comes from the Alderney wreck. (Alderney Maritime Trust)

Yet by the time when the greatest threat of the century arrived in the Channel, in 1588, one of the most noticeable problems facing both fleets was a shortage of ammunition. After three days of exchanges, Medina Sidonia wrote to Parma asking for '4 lb, 6 lb and 10 lb shot' because much of his 'had been expended in the successive fight'.[35] Howard was also keen for shot to be brought out from shore, but what he got in fact was men, a commodity he did not need. This difference of understanding in priorities highlights the change that was being effected in the war at sea. Those ashore still saw the battle as

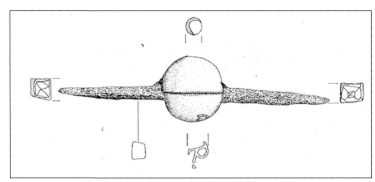

Bar shot was an incendiary device, the spikes inserted into the shot being wrapped around with pitch and set alight. This one was found on the Alderney wreck site. (Alderney Maritime Trust)

The ship's galley could be used to make lead shot using such moulds as this one found on the Mary Rose. (Mary Rose Trust)

being one of boarding and hand-to-hand fighting, which after several days of battle must have taken its toll; those at sea were fighting with the newer tactics of stand-off gunnery bombardments, where the expenditure was of iron and stone, not flesh and blood. The Privy Council even queried Howard's resolve in not boarding, asking: 'What causes are there why the Spanish navy hath not been boarded by the Queen's ships? And though some of the ships of Spain be thought too huge to be boarded by the English, yet some of the Queen's ships are thought very able to have boarded divers of the meaner ships of the Spanish navy.'[36]

There were advantages in communications not being instant: Howard would have had some time to calm down before making a retort. Ralegh, who was at court and was used as the queen's messenger to Howard just before the fireships were launched, seems to have kept quiet when this note was penned, but when it came to writing his *History of the World* he wrote in support of Howard's stand-off tactics, suggesting that, 'had he entangled himself with those great and powerful vessels, he had greatly endangered this kingdom of England'.

Gunpowder

Gunpowder was made by mixing roughly 75 per cent saltpetre (potassium nitrate) with equal amounts of charcoal and sulphur. For safety reasons these were ground separately and then combined, after which they were free to separate out in transit, as will any dry mix such as salt and pepper. However, re-mixing gunpowder was a risky business, especially on board a ship in action, and many a gun must have been discharged with an ineffectual mix. The problem was tackled by combining the ingredients in urine to make a paste, which was then dried into sheets and pounded back into grains which could be sieved to produce powder of differing coarseness suitable for weapons of different calibre. Urine became so important in propellant manufacture that cattle markets were compelled to have mud floors, which, every so often, were dug up and carted off to gunpowder factories. Although the instability of this gunpowder was well known, magazines to protect the kegs from spark and flame were not provided, and in 1514 *Mary Rose* sailed with twenty-one barrels of gunpowder in her hold – a lethal cargo store unprotected from flame.

When required, the gunpowder was either, and ideally, placed in the gun in cartridges of fixed amount, or spoon-fed through the barrels with long-handled ladles, each of which had a hemispherical scoop that could be filled and levelled to measure out the charge required. Loading by the latter method could not have been easy given that the gun would have had to be run inboard some distance before the loader could ease the ladle down the barrel. Just this one detail alone indicates the shortcomings of muzzle-loaders compared with breech-loaders. Experiments have shown that the idea of loading from outboard was a physical impossibility as well as too foolhardy to contemplate. In fact, so awkward was the ladle that Collado suggested that gun crews should practise using fine gravel instead of gunpowder, while Bourne stated flatly, 'I do see that there is no worse lading or charging of Ordnaunce than with a ladell', which he considered to be unhandy, inaccurate and

Ladling powder into a muzzle-loading gun was a tricky business and although each weapon had powder ladles designed to hold just the right amount of powder, the introduction of cartridges made the gunners' lives much easier. (Mary Rose Trust)

To fire effectively muzzle-loaders required ball, powder and wads to be successively driven home with a ramrod; this was a difficult task even with the guns run back inboard. (Mary Rose Trust)

With so many differing sizes of shot, gauges were required to ensure each gun was loaded with the correct ammunition. (Mary Rose Trust)

muzzle velocity, and hence range and striking force, would decrease rather than increase. Put simply, longer barrels did not deliver greater range.[37] Neither did the shot fit snugly and seal the barrel. Comparing guns recovered with the related shot in *Mary Rose* suggests that between half an inch and an inch was a common difference (called windage) between diameter of shot and gun calibre, causing a great deal of the explosive force to escape down the barrel ahead of the shot. This difference also meant that the shot careered eccentrically down the gun, exiting at a slightly different angle every time the gun was fired and with a vicious spin that curved it away from its target. What a longer brass barrel did deliver was greater safety for the user, because its vertical casting meant that a greater length created greater pressure and thus more solidity at the breech end. A preoccupation, almost an obsession, with length thus seems more likely to have been linked to the machismo of the purchaser than with the efficacy of the weapon; culverins were the Tudor E-Type Jaguars.

Range, whether maximum or effective, was a meaningless statistic in the days of smooth, flawed barrels, gunpowder of poor and uneven quality, no sighting or ranging instrument and a moving ship and target. Sighting from the breech end of a gun run out through a gunport in *Mary Rose* reveals very little of the world beyond, and even that, in a moving sea, is but a fleeting view. Aiming accurately at a ship further than one cable away would also be impossible, especially given the gaps in time between sighting, lighting the touch-hole and the shot discharging. Gun battles at sea were fought close whether or not the aim was to board, which it most often was. What changed was the form of the duel and the time selected for carrying out that boarding.

A battle at sea was won when an enemy surrendered, and he would do this, ideally,

dangerous, rather like the gunpowder itself. Paper cartridges were introduced early on, which would indicate that ladles were a reserve means of loading. *Mary Rose* had a chest full of 'carttuches' in 1514 and a roll of paper and six templates for making her own in 1545.

The powder itself had a marked and limiting effect on the efficiency of the weapons it served. Firstly, when it burned, less than half of the product was gaseous, the rest being solid and sooty. Secondly, the positive pressure on the shot of the explosive gases tailed off at about eight to ten feet from the powder charge. Beyond that distance

while his ship was still afloat and could be taken as a prize, with plunder being the reward for blood, sweat and toil. The idea that more powerful weapons led to a material change in this concept is erroneous. There were no such things as ship-killing weapons until the advent of the torpedo, explosive shell and high-trajectory shot. What the larger guns enabled a captain to do was kill men at greater range and behind thicker protection, allowing him to board, when he judged it right, with less opposition. Here, newer ship designs also influenced the decision to stand off, for the tumble-home, or curving-in topsides, of the galleons meant that, even when lying alongside, a considerable distance needed to be crossed from one ship to another, delaying the speed of entry while all the time lying open to a gunnery blast from the other vessel. Thus Winter, writing proudly to Walsingham once the Armada had been dispersed, stated:

> I deliver it unto your honour upon the credit of a poor gentleman that out of my ship [*Vanguard*] there was shot 500 shot of demi-cannon, culverin, and demi-culverin; and when I was furthest off in discharging any of the pieces, I was not out of shot of their harquebus, and at most times, within speech one of another[38]

– a claim supported by a Spaniard, who spoke of the English closing within a ' pike's-length asunder'.

Rates of Fire

Winter's note, quoted above, raises another issue which has been debated fiercely, namely the rate of fire from heavy guns. Two factors came into play here: the time it physically took a competent crew to reload their weapon safely following discharge; and, secondly, how quickly that gun could be brought back to bear on its target. The first depended on the use of such things as breech- or muzzle-loading, cooling down, recoil or hauling in and running out. The second depended on training, drill, the sea state, wind direction, the ship-handling of the master, his opponent and the presence of a gunner. The historian N A M Rodger implies that most ships had insufficient gunners to keep up a decent rate of fire, stating:

> The conclusion seems to be inescapable that however the guns were being reloaded, there were not enough men available to load all of them at once. We have to imagine teams of men moving from gun to gun. Reloading the whole armament, by whatever method, must have taken a long time, and there was no advantage in lingering within range of the enemy while one did so.[39]

This situation would have been acceptable if the recommended method of engaging an enemy had been followed on each occasion. This was to approach upwind from astern, firing, firstly, bow-chasers and then, as the ships drew level, each gun in turn, before steering away while firing the stern-chasers; then going about and returning to discharge the ordnance from the other side. The same manoeuvre was favoured by both naval and private ships alike, with *Amity* in 1592 being recorded as having given her whole broadside and then 'cast about, new charge' to fire from the other side. However, Cumberland, attempting to take *Black Bull of Hamburg* off Lisbon in 1592, was astonished by the strength of her broadside, which led to a very 'hot fight for a long while until the master and some of the company were slain and ... the ship much beaten, having received sundry shot ... and twice under water' surrendered. The account indicates that the two vessels lay beam-on and blasted rather than altered course to open and close the range.

Rodger, using Winter's report quoted above, estimates that it could have taken one and a half hours to reload and fire each of *Vanguard*'s thirty-four guns, but to extrapolate this from such evidence poses more questions than it answers. What, for a start, would have been the tactical implications of such tardy recharging? It gave a belligerent enemy time to counter-attack or a timorous one time to escape. There seems to be confusion between the time taken to reload and the time needed to re-aim and fire. The manoeuvre outlined above would take many minutes for a ship to achieve. During this time the gunners would have had plenty of time to reload and stand by to re-engage. It was thus the manoeuvring, not the reloading, that dictated the interval between discharges.

The descriptions of gun battles in Hakluyt and other contemporary accounts also indicate that firing, although not continuous from any one large-bore gun, took place at much shorter intervals. *The Complaynt of Scotland* of 1548 gives a vivid first-hand account:

> Then where I sat I heard the cannon and gun make many hideous crack – duf, duf, duf, duf, duf. The basilisks and falcons cried tirduf, tirduf, tirduf, tirduf, tirduf, tirduf. Then the small artillery cried tik, tik, tik, tik, tik. The reek, smoke, and the stink of the gunpowder filled the air ... burning in one bad fire which generated such murkiness and mist that I could not see my length from me.[40]

Hall considers that, on land, a culverin could fire seventy times a day, which could imply a safe rate of fire of one round every ten minutes.[41] At sea the drill would be more difficult, as would be aiming afresh at the target, but it need not have been much more infrequent.

A look at the guns recovered from *Mary Rose* would support, in a roundabout way, this notion of reasonably rapid fire. The fourteen guns on her main deck were a mix of bronze cannons, demi-cannons and culverins and wrought-iron port pieces. The upper deck had six wrought-iron guns and four bronze guns, four port pieces, two sakers and a falcon, while the castle deck held two demi-culverins, a mix confusing enough even if the ship had been in permanent commission with a long-standing crew. Given that no two guns were the same, and that the heavy weaponry included both breech-loading iron and muzzle-loading bronze guns, there must have been more likelihood of a circulating team of gunners making an error in loading than there would have been if each gun retained its own crew, even if aiming and firing was left to the master gunner. Indeed, although the latter was required to 'know the names of his pieces, their bore or height [diameter of shot], their weight, the weight of the shot, the weight of the powder, the goodness of powder, and how far every piece will carry, both at random and at point blank ...',[42] this was probably too much to ask of any man for such a vast number of disparate weapons during the heat of battle.

Another piece of evidence for allocated gun crews is that when a ship went into action, it did so with the minimum of sail necessary to preserve steerage way. This was done not only to keep the ship's movement to a minimum, so as to aid the aiming of the guns, but also to reduce the number of seamen exposed on the upper deck. What better use for those not so required than to have them work the guns? A third issue is that ships were laid up in time of peace, often, as in the case of *Mary Rose*, for many years, after which time it was not likely that a previous gunnery team would rejoin the same ship or have time to train up to proficiency in each weapon before action. Moreover, ordnance was offloaded when ships were laid up, with the same suite of guns unlikely to be provided on re-commissioning.

This well-known painting of the Battle of Gravelines at the climax of the 1588 Armada campaign, probably a design for a tapestry, shows a moderate amount of fire from the English ships, some firing more than one gun simultaneously. There is a distinct impression that the English are firing more frequently than the Spanish.
(National Maritime Museum BHC0262)

The Anthony Roll lists the crew of *Mary Rose* as 185 soldiers, 200 mariners and thirty gunners. Thirty gunners would be too many to form one frantic peripatetic gun crew and would be sufficient to man only five guns with a crew consisting completely of gunners, for, according to Hall, the number of men required per gun varied from six to eight depending on the type of weapon being serviced. Thirty-two carriage-mounted guns are listed for *Mary Rose* in the Anthony Roll among a total of ninety-one guns, many of which would be swivel pieces manned by one man. If the thirty professional gunners formed complete crews this would have given *Mary Rose* at least four crews made up totally of gunners. Without their ship going about and returning to present the opposite side, these teams should each have been able to bring a gun back into action in far less than an hour and a half. Yet what is more likely is that each gunner was allocated to a

particular gun and, under the supervision of the master gunner, trained the seamen who made up his crew. There is in fact a close link between the number of large guns carried and the number of gunners borne. Given that, a rate of fire commensurate with the contemporary accounts would have been easily achievable.

A telling argument in favour of having individual crews trained for each carriage gun is that no captain would tolerate his main armament falling silent during action while a frantic and frenetic band of gunners rushed around several decks reloading each weapon. Additionally, this major failing of heavy armament would be well known by any opponent, whose tactics would be to feint an attack close enough to draw off one salvo, knowing that he was then at liberty to close in with impunity. No evidence of such an obvious ploy exists. Indeed, the entry and control of Cadiz harbour by Drake in

1587, in the presence of a galley squadron, indicate an ability to keep up a withering rate of fire when necessity dictated.

Finally, given the limited maximum effective range of any gun and the fact that a 'long shot' was recognised as a lucky gamble, most commanders knew that close range was best. This is borne out by the fact that *Mary Rose*'s guns are canted to point out at right angles to her curved hull rather than in parallel to each other, so that no two guns could fire at a single ship target unless it was within about a cable. Bourne, in his preface to his book on gunnery, stated that a major defect of English gunnery was 'not knowing the distance to the mark', although how other nations achieved better range-finding is unclear.

The proximity of engagement while avoiding boarding is indicated in the words of a Spaniard written in 1574: 'The ordnance flush with the water should be at once discharged broadside on, and so damage their hull and confuse them with smoke. This is the English way of fighting and I have many times seen them do it to the French 30 years ago.'[43] Now, if smoke billowing sufficiently to confuse was the norm, then so must have been encounters of the close-quarters kind, and if this was the case then it would have been the skill of the master and not the gunner which counted the most.

Support for a more rapid rate of fire is provided by the Spanish accounts of their own ships in action during battles, all of which recognise that they were up to three times slower than the English in servicing their guns. When Medina Sidonia was isolated off Portland and receiving the full force of the heavy armament of the major English ships for an hour and a half, it was reported that his *San Martin* fired eighty shots from one side while the English discharged at least 500 rounds at him. The damage? The flagship lost her flagstaff and the stays to the main mast! This account by Calderon[44] is supported by another Spanish account, which states that *San Martin* 'returned the fire with so much gallantry that on one side alone she fired off a hundred shots'. The evidence thus supports the idea of rapid fire but at an ineffective range, creating a suspicion that it was strategy, not tactics, that controlled the English approach. Whichever it was, it was certainly not an example of ship-sinking weaponry in action.

Gunners

The need for qualified gunners to man the heavy ordnance that was being fitted on board naval vessels was immediately recognised and their expertise rewarded. The list of war expenses for April 1513 shows the payments for these specialists and includes, for example, for *Trinity Royal*, 5s per man per month for both mariners and the ship's forty gunners, but also a reward to the master gunner of a further 5s per month, 2s 6d for his mate and 20d to all other gunners.

As far as accuracy in firing was concerned, gunnery at sea was not an exact science. Too much variance in powder quality, dampness, size of shot and windage in the barrel, compounded with the movement of both firing ship and receiving ship and imprecision of ranging, meant that the only sure means of landing a shot on target was to be nearby. The good master gunner was, therefore, the one who made sure that

any damage from his weapon was confined to those outboard of the barrel and not, through accident, those firing it. Audley's instructions for master gunners in the army was thus just as relevant at sea in stipulating that the master had to be an 'expert and skilful in all points of cannonry', and to be able to pass on his knowledge to his subordinates.[45] He had to ensure that his heavy guns were 'well and strongly stocked, and mounted upon strong axle-trees and wheels well-shod and strongly bound with iron'. As well as instructing the gunners in the capability of their weapons, the master gunner had to impress on them the importance of carrying out safety measures when they took them over, such as checking that the barrel was clean and the touch-hole clear. The failure so to do could lead to misfiring or an exploding weapon, causing mayhem on board.

In these circumstances the best gunner would be the one who could fire his gun safely without endangering his crew. For this to be achieved two things were necessary: well-practised drills, and the loading of shot and powder within the safety limit of the weapon. The precautions were many, but obvious and simple. They included: the sponging-out of the gun to remove hot flammable material; the loading of stout cartridges which were not pricked through the vent hole until the shot had been rammed; priming only when ready; the removal of the cartridge, along with the charge and shot, if the action was delayed; and, the separation of the linstock and its slow match from the powder (another reason to use cartridges rather than loose gunpowder). William Bourne, recommending the use of cartridges, goes on to say:

> Gunners that do serve by the Sea must be very circumspect about their Powder in the time of service, and especially beware of their linstocks and candles for fear of their Powder ... then they may be set upright in some tube or barrel, and then they may take out one by one as need shall require, and to cover the barrel close again, that it may be without danger.[46]

To discharge a large gun safely and fire it accurately, speedily and with effect required a trained gun crew experienced in each of the weapons they had to use. (Mary Rose Trust)

The pride of a master-gunner can be seen in the way this linstock from the Mary Rose *has been lovingly carved. Note the burn marks from the fuze that would have been clutched in the dragon's jaws.* (Mary Rose Trust)

To which advice Ruscelli added the injunction that you cannot clean a piece too much for your own safety!

Gun Drills

In the preface to his work on gunnery of 1587 Bourne observes:

> We Englishmen have not been considered but of late day to become good Gunners, and the principall point that hath caused English men to be counted good Gunners, hath been, for that they are hardie or without feare about their ordnaunce: but for the knowledge in it, other nations and countries have tasted better thereof as the Italians French and Spaniardes, for that English men have had but little instructions but that they have learned of the Dutchmen or Flemings in the time of King Henry the eight. And the chiefest cause that English men are thought to be good Gunners is this, for that they are handsome about their Ordnance in ships on the Sea etc.

Bourne is absolutely right. For although Henry's 'great matter' of his divorce from Katherine led to the isolation of the English from the distribution of academic knowledge that was circulating around Europe on matters maritime, such as navigation and gunnery, the English gunner had the edge in practical experience, which he had gained not as a servant of the crown but as an adventurer, a pirate.

Although there is little evidence of royal ships carrying out practice firing drills, at the very least dry runs must have happened soon after a ship sailed, for operations for both breech- and muzzle-loaders could be fired safely and accurately only by a trained crew. Most drills would have been 'dry', because few vessels carried sufficient ordnance to allow for live-firing runs and fewer still were the opportunities for target practice. Those who wrote about gunnery were often theorists concerned mainly with shore-based ordnance, so they did not dwell long on the practicalities of firing a gun within the confines of a ship's deck. Here, the first problem was the fact that no two weapons, even of the same class, had the same characteristics. For each the calibre, weight of shot and amount of powder had to be ascertained and the men trained to provide these expeditiously. In contrast with land battles using siege weapons, where neither rate of fire nor manpower needed to be considered, at sea the pressure was on to deliver more with less in a smaller space. Peace-time drill would thus have been essential to achieve a fair standard of gunnery. Without documentary sources, an idea of the probable gun drills has had to be worked out by the firing of reconstructed guns. Much of our understanding has thus been drawn from the research carried out by Alexzandra Hildred

Breech-loading weapons also required an experienced crew to ensure that wedges were driven securely home so that they did not fly out and do more damage inboard than outboard. (Mary Rose Trust)

of the Mary Rose Trust in partnership with Nick Hall of the Royal Armouries, whose ideas on drill are summarised in Appendix 4.

Broadsides

The introduction of the gun-deck raises the question of whether or not these ships ever fired broadsides – in which all the guns on one side were fired together in a single volley. This is unlikely for many of the reasons discussed above, but principally because the gun barrels lay perpendicular not to the centre-line but to the curvature of the hull from which they extruded. This would mean that few guns could be brought to bear on an enemy vessel simultaneously unless the two ships were lying almost side by side. Then, of course, in extremis, such a discharge might take place. Far better was to fire a ripple of guns, with each one discharging as the firing ship sailed past slowly. Nevertheless, some take a statement by Lisle in 1545 that his galleasses handled the French galleys 'as well with their sides as with their prows' to suggest that the concept of a naval broadside began off Shoreham on 15 August 1545. If this were so, it was a grievous experiment, for, according to Corbett, the English units involved in the action 'had been so shaken by the weather and the shock of their guns that they were pronounced no longer serviceable without extensive repairs', although that great naval historian went on to say that 'Of all others the year 1545 best marks the birth of the English naval power; it is the year that most clearly displays the transition from oars to sails', by which he meant that the dominance of the galley in naval engagements was over, an idea that will be discussed later.[47]

Range

Another concern of modern researchers into medieval naval weapons is the range achieved by these guns. Two very different measurements are often quoted. The first is the maximum range of a gun, which in most instances would have been several thousand yards. In most situations this was a purely theoretical distance; what was far more important was the maximum *effective* range (MER) – the distance

The large forward-firing gun carried by galleys was an effective ship-sinking weapon provided the crew could close a ship under sail. They were therefore at their most lethal in calm or confined waters. Once galleons were fitted with effective bow and stern guns the supremacy of the galley was over, as Drake first showed in Cadiz harbour in 1587. This painting by Abraham Storck shows a Dutch galleon fighting off the concerted attack of a flotilla of galleys at musketry range. (Scala Archives)

from which a shot had a very high chance of hitting the target at which the gun had been aimed. This was substantially shorter than the maximum range for a number of reasons: while both ranges were affected by the muzzle velocity, windage, trajectory and the aerodynamics of the shot, the effective range had to take into account the aiming of the weapon (rudimentary at best), the height of the gun above the water-line, the sea state and the size and relative movement of the target. MER thus varied from engagement to engagement, but it was never very far. Most modern authorities quote 200 yards as a reasonable MER, but it was probably less than this, as contemporary comments by seamen themselves frequently indicate. The two most quoted are that by Sir Richard Hawkins, who stated, 'How much nearer, so much the better', and Monson's remark that 'he that

shooteth far off at sea had as good not shoot at all'. Some 200 years later Robins wrote (in 1747): 'ranging farther in distant cannonading is perhaps the least Pre-eminence of heavy Shot; for the Uncertainty in this Practice, especially at Sea, is so great, that it has been generally discountenanced by the most skilful Commanders, as tending only to waste Ammunition'.

In the 1595 Indies expedition, Thomas Maynard, somewhat ashamed to be on board the group that had abandoned Baskerville to make a fleeter passage home, noted in the encounter with the Spaniards that the ill-disciplined and incompetent gunners of *Foresight* 'popped away powder and shot away to no purpose for most ... would hardly have stricken Paul's steeple had it stood there'.[48]

Monson, indeed, suggested that 'a principal thing in a gunner at sea is to be a good helmsman and to call to him at the helm to loof or bear up to have his better level and to observe the heaving and setting of the sea'. The idea of 'firing on the upward roll' may not have been in use, but it was not far away. Obviously the stability of the ship influenced its efficacy as a gun platform at range, and this stability could be easily affected. In the sea chase described in *The Complaynt of Scotland,* it is stated that 'The master bid all his mariners and men of war hold themselves quietly at rest, by reason that the moving of the people within a ship stops her on her course.' If the ship's company was increased by the presence of companies of soldiers untrained in the way of the sea, the uncertain movement of the ship would have been further increased.

Monson was very critical of the desire to place more armament than a ship's design made either safe or practical. In his 'Naval Abuses' he drew attention to the 'Disability of ships ... occasioned by the great weight of ordnance which makes them laboursome and causes their weakness. And, considering how few gunners are allowed to every ship, it were better to leave some of these pieces at home than to pester the ship with them.'[49]

There are, then, indications that the MER was very short indeed. Guilmartin writes that siege guns ashore were placed within sixty yards of the walls they were battering – a dangerous proximity that could be justified only by effectiveness. He also refers to the term *quemaropa,* a Spanish word meaning 'clothing-burning range' and used to describe most vividly the range at which most galley gun fights took place. He then moves on to discuss point-blank range, a term from the Spanish *punto de blanco,* 'pointed at the target'. The reference to pointing concerned the gunner's system of aiming by sighting his target along the top of the barrel. The projectile, travelling the length of the bore, would then travel on an upward-moving trajectory until shot and sight line coincided at the point-blank range.[50]

The dictionary definition of 'point-blank' includes that of aiming with the target so close that it is unnecessary to make allowances for the drop in the course of the projectile, but also most people's under-standing of the word, which is firing at nearly zero range. Guilmartin indicates that this convergence of line of sight and line of flight took place at about 300 yards, but that is far too far to be considered point-blank in today's understanding. It also does not stand up to geometric study. The gunner's eye as he crouched down behind his weapon could be some twelve inches above the centre of the shot. By the time the shot had exited the bore its centre would be six inches below the sight-line. The extension of those two lines gives a point of convergence nearer to thirty-five yards than 300. This closer range is supported by the table reproduced in John Smith's *Sea Grammar,* an amended extract from which is shown below.

Taking a pace to be the equivalent of one yard, the table indicates a point-blank range that ties in with both the geometry and the general understanding of the term. The provision of such tables must indicate that 'point-blank range' had a practical as well as a theoretical purpose, and this can only be that it indicated a range at which ships' gunners might be expected to open fire on their target. Given the very limited visibility that they had available, squinting down the barrel through a small gunport on a moving ship, the point-blank distance probably also approximated to the range at which they first got a clear sighting of their target.

The Move to Mass Manufacture

Bronze was expensive, and an expanding navy needed cheap guns. These could only be produced from iron, but there had to be a change from wrought-iron to cast-iron manufacture before reliable muzzle-loading iron guns could be made. The transition took time, but by the end of the Tudor century cast-iron guns were in the ascendancy and the way was clear for standardisation and mass production. This development was aided by a sharp reduction in cost. Not only was iron under one-fifth of the price of bronze, but between 1565 and 1600 the cost of cast-iron guns fell from £10–£12 to £8–£9 per ton.[51] Along with this came the very necessary improvement by standardisation. *Mary Rose* had twenty-nine large guns, all different; the 100-gun

Characteristics and Ranges of Guns

Name of piece	Bore (in)	Weight of piece (lb)	Weight of shot (lb)	Weight of powder (lb)	Breadth of ladle (in)	Length of ladle (in)	Shot: point-blank range (paces)	Shot: random (paces)
Cannon	8	6,000	60	27	12	24	17	2,000
Demi-cannon	6½	4,000	30¼	18	9⅓	23¼	17	1,700
Culverin	5½	4,500	17⅓	12	8½	22⅓	20	2,500
Demi-culverin	4½	3,400	9⅓	8	6⅓	21	20	2,500
Bastard culverin	4	3,000	7	6¼	6	20	18	1,800
Sacre	3½	1,400	5⅓	5⅓	5½	18	17	1,700
Falcon	2½	660	2¼	2¼	4¼	15	15	1,500
Falconet	2	500	1¼	1¼	3¼	11¼	14	1,400
Serpentine	1½	400	¼	⅓	2½	10	13	1,300

HMS *Victory* was to have three classes of iron cannon. These iron guns were produced in English foundries sited mainly in the Kentish and Sussex Weald, where the raw materials were so readily available.

Thus a century which began with the English importing both ordnance and expertise ended with the nation becoming an exporter of large guns. The arms trade, which was to be of such enduring significance to the national economy, was underway, and then, as now, it was not influenced by ethical considerations, for guns were being sold to Spain even while the two nations were at war.

Close-Range Weapons

Given the limited effective range of the heavy ordnance, when the enemy was engaged it was inevitably at close quarters and often within the range of hand-held weapons, and so invariably bloody. It was then followed by a frenzy of hand-to-hand fighting as each ship tried either to board or to repel its opponents. It was a form of warfare that required both strong leadership and firm followership.

Henry, who had shown himself to be an enthusiastic supporter of change and improvement in heavy ordnance, also loved hand weapons; but he tried to delay rather than encourage change with these, for he had no wish to see the longbow, with which his ancestors had won renown, replaced with the harquebus or handgun, to which he had no romantic attachment and in which he had no personal proficiency. The changeover was thus slow, and took far longer than technological development by itself might have suggested, the projectile of choice remained the arrow fired from a longbow, the weapon that had slaughtered the French sailors at the battle of Sluys in 1340 and defeated their cavalry at Agincourt in 1415. A hundred years later *Mary Rose* sailed towards another anchored French fleet with some 400 bows and 3,000 arrows as a major part of her close-quarters armament.

Henry, a first-class archer himself, passed a law to ensure that all his countrymen, with the exception of clergy and judges, regularly practised at the butts which had to be set up at every town on the pain of a fine. Between the ages of seven and seventeen a boy had to be provided with a bow and two arrows, after which he became responsible for providing his own bow and four arrows; these were sold at a maximum rate, fixed by the government, of 3s 4d. Regular practice of the sport, including permission to use the butts on a Sunday, meant that most able-bodied men achieved an accuracy out to 200 yards by the age of twenty-four. One can imagine, therefore, that archery occupied a position which today might be held by compulsory golf. Unlike other universal legislation, it was apparently strictly enforced, for in 1554 the constable at Portsmouth was summoned for 'Not having inspected once a month the houses of their neighbours to see if every man and every boy from seven to sixty years of age have bows and

Throughout the sixteenth century the bow and arrow remained a major component in a warship's arsenal, being reliable, rapid-firing and lethal at close-quarters. (Mary Rose Trust)

arrows in their custody according to statute', while the town's chamberlain was punished for not making up the butts, where, on every holy day, everyone had to turn out to shoot or face a penalty of a halfpenny for each omission.

As war planning got underway, so the need for bows and arrows had to be met from both home and abroad, and indeed the bows themselves were now often not made from English yew. A finer grain and therefore a more 'whippy' and stronger stave could be made from trees grown in more southerly climates, and it was to there that Henry turned for his supplies. As early as 1510 he was writing to the doge requesting the export of 40,000 bows from Venice to be conveyed in whatever ships might be available. Although such arms trading was contrary to the laws of Venice, the Senate approved a partial permit.[52] The bows were a long time awaiting despatch. In May 1511 the contracted merchant, Piero da Cha da Pesaro, appeared before the Venetian Senate bemoaning the fact that the current war prevented him from taking up ships with which to honour his contract. The Senate gave him permission to hire foreign barks for the voyage, contrary to acts it had passed earlier forbidding such trade.[53] That embargo was overturned in 1514, when the Senate again allowed de Pesaro to send a large number of bows to England in foreign vessels, provided, to salve their consciences and to line their pockets, that he also sailed with 500 butts of Cretan wine and other Venetian goods.[54]

Henry was also scouring England and Wales for enough home-produced bows. In December 1511 the bowmaker John Wood was paid to ride through the southern counties as far as Bristol looking for hemp for bowstrings as well as ordering bows to be made.[55] At the same time William Huxley, Clerk of Ordnance, was riding into the Welsh borders to order bows to be made of 'wich hazel', the quality of which must have been suspect. Indeed, Lord Thomas Howard wrote to the Privy Council in June 1513 in response to a criticism that the fleet was wasting bows to say that: 'As touching the bows and arrows, I shall see them a little wasted as shall be possible. And where your lordships write that it is great marvelled where so great a number of bows and arrows be brought to so small a number, I have enquired the cause thereof; and as far as I can see, the greatest number were witch bows of whom few would abide the bending.'[56]

Being the ingratiating courtier that he was, Howard went on to say that the wastage probably took place during his brother's time as admiral but that he, of course, would take every step to ensure that losses were kept to a minimum. Given that the fleet had had one short major skirmish and one cutting-out operation since it had last been stored, the loss does seem surprisingly high. Perhaps (and it would be the only hint of this) the archers were being encouraged to keep up their exercises while at sea, where, of course, arrows could not be recovered. What seems apparent is that English yew bows of the right quality and quantity were not being provided to support the belligerent foreign policy. The reference to wych hazel is puzzling. Ordinary hazel splits when over-bent, as Howard indicated, but wych hazel is the beautiful shrub *hammamelis* of American origin. However, in Tudor times, the wych elm, which when coppiced resembled hazel, was commonly referred to as such and had stems which could be made into bows, albeit of an inferior quality.

The concern over the quality of bows was a constant. Writing from the army camp in France in 1543, Thomas Seymour complained: 'The bowstrings sent are so evil that they break with bending the bows, which bows are so weak that the soldiers complain. If the army shall continue any time, they will need stronger bows and better strings.'[57] It is only a snapshot, but the bows recovered from *Mary Rose* (there were no bowstrings salved) are of a quality above such reproach; but perhaps the skills necessary for maintaining such a high standard were becoming less common as hand-held firearms gained dominance.

The English retained the primacy of skill with this ancient and deadly weapon while its replacement was being introduced. Then, somewhat reluctantly at first but, inevitably, the hackbuss, or arquebus (the early musket), began appearing in the inventory of naval vessels. Henry did not favour the weapon. In December 1528 a proclamation was published forbidding the using or keeping of both cross-bows and handguns, as well as the playing of tennis, dice and other unlawful games, *contrary to the statutes for the maintenance of archery*. The additional sting was that the king's subjects were ordered to inform on any who disobeyed this statute.[58]

The sunset of the bow was thus a long one. During the Armada campaign, Drake, closing in on the disabled *Rosario*, discharged, along with twenty-five or thirty muskets, a volley of arrows. He had used the same mix of hand-weapons when drawing alongside *Cacafuego*, his rich prize in the Pacific, in 1579, with the same result – surrender. It was a clever combination, the guns providing smoke, noise and the whistle of shot to scare the crew into taking cover, and the far more accurate archers taking out any individual who might pose a threat or was about to take precipitous action. Bows were also handy for carrying in boats for landings when the surf might well dampen the harquebusiers' powder and fuze.

In June 1591 Elizabeth, railing against frivolous pastimes, required that 'archery [be] revived and practised; for by this ancient weapon hath our nation won great honour in time past. Moreover by this means those poor men whose living chiefly depends thereon, as bowers, fletchers, stringers and arrowhead maker, will be maintained and set to work in their vocations'.[59] The 1595 expedition to the Indies sailed with 174 longbows and 340 sheaves of arrows embarked, as well as 520 muskets and 220 calivers (another form of early musket), but by 1601 the end was in sight for the professional bowman, not because of the greater lethality of the musket, but because sturdy labourers with a lifelong training in archery were no longer available to bend bows, and it only took a few hours to train a puny soldier to fire a musket.

The admiration that was undoubtedly due to the archers for their deadly skill was enhanced by the gratitude of the soldiers, for, as well as

The first of hundreds of yew bows recovered from the Mary Rose, *in almost as good a condition as on the day the ship sank.* (Mary Rose Trust)

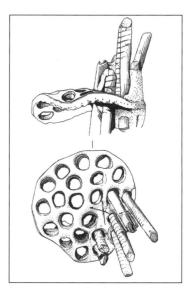

Each quiver had a leather spacer to protect the delicate goose-feather flights from being crushed against each other. (Mary Rose Trust)

Although over a thousand arrows were recovered from the Mary Rose, *salt water immersion had destroyed both the iron tips and feathered flights.* (Mary Rose Trust)

At close range archers fired at the opposing personnel, protected by moveable blinds. Above the archer anti-boarding netting can be seen, rigged in battle to protect the upper deck from enemy boarders. However, if the ship sank then the netting trapped those below it, as seems to have happened to the Mary Rose. (Mary Rose Trust)

taking life, the bow also provided protection. Many a soldier swinging on board the ship to which his own vessel had become grappled would have seen that all that was left for him to do was a mopping-up operation, cutting a few throats, disembowelling a few seamen and 'liberating' a few items of property, before returning to enjoy the glories of success, because the bowmen had done their work well.

The archers also provided defence for another group on board – the gunners. On the upper deck the guns were ranged behind a series of removable blinds that the archers could take out to give themselves a sighting line while protecting their bodies from return fire. A gunner, if he was to get any decent sight of his target, had also to remove the blind directly above his gun. This left him exposed, especially as the range reduced rapidly to the point of impact. To give him protection an archer stood on either side of the gun barrel, keeping an eye open for any enemy who might be aiming at the gun crew.

Wildfire

Bows were also used to discharge flaming arrows against an enemy's sails. The *Mary Rose* inventory of 1514 included:

74 arrows of wildfire
2 balls of wildfire
8 heads for arrows of wildfire
29 hooks for arrows of wildfire

She also had larger darts with wooden flights that could be hurled from close quarters, either into the rigging or down hatches. These had to be used with caution and control. If one of two ships grappled together caught alight, there was every chance that the other would be unable to cut herself free in time to avoid a mutual conflagration. This is what happened to *Regent* in 1512 once *Cordelière* caught fire, and several other instances are recorded. Yet the ability to use wildfire remained within the arsenal, and the 1595 Indies expedition included 144 longbow arrows for fireworks and 130 bows and arrows with fireworks.

Arquebuses

The introduction of the arquebus or hagbush to replace the bow was inevitable, albeit delayed, and by 1544 Henry was prepared to experiment. A royal proclamation of that year allowed:

... some number of his subjects skilled and exercised in the feat of shooting in handguns and hagbushes as well for the defence of the realm against enemies as annoying of the same in time of war ... gives licence and liberty to all and singular his majesty's subjects born within his grace's dominions being of age of sixteen and upwards that they and every of them from henceforth may lawfully shoot in handguns and hagbushes without incurring forfeiture loss or damage for the same[60]

– as long as practising was confined to butts away from inhabited spaces. However, peace in 1546 led to a rethink about this licence to

carry arms, and the statute was revoked and the carrying of guns once more limited. It may not be too fanciful to see in this proclamation the seed which sprang forth so sturdily in the American constitution.

The change was inevitable. England's stock of strong-armed and trained bow-benders and bowyers was in decline because of changes wrought by population movement, employment and the after-effects of plague and famine. It became much easier and cheaper to manufacture iron tubes, the user of which only needed a few hours' instruction before being placed in front of an enemy with a lethal weapon in his hands. Although the penetrative power of an arrow and a one-ounce ball into human flesh, even through chain-mail, was similar in close-quarters exchanges, the latter had an advantage, for whereas an arrow would pierce thin pavises it would get stuck in the woodwork, whereas a lead ball would pass on through with enough kinetic energy left to hurt someone sheltering behind. Many years later a musket-ball's most famous victim was to be Admiral Nelson at Trafalgar, but the handgun had established its reputation far earlier, accounting for both Richard Grenville in 1591 and Frobisher in 1594.

The Tudor arquebus was lengthy, heavy and unwieldy, but the introduction of the matchlock firing mechanism increased its reliability. No longer did the user have to thrust a length of glowing fuze into the flash pan, similar to the way the linstock was used for heavier weapons; now the slow match was grasped in a pair of jaws which, when the trigger was pulled, rotated downwards to make contact with the powder in the flash pan. All that the musketeer had to do was make sure his fuze stayed alight. If it did not, at close quarters, he was in difficulties. Drake's master gunner, Oliver, on raising his gun to

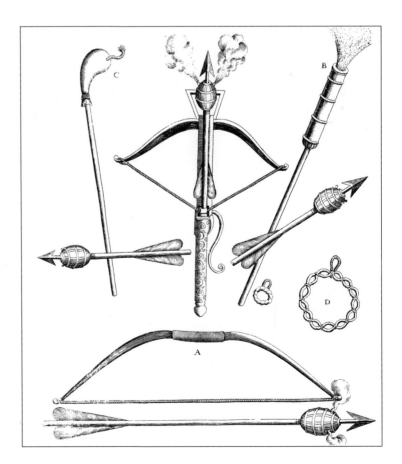

The fear and effect of fire onboard wooden ships was fully exploited within the range of weapons of war. These fiery weapons are illustrations from a contemporary treatise.

shoot a Patagonian Indian advancing with a bow with which he had already shot and killed one man, found his powder damp and, with no time to clear it, died when an arrow pierced him right through.

Cutting-Edged Weapons

The other hand-held weapons available on board retained a distinctly medieval appearance. They came in two categories: staffed and short-handled. The former were designed either to hook and cut an enemy's shrouds or to repel boarders; the latter included swords, the personal weapon of officers, and daggers, every seaman's constant companion and the one sharp-bladed instrument which was used daily for cutting rope, whittling wood and eating food. To keep these weapons sharp every ship carried both a grinder and whet-stones, which were often the personal possessions of the men. Knives, short for daily use and long for fighting, would normally have been sheathed, although some were worn as a fashion accessory, especially bollock knives, so named because of the double spherical form of their guard, which were often flaunted unsheathed. Carried in this fashion on board they would have been a hindrance to anyone working aloft, and so would have remained below deck until throats needed cutting.

Fireships

For those on board ship the greatest of all fears was fire. Once flames had taken hold, the primitive pumps and buckets available to fight the blaze were totally inadequate to save the ship. This combination of fear and effect made fire a great weapon if it could be controlled and directed. Setting fire to a vessel lying alongside by the use of flaming arrows or darts could make one's own vessel a part of the inferno, especially once gunpowder was ignited. Fire was therefore best deployed at a safe distance using unmanned vessels, but the problem

The most effective warship was the one whose fit of weapons enabled it to engage the enemy with effect from several hundred yards out to close in, giving the defenders no respite. This detail from the Storck painting reproduced earlier, shows arquebusiers in action.

was then one of accurate delivery, for ships that drift on wind and tide seldom fetch up where intended. Fireships were thus unguided missiles, best used in restricted waterways where they had no option but to float down on to their target.

In 1568 Hawkins's fleet at San Juan de Ulua was trapped in just such a restricted waterway, but gave such a good account of itself that it looked likely to be able to escape to sea relatively unscathed. Then both sides saw that the use of fire might turn the course of the engagement. For the Spanish, Vice-Admiral Ubilla loaded a large boat, lying upwind of the still-anchored English ships, with kegs of gunpowder and inflammable material and, lighting a fuze, cast her off. The fuze flared, fluttered and died.

Hawkins's French ally Captain Bland adopted a far riskier and more sacrificial approach born of despair. He tried to sail his ship, *Grace à Dieu*, up-wind of the Spanish, where he planned to grapple one of their vessels and set fire to his own ship before abandoning her.

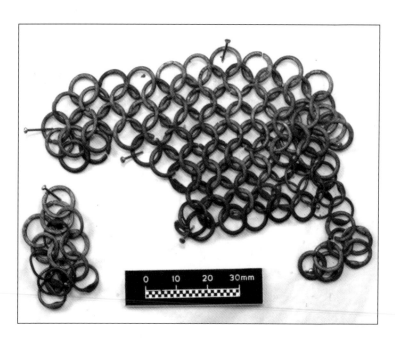

Chain-mail, although popular with soldiery in land battles, was weighty and its wearing guaranteed a drowning death to any wearer who was cast overboard. Although this example was found on the Mary Rose, sailors probably chose not to wear such protection. (Mary Rose Trust)

Only one sword (top) was recovered from Mary Rose but its weight and length of blade (as shown in reconstruction, centre) compared with a modern naval sword (bottom) indicates that the Tudor officer to whom it belongs was both tall and sturdily built.

The 'weapon' with which every seamen would have been most familiar was the knife, which he put to daily use in a number of tasks, from cutting rope to eating food. (Mary Rose Trust)

Spanish gunnery brought down her sails before she could reach her target, and she burned harmlessly away in the Channel. The initiative passed back to the Spanish, who this time selected a much larger vessel as a fireship and made sure she was well ablaze before casting her off for the short voyage towards *Minion*, which lay up-wind of Hawkins's flagship, *Jesus of Lubeck*. As she approached, she unleashed the secondary weapon in the fireship's arsenal – panic. Instead of waiting to fend off the fire–ship with long poles, the crew of *Minion* cut the lines securing them to *Jesus*, unfurled their sails and endeavoured to get underway. Seeing themselves on the point of abandonment, those on the deck of *Jesus*, including Hawkins himself, jumped on to the decks of the departing *Minion*, leaving their flagship and those still on board her, including Hawkins's eleven-year-old nephew Paul, to the devilment of Spain. Many of those on the overcrowded *Minion* would also fall into the hands of Spain when Hawkins was forced to land them on the coast of Mexico, to give at least those who remained on board a chance of reaching England. It was England's worst defeat of the cold war and was achieved largely from the fear of a fireship which, in the event, drifted by harmlessly.

It was not always so. At Antwerp in 1585 the Dutch released fireships filled with high explosive downstream to lie against the piers of a bridge, where they blew up, killing over 1,000 Spanish troops and devastating the land around. The fame and effect of these so-called 'hell-burners' spread far and wide. One group who knew the story very well consisted of the crews of the Spanish Armada. Some of them also believed that the inventor of those bombs, the Italian Frederico Giambelli, was in England in 1588. Aware of this rumour, and the threat to his fleet anchorage off Calais, Medina Sidonia ordered boats to be anchored upstream of his ships in order to grapple and tow clear any fireships drifting down from the English fleet. Also aware of the panic factor, Sidonia sent messengers to all his captains warning them of the threat, informing them of his countermeasures and ordering that no ship should slip its moorings unless directly in the path of a fireship that had got past his pinnaces.

The English prepared eight such vessels, offered up, patriotically, by Drake and Hawkins and a number of merchants, although the claims for compensation did seem to put a high value on the cost of the hulls and listed a curiously expensive cargo manifest! But whatever else was in the hold, there was no doubt that the remaining space was filled with explosives and combustibles. What is more, rather than leaving her course to the variables of tide and wind, each vessel had a volunteer crew on board to sail it towards the Spanish until prudence dictated that they should abandon their flaming charge and drop overboard into the rescue boats alongside. The enemy pinnaces dragged two away, but six drifted towards the fleet, the majority of which were not prepared to stay and play matadors with these flaming black bulls. They cut their cables and fled. The close disciplined formation that had been the Armada's greatest strength was wrecked, never to be re-assembled. Yet again fireships had proved that their greatest weapon was fear and not fire.

Six years later, in 1594, James Lancaster seized the port of Pernambuco in Brazil with the intention of transferring the cargo from a rich disabled carrack to his own small squadron. Driven from the town and its forts, the Portuguese inhabitants prepared five caravels, which they set alight and launched towards the English ships on a favourable tide and wind. For a moment it looked as though the caravels might outsail the protective group of six boats that Lancaster had sitting in the harbour, waiting to deal with just such a threat. At the last moment the crews of these boats 'So played the men when they saw the fires come near our ships that casting grapnels with iron chains on them, as every boat had one for that purpose, some they towed aground, and some they brought to anchor ... till all their force was burnt out.'[61] Note the attention to detail: the grapnel lines were of iron rather than rope to prevent the fire from burning through them.

From daggers to demi-cannons, Tudor warships were equipped to deliver damage and defend the coast. Today, devastating destruction can be wrought by the finger of one man, well out of contact with his target, releasing the technical skill of thousands. In the Tudor navy the ratios were reversed: the numbers were needed at the sharp end, and that was inevitably going to be at a dagger-blade's distance and at point-blank range. For all the hatred, torture and betrayal that the age wallowed in ashore, it seems that those who manned the guns and held the sword before their foemen at sea fought well, killed cleanly and died in a cause and a war in which they believed.

Close-up of the English fireship attack off Gravelines: in the end it was not the power of gunfire but the fear of fire itself which led to the dispersal and defeat of the Spanish Armada. (National Maritime Museum, detail from BHC0263)

Chapter Five

Feeding the Fleet

Is there any man among you which would proffer his son a stone if he asked him bread? Or if he asked fish would he proffer him a serpent?
Gospel according to St Matthew, Chapter 7, verses 9–10, Coverdale version, 1535

It was an age when if it moved, you ate it. In a proclamation setting the price of poultry in May 1544, the cost of the following wild fowl and poultry is listed: swan, crane, bustard, stork, heron, shoveller, peacock, pea-chicken, goose, egret, gull, dotterell (a type of plover), quail, sparrow, pigeon, mallard, teal, widgeon, woodcock, plover, snipe, lark and bunting.[1] At his daughter's wedding in 1582, Lord Burghley's guests consumed 1,000 gallons of wine, six veal calves, twenty-six deer, fifteen pigs, fourteen sheep, sixteen lambs, four kids, six hares, thirty-six swans, two storks, forty-one turkeys, 380 poultry (hens and chickens), forty-nine curlews, 135 mallards, 354 teal, 1,049 plovers, 124 knotts, 280 stint, 109 pheasants, 277 partridge, 615 cocks, 485 snipe, 840 larks, 21 gulls, 71 rabbits, twenty-three pigeons and two sturgeons, and all within three days. This is the same Lord Burghley who was to find it most difficult to provide food for the hundreds of English seamen dying in the streets of Margate six years later, having driven the Armada away from the shores of England.

These seamen were not as fussy as Burghley's guests, nor were the calls upon the skills of their cooks so varied. In the entire long century the menu card on board ship was to be based on just five main items; beef, biscuit, bread, salt cod and beer. This might seem mean as well as inadequate, yet for a great part of the twentieth century many seamen lived content on a self-imposed diet of beer, chips and tobacco – two of which essentials were unavailable to the sixteenth-century caterer. The provision of the victuals that they had was, by and large, a

Cardinal Wolsey, through his masterful management of provisioning, ensured that Henry VIII was able to maintain a permanent fleet of ships. (Wikimedia)

logistic triumph and not the disaster it is sometimes seen to be. The begetter of the fleet's logistic support was Thomas Wolsey, probably the only man in the kingdom capable of creating the enormous supply chain that a standing operational navy required. Comparison with Lloyd George, Minister of Munitions in the early part of the First World War, is favourable to both men, and yet the Welsh Wizard is renowned for his efforts while the master almoner's achievements are largely forgotten, even at Hampton Court. Nevertheless, by his success in keeping the navy in being, the corpulent cardinal can claim to be the man who kept alive Henry's vision of a standing navy.

The requirement to feed a navy was a new one. The English army had endeavoured to fight its wars on foreign soil where short rations could be supplemented by raiding nearby fields and farms, which were generally well stocked as the campaign season was a summer one. Baggage trains followed along agreed routes and store ships were unloaded at agreed ports. Yet few English generals managed their victualling satisfactorily. The Duke of Norfolk, besieging Montreuil in 1544, less than forty kilometres from English-held Calais, was forced to retreat through miles of starving peasantry with his own men famished and waterless. If it was difficult to provision the army with the resources available, how much harder it was to keep supplied an independently-operating navy whose movements were both uncertain and unknown. The navy had, for the most part, to be provisioned from national resources, with no guarantee of replenishment abroad. However, if opportunity arose then passing merchant ships and coastal towns and villages were seized and pillaged to supplement the sailors' diet. Thus Drake, on his circumnavigation, took every opportunity to intercept and plunder craft ranging from fishing boats to argosies, not just for cargoes of pecuniary value but for the food they had on board, and the same consideration was given on raids ashore.

It would be too simple to state that before Wolsey grasped the victualling problem all was chaos, but the evidence from Henry's early fleet deployments might suggest that this was indeed the case. Lord Darcy's expedition against the Moors in 1511 ended with the report that:

> Upon the deliberated sight of the great extremities and necessities that the King's army of archers stood in, as well for fault and lack of money, as especially victuals, the Lord Darcy delivered the said day at Cape St. Vincent, of his own proper money, to every captain, for the victualling of him and one hundred archers under his leading, £20 of English gold.[2]

Just a few months later the Marquess of Dorset repeated the shambles in Fontarabia in northern Spain, losing men to dysentery brought about by drunkenness. If the navy was to act as an effective arm of the king, then its supply chain needed to be examined and reformed. There was no one in the country, certainly among the nobility, capable of grasping the enormity of the problem and introducing a solution. Wolsey could. Wolsey did and, from 1511, Wolsey delivered and relished the challenge.

Wolsey's organisation involved appointing county purveyors to deliver certain commodities in bulk to contractors in the port towns. Special commissioners, such as John Dawtrey in Southampton, set the rates for purchase and also awarded contracts to specific brewers and bakers. This was not just a task for the counties on the southern sea coast. The sheriffs of Yorkshire and Lincolnshire were also told to proclaim that wheat and malt could not be exported but had to be sent to Southampton and Portsmouth for the provisioning of the fleet.[3] In an effort to forestall any 'futures' market being established, the proclamation also forbade suppliers in these counties to 'engross, forestall or regrate victuals'. Wolsey was both cornering the market and making himself the sole purchaser, an arrangement that would have caused much suffering in communities deprived of their harvest. In 1513–14 some 253 winter-fed oxen in Lincolnshire, along with 322 at Wisbech and 164 at Stamford and Peterborough, were purchased by the naval victualler for delivery to the fleet,[4] which would have placed the government in much the same position in relation to the provider as that which is complained about today in respect of supermarkets and the farming community. It had a major effect on retail prices. In May 1512 the Venetian ambassador reported that the salting of 25,000 oxen had raised the price of beef from 1d to 3d a pound. This was not a bad mark-up for those involved in setting prices – which the commissioners could do, for when purchasing for the king, they had to be sold goods at the price they set, and they then sold them on at another price they set.

A victualling account of 1514 gives an idea of the bulk involved and the sums needed to purchase it. It records the receipt of 1,000 barrels of flour at 10s and a further 3,611 barrels 4 bushels 3 pecks at 8s a barrel; forty quarters of wheat for brewing beer at 10s the quarter; 408 tons of empty beer barrels at 5s the ton; 7,845 quarters of malt at 5s 4d a quarter; 150 tons of beer at a £1 a ton; and 180 flitches of bacon for £13 10s.[5] The victualling bill for the period amounted to £25,625 6s 6d, a sum equivalent today (using Alison Weir's multiplier of 300[6]) to over £7,780,000!

The amount of food prepared and moved was thus staggering. The daily ration of beer, beef and biscuit for one man would have weighed about 5lb; when multiplied this by ninety, reflecting the need to provision for three months, this gives a total of 450lb per man. The naval forces assembled for major campaigns could number 10,000, making a staggering total victualling weight of four and a half million pounds that the commissioners had to find and transport to the ports. They would have needed some 1,500 wagons, 3,000 carters and 6,000 horses to move this bulk to the ports for storage or shipping either to the warships directly or to the fleet of victuallers which might be anchored some distance offshore, thus requiring many boats and boatmen to complete the transfer. Given these great numbers, much credit is due to the logistics team who managed the operation, and if some of them, like John Dawtrey, became rich in the process their wealth may not have been undeserved.

Once victuals had arrived at the quayside it was the purser's job to purchase them and have them transported on board. The post of purser was created by Henry in February 1512 in his order of 'Things to be done for the setting forth of the King's army by the sea'.[7] Among other provisions this stated that one 'substantial' person in every ship was to be appointed to oversee the king's victuals and 'control their expenditure by a rate delivered to them'. To achieve his task each

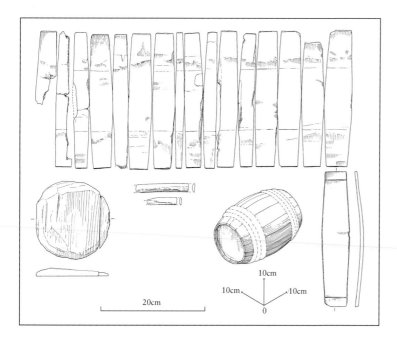

10cm

10cm   10cm

20cm

0

Barrels were the key to storage of both food and drink and ordnance stores. Ships had to have holds large enough to carry hundreds of barrels and the wine barrel, or 'tun', became the standard measure of a ship's capacity – its 'tunnage'. Since a shortage of barrels could severely curtail operations, they were greatly valued and a specialist cooper on board was responsible for their maintenance and dismantling the 'empties' to save space. (Mary Rose Trust)

John Dawtry made a fortune from being in charge of fleet victualling for Hampshire in Henry VIII's reign, as well as controlling customs and being the paymaster for Portsmouth-built warships. His wealth is demonstrated by his great house that still stands in Southampton. (Southampton City Council Heritage Services)

purser was provided with an allowance of about 1s 3d per man per week, or 2d a day. This may seem totally inadequate, but translated into today's prices it represents about £3 per man for two meals a day. The present allowance for sea-going ships in the Royal Navy is about £2.20, while in prisons it stands at about £2.30. Recent political debate has focused on increasing the allowance for one school meal a day to 50p per pupil per day.

The purser was expected to spend his allowance on the staple foodstuffs being prepared for delivery by the commissioner's agents, providing the following weekly rations per man:

7lb of biscuits
8lb of salt beef
¾lb of stock fish
⅜lb of butter
¾lb of cheese
7 gallons of beer

This was based on a twenty-eight-day month, with half rations on Fridays. A letter from William Cecil, Lord Burghley, to the Privy Council dated 13 March 1588 listed the menu on which the issue of rations was to be based:

Sunday	Flesh Day	Salt Beef
Monday	Bacon and Peas	
Tuesday	Flesh Day	Salt Beef
Wednesday	Fish Day	
Thursday	Flesh Day	Salt Beef
Friday	Fish Day	Half Rations
Saturday	Fish Day	

The introduction of three fish days for the fleet was followed by a short-term measure to introduce the concept nationwide. In 1593 Admiral William Winter introduced a bill to Parliament intended to make the nation, as well as the navy, eat fish on three rather than two days a week. The aim was to build up a reserve of fishermen who could be called upon to serve in the navy at times of emergency. Most of the measures were uncontentious, but the proposal to introduce yet

another national fish day, Wednesday, was contested so hotly that the sponsorship of the bill was moved from Winter to the far more influential William Cecil. In his address to the House at the third reading Cecil summed up the aims of a maritime life most cogently: 'The very ground that naturally serveth to breed mariners is the trade and conversation upon the sea which is divided into two sorts: the one is to carry and recarry merchandise; the other is to take fish: for the third, which is exercise of piracy, is detestable and cannot last.'[8]

Much of the fish came from Iceland and the Newfoundland Banks, which necessitated keeping a large fishing fleet. The proclamations of 1593, reissued in 1595, explained the necessity of fish days both to maintain fishermen, and therefore a pool of experienced seafarers, and also to stop the decay of coastal towns with their other important maritime trades. These were obvious considerations, but another was the government's concern with the effect that increased grazing was having on the countryside: its research had shown that one extra fish day a week in London alone would save 13,500 'beeves'.[9] The demand for fish was reflected in the price, with dried fish costs rising from £12 to £18 a last between 1585 and 1595.

In passing, Cecil was making out a strong case for the existence of a standing navy when the nation was at peace, for as long as the third activity that he mentioned persisted those occupied in the first two lawful occupations would require protection, while as long as they remained a threat, the pirates would need pursuing and deterring.

Cecil was content with the development of trade being carried in English hulls but saw that the fishing industry was in decline. Moreover, unlike other goods, fish had no obvious market abroad, because other nations had their own fishing fleets. The only way to halt the decline was to increase domestic consumption, hence the need for an extra fish day.

Members were not impressed. Many of them had recently enclosed land for stock and had great plans for selling their meat to the growing markets of the towns. They even resorted to playing the Catholic card, calling the measure 'Popish' and causing the sponsor to declare that it was unlawful for 'Cecil's Fast', as it came to be known, to be given a religious connotation. In the end, desperate to pass the measure, Cecil succeeded in doing so only by placing a self-inflicted flaw in his argument, stating that it was of such little practical significance that few would notice its existence. In that case, said the House

when the measure next came up for debate, we might as well rid ourselves of its irritation, which it duly did.

Fish days did, however, continue to be observed, and the rich were prepared to do their bit to help the ailing fishing industry. On 7 June 1594 the ten judges of the Court of Star Chamber were served ling, green-fish, salmon,

Pig and fish bones recovered from the Mary Rose *give some indication of the Tudor seaman's diet.* (Mary Rose Trust)

pike, gurnard, John Dory, carp, tench, knob-berd, grey-fish, plaice, perch, sole, conger, barbel, flounder, turbot, whiting, lobster, crab and prawns. Gastronomic greed, it seems, went hand in hand with the quest for financial gain. At sea, floating in waters abundant with all these species, the naval seamen were served salted cod, ling, skate and herring, while tunny and sturgeon were also provided for the officers. Fish was, of course, available very locally, and the artefacts recovered from *Mary Rose* include fishing tackle of the kind supplied to all deploying fleets: lines, hooks, nets, spears and harpoons.

The institution of a half ration day seems an ominous principle and scarcely the sort of policy to encourage a happy crew, especially when, given the unpredictable exigencies of life at sea, Friday could have been a day of great demand on a ship's company's energy, yet logic would suggest that this was the day when the cook was encouraged to use up the remains from earlier in the week and to produce a tasty and nutritious stew, so that the fare was actually something to look forward to as well as giving the purser an opportunity to dispose of the produce from less well-preserved barrels. This he was forced to do, for, as was stated in the indenture between Henry and Sir Edward Howard at the start of the sea campaign of 1512, each of the admiral's eighteen ships was required to sail with three months' victuals, which they were to embark off Cowes and which had to last until the fleet returned to Southampton.[10] The only relief was the presence of two small crayers which were to act as re-supply boats.

The daily calorific value of this vitamin-deficient diet, including the beer, has been estimated at between 4,265 and 5,132 kilocalories,[11] scarcely enough to keep active men healthy, especially if the effects of cold, wet and wind are taken into account. Commanders, even if unschooled in the science of diet and vitamins, would have been well aware that trying to work a ship with a weak crew was unsatisfactory and dangerous, and the margins between fitness and illness were small even in English coastal waters, where the problems of supply might be thought to have been minimal. So the pressure from sea upon the suppliers was, from earliest times, intense. By 1562 the purveyancing scheme introduced by Wolsey was creaking at the seams and Edward Baeshe, the navy victualler, proposed replacing it with a system of bargains with the brewers, bakers and butchers.

Wolsey's arrangements were initially accepted by the navy even when, in the second year of the war, Sir Edward Howard was forced to sail from the Thames not fully stored and wrote to Wolsey in March 1513:

> Master Almoner, in my heartiest wise I can recommend me unto you. And I have received your letter, whereby I perceive that you have sent my fellow Kerby with a clerk with him to take a view how much victual we have here. Sir, without I should lose a tide, it cannot be. And you shall have as good a certainty there at London of the deliveries of the victual which have delivered the pursers upon their bills to them made as much victual as is come.[12]

A reconstruction of the cook-room of the Mary Rose. *An interesting feature is the dangle-spit, which allowed the roasting of limited amounts of meat.*
(Mary Rose Trust)

Howard made the error of leaving his pursers behind to chase up the tardy victuals and consequently, later in his campaign, had no clear idea as to which ships were adequately stored and which were not. The failure to deliver in port did lead to the first occasion on which ships were replenished at sea, a procedure which became traditional for those deployed away from their base port.

By the beginning of April, Howard, while reporting his eagerness to get to grips with the French, showed that he had lost patience with the supply train, telling Wolsey:

> I assure you was never an army so falsely victualled. They that received their proportion for 2 months' flesh cannot bring about for 5 weeks, for the barrels be full of salt; and when the pieces keepeth the number, where they should be penny pieces they be scant halfpenny pieces, and where 2 pieces should make a mess, 3 will do but serve. Also, many came out of Thames but with a month's beer, trusting that the victuallers should bring the rest, ad here cometh none.[13]

A week later, seeing no evidence of improvement, Howard went over Wolsey's head and wrote to the king voicing his complaint in a way that the monarch, eager for action, would comprehend:

> Sir, we lose no time, I warrant you, for we think upon none other thing but how we may best grieve our enemies. If victual serve us, as your men and ships are determined, we shall this year make a bare coast all the realm of France that boundeth on the sea coast, which shall never recover in our days. Therefore, for no cost sparing let provision be made, for it is a well spent penny that saveth a pound, for [...] was wont to be spent in 3 or 4 year on the sea with one expense now, we shall do more good than in 4 year by driblet. Sir, I remit all the further order of this great matter to your noble wisdom and discreet order of your wise councillors.[14]

A cleverer way of making his point, appealing to the king's wisdom, vanity, supreme command and desire to damage the French, would have been hard to imagine. Yet the letter does not seem to have had much effect on Wolsey's organisation. Throughout May and June, Lord Thomas Howard, having been appointed Lord Admiral on the death in action of Edward, was writing to Wolsey complaining that he had his fleet with soldiery embarked uncomfortable in the exposed anchorage at Plymouth while their victuals lay at Southampton, unable to sail west because of contrary winds.

Even when the fleet had worked its way east into the tidal reaches of the Solent other problems arose. Firstly, there were not specialist boats to transport the victuals out to the ships:

> And as touching my departure hence, I assure your lordship, I tarry for nothing save only for lading of beer, which is slowest work that ever a man saw. There is but two cranes and the crayers that shall be laden with them must come in at a full sea and at a full sea go out. Wherefore, if your lordships see not another provi-

sion for lading beer against the next re-victualling I fear me we shall spend half or we get hence.[15]

Howard's practical solution was for some lighters to be brought round from the Thames, and he also suggested that if this course was followed they would require additional strakes to make them more seaworthy once outside the shelter of the river.

There were other problems over which Howard and Wolsey saw fit to quarrel. Nearly all the supplies were embarked in barrels, meaning that space had to be found on board for a very great number. *Mary Rose* is thought to have had between 120 and 150 of them when she sank off Portsmouth,[16] and presumably many more would have been taken on if she was expected to be heading for the French coast. As well as consumables, the casks would have held ship stores such as candle, tallow, pitch and tar, gunpowder and tampions. Empty casks even when dismantled, which they usually were, take up a lot of room and in tight storage conditions need to be removed and returned to make way for new. However, that is a time-consuming task on board ship, while holding them on deck until a suitable boat arrives to carry them away clutters up gangways. Sailors have always found it far simpler to throw them overboard or even burn them, which leads to a shortage ashore for re-provisioning, and this is what happened in

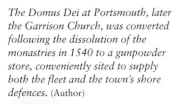

Lord Admiral Thomas Howard loathed the upstart Thomas Wolsey but both men set aside their hatred in the common aim of establishing an effective fighting navy.

The Domus Dei at Portsmouth, later the Garrison Church, was converted following the dissolution of the monastries in 1540 to a gunpowder store, conveniently sited to supply both the fleet and the town's shore defences. (Author)

Thomas Howard's fleet.

The first indication of the problem was voiced in a letter to Wolsey from John Dawtrey, who informed him that of 756 pipes (large casks, equivalent to four barrels or 105 gallons) of store delivered to the fleet only eighty foists (or casks) had been returned, making it almost impossible to keep up the supply.[17] Wolsey fired off a letter almost immediately to Howard:

My lord, I assure you it is not possible to furnish your re-vict-ualing if foists [barrels] be not more plenteously brought from the navy to Hampton than they be, which is a great lack and default, for ye cannot be provided elsewhere of any foists for money. And if the foists amongst the navy be not kept and reserved, but waste-fully burnt and broken as I hear say they be, ye cannot be sufficiently re-victualed to tarry any longer on the sea, for whereas ships have received 10 weeks past 756 pipes, they have redelivered scantily 80 foists of them. What as it appeareth is done by some lewd persons that would not have the King's navy continue any longer on the Sea. And therefore, My lord, for God's sake, look well to this matter so that such substantial order may be taken that the empty foists may be continually rescued.[18]

This was received frostily by the noble lord, who responded in the letter quoted earlier to the Privy Council, using the opportunity to crit-icise indirectly the almoner over the supply of bows:

And as touching the receiving of bows and arrows, I shall see them as little wasted as shall be possible. And where your lordships write that it is great marveled where so great a number of bows and arrows be brought to so small a number, I have enquired the causes thereof: and, as far as I can see, the greatest number were witch bows, of whom few would abide the bending. But as for that was done before my time, I cannot call again, but from hence-forth, if I do not the best I can to keep everything from waste, I am worthy blame, which I trust I shall not deserve.

And as touching the safe keeping of foists, assuredly, before my coming was great waste, and since my coming I trust few or never one hath been wasted, nor shall be.[19]

This is typical Howard, justifying himself, blaming someone else, in this case his dead brother, promising better and discrediting an enemy, Wolsey – masterly!

The vital importance of foists continued throughout the period. In 1586, with the Spanish war scarcely underway, Burghley ordered that the exporting of casks and clapboard (oak planks from which they were made) was to stop and that, in addition, for every seven tons of beer exported, merchants had to return with 200 clapboards.[20] Among the achievements of Drake in singeing the King of Spain's beard in 1587, his capture of barrel staves has been seen as a crucial blow to the Spanish state of preparedness.

Victualling was to create one of the century's perennial problems. In the war of 1522–5 Howard again corresponded with the king:

... to advertise your highness how your grace is deceived for the furniture of victual for your army, where it was promised that by the last day of May we should have had the whole complement for 5,000 men from Portsmouth of beer, and from Hampton of all other victual, with much difficulty we be furnished now, which is the 20 day of June, from Hampton of flesh, fish and biscuit for the said two months, and from Portsmouth by no means he can have none than for one month of beer ... Most humbly beseeching your grace to consider that it shall not be possible for me and the company here to accomplish all that we be determined to attempt unless we be better furnished with victuals than we be as yet.[21]

Such a chain of correspondence has links made from common alloys, weakened by the flaws of incompetence and malpractice. Often the admirals or individual captains themselves had to purchase food to keep their men supplied. The king's grants of July 1512 included a payment of £50 to Sir Thomas Knyvet for the provision of biscuit, beer and others victuals a well as the hire of hoys for their transportation.[22] Whether the ill-fated Knyvet ever received any money is a matter of conjecture, because on 10 August he was blown up along with the rest of his crew in the massive explosion that tore apart his ship, *Regent*, and the Breton flagship, *Cordelière*, to which she was grappled.

Victuallers had their moments of excitement too. In May 1513 Sir Edward Echingham reported to Wolsey that on his outward passage he had been approached by three French men-of-war. It is worth recording his reaction:

I comforted my folks and made them to harness; and because I had no rails upon my deck I coiled a cable around about, breast high, and likewise in the waist, and so hanged upon the cable, mattresses, dogswaynes, and such bedding a I had within board, and set out my marris pikes and my fighting sails all ready to encounter them with such poor ordnance as I had.[23]

This so scared the French that they made off, only to be chased in turn by Echingham until they gained the shelter of the shore.

Victualling remained big business. In September 1545 Thomas Rolfe at Dover received 30,000lb of biscuit from *Anne of London* but lacked the £6 to cover the freightage. And it was not only over beer that the sailors could be choosy: a few weeks later the victualler John Lee, writing to Vice-Admiral Sir Thomas Clere, mentioned that 'if the mariners had their own way they would have no other biscuit but that which was baked at the Maison Dieu'.[24] At a price of 10s a hundred this was a sizeable and profitable order. He also told the admiral that he was waiting for the command to slaughter forty to sixty bullocks for both fresh and salted beef for the fleet to cover fourteen days' victualling.

The problem of post-crisis victualling was also a feature of the entire century. When the threat of a French invasion lifted in August 1545 Lisle complained that if victuals did not arrive soon his crews would have to drink water (presumably non-potable) and that he had sent over to some of them a re-supply of his own ship's beer. To alleviate his

needs he commandeered some grain ships heading for Lisbon, including a great Danish vessel whose construction he could only admire. It was not only victuals that were in short supply, for Lisle also confiscated some coal being shipped to La Rochelle because the smiths at Portsmouth had none. This was important, for not only were the smiths involved with manufacturing bits and pieces to assist with the raising of *Mary Rose* but several vessels – Lisle listed *Mistress*, *Galley Subtle* and *Forsyte* – were in need of repairs, while even more might need attention if another storm was experienced. Lisle did, however, take comfort in the supposition that, if the English were in sore need, so likewise must be the French.[25] He reinforced this view in a letter to the king that same day, stating that intelligence was suggesting that the French fleet had dispersed to several Channel ports to land 'great numbers of sick, and the army cannot return to sea for lack of victual and men'; and the men it was said, were saying that they would rather hang than sail again.[26] Other issues at this time showed that there was not always a clear understanding between victuallers and victualled. At the end of July Lisle complained that the Lord Privy Seal had sent him two barks from Middlesbrough that had arrived unvictualled; he remarked wryly to his friend Suffolk that 'if the rest come thus victualled they will do small service, considering the scarcity of victual here', and, as he went on to comment, such scarcity produced illness with 'a great disease fallen amongst the soldiers and marines almost in every ship ... the swelling in their heads and faces and in their legs and divers of them with the bloody flux'.[27] Even before this note the supportive Suffolk had informed the Privy Council that 'Lockyer, of Bristol, a very good captain, one of the Guard is dead. Francis Finglos, captain of Sampson, is departed hence sore sick, and Sir William Woodhouse is very sick.'[28]

Towards the end of August 1545 Lisle wrote to the king to explain that it was far easier for his fleet to be re-victualled at Portsmouth than at Dover or the Downs, where it was 'impossible to victual when the weather is foul', but, as so often, he asked the king to decide the issue. He did, however, appear to be taking desperate, and dubious, measures to keep his fleet fed. On 16 September the Privy Council ordered him to restore seventeen lasts of herring to Adrian Gelder of Flushing, an unspecified amount of herring to Henry Cornely, also of Flushing, and a hoy laden with herring, pitch and tar to a Peter de Snygere.[29]

A bread paddle from the Mary Rose. *To keep a crew well fed it is likely that bread was baked on most days of the week.* (Mary Rose Trust)

By the end of Henry's reign the problem of deficiencies in victualling supply was being grasped by William Gonson, who used his own agents to arrange delivery. This seems to have reduced fraud and led to the appointment of a London agent, the highly experienced Edward Baeshe, as Surveyor of Victuals in 1550. Although considered to be a member of the Navy Board, Baeshe retained a financial independence but was required to submit accounts. These showed that in his first twenty-seven months he spent £17,572 on victuals and received £17,780 from the Privy Council. In 1557 the Council for Marine Causes ordered an audit of the victuals being carried in the sea-going fleet, as a result of which the Lord Treasurer, the Marquess of Winchester, assumed direct control of the victualling process and introduced the idea of keeping 'a mass of victuals in readiness to serve for one thousand men for a month'.[30] The audit also resulted in another Howard, the First Baron Effingham, being dismissed as Lord Admiral while Baeshe, who seems to have managed his most difficult role free of criticism and temptation, was told to account for the fleet's victualling costs separately, a directive which led to his creating his own bureaucratic department complete with headquarters on Tower Hill. However, the costs of this arrangement grew apace, and in 1565 a contractual arrangement was instigated whereby Baeshe was to receive an annual payment equivalent to 4½d per day for each man in harbour and 5d for every man at sea. With this sum he had to provide every sailor with a daily allowance based on the following menu:

Flesh Days

Sunday	2lb fresh beef or half a pound salt beef or
Monday	half a pound of bacon
Tuesday	1lb biscuit or bread
Thursday	1 gallon of beer

Fish Days

Wednesday	Quarter of stockfish or four herring, ¼lb butter and ½lb cheese
Friday	1lb biscuit or bread
Saturday	1 gallon of beer

If deployed away for any length of time, few ships were able to carry sufficient provisions. This drawing of Winter's fleet at Smerwick shows a group of victuallers anchored clear of the fighting. (National Archives, Kew)

Baeshe also undertook to provide other stock goods such as firewood and candles, for which he received an additional monthly supplement. In a typical Tudor arrangement, he was also given, as a sweetener, the export licence to ship out the hides from the cattle slaughtered for the navy for his own profit; as these amounted to 1,000 a year this was a decent source of income even if its origins stank.[31]

The Surveyor of Victuals was another of those long-lived naval administrators who provided the quiet continuity that was so necessary to ensure the survival of the Navy Royal, especially through the turbulent years between Henry's death and Elizabeth's succession. When he died in 1587 he had been in harness for thirty-six years and, sadly, it was his last years that proved personally the most difficult when store fires and an embargo on exports hurt his pocket. He had in his time also to browbeat the counties to release the provisions that he needed, giving many a well-placed courtier an excuse to complain about his procedures and to hint darkly at malfeasance. There was no evidence of this, and the anguish first heard with the Howard brothers in the first French wars diminished until the arrival of Baeshe's successor just ahead of the major battle with Spain in 1588.

When the threatened war with Spain materialised in 1585, Baeshe was faced with an enormous task, for not only had he to victual the royal ships for three months at a time, but he had an additional fleet of merchant vessels, some twenty-two, to care and cater for. One year into the war he reported not only a dearth of victuals but a murrain among the nation's cattle, and by 1588 there were open discussions about reducing the victualling costs by providing substitutes for beef. Soon the pressures began to tell, and by July 1586 Baeshe was petitioning Walsingham to be discharged from the 'hard bargain' to which he was signed up and which required him to victual the fleet for the sum agreed in 1573. This meant that he was submitting bills for victuals alone of around £12,500 to supply twelve ships and twelve pinnaces for four months,[32] a huge sum to find and one representing a mountain of food and a lake of beer. It may be unsurprising that Baeshe, who had held the post of victualler for so long, died in 1587. Was he worn out by the many years of provisioning, of criticism and accusation? Over in Spain, the old victor of Lepanto, Don Alvaro de Bazan, Marquis of Santa Cruz, died on 9 February 1588, tired out by preparing the fleet in which he would not now sail. Both men, in their very different capacities, had served the maritime interests of their nation well; now they would both die exhausted before the great trial, whose result would be to some extent predetermined because Baeshe's bureaucracy had the beating of Bazan's belligerence. Spain had no arrangement similar to that which had developed in England: the Armada sailed under-victualled, having consumed over and above its allowance while in harbour, and there were simply not enough casks in which to store provisions. Unlike James Quarles, Baeshe's successor, the Spanish had not sat down and estimated how many would be needed to provision 10,000 men for three months.

It is one of history's little ironies that, with the navy preparing for a major battle with the Spanish, the correspondence to the court was signed by a Howard, just as it was in the French campaigns sixty years earlier, and that the greatest cause of complaint remained exactly the same: victuals, or rather the lack of them. Out of context it would be difficult to tell which pleading epistle came from which Howard, for whatever administrative improvements may have been made, the fact remained that the sovereign's sailors went to sea under threat of starvation. Part of the problem in the later years was the Bishop of Winchester's introduction of victualling for just one month. Howard wished for a minimum of six weeks, telling Walsingham, 'This one month's victuals is very ill, and may breed danger and no saving to Her Majesty; for the ship spend lightly seven or eight days in coming to meet their victual and in taking of it in; and if the enemy know of that time, judge you what they may attempt.'

Drake, in his famous letter to Elizabeth requesting permission to fall upon the Armada while it lay in Spanish harbours, thus gaining 'the advantage of time and place [which] in all martial actions is half the victory', was also keen to clarify the problems that lack of victuals might cause to his plan:

> Wherefore if Your Majesty will command me away with those ships which are here already and the rest to follow with all possible expedition, I hold it in my poor opinion the unrest and best course; and that they bring with them victuals sufficient for themselves and us to the intent the service be not utterly lost for the want thereof ... for an Englishman being far from his country and seeing a present want of victuals to ensue and perceiving no benefits to be looked for, but only blows, will hardly be brought to stay. I have order but for two month's victuals ... whereof one whole month may be spent before we come there; the other month's victuals will be thought with the least to bring us back again. Here may the whole service and honour be lost for the sparing of a few crowns.[33]

The importance of this can be judged by the lengthy and largiloquent language that the not over-loquacious Drake used. At his most pithy he was devastating: his statement that '... as long as we have victuals to live upon that coast, they shall be fought with' echoed the sentiments of Edward Howard almost eighty years earlier. The Lord Admiral, Charles Howard, as cousin to the queen, could allow his correspondence to be more barbed than Drake's when he wrote from Plymouth:

Ship's galleys were multi-functional and flexible, a fact that only came to light once a reproduction cook-room had been built and put to use. (Mary Rose Trust)

There is here the gallantest company of captains, soldiers and mariners that I think was ever seen in England. It were a pity that they should lack meat when they are so desirous to spend their lives in Her Majesty's service ... I will never go again to such a place of service but I will carry my victuals with me and not trust to careless men behind me. We came away with scarce a month's victuals; it had been little enough but to have gone to Flushing. We think it should be marvelled how we keep our men from running away, for the worst men in the fleet know how long they are victualled, but I thank God as yet we are not troubled with mutinies, nor I hope shall be, for I see men kindly handled will run through fire and water.[34]

Quarles had soon found himself in trouble, for once he had, at last, been granted £25,000 to victual 10,000 men for three months, the food was tardy in arriving at the jetties. Part of the reason can be traced back to the court's traditional parsimony: Howard had to remind Secretary Burghley forcefully that the fleet needed more than one month's supplies and that Henry VIII never made less than six weeks' provisions available, whereas now it was in great danger of lacking victuals 'at time of service'.[35] In May, with the Armada soon expected, Howard wrote again to complain that the provisions promised by Quarles had not appeared to refresh a wanting fleet.

Howard even hinted, in an earlier angry letter, that the logisticians could be playing into Spanish hands, surmising that the enemy might well be aiming to delay their departure until they knew that the English fleet was on starvation rations. The spy system may well have been able to furnish Medina Sidonia with such information, but he was hardly going to persuade his monarch, champing at the bit in the Escorial, to allow him to postpone yet again the enterprise against England on the off-chance that famine would overcome the opposing fleet rather than force of arms.

The state might have seemed unwilling to pay and provide, but the underlying cause was that often the nation's farms were hard pressed to feed an army at sea. Anchored in Plymouth Sound awaiting the Spanish Armada's arrival, Howard, despairing of provisions arriving from London, sent the local commissioner, Marmaduke Darell, into the Devon countryside to obtain supplies. He was not very successful, for a series of bad harvests had reduced the grain available so much that the price had trebled while, of course, that year's harvest had yet to be gathered in. Some salted beef could be made available but not for several weeks, as the farmers and butchers had not anticipated the demand. Rather than consume all their food while swinging idly at anchor, Howard and Drake itched to get to sea, echoing each other in their letters; with only three days' supplies remaining Howard used the privilege of rank and relationship to tell the queen and her councillors just what he thought of their efforts, stating: '... we have been more

Around England galley fires were probably fed birch logs; each day bellows would have been needed to stir the embers back to life. (Mary Rose Trust)

careful of Her Majesty's charges than our own lives as may well appear by the scantyings which we have made ... I am sorry that Her Majesty will not thoroughly awake in this perilous and most dangerous time.'

Shortly after that letter was despatched the victualling fleet entered and, as Howard reported, 'They were no sooner come in, though it were at night, but we went all to work to get in our victuals which I hope shall be done in 24 hours, for no man shall sleep nor eat till it be dispatched so that, God willing, we shall be under sail tomorrow morning ...'[36]

Their weather-frustrated passage to seek out and destroy the Armada before it reached the Channel succeeded only in using up precious supplies and losing more sailors to illness. By the time the false alarms and failed forays were over and the Armada eventually hove into sight, Howard sailed from Plymouth to meet it with just ten days of provisions on board.

When it was all over Captain Henry Whyte, who surrendered his own vessel up for use as a fireship at Calais, wrote to Walsingham, seeking compensation for 'being beggared in the queen's service' but also to state, 'our parsimony at home hath bereaved us of the famoustest victory that ever our nation had at sea'.[37] It had been, of course a far greater victory than Captain Whyte realised, but his chagrin and frustration are palpable and, given his own circumstances, were justified.

Sir Thomas Henege was even pithier. In his complaint about the absence of victuals he states that the Lord Admiral was forced to eat beans and that many of the men had 'to drink their own water [urine]',[38] a contingency that, although often cited as being resorted to by those adrift for many weeks in lifeboats, is astounding in a fleet just a few miles from its own coast. As Howard wrote again to Walsingham, 'it is a pitiful to have men starve after such a service', and he added a wise warning: 'As we are like to have more of such service the men must be better cared for.'[39] Faced with such obvious criticism, Quarles introduced a system of providing certificates of wholesomeness of his victuals. After all he should have been able to select the country's finest produce, for, as Ralegh complained in 1591, the victualler could 'take up goods at the Queen's price for victualling while others have to pay more',[40] which arrangement must have made men such as Dawtrey, Baeshe and Quarles comfortably off and of more than average girth. Ralegh, who had his own sinecure, mainly that of licensing the wine trade, was not the person most likely to highlight abuse unless he himself was being hurt in his deep pockets.

Yet the stark truth is that when twice faced with an invasion threat that required the whole fleet to mobilise, English victualling arrangements were incapable of provisioning the mariners for even a month at sea. Lisle sailed out of Portsmouth on 19 July 1545 to meet the French, and by August he was reporting short rations and disease. Howard brought the western squadron out of Plymouth on 30 July to meet the Spanish, and by 20 August he was reporting to Burghley, 'Sickness and mortality begins wonderfully to grow amongst us; and it is a most pitiful sight to see, here at Margate, how the men, having no place to receive them into here, die in the streets.'[41]

One is left with the inescapable impression that the two longest-serving Tudors monarchs, whose reliance on armies at sea and on land

Liquid, whether wine, beer or water, was a precious commodity onboard and many individuals would have kept a supply in pottery jars or leather bottles to supplement that which was served out of barrels. (Mary Rose Trust)

had been great, cared not a fig for the plight of their serving poor. The contrast between victorious England and defeated Spain could not be more striking.

Ahead of the Armada's departure, arrangements had already been made at Corunna, to which the fleet had been directed to return, to stockpile supplies for the homecoming. This included not only food, but also clothing and medicine, while doctors and hospitals were detailed to stand by to provide whatever treatment might be needed. This was caring, careful contingency planning far in advance of anything contemplated by England. When it was obvious that the scattered, shattered fleet was going to put into whatever port the sinking hulls could reach, emergency measures were swiftly implemented:

... within a day of Medina Sidonia's arrival [at Santander] the first relief column was threading its way by mule train across the mountains from Burgos. Lights were erected on the northern coast to guide remaining stragglers. The provisions collected in Corunna were redistributed to other ports, where they would be most useful, and pleas went out from the king to every potential source of help in the kingdom ... Burgos was first in the field ... Logroño and Valladolid were not laggard. It took the Council of Logroño only nine days ... to dispatch a thirty-strong mule train with 1,533 lb. of basic rations, 520 lb. of almonds, 525 lb. of sugar, 289 lb. of preserves, 2,510 lb. of eating apples, 479lb. of cooking pears, 619 lb. of pomegranates, 1,146 pints of sweet oil, 1,305 bolt of linen for bandages, 150 pairs of leather shoes, 72 pair of hose, 100 baskets of bootlace, 30 counterpanes ... for hospital beds, 500 ducats to by mattresses. Valladolid [sent] a wagon train ... loaded with preserves, pumpkin, sweet biscuits, quince jelly, good white wine, medicines, and luxuries and doctors and grave and learned surgeons of this city, each one duly examined to establish that they are persons practised in their art.[42]

It is not only the speed of response that impresses. The food, luxury items in England's basic cuisine, was precisely that which would serve the sick, starving, scurvy-struck seamen best. There is no indication that London and the towns of Kent responded in like manner – not even with a single apple or cherry from their famous orchards. Howard was left to sort out his fleet's salvation. He ordered ships, like *Elizabeth Jonas*, which had lost 200 men out of a complement of 500, to be fumigated and provided from his own resources a payment of £7 to be distributed among the sick. His problems were identical to Sidonia's; he begged for clothes to replace the rags with which his naked sailors were trying so desperately to preserve both their modesty and their dignity. To little avail. Margate, which could have seen its citizens slain by Parma's troops, watched as the sailors who had saved it died in its streets. Howard continued his plea for help, writing to the Privy Council:

> As I left some of the ships at my coming up, so I do find, by their reports that have looked deeply into it, that the most part of the fleet is grievously infected and die daily, falling sick in the ships by numbers; and that the ships of themselves be so infectious, and so corrupted, as it is thought to be a very plague; and we find that the fresh men that we draw into our ships are infected one day and die the next, so as many of the ships have hardly enough men to weigh their anchors; for my Lord Thomas Howard, my Lord Sheffield, and some five or six other ships, being at Margate, and the wind ill for that road, are so weakly manned by the reason of sickness, and mortality, as they were not able to weigh their anchors to come as we are.[43]

In these circumstances Howard had to lay up half his fleet and discharge the crews. He, more than the court, realised that the council's parsimony was gambling with the nation's future safety:

> ... for the loss of mariners will be so great as neither the realm

shall be able to help it and it will be greater offence to us than the enemy was able to lay upon us; and will be in a very short time answerable to their loss, besides the unfurnishing of the realm of such needful and most necessary men in a commonwealth.[44]

This was getting to the heart of the matter. England was a small country with a small population, few of whom were seamen. Reduce that pool of labour through avoidable mortality, delay paying the survivors or their dependents, and persuade others not to volunteer because of such treatment, and future calls to arms would not be met with an adequate and enthusiastic response. Poor provision of food, lack of medical care, absence of pay: this could have been the fate of prisoners of war, but it was the treatment for heroes. Howard railed, 'My Lords, I must deliver unto your Lordships the great discontentments of men here, which I and the rest do perceive to be amongst them, who well hoped, after this so good service, to have received the whole pay, and finding it to come this scantily among them, it breeds a marvellous alteration amongst them', and re-emphasised his strategic point that 'It were too pitiful to have men starve after such a purpose ... for we are to look to have more of these services; and if men should not be cared for better than to let them starve and die miserably, we should very hardly get men to serve.'[45]

That men continued to come forward when required is more a reflection on the general condition of the English poor than evidence of the promise of any believable incentive held out by the administrators. Burghley saw no reason to question this state of the nation, even remarking that an increase of dying seamen would help reduce the pay that was grudgingly having to be provided. The English sick and wounded eventually received £80 to be distributed among them, while the volunteer crew of the fireships, whose actions had been so decisive, were given the total grant of £5 to be spread among the survivors. This insensitive treatment was not unusual. When the treasure ship *Madre de Dios* was brought into Dartmouth the queen thought it fitting to award the seamen who seized her £1 each as a fair share in the fabulously wealthy prize. Any who were found to have helped themselves were jailed.

An attempt to divert criticism from a monarch who cared little for others can be deflected by reference to the way in which she treated her most faithful servant, Francis Walsingham, who, when mourning the loss of his son-in-law Sir Philip Sydney, who had died heroically at Zutphen in the Netherlands, as well as that of Sydney's parents and his own daughter's still-born child, appealed to Elizabeth for help to settle Sydney's debts but found her ears closed. Her true aim was to preserve her throne and her own being; concerns outside that were peripheral, but if she could achieve her aim with a pretence of loving care she could act the part with theatrical and gracious insincerity. The poor had their place, and if she was forced to pay some of them to risk their lives to defend her realm she preferred that they did so out of sound and sight.

The contemporary criticism of the English victualling has to be tempered by other considerations. Firstly, in the absence of the corre-

Senior officers would join ships with their own retinue and dinner services, mostly made of pewter, like these examples. (Mary Rose Trust)

spondence one has to accept that the navy successfully drove off the two greatest invasion forces that the nation had ever faced, one of which kept the English ships in a state of prolonged readiness that would have strained lesser organisations beyond breaking point. Secondly, and this is particularly apposite when criticising Elizabeth and her parsimonious court, short rations have the unanticipated consequence of providing fresher food. Being victualled for three months might seem both comforting and sensible but, faced with the contents of the casks containing the oldest supplies, consumers might have preferred a less lengthy and more frequent supply regime. Howard and Drake might have despaired, but what little food was being brought in from the local Devon countryside to augment their meagre resources had the advantage of freshness.

Thirdly, and most importantly, the English supply chain might have been suspect, but it was far better than the arrangements among her enemies for the duration of the active engagements. Although Drake's destruction of boatloads of barrel-staves is credited with disrupting the Spanish Armada's storage arrangements, and the spat between Wolsey and Thomas Howard earlier in the century has shown how important empty barrels were for supplies, Philip's fleet had other more major problems that it failed to overcome. On board the Spanish ships, messing arrangements were based, as with the English, on a group of six to twelve comrades, one of whom was responsible for their food. But whereas in the English system 'the cook for the mess' collected prepared meals from the galley, in the Spanish system he was responsible for the cooking as well, a recipe for chaos. Indeed the Spanish ships were considered to be 'foul and beastly, like hog-ties and sheep-cots' in comparison with the English ones.[46] Their supply problems were, in fact, greater than those faced by Howard, and in adverse weather they manifested themselves embarrassingly and worryingly early in the voyage. Slipping downstream from Lisbon on 11 May, Sidonia's Armada did not disembogue from the Tagus until 28 May to reach Finisterre on 14 June, by which time his captains were reporting severe victualling difficulties, with corrupt and inedible supplies. Although Philip had ordered them to sail with six months' stores embarked they sailed with just four months' provisions, and these were already rotting – which is not surprising, for the long preparation before departure meant that some barrels had lain in the holds for a year or more. Many barrels had been made of green wood in an effort to overcome the shortage imposed by Drake's deprivations, and because he had also disrupted and destroyed the tunny fisheries, salted fish no longer formed the reliable dietary staple. Off Finisterre barrels of stinking tunny, sardines and meat were cast over the side as contagion took hold of the poisoned men. On 19 June Medina Sidonia ordered the fleet to enter Corunna to replenish, only to have a sudden gale drive many of his ships back out to sea, where their weakened crews had to struggle with a fierce tempest while trying to manage the onset of dysentery and even scurvy – and all this in ships still only a few leagues from a land where lemons and olives grew in abundance, their anti-scorbic properties suspected by some but disregarded by most. In the early morning of 20 July the great Armada sailed from Corunna, probably with the bacillus of its own destruction as present in its victualling deficiencies as it was in the dysentery and the 'bloody flux'.

Even the humblest wooden spoon was made with care, often by the ship's carpenter or even by an individual for his own use. (Mary Rose Trust)

Pewter, and occasionally silver, spoons would have graced the officers' table. (Mary Rose Trust)

The problem was, however, not solely caused by poor and tardy provision. Ship design that gave too little room in the hold, and manning levels that could be as crowded as one man per ton weight, both contributed to the straitened circumstances that naval crews so often found themselves in. By contrast, good victuals and the fair sharing of the same kept many a crew willing to endure great hardship. Evidence of a well-victualled ship would have encouraged seamen to sail in that particular vessel, while, conversely, some captains such as Drake had a reputation for sailing when not fully victualled, with the expectation of picking up supplies, a reputation which his ability to return with plundered wealth had to counteract. When there was no booty, as in the 1595 expedition, the lack of food must have been harder to bear. Thomas Maynard tells of his ship's company being reduced to 'a very hard allowance' with four men (a mess) sharing one quart of beer and one cake of biscuit each morning, and for dinner and supper one quart of beer, two cakes of biscuit and two cans of water with a pint of peas or half a pint of rice.

Beer

As the fifteenth century drew to its close the traditional English brew of ale was being challenged by the introduction of beer based on continental recipes that included hops. Ale production was a simple and cottage-based process, using just malted barley, water and yeast. This produced a heavy sweet drink which needed to be consumed within a short time before it went off. To change the liquor into beer required the ale to be boiled up with hops before fermentation took place. The resultant drink, with its famous bitter flavour, could be stored for longer, which made it far better than ale for provisioning ships. A product with a prolonged 'shelf life' encouraged larger-scale manufacture, as did the fact that beer brewing was a cheaper process requiring far less malt than did ale. The boiling process also sterilised the liquid,

A leather bottle from the Mary Rose. *It possibly had a cord attached so it could be hung in a convenient place.* (Mary Rose Trust)

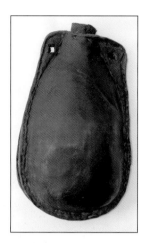

This leather flask seems to be designed to be carried at the hip. (Mary Rose Trust)

while its alcoholic content had mild antiseptic properties. Thus as a standing fleet came into being, so a way of provisioning it with a drink that could be stored in barrels for longer and was safer to drink than either water or ale became readily available. Of course, beer was also both bulky to transport and liable to spoil in transit, facts that encouraged the growth of port-based breweries to supply the fleet.

At the beginning of Henry's reign there was one brewery in Portsmouth, the Greyhound, built by his father to provide beer to his ships and the workforce at the new dockyard. Finding its output inadequate to equip his forces for war with France in 1512, Henry ordered four more breweries to be built in the town. These, the Rose, Lyon, Dragon and White Hart, were grouped around the town pond, the water from which, as it was also used as a laundry and as a trough for farm animals, must have lent an original flavour to the beer. Whatever the taste, it was favourably received, with Thomas Howard telling the Privy Council in a letter of June 1513 that the brew houses were the 'goodliest' that he had ever seen.[47] Howard's problem, and there was always one with Howard while he was Lord Admiral, was that he could not load the barrels quickly enough, and he justified his tardy departure from Portsmouth by stating that the 'lading of beer ... is the slowest work that man saw'. To prevent the unstowed beer from going off while he awaited additional boats from London to help with its embarkation he 'commanded William Pawne [who had built the breweries] to cause great trenches to be digged and to be covered with some boards, turves, sedges, and such stuff as may be gotten, to keep the heat therefrom'. The problem of storage was soon addressed, with the king ordering ten storage houses to be built in Portsmouth in response to Howard's letter.

With Portsmouth brewing satisfactory beer, a hint of competitiveness and comparison began to creep in. Howard, pleased with Pompey's beer, told the council that the beer that had arrived from London was mostly 'unable stuff ... small as penny ale and as sour as a crab' and that although he did not know what the king had paid for it he was sure that their lordships would 'see the brewers punished'.[48]

London beer was not always so much disdained. The regions of the country brewed their beer in different ways and, as always, those

who drank it had their own opinions as to which was best. In May 1513 a group of West Countrymen wrote to the Privy Council to complain that the admiral had, contrary to the king's command, ordered that no more West Country beer was to be brewed for the fleet as, 'being made of oaten malt, it will not keep so well as that made of barley malt', and that the soldiers were not as willing to drink it as they were to drink the London beer. The complainants went on to point out that the sailors had been quite content to drink it over in Brittany and had consumed twenty-five tuns in the twelve days since their return, only to turn their noses up at it once the London beer arrived.[49]

More often than not complaints about the beer were justified. On 26 August 1588 Charles Howard wrote to Walsingham:

> The mariners have a conceit and I think it true and so do all the captains here, that sour drink hath been a great cause of this infection amongst us; and, Sir, for my own part I know not which way to deal with the mariners to make them rest contented with sour beer, for nothing doth displease them more[50]

– a sentiment to which most modern seafarers would say 'amen'. Howard changed his brewer to one who used more hops; the government, less concerned with collywobbles than with cost, tried to mix new beer with the old and re-brew it. The record is silent as to how this new ale was received. Howard's complaint may have been the result of savings being made by James Quarles, who was charging for beer at a penny three farthings a gallon instead of the halfpenny a quart which was the going rate ashore.

Occasionally the *force majeur* of the weather meant that beer could not be delivered. For example, it is recorded that in September 1513 two brewers of Sandwich had to be paid to provide the fleet with beer off the Downs, where Surrey was waiting for the Scots fleet but to which anchorage beer could not be shipped from the usual places because of contrary winds.[51]

Beer could, of course, create problems with sailors and dockers, as it always has done. In September 1535 Lord Lisle was informed by

Wooden tankards, waterproofed with pitch, were personal items and carried the marks of the owner. (Mary Rose Trust)

This pewter tankard from the Mary Rose *has an unusual design and was probably a valuable and favoured drinking piece.* (Mary Rose Trust)

letter that 'Your man Candelar is so drunken ever night that he causes great trouble, and has hurt one of your chief carpenters; otherwise your ship would have been with you before this.'[52] A few years later, in June 1539 the Admiralty Court presided over a case of assault and theft brought by a Portuguese merchant, whose ship had been boarded by a group of drunken seamen from *Mary Rose*. They had driven the crew below with the flats of their swords and rowed away with a boat-load of cloth, much of which was abandoned on the muddy foreshore.[53]

However, the absence of beer was a greater problem. Stored water very soon went off, and whenever possible ships away from England would anchor where fresh streams flowed into the sea so that the lengthy and tiresome task of floating barrels ashore to top up and return could be accomplished. In 1522 Thomas Howard struck up an attitude of bravado by writing to Wolsey that he would descend on the Trade (Ushant) and remain there, 'as long as we have any beer left, though in our return we should drink water'.[54]

With many West Countrymen embarked it is not surprising that cider was also carried, yet in Drake's final voyage of 1595 the fleet stored 1,533 tuns of beer and just two and a half tuns of cider. The difference was in part explained by the cost, for beer was charged at 40s to 60s per tun while cider cost £4 a tun. Wine was much more expensive, with the prices for that voyage ranging from £30 a tun for Muscatel to £8 a tun for some Spanish plonk.

Platters

Markings on wooden plates and tankards raised with *Mary Rose* indicate that sailors held their own personal platters, but these may have been bought in bulk and issued to the individuals once they joined. Among the items costed by Roger Basing in submitting his accounts for his voyage to Bordeaux to collect wine for the king in the king's ships *Minion* and *Mary Guildford* were seven tankards, eight cups, a dozen trenchers and two trays for meat.[55] However, other inventories record few items being provided by the state. It may be that the large wooden bowls used to collect rations for a 'mess' of seamen were issued but seamen had to provide both their own plates, drinking bowls and tankards.

The admirals and captains did not eat off anything as common as wood. Instead they brought their own pewter dinner services with them, and, once more, it is the finds from *Mary Rose*, which include both Carew and Lisle marked plates, that give us the best surviving collection of these items. A *bon viveur* like Drake ensured that his guests, whether voluntary or captive, enjoyed eating from his excellent tableware.

Pay

It can be assumed that Wolsey made a great deal from the victualling regime that he initiated, but so did those to whom he entrusted its execution. In 1514 John Dawtrey, at Southampton, raised bills that covered not only victualling the fleet, but also the 'transporting of the French Queen to France'; 'wages and conduct of the army sent to sea'; payment for the carriage of wood; wages for the victualling ships including three Spanish vessels; the hire of ships and anchors; keeping the garrison at Portmouth; keeping the king's ship over winter; and

Ship's companies ate their meals from wooden trenchers, bowls and dishes which also carried ownership marks. (Mary Rose Trust)

payment for masts and mercenaries, for beer and baking houses and for repairs to gates and ditches. The sum involved totalled £86,719 2s 1d; even excluding the one penny this would be about £25 million in today's money. It was an enormous sum to account for, and one for which the two-man book-keeping team serving Dawtrey deserved full credit. That was not all, however, for in the document Dawtrey submitted an account for 'sundry payments for which the accomptant has no warrant',[56] that is, incidental expenses for which no documentation existed. This too is no small bill, and the items listed would have been difficult to verify including, as they did,

> Payments for biscuits and western fish in a great storm lost; loss in sale of wheat after the wars; for wages to John Dawtrey and his two clerks; wages of brewers, millers, beer-clerks, mill-makers, coopers, surveyors, master-brewers, horse-keepers and smiths; expenses relating to the carriage of beer, the rent of houses and for building the great store-house at Portsmouth and repairing other buildings; post-war losses in sales of mill and dray-horses, wheat, malt, oats and hops and for the loss of some of these items at sea.

The amount claimed here was £5,007 15s 5d, or £1.5 million in today's terms (based on Alison Weir's multiplier of 300), and all without documentation – it is no wonder that Dawtrey eventually became a Member of Parliament and the builder of the most stately house in all Southampton![57]

Settlement appears to have been swift, for the records show that on 14 July 1515 Dawtrey had received from the exchequer the sum of £97,214 8s (£29.1 million) against a bill of £93,826. It is good to note that this included a payment of £214 8s to Richard Palshyd, 'being the produce of the king's beer sold by him'.

Further down the food chain, the returns were not so splendid, and if any one issue demonstrates both the level of management skill achieved by the Tudor state and its parsimony towards its servants, as opposed to its generous grants to its favourites, it is the naval accounts, which list in great detail what was to be paid and to whom. For example, that drawn up in October 1512 for the three months from Saturday 17 April to 8 July began with the flagship, thus:

> The *Marie Roose* [sic]: – First to Sir Edward Howard, knight, chief captain and admiral of the Fleet for his wages and victuals at 10s. a day by the said 3 months amounting to £42. Also to Sir Thomas Wyndham knight for his victuals and wages at 18d. by the day by the said 3 months, £6 6s. Also for the wages and victuals of two lodesmen alias pilots each of them at 20s. a month for the said 3 months £6. Also for the victuals of 411 soldiers, 206 mariners, 120 gunners 20 and 20 servitors, in the same ship, every man at 5s. a month by the same time £308 5s. Also for wages of the same 411 persons every man at 5s. a month by the said time – £308 5s. Also for 34 deadshares at 5s. a share by the said time £25 17s 6d.[58]

Thus the admiral received in one day twice as much pay as his seamen collected in one month, although this pay gap was to decrease as the century moved on.

That neat summary of pay is, possibly, just too neat. The three months concerned began right at the start of the reckonable naval service and included several skirmishes with the French on land as well as at sea. It is highly unlikely that crew numbers remained the same throughout, or indeed that new men did not join and others depart. Sickness, injury, desertion and death must have been influences; if they were they are not reflected in the pay-roll. Someone must have made a few extra shillings other than from the dead shares, the wages of non-existent crew included on the pay-roll to boost earnings.

A long document of 1513 lists the dead shares for all the ships in the navy, with, for example, *Trinity Sovereign* being allocated thirty-eight, including seven to the master, two to his mate, eight for the four quartermasters, four for their mates, two to the boatswain and one to his mate, one to the coxswain and a half to his mate, and one each to the master carpenter, the caulker, the steward and the purser, with a half to each of their mates. The pilots shared six. The ordinary seamen, as so often, were excluded.[59]

Supply and demand are reflected in the level of wages that the government had to pay its sailors. In 1512, while an ordinary seaman was receiving five shillings a month along with a coat, conduct money, a sort of travel expenses of 6d per day and free board, a labourer was lucky to get 4d per day, from which he had to feed and clothe his family. In 1543, although, in an effort to retain mariners, they were exempted from service in the army, conditions ashore were improving and many of them absconded. The king was not prepared to allow this desertion to take place and on 24 January 1545 a proclamation was issued that stated:

> Forasmuch as mariners and soldiers serving in the king's ships have at times past and yet continually do, use not only unlawfully to depart from their ships unto the towns near ... His Majesty's pleasure and straight commandment is that no mariner or soldier ... depart or go from their ships without testimonial signed with their captain's hands ... upon pain of death.

However, seamen's wages were also increased to 6s 8d for a twenty-eight-day month to keep the employment competitive – just. Yet for this sum, men of several nationalities were prepared to serve in Henry's fleet. Paying them on time was, however, as always, a different matter. In April 1513 John Dawtrey complained to Wolsey that he lacked money to pay wages a month in advance as agreed and that his money 'goes away very fast' for many reasons,[60] while in June 1515 Thomas Howard, emboldened now as Earl of Surrey, complained to Wolsey that William Ellecar, his victualler in *Mary James*, had been unpaid for six weeks' victuals. It was not an infrequent occurrence.

It did not take long for that Henry's threat to deserters to be forgotten. Mary had to issue a very similar proclamation in 1557:

> ... no small number of the best and ablest of the said shipmasters, mariners, gunners, seafaring men and watermen, contrary to the obedience and duty of good subjects, not regarding the premises but in contempt thereof, have withdrawn themselves from her highness' said service, and by colourable means conveyed themselves into divers good ships and other vessels lately set forth towards outward realms and places in voyages for traffic and merchandise, and also in adventuring and warfare.

As might be expected, 'pain of death' featured yet again as the 'reward' for non-compliance.

Even so the ships sailed and the seamen did their duty. It was Elizabeth's genius to incorporate 'colourable' activities 'in adventuring and warfare' into the state's own mission, and she was not required to issue a similar edict until 1592.

When war offered the opportunity of plunder, seamen's wages could be boosted by the legal allocation of one-third of the cargo's value to be split among them, plus their gains from pillage, a recognised term for items that were found lying on the deck of the prize but did not constitute cargo. Because they could range from a cutlass to a set of clothes there were frequent mutinous outbreaks as a crews argued over who had snatched up what. The more senior did not, of course, have to besmirch themselves in such squabbles: the sovereign was entitled to one-fifth of the value from reprisal prizes, and the Lord Admiral one tenth, an arrangement which could leave the investors with little to cover their expenses, let alone make a profit, and therefore encouraged fraud.

Henry's great decision to keep his fleet laid up in time of peace meant that money had also to be found for the ship-keepers. Thus it is recorded that in January 1530 Thomas Jermyn, Spert's deputy, paid 'Henry Grace de [sic] Dieu – For wages and victuals of 75 shipkeepers keeping the ship in the haven of Portsmouth for 10 months, at the rate of 10s 4d. a man per month, with two dead shares for the master, at 10s per month and one for the boatswain at 5s[61] – which indicates a strong wage inflation between 1514 and 1530. Those who were paid off and then recalled received conduct money of 6d per man for every twelve miles, which gives some idea of the state of the nation's roads and the daily rate of progress that could be made upon them. This not only made the gathering of seamen in a timely manner difficult but rendered their recall, should they be discharged prematurely, even harder. Elizabeth was always keener to get them off her books than her father was. Henry in September 1545, when the threat of invasion had almost certainly passed, was still cautious about relaxing his guard, and although he allowed the discharge of the army 'because often

When provisions allowed, the officers ensured that the standard diet was supplemented with foodstuffs more suited to their background. This reconstruction of an officers' table is based on objects found with the Mary Rose.
(Mary Rose Trust)

times attempts be sudden and the mariners being once scaled it shall be very hard to have them gathered again', he required between 1,000 and 1,500 of the mariners to 'remain' in place of other soldiers.[62]

After twenty inflationary years, Hawkins pleaded successfully in 1582 for the seamen's wages to be raised to 10s per month. He also introduced scales of pay to encourage promotion and retention, with the master of the largest ship, *Triumph*, receiving £2 1s 8d per month and that of the smallest, *Merlin*, getting £1 1s 8d. It is worth reflecting that the differential between those on the highest pay scale and those on the lowest, just over 4:1, was not very different from that which pertains today between a naval captain and his most junior crew member. This pay rate did not draw hundreds to the ports at time of need, but it did make the impressment by magistrates, JPs or other officials easier to enforce. The fact that men were paid conduct money to travel to their call-up ports unescorted is ample evidence that the system was accepted by both parties. Yet on occasion, wages were not settled when due, causing great hardship. In 1596 the Lord Chancellor, Sir John Fortescue, wrote to Cecil about those who had returned from the Indies voyage, 'If you saw the number being poor miserable creatures hanging at my gate who neither have meat or clothes it would pity your heart.'

Rather than being embarrassed into action, the state found an excuse not to pay three weeks' worth of wages due and also proposed charging the mariners for the shoes and clothing that had been issued to them for free.

Nevertheless, despite such occasional harsh treatment, the majority of sailors saw no reason to risk their lives in departing for what was a harder, and often more lawless, unpredictable life ashore. Indeed, for many the very part-time nature of naval employment must have offered a seasonal boost to their wages. Tudor England had several series of bad harvests and the occasional famine. Later, enclosure of common land, rack-renting and the harsh treatment of vagrancy meant that for the agrarian poor, who constituted most of England's population of four million, scraping a livelihood was hard. Kett's rebellion of 1549 was just one expression of the frustration of an under-privileged class. The seaman was far better cared and catered for.

Half-sovereigns from the Mary Rose. *To avoid theft and gambling ships' companies were not encouraged to carry money onboard; much of the coinage would therefore have belonged to the officers or the purser, with the sailors being paid on discharge. To enable some onboard transactions to take place jetons were sometimes carried, their worth only being recognised within the ship.*
(Mary Rose Trust)

Chapter Six

Command and Control and the Company

Yet therein now doth lodge a noble peer,

Great England's glory and the world's wide wonder,

Whose dreadful name late through all Spain did thunder,

And Hercules' two pillars standing near

Did make to quake and fear.

Fair branch of honour, flower of chivalry,

That fillest England with thy triumph's fame,

Joy have thou of thy noble victory,

And endless happiness of thine own name

That promiseth the same;

That through thy prowess and victorious arms,

Thy country may be freed from foreign harms;

And great Elisa's glorious name may ring

Through all the world, filled with thy wide alarms.

Edmund Spenser, Prothalamion

Henry Tudor worked for peace. His son Henry wanted war, for of all his ambitions when he came to the throne that of becoming distinguished on the battlefield was the most dominant. Only by successfully campaigning could he claim his place among the crowned heads of Europe as a supreme example of the warrior prince. With such belligerent ambitions he spent six years of his forty-six-year reign in mostly desultory campaigning, bankrupting the nation for no gain and leaving it in an isolated position politically and religiously that meant trouble for his successors. Edward and Mary both had to fight wars that they would have preferred not to wage, while Elizabeth, who desired peace, spent eighteen years of her forty-two-year reign in open conflict, with a further ten years of cold, or rather lukewarm, war.

Henry's love of combat never reached the stage at which he desired to lead his warships into battle, but his inexperience did not affect his belief in his innate maritime strategic and tactical sense: he enjoyed not just the pomp of command but also directing his forces, from a safe and shore-based distance. At the start of his reign he had his two new vessels *Mary Rose* and *Peter Pomegranate* dressed with flags for their passage up the Thames, and he loved to make an event of any new launch. So when *Great Galley* was completed at

Greenwich, the king dined there and took on the role of pilot dressed, according to the French observer De Bapaume, in 'a sailor's coat and trousers made of cloth of gold, and a gold chain with the inscription "Dieu et mon Droit", to which was suspended a whistle which he blew nearly a loud as a trumpet'.[1]

Henry also feted the Emperor Charles V on board *Mary Rose*, and although going on any voyage lengthier than the crossing to Calais from Dover was not his style, he did like to dine with his admirals on board in harbour, as for example on 18 July 1545, the day before *Mary Rose* was lost, when he appointed Sir George Carew the fleet's vice-admiral and hung a golden boatswain's call around his neck as his badge of office. Doubtless too tactics were discussed, with the commanders having to listen to the wisdom of their land-based lord. Sadly, the Lord Admiral, Lisle, Dudley that was, was too much in awe to contradict his king, who kept the orders and advice coming through the Privy Council, when all the while Lisle was trying to drive the French invasion fleet away.

Thus on 21 July the admiral was told 'that in sending forth row vessels he should take heed lest the galleys cut between them and home and if the French continue to land men in the Isle of Wight and so disfurbish their galleys he might essay some attempt against them'.[2]

Lisle responded with a letter in which he raised the idea of trying to drive the French fleet on to the Owers shallows, but stated that before he did so he would discuss the matter with the king, because 'being so near the fountain it were little joy to die for thirst',[3] an example of sycophancy in the Thomas Howard tradition!

When the royal party departed from Portsmouth on 2 August, Henry looked back over the Solent and had Secretary Paget write to Lisle that His Majesty found fault with the lie of the ships and wished that they should repair to the straits opposite St Helens and lie where His Majesty had directed. A day later the query was as to when Portsmouth would be sufficiently fortified to be 'tenable' in the absence of the fleet. Next came a tactical idea of sending some ships to lie between the galleys and the fleet off Seaford. This was one suggestion too many, and Lisle, taking care to involve Suffolk, the king's long-time friend and the land commander, in his reply, told His Majesty, gently, that it was not an expeditious idea to divide the king's fleet, for the galleys would gain an advantage should the ships be becalmed, and if the winds remained as at present then the ships would be unable to regain the safety of Portsmouth, becoming trapped by the French fleet.[4] By 5 August Lisle was having to tell Paget that 'The King's pleasure to have certain of his ships made to row, to attend upon the French galleys, should be done as far as stuff and time permit; but all the shipwrights have been so occupied with making engines to bring up *Mary Rose* that they have no leisure for other things.'[5]

A few days later Lisle had to inform the king that all the ship commanders remained as His Majesty had appointed them except for Peter Carew, who seemed to have pleaded for a ship in which he could board the enemy; and those who had gone sick or, in one case, had died. Lisle also had to explain that a shortage of suitable high-born commanders had forced him to put 'mean' men in command of the 'mean' ships, the experienced John Winter, if he recovered his health, in *Matthew Gonson*, and that William Tyrell, not the obvious choice by rank, was the man best suited to command all the rowing

Had he not been the vice-admiral onboard Mary Rose *when she sunk in 1545 few would have heard of Sir George Carew, shown here in a sketch by Holbein.*
(Bridgeman Art Library)

squadrons because he understood galley warfare.[6] In just those few days, while the Lord Admiral was defending the nation against the greatest threat that had arisen during the king's reign, the latter kept up a stream of correspondence, none of which was of tactical use or strategic significance.

Later that August, with the French presumed to be in the Narrow Seas, Lisle wrote in response to instructions received from the council that he was sending them a list of his ships and their captains and that the reason, 'that certain names of captains are altered from the King's last determination is that Winter is taken with a fervent burning ague and that putting another in his place alters many others'.[7] Lisle, it appears, also risked sarcasm, for in commenting on his fighting instructions, a copy of which he enclosed, he begged that they might be taken in good part as he thought of himself to be 'one void of all knowledge in such affair', who if he had the experience 'would keep as good order as the Admiral of France', adding that he trusted that their own good purpose would serve them better than the Frenchman's knowledge and vainglory. Lisle knew that Henry knew that D'Annebault, his opposite number, had little or no sea experience. Yet the Lord Admiral was often painfully subordinate and self-effacing. On 17 September 1545, in a letter in which he explained that he might not be able to despatch Seymour immediately to support Boulogne because the latter was very 'evil at ease', he went on to say, 'I would the King had appointed me to serve in the meanest room under some nobleman of reputation for all the world knows that I am not of estimation for so weighty a charge. I should do better service as directed than director; for directions in great affairs appertain to such as have great credit and are feared.'[8]

And this from the man who, in a few years, would endeavour to rule the nation!

Henry's instruction to subordinate commanders could be even more detailed. In August 1545 Vice-Admiral Sir Thomas Clere was told precisely what to do on patrol in the Narrow Seas:

> to traverse the seas for the defence of the King's subjects, and endeavour to take the King's enemies, either Frenchmen or Scots. Ships of any other nation he shall gently enter and, if he find, by charter party, that neither lading nor vessels belong to enemies, he shall suffer them to pass without taking anything from them. This is important and any violation of it will be punished. Leaving always a convenient number of his fleet to guard the passage between Dover, Calais and Boulogne, he shall send the lesser vessels to Etaples and St. Valleries to burn or bring away ships laden with victuals; doing this twice a week at the least. The great ships must keep the deep seas and not venture to the enemy's coast, least in the case of storms, they may not win our ports on this side.[9]

Leaving aside, in this wind-dictated age, the impossibility of guaranteeing a twice-weekly cross-Channel sailing, these instructions are

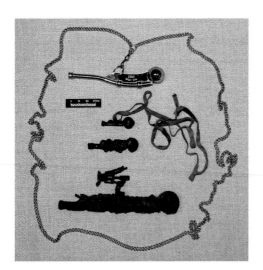

From the Lord High Admiral to a boatswain's mate the wearing of a bosun's call was a symbol of authority while its shrill notes can still be heard in ships of the Royal Navy today. These examples from the Mary Rose *are displayed alongside a modern version.*
(Mary Rose Trust)

Queen Mary and Philip II. Although subject to almost universal denigration for her religious and political policies, Mary, through her marriage to Philip of Spain, reopened the cultural links with mainland Europe that allowed England to access to new ideas on navigation and cartography.
(National Maritime Museum BHC2952)

noteworthy for two reasons. Firstly, the gentle treatment of non-belligerents, which was not always practised, shows Henry's awareness of his isolation among the nations of Europe and his desire not to create the excuse for an armed alliance against him; and, secondly, Henry's need to explain simple issues of tactics to his sea commanders, much, it may be presumed, to their annoyance.

Edward, crowned young and dying youthful, had no opportunity to show his potential talent as a commander-in-chief, but there is a tantalising snippet about a visit he made to Greenwich with the French ambassador to inspect *Great Harry*, which, as his flagship, had been renamed *Edward* on his succession, that indicates that he was as supportive of the Navy Royal as his father had been. He also, unlike his relatives, seemed interested in astronomy and, although this was a faith-based interest, was presented with astronomical instruments, such as a quadrant in 1551, to aid his understanding of the principles of the movement of heavenly bodies. Perhaps, had he lived, England would have had a monarch who would have encouraged his countrymen to seek out new lands. The key naval event of his short reign occurred when William Winter took a fleet into the Forth during the winter to destroy a French fleet lying there, thus proving that a well-managed professional navy could keep the seas in all weathers.

Mary owed her fleet a favour. In the turbulent days between Edward's death and Mary's arrival in London, Lisle, self-promoted to Duke of Northumberland, endeavoured to use the navy to support his coup. It was to be the only occasion on which the fleet was to be involved in internal politics and it failed. The duke despatched six ships with almost 1,000 men on board to Great Yarmouth, from where he expected them to land and seize Mary, who was gathering her supporters at nearby Framlingham Castle. Northumberland's first error was to replace the tried and trusted ship's captains with his own men, of whom the sailors knew little. Bad weather then scattered the ships, with the commander, Gilbert Grice, being forced to take shelter

in Lowestoft Roads before sailing on to Harwich, where lack of wages and promises of recompense from Sir Henry Jerningham resulted in a bloodless mutiny by the fleet, and indeed its captains declaring for Mary, the legitimate queen who was to prove herself to be a decisive although unlucky commander-in-chief.

Mary had almost been shamed into reversing the halt in the mid-century decline of the royal fleet. In 1555, when Charles V had indicated that he would like to travel from Flanders to Spain, his son and Mary's alien husband, Philip, was asked to provide a twelve-ship naval escort, only to be informed that England could not do so without much longer notice. Philip, much to the irritation of its members, came before the Privy Council to inform them that 'England's chief defence depends upon the navy being always ready to defend the realm against invasion, so that it is right that the ships shall not only be fit for sea, but instantly available.'[10]

That his words were acted upon he might ruefully have realised in 1588, but the reaction was more immediate, for later that same year there were thirty naval ships ready for sea, and when war was declared against France in 1557, Mary had twenty-four royal ships operational. This total compared with the twenty-nine that Henry, after years of building and months of warning, had to repulse the full-scale French invasion force in 1545.

Mary was also responsible, in January 1557, for a royal warrant that required the exchequer to '... have the sum of £14,000 by year to be advanced half-yearly to Benjamin Gonson, treasurer of the Admiralty, to be by him defrayed in such sort as shall be prescribed unto him by the said Lord Treasurer, with the advice of the Lord Admiral'.[11]

This was the financial keel on which the growth, strength and sustainability of the future navy would be built. The control to be exercised by the Lord Treasurer, the Marquess of Winchester, reflected the findings of a 'secret muster' of the ships and mariners which had voiced disquiet over slack administration. Later that same year Peter Pett, the first of a long-serving family of shipwrights, was appointed as the second royal master shipwright. Mary thus ensured that the fleet remained seaworthy and responsive through her decisive actions and ability to delegate.

At the end of May 1557 Mary ordered Lord Clinton to sea with twenty ships. Four of these were to patrol the Narrow Seas but the remainder were to be taken on a plundering raid along the French coast, although Clinton was told not to begin hostilities before 7 June, on which date the queen's herald would hand the declaration of war to the French king. Thus Mary seized the nautical initiative, ensuring that by the time war broke out she commanded the Channel and especially the Dover Straits, out from which Clinton was forbidden to venture unless driven from his station by foul weather or hot pursuit. As was so often the case aggressive action was to be tempered with caution, and the admiral was told that when 'taking the enemy he should be in great hope and without danger' while ensuring that the queen's subjects and friends could pass unmolested upon the sea and that the coastal littoral would also be free from harm.[12]

Clinton was no Edward Howard or Drake, but he was dutiful and reliable and, taking the queen's advice, avoided the Trade as he considered it to be 'too dangerous to enter ... for there are a great many

Edward Fiennes, Lord Clinton, survived court turbulence to serve several monarchs as Lord Admiral dutifully but without distinction.
(National Maritime Museum BHC2841)

had been businesslike and calm although she was always behind the rapidly moving events. On 8 January she ordered Sir William Woodhouse to ensure he had command over the Narrow Seas to prevent enemy reinforcements from arriving by sea and allowing English forces to sail unmolested across. The next day she ordered the shires to provide the men for the relieving force and, on learning that the town had fallen, immediately changed the disembarkation port to Dunkirk; she then agreed before the month was out to allow the larger vessels, whose presence in the Narrow Seas was no longer vital, to return to the Thames for repairs. With the location and the speedy onset of these disastrous events Mary was dealing with a situation very similar to that of Dunkirk in 1940, but she handled it well and decisively and did not rage at her commanders in public or on paper. Throughout her naval wars she issued clear and unambiguous commands and allowed her admirals to operate free of interference. Elizabeth's much more irritating ways are well known, and so just one example may suffice by way of contrast. Near the end of her reign she ordered Sir Richard Leveson in *Repulse* to take a squadron of nine ships in February 1602 'to intercept the Spanish off Ireland or between North Cape and Lisbon', with 'our first point being to defend our kingdom, the next is to obtain some profit towards the maintenance of our great charge by taking either the outward or the homeward-bound Indies fleet'.[13] Poor Leveson was being given half an ocean to patrol with every chance of failing in one of his several contradictory missions. Nevertheless he was anxious to get to sea and in a phrase that is worth a thousand words told Burghley that the delays to which he was being subject did his name no good, so that 'I now sit upon thorns'. Many Tudor commanders would know precisely what he meant.

This contrast between Mary's and Elizabeth's instructions embraces their different approaches to prizes and other benefits. Elizabeth told Leveson in 1601 to ensure that in every prize he took he kept the bill of lading so that there would be a check against those who 'break the bulk' and are thus guilty of embezzlement. Mary, on the other hand, invited the Lord Admiral in 1558 to sell off any prizes which had been long unsold since, with the greater part of their cargo gone, they would be of little profit to the crown. He could then pay any monies raised to the exchequer, but only after he had subtracted 'such shares as by just and ancient order has been allowed to all as have their interests therein'.[14] From the written record there is little doubt as to which of these rulers was the easier for the admirals to serve.

Elizabeth's greatest asset as commander-in-chief was that she was a woman. Barred by her sex from leading an army into action, she could sense and control the ambitions of her erstwhile champions and not be taken in by their dreams of unachievable glory, while they could endure her constant inconsistencies by putting them down to feminine whims. Many writers liken her spirit to that of her father, but she had more, thank goodness, of the dull vision of Henry Tudor than of the glamorous vices of Henry VIII. What she was adept at was appearing glorious while advocating caution. Although her incompetent favourites cost her more dearly than did Henry's equivalent, Suffolk, she could recall and chide her champions in a way that allowed male warrior feathers to unruffle in time, apart from, of course, the worthless strutting bantam Essex, who managed to scale heights of incompetence in command both at sea and on land. Elizabeth could,

rocks, and very ill coming out'. Sticking to his brief, he sailed along the French Channel coast chasing the occasional ship into Dieppe or Boulogne and capturing a few poor sailors. It was neither a glorious nor a wealth-creating deployment but it achieved its goal, in part because Mary had laid down only the one objective and had not either provided caveats concerning bounty or changed her mind, as her sister would so frequently do.

The letters from Mary's pen were numerous but they were short, clear and never contradictory until Philip messed her about by delaying his return to England in 1557. Before that sad moment she was all positive. In July she ordered the treasurer and comptroller of the navy to get *Pauncy*, *Sacrette* and *Mary Fortune* to sea within seventeen days to patrol the Channel. Mary's mind then turned to other deployments, and she ordered Sir John Clere to take nine ships to escort the returning Iceland fishing fleet while another squadron, commanded by Sir William Woodhouse in *Great Bark*, was to continue to patrol the Narrow Seas. The year ended with the fleet achieving, unspectacularly, all that the queen had asked of it, apart from losing Clere himself in the surf off Orkney. One day later, however, the loss was of a far greater magnitude.

For on 1 January 1558 Calais fell after a lightning strike by the French across frozen marshes. Mary's response, as the threat built up,

Elizabeth was rightly proud of how her small nation had defeated the might of Spain, as this 'Armada' portrait shows: her treatment of her victorious crews was, however, disgraceful. (Wikimedia)

may move you to take any other course than by these our instructions you are directed, we therefore think it most expedient to refer you therein to your own judgement and discretion, to do that thing you may think may be best tended to the advancement of our service.'[16]

Given evenly balanced sides, it is the commander with the freedom to use his initiative who is likely to win the day. No such freedom was granted by Philip, whose commanders, both Parma and Medina Sidonia, had a far more complex task to attempt far further from home. In February 1940, when it was known that the German auxiliary *Altmark* with British prisoners of war on board was in neutral Norway's waters, the Admiralty sent the captain of *Cossack* the following order: '*Altmark* your objective, act accordingly.' If we allow for Tudor grandiloquence and substitute Armada for *Altmark*, we have Howard's final instructions. Generally, however, the Lord Admirals were not blessed with such brevity of direction.

Sea Lords

Given the high esteem in which command was held and the fact that the monarch never considered exercising personal command at sea, great importance was attached to appointing the Lord Admiral and when it did not revert to a sinecure, the post was usually given to a scion of the most noble of families, such as the Howards or Seymours, or a personal favourite of the king, such as Lisle. The holder of the post, as an earl, took precedence over all bar the Great Chamberlain,

however, advance leaders who were not from the nobility, the traditional source of military commanders. In the army this meant that Norris and Baskerville could use their talents to the full and, of course, at sea it gave full rein to Drake, Grenville, Hawkins and Frobisher. Not that they too did not feel her wrath when they failed to carry out her commands.

When Drake and Norris, in their follow-up to the Armada campaign, failed to descend on the Spanish fleet known to be at Santander, but instead dawdled before Vigo, the queen's words spat full scorn as she chided her joint commanders for 'perverting the primary object of the expedition which was to have burnt the King of Spain's navy and shipping in the ports where they lay'.[15] She then issued a warning that they should 'not suffer themselves to be transported with an haviour of vainglory, which will obfuscate the eyes of their judgement', which left them in no doubt as to her ire, but it did not change the fact that the voyage was one with several missions and failed because these were not complementary ones.

Yet in 1588 at the greatest point of crisis in her reign Elizabeth acted with all the genius of a successful commander-in-chief. This was not with the brave but empty words at Tilbury, but in her final orders to her commanders at sea. Having frustrated and prevented them from carrying out the forward policy they advocated and changed her mind too readily and frequently to assist in their endeavours, when the time came she gave them what they needed, a free hand, instructing Howard: 'Lastly, forasmuch as there may fall out many accidents that

Elizabeth's lengthy indulgence of her youthful favourite, the Earl of Essex, is a mystery. Ashore in Ireland, and afloat off the Azores, he showed none of the leadership qualities that a man graced with his rank was expected to display. (National Maritime Museum BHC2681)

Lord Steward and Earl Marshal, much to the chagrin of Essex when Howard of Effingham was appointed Earl of Nottingham and his senior in 1597. This made the rank an important and rewarding one, best exercised when granted to those who knew the sea rather than given as a gift to those who had fawned at court. In the Tudor period we see this responsible position not being awarded on the basis of rank alone but rank being accorded to those appointed. It was not a smooth transition, however. Henry's appointment of his illegitimate son, the young Duke of Richmond, to be Lord Admiral was a reversion to the medieval that lasted until the young man's death in 1536, when the elevation of Fitzwilliam once again placed an experienced sailor in authority. Yet it remained harder for a simple sailor, say a Drake or Hawkins, to rise through the social ranks than for a salt sea one, and the age when a Lord High Admiral or First Sea Lord was appointed solely on merit was still many years away.

The Norfolks

While one dysfunctional nuclear family reigned over sixteenth-century England, another more extended one ruled over her waves for much of the same period. Indeed, the Howard link with the sea predated that Norfolk family's elevation to both its eponymous peerage and the Tudor accession, while its continued involvement in things maritime outlasted Elizabeth. The First Duke of Norfolk had held the post under Richard III until his death at Bosworth Field. Then the Tudor dynasty saw four more of the family, two Norfolks and two Effinghams, become Lord Admirals, while several others became admirals – a feat that cannot be matched by any other family in English history.

The Norfolk family tradition was based on a life of service to the sovereign, ending in execution for becoming too uppity. There is little doubt that they did feel more blue-blooded than the Welshman's brood; they just lacked the survival techniques to keep quiet about it. So although the scheming, slippery Third Duke's life was spared simply because Henry VIII died the night before his intended execution, his son Henry was axed. Later several others went the self-same way. Shakespeare was wrong: it was not the head that bore the crown that lay uneasy, it was the heads of those who served that were at greater risk.

If the Howards carried an air of bruised potential in their dealings with their monarch they felt nothing but scorn for those who aspired to scramble to their heights. Their greatest bone of contention was not the orders that they received but the people who gave them, especially in Henry's time, when the king saw no wrong in promoting and delegating authority to servants such as Wolsey and Thomas Cromwell, both of whom by brilliance rose well above the position that birth had bestowed upon them. Thomas Howard, a fawning pit-bull, brushed against their legs until the time was right to bite. This loathing is very apparent in the letters which the blue-blooded snob sent to Wolsey, the venom-mouthed butcher's cur, as Shakespeare has it, who was his administrative and intellectual superior, during the French wars of 1512–14. In June 1513 he wrote:

> Master Almoner, with all my heart I recommend me unto you. Good Master Almoner, I have found you so kind unto me that methink I can do no less than to write unto you from time to time of all my causes. So it is, though I be unable thereof, it hath pleased the King's grace to give me this great room and authority more meet for a wise, expert man than me. But since it hath pleased his grace to admit me there unto, as far as my poor wit can extend, I shall endeavour myself from time to time to do all manner of service where I shall think to deserve his most desired favour. And, good Master Almoner, as my most singular trust is in you, send me both now and at all times your good advice and counsel, assuring you that never poor gentleman was in greater fear to take rebuke and ill report than I am of such a knoweth not what may be done, which generally be the greatest number, and for many causes, of which I shall rehearse a part.[17]

The letter ends with more sycophancy:

> Master Almoner, all the premises and all other my cause I remit to your wisdom, fully trusting that you will not only from time to time give me your good advice and counsel, but also with your friendly words withstand all ill reports undeserved made of me, as my singular trust is in you. And thus Our Lord have you in his tuition.

The insincerity drips from the page, but with Wolsey having the king's ear Howard was not going to risk expressing his true feelings. These were well expressed by Shakespeare, who put into his mouth these warning words to Buckingham as the cardinal approached:

> ... You know his nature,
> That he's revengeful; and I know his sword
> Hath a sharp edge: it's long and't may be said
> It reaches far, and where 'twill not extend,
> Thither he darts it. Bosom it up my counsel,
> You'll find it wholesome. Lo, where comes the rock
> That I advise your shunning.[18]

The early correspondence shows Howard to have been very good at 'bosoming up', but by August 1522, when the country was once again at war, Wolsey's hold was loosening and the fear in which he was held by the admirals had so much weakened that they were prepared to be querulous. In August Wolsey sent to Vice-Admiral Fitzwilliam, on board *Mary Rose*, a letter setting out the ships, their captains and the crew numbers that he expected to be at sea. Instead of endeavouring to comply, as would have happened eight year earlier, Fitzwilliam answered by return with a letter stating that Lord Admiral Howard had already 'appointed as well the ships as the captains and number of men to keep the sea', a copy of which Fitzwilliam enclosed with the statement that it was not possible to change them.[19] The letter goes on to question every other directive received from Wolsey, giving for each a short, snappy reason why a different course of action was necessary. It is thus not surprising that when Wolsey did finally fall from grace, Norfolk, as Howard had become, was one of the leading plotters in his downfall, nor that when his successor, the equally humbly born Thomas Cromwell, was vulnerable, Norfolk and Fitzwilliam, by then Earl of Southampton, were his cruel gloating judges. Neither is it surprising that Cromwell's fate was sealed once Henry had elevated him to the high position of nobility as Earl of Essex, a position to which the noble families considered that he had no right by birth. Of greater importance is the fact that the infant Navy Royal survived because two men, who loathed each other, put aside personal animosity to raise the newborn child.

After Henry's second French war in 1524, Norfolk hung up his sea-boots and returned to court to act as pander to the king in respect of his two nieces, Anne Boleyn and Katherine Howard. The office of Lord Admiral reverted to a sinecure, being granted in 1525 to the king's only acknowledged illegitimate son, Henry Fitzroy, then aged six. His tenure ended with his death in 1536 and, because it coincided with a prolonged period of peace, he was not required to exercise his youthful wisdom in matters maritime. His successor, a belated appointment, was Thomas Howard's faithful deputy, William Fitzwilliam, who was elevated to be the First Earl of Southampton, thereby becoming, of Lord Admirals, also the first first, for six of his seven successors were also to become the founding holders of an earldom, illustrating not only the importance of the post but also the increase in titled positions created by the Tudors. Most, like Fitzwilliam, were also appointed to titles over which they had no sway; his grant of 16 August 1536, for example, proclaimed that he was to be 'Admiral of England, Wales, Ireland, Normandy, Gascony and Acquitaine, Calais and the marches thereof',[20] a folly in keeping with Henry's idea of his own grandeur.

Fitzwilliam's sea service had begun in the first French war when he was selected from the king's sporting companions to take command of a royal ship. In the fight that ended with Edward Howard's death he was himself wounded by an arrow, but his injuries were not sufficient to prevent him from joining the king in France later that year and being knighted for his services at the siege of Tournai. It was his sea-service potential that appealed to the king, however, for a little while later he was appointed vice-admiral, a rank that he held while being attached to Wolsey's household for a number of years until, with the outbreak of war in 1522, he sailed again as Thomas Howard's second-in-command with special responsibility for the Narrow Seas. His main task in this campaign was to prevent the Duke of Albany from reaching Scotland from France, and the force that he had to carry out this task was captained by many of the major players in Tudor naval affairs including Sir Francis Bryan, Sir Anthony Poynz, John Hopton, William Gonson and Anthony Knyvet, a gathering of drive and experience that would have hammered hard any Franco-Scottish convoy voyaging northwards. Unfortunately, they were not given the opportu-

Although he was a competent commander, the naval career of William Fitzwilliam, Earl of Southampton, ended abruptly, after he had praised Anne of Cleves, whom he escorted from Calais to Deal, for her failed marriage to Henry VIII. (Bridgeman Art Library)

nity so to do, for with errant timing Fitzwilliam allowed a craving for fish to get the better of his judgement and led his fleet on a raid of the French fishing port of Le Tréport, which gave an opportunity for the Duke of Albany to slip past the blockade and sail from France through the Irish Sea to Scotland, where, luckily for the English, he and his Scottish supporters failed to gain any advantage from his presence. But Henry was not amused, and Fitzwilliam found himself sent to Calais to command the garrison at Guisnes, a form of internal exile. However, it was a temporary distancing, for he was soon on the rise again, becoming Chancellor of the Duchy of Lancaster and, for a while, Lord Privy Seal. On the Duke of Richmond's death he was appointed Lord Admiral, and in 1539 he was at sea both to respond to a French invasion scare and to escort the unfortunate Anne of Cleves from Calais to Dover for her meeting and marriage with Henry. A delay at Calais, caused by bad weather, meant that Fitzwilliam spent almost as much time in Anne's company as would the king himself. Ill-advisedly, he took this opportunity to write to the king in praise of Anne's looks. Henry, noting his admiral's lack of judgement, fired him on 28 July 1540, the date on which he had Cromwell executed for the same lack of taste and married Katherine Howard, the youthful offering of her pandering uncle, Norfolk – a cynical trilogy of actions that was fully in keeping with the king's character. Although Fitzwilliam's naval career was thus ended, he did die in harness, at Newcastle upon Tyne, once more subordinate to the Duke of Norfolk, during the march against Scotland in October 1542, missing a grudge match, for his elder brother had fallen at Flodden Field in 1515 also while serving with Thomas Howard.

John Lord Russell, the First Earl of Bedford and Fitzwilliam's successor, had like him been a youthful companion of the king and an excellent jouster and jester, but in Henry's first war he went not to sea, but with him to France, where he fought well at the sieges of Tournai and Thérouanne. It was in another attack on a township, that of Morlaix, that he experienced his first sea service when he sailed there with Thomas Howard, being injured outside the town walls. Foreign travel in the king's service then occupied him until his return to court in time to participate in Wolsey's fall, when he, to his credit and almost alone among the king's coterie, spoke up for the disgraced cardinal and showed him some kindness. Over the next few years his work suppressing rebels and monasteries scarcely equipped him for his appointment as Lord Admiral in 1540, and he was probably relieved to hand over that role with its responsibilities to Edward Seymour, brother to Henry's latest queen, in 1542. When a new war broke out

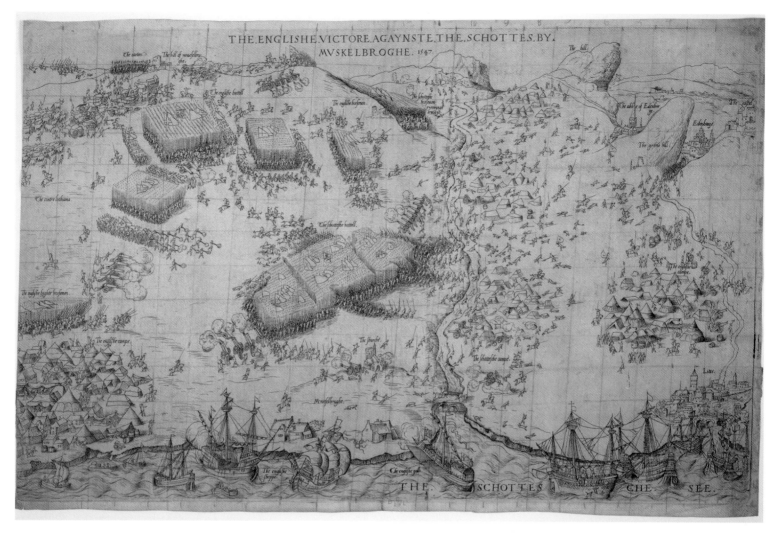

The battle of Pinkie, 1547. Lord Clinton's fleet is shown in close support of the army, firing on Scottish positions from inshore. (British Library)

he was given command of the vanguard of the army in the invasion of France in 1544, a position on land far more comfortable for him than the equivalent at sea.

Clinton

In Lord Admiral Edward Fiennes, Lord Clinton and First Earl of Lincoln, the navy gained its own Vicar of Bray. He went to sea for the first time aged thirty-two but made the career-enhancing move of marrying Elizabeth Blount, mistress to Henry VIII and mother of the king's bastard and Lord Admiral, Henry Fitzroy. His advantageous marriages continued when, on Elizabeth's death, he married the niece of John Dudley, Lord Lisle, another favourite of the king. At the start of Edward's reign Clinton commanded the English fleet for the invasion of Scotland, providing useful support from offshore at the battle of Pinkie in September 1547. That apart, loyalty, rather than service, led to him being appointed Governor of Boulogne, whose successful defence and negotiated handing back to France led to his being appointed Lord Admiral for life in 1550. A miscalculation when he backed Northumberland against Mary and lost his post was pardoned and favour restored when he raised a force to march out and confront

Wyatt's rebels, thus earning grudging respect from King Philip, who considered that, 'although the admiral is a double-dealer and principally concerned with his own interests, he has more authority than anyone else …'. With Elizabeth on the throne, Clinton sided with either Cecil or Robert Dudley, as best suited him, while occasionally sailing on unsuccessful voyages around the coast both to Brittany and Normandy and to provide succour to Le Havre, which surrendered two days before he arrived. He was created Earl of Lincoln in 1572, 'for services to Henry VIII, Edward VI, Queen Mary and the present Queen'. No other crown servant could match that, and although few Lord Admirals achieved so little operationally, Clinton showed that the head of the navy could be a political and administrative post rather than an operational one. He was the precursor of the First Lord of the Admiralty, not the First Sea Lord.

Charles Howard, Second Baron of Effingham and First Earl of Nottingham

In the latter part of the century the Dukes of Norfolk resumed the family tradition of placing their heads on the block. Faced with such perversity, the sovereigns moved their selection of Lord Admirals to a cadet branch of the family, the descendants of Thomas Howard's second marriage to Agnes Tilney, whose eldest son, William, became Lord Admiral and the first Baron Howard of Effingham. His period of command, from 1554 to 1558, covered the transition from Mary to Elizabeth and the fall of Calais, and ended with the return of his predecessor, Clinton. Neither brilliant nor incompetent, William Howard made his greatest contribution to the development of the Royal Navy by doing nothing to preclude his competent son from being appointed Lord Admiral when his time came.

Charles Howard was the most successful Howard seaman, and the only one of the family who can be considered in the same illustrious company as Drake. That he owed his appointment to his position as Elizabeth's uncle, rather than a successful sea commander, he would probably have admitted, but this proclaims rather than detracts from the fact that he was in command when the English fleet achieved its two greatest victories – the defeat of the Spanish Armada in 1588 and the raid on Cadiz in 1596. Indeed, given the fact that in the first campaign he had to command the free-spirited pirates Drake, Hawkins and Frobisher, while in the latter he had to control the royal rivals Ralegh and Essex, his social status aided rather than hindered his position. The best modern analogy would be that of General Eisenhower being made Supreme Allied Commander over the bristly Patton and Montgomery.

It could still have gone horribly wrong without Effingham's virtues. As far as his commanders were concerned he consulted, listened, elected, supported, showed no favouritism, criticised in private and praised in public. With his masters he inspected their ships and praised their qualities and state of preparedness. For his men he fought fiercely for their pay and victuals and gave of his own to ease their deprivation. Moreover, in each of these activities he had no hesitation in passing on his views to queen and court even if they were critical of his superiors – unlike his father he was no sycophant.

At the beginning of the Armada campaign Howard had held to the view that the fleet should be divided almost equally into two squadrons, one at each end of the Channel. Having joined Drake in Plymouth, however, he allowed himself to be influenced to bring the majority of his force to Plymouth and then lobbied the queen furiously for permission to sail, having again been persuaded by the experienced sea commanders that this was the right way to deploy his units. When, on the first night of contact, Drake failed the fleet by dousing his leading light and going in search of plunder, Howard treated him as a prodigal son on his return; he could have had him hung. Then when the fight was over it was Howard who kept up the protests that his starving, ragged, dying men were being shamefully treated by being denied victuals and pay.

At Cadiz the same qualities of quiet control kept the amphibious commanders together so that, although command was shared, a most heinous practice, there was never any doubt about the person on whose shoulders wisdom lay. Andrew Lambert includes Howard of Effingham among his list of ten great admirals for the following reasons:

Lord Howard of Effingham was no seaman: he was a great leader who held together a disparate collection of self-interested and self-

The Tudors' most successful Lord Admiral, Charles Howard of Effingham, Earl of Nottingham, commanded both against the Armada and in the Cadiz raid of 1596. As Elizabeth's uncle he had the prestige to dominate his subordinate commanders and also the opportunity to speak to the queen in a way that others might not have risked. Avarice and nepotism blotted the latter years of his lengthy career. (National Maritime Museum BHC2786)

willed men, ensuring they worked together in harmony. He used rank and authority to control and conciliate ill-assorted captains and make them an effective fighting force ... In battle he provided the voice of sense and reason, avoiding unnecessary risk and ensuring orders were executed with a nicely judged combination of obedience and initiative ... He resisted the temptation to chase glory [and] was safe, reliable and perfectly capable of acting the grandee. In addition he knew that great navies were made by men, not ships.[21]

Sadly, he was, as the elderly and unassailable Earl of Nottingham and Lord Admiral, to use his position to line his pockets and those of his relatives: a sad and sordid blot on an otherwise shining escutcheon.

Dudley and the Brothers Seymour

Edward and Thomas Seymour were the second set of brothers to hold the position of Lord Admiral, a rank granted not because they were sailors but because their sister, Jane, had become the king's favourite wife. Their tenure was short and was separated by the four-year appointment between 1543 and 1547 of John Dudley, Lord Lisle, who brought to the post a man experienced in sea command just in time to meet the greatest amphibious threat to England since 1066. Dudley was to hold the post twice, the first time with distinction, the second merely as a way of gaining power in his struggle with the Seymours to control the protectorate of Edward VI.

Dudley's earlier sea career is covered elsewhere. In January 1543 he was the only man in the kingdom who both could draw up a rational plan for repelling the French and had sufficient experience and authority to manage the maritime concepts of the king. His opportunity for greatness came in 1545 when the French arrived off Portsmouth. He failed to engage, but he protected the shore, thus not winning renown but not losing a fleet either. In fact he probably provided as great a service to the establishment of a permanent navy ashore as an admiral would afloat. In 1545 and 1546 the appointments of what was to become the Navy Board involved each appointee having responsibility for a particular aspect of naval administration. This placed the English navy way ahead of any of its continental rivals and created a concept of corporate responsibility and administrative authority. In neither of these activities had Henry himself ever shown much interest, and it is most likely that this major step forward was introduced by Lisle rather than the king.

The best benefit that the Seymours offer to naval history is to show how senior the position of Lord Admiral was in Tudor England. Henry had, for example, in a reversion to benefice, appointed his bastard son, Henry Fitzroy, to the position at the age of six. The Seymours were the brothers of Henry's beloved third wife, Jane, which made them Edward VI's uncles, while Thomas married Henry's sixth and surviving wife Katherine Parr. It is during this relationship that he is best remembered, for attempting to be overly avuncular with the nubile Elizabeth and then trying to kidnap the king, her brother Edward. For the latter act he lost his head, having been condemned by his own brother. These asinine activities would not have surprised those who had served with him at sea, although he covered up his incompetence in the words that he had inscribed on the tomb of his wife, Queen Katherine Parr:

> A wife by every nuptial virtue known,
> And faithful partner once of Henry's throne.
> To Seymour next her plighted hand she yields –
> Seymour, who Neptune's trident justly wields

– words which mark a smooth transition from charming truth to unjust flattery, for the incompetent ambitious Thomas Seymour used his position as Lord Admiral to increase his wealth by supporting a haven for his pirates in the Scilly Isles, which he had purchased for this purpose, even though his official position required him to prosecute such lawbreakers. His own lawbreaking, brought about by coveting his brother's position and authority as Lord Protector, ended with his execution for his undoubted treasonable plotting; at his trial King Edward said in agreement, 'We do perceive that there is great things objected and laid to my Lord Admiral mine uncle – and they tend to treason', thus dispassionately condemning an admiral and an uncle who had shown him much kindness. Even his death was summed up but briefly in the king's diary: 'The Lord Sudeley, Admiral of England, was condemned to death, and died the March ensuing.'[22]

Before being appointed Lord Admiral, Thomas Seymour had served some time at sea in Henry's reign. In 1537 it was noted that he went to sea under Sir John Dudley, another of those who was later to condemn him to death, in the anti-piracy operations dealt with in a later chapter. Evidently, it was the opportunities to get rich pursuing plunder rather than pirates that impressed Seymour.

Back at sea during the war over Boulogne, Thomas Seymour was commanded to convoy supplies to that besieged garrison. The detailed correspondence between him and the Privy Council about the way in which he was carrying out the task is one of the few exchanges between the king and his sea commanders in which the monarch's ire with his admiral is clearly spelled out. To be fair to Seymour, the king was being kept informed of much Scottish naval activity in the North Sea, where the Scots seemed to be taking English vessels with impunity; he did not want further problems in the Channel.

Seymour was appointed admiral of the ships to serve in the Channel on 29 October 1544, an appointment that then required a deal of discussion as to who was in command of what ships and where they were to assemble. The final instruction to Seymour was, however, clear enough. He was 'above all things' to convoy victuals to the garrison at Boulogne. Then, while remaining in control of the Narrow Seas with the great ships, he was he was to send the smaller vessels to attack the enemy fleet laid up at Etaples. Finally he was to collect further provisions at Portsmouth to convoy again to Boulogne. His aim was to 'endeavour himself to endommage th'ennemies by all wayes and mean possible'.[23] Minor amendments to Seymour's orders, on 4 November, reinforced the idea that he was to 'lose no time, but by all ways and means employ yourselves to th'annoyance of th'enemies to th'uttermost, with such respect to your own safeguard as appertaineth'.[24]

Seymour seemed to take the first directive to heart, for, with a few excuses about thick mist and gales, he replied on 6 November that there were seventeen men-of-war at Etaples. One anticipates that he was going to attack them only to find he took the final piece of Henry's directive as being the weightier and excused his action by stating that 'the masters doubt the enterprise of Etaples: a good ship may not come near the shore by 7 miles and with any great gale at the North West it would be difficult to recover the seas'.[25]

Nevertheless the English had command of the Channel, making it possible for the Privy Council at Calais to pledge to send by sea a fortnight's victuals for 2,000 men in dire need at Boulogne as soon as the wind was favourable. The strategists at Calais also saw that for Boulogne to survive the winter all that was necessary was to keep command of the sea, 'wherein Henry, especially in winter, has more

Thomas Seymour did little in his sea career to justify his appointment as Lord Admiral, a position he owed to his sister's marriage to Henry VIII. Incompetent scheming led to his execution, a fate he shared with two other Tudor Lord Admirals. (National Maritime Museum BHC3021)

succours of his navy than the enemy has'.[26]

Bad weather prevented Seymour from either attacking Etaples or re-victualling Boulogne. Nevertheless on 8 November the king approved his idea of launching an attack on Brittany. The next day Seymour wrote again to the Privy Council explaining that 'as sore a storm as ever' he saw had driven him into the Solent while others of his fleet were heading as far west as Dartmouth, their mission unaccomplished.[27] At this Henry exploded. The council wrote tersely to the underachieving windswept admiral:

> Upon seeing your letters of the 9th inst., the King commands us to write to you that you have not had such respect to his pleasure, signified by our memorial and letters, as the importance of the affairs required. For, where you were told that your chief charge was to see victuals safely wafted to Boulogne, you appear not to know what is become of the victuals, and have gone thence leaving them in danger of the enemies. And where you were to
>
> burn and bring away such ships as you found about Etaples, and afterwards, in passing towards Portsmouth, to take the fishermen;

although the wind and time served well, you passed to Portsmouth without either going to Etaples or annoying the fishermen. You are with speed to take order that the 14 ships appointed to keep the Narrow Seas, may be despatched thither with command to take the said fishermen on their way, if the wind serve.[28]

As blasts go that hurricane force one would, one might have thought, curtailed any thought Thomas Seymour might have had of advancement, but he was the late queen's brother. Unrepentant, he wrote back to say that as he had heard that the seas were clear he was sending the victuals from Portsmouth to Boulogne escorted by nine ships with 940 men and he would remain at Portsmouth awaiting further instructions.[29] On 13 November the Privy Council wrote to him that the king 'likes your advice' and then provided him with his new set of orders. Amicability restored, Seymour adopted a more obedient and humble tone and responded, also on 13 November, with a lengthy and detailed letter explaining precisely what he had done, intended to do, which did not include an all-too-risky attack on Etaples, and the effect of the wintry weather on his fleet. Humble pie did not exclude the customary

111

complaint about insufficient victuals, casks or wages. Two days later he was even enquiring what he should do with '24 French varlets taken in fishing boats', a group of unfortunates to whom, previously, he would have given short shrift as being unworthy of the king's attention.[30]

This episode covering a few weeks in October and November serves to show two things: firstly, even allowing for the occasional crossing of letters, how readily the Privy Council in London and an admiral at sea could keep in touch and, secondly, how the sovereign still depended on a small group of nobles to serve him in senior posts and how reluctant he was to dismiss them for reasons other than traitorous ones – a charge that saw not only Seymour's head fall but also that of his successor, John Dudley, Henry's Viscount Lisle, by then Earl of Warwick and heading upwards to become the Duke of Northumberland, whose own scheming was to also end with his execution.

The statistics are remarkable. Of the eleven individuals who held the post of Lord Admiral in Tudor England, three, the Seymours and Dudley, were executed; one, Thomas Howard, only escaped execution on Henry's death; one, Edward Howard, died in action and one, Fitzwilliam, died on campaign, which does indicate that politics was a far more deadly arena than the battlefield. And yet, despite this century of turmoil, leaving aside the Earl of Richmond's period in office, two holders, Clinton and Howard of Effingham, presided as Lord Admiral for over half a century (Clinton from 1550 to 1554 and 1558 to 1585 and Howard from 1585 until 1619), bringing a much-needed continuity to nurse and instruct the growing naval child.

Sea Wolves

While the sea lords could be drawn from the upper ranks of the aristocracy, Henry had a problem with his subordinate sea captains. Desiring to create a standing navy, he had no naval college to which an aspiring commander might be sent to learn the ropes. His army generals might be considered to have had a life of training, for that was what the chase and the joust and archery were considered to be, but giving these rather bone-headed incompetents command of the sovereign's most expensive single items of military expenditure, for which they had neither training nor obvious aptitude, was a gamble. With such a dearth of experience Henry had to turn to his newly formed 'King's Spears', the younger members of the nobility whom, in 1509, he had banded together to form his bodyguard of fifty, each of whom was supported by two archers, a cavalryman and a mounted attendant.[31] Each 'Spear', together with his entourage of four, was paid 3s 4d per day which meant, usefully, that they did not need wages when appointed to sea command, as many of them were, to serve under Sir Edward Howard.[32] Among them was the king's great jousting favourite, Thomas Knyvett, a prankster and popular champion and brother-in-law to the Lord Admiral, who was to lose his life when *Regent* blew up alongside *Cordelière* off Brest in 1512. Thomas Wyndeham, another 'Spear', was obviously suited to the life at sea, for, having been sent there in 1510, he was Edward Howard's flag captain in *Mary Rose* in 1512 and rose to be fleet treasurer, Vice-Admiral and the captain of *Henry Grace à Dieu*. His son, another Thomas, commanded the squadron that attacked the Scots in the Firth of Forth in 1544. Arthur Plantagenet, another 'Spear' with an illustrious pedigree, managed to run his ship aground on the rocks off Brest, but, that

accident apart, the inexperienced commanders seem to have done well, thanks, it must be said, to the very professional, and generally anonymous, ships' masters who would have advised and guided them. There can be little doubt that without such professional advice these amateurs would have been given a very hard time by the professional commanders and seamen such as Portzmoguer and Prégent who led the French. Many of Henry's masters were to achieve not just command of the great flagship *Henry Grace à Dieu* but also administrative posts of importance, as did Spert, Gonson and Winter, their expertise leavening the rising Navy Royal.

Mary's reign saw the beginning of a change in the selection of commanders for the royal fleet. In July 1557 she sent out a letter to a number of her gentlemen stating that Sir William Woodhouse lacked sea captains and that they were to repair to Dover to serve in this capacity. The following year her similar summons contained the words 'for the good opinion we have of your faithfulness and experience in service on the seas'; it was a phrase her father could not have used and her sister never had to. For by Elizabeth's time the state was able to appoint commanders who, having learned the art of warfare while trading or plundering for their own benefit, now saw advantages in lending the navy their skills. These included those such as Drake, Hawkins, Frobisher and Monson who were patriots as well as pirates, and men like Winter, Leveson and Monsell whose careers had been spent mostly in the service of the state. Although coming from different backgrounds, they had a mutual regard for each other's professionalism and a shared liking for prizes.

There is one occasional sailor who, it seems, is always mentioned whenever the Tudor navy is discussed: the golden-tongued, silver-penned, thirsty-pocketed braggart Walter Ralegh. Just below the Ministry of Defence in Whitehall a diminutive statue of the popinjay stands, its size commensurate with his achievement, its position, as the only Tudor seaman to be so honoured, reflecting his pomposity. Leaving aside his execrable venture capital voyages to Guyana and trips to his great estates in Ireland, Walter Ralegh would appear to have spent only short periods at sea, as shown in the table below – which for any other naval officer, let alone admiral, would scarcely be a dog watch.

The Sea Service of Sir Walter Ralegh

Date	Ship	Voyage	Time at sea
September 1578	*Falcon*	Western Approaches	2 days
November 1578	?	Western Approaches	11 days
July 1588	?	Armada Messenger	2 days
June 1596	*Warspite*	Cadiz	2 months
July 1597	*Warspite*	Azores	3 months

Supreme in the Tudor naval hagiography, Drake's fluctuating fortunes as a commander demonstrated that he was best when acting as a free spirit rather than when encumbered by major command with set objectives. No English seaman, until Captain Cook, two centuries later, had such a feel for the maritime environment. (National Maritime Museum BHC2662)

'The courtier's wit, the poet's words, could not be weighed with the experienced sailor's eye to bring the balance of judgement down in favour of Ralegh being a good admiral or competent commander.' Drive and bravery he possessed in plenty and put to good use at Cadiz, but he was never one whom the call of the sea could seduce from the glamour of the court.

Two naval pirates worthier of acclaim were Sir Richard Leveson and Sir William Monson. Leveson, whose father was a privateer, gained advantage by marrying Margaret Howard, the daughter of the Lord Admiral, but proved himself worthy of his post. Having fought as a volunteer against the Armada, he captained *Truelove* in the 1596 Cadiz expedition, becoming, along with Monson one of the sixty-six knights dubbed so extravagantly by Essex. The next year he was a vice-admiral on the Azores expedition before returning to command the winter guard ships, during which time he captured ten Hamburg ships bound for Lisbon. In 1599 he was criticised for failing to intercept Spinola's galley squadron in the Channel although storms had driven him off station. Three years later he achieved his revenge, with riches, off Cezimbra when, with his own ship blown out to sea, his vice-admiral, Monson, drove Spinola's galleys away and negotiated the surrender of the wealthy carrack *San Valentino*. For this action the Lord Treasurer demanded £40,000 from Leveson's estate but settled

for £500 after an investigation found Leveson to be an honest man and one who did not accept bribes. The words on his tomb in Wolverhampton thus touch on the truth when they state: 'Here lieth the body of Perfection's glory; Fame's own world wonder and the ocean's story.'

Much more of a rogue was Monson, who ran away to sea at sixteen and experienced enough adventures for three incident-packed lives. Those ships he boarded had a habit of being recaptured with Monson barely making his escape, until his luck failed in 1590 and he was seized and sent to the galleys, from where he managed to work his release in 1592. Monson was one of Cumberland's pirates and served him well, although he did later challenge the earl to a duel over an alleged slight, a rendezvous that Cumberland failed to keep. By 1594 Monson was serving with Drake and Essex, after which he became Leveson's vice-admiral, taking great pride in his blasting the galleys away at Cezimbra. On return from this deployment he was given command of his own squadron to effect an Anglo-Dutch attack on the Spanish fleet, an assault that almost ended in disaster when the Dutchless Monson found himself pitted against a vastly superior Spanish fleet. His later career lies beyond the range of this book apart from the fact that he became an extraordinarily prolific author, writing on all things naval. The output is variable in quality and reliability, but its existence in published form gives us as many insights to the activities of the Tudor navy, as do the state papers.[33]

The exploits and activities at sea of men such as Leveson and Monson, along with the latter's accounts, should place them on a pedestal somewhat higher than their flashy comrade Sir Walter Ralegh, but he had the status of a 'celeb' and they did not. Only one 'Sea Wolf' had that star ingredient and that was Sir Francis Drake. His exploits are well documented in many works, both fiction and non-fiction, poetry and prose;[34] his life and work infuse this book.

Right Sir Richard Leveson is one of the unsung heroes of the later Tudor years. Completing the destruction of the galley threat, he commanded in a way that heralded the development of a more professional navy in the seventeenth century. This statue, that survived Parliamentary attempts to destroy it, stands by his magnificent tomb in St Peters, Wolverhampton. The son of a pirate, he joined the maritime hierarchy by marrying Elizabeth, the daughter of Lord Admiral Charles Howard of Effingham. (Author)

Left Silver-tongued and good-looking, courtly not nautical attributes, Walter Ralegh, was dashing, brave and inexperienced at sea, his own actions being flattered by comparison with the incompetent Essex with whom he sailed on major deployments. (National Maritime Museum PU4684)

James Lancaster's incident-packed career, from shipwreck and castaway to plunder beyond the dreams of avarice, marked the transition from privateering to legitimate trade. In his first expedition on behalf of the East India Company, he sailed in Red Dragon, *which as* Scourge of Malice, *had been built for the Earl of Cumberland to go raiding.* (National Maritime Museum BHC2828)

Seamen

Although a system of benign impressment, whereby seafarers were summoned to make their way independently to a mustering port and paid conduct money so to do, existed for most of the century, it was never easy to find sufficient sailors when a full muster of vessels was required.

This is not surprising, for a four-masted sailing ship required a large crew. In 1513 the fleet of twenty-four ships with a combined portage of 8,460 tonnes was manned by 6,480 men, including soldiers, an average of one man for every 1.3 tonnes.[35] This ratio did not change much during the century: in August 1535 Lord Lisle's agent, James Hakysworth, wrote to him to bemoan the fact that not only had the ship's master he wanted gone elsewhere but 'all the good mariners are already shipped'.[36]

As men meant wages and such expenditure was always close to the Tudors' minds, a good record exists of how many men were provided for many of the ships in commission. The table below shows an extract from the list of ships 'appointed for the Narrow Seas' in 1546.[37]

Ships Appointed to the Narrow Seas, 1546

Ship	Tonnage	Crew
Henry Grace à Dieu	1,000	700
Great Venetian	800	450
Jesus of Lubeck	700	350
Salamander	240	220
Minion	300	220
Shallop Reneger	25	25

Samuel Johnson's cynical statement that life at sea was no better than being in jail but with the additional chance of drowning reflected a view that among all the nasty, brutish and short occupations of the human race being a seamen was pretty near the bottom. Yet this was not so. Life ashore for the labouring classes was no easy alternative. A statute of 1495 laid down that the working day from mid-March to mid-September would run from 0900 to 2000 with half an hour for breakfast and an hour and a half for lunch and a nap, although the siesta was allowable only from mid-May to mid-August. In the winter the work started with the springing of the day and ran until nightfall. There was no such thing as a weekend. This gave a sixty-nine-hour week for six months and a seventy-five-hour one for the other six. There were, of course, holy days, but a decree of 1522 reduced these to twenty-seven unpaid days. The record of the building of Somerset House between 1547 and 1552 shows that the work was continuous with no days taken off, during which period a labourer might have been lucky to receive 5d per day.

These labouring conditions made a life at sea, with the day divided into watches and food provided although of uncertain quality, a sensible alternative career. There were other advantages, as anyone who has spent time in the villages of a developing country will be well aware. At sea the sailor did not have to wade through mud for six months of the year or be choked with dust for another three. And, as always, there were companions with whom to share hardship and a system of dispensing justice which was less arbitrary and vicious than that which could be experienced ashore. So Luke Fox's comment that life at sea consisted of 'cold and salt meat, broken sleep, mouldy bread, dead beer, wet clothes and want of fire' needs to be set against any similarly jaundiced comment about life ashore.[38] A vivid account of the destitution that the indigent found themselves in is given by Harrison, who, quoting from contemporary reports of the invasion scare muster of 1592, stated that of fifty men provided by the county of Bedford, fourteen were incapable and all were evilly apparelled, while of a similar number from Cambridge, ten were insufficient and most were 'ill and nakedly apparelled, wanting doublets, hose, stockings, shirts and shoes'.[39] The army may not have been sent the counties' finest but there is sufficient evidence here to suspect that poverty was now widespread. At least the seamen were clothed and shod.

The contrast between sea and shore service is vividly illustrated by an event in 1544, when Henry wished those who had been serving in the army at sea against the Scots to transfer over to France immediately for land duties. The commanders protested directly to the king that, although they were most willing to serve, it would be impossible to provide the number demanded unless they had an opportunity to go home on leave first to recuperate and re-clothe themselves. They had spent all their money and, as they had been at sea, they had neither tents nor pavilions. Their soldiers had 'lain nightly in their clothes for two months', with the last fortnight being in the field with no cover so that most of them, through 'cold and great travail and scant victualling', were diseased, swollen-legged, weary and in rags with no money to clothe themselves.[40]

But sailors cost money and it was every monarch's wish not to have to feed mouths that could dine elsewhere. Elizabeth was the extreme exponent of discharging and rehiring and, through so doing, was very lucky not to make a serious miscalculation as to when the Armada might arrive. As it was her behaviour drew forth a rebuke, via Walsingham, from Lord Admiral Howard in *White Bear* who was anxiously, in February 1588, watching for a fleet in Dunkirk to break out and head for Scotland as he lay unmanned. As so often, his language was pithily punchy. Having explained that he believed that Scotland was 'the mark they will shoot at' he went on to say that 'he would rather be torn to pieces by wild horses than that the enemy should pass through to Scotland'; however, the 'evil policy' of reducing the numbers of men in the fleet had meant that 'the enemy now make but little reckoning of us and knows that we are but like bears tied to stakes, and they may come like dogs to offend us'.[41]

Charles Howard was also concerned with ensuring that those men he did have embarked were paid and so, at the start of the Armada campaign, he asked that the sailors in the fleet sailing from Queenborough be paid six weeks' wages in advance, as 'the late bitter time hath sharply handled these men' who had shivered their ways through weeks of waiting.

Impressment

Many of those quite content with the concept of conscription express concern over the idea of impressment, which was just an earlier and more necessary form of forced recruitment

Although at the time only the wealthy had their likenesses portrayed, modern scientific techniques have enabled these portraits of crew members from the Mary Rose *to be reconstructed with great accuracy from skulls raised from the wreck. From their location onboard, their skeletal development, injuries, and the tools that lay close by, it is thought that one was a bosun and another a gunner. Dental analysis has revealed that many of the crew of* Mary Rose *were not English; the gunner, for example, probably grew up in Spain.* (Windfall Films)

for both masters and men. In the great war against Spain both nations haemorrhaged seamen but England, with a much smaller population and with its mariners confined to a narrow coastal selvage, could least afford to lose them. So when threats arose manning the fleet in a timely fashion was paramount. Lists were kept and impressment used when necessary, with severe punishment threatened for any seaman who made himself scarce in his port town rather than be ordered to report to the fleet. Letters were sent out to the local justices and sheriffs asking them to provide such manpower. One written in 1539 deserves to be quoted for its introductory invective alone. It was sent to Lord Mordaunt and twenty others. In it Henry stated that having been informed that 'The most persistent idol, enemy of all truth and usurpator of princes, the Bishop of Rome, is minded to seek all ways possible to rob and spoil the realm and invert the good religion of the same' he asked his lordship to furnish forty able persons to do duty on the sea, as many to be archers and gunners as possible and that they were to be ready at an hour's warning when called upon by the Earl of Southampton (the Lord Admiral, Fitzwilliam).[42] As the century drew to a close, manning, from masters' mates and pilots to ordinary seamen, became difficult. What is more, many of those impressed no longer had the skills necessary for the work. Both Ralegh and Essex scoured the stews and dives of London to winkle out loafers but the latter reported that 'men utterly insufficient and unserviceable taken up by the pressmasters in mariners' clothes, do not know one rope in the ship ...'.[43]

In January 1602 the need to impress for a major fleet deployment became most obvious and the Privy Council came up with a suggestion for the 'redress of the inconvenience arising from the impress of mariners' in the form of a proclamation requiring:

1. That in all maritime counties a yearly register of seafarers be made.
2. That all households that followed the sea should be listed, with the children, servants and parents of seafarers included.
3. That copies of this register should be held by JPs and passed to the vice-admirals of the counties and then forwarded through them to the Lord Admiral.

Canaries during the Indies voyage of 1595, one was a Frenchman born in Angers and one a Pole born in Danzig, although the latter claimed to have been impressed after being captured at sea by the English, but it can be assumed that the nationals of many other countries found life at sea in an English warship more tolerable than that ashore in their own land.

Capture

When Grenville, in 1591, told his men that it was 'better to fall into the hand of God than into the hand of Spain', he was not exaggerating the stark choice before them. All who were captured could anticipate lengthy interrogation and imprisonment, many the Inquisition and immolation. With no Geneva Convention, but all the hatred of a split communion, few were treated well or ultimately released. Most of the crew of *Hope*, captured in 1595, were flogged or starved to death in the galleys, a fate from which the ever wily Monson wheedled his way out. The tale of Hawkins's men, abandoned either at San Juan de Ulua or on the coast of Mexico, is one of forced marches and slavery (from which Miles Philip, almost alone, escaped after sixteen years[45]), deprivation and pain, while to get a few released Hawkins had to resort to deals verging on espionage and, possibly, treachery, the depths of which remain uncharted. A few escaped, but more were captured in the attempt. The cruelty of dashing prisoners' hopes, however hard the original sentence, was also practised. In 1580 Oxenham and Butler were 'sentenced to perpetual captivity ... in His Majesty's galleys, in service at the oars without wages', only to be taken out and hanged. Youth was one of the few extenuations. John Drake, the admiral's cartographical companion during the circumnavigation, was captured aged twenty-two in 1584, having sailed to South America with Fenton. He was to spend the rest of his life confined to a monastery, the last possible mention of him being in 1650, when he would have been over eighty.[46] Occasionally the state interfered; on one occasion the navy was told to seize several Spanish seamen of 'the best sort' to hand over as bargaining chips to the wives of captured English sailors; given their renowned 'Spanish graces' one wonders if all the substitutions were made.

Ironically, Grenville's crew were treated with courtesy and not double-crossed, their amazing defence of one against fifty-three winning them admiration and freedom. Among the despatches sent to England in a pinnace from *Revenge* before that last fight was a letter home from Philip Gawdy, a volunteer, stating that not only had he 'never had my health better in my life' but that he liked, 'the sea and the sea life, and the company at sea, as well as any that ever I lived withal. The place is good and healthful to a willing mind.'[47] Captured by the Spanish and then treated well and released early, he probably never experienced anything subsequently to make him change his opinion.

4. That no seafaring man on pain of imprisonment should send his sons or servants away from the coast without notice to the register keeper.

5. That the vice-admirals should keep themselves up to date with their counties by making frequent tours.

6. That when an impress summons was made the parish officers were to be responsible for delivering the seamen from their community.

7. That a note should be made of other onboard ships at the time, and that they were also to be impressed.[44]

The need for a register was not a result of a dearth of mariners but the consequence of the success of the corsairs, whose fleets had grown along with the rewards, which could, on a good voyage, far exceed what a sailor might earn on board a royal naval vessel. The new century was to see a rise in merchant shipping as England entered new market and challenged for its control. Impressment was going to be a feature of port life for a long time, until piracy and privateering ended, and life in factories became miserable enough to make men turn once more to the sea for a healthier and nobler life.

Not all the Navy Royal's seamen were English or even British. Studies of tooth enamel from the skulls raised with *Mary Rose* indicate the presence of many southern Europeans on board that ship in 1545. Among three prisoners captured and interrogated by the Spanish in the

Chapter Seven

A Sailor's Life

Some coffin'd in their cabins lie, equally

Griev'd that they are not dead, and yet must die;

And as sin-burd'ned souls from grave will creep,

At the last day, some forth their cabins peep:

And tremblingly ask what news, and do hear so,

Like jealous husbands, what they would not know.

Some sitting on the hatches, would seem there,

With hideous gazing to fear away fear.

Then note that the ship's sicknesses, the Mast

Shake's with this ague, and the Hold and waist

With a salt dropsie clog'd, and all our tacklings

Snapping, like too-high-stretched treble strings.

And from the totter'd sails, rags drop down so,

As from one hang'd in chains, a year ago.

Even our Ordinance plac'd for our defence,

Strive to break loose, and 'scape away from thence.

Pumping hath tir'd our men, and what's the gain?

Seas into seas thrown, we suck in again.

John Donne, 'The Storme'

If it were possible to breathe life into the bones of one of the sailors from *Mary Rose* and to place him on the gun-deck of HMS *Victory* he would immediately be familiar with his surroundings and, in a day or two, be able to understand and share in the routine. Move him then to the same deck in HMS *Warrior*, launched in 1860 as the nation's first ironclad warship, and he would settle in as easily as he had done in Nelson's flagship. In few other walks of life has this continuity of conditions lasted for so long. The industrial revolution had little impact, and it was not until the major changes brought about by the steam turbine and the trainable gun turret that the seamen's life changed, and that was after HMS *Warrior* entered the reserve fleet in 1882.

There was one major difference in the life of the Tudor naval seaman from that of his successors: his job was both part-time and non-permanent. When the ships returned to harbour in the autumn or at the end of a crisis he would be laid off and sent home. Generally this

A Venetian illustration from 1598 of the English seaman's attire worn while serving in far northern waters – note the fur cap. A seaman's basic garb varied little: a linen or wool shirt, a leather jerkin, breeches, wool hose and a hat, all of which they generally supplied themselves.

arrangement of seasonal employment worked well. Back in their home towns the men would soon pick up work on the fishing boats or on merchant ships, and they would have had the balance of their wages to keep them and their families fed until they resumed employment. When wages were paid promptly there were few problems with the system, and it was disease and hunger that led to most deserting their ships before they had official permission to depart. Of course, concerns over family matters – pregnant wives, ill parents, starving children – led to some absconding or endeavouring to avoid call-up but this is true of every age and every nation and such absenteeism is not a reflection, at least in Tudor times, of grim conditions on board ship. So when the summons went out from magistrate or sheriff the seamen gathered their things, said their farewells and set off along the roads to the ports.

They travelled light. It was a time when few, other than the wealthy, owned anything other than the tools of their trade and essential household kitchen items. If they carried anything along the road, it would have been a tankard, plate and spoon, a few toiletry items, such as a comb, and a needle and thread. The religious might have had some prayer beads, and the better-off and better-educated a devotional book. Most would also have had a purse of some description to hold their travelling expenses of sixpence a day and their pay at the end of their employment. All in all, they had few enough items to wrap up in a bundle, while a knife, the only essential tool of their trade, probably hung from their belt.

The clothes they wore would be those in which they would serve and consisted of a rough woollen or linen undershirt, a leather jerkin, breeches and a hat. Their status and poverty would have meant that these were of the coarsest fibre, for the wealth of the nation and its merchants depended on the export of good-quality wool and cloth to Europe. Once donned the shirt would seldom come off except to be patched, for it was too important an item to be discarded once ripped or stained.

Over the shirt, especially on deck, a sleeveless leather jerkin would have provided some protection against the wind and the spray. The jerkins were again of the simplest design, consisting of a bodice and a short skirt, generally fastened at the front by laces with aiglets at their ends to prevent fraying. Laces, rather than buttons, made sense on board as, should they part, there was always plenty of string or twine with which to replace them. The sheep's wool or calfskin jerkin could often be turned inside out to even out the wear, a common practice, as the term 'turncoat' or Shakespeare's line 'A plague of my opinion one may wear it on both sides like a leather jerkin' makes clear.

There was an advantage in joining a ship that was being newly commissioned, for in such cases an issue was sometimes made of new clothing to make a good impression. Thus in July 1511 Sir John Daunce, a teller at the Exchequer, paid:

Richard Palshide, one of our customers in the port of Southampton, these parcels ensuring: first, for 24 coats of white and green for 24 soldiers for the sure conducting of our ship called *Mary Rose* from Portsmouth, to the Thames of London, and 6 coats of white and green for the master, 4 quartermasters and the boatswain at 6s 10d per coat.[1]

The price paid indicates that these were very special items made in the Tudor colours. Usually the crew could expect something much cheaper. In 1512 Edward Howard indented for jerkins for his mariners at 20d each, which must have involved a very standard 'one size fits all' tailoring. Nevertheless they were free and would have provided a welcome change of clothing to those coming off watch soaked to the skin. Like every other item of clothing, jerkins would have been patched and repaired and kept until they just fell apart, which in extreme conditions they did. On 28 August 1545, with the French invasion no longer an immediate threat, Lisle wrote to the king that: '...You shall understand that men in this army decay very sore, and those that be whole be very unsightly having not a rag to hang on their backs.'

Forty years after this Charles Howard was to write to his sovereign in similar circumstance, with the Armada driven north, that he had an urgent need for new hose, doublets, shirts and shoes, 'for else, in a very short time, I look to see most of the mariners go naked'.

In better times the mariners covered their nakedness with breeches, which were either tied around the waist or attached to the undershirt with laces threaded through eyelets. These would have covered the thighs and been tied once again above the knee. In cold weather woollen hose, large socks, would have been pulled up over the lower leg.

On deck the seamen would have moved barefoot, their toes providing a surer grip than any footwear and being used in a prehensile fashion when climbing the rigging. Most shoes at the time were made of leather, a material that becomes slimy, slippery and uncomfortable when wet. Shoes would thus have been stowed below and used as slippers (most were slip-on style) when wandering around the lower deck off watch – a sensible precaution against splinters. The discovery of a bag of shoes in *Mary Rose* indicates that these might have been issued to the crew. Drake sailed in 1595 with 172 dozen and 10 pairs of shoes costing between 15d and 19d per pair, mostly for issue to Baskerville's soldiers. Nevertheless, during their failed march on Panama the soldiers suffered miserably in the muddy conditions; many ended walking barefoot and offering up to 30s to buy a pair of shoes.

Most of the shoes were well made, being welted, a form of shoemaking only introduced at the beginning of the sixteenth century which was both better lasting and more waterproof than the traditional turn shoe with its all-in-one sole. Senior officers, for the most part, would have walked the deck in thigh boots, while, between these two extremes, some of the officers would have worn ankle boots with buckles or laces, not good for climbing and hauling but most comfortable for those in a supervisory position on deck.

From items such as this jerkin recovered from the Mary Rose *the way Tudor seamen dressed has been carefully established.* (Mary Rose Trust)

Shoes were one of the few items of clothing that were occasionally purchased centrally and then stowed onboard, as they were for Drake's final voyage. Most crew would have kept their footwear below decks, preferring to work in the open in bare feet. (Mary Rose Trust)

Headgear was one of those items the choice of which was governed by Tudor dress regulations. Not that the poor needed to worry much about these, for, as a contemporary satire, 'The Ballad of the Caps', stated:

> The Sea-man with his thrum doth stand
> On higher parts than all the land
> For any Cap, what ere it bee,
> Is still the sign of some degree.

Thrum caps were made from the waste from the weavers' looms and were thus mostly home-made; this exempted them from the charge laid down in an Act of 1512, which established a national price for headgear depending on the quality of wool used. Homespun they may have been, but they were warm and waterproof, as were some of the more sophisticated hats knitted at home.

The Boatswain

In charge of the men for their daily round of tasks were the boatswains, who, unlike the senior officers, had risen from the ranks of seamen and commanded respect from their experience, not their social status. John Smith wrote a vivid first-hand account of the boatswain's role which can scarcely be bettered. He states that the boatswain had:

> ... the charge of all the cordage, tackling, sails, fid and marline spikes, needles, twine, sailcloth, and rigging the ship. His mate has the command of the long boat, for setting forth of anchors, weighing and fetching it home, warping, towing or mooring ... As the master is to be abaft the mast so the boatswain, and all the common sailors under his command, are to be afore the mast ... As the master commands the tacking of the ship, the hoisting or striking the yard, the taking in or putting forth the sails, upon the winding of the master's whistle the boatswain takes it with his,

and sets the sailors with courage to do their work, every one of them knowing by their whistle what they are to do. The boatswain is to see the shroud and other ropes set taut, the deep sea line and plummet in readiness against their coming to soundings, and the tallowed ... And to conclude, his and his mate's work is never at an end, for it is impossible to repeat all the offices that are put upon them.[2]

The Quartermaster

The quartermasters' role, according to Smith, was concentrated below decks, ensuring that the ship was securely stowed and the ballast turned and 'rummaged' (cleaned) as its state indicated. They also took take charge of fishing and needed to have available not only nets but fish hooks, spears and harpoons for catching not only sprats and mackerel but even dolphin, an indicator of how the standard issue of rations was supplemented. Later quartermasters took charge of the whipstaff and steered the ship.

One can see here the way an efficient ship's crew worked. The relationship of master, boatswain, his mates, the carpenter and the crew was paramount, and it would be a foolish captain indeed who did not treat his boatswain with respect and encourage him to relax if his work ever gave him an opportunity so to do.

Apart from certain difference in clothing, the supervisors would have carried as both a badge of office and an aid to the giving of orders a 'boatswain's call', the whistle to which Smith refers, hung on a ribbon or chain around the neck. This simple whistle was such a quintessential item of the mariner that its wearers ranged from the boatswain to the admiral and even the sovereign himself. The inventory of Henry lists a number of gold whistles adorned with precious stones; he was fond of blowing them with all his might when his ships were being commissioned, so much so that the call was another item the wearing of which was strictly ordered, Henry laying down in the Excess in Apparel Act of 1532 that 'Masters of the ships or other vessels and mariners to wear whistles of silver, with the chain of silver to hang the same upon.'

It was from his own collection of gold calls that he appointed Sir George Carew Vice-Admiral of his navy, for, just before the latter sailed and was drowned in *Mary Rose*, the king took '... his chain from his neck, with a great whistle of gold pendant to the same, and did put it about the neck of the said Sir George Carew, giving him also therewith many good and

Even in daytime it was gloomy below decks and lanterns, their hours of use strictly controlled, would have provide the only source of light, especially when the hatches were battened down. (Mary Rose Trust)

comfortable words'. Portraits of other admirals, such as Frobisher and Clinton, also show them wearing their boatswain's calls.

Yet the most important role for the call was the practical one of using its shrill notes to carry above the sound of weather and gunfire to pass orders to seamen working the sails. Although the number of notes was strictly limited, a series of trills and short and long blasts gave the call its necessary vocabulary. The use of the whistle became well known even away from the sea. Shakespeare refers to it in *Henry V*:

... behold
Upon the hempen tackle ship-boys climbing,
Hear the shrill whistle, which doth order give
To sounds confused.

It was with the sound of that whistle that the day began on board for those sleeping below. 'Call the hands' at 0700 gave the off watch crew time to carry out their cursory ablutions and grab something to eat before the sound of eight bells summoned them to relieve those who had worked the morning watch.

That watch, as soon as daylight came, would have squared off the upper deck, coiling and tidying ropes and swilling out and scrubbing the deck itself. Their reliefs, once the ship had settled on to her course for the forenoon watch, would have been occupied in tensioning the standing rigging, patching sails, spicing rope and even helping the carpenter with the making of replacement blocks or the far simpler dead-eyes. A wooden sailing ship at sea was in constant need of such husbandry to prevent canvas from splitting or ropes parting at critical moments when they could no longer take the strain being placed upon them. With a good seaman's eye the boatswain could see what ropes need tensioning or what rigging was fraying; down below the carpenter had a harder task ensuring that the ship's seams were still waterproof and her timbers sound.

The Carpenter

The shipwright or carpenter was a key professional, having served an apprenticeship, and had his own cabin and workshop. His responsibilities ranged from the top of the masts to the bottom of the keel, and he had to have the ability not only to make and mend most of the fixtures and fittings in this wooden world but also to make emergency repairs while the ship was being pounded by the sea or enemy fire. The crew relied on the master to con the ship safely, but should fell circumstance mean that his best endeavours failed then it was often only the carpenter who could keep them alive, which in extreme cases might mean building a boat from whatever material was available. In action the carpenter and his mates were the damage-control team, and that was another hazardous responsibility. John Smith's captain ordered during a lull in the action:

'Master, let us breathe and refresh a little, sling a man over boord to stop the leakes.' That is, to trusse him up about the middle in a peece of canvas, and a rope to keepe him from sinking, and his arms at liberty; with a malet in one hand, & a plug lapped in Okum and a well-tarred tarpawling clout in the other, which he will quickly beat into the holes the bullets made.[3]

With such enormous responsibilities and such a range of circumstances

With tools such as these a ship's carpenter waged a constant battle to keep his vessel seaworthy and its fittings and fixtures in good repair. (Mary Rose Trust)

Each carpenter had numerous planes, enabling him to work on items ranging from ship's timbers to bows and arrows. (Mary Rose Trust)

A carpenter's brace from the Mary Rose. (Mary Rose Trust)

Every seaman carried a working knife and these, and other blades, were kept sharp with a whetstone, which was housed in a wooden holder, like this example from the Mary Rose. (Mary Rose Trust)

Although seamen repaired, if not made, their own clothes, these thimbles probably belonged to the sailmaker. (Mary Rose Trust)

which might require their application it is not surprising that the carpenter's tool box contained a most comprehensive set of tools, most of which, as befitted a craftsman, were his own personal items, and their form would be readily identifiable by anyone working with wood today.

A variety of saws, planes, braces and bits, augers, rules, chisels, mallets and hammers would have been assembled in his tool boxes, and when he was doing his daily rounds of the ship, peering and probing into the darkest recesses, he would have carried a number of these in an ingenious wooden holder on his belt. His knives and chisels would have been kept sharp by use of a grinding wheel and a number of whetstones, the former also being used to sharpen swords, axes and bill hooks prior to action.

Away from harbour the carpenter would have supervised the caulking of the ship using frayed rope unravelled by the seamen and pitch carried in barrels on board. On longer voyages, when the ship needed to be careened and the side scraped and tarred, this messy whole-ship evolution would also have been supervised by the carpenter or shipwright.

Storm damage was another hazard which the carpenter needed to be competent to handle. If masts split or yards snapped then he had to make a jury rig, often in the teeth of a gale if the ship was being driven into danger. The debris needed to be chopped away with an axe and a new mast made from spare timber or a yard, often by fishing broken spars together. Here was a man then who needed to combine craftsmanship with ingenuity if he was to serve well those whose lives depended on his skills.

The Barber-Surgeon

The arrival of another professional lifesaver would have indicated to those on board that they were sailing into action. This was the barber-surgeon, whose appointment to the fleet was probably a direct result of Henry's deep interest in his fighting navy. In 1513 Wolsey told Dauncey to pay two months' wages for twenty-four 'surgeons appointed to the sea', so that from the start of the Tudor wars seamen were provided with medical support superior to that which accompanied the land-based soldiery.[4]

By the sixteenth century professional medicine was practised by three identifiable groups: university-trained physicians, apothecaries and barber-surgeons. The seamen would not have come across any of these in their sea ports and fishing villages, where a midwife and a quack would have dispensed any medicine and dealt with injury while the blacksmith doubled up as the dentist, extractions only. The presence on board of a professional who could dispense medicine, set broken bones and keep him clean-shaven would have impressed and, before battle, calmed, the inexperienced sailor. Yet the barber-surgeons were not always the most experienced of their profession. In 1595 Daniel Equisman, the barber-surgeon of *Solomon,* was captured in the Canaries at the start of the Drake and Hawkins deployment. Under interrogation he stated his age to be twenty-three, which would seem very young to be fully qualified.

Barber-surgeons already belonged to a guild that Henry had recognised by presenting it with a set of gold and silver instruments. Members of the guild had been available for military deployments for many years, and when hostilities broke out were impressed with a payment befitting their status. In 1513 Lord Ferrers was paying the chief surgeon in the fleet 13s 4d per month, the next most skilled 10s, and the remainder 8s. They remained a part of a ship's wartime complement throughout the century with a system that allowed for their call-up in time of conflict, often through impressments, but on good terms. They too were not immune to danger; Drake's barber-surgeon in *Golden Hind* was killed by Indians; the chief surgeon of his 1595 expedition, James Wood, died off Porto Bello.

John Smith stated that the 'Chirugion' needed to present his certificate from the Barber-Surgeons' Hall on joining his ship and also show that he came with a chest well furnished, 'as may be proper for the clime you go for, which neglect hath been the loss of many a man's life'. Such well-equipped chests, containing both instruments and ointments, have been recovered from *Mary Rose,* indicating that there was no such neglect; thanks to them we have an excellent mid-century record of the state of maritime medicine, and it is not unsophisticated.

Among the medical stores were numerous wooden ointment canisters, glass phials, a bleeding bowl and a robust syringe which, although it could be used in the treatment of venereal disease or for implanting suppositories, was probably for draining wounds. Most were found in a well-made chest in the barber-surgeon's cabin, which would have served as a consulting room as well as a sleeping cabin. Among the many other items in the chest such as razors and bandages was a unique wooden feeding bottle, with a teat-like screw top that would have been used to feed the very sick or those with facial injuries. The composition of the ointments included resins, beeswax, mineral oils, plant oils and animal fats, reflecting the latest advances in treatment for gunshot wounds, broken and fractured bones, sprains, minor abrasions and other common ailments. A similar stock of ointments was provided for all expeditions. The invoice for the 1595 Indies deployment lists many pounds' weight of ointments and concludes with 'Divers other provisions for physic and chirugery for the

This chest probably belonged to the Mary Rose's *surgeon; some of its contents are arrayed in front.* (Mary Rose Trust)

A syringe from the surgeon's 'tool kit'.
(Mary Rose Trust)

furnishing of two chest more ... sundry other drugs made up in two other chests ... money paid to divers surgeons above their wages for the supplying of their chests ... two spare chests for the relief of the whole fleet',[5] which, given the losses, would have been most necessary.

Of course, the real reason for carrying a professional surgeon on board was to care for those damaged in battle. To attend to the injured the surgeon had available a number of instruments, which are identifiable in the *Mary Rose* collection, even though the blades have eroded away leaving just the handles. It is also possible to examine works on medical practice dating from the mid-century and see if the ship's equipment indicates a match with the latest professional thinking. Thus William Clowes, writing towards the end of the century, considered that a surgeon should have available for treating his patients:

A sharp amputation saw: for cutting bone
A sharp curved incision knife: for cutting skin and flesh
A trepan with a screw mechanism: to lift pieces of depressed skull bone
Probes of silver, lead and tin, or wood: for finding foreign bodies in deep wounds
A syringe: for irrigating wounds with wine or vinegar
A *Dilator*, with three prongs and an expanding mechanism: to hold wounds open
Forceps
Two buttons soaked in vinegar and cautery irons: to stop bleeding
Splints and tapes
Cupping glasses
A chafing dish: to heat cautery irons and for making ointments
A Pestle and Mortar
Needles
Silk thread
Bandages[6]

In addition to these, and useful in the barber's role as well as that of the surgeon, would have been scissors, razors, whetstones and a shaving basin. For minor amputations there would have been a wooden mallet heavy enough to provide the force to sever a finger or toe.

Clowes's *Book of Observations*, published in 1596, detailed the treatment of gunpowder burns, musket-ball wounds and other wartime injuries as well as the sailors' peace-time ailment of venereal disease, which alone would have made it a standard text for naval surgeons. Certainly, the *Mary Rose* inventory mentions most of the items on Clowes's list.

Among the daily complaints with which the barber-surgeon had to deal would have been toothache. Indeed a law of Henry VIII permitted only registered barber-surgeons to practise dentistry. An examination of the skulls raised from *Mary Rose* indicates that a number of the

sailors suffered from caries or gum disease. There are many missing teeth and signs of extractions. That having been said, there are also examples of extremely good dental arches forming an almost perfect curve of teeth. The main finding was that at least 10 per cent of the crew could have been in pain from dental disease at any one time.[7] The presence of a barber-surgeon would have been a great comfort carrying with it the hope, if not the actuality, of relief in a more professional way than that offered by the blacksmith in village England.

The barber-surgeons would also have been well-read at a time when the writings of other professionals were being printed, translated and distributed for the first time. Thus the Tudor seamen had the services of men at the forefront of their profession who were learning more as the century progressed. Yet medical advances were uneven. Surgery, including amputation, was well developed but little was understood about hygiene, infection, sterilisation or shock, so that in many cases the operation was a success but the patient died. Thus the ability to heal wounds, amputate limbs, mend bones and cure or ameliorate toothache has to be balanced by the almost total ignorance regarding the prevention and treatment of sickness and disease, which killed more sailors than either accident or action damage.

Many believed that the infections that followed penetrating wounds from arrows or shot were caused by poison or inherently toxic gunpowder rather than being the result of imbedded foreign material, such as cloth, that set up inflammation and contamination. The result could be a lingering, painful and smelly death. Martin Frobisher, landing at Brest Roads in 1594 to support the final assault on the Spanish fort El Leon, built by the Spanish to control the entrance to the harbour, 'was shot in the side, the wound being not mortal in itself, but swords or guns have not made mortal wounds then proved in the careless or skilless surgeon, as here came to pass'.[8]

This was unfair, for with just two surgeons to tend to the whole force, a wound from which the bullet had been extracted was probably thought to need no further professional attention compared with the other ghastly injuries incurred. Initially, it would appear that Frobisher himself just felt inconvenienced, and probably only temporarily. In his report of the proceedings to Howard he made light of the matter, stating: 'I was shot in with a bullet along the huckell bone. So as I was driven to have an infusion made to take out the bullet. So I am neither to go nor ride [with Sir John Norris]'. Instead his main concern was, as so often, with the fleet commanders' victuals: 'Sir John Norris would willingly have some five hundred of sailors for his better strength ... which I would very willingly have done if we had victuals to continue our fleet here for the time ... we will do what we are able, if we had victuals it were easily done, but here is non to be had ...'.[9] Sadly, the bullet had driven a wad of cloth into the wound, where it was not found, and the tell-tale smell of corruption was apparent

Most seamen carried few personal possessions with them and what they had was mainly linked to the repair of clothing and the eating of meals with the occasional religious charm or keepsake. This collection from a variety of locations in the Mary Rose *shows how varied even such a limited group of items can become.* (Mary Rose Trust)

before the ships reached Plymouth. With the wound high up on his upper leg, even a risky amputation was not an option. The victorious commander died on 22 November, fifteen days after receiving his fatal wound.

Yet in the general run of things serious injury was as rare as it was on land; *Before the Mast* states that 'Evidence from skeletal remains from the *Mary Rose* revealed only a small number of healed fractures, few of which involved major bones, tending to confirm that severe fracture led to discharge from active service',[10] when, in fact, they probably confirm the limited incidence of such breaks, especially in a crew that had been on board that particular ship for only a matter of weeks.

The skeletal remains from *Mary Rose* do in fact indicate that she was manned by a young and healthy crew, some of whom showed signs of having suffered from childhood diseases caused by vitamin deficiency, but who showed few signs of occupational stress such as fractures except in one instance. In England all males were required to practise archery between the ages of seven and seventeen. Those who became professional would have practised for longer and put far more strain on their bodies, for the great war bows had a draw weight of up to 165lb. The result seems to have been the prevalence of a traumatic abnormality called *os acromiale* in which the bones of the scapula fail to fuse, something which they do normally before the age of twenty.

As with infection caused through battle injury, so with a host of other ailments, the barber-surgeons could only respond to the limit of their understanding, often failing not through their own shortcomings but because of widespread ignorance about how disease was caused and spread. This ignorance caused a deadly drain on manpower that the navy found hard to stem and some ships found impossible to manage.

Anther major cause of illness was the frequent post-combat neglect to which the fleets were subjected. As the French invasion scare of 1545 receded, Lisle was immediately faced with a major outbreak of disease caused by his men's long confinement in fetid living condi-

tions. On 1 August he wrote to Suffolk, the army commander at Portsmouth:

> ... there is a great disease fallen among the soldiers and mariners almost in every ship, in such sort that if the same should continue, which God forbid, we should have need to be newly refreshed with men. The disease is swelling in their heads and faces and legs, and divers of them with the bloody flux ...[11]

There was no remedy, and on 28 August he wrote to the King in Council, via Paget, that 'his men decayeth very sore, and those that be whole be very unsightly, having not a rag to hang upon their backs', and that 'had he tarried longer away there would have been little order in this army; for soldiers and captains wax weary of each other because both are weary of the ships'.[12] A fortnight later Lisle and Thomas Seymour were writing to inform the king that 'the plague reigns sore in this army and that divers of the ships appointed to keep the Narrow Seas with Seymour are infected'. Yet, rather than sort out the dilemma posed by the fact that the infected ships were not able to be despatched because none were willing to enter them and their own sailors were not able to be placed in other vessels, the two admirals asked for instructions from the king, thus, yet again, illustrating the unwillingness of Henry's commanders to take straightforward operational and administrative decisions. It was quite clear that they were facing a major dilemma: 'As plague begins to be universal in the army, they will muster only those in ships not infected and try to preserve them; albeit there is no certainty, for they fall sick nightly ... The clean men mount to few, compared with the number that the king wishes to be sent to Calais.' They list *Pauncy*, *Mary Hambro*, *Lese Galley*, *Pelycane*, *Salamander*, *Unicorn*, *Swallow*, *Falcon Lisle*, *Evangelist Jud*, *Phoenix* and *George of Totnes*.[13]

A few days later Lisle gave the Privy Council a summary of his numbers. On 4 September he had returned from a raid on Le Tréport with 12,000 men. By 14 September only 8,488 of these were healthy, and from these he had discharged several hundred fishermen to return to their task (it being reported that many women had had to go out fishing in their absence). After removing men from the infected ships, he was left with just 4,784 for sea service with him, with 900 for the other squadrons and 705 as a reserve to replace those who were bound to fall ill over the next few weeks. It was worse ashore, with just 500 men fit to garrison the Isle of Wight and none at Portsmouth, where all

One very personal touch from the artefacts discovered in the Mary Rose *was a collection of gunners' linstocks, each carved and decorated individually.* (Mary Rose Trust)

were 'full of sickness'.[14] Edward Vaughan, writing from Portsmouth, told the council that the infected town needed some expert physicians, for they lacked even enough fit men to draw the chain across the harbour mouth should the French reappear. Vaughan emphasised his own duteous position by closing with: 'The writer is himself so light of head and in such fever that, if he had not thought it his duty, he would be loth to set pen to the book.'[15]

By October the Privy Council were concerned enough to order Thomas Seymour to 'enter some clean and uninfected vessel and sail with the whole navy to Portsmouth'.[16]

The disease continued. On 25 April 1546 Lord William Howard, in Great Venetian, entered Portsmouth with a number of captured vessels taken from a convoy of a hundred hulks. He had noticed that sundry men had died on board but considered it normal attrition until on the 26th two men who were fit at 7am were dead by 10am and another fourteen were reported ill. Hastening over to *Pauncy*, he was made unwelcome by those who suspected plague, a fact supported by reports of further deaths throughout the fleet, although he 'wot not whereof'.[17]

A very similar story emerges from the 1588 campaign, with Howard of Effingham writing to Burghley from Margate Roads on 18 August that it was 'a most pitiful sight to see, here at Margate, how the men, having no place to receive them into here, die in the streets'.[18]

Howard had landed his men into the town but only barns and outhouses were made available for his sick mariners. More English sailors thus died in the streets of Margate during the Armada campaign than were lost in enemy action at sea, a fact that does not feature in the town's promotional literature!

Howard reported that:

> Sickness and morality begin wonderfully to grow amongst us ... the *Elizabeth Jonas*, which hath done as well as ever any ship did in any service, hath had a great infection in her from the beginning, so as of the 500 men which she carried out, by the time we had been in Plymouth three weeks or a month there were dead of them 200 and above, so as I was driven to send all the rest of her men ashore, to take out her ballast and to make fire in her of wet broom three or four days together, and so hoped thereby to have cleansed her of her infection, and thereupon got new men, very tall and able as ever I saw, and put them into her. Now the infection is broken out in greater extremity than ever it did before, and they die and sicken faster than ever they did, so I am driven of force to send her to Chatham.[19]

Other ships were faring almost as badly while Howard, like Lisle before him, was also worried by the ragged nakedness of the crews and implored the council to provide new hose, shirts and shoes.

The fact that English sailors were dying in droves in their base ports even before the arrival of the Armada is a shocking indictment seldom mentioned, but it does place in perspective the problems experienced by the Spanish in port prior to departure.

Yet however shocking the losses were and however callous the reaction of the council, the English were, on each occasion when invasion threatened, better off than their opponents. The ships of the French fleet were diseased even while they were landing troops on the

A collection of items used for tarring the ship's sides and decks. The battle against leaks was waged on most days with few ships ever achieving total watertight integrity. (Mary Rose Trust)

Isle of Wight in 1545 and could not long have remained anchored off that coast. Medina Sidonia was reporting contagion before he sailed from Corunna, and there is no doubt that some of the groundings that took place on the long voyage home were the result of ships no longer having sufficient strength to man their vessels. One ran aground in Laredo harbour, simply because there were not enough hands to lower the sails or let go the anchors. On *San Martin* some 180 of the crew died from disease before she entered Santander on 23 September, and many more died after she berthed. By mid-October the two senior fighting admirals of Spain, Recalde and Oquendo, were also dead, having fought the English and the elements to total exhaustion. A year later, with the English counter-offensive led by Drake and Norris to destroy the surviving Spanish ships and place the pretender Don Antonio on the Portuguese throne at Lisbon, of the 16,000 men who sailed from Plymouth over 10,000 did not return and, although the army fought several skirmishes, the majority of the casualties succumbed to disease or malnutrition.

The problem was that, for all their technical skills, the barber-surgeons had no idea about either the cause of disease or the measures necessary to contain its spread. Ships are crowded places and contagion can spread rapidly. Even today cruise ships are reported as having to return to port because of an outbreak of food-poisoning or Legionnaire's disease or something similar. If, with all the medical advances, such illnesses are still commonplace, it is hardly surprising that the crowded decks of Tudor warships had frequent epidemics. Yet conditions ashore were often worse, especially when the growing number of dispossessed flooded into London in the latter half of the century. Plague, although not endemic, was a frequent visitor to both town and country. In 1597 one-third of the citizens of Norwich died from it; in 1563 over 20,000 died in and around London; in 1593 the figure was 18,000, and in 1603 it rose to 30,000. As with all major epidemics it was the poor in their crowded unsanitary hovels, from which they could not, like the court, escape, who suffered most, the very socio-economic group from which sailors were drawn. Even if they were free from plague, as many in the country were, the enclosure of open fields, the increase in rent, the evictions for non-payment of arrears or to create parkland left many families landless and homeless, prey to the harsh treatment that a Christian nation felt fit to grant its their poor. In Edward's reign the price of food in London rose by over 90 per cent, while the latter quarter of the century saw failing harvests and the spectre of famine, which by weakening the wretched made them succumb to other diseases. The sailors in the Navy Royal were not immune to these forces but they were, as long as the state acknowledged its duty to feed them, protected from both dearth and deprivation. This left Monson bemused by the fact that so many sailors chose the precarious life in crowded unsanitary privateers rather than serve her Majesty, 'where the pay is certain, their diet plentiful, and their labour not so great'.[20]

In future centuries, long naval voyages would be overshadowed by the curse of scurvy caused by a lack of fresh fruit and vegetables. Even then, comparisons with these later voyages would cast the Tudors in a good light. Drake's circumnavigation in the 1570s and Anson's in the 1740s sailed over similar routes and both seized one major prize before returning with just one ship from the several that had left England, but the death toll in Anson's vessels far exceeded that experienced by Drake. Overcrowding and wet, stormy weather in the southern ocean all contributed to the losses, but Drake's penultimate leg, a 9,000-mile, 118-day non-stop sail from Java to Sierra Leone, where he arrived with just eight pints of water and having lost just one man, was a feat that Anson could not have emulated. Admiral Vernon, revisiting Cartagena in 1741 with similar intentions to those of Drake in 1586, lost thousands of men during his expedition, and it has been estimated that in 1810, some 50 per cent of the navy's casualties were caused by disease, even after the causes of and remedy for scurvy had been identified.

The mystery of the cause of scurvy remained until almost the time of Captain Cook, yet Drake's circumnavigation had taken place without any deaths from dietary deficiency and, in 1601, James Lancaster, sailing on the first East India Company voyage, insisted on departing with sufficient store of lemons on board to give each man three spoonfuls of juice each day to avoid 'the plague of the sea'. Even on Cavendish's last voyage, Captain John Davis reported that, in the Straits of Magellan, the crew came across the significantly named 'scurvy grass', 'which we fried with eggs, using train oil instead of butter. This herb did so purge the blood, that it took away all kinds of swellings, of which many died, and restored us to perfect health of body, so that we were in as good a case as when we came first out of England.'[21] Was the efficacy of these readily available antiscorbutics forgotten in the century that followed?

Personal hygiene and unsanitary ships have been blamed for many of the illnesses that broke out on board ship, yet even this assumption has to be treated with some reserve. *Mary Rose* yielded over eighty combs, sufficient to indicate that the majority of the crew possessed one of these superbly crafted simple items. Although all were made of boxwood and had the same double-sided form, with the teeth on one side (the nit-side) being much finer and closer than on the other, within

Sufficient examples were recovered from the Mary Rose *to indicate that each sailor carried his own personal comb; what is more, no two of these everyday items, made from boxwood, are the same, which suggests the great pride in creation even of the mundane before mass production.* (Mary Rose Trust)

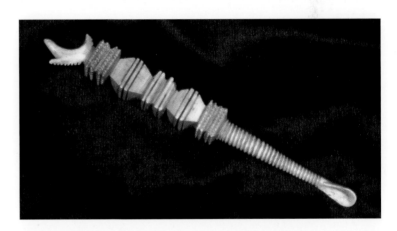

Ear-scoops also show a high level of personal hygiene; furthermore, ear-wax was useful for waxing thread for stitching leather shoes and jerkins. (Mary Rose Trust)

this commonality lies a wealth of difference so that no two are the same – an indicator of the pride taken by the maker. If the men paid that much attention to their hair it can be presumed that other areas of their body were granted equal care. The presence of shaving sticks and razors indicates that they were well shaved, and ear-scoops and manicure sets suggest that grooming was important – ear-wax anyway would have been useful for waxing thread.

That keeping the decks shipshape was a common requirement can be seen in the guidelines issued by Sebastian Cabot to those hoping to sail to Cathay in which he states: 'No liquor to be spilt on the ballast, nor filthiness [excrement] to be left within board: the cook room, and all other places to be kept clean for the better heath of the company ... the sick to be tended, comforted and holpen in the time of infirmity, and every manner of person, without respect, to bear another's burden',[22] which indicates that ship's company were not a lumpen group of the great unwashed, as is sometimes inferred.

Among the aristocracy manicure sets, such as this one from the Mary Rose, *would have been in common use to maintain the standard of grooming thought appropriate to life at Court, but they were probably not put to as much use at sea.* (Mary Rose Trust)

It is in the defecating department that a question mark arises. In the fore-part of the ship, the beak-head, boxes were secured on which seamen could sit to relieve themselves, but how many ventured up to the 'heads' when the weather was foul can only be guessed. Rather, in such conditions, use a bucket and throw the contents overboard, while urinating could be carried out by swinging outboard while hanging on to the rigging. The heads themselves relied on the action of the waves to cleanse them but this was seldom totally efficacious, and so a seaman had to be detailed off for that less than pleasant job. The choice was made, according to John Smith, in a way that would appeal to the crew's sense of fair play: 'The Liar is to hold his place but for a week, and he that is first taken with a lie every Monday is so proclaimed at the main mast by a general cry of; "A liar, a liar, a liar!"; he is under the Swabber and only to clean the beakhead chains.'[23]

Elsewhere on board there was a 'daille', a trough-shaped timber used to discharge waste water via a pump from the bilge, and this would have had an ablutionary use as well. Officers would have used a 'piss-pot' in the privacy of their cabins.

On dark, wet days many would have relived themselves into the hold, adding to the fetid nature of this area; this arrangement would not have helped the recovery of the sick, who were often laid upon the ballast in the bilge to keep them safe and out of the way. Evidence from *Mary Rose* indicates that at the time the ship capsized there were many seamen in the hold.[24] It can be presumed that none of these were battle casualties, but could they have needed treatment for another reason? Watt hypothesises that they might have been among the earliest victims of the dysentery which, as Lisle reported to the king on 2 August, had struck the fleet and caused great sickness.[25] If so, Watt

goes on, the ship's company might not have been able to react with alacrity to the problems that so fatally struck her on 19 July 1545. It was in the dark and the stench of *Revenge*'s hold, amid the noise and flame of battle, that Grenville in 1591 laid the ninety men or more who had been sick ashore, an experience which must have terrified them. However, in their case, the ballast might have been cleaner than it had been, for the fleet had come into Flores specifically to 'rummage', that is, to dig out the stenching shingle and replace it with new shingle brought out from the shore.

The healthy crew most often slept upon the deck using whatever was available for pillows and added comfort. Straw mattresses were discouraged as a fire risk, so for those who did not have cabins and bunks sleep was not a comfortable experience until, late in the century, the introduction of hammocks, or brazil beds, first reported by Hawkins in the villages of the Indies, made as great a leap forward in sleeping arrangements at sea as did the sprung mattress many year later ashore. Hawkins's last expedition, in 1595, sailed with 927 brazil beds embarked, each priced at 4s 6d.[26]

It was not pleasant, but not that far different from campaigning conditions ashore, where an army could be encamped surrounded by the stench of the living, dying and dead. Elis Gruffudd, describing conditions in France in 1544, wrote of the:

> ... stink of the carrion of the mares and the horses that died among the host which were left to rot on the ground for want of anyone to bury them as the discipline of a host demands. This stench struck within and filled the vital senses and spirits with rotten air which made great havoc with the heart and the mind, and for all these reasons, as well as the displeasure of God, there fell a great pestilence among the soldiers.[27]

It was not only the campaign trail that produced less pleasant conditions than those at sea. In a hot dry summer an English village would have had dust and chaff blowing everywhere, while in winter the streets turned into thick, muddy troughs into which animal and human manure were slurped. Beneath a sailor's feet lay clean decks, the sea air was fresh, and a readily available bucket of seawater washed both a man and his clothes. All in all it was not as bad a life as some accounts suggest.

Although a modern photograph, this picture of a mess deck in Matthew *gives some idea how crowded life below decks was in a Tudor ship.* (Matthew of Bristol)

Cooking

There were at least two other factors that made life on board compare favourably to that ashore. The first was food. It was guaranteed, it did not have to be worked for, and there was a cook to prepare and serve it. At least, when the victualling arrangements went well this was what was intended. Short rations happened, while on some voyages food ran out completely, but so it could in rural England, which was a land of famine as well as plenty. Ann Stirland found evidence of adolescent scurvy and other signs of childhood malnutrition in the bones and the teeth of the crew of *Mary Rose* but little evidence of similar adult illnesses, so many of those serving on board such naval vessels may have enjoyed the best meals of their lives.[28] Down in the hold, from where it was to be moved at the end of the century, the galley range, consisting of one or two wood-burning cauldrons laid directly on to the ballast, provided not only food but a warm area in which to dry out when coming off watch. Although at first glance such cauldrons appear primitive and suitable only to produce a stew, Chris Dobbs of the Mary Rose Trust rebuilt one from the evidence lifted with the ship and found that it could be used for roasting, baking and bread making.

Food was cooked centrally, and when meals were served each mess, of four to six men, sent a member below to collect their share, which was eaten either on the upper deck, when the weather or daylight permitted, or in the gloom of the main deck, where lanterns, their candle light dimmed by having to shine through horn slots, were the only source of light if the gunports were closed and the hatch gratings in place. The quality of the food depended on both the cook's skill and the length of time for the ship had been at sea. It was felt desirable to victual naval vessels for three months, at the end of which time perishable produce, such as salted meat in barrels, was far from appetising. Yet however unwholesome the food became it had to provide sufficient calories to carry out work with alacrity, especially when life depended on it.

Sebastian Cabot's draft orders suggested that:

> The steward and cook of every ship to render to the captain weekly (or oftener) a just and plain account of expenses of the victuals, as well as flesh, fish, biscuit, meat, or bread, as also beer, wine, oil, or vinegar, and all other kind of victualling under their charge, that no waste be made otherwise than reason and necessity shall command.[29]

Leaving aside the possible sting in the tail, such a regime, if properly followed, should have guaranteed the crew the best food available from the provisions on board.

A caring purser and good cook would also supplement the menu with whatever was available locally. Away from England foraging parties could catch such exotics as penguin and pick foreign fruits, but England itself was a nation that was growing because, in most years, there was a surplus with which to feed the population. Vegetables, disdained by the gentry, would have been appreciated by the sailors along with such marshland plants as samphire. Many would fish in seas where mackerel and herring abounded, guaranteeing a good catch. It would be wrong, therefore, to assume that the limited range of food supplied translated into an equally limited menu. The adapt-

Backgammon (or more accurately tabula) was a favoured game at Court, so this table, found in the Mary Rose, *probably belonged to one of the officers.*
(Mary Rose Trust)

Captains were under strict orders to discourage any sort of gambling among the crew, so backgammon was probably a game played mostly by the officers.
(Mary Rose Trust)

ability of the galley range and the ingenuity of the cook and the purser would, in a good ship, have provided seamen with better fare than they were likely to find available to them ashore. Coupled with this, long periods in harbour or on slow passage and a watch system that gave them regular time off would have given many seamen a far more pleasant life than they would have experienced in the fields.

The watch system was devised around dividing the crew into port and starboard watches also compared favourably with rising with the sun and working until nightfall. With each watch lasting four hours, there was plenty of time for rest. John Smith details how the watch system was organised at the start of a voyage:

The Captaine or Master commands the Boatswaine to call up the company. The Master, being chiefe of the Starboard watch, doth call one, and his right hand Mate on the Larboord doth call another, and so forward, till they be divided in two parts. Then each man is to chuse his Mate, Consort, or Comrade, and then devide them into squadrons according to your number and burthen of your ship as you see occasion. These are to take their turnes at the Helme, trim sailes, pumpe, and doe all duties each halfe, or each squadron for eight Glasses or foure houre, which is a watch ... The next is, to mess them foure to a messe, and then give each messe a quarter Can of beere, a basket of bread to stay their stomacks till the Kettle be boiled, that they may first goe to prayer, then to supper; and at six a'clocke sing a Psalme, say a Prayer, and then the Master with his side begins the watch. Then all the rest may doe what they will till midnight; and then his Mate with his Larboord men, with a Psalme and a Prayer, releeve them till foure in the morning. And so from eight to twelve each other, except some flaw of winde come – some storme or gust – or some accident that requires the helpe of all hands, which commonly, after such good cheere, in most voyages doth happen.30

Minute dice indicate that the crew of the Mary Rose *overcame the ban on gambling by possessing dice which could be readily concealed.* (Mary Rose Trust)

Manning was thus a simple business; what varied greatly was the number of people on board, and this depended very much on the business in hand. When that business was war an influx of soldiers made the normally cramped living conditions disagreeably uncomfortable, and good management would have been needed to ensure that disturbances did not break out on board.

The off watch crew in the evening had time to listen to music and play games. Recreation on board ship has always been a matter of self-help based on communal song and dance, horseplay and games. Those from *Mary Rose* included a merels (or nine men's morris) board carved on to the end of an oak cask, the remains of another board carved with a square pattern similar to a draughts board, a single bone domino and a number of dice also cut from bone on which the numbers are still clearly legible.31 The most complete and recognisable game board was for the playing of tabula, an early form of backgammon. This was found in the carpenter's cabin along with eight poplar counters and a leather shaker for the dice. All of these games became more exciting if they involved gambling, an activity that, despite legislation and direct orders,32 formed an important part of daily entertainment. The reason for a ban was explained in the very sensible words of Sebastian Cabot: 'Dicing, carding, tabling nor other devilish games to be frequented, whereby ensueth not only poverty to the players, but also strife, variance, brawling, fighting and oftentimes murder to the utter destruction of the parties ...'33 This may explain why the dice recovered from *Mary Rose* are small enough to be concealed instantly if a game was disturbed by a patrolling officer. 'Orders is orders', but sailors is sailors.

Music provided the other form of entertainment, varying from the wistful sentimental song sung by a single sailor with a sweet voice, and the shanty accompanied by the fiddle to jolly along such tasks as weighing anchor, to the small orchestra that would play for the officers as they dined. *Mary Rose* yielded ten musical instruments, many of which are the only survivors from the period. They include two fiddles, a 'still' shawm (an early oboe), a tabor (drum) and three tabor pipes.34 No trumpets were recovered, although it is known that admirals would have included trumpeters in their entourage along with drummers. The Indies voyage of 1595 was provided with 'sundry instruments of music for 8 musicians and nine trumpeters'.

The one-man band of pipe and tabor provided the usual musical accompaniment for rustic English dances. The pipe was held in the left hand and the tabor beaten with the right. The obvious feature of the

Whatever bans were or were not enforced, there can be little doubt that seamen off watch relaxed playing games of chance. (Mary Rose Trust)

pipe is that its three holes are at the extreme end of the pipe, requiring the player to have a very long left arm.

The 'still' shawm was a more sophisticated instrument, and its recovery and the reconstruction of a replica solved a musical puzzle concerning the two known forms of this instrument, a strident standard version and a quieter development with a thumb hole and a bore that induced a softer sound.

Fiddles have always been the instrument for creating cheer and accompanying hard work, and they provided the music to sing shanties which were linked to and sung only during specific evolutions. As most of these, such as hoisting a yard or raising an anchor, required the concerted application of co-ordinated manpower, the music reflected the muscular rhythms required, the equivalent of the 'two, six, heave' order of the master gunner to his crew. Time and the fact that many a tune was picked up by ear and the words learned by rote mean that working shanties from the period have not survived but they are mentioned in 'The Pilgrims', a ballad about a sea voyage written in the reign of Henry VI. Another reason for their demise was that they were often ribald, crude and full of sexual references and obscure nautical terminology – which, along with the fact that each song was probably modified to suit each ship, did not encourage their recording on paper.

Sea songs had a longer life and often expressed the seaman's view on contemporary events as well as his yearning for home.[35] One of the earliest extant is the song of John Dory, which tells of a Cornish galleasse's capture of a French privateer. A ship's company's pride in their 'swift swimming' ship and 'master excellent in skill', as well as their desire to return home to 'friends linked in love, and cans filled with wine, ale and beer', are the theme of a 1576 sea song which, although written for a stage comedy, *Common Conditions*, has a whiff of sea air about it.

It was the great events that drew the greatest response from the ballad writers. Drake's circumnavigation was celebrated in several songs, while between June and November 1588 twenty-four ballads about the fight with the Spanish Armada were listed in the Stationer's Register; how many more unregistered ones were also composed it is impossible to say, but many would have been heard first on the deck of a queen's ship.

Time ashore while on deployment was a good occasion for relaxation and games, as is very evident from the accounts of Drake's passage up the coast of the Americas and earlier in the Gulf of Darien; here, while his ship was being careened, the crew appear to have worked day about, with one watch attending to the ship's overhaul while the other played sport and the archers practised at butts.

A relaxed atmosphere would have worked best, but discipline was there to be enforced and obeyed. The origins of the code of conduct for the English navy dated back well over a century to the rules that were put in place to codify behaviour among those crews sailing on the annual voyage to collect wine from Gascony. It was on these rules, the Laws of Oleron, that Thomas Audley relied when writing, at Henry's command, the 'Booke of Orders for the Warre both by Land and Sea',[36] which endeavoured to codify both discipline and tactics to be used at sea. Audley's background as a landsman and a lawyer (he was Speaker of the House of Commons when he wrote his book and

The sound of pipe and tabor, shown here in Henry VII's Psalter, would have been familiar onboard ship where music was used both for pleasure and for accompanying some of the major, lengthy and exhausting evolutions such as weighing anchor.
(British Library)

The earliest documented sea-songs and shanties emerged from the Tudor age with major events, such as Drake's raid on Cadiz, or the defeat of the Armada, leading to a great outpouring of songs and music.
(Mary Rose Trust)

The shawm was known to be a Tudor musical instrument but none had been seen or heard until one was recovered from the wreck of the Mary Rose *and a working reproduction made.* (Mary Rose Trust)

became Lord Chancellor) is very evident in the work, which reflects far more what he would have gleaned from medieval tradition than the practical experience of seamen.

The part of Audley's work that covers discipline must have seemed quaint even to his seafaring contemporaries, but there is one most significant passage that has remained law ever since, and that is the requirement to pin the 'Articles of War' up in every warship where they can be read by the ship's company and, indeed, have to be read out by a commanding officer on every commission.

Discipline

First the laws will be written what every man ought to do in the ship towards his captain to be set in the main mast in parchment and read as occasion serve.

If any man kill another within the ship, he that doeth the deed shall be bound quick to the dead man, and so be cast into the sea, and a piece of ordnance shot off after they be thrown into the sea.

If any man draw a weapon within the ship to strike his captain he shall lose his right hand.

If any man within the ship draweth any weapon, or causeth tumult, or likelihood of murder or bloodied within the ship he shall lose his right hand as is said before.

If any man within the ship steal or pick money or clothes within the ship duly proved, he shall be three times dipped at the bowsprit and let down two fathoms within the water, and kept on a line, and at the next shore towed a land bound to the boat's stern with a loaf of bread and a can of beer and banished the King's ship forever.

If any man within the ship do sleep his watch four times and so proved, this to be his punishment, the first time he shall be headed at the main mast with a bucket of water poured on his head.

The second time he shall be armed, his hands hauled up by a rope and two buckets of water poured into his sleeves.

The third time he shall be bound to the main mast with certain gun chambers to his arms and as much pain to his body as the captain will.

The fourth time and last punishment being taken asleep he shall be hanged on the bowsprit end of the ship in a basket with a can of beer, a loaf of bread, and a sharp knife, thus to hang there till he starve or cut himself into the sea.

Command and Control

All captains must be obedient to their admiral. If any be stubborn the admiral shall put him ashore and put another in his place and write to the king and his council of his faults truly and without malice.

And if he did an exploit without consent of the captains and proved well, the King ought to put him out of his place for purposing a matter of such charge of his own brain whereby all the fleet might fall into the hands of the enemy and the destruction of the king's people.

Tactics

The admiral ought to have this order before he join battle with the enemy, that all his ships shall bear a flag at the mizzen top, and he himself in the fore mast beside the main mast that every man may know his own fleet by that token, if he see a hard match with the enemy, and be to leeward, then to gather and seem to flee, and flee indeed, for this purpose until the enemy draw within gun shot, and when the enemy doth shoot then shoot again, and make all the smoke he can to the intent that the enemy shall not see the ships and sudden haul up his cable aboard, and haul the wind of the enemy, and by this policy if it be possible to win the weather gauge of the enemy, and then he hath a great advantage, and this may well be done if it be well foreseen aforehand, and every captain and master made privy to it beforehand at whatsoever time any such disadvantage shall happen.

Firefighting

That no captain suffer any bedstraw within the ship when he shall fight with the enemy for it is perilous for firework and that the said captain cause two hogsheads to be cast a sounder in the middle and chained to the side of the orlop afore the mast, that the soldiers and mariners may piss in them, and so being full of urine to spend the firework with that shall come out of the enemy, two or three pieces of old sail ready to wet in the piss and always put it on the firework as need shall require.

Damage Control

The captain does appoint a discrete carpenter to make search in the whole of his ship in the time of his fight to see that if any shot be come in near the bowching places, and that there be in every ship some salt hide and lead to stop the holes, for if these things want and be not careful looked for many ships be put to the founder and utterly cast away.

Boarding

In case you board your enemy, enter not until you see the smoke gone, and the shot of all your pieces, your portpieces, the piece of hailshot, crossbowshot, to lighten his cage deck, and if you see his deck will rid then enter with your best men, but first win his top in anywise if it be possible. In case you see there come rescue bulge [scuttle] the enemy ship but first take the captain, certain of the best with him, the rest be committed to the sea, for else they will turn upon you to your confusion.

Booty

If any captain take any merchant he may not break any bolt until the admiral see what is in the ship, but nail up the hatches, that nothing be embezzled, and all thing under the lower loop is the king's and all that is under upper loop is the mariners and the soldiers to be indifferently divided by the admiral except treasure.

Audley's proposed punishments for the tired watch-keeper appear first quaint and then brutal, beginning as they do with an attempt to give the weary man pneumonia and then having him, so it seems, choose between starvation, suicide or drowning. But even this option may not have been as severe as it appears. A similar punishment existed at Calais for the same offence, with the moat being used instead of the sea, but here a boat was manned below the basket to drag the falling man on board before he drowned; one can assume that a like arrangement might have been used at sea.

The most practical of Audley's orders were those that applied to damage control and firefighting. Although urine slopping around the deck of a wallowing ship may not have been too pleasant for the bare-footed mariner, having a ship's urinal so readily available was such an excellent idea that the arrangement may have been kept in place at times other than combat, for it would have saved a climb out into the heads as well as acting as a permanent fire-extinguisher: fire was as likely to break out in peace as in war.

Religion

The more contemplative and educated on board ship would have read, but probably from a choice limited to the Bible, Psalter and latterly the Prayer Book. The beautifully embossed leather book covers recovered from *Mary Rose* carry religious texts, one from 1 Peter 1:25, 'Verbum Domini Manet' ('the Word of the Lord endureth for ever') and the other from Psalm 101, 'Domini Exaudi Orationem Meam et Clamor Meus ad Te Veniat' ('O Lord, hear my prayer, and let my cry come unto thee'). Neither text gives a clue as to the religious leanings of the owner, although the quotation from Peter attuned with the Lutheran idea that it was the Word that was important, not the priestly interpretation.

The spiritual needs of those who could not read were never forgotten. Cabot's blueprint states: 'Morning and evening prayer, with other common services appointed by the King's Majesty ... to be read and said in every ship daily by the minister in the admiral ... or some other learned person in their ships, and the Bible to be read devoutly and Christianly to God's honour.'[37]

The fact that the Indies expedition of 1595 was supplied with just one Bible, twenty-five psalters and two service books reinforces the idea that a priest was carried in the flagship and transferred around the fleet, similar to the arrangement in force in the modern navy.

Mary Rose first sailed under a Catholic king and sank under the gaze of the same, but by then reformist, one. History hints at the turbulence caused by Henry's Act of Supremacy and adaptation of 'Lutheran' views, yet there is little in the book covers and the eight sets of beaded 'paternosters' with their hanging crucifixes to indicate that those on board had changed either their views or their rites. In this timing might have been everything, for the banning of recitations with a rosary did not take place until 1547, and thus sailors nervously fingering their beads and mumbling their Lord's Prayer before the ship sailed to meet the French in the Solent might well have done so openly without fear of a lecture.

This attitude of 'he who is not against us is for us', apparent from the *Mary Rose* artefacts, did not last for long. Elizabeth's commanders were often holders of strong reformist religious views. On Hawkins's slaving voyages the mate summoned the crew to the main mast twice a day, where they knelt, said prayers, recited a psalm and proclaimed the Creed. To this was added, on Sunday, a reading from the gospel or epistle and a short (at least one hopes it was short) homily. This was an occasion for 'clear lower deck', with that order being enforced by a whip or knout. Now, far from the telling of beads being tolerated, a

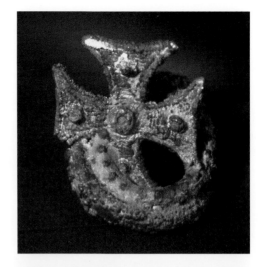

A silver cross pendant, fused to two rings, recovered from the Mary Rose *shows that then as now religious object were worn as personal jewellery.* (Mary Rose Trust)

Throughout the age most published books were on religious subjects, their content hinted at by texts embossed on the leather covers.

The age passed from one where the carrying of rosaries or paternosters was encouraged to one where the possession of such items was frowned upon or even punished. (Author)

seaman who crossed himself before taking over the helm was roundly and openly condemned.[38] Giusepe de Parraces in his deposition after his release by Drake stated that 'There was a crucifix in Rodrigo Tello's bark which they broke to pieces, trod under foot and cast into the sea',[39] but went on to say that during their time on board *Golden Hind*

At the taking of Cadiz in 1596 English soldiery fired at a picture of the Virgin Mary that stood guardian over one of the town's gates. They must have been poor shots for the undamaged picture was later removed (the gatehouse is now plain) and placed out of harm's way in its own dedicated chapel within the walls beside the gate. Such religious intolerance waxed and waned depending on the control of the land commander; most discouraged landing parties from such desecration but many even allowed churches to be razed to the ground. (Author)

he and his companions were told that, if they did not wish to witness 'Luthern ceremonies' they 'could withdraw to the prow or the poop', and moreover they were allowed to 'tell their Christian beads'. This illustration of greater tolerance being shown to those outside the group than to those within was ever and remains a strange feature of religion.

Strange also were Drake's occasional services as reported by some of his uncomprehending captives, such as Fransisco Gomez Rengifo, the factor of Guatulco, who recounted a gathering where:

Francis Drake had a table placed on deck at the poop of the vessel and, at its head, on the deck, a small box and an embroidered cushion. He then sent for a book of the size of the *Lives of the Saints* and all this was in place struck the table twice with the palm of his hand. Then, immediately nine Englishmen, with nine small books of the size of a breviary, joined him ... Then the said Francis Drake crossed his hand and, kneeling on the cushion and small box, lifted his eyes to heaven and remained in that attitude for about a quarter of an hour.[40]

This was followed by an hour-long recital of the psalms, after which four viols were produced to whose accompaniment the crew sang 'lamentations'. The service ended with one of the ship's boys performing a dance. Strange although this might have seen to the Catholic Iberians, Drake's most important hostage, the Portuguese pilot Nuño da Silva, on occasions did not retire but stayed to witness. For this he suffered greatly after his dumping ashore in Spanish America, being brought before the local Inquisition accused of joining in the rites and ceremonies of the 'English Lutherans' and even listening to Francis Fletcher's sermons. He was tortured, found guilty and sentenced to make a public confession in the auto-da-fé of 1582 before being banished to Spain later that year.

Drake was a zealot. On the positive side of this he ensured that a well-educated priest, Francis Fletcher, accompanied him on his circumnavigation, which has given us a record of the voyage.[41] On the negative, we have an insight into Drake's temper when he 'excommunicated' Fletcher for suggesting that *Golden Hind*'s grounding in the Philippines was God's judgement on the crew's buccaneering behaviour. Fletcher merely had to endure Drake putting him in leg-irons and shouting at him, 'Francis Fletcher, I do here excommunicate thee out

This delightful ebony angel from the Mary Rose *probably ornamented a small casket.* (Mary Rose Trust)

of ye Church of God, and from all the benefits and graces thereof, and I denounce thee to the devil and all his angels', before being released when his captain's anger calmed, although he had to walk the deck with an arm-band stating, 'Francis Fletcher, ye falseth knave that liveth'. Many of his fellow countrymen who were captured and accused by the Spanish ended up being burnt for their faith.

Fletcher's tactlessness was not unique. On Fenton's voyage the chaplain preached that plunder was not supported by scriptural teachings; it was probably not his most-appreciated sermon. Priests also sailed both against the Armada and on the 1596 Cadiz expedition, where one was selected to preach in the cathedral while the city was being plundered; his text must have been carefully chosen.

As evening darkened over the sea, mariners, of whichever creed, committed themselves to God's care. Jehan Bytharne, writing in his *Book of War by Sea and by Land* in 1543, stated that the men should muster to 'Sing the evening hymn to our Lady before her image, and then put out all the lights in the ship except for those in the cabins of the gentlemen who may have lamps trimmed with water covering the oil, but neither candles or any other kind of light', a combination of sanctity, privilege and practical seamanship that would have been understood by Drake even if the object of veneration offended.

The orders for the Azores voyage of 1596 stated: 'First you take a special care to serve God, by using a common prayer twice a day ... except urgent cause enforce the contrary', and then added the wise command that 'no man dispute matters of religion'.

Among the thirty-one orders issued by Howard and Essex four concerned themselves with living at ease in crowded company:

You shall forbid swearing, brawling, diceing and such like disorders as may breed contention ...
Picking and stealing you shall severely punish ...
Special care should be taken to avoid fire.
The ships should be washed daily.

Thus, as the sun set and the sounds on board were limited to the slosh of the sea, the creaking of the timbers and the wind in the rigging, so those off watch would have retired to sleep, for the most part uncomfortable but content.

Chapter Eight

Pilotage, Navigation and Seamanship

Sir Drake! whom well the world's end knew;

Which thou dids't compass round,

And whom both poles of heaven once saw,

Which North and South do bound.

The stars above would make thee known,

If men here silent were;

The sun himself cannot forget

His fellow traveller.

Anon, 'Sir Francis Drake'

The motto of the city of Portsmouth, 'Heaven's light our guide', is a true reflection of the importance of the sun, moon and stars to the many pilots and navigators who have arrived and departed from this great naval port. Close inshore they needed to know how the phases of the moon were affecting the tides; some leagues off from land, the height of the sun would indicate their latitude while the position of Polaris would indicate where north lay.

The safe passage of a ship at sea was based on three consecutive skills. Firstly, and lastly, there was 'pilotage', the guiding of a vessel in ports and harbours and past shoals and mud-flats and rocks. Secondly, there was the coastal passage planning which enabled a master to take a ship from port to port in a safe and timely manner, and thirdly, there were the skills of navigation, the science needed to take a ship across an ocean to the desired landfall. For the first of these local knowledge of

the sea bed and shore, tidal streams and currents was essential, but this came from experience, and the art was a visual one seldom having to resort to instrumentation. For the second, experience had to be reinforced by notebooks, charts and a few basic instruments to judge course, tide times, depth and speed made good. Navigation tools of precision and accurate tables for celestial interpretation distinguish the ocean-going science. In the first half of the century the first two skills dominated most English sea-going ventures but gradually, as Polar expeditions, West Indies raids and Pacific voyages took place, some masters were required to learn the art of celestial navigation and become acquainted with the instruments that enabled accurate observations to be taken. However, at the end of the sixteenth century few English sailing masters understood blue-water navigation; their skills remained firmly those of pilotage, and there was no school at which navigation was taught. How many had acquired oceanic competence by 1603 is not known, but if a suggestion of a few dozen were proposed it would be interesting to know the reason for gainsaying this.

PILOTAGE

Passage Planning

The naval master planning his voyage prior to setting sail would first consult his notebook, for, as befitted a navy whose seamen served their apprenticeship plying familiar coastal waters, the tools of the master's trade were simple and satisfactory for their limited purpose. Of these,

Navigational instruments from the Mary Rose. *For over half of the sixteenth century most naval ship's masters would have needed few instruments to make a safe journey around the coast. The broken slate protractor might well have been used as a tidal reckoning, allowing ephemeral markings, in chalk, to be wiped away.* (Mary Rose Trust)

by far the most important was a trained eye; as Nathaniel Butler wrote in his *Dialogical Discourses*:

> a good pilot is required when sailing in or out of any river or haven to be sufficiently acquainted along the reach from buoy to buoy, or beacon to beacon, and that he be a diligent observer of all the cape, points, steeple and all other marks, and to know the mouth of the haven and the depth of water both inside and outside. When the ship is in the offing he should note what hills or downs, towns and castle are first seen and to portrait these forms with a pen upon several stakes of the compass as they change their forms and manner of posture in sailing by them.[1]

The notebook in which the pilot drew and noted his observations became known as a 'rutter', and in the sixteenth century these books were produced for purchase by others, thus enabling masters to sail safely in waters with which they were not acquainted.

It was considered essential for each 'rutter' to include the following: the magnetic compass courses between ports and capes; the distance between such capes in 'kennings' of twenty miles; the range at which such headlands became visible and identifiable from the deck; the direction of tidal streams; the times of high water and full and new moon at major ports, headlands and channels; and the 'establishment' at these ports as well as the soundings. In addition a master would note the characteristics of the sea bed at various depths as he approached the coast or a port and would also carry sea-cards, outline maps with the names of the ports and compass roses with radiating lines to indicate the courses to be steered. The first recorded 'rutter of the sea' appeared in 1502 and gave the directions for wine merchants sailing to Bordeaux as well as extending the voyage to Cadiz.

In 1528 a 'rutter of the sea' translated and published by Robert Copland contained the following information:

> The course to the race of [the] Seine into Flanders and the tidal streams around Britain
> Routes and courses from the race of Seine to Flanders
> Entering harbour directions for Normandy
> Routes from Scilly and England to Flanders
> Directions for entering certain English harbours
> The location and distances between harbours in England, Brittany and Normandy
> Soundings to be anticipated coming from Spain, the Levant and Portugal to Ushant
> The kennings from Scilly and England to Flanders
> Floods and ebbs from Cape Cornwall [Land's End] to Wales and along the coast

and, as an annexe, the Laws of Oleron.

Leaving Harbour

With his passage planned, the departing master would then muster the tools of his trade, which were very different from and more rudimentary than those required for ocean navigation. Yet simple as they might have been, they were time-proven to be effective. The full suite recovered from *Mary Rose* consisted of a compass, sounding line, log-line, traverse board, sand-glass and dividers. Each, although used inde-

A traverse board allowed a day's passage, with all its alterations of course and speed, to be calculated with some accuracy to work out the distance and direction travelled during the course of a day's sailing. (National Maritime Museum E0437)

pendently, supported and confirmed information gleaned from the others.

The next consideration of the master would be at what time he should slip and proceed. Invariably he would want to depart on an ebbing tide, whose stream would carry him out into waters where the tidal stream slackened and the separating shores gave him room to unfurl sufficient sails to give him steerage way. If necessity required him to sail against the tide and wind, as happened when the Spanish Armada arrived in the Channel with the English fleet 'trapped' in Plymouth, he had either to get boats to tow him out or painstakingly row out with a kedge anchor and drop it so that he could haul himself up to it, when it would be raised and rowed out again for the whole exhausting process to be repeated. In Portsmouth boats were kept available to tow ships out of harbour through the narrow entrance when contrary winds prevented their departure under sail; there were constant arguments between town and navy over who should pay the boatmen.

Even when departing on the ebb the master needed to be aware of the state of the tide. Obviously he had local knowledge available, but to be certain in his own mind he would have to have an idea of the phases of the moon and their effect on the tide. The main concern of the mariners entering and leaving ports such as London was not, except in times of fog, where precisely they were, but how much water lay beneath their hulls and in what direction the current might be pushing them. Both of these were dictated by the phases of the moon, and it was this heavenly body which interested them far more than the sun and stars, the knowledge of whose position indicated latitude to their offshore peers.

Luckily, the moon's behaviour was accurately predictable by anyone who had been taught the equally formulaic lunar calendar. High water at a port occurs theoretically when the moon is due south,

As this detail from a tapestry in Seville shows, boats were often used to help hoist anchor or to warp ships out of harbour. (Author)

but local anomalies such as the shape of the coast can delay or advance its onset. This time discrepancy can be measured and was recorded as the 'establishment' of the port; at Portsmouth, for example, high water occurs when the full moon bears south-east by south. The moon's movement across the sky, and thus the timing of high and low water, is retarded by forty-five minutes each day from full moon. This coincided with one degree on the thirty-two-degree compass rose if its face was used as a clock. So by knowing the establishment of a port and the age of the moon, and then adding a compass point, starting at the establishment bearing, for each forty-five-minute retardation of the tide, the master could estimate the time of high water for each day. Local knowledge, and information recorded in a rutter, then informed the pilot as to the direction and strength of tidal stream to be expected in the environs of the major ports. This was not just a point of general information. In a port such as Bristol with a huge tidal range and a long channel leading to the sea, it was possible to enter the river with water beneath one's keel only to run aground mid-channel before reaching the docks.

Buoys, Sea-Marks and Trinity House

Leaving and entering harbour brought a ship to its closest proximity to danger on a safe and incident-free voyage. To help in keeping it this way many ports established sea-marks, but this was not a controlled procedure and was not required of the local authorities. Then, in 1514, Henry granted a royal charter to the brethren of Trinity House, Deptford, so that 'they might regulate the pilotage of ships in the King's stream'. The charter would have been linked to Henry's decision both to increase the size of his navy and to have his ships built in the Thames and maintained at Deptford but it addressed other concerns as well. The preamble stated that the practice of pilotship in rivers by young men who were unwilling to take the labour and adventure of learning the seaman's craft on the high seas was likely to cause a scarcity of mariners, and so; 'this your realm which heretofore hath flourished with a navy to all other land dreadful shall be left destitute of cunning masters and mariners'. It also complained that many Scots,

139

North Foreland's towering chalk cliffs were a great obstacle to those heading for the Channel from the Thames. They would also have presented a major challenge to Philip II's Armada had they been able to head for his favoured landing spot at nearby Margate. (Author)

Flemings and French lodesmen, having learned the secrets of the king's streams, had reached as far as Gravesend in time of war, causing much embarrassment to the realm. It would appear from this that Henry was concerned as much with war as with peaceful trade.[2] This is clear from the fact that the first, and longest-serving, master of Trinity House was Thomas Spert, who had commanded both *Mary Rose* and *Henry Grace à Dieu* and was thus fully versed in the requirements of the Navy Royal as well as the merchant fleet. It was also apparent in that Trinity House was opposed to the introduction of navigation lights around the coast, fearing that they would lead to betrayal in time of war and spying in time of peace. Certainly, in July 1545 the Privy Council was informed that the beacons and other marks which lead into the Thames had been taken down to deter the French from finding their way upstream, for, as Suffolk was informed by the shipmasters:

> If the beacon standing in the sea at the Spanish Knock be taken away, no stranger can or dare bring any ship of charge over the Land's End [North Foreland]. Also that if the two beacons standing upon Whitestaple Weares, the one on the north side of the channel of the East Swale, and the other on the Beacon Weares on the south side of the said channel, were taken away, no stranger dare bring a ship into the East Swale.[3]

Given the newness of beacons and the many years for which that 'strangers' had traded into London, this proposal seems somewhat dubious, but the strategy of dousing lights and removing beacons existed until the time of satellite navigation and beyond.

But by 1565 concern was being expressed that '... by the destroying of certain steeples, woods and other marks ... diverse ships ... by the lack of such sea-marks have of late years miscarried, perished and been lost in the sea, to the destruction and hurt of the common weal and the perishing of no small number of people'. In response the Seamarks Act of 1566 entrusted Trinity House to set up 'so many beacons, marks and signs for the sea ... whereby the danger may be avoided and escaped and ships the better come into their ports without peril', while any found guilty of destroying a sea-mark became liable for a fine of £100.

By 1594 Trinity House was running short of funds, and the Lord Admiral, in a move unusual for the age, surrendered his right to 'ballastage', the sale of dredged gravel for use a ballast by ships discharging at London, to help fund Trinity House.

Another concern lay behind the slow introduction of lighthouses. Trinity House felt that a mariner who trusted on lights that could be seen three leagues off on a clear night might, on a wet, stormy night, close the coast to pick up the light, only doing so at the last moment when he was almost on the rocks. This viewpoint delayed the introduction of a system of coastal lights. The first were provided at Newcastle by the local Trinity House, which made funding available in October 1536 'to maintain two towers either side of the port entrance with a perpetual light to be nightly maintained'. But Trinity House of Deptford did not fund a light until 1609, when one was erected at Lowestoft. So in navigational aids, as in so much else, the Tudor approach was to cause a delay of many years between an idea and its execution.

The Magnetic Compass

Once open water was reached the master could fully set his sails and select a magnetic compass course for the helmsman to steer to keep the ship clear of the next headland.

The Tudor magnetic compass consisted of a card on to which were painted the thirty-two points of the compass, with north being distinguished by the letter T or a fleur-de-lis. Beneath the card and aligned north–south was stuck a flat magnetised needle. The card was then suspended on a central pin, which enabled it to 'float' freely within a box on which a marking showed where it needed to be lined up with the ship's or boat's head. To avoid the problem of the needle sticking to the pivot pin, often two needles were used, joined at the ends but

Sophisticated as they were, the box compass, like this one from the Mary Rose, *was one of the first truly navigational items to be widely distributed among ships.* (Mary Rose Trust)

A fine example of a box compass from the National Maritime Museum's collection. (National Maritime Museum D9602)

separated at the middle so that they could turn more freely. A further sophistication was to mount the box on gimbals of brass so that the compass could remain relatively level while the ship rolled around. The compass was mounted in a wooden binnacle, constructed with wooden dowels so no iron would affect the compass needle, and fixed in front of the steersman with a light close by so that he could steer by night, although John Smith makes reference to a 'dark compass' with the points picked out in white, 'to be seen when we steer by night without any lights'. The compass boxes themselves could be opened to enable the pilot to re-magnetise the needle by stroking it with a lodestone. On the deck above, the officer of the watch would have yet another compass to observe, which allowed him to shout down the direction to steer to the man on the whipstaff. Further compasses were kept in the ship's boats; a ship like *Mary Rose* had at least five in use along with some spares.

The Log-Line

The estimate of the ship's speed was made by using a log-line. The earliest description of this knotted line was made by William Bourne in his *A Regiment for the Sea* of 1577, in which he states:

> ... to know the ship's way, some do use ... a piece of wood, and a line to veer out overboard, with a small line of great length which they make fast at one end, and at the other end and middle they have a piece of a line which they make fast with a small thread to stand like unto a crowsfoot: for this purpose that it should drive astern as fast as the ship doth go away from it, always having the line so ready that it goeth out as fast as the ship goeth. In like manner they have either a minute or hour glass, or else a known part of an hour by some number of words, or such other like, so that the line being veered out and stopped just with that time that the glass is out, the number or words spoken, which done, they haul in the log or piece of wood again, and look how many fathoms the ship hath gone in the time: that being known, what part of a league soever it be, they multiply the number of fathoms by the portion of time or part of an hour ...[4]

Thus if the time measurement used was a thirty-second glass the length of line run out had to be multiplied by 120 to get an equivalent in miles per hour. This was simplified when the line was knotted at distances along its length equivalent to a nautical mile an hour; this worked out at a knot every fifty-one feet (multiplied by 120 to give a nautical mile of 2,040 yards). All the log man had to do then was to haul the line in and count the number of knots and the little bit left over to report the speed of the ship – in knots.

The date when the log-line came into use was, however, much earlier than Bourne's work, for one was found in *Mary Rose* along with the reel on which it was wound, which included a projection that allowed the reel to be checked at the allocated time by braking it against the stern rail.[5]

The ship's officer of the watch would have kept a record of the course and speed made good, marking them on a chart or traverse board. This latter consisted of a circular board, from the centre of which radiated lines of holes into which a peg could be placed to indicate the direction sailed in the past half-hour. At the end of the watch

the direction between the first and last pegs could be measured off with dividers and the estimated speed made good noted, with the resultant information transferred to a chart or log-book so that the ship's position could be estimated and her course adjusted to allow for the effect of wind and tidal stream.

The Sand-Glass and Timekeeping

Time-telling, both actual and relative, was thus another important ingredient in the art of safe navigation. Well-made hour-glasses and half-hour-glasses were accurate, and the process of keeping the time would have begun with setting the sand to run at noon at the port of departure. Two such running glasses are recorded in the 1514 inventory of *Mary Rose* but she, like all vessels, would have had more than this, including smaller glasses to record the thirty-second period when the log-line was run out, although in this latter case the timing might have been measured by a regular voiced count or even a recitation such as the Lord's Prayer, which can be said in exactly thirty seconds. All naval vessels were supplied with both compasses and sand-glasses to record the passing of time. In 1526 Sir John Daunce, the treasurer,

To provide a standard drag through the water log-lines were fitted with a triangular float that exerted an even pull. (Mary Rose Trust)

In this recreated log-reel one of the knots indicating speed/distance can be seen on the reel while the braking projection can be seen pointing upwards. As the sand on the thirty-second time-glass ran out, the reel would have been thrust onto the gunwale to brake its spinning. This photograph was taken from the stern of HMS Warrior *whose crew would have been familiar with such methods of measuring their ship's speed three centuries after its introduction.* (Mary Rose Trust)

The recovery of this original log-reel from the Mary Rose *established the fact that such instruments were in use much earlier than had previously been believed.* (Mary Rose Trust)

recorded paying for six dozen of the former and 160 of the latter to supply the fleet.[6]

Every half-hour on the turning of the glass the ship's bell was sounded: one bell for the first half-hour of the watch, up to eight bells on the fourth hour signifying the watch change. The ship's bell, therefore, marked the time of day as regularly as a church bell might ashore.

In open waters ships equipped with the necessary instrumentation might each day measure the meridian passage of the sun and check their own time-keeping against this infallible marker of noon but in coastal waters such accuracy would not have been necessary. Ships would also have had sun-dials, while some of the officers carried pocket dials complete with a hinged gnomen and a small magnet to set them up north–south. Several of these miniature masterpieces were recovered from *Mary Rose* with the gnomen angled for a northern European latitude.

At night the time could be estimated by measuring, with an instrument called a *nocturnal,* the movement of the stars of the Great Bear (or Plough) constellation circling around Polaris. A nocturnal consisted of three concentric discs, the outer one engraved as a calendar, the middle one marked with an hour scale, and the inner one fitted with a long arm. When required the hour disk was moved until midnight lined up with the date, Polaris was sighted through a hole in the centre, and the arm moved to line up with the guard star selected to give a reading of time.

Thus day and night the master could record his ship's position and the influence of wind, tide and current upon his desired course, and could make allowances to correct the effect of those forces. Then, when the position was reached to alter course for his destination, other instruments would be brought into use to ensure that the ship remained in safe waters as she closed the shore. The most important of these was the sounding line.

The Sounding Line

Knowing the time of high water was important close to a port, but what the pilot needed to know most was the depth of water beneath his keel. This he found out by heaving a line, weighted at the end with lead, over the side. For ease of measurement the line was knotted at a stretched arm's length, six feet, or one fathom (from the Old English word meaning 'embrace'). The leaded weight was indented at its base so that a lump of tallow could be inserted, on to which material from the sea bed would stick. Local knowledge or information in a rutter could then be used to indicate where the ship

Pocket sundials were the Rolex watches of their day: sophisticated and designed with accuracy, they were probably more use as an ornament than for telling the time at sea. (Mary Rose Trust)

At night the rotation of the Plough or Great Bear around Polaris gave an opportunity to tell the time provided an instrument as sophisticated as this nocturnal was available. (National Maritime Museum D9091)

Ships needed to carry numerous leads for sounding out the depth: heavy ones for deep waters and lighter ones, which could be cast and recovered speedily, for close inshore. In addition, many would be replacements for those lost through the line snagging on rocks or other obstructions. (Mary Rose Trust)

might be, depending on whether the tallow showed mud, or sand or shell etc. Copland, for example, stated in his work of 1528 that when entering the Channel: 'when you be at 10 or 15 fathoms you shall find white sand and white soft worm and you shall be very nigh to the Lizard'.

Naval vessels were provided with two types of sounding line, marked with a variety of knots and coloured cloths to identify easily the depth being indicated, and to speed up the process of reporting this to the pilot. *Mary Rose* yielded eight sounding leads and two examples of marked hand lines, the earliest discovered. The inventories of naval vessels always included the number of sounding leads on board; for *Henry Grace à Dieu* this was six. The 1595 Indies expedition sailed loaded with over four hundred-weight of spare sounding leads, indicating that in coral seas of unknown depth losses were frequent.

The two types of lead were designed for different occasions. The shorter sort, with a lighter weight, was used in coastal waters, enabling the leadsman to take frequent soundings. The longer and heavier one (also called the dipsie line) was used when approaching land from the open sea. This second one was critical when the navigator was unsure of his position or was approaching an unknown coast. Richard Hawkins described an alarming occasion in the South Atlantic which would have been familiar to many:

> The next day ... it seemed to me that the colour of the sea was different from that of the days past ... the captain and master of my ship ... made answer, that all the lines in our ship could not fetch ground: for we could not be less than three-score and ten league off the coast, which all that kept reckoning in the ship agreed upon, and myself was of the same opinion. And so we applied ourselves to serve God, but all the time the service endured, my heart could not be at rest ... Our prayers ended, I commanded a lead and line be brought, and heaving the lead in fourteen fathoms, we had ground, which put us all a maze, and sending men into the top, presently discovered the land of Guinea some five leagues from us ... Here is to be noted, that the error which we fell into in our accounts, was such as all men fall into where are currents that set east or west, and are not known, for that there is no certain rule yet practised for trial of the longitude.[7]

Hawkins's actions were too timely for this event to be described as a lucky escape, but it does also illustrate another facet of navigation – the 'gut' feeling of the pilot. Neither scientific nor quantifiable, this feeling in the water on many occasions prevented disaster; it was an asset that all great navigators had, Drake included. On occasion, however, it failed even him. On Saturday 9 January 1580 *Golden Hind* had at all but completed a hazardous passage between Celebes and the Moluccas and was heading out into the open sea when ship struck hard against a coral reef and ran firmly aground. Good damage control, seamanship and leadership, along with a solid hull, got her off, but the voyage could have ended there in unknown, uncharted seas as easily as it could do for those approaching the Channel coast in foul weather with no recent sighting or soundings. Science and observation were improving navigation, but until the sea and its dangers were charted, ships would continue to run aground where no land was expected. Later the navy's hydrographic arm was to carry out the enormous but essential work that would make the seas safe.

Drake recovered and his voyage was a success. On other occasions poor pilotage, even if the ship was saved, could have significant effects. In June 1585 Simon Fernandez, a Portuguese pilot in the pay of the English, chose to con the Virginian expedition into Pimlico Sound through a channel he had not used before. The result was that *Tyger* grounded and sprang several leaks which ruined most of the expedition's precious stores. From that moment it was catch-up time for Ralph Lane and the colonists and they never did catch up, abandoning their precarious toe-hold on American soil at the earliest opportunity, when Drake visited one year later.

Thus with his rutter and his instruments the master should have been able to conduct both a safe passage, weather as always permitting, and a safe entry into harbour. As the century progressed, the first printed pilots became available, and not before time. The 1528 *Rutter of the Sea* did not even have sufficient information for the navy to sail over to Holland to collect Anne of Cleves for her marriage to Henry. In 1541 Richard Proude published *The New Rutter of the Sea for North Partes*, a translation from the Dutch, which was probably linked to James V's circumnavigation of his Scottish kingdom the previous year. Eventually the process would lead to the publication of the detailed 'Admiralty Pilots', for it was upon the navy that the task of providing charts and directions for safe navigation the world over was to be placed. The Tudors began that challenge and that responsibility. Printing thus enabled many more masters to gain foreknowledge of a coastline which they had never visited, although many remained distrustful of such aids, William Bourne scornfully recording, 'I am of the opinion that a number of these doeth but grope as a blind man doth ...'.

Pilots

If rutters were not available or trusted, then local pilots could be employed, as they were throughout the period. In 1514 a pilot, John Wodlas, submitted an account to the Privy Council for 'conveying of the King's ships', which included taking:

> ... *Mary Rose* out of Harwich haven over a danger in the sea called the Naze, and incontinent after, continued to conduct and ring the same ship over again into Harwich haven; and within five days ... to conduct ... the said ship out of the said haven through a place called the Slade to meet with the King's grace coming from Calais-

ward ... And then ... conveyed her out of the Downs through the lack Deeps into Thames ...[8]

Among the royal grants made for 1540 was one made to John Bartelot for 'reversion for the safe conduct and pilotage of the king's ships through a place called "the Blakedeeps" and for his labour and skill in finding a new channel there by which many serious dangers are avoided in navigation of an annuity of £20 now held for life'.

In further-flung places local pilots were obviously most useful if they could be found. Drake's capture of the Portuguese master and pilot Nuño da Silva proved to be of inestimable value during his circumnavigation. Later, during the West Indies raid of 1585–6, Drake captured a Greek pilot on board a Spanish ship heading for Santo Domingo and 'persuaded' him, as a New Year's Day present to the English, to guide his ships into the harbour. One hopes that, given the paucity of the plunder, a small sum was set aside as a reward.

NAVIGATION

While pilotage was an apprenticeship trade, its art passed on through experience, navigation was a science that had to be taught, and when Henry divorced Katherine of Aragon he separated England from a Europe where this science was emerging. The evidence of this can be seen in the development of forts rather than ports along the south coast, but the barriers were also raised in intellectual terms, and the effect was to delay the introduction of new learning that was underway on the continent.

A School of Navigation

In 1503 Ferdinand of Aragon created a school of navigation, the Casa de la Contratación (House of Commerce), in Seville, basing it on the earlier Portuguese foundation, by Duarte, the brother of Prince Henry the Navigator, of the Casa de India (originally the Cas de Mina e Guiné). Its objective was to 'stimulate, direct, and control traffic with the New World'. Just how far behind this contemporary English royal thinking was may be judged by comparing that aim with that of Henry's Trinity House: while the Iberians were planning voyages to the furthest shores, the English began to chart and mark, quite necessarily, the mud banks back home. Ironically, Trinity House, with its humble origins, outlasted all the great Iberian navigational schools and eventually provided the better service to mariners from all nations, but in Henry's reign it limited its activities to serving English ship masters in their home waters.

The presence of dividers, like these recovered from the Mary Rose, *presupposes the existence of charts on which to measure distances.*
(Mary Rose Trust)

In Edward's time some advances in navigational learning were made, but it was Mary who, as a result of her marriage to Philip of Spain, re-opened the intellectual channels, and the mid-point of the century therefore saw a sudden flourish of the scholarship necessary to develop the science of navigation. Its mathematical grounding was provided by Robert Recorde's *The Pathway to Knowledge*, published in 1551. Information on the New World was spread by Richard Eden's *A Treatise of the New India*, printed in 1553, and followed up in 1554 with a translation of Peter Martyr's *Decades of the New World*, which described the route across the Atlantic Ocean. In 1558 Mary authorised the experienced Stephen Borough to travel to the Casa de Contratación to see how Philip's navigators learned their trade. Borough returned to England bursting with the desire to establish a similar professional organisation in his own country. He also brought with him a number of Spanish books and charts, one of which, Martin Cortes's *Arte de navegar*, was translated by Richard Eden and gave to English mariners exactly what it said on the cover. For the first time there was a document in English that was available to those who wished to develop their skills; one can assume that an early purchaser was Francis Drake. The future circumnavigator may also have obtained copies of other works: in 1559 William Cunningham published the first book in English on cosmography, *The Cosmographical Glass*, which also showed that English intellectual ideas existed, if only they were encouraged, by pursuing the idea of estimating longitude through the use of a chronometer.

Borough may also have been responsible for bringing to England a copy of Battista Testarossa's *Brieve compendidio de larte del navegar*,[9] a publication the erudition of which just served to show how backward the English were in matters navigational. This was shortly to change, for the otherwise barren marriage of Mary and Philip had given birth to an interest in the skills needed to venture out into distant waters. For it cannot be mere coincidence that Mary's reign marks a watershed between the haven-hugging passages of Henry's fleet and the merchant-adventurer-led, but royal-approved, ocean voyages soon to be undertaken.

Sadly for Borough, by the time he was ready to present his ideas to the queen it was no longer Mary but Elizabeth who was his mistress. To her he presented a 'Petition for the Creation of the Office of "Pilot Major"', concerning a post for which, naturally, he considered himself to be the best candidate. She was impressed by his idea that no one should be placed in charge of a royal ship unless he had been first examined through a series of tests taken during his progress from boy to master and pilot. So in 1564 Elizabeth had drafted a document proposing to appoint a 'man skilful in marine affairs, to be the Chief Pilot of this our realm' but, being Elizabeth, she hedged her bets by inviting the submission of critical comment. When Trinity House, jealous of its own authority, did so, Borough's plan was discarded, although as he himself later became master of Trinity House one can assume there were no hard feelings. Although his proposals were rejected, Borough was nevertheless correct in his premise about English navigational backwardness. Leaving aside the apparently self-taught Drake and cavalier Cavendish, few other seamen showed a flair for the blue-water skills. Borough himself had to arrange for Martin Frobisher to receive lessons in the art of naviga-

This magnificent astrolabe is believed to have been presented to Henry VIII: a most accurate celestial navigation instrument for a land-based monarch with a coastal navy. (British Museum)

tion from the nation's acknowledged expert, John Dee, before it was felt safe to despatch him to search for the north-west passage.

Dee was one of the few men in the nation whose work and interest in navigation could be considered on a par with those studying in mainland Europe. He also advocated the establishment of a 'British Empire', a name which he coined, in whose creation the navy and its navigators would need to play a role. In 1577 Dee was the first person in the country to describe a 'Petty Navy Royal' and the size and shape it should take, rather than allowing the fleet to grow, or shrink, piecemeal; he thus became the first person to see that to achieve greatness the nation needed both a fighting navy and an hydrographic one with all its officers trained in the navigational sciences.

Frobisher's ineptness as a pupil deserves a certain amount of sympathy, for this ill-educated gruff Yorkshire man was being taught the rudiments of 'spherical trigonometry', a phrase which still strikes fear into trainee navigating officers with A levels and degrees. A short

This chart of the Thames estuary was produced to assist those planning the passage of Anne of Cleves from the low countries to London. Unsophisticated as it is, the existence of such information worried Henry VIII, who was developing great fears about a foreign invasion. (British Library)

quote from Waters, dealing with the early attempts to determine longitude, may suffice to illustrate this:

> ... the First point of Aries was used as a datum point. Astronomically, the half-meridian passing through it served just as the meridian of Greenwich does today for terrestrial longitude. By observing the position and time of transit of planets and stars at the equinoxes, their declination and right ascension, their angular distance measured in time from the First Point of Aries can be recorded in an almanac or plotted on a star map. This makes it possible to find longitude by the occultations of the planets by the moon's disc, that is by observations made when the declination and right ascension of the moon and planet are identical.[10]

Leaving the Land Behind

There had been English-backed attempts before Frobisher to explore beyond the known world, and they began early very soon after 1492, when Columbus sailed the ocean blue and reached the central Americas. In 1497 John Cabot did likewise and discovered new-found land in the north. Five years in time and the length of a continent separated the voyage of these two adventurers, both undertaken by men foreign to the nations that sponsored them. One hundred years later, the Spanish had conquered three kingdoms, established many towns and travelled many miles, and were despatching year on year a convoy of ships to Seville, any one of which was weighed down with a king's ransom. A hundred years after Cabot the single enigmatic word 'CROATOAN', carved on a post in an abandoned settlement, was all that was left to show that the English had ever been to the Americas. The story of English colonisation, whether near home in Ireland or on the far side of the Atlantic Ocean, was a story of disaster and the underachievement of greedy men with

The frontispiece to John Dee's treatise on navigation published in 1577.

blinkers, seldom a satisfactory combination.

Success was achievable, available and anticipated. Henry Tudor, so often considered a domestic dullard, offered it to Cabot in phrases that are worth relating in full to show their vision:

> The King, to all ... Greetings. Be it known and made manifest that we have given and granted as by thee presents we give and grant, for us and our heirs, to our well-beloved John Cabot, citizen of Venice ... full and free authority, faculty and power to sail to all parts, regions and coasts of the eastern, western and northern sea, under our banners, flags and ensigns, with five ship or vessels of whatsoever burden and quality they may be, and with so many and with such mariners and men as they may wish to take with them ... to find, discover and investigate whatsoever islands, countries, regions or provinces of heathens and infidels, in whatsoever part of the world placed, which before this time were unknown to all Christians. We have also granted ... licence to set up our aforesaid banners and ensigns in any town, city, castle, island or mainland whatsoever, newly found by them. And that the afore-mentioned John ... may conquer, occupy and possess whatsoever such towns, castles, cities and islands by them thus discovered that they may be able to conquer, occupy and posses, as our vassals and governors, lieutenants and deputies therein, acquiring for us the dominions, title and jurisdiction of the same towns, castle, cities, islands and mainlands so discovered ...[11]

Deliberately omitted was the coast of any southern sea, for in just four years Spain's rights to the land from greater Florida south had apparently already made themselves manifest. When the Houses of Tudor and Aragon agreed to link their dynasties through the betrothal of Arthur, Prince of Wales, to Katherine, Princess of Aragon, in 1489 the opportunity for an alliance and a partnership in the New World was not a part of the marriage settlement. Indeed, a papal bull issued by the Spanish Borgia Pope, Alexander VI, on 4 May 1493 drew a demarcation line along the meridian one hundred leagues west of the Azores that granted the lands to the east to Portugal and those of the west to Spain. Reinforced by the more famous Treaty of Tordesillas in 1494, this dividing line condemned the English to bang their heads against an ice wall as they searched for a passage that, by either a north-west or a north-east route, would lead them to the riches of Cathay by outflanking the Iberian grant. The terms of Tordesillas thus made the English polar explorers and lengthy voyagers. Unavailing as these icy quests may have been, they were to lead, in the north, to the explo-

This beautiful Italian compass of 1570 shows how advanced European mainland producers were in comparison with most of their English contemporaries. (National Maritime Museum D8908-1)

ration and settlement of Canada, and in the south, to the discovery of Australia and New Zealand. The legacy of Tordesillas includes both Captain Scott's Antarctic tragedy and Darwin's Galapagos triumph, and both of these involved the Royal Navy which had taken the lead in charting the coasts of the world.

The English were slow to grasp the challenge of Tordesillas as, straining their eyes for a view of Cathay on the horizon, they failed to focus on the opportunities floating past along the nearer shoreline of North America. They were also only considering the short-term gain of great wealth, through either trade or mining. Whether in Guiana or Labrador, their greed saw gold in the rocks beneath their feet. They loaded their ships with it and dreamed of wealth on the voyage home, only to wake up as the assayers pronounced their cargo worthless.

Were they naive? Probably. Yet imagine a community where the highest hills ever seen were on Dartmoor; the widest river crossed was the Thames or Tamar; the hottest day experienced an English summer; the coldest a February freeze; the thickest ice that on the village pond; the greatest downpour a thunderstorm; the mightiest tree an oak, the tallest a Scots Pine. Then take those people, with no picture books or accounts of adventures other than those in the Bible, on voyages where they saw snow-capped islands, the night fires of volcanoes, coasts where cliffs of ice broke off into the sea, rivers over thirty miles wide, seas where monsters the length of their craft broke surface alongside them, where fishes flew and birds swam, and lands where wondrous fruit fell ripe into their laps. Take them to places where the sun passed to the north of them, where darkness could last all day, where savages wore paint for clothing, where narwhals' with horns resembled unicorns and dugongs (with imagination!) recalled mermaids, and then it is no wonder that they returned talking, like Shakespeare's Othello, of:

... the Cannibals that each other eat,
The Anthropophagi, and men whose heads
Do grow beneath their shoulders.

These tales did the rounds of county as well as court, for the experience of England's monarchs was just as geographically confined as that of their subjects. What is dispiriting is that every gulf, every glade, every river, every strait was assessed by the state on two things alone. Did it lead to either Cathay or gold? None did, but the head-banging continued wherever the remote geographical chance might make the passage feasible or the fabled mines a reality. Sadly, this hope of gain devalued the real opportunities offered in lands where the dream was unrealisable but the reality worthwhile.

This failure began where it should not have done – with John Cabot, who on 24 June 1497 after a thirty-five-day voyage from Bristol, rowed ashore to the coast of Newfoundland and raised the banners to which Henry Tudor had referred. The crew followed a path inland 'the shooting distance of a cross-bow' and then returned, rather scared, to the shore, where they filled their water-barrels and went back on board. And that, although the ship spent a month sailing along the coast, was the only occasion on which any of the voyagers set foot ashore. So much for conquering towns! Now it might be argued quite fairly that Cabot's crew of twenty or so Bristol seamen were not competent to conquer castles, for although the king had

This reconstruction of Cabot's Matthew *celebrates the first hesitant steps taken by the English in overseas exploration. Its tiny size underlines the risks involved in early transatlantic voyages.* (Matthew of Bristol)

allowed him to take five ships, this had ended up as a solo voyage, yet his subsequent voyage in 1498, in which five ships did sail, was also equipped to trade (with that elusive chimera the Orient) but not to settle and seize new lands. Sadly, it came to nothing. One ship turned back and reached Ireland, and all the others disappeared, setting another trend for English exploration which was hardly going to inspire those who considered following.[12]

With Cabot's disappearance, English enthusiasm for oceanic voyages of discovery and settlement also faded, almost to nothing. Three sovereigns came and went seeing no city more distant to conquer than Boulogne and no town worth controlling more important than Calais, no territory over which to exert authority than Ireland.

Although Henry did not pick up the baton handed to him by his father, through the exploratory work by John Cabot, he did venture some ships abroad once his first aim, war with France, had been concluded. In 1517 John Rut in the king's ship, *Mary Guildford*, sailed with *Samson* to seek a route to Cathay via a north-west passage. The result was another chapter in the heroic and useless battering of English vessels against the pack ice of the north. *Sampson* was lost, and Rut, having reached 64 degrees north, was driven back by icebergs and returned to England via the dog-leg route of Santa Domingo with nothing achieved. His crew could count themselves lucky: another attempt to find a northern route, by Richard Hore in 1536, descended into cannibalism before the survivors, probably chubbier than most such voyagers, came home. Eventually the reawakening of interest in distant lands came through the alliance of a visionary writer, Richard Hakluyt, a visionary scientist, John Dee, and a visionary chancer, Walter Ralegh.

It was Walter Ralegh's half-brother, Humphrey Gilbert, who had the idea of continuing where Cabot had so inopportunely finished. He had written a proselytising pamphlet, *Discourse to Prove a Passage by the North West to Cathay*, which was then later produced to provide the propaganda necessary to encourage investment in Martin Frobisher's three voyages to the north-west (1576–9), from which he was to return with one kayak, two Inuit, a thousand tons of aggregate that contained not one grain of gold and the dubious and false evidence of a strait of clear water leading towards Cathay. This report raises a tantalising question regarding the timing of Frobisher's journeys: if one of the return routes being contemplated by Drake, who was also just about to sail to the Pacific on a southerly route, was via the north-west passage, the Straits of Anian, was Frobisher being despatched to work his way through from the east to effect a rendezvous and to guide the great man home? That is supposition, but it was believed credible by none other than the great map-maker Ferdinand Mercator. Frobisher, however, returned without Drake but with myths to confuse and divert for years to come. The first myth was that 'There he saw far the two headlands at the furthest end of the straits and no likelihood of any land to the northward of them and the great open sea between them, which ... they judged to be the West Sea [Pacific] whereby to pass to Cathay and to the East Indies.'[13] Frobisher's other diverting myth was that he had discovered gold; future hydrographic exploration in the north-west was delayed while he went off to bring hundreds of tons of useless non-gold-bearing rock back to London and a future as the capital's most expensive aggregate.

Humphrey Gilbert, however, returned to the idea first made manifest in Cabot's grant – colonisation. In his letters patent Elizabeth granted him the right 'to discover, search, find out and view such remote heathen and barbarous lands, countries and territories not actually possessed of any Christian prince or people', and to settle these with people who would enjoy the full right and privileges, 'in such like ample manner and form as if they were born and personally resident within our aid realm of England'. Two hundred year later the abrogation of those rights produced the battle cry 'no taxation without representation' and the cessation of subjection to Elizabeth's own heirs.

Ralegh joined the expedition that Gilbert put together to action his letter patent. His fleet of 365 men in ten ships sailed out of Dartmouth on 26 September 1578, a date very late in the Atlantic's weather calendar. The equinoctial gales drove them back into Plymouth, at which point three ships took their leave. Unperturbed, or stupid, the remainder set off once again on 19 November, only to be driven back this time to Dartmouth, their home port, where, with winter settling in, the temptation of home fires kept them from further adventure that year. All, that is, except the young Walter Ralegh, who stayed at sea to chance his arm in the queen's elderly 26-gun pinnace *Falcon* against a group of Spaniards. The exchange over, the defeated Ralegh limped home in his badly damaged ship, on which several had died and many been wounded thanks to the captain's untrained impetuosity. This was a trait of character which lasted his lifetime and which often, as in this case, ended in losses to his company but his own survival.

While Gilbert's and Frobisher's sponsors were coming to terms with their failure, the greatest voyage of the century by the greatest mariner of the age was underway, and it is in this, Drake's circumnav-

Drawn to record the state of England's coastal defences, this map is one of the earliest in existence to show the complete Channel coast. This section covers Plymouth to Exeter. (British Library)

igation, that the capabilities and limitations of open ocean theory were to be practically demonstrated.

Global Charts and Ocean Passage Instruments

Although much lay undiscovered and unanticipated over the horizon, cartographers were endeavouring to make sense of the world beyond the known. So along with the theory and instruction in navigation went the production of charts and guides of the whole world, a development that involved the Low Countries but still not England. All the cartographers engaged in this task were hampered by an error made many centuries earlier over the true measurement of the circumference of the earth. Although this had been worked out with extraordinary accuracy in 250 BC, the Europeans of the fifteenth and sixteenth centuries chose to base their concepts on the later ideas of Ptolemy, who underestimated the circumference by some 6,000 miles. The practical effect was that Cathay was considered to lie in the region actually occupied by North and Central America, to the confusion and occasional despair of all who ventured to discover it from the north, while those entering the Pacific from the south and expecting to reach China in a few days, such as Magellan, found themselves at sea in open waters for months.

Sixteenth-century navigators and cartographers were thus trying to finish a jigsaw in which certain pieces were joined together but their positions relative to other chunks were unknown, as was the size of the final picture. The genius of Mercator laid the world's surface out in a practical and workable form, but even he was unable to do any more than guess where the pieces upon it might be placed. Much then was hypothesis and would remain so until men ventured out into the unknown and reported back with accurate charts and global positions. The challenge to complete the jigsaw by exploration rather than reflection had, with the exception of the north-west and north-east passages, not been taken up by the English, but as more seamen dared to venture out of sight of land the realisation that there was much to learn about navigation slowly dawned, though not without cynicism and prejudice about the new ways. William Bourne scorned the old men for 'saying they care not for their sheep's skins [charts], for he could keep a better account upon a board. And when they did take the latitude, they would call them star shooters and sun shooters, and would ask if they had struck it.'[14]

For any exploratory venture into unknown and distant waters to be a success, the navigator needed to know where he had been, how he got there, and how to pass on that information to those who might follow. For this reason many endeavoured to add to the theory with recorded fact. In 1556 William Borough was to use the sketches and notes made by his brother Stephen during his voyage to the White Sea to produce a rutter for these parts, while he did much scientific planning for the aborted 1568 voyage to the same area, including the provision of an instrument for measuring horizontal angles and bearings so as to produce accurate charts. This instrument eventually accompanied the 1580 Pet and Jackman voyage which sailed once the Lok and Frobisher north-west passage enterprise had ended in failure. Drawings might help identify a place once an expedition had arrived, but to steer for a previously reported landfall with any hope of success required accurate celestial observations to determine and record the

When globes first began to appear the only land masses that could be positioned on them with any degree of accuracy were those of Europe and the Atlantic coast of Africa; although the longitude of the Americas was fairly well known, the size of the Pacific and what land might lie within its boundaries was only guesswork, as was the existence or otherwise of a north-west passage. (National Maritime Museum D7693-A)

Surprisingly, the heavens could be mapped with greater accuracy – as shown on this globe – than many of the lands upon earth. (National Maritime Museum D7694-A)

latitude and longitude of bays and headlands. Sadly the ability to determine longitude with any certainty remained elusive until an accurate chronometer was produced after centuries of trial and error and design competitions.

John Smith wrote:

To learn to observe the Altitude, Latitude, Longitude, Amplitude, the variation of the Compass, the Sun's Azimuth and Almicanter [the common altitude of certain stars]; to shift the Sun and Moon, and know your tides, your Rhumbs [lines intersecting meridians at the same angle, helping to work out the most direct course to be steered], prick your Card, say your Compass, and get some of these books; but practice is best.

Master Wright's errors of Navigation
Master Tapp's seaman's calendar
The Art of Navigation

The Sea Regiment
The Seaman's secret
Waggoner
Master Gunter's work
The Seaman's glass for the scale
The New Attracter for variation
Master Wright for use of the Globe
Master Hughes for the same.[15]

The publication dates of the listed works confirm that it was towards the end of the sixteenth century that the study of navigation became a serious subject in England, but it still relied on the work of mainland European academics for its scientific rather than descriptive input. Late although the published dates of these works may have been, the thoughts behind them and the knowledge that they would impart were probably available to those like Drake, anxious to absorb the latest thinking before steering into seas where no Englishman had ever ventured.

Drake's Circumnavigation

If Britain was to announce to the world that it had sent a man to the moon, and that his spacecraft had reached Mars and then disappeared until the astronaut returned to earth successfully, then one might get an idea of the impact that Drake's circumnavigation had on the European world. Only once before had such a voyage been undertaken, and that had been led by Magellan, who had been killed half way around. But that had been seventy-six years earlier, and besides Magellan had been Portuguese and might be expected to know something about long-distance voyages. What did the English, confined to their Channel coast, know about such matters?

It is thus no wonder then that the apotheosis of Tudor naval voyages was Drake's circumnavigation of 1577–80. Much has been written on the aims of the voyage: was it to discover new lands unclaimed by either Spain or Portugal on which to establish English colonies; was it to enter the Straits of Anian from the west; was it to disconcert the Spanish and to seize their goods? As far as Drake was concerned there was only one main aim. He was a corsair and one with a grievance born of the fight at San Juan de Ulua in 1568, when he and his cousin John Hawkins, with just two overcrowded ships, managed to escape from the harbour after a treacherous attack by the Spanish. Frankly, given the commander, his strong Protestant faith and the grudge that he bore, Drake could only have had one object in mind – restitution, or to be less refined, plunder. There were often, in the course of his career, differences between what Drake was ordered to do, what others expected him to do, and what he decided to do, the latter being a concept that could change as circumstance and opportunity altered, but for his circumnavigation recompense and revenge were powerful enough aims. The question that few address is this: where did Drake get the information that he needed to plan such an odyssey? And with this query comes an added question: what was Drake doing in 1574? He may just have devoted his time to study, for he had a lot to learn. It was not just a matter of the theory of celestial navigation, much of which was available in

printed form such as the tables of declination. Most importantly he had to obtain and use the instruments that converted theory into a position on a wide and empty ocean, and the best way to do this was to go to sea; Drake may well have done just this in his 'gap' year. His easiest navigational task was to estimate was latitude.

Latitude

Ascertaining latitude depended on measuring either Polaris or the angle subtended between the sun, the observer's position and the horizon at local midday, when the sun was at its zenith or highest point. Tables of declination to convert this angle to latitude had been produced as early as 1475, while in 1537 the Spaniard Pedro Nunes published a sum of all knowledge in his *Tratado da sphera com a theoretica do sol e da lua*, which also introduced the concept of the 'great circle route', which showed seamen how to work out the shortest distances across the oceans. Along with these intellectual developments came the Iberian desire to impart such knowledge through schools and examinations for pilots, which produced such works as *Arte de navegar*, written in 1545 by Pedro de Medina, a cosmographer on the staff of the Casa de Contratción in Seville, which was widely translated within mainland Europe. Along with the theory, the production of navigational instruments was covered in Martin Cortés's book *Breve compendio de la sphere y de la arte de navegar*, the information in which became available in England following Mary's marriage to Philip of Spain.

By the time of Drake's circumnavigation the Iberians had fused Greek theory with Arabic instrumentation to develop instruments of their own with which to measure the altitude of Polaris, the Pole Star, and the sun, which gave an indication of latitude, while the bearing of both could also give an idea of compass directions.

In the sixteenth century the bearing of Polaris was not as close to true north as it is today. It varied by three and a half degrees and appeared to circle the Pole every twenty-four hours. To allow for this, mariners were encouraged to observe Polaris with the guard star of the Little Bear in the same relative position on each occasion. Tables were soon available to help with the correction to true north. Calculations based on the altitude of Polaris also gave an indication of latitude in the northern ocean until, as one journeyed south, that star failed to appear above the northern horizon. This altitude was measured by using a quadrant.

The Sea Quadrant

The sea quadrant was a quarter-segment of a circle, along one straight side of which two eye-holes were placed to line up with and observe

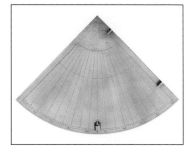

It took decades to create an accurate, and optically safe, way to measure the angle subtended between the sun and the horizon and thus make a start on measuring a ship's latitude. Early quadrants were so unwieldy that the navigator had to be rowed ashore to set the instrument up to read the angle cut by the plumb line that hung from the vertex when the sighting was made.
(National Maritime Museum F6429-001)

Polaris. From the end furthest from the observer hung a plumb line, which would dissect a scale on the graduated curved edge at a point depending on the angle at which the observation was being made, thus giving a reading of latitude. Soon the fact that certain ports or headlands coincided with particular degrees of latitude led to these references being marked on the quadrant. This was most useful for Atlantic crossings, where the navigator used to sail north or south until he could measure that he was in the right latitude, at which time he would turn east or west and 'run down the latitude' knowing that his destination lay at the end of this imaginary line, while all he had to do was take the measurement of Polaris and adjust his course accordingly. What he could not estimate accurately was how far he had to travel, a problem unsolved until the production of a good time-piece allowed longitude to be calculated.

The Sea Astrolabe

The next navigational instrument to be developed was the sea astrolabe, the simplification of a land survey instrument for use at sea. This was a circular disc with a ring to suspend it from the top and a solid or weighted bottom to keep it steady while the wind buffeted and the ship rocked. Observations of the sun or stars were made through looking through pin-holes placed along an alidade, a movable arm pivoted in the centre of the ring, allowing readings to be taken from the graduated arc of the instrument. Bartholomew Diaz and Vasco da Gama both used astrolabes, the method of construction of which was described by Marin Cortés in 1545. Between 1550 and 1580 design improvements made the instrument easier to use at sea. Its great benefit for sun sights was that it could be hung vertically and the alidade adjusted until a pin-prick of light appeared on the deck as the

The mariner's astrolabe marked a great leap forward not least because it allowed the observer to line up the two sighting holes on the sun until light passed through the lower one without having to squint directly at the sun itself. The instrument was designed to be suspended from a convenient high point and weighted at the base to reduce its own motion on a rolling ship. (National Maritime Museum neg 8450)

sun pierced both viewing holes, thus avoiding the observer having to look into that blinding light while still obtaining an accurate reading (to within one tenth of a degree) from the engraved scale.

The disappearance of Polaris below the horizon on southern voyages encouraged mariners to turn their attention to sun sights. Here difficulties arose for two reasons. The first was the very practical one referred to above, whereby some instruments required the user to look directly at the sun, whose apparent movement between the tropics as the year progressed caused the second problem, in that its noonday altitude varied not only with the position of the observer but with the day of the year on which the measurement was made, because of the sun's apparent travel between the two tropics. For example, Drake in his circumnavigation crossed the equator, Tropic of Cancer and Tropic of Capricorn four times. On each of these days, as on every other during the voyage, he would have worked out the ship's position by measuring the angle of the sun at midday. But he would have had to add to or subtract from this measurement a figure equivalent to the sun's apparent position (declination) north or south of the equator as it appeared to move between the Tropics, the calculation being based on the relative position of the sun, the equator and the ship. This is shown in the two tables overleaf.

To find his latitude using the sun Drake needed to be aware of the time of local midday. This was not easy in a ship where the sand-glass was the only timepiece on board. So as midday approached, a series of readings had to be made until the observer was confident that the sun had passed its zenith. This

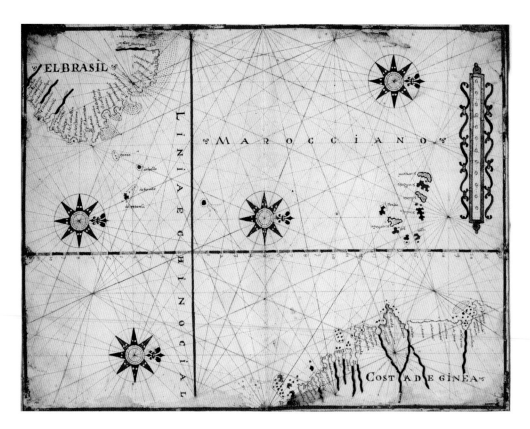

As demonstrated by this chart, by the end of the sixteenth century mariners crossing the Atlantic could be fairly certain of where they would make landfall in the Americas. A knowledge of currents and wind patterns had also grown up and been disseminated, making navigation more reliable. (National Maritime Museum F1404)

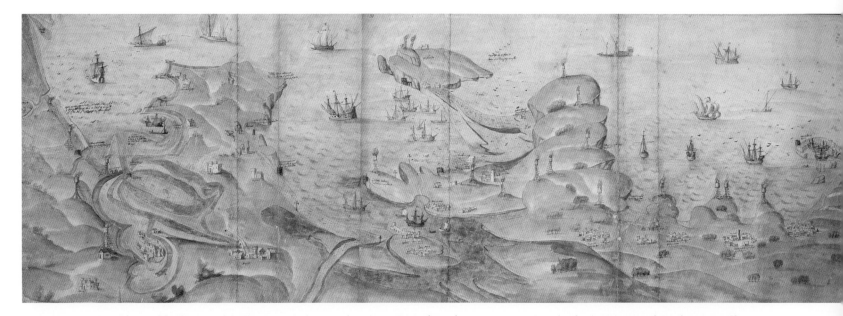

Contemporary pictorial maps like this one of the Dorset coast from Poole to Lyme Regis showed many inaccuracies and at best were vague about the topography, so it is not surprising that many masters relied on personal observations in their notebooks rather than charts to ensure the safety of their ship. The beacons were more of a warning system against invasion than a navigational aid. (British Library)

meant that the exact moment of solar meridian might not be recorded, for unsteadiness on a rocking vessel, or a passing cloud, could interfere with or upset the measurement so that the navigator might have to extrapolate from a series of readings. This done, he then had to do a sum using a set of declination tables.

Although the first known description in English as to how to convert solar altitude into observer's latitude did not appear until 1595, when John Davis explained with clarity what had been up until then obscure, it must be assumed that Drake had already acquired the arcane art.

The Cross-Staff and Back-Staff

In their quest for latitude the first navigators must have blinded themselves by staring at the sun: indeed some instructions advised only looking at the orb through cloud or smoked glass. The Portuguese developed a simple, cheap instrument for doing this, the cross-staff, which consisted of a long pole along which a sliding cross-piece with a hole in the middle was moved until the observer looking down it could place the bottom end on the horizon and the top edge on a star or

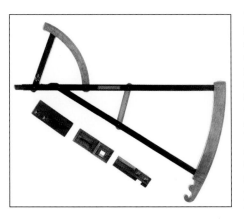

With the back-staff accurate measurements could be made of the sun's position without looking at it directly. This was the first navigational instrument designed by a user, the Tudor navigator Captain Davis, who described it in his 1595 book The Seaman's Secrets. *The angle of the sun was measured by sliding cross-pieces along a graduated staff.* (National Maritime Museum F6840-001)

bottom edge of the sun. A reading was then made from a scale engraved on the pole. While the Portuguese were using cross-staffs to measure the altitude of Polaris by 1515, practical difficulties delayed its use for sun sights. In England William Bourne explained how to use the cross-staff in 1574, but by 1595 John Davis was describing his own invention, the back-staff, which allowed measurement to be made of the sun while one's back was turned to it by lining up its shadow with the horizon.

At the time of Drake's circumnavigation the back-staff was not available, and he would have had to rely on the cross-staff for Pole Star sightings and an astrolabe for readings of solar altitude. He also needed the most up-to-date charts and some feeling for his longitude, which, at this stage, without accurate timepieces, it was not possible to commute.

Longitude

On three occasions on his long voyage the knowledge of his rough longitude would have been critical for Drake. Firstly, on turning north having overcome the storms that greeted his arrival in the Pacific through the Straits of Magellan, he needed to know how far he was from the coast of South America; secondly, in his search for the opening of the Straits of Anian, he needed to be able to estimate how long the journey home via that route might be; and, thirdly, having decided to return home across both the Pacific and Indian oceans, he needed to know for how long he would be away from land.

Drake departed from Plymouth in November 1577 with as good a collection of instruments, charts and first-hand accounts as he could obtain. What he lacked was a pilot with local knowledge of the South Atlantic. This defect was remedied when the Portuguese navigator Nuño da Silva was captured off the Cape Verde Islands and kept on board until Drake was ready to sail across the Pacific. In the deposition he made after capture and interrogation by the Spanish da Silva stated:

Significant Dates during Drake's Circumnavigation

Position

Tropic of Cancer	15 January 1578	29 April 1579	26 August 1579	26 August 1580
Equator	21 February 1578	1 March 1579	10 November 1579	14 July 1580
Tropic of Capricorn	22 March 1578	28 January 1579	30 May 1580	30 June 1580

The Sun's Declination on the above dates

Position

Tropic of Cancer	South 21° 11′	North 14° 40′	North 10° 10′	North 10° 11′
Equator	South 10° 40′	South 7° 20′	South 17° 19′	North 21° 34′
Tropic of Capricorn	North 0° 53′	South 18° 17′	North 21° 52′	North 23° 07′

Notes 1. When Drake crossed the Tropic of Capricorn on 22 March 1578, it was almost the time of the equinox with the sun almost overhead at the equator.

2. On 30 June 1580 Drake crossed the Tropic of Cancer, very close to the time of the northern hemisphere's summer solstice, with the sun almost overhead of the *Golden Hind*.

Francis Drake carried with him three books on navigation. One of these was in French, another in English and the third was Magellan's *Discovery* ... Drake kept a book in which he entered his navigation and in which he delineated birds, trees and sea-lions. He is adept in painting and has with him a boy, a relative of his [John Drake, his cousin] who is a great painter. When they both shut themselves up in his cabin they were always painting.[16]

This desire to record remained with Drake up to and including his last voyage, from which just a few sketches survive. This is more than remains of the ones to which da Silva refers. They were handed to the queen, who shortly afterwards lost these priceless documents, yet another indication that Tudor monarchs might have been well educated but lacked vision, intelligence and great minds.

From Cape Verde onwards any craft that came Drake's way was likely to be stopped and searched and relieved of its cargo, including charts, navigational instruments and, most importantly, pilots. One of these reported that Drake had a chart some ten metres long that he had made for him in Lisbon for 800 *cruzados* (had the corsair visited that port during his planning phase?) and that one of the routes that he was contemplating using to return home was via Norway. This was a fantastical suggestion as it involved traversing the whole of Russia, of which only the first few leagues around Nova Zemblya were known to the English.

Nuño da Silva had sailed frequently to Brazil and knew the coast well. Drake and he soon established a good professional working relationship, which enabled the former to copy the Portuguese's charts and translate his sailing directions. He was also reported to have had great expertise in the 'determination of latitude by observation', a skill that Drake would have found most useful when he was driven far south after his exit from the Straits of Magellan. Shortly after passing through these straits, violent storms drove him far south after his exit

from the Straits of Magellan, enabling him to establish that South America was not contiguous with the southern continent. He had discovered Cape Horn and another route into the Pacific – something to remember when the time came to return home and, strangely, really his only cartographic discovery of any significance.

Turning north, the voyagers remained in uncharted waters. Even Nuño da Silva had no knowledge of these seas, and the *Golden Hind* was in danger of wandering out far into the Pacific. This was a dangerous course at this stage because the men were already showing signs of scurvy and were in desperate need of fresh supplies. A bold alteration of course brought the ship back to the coast off the island of Mocha, where a hostile reception did not materialise until the English had fed and watered and replenished their ship.

From then on the passage north turned into a triumph. Drake was a fox in a hen house whose floating chickens could almost be plucked at will and whose administrative guardians were both hopeless and helpless when faced with this wily intruder. Out-gunned and out-thought, the Spaniards could only plan onslaughts, which they were incapable or too timid to execute; blame others for their inefficiency; and close the obvious exits from their ocean to prevent Drake's escape with his great booty. Even here they second-guessed wrongly, and Drake continued his voyage up the coast of the Americas unhindered by Spanish pursuers.

The North-West Passage

What Frobisher was attempting to do from the Atlantic, Drake, under greater pressure, was contemplating achieving from the totally unknown Pacific coast. He was aware of the contradictory views on the existence of a navigable north-west passage, but at the time of his departure, most mariners and map-makers favoured the idea that the passage was navigable. Yet if he were to attempt the passage himself from the west, the distance that he might have to travel in icy northern waters through the straits, if indeed they even existed, would depend on the longitude of their opening, and from this he would be able to judge whether their latitude, and the season of the year, gave him a chance of a safe passage home. As the coast of North America steadfastly refused to veer to the north-east, so his desire to try his luck by finding the straits must have diminished. His chaplain, Francis Fletcher, noted that the signs of a navigable passage were not good and:

> From these reasons we conjecture that either there is no passage at all through these Northern coasts (which is most likely), or if there be, that yet it is unnavigable. Add that, though we searched the coast diligently, even unto 48 degrees, yet found we not the land to trend so much as one point in any place toward the East, but rather running on continually North-West, as if it were directly to Asia.

– a fact reinforced by the lack of any current that could indicate such a passage. Fletcher's comment about the trend towards Asia, surprisingly accurate, reinforces the idea that exploration was not uppermost in Drake's mind at this time. To have followed the coast until it curved to Cathay would have been an extraordinary undertaking, yet Drake may even have considered so doing when, in the port of Guatulco in Central America, he had produced a chart and told Nuño da Silva that if he failed to find the Straits of Anian he would have to go back via China. This may have been a ploy to fool the Spaniards into whose ungentle hands Drake abandoned his unfortunate pilot that very day, knowing that he would be thoroughly interrogated by the Spaniards as to the corsair's plans. This callous dumping of his pilot achieved the required end. Da Silva, under torture, confused the Spaniards, several of whom were convinced that he had been landed to 'proclaim and persuade people ... that the Corsair was going to return by China or the Straits "de los Bacallaos"'.[17] Accused of heresy because he had taken part in a 'Lutheran' mass on board *Golden Hind,* da Silva suffered great indignities until he was eventually sent back to Europe in 1582 and released by Philip of Spain.[18] His log and his depositions before his interrogators, discovered in the twentieth century by Zelia Nuttall, give us the best insight we have into life on board during the epic voyage and, by association, the clearest description of the Tudor navy at sea in Elizabeth's reign.

In fact Drake was having none of it. 'Safe seas' was to be his motto for the remainder of the voyage, and the evidence of his eyes must have made him decide that Ortelius's northern chart, with its Straits of Anian and open Arctic Ocean, was seriously incorrect.

Just where he made landfall on the coast of North America and how far up the coast he travelled is a source of much speculation, with some suggesting that he reached Alaska while others have his northernmost advance concluding at around forty-two degrees north.[19] The contemporary problem was that this part of the voyage appears to have been cloaked in secrecy and subject to censorship to protect the information that the English had gained from Spanish eyes. Indeed, much to the consternation of the major cartographers, Drake was made to keep his own counsel. In December 1580 Mercator wrote in response to a letter full of frustration that he had received from Ortelius:

> Thank you for the dispatch about the new English voyage on which you have previously sent me reports through Rombold ... I

am persuaded that there can be no reason for so carefully concealing the course followed during this voyage, nor for putting out differing accounts of the route taken and the area visited, other than they may have found very wealthy regions never yet discovered by Europeans, not even by those who have sailed the Ocean on the Indies voyage.[20]

Eventually, and probably without too much soul-searching, Drake decided upon a crossing of the Pacific to the Spice Islands. On this leg of his journey he could have been left thousands of miles from land without food and water if he had relied on the chart drawn by Ortelius, which showed eighty-seven degrees of longitude between Acapulco and the Moluccas when in fact the true distance was 140 degrees. This was an error equivalent to 3,500 nautical miles or a month's sailing at a good speed of 120 miles a day. It must be said in Drake's favour that he had captured some pilots who had made the journey on several occasions, so he may have considered their knowledge more reliable than that of his charts. Finally, he had to sail across an uncharted ocean, from Java to the Cape of Good Hope, an effortless and fast journey that took only fifty-six days but in which the longitudinal difference between the point of departure and the destination would not have been known.

Like so many lengthy voyages, this one was mainly incident-free but the one incident that did occur nearly ended in disaster. On 9 January, off the Celebes, *Golden Hind* went firmly aground on a coral reef. Lightening the ship of her main armament failed to lift her off, so food and stores – in fact, most items other than the deep-loaded bullion ballast – were jettisoned, but all to no avail. Then, with all hope gone, a fresh wind blew and the ship slipped off her rocky berth into deeper water. Surprisingly little damage seemed to have been done, so after stopping off to replenish the jettisoned stores, and probably to gain sailing directions, Drake passed through the beautiful archipelagos of the East Indies and was soon in the Indian Ocean and heading for the Cape of Good Hope, which took several weeks to round, before he could turn north for England, home and glory. A non-stop voyage between Java, which he left on 26 March 1580, and

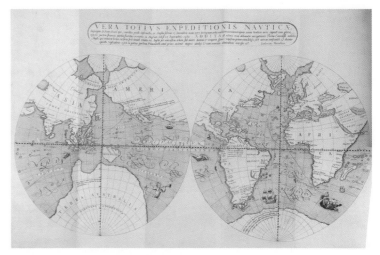

The track of Drake's circumnavigation shown on two hemispheres. From The World Encompassed. *(Royal Naval Museum, Portsmouth)*

Sierra Leone, a short watering stop on 22 July, during which just one man was lost, is proof enough of his all-encompassing skills. On 26 September 1580, after an epic voyage of over three years, *Golden Hind* entered Plymouth Sound, where the first words spoken by her captain to the welcoming party were 'Does the queen still live?' His life depended on the answer; his loot would influence his fate.

What loot it was. From the laden holds of *Golden Hind* emerged £600,000 in gold, silver and precious jewels, cloves and other spices, of which the queen received £160,000 – a cheap enough bribe with which to avoid a beheading. The other investors received a return of almost 5,000 per cent, which some invested in the new Levant Company; Drake's circumnavigation thus led to the expansion of overseas trade away from the Iberian-controlled Indies.

After Drake

Drake's epic voyage was not followed up by the English crown with the same enthusiasm that had been given to building upon the early voyages of the Spanish and Portuguese explorers. In June 1583 Sir Humphrey Gilbert sailed across the Atlantic to Newfoundland and took possession, in the queen's name, of the land around St John's, much to the bemusement of the Breton and Iberian fishermen present.

When Drake planned his circumnavigation he had to rely on global charts such as this one dated to 1567 which was made by Nicolas Desliens across the Channel in Dieppe. Note that it shows much of the Pacific occupied by a vast continent-sized Java. (National Maritime Museum C4575)

However, he perished on the voyage home, and the survivors were disillusioned. Even the enthusiastic Richard Hakluyt felt obliged to write: 'all the men tired with the tediousness of so unprofitable a voyage to their seeming: much toil and labour, hard diet and continual hazard of life was unrecompensed'.[21]

Between 1586 and 1588 Thomas Cavendish sailed around the world in an almost copy-book repeat of Drake's voyage. Epic although this also was, it was a private venture and thus outside the scope of this work. However, it was covered in some detail by Hakluyt, who wanted to shame the English into making more exploratory voyages. In the dedication of the first edition of *The Principal Voyages, Traffiques and Discoveries of the English Nation*, published in 1589, he wrote that during his time in France, 'I both heard in speech and read in books other nations miraculously extolled for their discoveries and notable enterprises by sea, but the English of all others for their sluggish security, and continual neglect of the like attempts especially in so long and happy a time of peace, either ignominiously reported, or exceedingly condemned.'

Hakluyt put the reason for this slothfulness down to 'the huge toil and the small profit' involved. This was the rotten kernel of the mainly sound nut of the queen's policy of venture capitalism – unless investors got a worthwhile return they were not willing to take a risk. With such commercial considerations taking precedence it is not surprising that the great age of English naval exploration lay some years ahead. Nevertheless it was the Tudors who sailed the first leagues on what

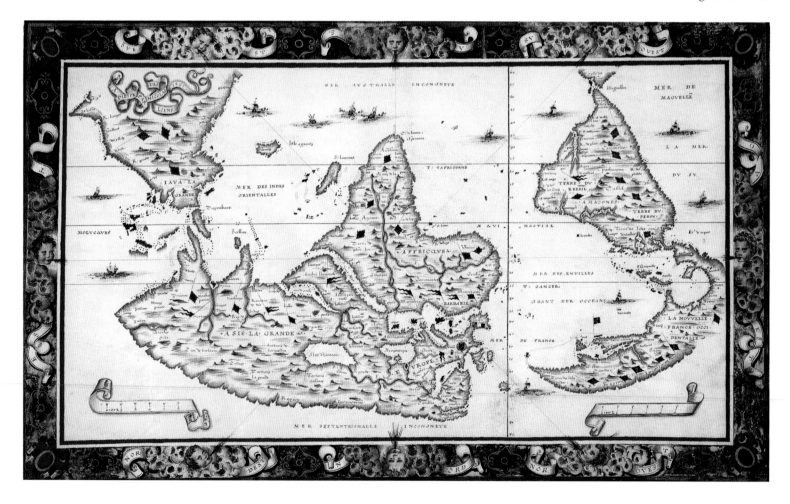

was to become an everlasting journey. Hakluyt realised that the promise of trade and the hope for gain had to be the up-front bribes, and so, rather disingenuously, he stated that as 'our chief desire is to find ample vent for our woollen goods', the best place to head to would be Japan and northern China, to which, of course, popular opinion held that the best theoretical routes were the northern passages, which thus needed to be explored. Yet without the ability to record longitude accurately it was not possible to provide the necessary information about bays and headlands and open waters that those following behind would need.

However, when it came to the turn of Ralegh, the natural successor to his relative Humphrey Gilbert, to go exploring, he too was seduced and turned into a liar by the lure of gold. The Guiana that he chose to explore, and to which he returned in a vain effort to save his life, had no mine, was not El Dorado, but anyone reading his reports would have imagined that it would be if only further effort was made to explore just one more bend in the river.

Tudor colonies, beyond Ireland, would survive only if a rich mine, costly spice or sea passage to Cathay made a good return on investment. Tobacco was the only crop that might make money, and even here the English were unlucky. The 'weed' exported from Virginia was *Nicotiana rustica*, a far less pleasant leaf than *Nicotiana tobacum*, which indicated its superiority by giving its name to the product. Unfortunately tobacum grew best in the Spanish-controlled areas of the New World, as a result of which as the smoking habit spread in

England people paid Spanish merchants, not English settlers, for their smoke. It was not until 1609 that John Rolfe, salvaging a seed packet of *tobacum* from the wrecked *Sea Venture* in the Bermudas, was able to introduce the superior plant to Virginia.

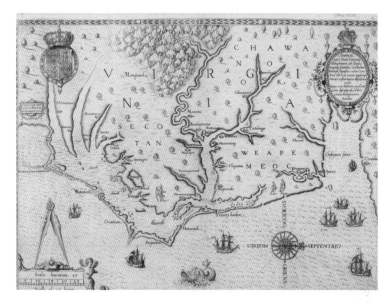

An engraved version of by Theodore de Bry of John White's map of Virginia, originally drawn about 1585. White was a member of Ralegh's short-lived colony at Roanoke, and later governor of the 1587 settlement. (National Maritime Museum PX7335)

The latest visualisation of the Mary Rose *in her heyday, by the well-known marine artist Geoff Hunt. Based on recently unearthed documentary evidence that proved the ship had two full decks abaft the mainmast, it tends to confirm the general features of the ship so naively depicted in the Anthony Anthony illustration – in particular the height of the castles. However, these latter were lightly constructed and, in the case of the forecastle, very narrow, so they did not add as much topweight as often assumed.*
(Mary Rose Trust)

SEAMANSHIP

Drake had proved himself an extraordinarily competent ship-handler, but the art of ship-handling for a naval vessel required adaptation for differing circumstances. Firstly, there was the management of the sailing plan while on independent passage or in unformed company. Secondly, there was the need to adjust this plan to take into account the movements of vessels close by when in formation; and finally, closing an enemy and engaging successfully needed an understanding of sea warfare that also depended on whether the fight was between two ships or a fleet of ships. It was the art of handling a ship in all these circumstances that distinguished the great master from the adequate and the successful commander from the less fortunate. Taking all this into consideration, Drake is peerless as the consummate manager of a private vessel, but it would be churlish not to recognise the passage of the Armada from the Scillies to Calais as the most magnificent example of fleet command and control during the age.

In all circumstances it was the art of managing sails to achieve the aim that was all-important. With all sails set *Mary Rose* had a sail area of just under 900 square metres. This can be compared with 112 square metres for a Viking long ship, 650 square metres for the magnificent 'J' Class yachts of the 1920s; 278 for a typical Americas Cup competitor and 270 for Ellen MacArthur's record-breaking single-handed round-the-world catamaran, while HMS *Victory* could set almost an hectare of canvas. One indication of the improvement in mechanical aids to sailing is the ratio of sail area to vessel weight (in tonnes) to manpower, which for *Mary Rose* is 900:700:500 while for Ellen MacArthur's boat it is a stunning 270:8.3:1. Paradoxically, the greater the crew needed to handle the sails, the more professional knowledge was necessary to control any evolution such as tacking or reefing.

The great ships of the Tudor navy had either three or four masts, with the sternmost two rigged with lateen sails, which much improved their steering. Thus the main sail gave the ship its motive power; the foresail, shielded from the wind, added little to the speed but made tacking easier, while the lateen sails aft enabled the ship to sail closer to the wind and assisted with steering as well as adding significantly to the ship's speed when sailing down wind. Additional help in tacking or altering course could be achieved by use of the spritsail, a small sail supported by the bowsprit which, because of its forward position, could exert a good turning moment. Higher up each mast, topsails, high above the turbulence created by the larger sails, could add power greater than their relative size might suggest. As far as ship-handling was concerned, the master of a ship with four masts and numerous yards could select from a large number of available combinations in order to get the best out of his ship and his men and to pursue an enemy or keep station on a commander. This skill could be learned only at sea, and it required a long apprenticeship.

Thus the warships that were being built or purchased for the Navy Royal were moving towards the designs that would reach their military zenith in the Napoleonic Wars and their commercial apotheosis in clipper ships such as *Cutty Sark*.

As important as the size and location of the sails themselves were the way in which they were rigged and how the ropes and lines attached to them were handled. Square in shape they may have been, but setting them square, at right angles to a stern wind, was only one way of rigging them on passage. The masters would have been well aware of how best to use the laws of laminar flow, which dictated that the suction forces acting on the leeward side of a sail were mechanically more efficient than the straightforward 'push' of the air on the windward side. Moreover, by taking the leading edge of the sail forward and the other end aft, the sails could behave much more like those on a vessel that was rigged fore and aft and could allow the ship to be sailed closer to the wind. The 'bowline', a length of rope by which the leading edge of the sail could be hauled taut, was another new feature that was to improve sailing ability, but even with this few vessels could sail closer that six points from the direction of the wind.

No two vessels handled the same and none behaved consistently during a voyage. When in company, the need to sail at the same course and speed of another ship required the master not to follow slavishly the sails rigged on his neighbour but to have a full understanding of how and why that ship was maintaining its track. If there was a need for a boat transfer, that meant the admiral heaving to and the remainder of his ship closing him, and it also required a great knowledge of how best to keep station. A ship could reduce sail and then heave to itself by backing the sails on either the fore or the main mast, usually the latter. This meant that the wind acting on the main sails tended to push her astern, while an equal and opposite effect was produced on the fore sails – effectively achieving a state of equilibrium. With more sails set speed a ship could be slowed down by 'shivering' the sails on one mast – again probably the main. This involved aligning the yards with the wind so that it expressively caused the sails to shiver and not impart any motion to the vessel. Doing this in a large fleet of vastly different vessels, including some with newly scraped hulls and some dragging weed along with them, was not an easy evolution. And over all of this activity the wind – its absence, presence, fickleness, changeability, strength and direction – always exerted an influence that not even the best-rigged and -sailed vessel could overcome. Whether mid-ocean calms and the fear of starvation, inshore gales and the fear of shipwreck, or close-quarters evolutions and the fear of collision, the masters' first consideration was wind direction and speed. The fact that they achieved what they did as a matter of routine says much about their skill and made them fully deserve their title and accolade of master.

In March 1513 Sir Edward Howard, the newly-appointed Lord Admiral brought his fleet to sea from their winter haven in the Thames and ordered an evolution to shake down the crews, brush away the winter cobwebs and see how his ships and their masters, commanders and crews performed. The race he set in being was the first occasion on which an English admiral had commanded his fleet to carry out any such training activity and demonstrates how far ahead of his times young Howard was.

It was a blustery day with a strong east-north-easterly wind that had forced the ships to anchor off Margate. Now, with a change in direction, they got underway with the aim of arriving just north of the Downs by nightfall. The waters through which they had to sail were shoaly and shallow, and with the added incentive of a race the masters needed all their local knowledge to avoid the ignominy of grounding. In his letter to the king written that evening, Sir Edward can scarcely

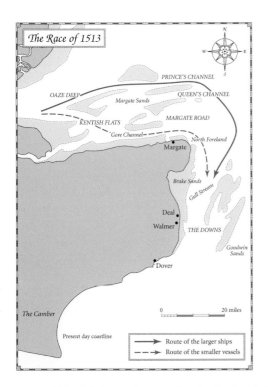

When Edward Howard ordered the fleet to race from Margate to the Downs in 1513 he was testing the navigational and seamanship skills of the ships' masters, for these shoaly waters are unforgiving and the tides at times treacherous. (Map by Peter Wilkinson)

The wind had allowed for an exhilarating race, with bonnets being attached and the waters washing over the gunwales as the vessels heeled over. Apart from *Mary Rose*, the star of the show, Howard had been impressed by the three Bristol ships, but decidedly underwhelmed by the way the king's own *Katherine Fortileza* and *Christ*, 'one of the worst that day', had performed, although he felt that the former could be remedied, 'well enough that she shall follow with the best', putting her deficiencies down to her being overladen and top-heavy. It was not to be, and *Katherine Fortileza* was ever a sad ship.

By 1522 the darling of the fleet was *Henry Grace à Dieu*, which, Fitzwilliam informed the king, 'sailed as well as any ship that was in the fleet, and rather better, and weathered them all save *Mary Rose*. And if she go by a wind, I assure your grace, there will be hard choice between *Mary Rose* and her, and next them the *Galley*.'[23]

It is very difficult to be precise about any speeds reached by Tudor ships because of the effect of wind direction in relation to the course desired and the increased distance covered through tacking or even anchoring if wind and tide conspired to be adverse. We do, however, have one straight-line passage which we can be certain was an uninterrupted one. On the evening of 30 June Lord Thomas Howard sailed his fleet out of Dartmouth, arriving in the Bay of Morlaix before dusk the following day. He thus covered some 145 miles in thirty hours, which would give an average speed made good of five knots.

Coastal passages could always cause frustrations. Thomas Howard was unable to bring the fleet from Plymouth to Southampton to re-victual in 1514 because of the wind direction, while all the time he remained at anchor his ships were buffeted by strong winds and in danger of being blown against each other.[24] On the other hand Vice-Admiral William Fitzwilliam, endeavouring to pass west down the Channel in June 1522, informed the king that 'Monday the wind came to the West and by North, and so we have made sail, purposing to have stopped at every flood, and so to have plied to Hampton with the tides',[25] a laboriously slow progress involving anchoring while the tidal current ran eastwards and then weighing to allow the ebb tide to carry them a few miles west until it turned once more, forcing them to anchor once again.

If the weather was a continuous hazard at sea, its effect in delaying supplies reaching outstations such as Broughty Castle or Boulogne could cause much stress to a beleaguered garrison or, in the

conceal his delight at the way the day had unfolded:

> All such ships as made sail even together with ... your good ship [*Mary Rose*], the flower, I trow, of all ships that ever sailed ... left her in flight ... And, Sir, then our course changed and went hard upon a bowline ... Sir, she is the noblest ship of sail and great ship at this hour that I trowe in Christendom. A ship of 100 to will not be sooner at her ... When I came to an anchor, I called for pen and ink to mark what ships came to me, for they came all by me to an anchor.[22]

It would appear that, even allowing the little ships an inshore and shorter passage and starting astern of many of the great ships, *Mary Rose* had outsailed them all on a course which meant sailing both close-hauled and with the wind astern. The excitement did not end with the evening's anchorage, for that night a wind blew up:

> ... so strainably that we could ride no longer there without great danger so we weighed to get us into the Downs through the Gull Stream. And when we were in the midst, between the Brakes and the Goodwin, the wind veered out again to the West-South-West, where we were fain to make with your great ships three or four turns, and God knoweth ... channel at low water ... I fetched the Downs with many turns, and thanked be to God I ... at an anchor fast.

Towards the end of the letter Howard reveals not only that he had promised the king to conduct such a trial but that it had turned out to be a real test of ship-handling and seamanship:

> I beseech your grace not to be miscontent that I make so long a matter in writing to you, and of no matter of substance, but that you commanded me to send your grace word how every ship did sail, and this same way was the best trial that could be, for we went both slacking and by a bowline, and a ... course and a bonnet, in such wise that few ships lacked no water in over the lee wales.

Anchors, of which most ships had several weighty examples, not only enabled a ship to ride out a storm safely when close inland but, when contrary tides were flowing and the wind unfavourable, allowed a master to ride out an adverse tide and slip downstream once it had turned. This picture shows one raised from the Mary Rose. *(Mary Rose Trust)*

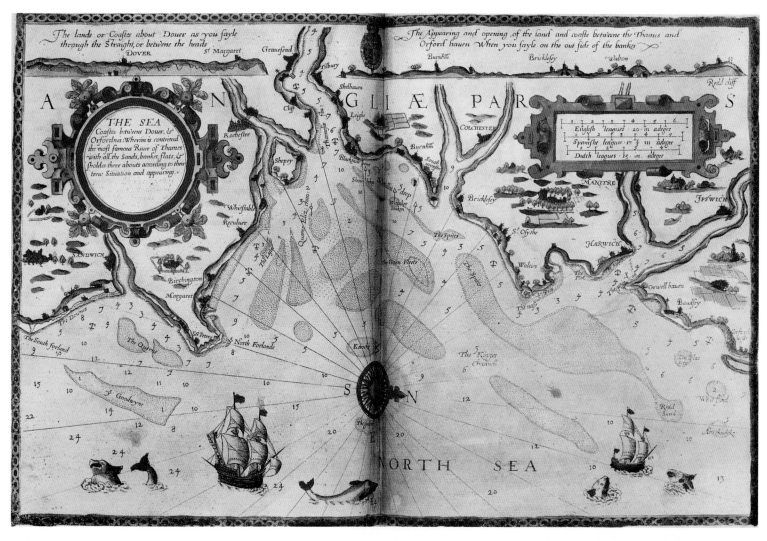

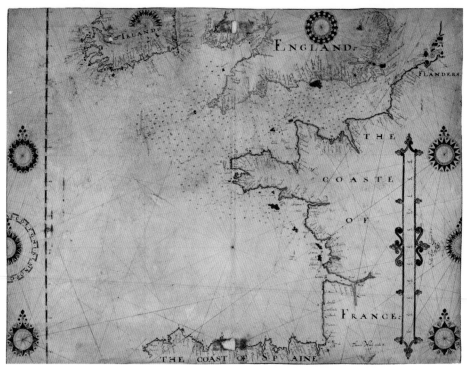

As this 1596 chart by Thomas Hood shows clearly, by the end of the century English cartographers were producing charts the equal to any being made in Europe. Note the emphasis on the sandbanks of the Goodwins and Thames estuary. Nevertheless, such charts served as guidance and warning to mariners rather than for plotting their position with any degree of accuracy. (National Maritime Museum F8009)

Another of Thomas Hood's charts produced in 1596, it covers the Channel approaches and the Bay of Biscay – still the centre of English interest, despite occasional naval operations as far off as Cadiz and the Azores. (National Maritime Museum K1035)

case of Calais, contribute to its loss. During one re-supply voyage to Boulogne in November 1544 Thomas Seymour's squadron were struck by a gale. What happened next is worth recounting in detail as it shows how fragile life at sea could be in winter weather:

That night the wind veered to North East so extreme that we were fain to forsake Bolen road and go westward under sail, until half-an-hour before day, when the wind rose so high that such a were not fast aboard the shore was fain to go run, of the which I was one, the *Minion*, the *Salamander* with 5 other sail. And it was as much as we could do for our lives to get sight of the Isle of Wight before night, and it was an hour within night or I could get in. Three hulks that came after me could not get sight thereof until they were in a bay on the East side of the Isle, of the which Mr. Stowd, Bramston and Batterbee of the Guard (God rest their souls) was in one of them [*Christopher* of Bremen] which hulk brake all her anchors and cables and she brake all to pieces on the shore, and but 41 of 300 saved alive. The other two rode out the storm, which lasted all that night and the next day. My brother and John Robert of the Guard tried the seas all the first night and the next day came into Dartmouth haven; where my brother's hulk [*Lion*] struck on a rock and broke all to pieces, but, God be praised, all the men were saved saving three. And another new hulk that tried the seas that night brake three of her beams and with much ado came into the Wight ... As yet I hear no word what is become of the *Great Shallop*, the *Falcon* and a crayer of 50 ton of mine. The King's Highness nor few others that had any ship in this fleet but the ordnance flew about and shook the ships, by reason of the 'hollows' of the seas, that they were strained continually to pump, especially the *Swallow*, the *New Barke*, the *Trinity Henry* and *Sweepstake*.[26]

Thomas being Thomas and Henry being Henry, the letter would not have been complete without the former excusing any inaction on his behalf by blaming the weather and inviting all his captains and masters to do likewise. Yet matters could have been worse. In another letter, in which the loss of *Christopher* is also reported, Seymour states that both *Trinity Harry* and *Sweepstake* were leaking so badly that they needed to 'be brought aground'.[27]

As the century progressed this frustration with wind and tide remained. On 26 December 1559 William Winter sailed with a fleet of twelve ships from Queenborough, in the Thames estuary, with the Firth of Forth his objective, in response to the rumour of the departure of a French fleet for Scotland. Two days later, off Harwich, a north-easterly forced the group to shelter in Yarmouth Roads, which they did for five days. The wind then blew so 'strainably' that they were forced to slip their anchors and cables and ride out the gale at sea before drifting back to Harwich to effect repairs. Back at sea on 11 January, they reached Yarmouth again the next day, thus sailing 220 miles in seventeen days and progressing only a hundred. Although the same storm had scattered the French, Winter continued and raced north, covering the next 130 miles in just nineteen hours before being impeded by another gale off Flamborough Head, which drove his group to take shelter in the mouth of the Humber. The storm had not abated when they set sail again, and this time in its ferocity it stove in

all the ships' boats being towed astern and dispersed the fleet, so that Winter was able to lead only seven of them into the very tricky sheltered anchorage near Bamburgh Castle. From there the fleet sailed on to reach the Firth of Forth on 22 January before going into action the next day and capturing the galleys *Trywright* and *Speedwell*, which were added to the royal fleet. Other shipping in the Forth was driven ashore, and thus the war ended with a satisfactory conclusion for the navy, which was left only with the task of ferrying 3,613 Frenchmen, 267 of their women, and 315 children back to France.

Winter, a good seaman, had used his knowledge of the North Sea coast to advantage and thus ensured the safety of his force. When similar adverse conditions arose in unfamiliar seas the outcome was seldom as felicitous. In August 1568 John Hawkins brought his slave-trading fleet out from Cartagena in New Spain with the aim of sailing home through seas on which he had never previously ventured. A successful passage would have required him to navigate his force through both the Yucatan and Florida Channel at a time when storms could be anticipated. To add to Hawkins's concerns, he was sailing in *Jesus of Lubeck*, a bulky, weatherly and elderly royal ship which with *Minion* had been hired from the queen. *Jesus* had been taken by William Winter on a trading voyage to the Levant, but by the time Hawkins took command of her she was a leaky, creaky tub with rotting timbers; her only advantage had been that he could cram more slaves into her capacious hold. Now her poor shape and handling qualities would prove his nemesis.

A fair passage brought the fleet close to the Isle of Pines, off mainland Cuba, from where the ships turned west to enter the Yucatan Channel. It was the hurricane season. In a vivid description Rayner Unwin explains what happened next:

The sky, which had been benign and cloudless, became lowering and a series of squalls, each more tempestuous than the last, drove up from the south-east, blotting out the shoreline and enveloping the ships in hard-flung bursts of rain. At the first onset the crews were sent aloft to reef and furl the canvas, but several sails were carried away before they could be secured, and their flapping remain were cut from the yards ... The wind and blinding scud showed no sign of abating. The sea, that had been whipped up into a confused froth of waves, beat against the plank with an increasing rhythm ... Visibility was poor, and at times the fume of the sea and the driving rain seemed to encase and isolate each separate vessel – almost to suffocate it with water. Two or three men struggled with each whipstaff, endeavouring to hold a course ... various captains grew apprehensive lest they be forced on to a lee shore, and urged their rain-blinded look-out to increasing vigilance.[28]

Hawkins in the queen's ancient cranky ship not only knew but could feel and see in the sprung timber around him that *Jesus* could take very little more of this punishment. He abandoned his course towards the open sea and for days, with the leadsmen in the chains constantly calling out the depth, he led his fleet along the coast until, after another hurricane, it was forced to take shelter in San Juan de Ulua to effect repairs, arriving just days ahead of the new Viceroy of New Spain, Don Martin Enriquez, who had no wish to begin his period in office by tolerating the presence of interloping 'Lutherans'. The aftermath and aftertaste of the battle that followed would radically change the course of Tudor naval history. Once again it was the elements that were determining the condition of men, especially mariners.

Yet it is the ability of Tudor vessels to survive in ferocious seas that, time after time, amazes. Most losses in bad weather seem to have been of minor vessels. *Marigold*, the vessel lost in the maelstrom off Cape Horn endured by Drake's expedition in September 1578, was only a thirty-tonne bark. In 1583 Sir Humphrey Gilbert, sitting calmly with his book and proclaiming that they were as near to heaven by sea as by land, was lost when his ten-tonne frigate *Squirrel* was overwhelmed by an Atlantic gale. Even when sickness had left few on board capable of setting or, more importantly, furling a sail, given sufficient sea-room, ships survived, a credit to their builders and handlers. In such conditions the carracks came into their own, although not by design. It was found that, with all sails furled and the tiller lashed to leeward, they could comfortably lie 'ahull' in a heavy sea as long as there was plenty of open sea to downwind.[29]

The winds of the Channel had a major bearing on operations, the essence of which was that a wind that blew an enemy towards England could prevent the English sailing out to meet them. Conversely, an English admiral could turn over in his bunk at night knowing that a north-easterly wind was keeping his enemies trapped below Ushant. The winds of the Armada campaign best illustrate this. Drake, ever anxious to take the fight to the enemy, was kept frustrated inside Plymouth Sound by the wind that he knew was blowing the Spaniards towards his shores. Yet Medina Sidonia had suffered equal frustration earlier when a northerly wind kept him in Corunna but blew Drake southward until it, fortuitously, died down just short of the Spanish coast.

There being no school where the aspiring sailor could learn the theory of sailing, the only college was that provided by time at sea itself. A future master would have crewed from an early age and progressed as his abilities came to be noticed by his superiors. Drake can provide us with a typical progression. Mudlarking as a child was succeeded by handling small boats, followed by apprenticeship with the owner of a small coastal bark plying the Thames estuary and occasionally crossing the Narrow Seas. These were gentle but difficult waters in which to learn the essentials of pilotage, for although the coast lies low and featureless and the mud banks are many, movable and shallow-lying, especially at low water in a region of significant tidal range, for a young apprentice they are also kindly and forgiving waters as, lacking rocks, they will allow the occasional grounded vessel to refloat with little damage done to anything other than pride. Having inherited the bark from his childless master, Drake was in a position to sell it and return to the West Country, where his skills enabled him to gain passage with the Hawkins fleet which was about to take the coast-hugging English out into unknown seas to ship new cargoes. Drake was in a position to start his study of blue waters. This background would have been a familiar one to many of the masters who so successfully manned the sovereign's ships: what was to

be new was that several of these common sailors would break into the realm of high command, previously the preserve of the courtier, and that their presence and status would not be resented by those who believed their birth made them their betters. Eventually it dawned upon the nation that to handle a ship to its greatest potential did require all who aspired to command to undergo a similar apprenticeship afloat. The army could be commanded by ranking amateurs; it did after all require little technical knowledge. The navy was different. It could take a lifetime to gain full competency, and because of this it was later realised that training had to begin early. Nelson went to sea at fourteen, as did both Cook and Fitzroy. In the sixteenth century royal appointees might never have set foot on board a ship until they arrived in command. The whole ship's company, in these circumstances, had to trust that their master had the necessary experience to compensate; generally he did.

The result of good ship-handling can be seen in the record of how few naval ships were lost despite the years of war, poor or non-existent charts and ventures into strange seas; these area outlined in the table opposite.

If one extracts from the list those that were lost when on 'hire' then the survival rate becomes even more commendable. Against this, however, has to be set the loss of ships taken up from trade, such as Arthur Plantagenet's *Nicholas of Hampton*, which he drove on to the rocks off Brest in 1513, and the victualler sunk by Pregent's galleys at around the same time. There is no full record of these but it can be assumed that, while in naval service, few indeed were lost.

A helmsman steering a ship by means of a whipstaff lacked the subtlety of control that came with the introduction of the ship's wheel. Moreover, because the steersmen were below deck they had to obey a relayed command, with the delay that caused, and were unable to point the ship's head other than by following a jerky compass needle. Nevertheless, the fact that skilful use of sail and tiller together allowed for delicate manoeuvring is evident from the way vessels were handled both when in company and in close quarters with an enemy.

There has been much debate over the importance to warships of gaining the weather gage prior to a fight. For most commentators Howard established his dominance over the Spanish by warping out of Plymouth and clawing his way across the face of the Armada to place his fleet up wind, but it was not necessarily so. One argument put forward is that a ship with the weather gage heeled over in such a way that her fire could be directed low down upon an enemy's hull, while the foe to lee was forced by the same heel to fire high and possibly harmlessly. This ignored both the fact that heel was a correctable characteristic and that any noticeable swell would affect both ships equally, making the aiming of guns dependent on good timing when the ship was momentarily steady in her roll. In the fight between Captain Towerson's *Tiger* and the Portuguese off Guinea in 1557, the Englishman, gaining the weather gage, found that he could not use his

Between the hourglass and the watch bell (this one is from the Mary Rose*), even without clocks, the daily routine onboard ran smoothly with the turn over of watches being well regulated.*
(Mary Rose Trust)

Ships Lost in the Tudor Navy [30]

Reign	Total No of ships	Battle	Fire	Wrecked	Captured	Storm	Lost at sea
Henry VII	15		Mary and John				
Henry VIII	106	Regent 1513 Mary Rose 1545		Anne Gallant 1518 John Baptist 1534 Great Elizabeth 1514	Christ 1515 Roo 1547		Henry Galley 1513
Edward VI	74				Black Galley 1549 Brigantine 1552	(Moon 1553) Lion	Lion 1552
Mary	42		Henry Grace à Dieu 1553	Edward Bonaventure 1556			
Elizabeth	114	Revenge 1591		Delight 1583 Greyhound 1562	Flower de Luce 1562 (Jesus of Lubeck 1568) (Dainty 1594) Francis 1595	Pegasus 1599 Lion's Whelp 1591	Dennis 1578 Makeshift 1591

main armament because 'our ship as so weak in the side that she laid all her ordnance in the sea'.[31] Conversely, the Portuguese to leeward were able both to bring down the mast of Towerson's French ally and to hole that vessel, presumably using the swell and their leeward position to advantage. To give such gunners the best weapon platform from which to fire ships would reduce their sail area to just topsails and fore sail to retain steerage way but not be over-frisky. This sail plan is clearly indicated in the Cowdray print of the battle of the Solent in 1545. Not only would carrying more canvas increase the roll but it required more hands on deck to manage the sails rather than assisting in the gunnery or standing by to board. Conversely, ships under reduced canvas, making little headway would be inclined to roll more than if they were almost beam on to the sea. Thus it was roll than was the main problem and not heel.

A fleet that knew its ships could outsail its enemy might also not elect to close from windward. If it lay to leeward its superior's sailing ability would permit it to cut off an enemy trying to sail away to windward while its own position denied an escape to leeward. If it came to boarding, then, in any sort of sea, getting under the lee of an enemy would reduce the motion for the boarding party as they endeavoured to swing across, usually from the bow because the curve of the ship's sides meant that even if they were lying alongside a considerable gap existed at the level of the upper deck and, what is more, a gap that scarily opened and closed with no certain timing.

On six occasions only did the English meet their enemies at sea when both sides had fleet size forces available to them to deploy. In 1512, off Brest, the French admiral chose to cut and run, leaving Cordelière to face the foe alone. In 1545, almost it seems by mutual unspoken consent, Lisle and D'Annebault failed to exchange much more than insults both in the battle of the Solent and off Sussex a few days later. In 1591 the cautious Lord Thomas Howard chose to 'sail away from the Spanish fleet that day', leaving Sir Richard Grenville to his fate and his fame. Baskerville, a military man in command only because both Drake and Hawkins had died, also wisely avoided battle in 1595. Only off Gravelines, in 1588, did the English actually close

In this detail from the Cowdray print of the 1545 battle of the Solent, Henry Grace á Dieu can be seen approaching the enemy under just enough sail to maintain steerage way, thus giving her gunners a more stable weapon platform from which to take aim.

the enemy with sufficient determination and within effective range to fight what can be described as a fleet battle. In those shoal waters the experienced English masters handled their ships with the skill that only a life at sea in coastal waters could have given them, and they brought their ships out of battle in good shape to pursue the dispirited and damaged Spanish.

Up until that moment the seamanship stars of the Armada campaign had been the Spanish, for it would be wrong to view their fleet as one characterised by inexperienced leadership, unsound management and poor seamanship. Indeed, if Drake's circumnavigation marked the apex of individual seamanship in the age, the passage of the Armada from the Scillies to Calais was the pinnacle of fleet seamanship and management unsurpassed in the century. The problem facing Medina Sidonia is best summarised by an extract from a study of the art of sailing warfare written several centuries later when ship design, signalling development and many years of experience should have made the task of fleet commanders that much easier. Referring to the problem of station-keeping, Sam Willis writes:

> ... the inherent nature of the problems of sailing fleet cohesion and unity ensured that the problems of ship handling in a fleet were not solved by improvements over time, but merely eased. There was no glorious chapter of absolute control, because it was the very nature of sailing warfare that absolute control was unachievable. To attain unity and cohesion was the holy grail of fleet performance, not its defining characteristic. The best that could be expected in a sailing fleets was, '... for vessels of nearly equal size, placed at nearly equal intervals from each other – sailing, at nearly equal angles from the wind, and going pretty nearly at the same rate', and instructions issued 'in case of separation by bad weather or unavoidable accident' do not represent over-cautious and pessimistic commanders covering all eventualities, but were a fundamental and principal requirement for any number of ships sailing in company.[32]

To judge from that honest summary, between 29 July and 6 August 1588 the Spanish achieved the command and control of an amorphous mass of shipping and held it together as a cohesive formation in a way that would have made a Vernon, Anson or Kempenfeld proud. What is more, the Spanish achieved this while on passage through a narrowing Channel, which restricted movement, under the influence of strong tidal streams and in the presence of a hostile force which impeded readjustment. This was sea-shepherding at its best, and no other convoy in the annals of sea warfare can be said to have been so well handled in such unfavourable circumstances.

Sidonia also had to manage ships that were not designed to sail in these northern waters and had demonstrated their shortcomings in the storms that had scattered them in Biscay. It is the Armada's losses, while scattered and homeward bound, that have gained it its infamy, but the main casualties were vessels such as the Levanters that had been built for the safer waters of the Mediterranean, venturing out beyond Gibraltar only on trading voyages when their thinner frames

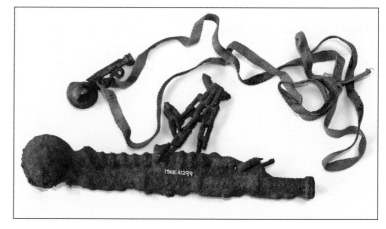

Examples of bosun's calls recovered from the Mary Rose. *An essential tool for command and discipline on board, they also became a recognised symbol of naval service.* (Mary Rose Trust)

and lighter construction could be compensated for by running before the weather or seeking shelter in port, their schedule of less importance than their safety. Eighty per cent of the Mediterranean-built vessels were lost, while only one of the galleons of Castille failed to return.

Each ship in the Armada's crescent-shaped convoy needed to be constantly vigilant, both to keep station and to prevent close-quarters situations from developing. The fleet, like any convoy, had to travel at the speed of its slowest vessel, but which ship this was would vary with the wind direction, the state of the tide and the currents inshore and in the offing. Allowance had to be made for ships to tack or wear, to increase speed or slow down, to heave to for transfers or to receive orders and to get underway again without blocking the way or forcing an alteration of course on those astern. One ship's sail plan might be inappropriate even for one of a similar class, depending on her lading and its distribution. On top of all this was the necessity for the watch-keeping officers to be able to judge the distance of not only the ships immediately ahead and astern of them but also those on their beam, and to be prepared to take avoiding action, should this be necessary, in a safe and timely manner. A modern analogy would be attempting to keep a steady speed on a crowded three-lane motorway while, at the same time, aiming to keep the same vehicles on the right-hand and left-hand sides with, of course, the motorway itself moving underneath all the vehicles, none of whom possess brakes, while incidentally weighing several hundred tons. In these crowded conditions it is unlikely that the distances between the vessels in the Armada, either ahead, astern or abeam, were less than two cables (400 yards), meaning that the fleet occupied a vast sea area which added to the problem of communications as well as ship-handling.

Given the circumstances, then, and the composition of the fleet, the Armada of 1588 cannot be criticised for the way in which it was handled. What is surprising is that only one accident was serious enough to lead to a vessel being lost, and even that was through capture rather than the initial collision. This is a record of which ship-handlers on either side and in any age would have been proud.

The tight and disciplined crescent formation that the Spanish Armada adopted for its passage up the Channel required many individual acts of expert seamanship for it to be maintained. It was probably a feat that the English, not used to sailing in convoy, would have been unable to emulate. (National Maritime Museum F8040)

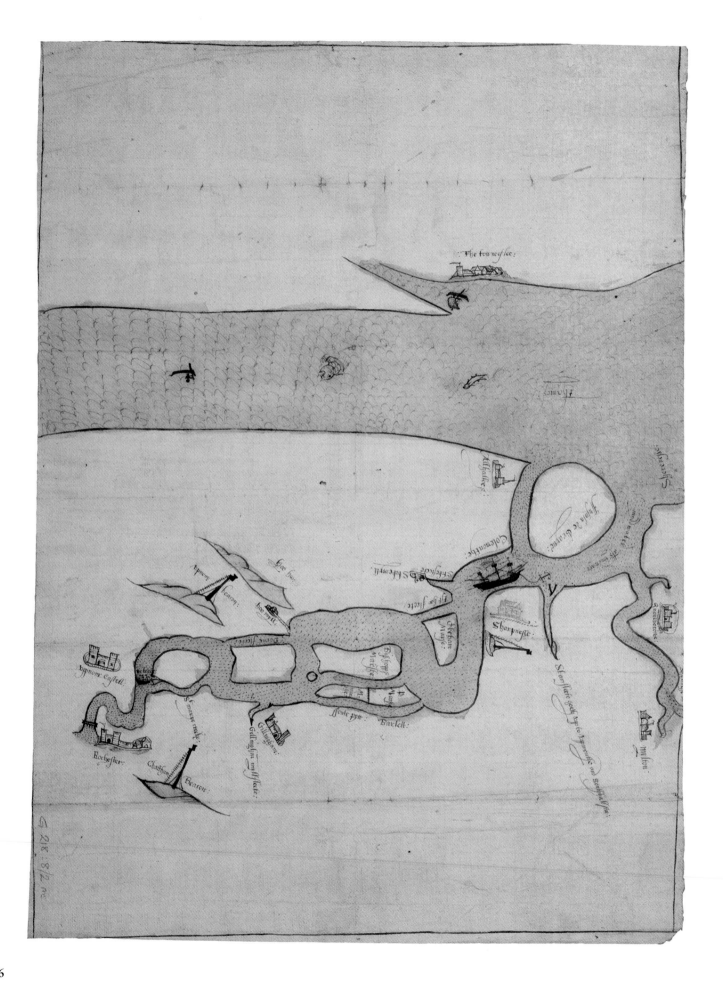

Chapter Nine

Havens and Harbours

... bring forth the soldiers of our prize,
For whilst our pinnace anchors in the downs,
Here shall they make their ransom on the sand.
Shakespeare, Henry VI Part II

The Tudor navy was a home fleet with its support centred upon Kent, while Portsmouth and Plymouth became its forward operating bases. Kent, wherein lie most of the Cinque Ports which had originally provided English monarchs with shipping when they required it, is England's eastern elbow, and its proximity to the Continent established its dominance. However, it was not a position that always found favour with it citizens, the leading members of whom complained late in the century that they had to 'bear a great burden of the soldiers of other ships, who lie there for want of wind and shipping'. Grumbling got them nowhere, and the county and its main rivers, the Thames and Medway, became the birthplace of many Tudor warships, and their home when not at sea.

The Thames

The Tudor monarchs were not great travellers. After Henry Tudor had returned from his enforced exile in 1485, with the exception of his son's military expeditions to the French coast the sovereigns confined themselves to England and mainly its south-east corner. This London-based existence also allowed them to keep close at hand those matters that they held dearest. This applied very much to their shipping. Henry Tudor kept his fleet at Deptford, in the crowded little creek which would have become a most familiar sight to his son, Henry, who was born nearby at Greenwich. The latter selected Deptford, and Woolwich, a few miles downstream, as the sites for his dockyards on the Thames, which enabled him to visit his ships with ease. He delighted in so doing and made of any launch an occasion for partying

The wide and welcoming Thames is contrasted here with the narrow and windy Medway, its passage for shipping aided by the placing of several very conspicuous beacons, while two pinnaces and several forts protect the shipping seen lying at Upnor. An anonymous chart made about 1590. (National Maritime Museum K1040)

and pomp, with the additional aim and advantage of impressing on foreign ambassadors the naval strength of his nation. With such advantages it is no wonder that the shipyards, rope walks and store-houses on the Thames were developed and kept busy with both shipbuilding and repairs. With the royal arsenal at the Tower, the convenience of fitting out and decommissioning artillery here was an added advantage, and the yards maintained their primary position well into the following century.

The Medway

Gillingham and Chatham, which was to develop into a major naval base, began to be important in the latter half of the century. In 1547 Robert Legge's accounts for naval stores during that year showed that £484 was spent at Colne, £1,211 at Portsmouth, £1,631 at Harwich, £3,439 at Woolwich, £4,167 at Gillingham and a massive £18,824 at Deptford.[1] Yet Deptford had its limitations as an anchorage, and in 1550 the Privy Council approved a plan for all ships to be laid up at Gillingham, including those at present at Portsmouth. One unforeseen and very important result of this policy was that Edmund Drake, fleeing Devon a fugitive as much from justice as from religious perse-cution, was able to get work there preaching to the bored sailors acting a ship-keepers and so introduced his son Francis to the life afloat. Chatham may have gained the floating hulks, but the docks and workshops remained at Deptford until Stuart times.

By 1578 a workforce of about 150 were building and repairing nearly two dozen ships on the Medway, while the provision of accom-modation for the members of the Navy Board emphasised Chatham's growing importance. Hawkins also had a new mast pond dug out at Chatham, whose burgeoning infrastructure was defended by the building of both Upnor Castle and a chain laid across the river, similar

to the one that could be hauled across the entrance to Portsmouth harbour. The Upnor chain, which, together with its winding gear, cost £290, had been provided after the government had discovered, in the Ridolfi plot investigations, a proposal that the King of Spain burn the ships moored off Rochester – an idea which the Dutch were to follow up in the next century. The chain necessitated additional fortifications both to protect its wheelhouse and to cut off alternative passages past it, such as St Mary's Creek. Downstream, Hawkins erected a line of warning beacons and arranged for their manning, measures that added further to the expenses; in its first year of operation the chain and its ancillary defences cost a staggering £1,500.

The Downs

The paucity of good southern harbours has no better illustration than the fact that the treacherous waters of the Downs off the east Kent coast provided a fleet anchorage for the Royal Navy for centuries. So notorious was this sea area that its most ill-famed shallows are mentioned in Shakespeare's *The Merchant of Venice* as being contributory to Antonio's downfall, as Salerio reports: '... Antonio hath a ship of rich lading wrecked on the narrow seas – the Goodwins I think they call the place – a very dangerous flat, and fatal, where the carcasses of many a tall ship lie buried ...' – so dangerous in fact that they claim the distinction of being the scene for Britain's greatest single loss of shipping in one incident, when the great hurricane of 1703 wrecked eighty ships anchored there, including ten naval vessels. Yet their shifting shallow sands served as a breakwater for easterly gales, while the land protected those at anchor from westerlies. Nevertheless only foolish masters would not have posted a wary anchor watch while in those waters. Arriving at the anchorage could also be difficult with a contrary wind, as was made clear in Edward Howard's letter of March 1513, quoted in Chapter 8.

The fleet did not always have a master on board with the local knowledge to sail these dangerous waters safely. In 1514 a pilot, John Wodlas, billed the Privy Council for pilotage dues for guiding *Mary Rose* through these waters to meet the king returning from France and then to take the ship out of the Downs and through the Black Deeps into the Thames.[2] This may well have reflected the fact that the less experienced and more cautious Thomas Howard, Earl of Surrey, was now the admiral, Edward having been killed some weeks earlier.

In November 1545 three Spanish and Portuguese ships, *St John*, *St Peter* and *St Saviour*, were apparently grounded on the Goodwins on the same day with some loss of life and, inevitably, much loss of cargo both to the sea and to scavengers.[3] In such circumstances, rescue of the crew was all that their masters could hope for; local avarice took care of the rest. The Lord Warden of the Cinque Ports considered the Goodwin Sands to be in his bailiwick; there are records to show that ships that grounded there were charged for 'compensation for the use of his sands and damage to them'!

A year later it was almost the turn of the Lord Admiral to be wrecked. In April Lisle, on board the twenty-tonne pinnace *Saker*, was

A later painting of the Downs showing the anchorage. Henry VIII built three forts, at Deal, Walmer and Sandown, to 'keep the Downs'; the last has disappeared but the others survive and can be seen in this painting. (British Museum).

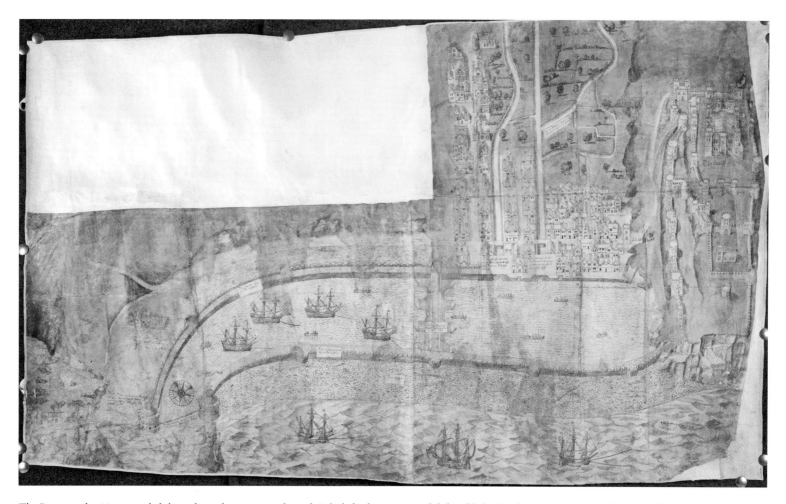

The Dover authorities struggled throughout the century to keep their little harbour open and defensible but its shortcomings meant that it would never develop as a naval port of any significance. In this sixteenth-century pictorial map, the harbour is bounded by a sand and shingle spit which is walled, with towers and a chain at the entrance. (British Library)

caught in a violent storm on leaving Calais and had much difficulty 'to fetch the Downs and avoid being cast upon Goodwin'. He presumed his consort, a new shallop, 'to be swallowed in the least of a great number of seas that came over her' but she went through it all and was at anchor in the Downs 'as soon as they'.[4] Back at Calais they had supposed their admiral drowned. The experience may have influenced Lisle to suggest, as he did, that the French threat was so limited that seven or eight of the great ships might return to port and 'be safe from tempests and yet ready when required'.[5]

In 1580 a proposal was made to erect a beacon and refuge upon the sands large enough to shelter up to forty shipwrecked men, but it came to nothing. Of more value, locally, was the opportunity for looting vessels that fell foul of the Goodwins: in November 1592 alone two Dutch ships and one English ship were completely stripped of goods, sails and rigging.[6]

Apart from the fear of shoals and shore engendered by adverse winds in the Downs, their presence could hamper onward passage down Channel. In June 1522 Vice-Admiral William Fitzwilliam complained by letter to the king that he had tried to sail down the Channel but been driven back to the Downs, with little hope of progressing west until the weather changed.[7] Such unplanned stays caused the usual problems with victuals being in the wrong place and,

in the Downs, harder to embark from boats on the steep pebbly beach by Deal. The Downs anchorage did have a strategic role in that a fleet lying here was well positioned to escort the army to Calais as it did in 1513, 1522 and 1544 and keep an eye on enemy shipping gathering either in northern France or in the ports of the Low Countries.

Dover

Dover was the sea gate from northern Europe into England and the only major cross-Channel port. While the English held Calais, traffic constantly moved between these two harbours, and when war was in progress it was from Dover that armies and reinforcements departed. Rich pickings thus lay here for any pirate to seize or any hostile state to disrupt, and the havens from which those threats could emerge had but recently crept closer. For most of the previous century the Pale of Calais had been surrounded by the lands of the Dukes of Burgundy, uncomfortable vassals of the King of France, whom England could woo in friendly fashion. But in 1477 Louis XI took advantage of the death in battle of Duke Charles of Burgundy to seize his lands, bringing hostile France to the narrowest part of the Channel coast and the borders of Calais. From that date on the Narrow Seas became the most important stretch of water in British history, and the keel of naval strategy was laid upon their command and control.

Unfortunately Dover was too shallow a port from which to dominate the seaway and the Downs too poor a place to lie at anchor. Dover did however have a high and formidable castle from where, as Sir Thomas Cheyne informed Cromwell in 1539, a better watch could be kept on all ships that passed through the Narrow Seas than by any boat or ship at sea.[8]

Given Dover's importance, it might be considered surprising that a fleet of ships was not based there to provide a permanent patrol in the Straits. The problem was that the small natural harbour, 'Paradise', was never deep and was constantly in danger of being filled up with silt and blocked off by shingle. In 1530 the entrance was destroyed by a gale and the crown was asked to provide £300 for its clearance. Three year later the mayor wrote to Cromwell that the harbour had ceased to exist and that unless some remedy was found the towns-people would have to forsake the town. That petition led to work beginning to build a 770-foot pier to deflect the shingle, but this had to be abandoned when the difficulties of piling into the deep water offshore became insurmountable. By 1534 the citizens were complaining that whereas once they had had twenty ships and small craft now the harbour was closed to them all.[9]

The harbour itself seems to have been in a constant state of disrepair. In January 1537 the result of nine months' work was dismissed because the supervisors had begun the work with no experience, 'but even as the blindman casts his staff; and so hath builded unto this day, thinking that he hath done well and is clean deceived'.[10] The work on the jetties and in the harbour itself was judged to be 'in small effect' because the four mariners, who were good seamen, understood nothing about building work while, so the writer implies, the foreman was fiddling the books, and the expenditure, listed in detail, was either insufficient, unnecessary or incompetently spent. This inefficiency brought the wrath of Thomas Cromwell about the ears of the Surveyor of the King's Works at Dover, John Thompson, who was told clearly that he had to 'do better service this winter than had been done in the summer'. What he did achieve is questionable, especially as he later wrote to complain of unforeseen bills raised by one of the contractors,

who was 'blind in one eye and can scarcely see from the other'. As far as Thompson was concerned the workmen that he had been allocated were not up to the job.

Aware of the importance of the port and the costs involved in keeping it open, Mary in 1553 gave the townspeople a monopoly of shipping and ferrying from the port. The petitions continued, and in Elizabeth's reign, by which time the harbour was open only to ships drawing less than four feet, the town proved to her 'how needful for this realm such a haven is in that place, which is at the point where the seas are narrowest and may for the apt situation thereof be accounted as one of the eyes of our country'.[11]

The result was that in 1579 a bold new plan with two jetties was proposed. This included a scheme to dam the waters entering 'Paradise' to form a pool which would be used to sluice out the silt in the harbour: ingenious, but at £18,200 it was too expensive. Instead a more modest proposal supported by Walter Ralegh was adopted in 1581. It too proved difficult, although work did begin on building a sluice gate across 'Paradise' and a new harbour below it called 'Great Paradise'. Yet again the workforce proved unable to challenge the elements: in 1584 the sea walls were breached and, to save money, the workers were discharged before the repairs were carried out. This time the deficiencies were swiftly remedied and a new 110-foot-long wall built to 'stand in the sea against the force of the waves'.[12] But, rather like that at Portsmouth, the work yet again may not have been up to scratch, for in 1588, Sir William Wyndham, in *Vanguard*, was expressing great dissatisfaction with the new harbour at Dover.[13]

The town of Dover, meanwhile, was taking on all the attributes of a naval port. In 1546 an Act of Henry was introduced to regulate the 'victuallers called tipllers', ordering that they hang out signs, keep good rule, exclude loose women and misruled persons, and throw out of their houses all dice, playing cards and tables. Twenty-seven such properties were listed in addition to ten inns, which were licensed to retail both bread and beer as well as feed for horses. As far as the port itself was concerned, all those who had shoreside frontages were ordered to scour their stretch of water, while all were forbidden to 'cast filth into the said river', an indication of the problem of water depth that always existed at Dover.[14]

The Cinque Ports

By the time Henry Tudor came to the throne, silt had settled the fate of the historic Cinque Ports, and their role in the century was more one of defending their privileges than of delivering on their responsibilities. Henry called upon them three times to provide shipping, but this was for transporting horses and store rather than the traditional ships for war. Most accounts of the Spanish Armada campaign do not even list them in their indexes. This is not surprising because the demands on their shipping were very small; Dover, for example, was asked only to provide a hundred tons of shipping, a task which it was unable to meet without the support of the eager burgers of Faversham, who hired the thirty-eight-tonne local vessel *Hazard* for the duration.

In this recent view of the lower town from Dover castle walls, the sand spit that constantly closed off the natural harbour at Dover can be clearly seen, now enclosing the marina. The modern port was built outside it by creating a large breakwater. (Author)

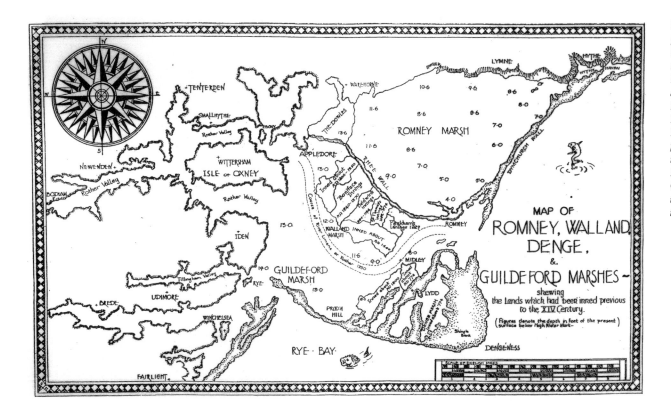

Along with her hire a crew of thirty men was recruited with a wage bill of £49 6s, covering wages that ranged from £8 4s for the captain and £3 for the master gunner to 10s for the boy seamen and the trumpeter.

In December 1595 the Cinque Ports were ordered by the Privy Council to provide four ships above 160 tonnes each to be available for service by 31 May and with victuals for five months.[15] This was for the attack on Spain known as the Counter-Armada, which was to climax in Essex's and Ralegh's famous assault of Cadiz. Yet even a demand of less than one ship per port was considered too great a burden, and the ports protested against the imposition.[16] In response the Privy Council reduced the core Cinque Port levy to two ships and two hoys, while Dover, Sandwich and Hythe were separately to provide two more ships of 160 tonnes. The state of the ports can be gauged by the fact that one of the vessels selected for the Cinque Ports' contribution, *Vineyard*, was chosen for them by Admiral Lord Howard, who had seen her lying at her berth in Deptford, and, further indication, Howard's letter was written to jog the tardy Lord Warden of the Cinque Ports into providing the crew for the ship.[17]

The silting-up of the Cinque Ports and the eastern Channel coast was not just a problem for trade and ship provision, for it left the Navy Royal with no safe haven between Portsmouth and the uncomfortable Downs. The one sheltered haven, the area below Romney Marsh where Dungeness now protrudes into the sea, was a bay known then as the Camber, through which vessels built at Smallhythe passed on their maiden voyages. In May 1514 the pilot John Wodlas anchored here to ride out a storm in the unfortunate *Salvator of Lubeck*, renamed *Great Elizabeth*, which had recently been purchased by the king but which was to be lost shortly afterwards while escorting Princess Mary to Calais for her marriage to the French king. In June 1522 Vice-Admiral Fitzwilliam also anchored here and sent the masters of *Mary Rose* and *Peter Pomegranate* into the haven to take soundings, along with a team from Rye, to see whether or not sufficient depth of water was available to lay up the *Great Harry* during the winter.[18] There was not, and little more is heard about this haven, which rapidly silted up and finally disappeared.

Portsmouth

Portsmouth, together with Portchester, had been a traditional muster point for English troops sailing to France. It provided the safest haven for ships to lie up, inside the harbour, and a sheltered anchorage at Spithead for operational vessels to assemble secure behind the great bulwark of the Isle of Wight. To this traditional role Henry Tudor added the further one of a dockyard and a shipbuilding centre, a move from the domination of the Thames that his son soon scotched. It was thus her importance as a fleet anchorage that led to the creation of major defence works that would make the town the best defended in Europe.

The principal natural defence of the harbour itself was its narrow entrance, even narrower before dredging could widen the channel, between the fortifications. What was equally important, however, was to ensure that no enemy could land at Southsea and outflank the harbour defences. This required the town itself to be protected with a wall, estimated at 1530 tailor's yards around. Impressed by these walls, in 1514 Thomas Howard informed the Privy Council that Portsmouth was 'the best fortified thing with bulwarks, trenches and great pieces of artillery thick laid in them that I ever saw or heard of' and that should the French, who were suspected of embarking an army, know this they would not dare enter the haven.[19] The port was soon to be fortified further by the arrival of 138 Flemish gunners hired at 6d per day.[20]

The improvement in fortifications continued throughout the

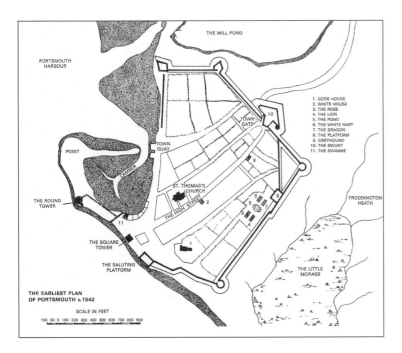

One of the earliest street maps of an English town, this map of Portsmouth shows clearly the narrow entrance to the harbour, and the large camber, the main port, lying behind the Round and Square Towers with their protective palisade. The easternmost cluster of four building grouped around a pond are the breweries that Henry VIII ordered to be built. (Mary Rose Trust)

century, and in 1539 Fitzwilliam, while reporting his interception of contraband shipping in the Solent, also stated that he had ordered two towers to be built at Cowes to command the central part of that water,[21] while at the same time Hurst Castle was built to guard its western approaches. But building and maintaining were not the same thing, and in February 1541 the French ambassador, Marillac, informed Francis I that 'most of the ramparts made about Southampton and Portsmouth have fallen, which shows that the work had been hurriedly done because of the fear of war two years ago'.

By 1544 fresh work was well underway, but it was a race to complete it before the much-anticipated French assault, for the usual lack of money to feed and pay the labourers was slowing work down. Then bad weather in May delayed the transport of stone and chalk from the Isle of Wight for the making of lime as well. Yet by mid-June Sir Anthony Knyvet seemed confident that both the new work and the repairs were well in hand, although French shipping activity off the Needles was causing some concern.[22] This was also the case a few days later, when he wrote again to the king stating that, although the new fortress (Southsea Castle) would be ready to receive its armament in twelve days' time, only two small sakers had been delivered and he lacked the minimum 'twenty great pieces of brass and iron' considered essential for its defence.[23] However, warming to the subject of inadequacy, a note entitled 'A view of things needful to be considered for the safety of Portsmouth', written almost immediately after the previous letter, concentrated on the town's defensive deficiencies. Pointing out that Portsmouth was one of the chief ports of the realm and one that great ships can enter at any state of the tide, the writer reminded the reader that it was also just a day's sailing from the major French Channel ports and yet remained badly manned to ward off a sudden

attack. Its armament included guns made for the old *Great Harry* (Henry V's ship!), eight gunners, compared with a hundred in the first French war and fifty in the previous one, and just a hundred able-bodied citizens to defend the decayed ramparts. The writer ended by begging 'your good lordships' to be 'mean to the King's Majesty that some number of men ... be sent to repair the decayed walls ... now in time of war'.[24] Reading this one wonders whether if, a year later, the French had landed on Portsea Island instead of the Isle of Wight they might have wrought more damage than they did.

That French assault of 1545 gave Sir Anthony Browne, Master of the King's Horse, an excuse to commission a picture showing him riding very close to Henry on Southsea Common while the English fleet moved out of Portsmouth to confront the enemy off Saint Helen's, during which passage *Mary Rose* capsized and sank in full view of the king. The resultant work was one of genius and it does give, inter alia, a very clear picture of how contemporary Portsmouth, with its fortification and breweries, must have looked.

Five year later Portsmouth was visited by King Edward, who recorded that he:

> Found the bulwarks chargeable, massy, well rampaired but ill-fashioned, ill-flanked, and set in unmeet places ... the town weak in comparison of what it ought to be ... the haven notable, great, and standing by nature easy to be fortified, and for the more strength thereof we have devised two strong castles on either side of the haven, at the mouth thereof; for at the mouth of the haven is not past ten score over, but in the middle is almost a mile over; and in length, for a mile and a half, able to bear the greatest ship in Christendom.[25]

– a most accurate summary and one that shows the young king had many interests in common with his father.

Although Portsmouth failed to develop its full potential during Henry's reign, in part because of the king's desire to be able to make frequent visits to his ships as they were built and maintained, Philip of Spain, when married to Mary, had no such attachment, and for him the advantages of Portsmouth were obvious. In 1555, with international relations reasonably quiet, Mary invited the Privy Council to bring the larger ships into the Thames to repair storm damage and to

The skilled artist of the Cowdray print has shown all the features of Portsmouth town that are depicted in the earlier map. Note the breweries and the beacon on top of the tower of Saint Thomas's church (now the cathedral). Also visible, beside the Round Tower is the capstan that wound the chain across the harbour mouth.

The Round Tower at Portsmouth guarded the northern side of the narrow harbour entrance. Its origins are pre-Tudor but it was rebuilt and strengthened during the sixteenth century. However, for much of that time it lacked both ordnance and soldiery to defend it. (Author)

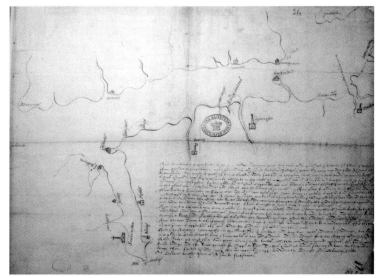

The defences of Portsmouth and the Solent developed throughout the century making it eventually the most heavily defended town in Europe. This official survey shows the state of the defences in 1587. (National Archives, Kew)

leave just a few of the smaller ships in the Narrow Seas. Philip, who was shown the note, appended in the margin that, although he was in agreement, he was concerned because 'as England's chief defence consists in her ships being always ready and in good order to resist an invasion', and as passage out of the Thames was always difficult there must be advantage in basing the fleet at Portsmouth. Thirty-three years later he received ample demonstration of the efficiency of that chief defence; one wonders whether he just forgot its efficacy or whether years of being an autocrat had made him convinced of his own-God supported invincibility. He did not get his own way with Portsmouth either, and neglect of the town continued: a report on the garrison in 1557 informed Mary that it consisted of a captain in the tower supported by just two soldiers.[26] Given this parlous state of the defences it is no surprise that the fleet was slowly removed to the Medway.

Throughout the middle years of the 1580s the fortifications of Portsmouth were improved, but in what would seem to have been a desultory fashion. First the camber was enclosed, and then the slaughterhouse was repaired and a pond new made indicating, the port's continuing importance as a victualling base.[27] Yet despite the work, Burghley was informed by the Earl of Sussex in November 1587 that he did not dare fire off a cannon from the tower at Portsmouth to celebrate the queen's birthday as he feared that the whole edifice would collapse, being 'too old and rotten'.[28] Perhaps it was this suspect quality that created another typical Tudor government ploy – the failure to pay wages when due. At Portsmouth it took two reminders before Burghley in December 1588 authorised payment to the artisans of their wages which they had not received since April.

The Central Channel

Between Portsmouth and Plymouth the paucity of fleet anchors was almost as bad as it was east of the Solent. This is ironic given the fact that Poole harbour was the largest natural harbour in the then known

world, but Poole, into which the river Piddle trickled, was more a puddle than a pool and was never suited to offering protection for sea-going vessels.

Thomas Howard, Earl of Surrey, thought in 1522 that he had discovered a usable haven. Anchoring his fleet off Dartmouth for afternoon refreshment with a few friends, he was delighted by what he saw beyond the narrow, well-defended harbour entrance – so much so that he wrote in fulsome praise of the port to the king and despatched the town's mayor, Nicholas Semer, to deliver the letter in person.

Surrey reported that he had never seen 'a goodlier haven' or one with such secure provision for winter laying-up of the fleet. True, he realised that an enemy might land at Tor Bay and attack the port from that direction, but that contingency, as he saw it, could be addressed by the building of a fort, the clearing of some woodland and the building of a wall which 'will cost no great money'. Surrey, also impressed by the close proximity of at least 2,000 'goodly oaks' on the king's park at Dartington, considered that this and other attributes

Although exaggerated, the shallowness of Poole harbour is very evident in this detail from a contemporary map and the port became a haven for pirate vessels rather than naval ships. (British Library)

In 1522 Lord Admiral Howard, Earl of Surrey, wrote to Henry recommending that Dartmouth be developed as a naval port. The harbour does provide a sheltered haven but its easily defended entrance is also too narrow to be safely negotiated in foul weather or adverse seas. Detail from a contemporary map. (British Library)

should remain at Plymouth until joined by Charles Brandon with a new army for Brittany. On 13 May he wrote to the king stating that:

> Whereas your grace willeth me to remain here till my said cousin Sir Charles' coming hither; Sir, under your correction, it is not to be done, for divers causes. One is we lie here in the most dangerous haven of England for so many ships, and lie moored together in strait room, and divers of your ships hath been in great danger, and nightly fall together; howbeit, God be thanked, there is no hurt done. Also, the wind blowing any part off the South, it is impossible to get hence.[30]

Howard's normal pedestrian style reflected the writing skills of a man who boasted of never having read a book, but this small passage vividly conjures up the worry of the ship masters and the bustling activity of the crews as they tried to fend off vessels that were slewing around on their moorings and crashing hulls, masts and rigging together through lengthy days and longer sleepless nights.

Howard went on to explain that for Brandon to come to Plymouth from Southampton, where his army was mustering, would take him way off his course for France and, if the wind continued southerly, might also bottle him up in the Sound, where before too long he also would run short of victuals. This latter point highlighted another shortcoming of Plymouth, whose westerly location and less abundant hinterland meant that it could not be as readily re-supplied as Portsmouth and Southampton.

In fact Howard's concerns had already been addressed by the king, for in a letter dated the same day to both Lord Lisle (he crossed out Lisle's previous name, Sir Charles Brandon) and Lord Howard, His Majesty crossed out the order for Lisle 'to take shipping at Southampton and resort to Plymouth or Dartmouth where the King's navy is' and replaced it with a line telling him to 'join the Admiral at Southampton'.[31]

The wind would have none of it, so although Howard told the king that if the wind served him, 'I will not fail to draw to Hamptonward', he failed and the next day, in typical Howard fashion, he began the excuses, writing to the king: '... we lie in the worst haven in England to get out of, for our army lieth in three parts, and all within Plymouth Sound, so that no wind save only North can bring us all forth without warping. I pray God bring the wind out of the South, or else none of us can get forth.'[32]

Equally concerned that Wolsey might misinterpret his inactivity as sloth, Howard wrote to him in a similar vein the next day, stating that although the wind direction was ideal for his passage it 'bloweth so sore' that the fleet could not get out of the Cattewater as it was 'full in our way.' He then added, 'Wherefore, I heartily desire you to call unto you some mariner that knoweth this coast, and then I doubt not you shall know there is nothing undone that may be done',[33] a rider that sheds much light on the mentality of this deeply distrusting, cautious and scheming soul.

On 15 May Howard reported that the fleet was under sail, but by 16 May he had to tell Wolsey that the wind had changed again at the last minute and the ships were back in the Sound. On 18 May, in a letter to the king, he gave another vivid picture of the position that he found himself to be in:

would make Dartmouth far cheaper to maintain than Portsmouth.[29] Luckily, the king listened deafly to the mayor's presentation, and Portsmouth remained the major south-coast dockyard, with Plymouth a forward operating base.

Plymouth

Travellers crossing the Tamar into Cornwall from Devon and looking down at the fleet lying peacefully at berths along the east bank of the river might imagine that this calm port had always been available for the English navy. But it was not always so. Before the move into the Tamar took place, the ships used to lie in the small bay of the Cattewater, where the River Plym discharged into the waters of Plymouth Sound. Here, before the great breakwater was built to protect the Sound from the large rollers that ran in on a south-westerly gale, ships could have an uncomfortable stay; Thomas Howard had no sooner arrived to take up his post as Lord Admiral in May 1513, following the death of his brother, than he was anxious to sail away.

Howard's desire was to be frustrated by the very weather that made Plymouth a poor naval port, albeit an excellent forward operating base, while the additional problems that he was experiencing led this most sycophantic of courtiers to challenge the king's orders that he

Beseeching your grace to take no displeasure that they, the victuallers, nor the residue of your army, departeth not hence, for I assure your grace, as yet it is not possible. We be all ready, and have been these six days; and now these two or three days past, the wind blowing at West-South-West, which is the best wind possible to bring us to Hampton, hath and yet doth blow so strainable that we have been forced every man to lay out shot, anchors and all, and have broken many anchors and cables. Assuring your grace that whosoever bought your new cables hath done you shrewd service, for they be made of the worst stuff that ever man saw ...[34]

adding for good measure that he would send the king a sample.

This is a vintage Howard: it includes in a few sentences an exoneration (his), a justification and a blame (on someone else). His choice of wording for the latter part illustrates his guile, for he did not place the blame on the cable manufacturer, who could indeed be a foreigner, but squarely on the purchaser, hoping that it was Wolsey who had authorised the contract; such small pin-pricks would suffice for the present until opportunity and confidence produced the dagger to stab the cardinal in the back. The records show that John Dawtrey, Wolsey's commissioner at Southampton, had signed for a delivery of Italian cables the previous March, and there would have been many other such deliveries organised.[35]

Two days later, Howard 'scribbled at Plymouth' a note to his 'beloved' master almoner while 'warping with much pain from Cattewater to the Sound'. In this letter, with its usual hypocritical ingratiations, as well as asking Wolsey to 'think no default in me of our long abode here, which is the most sorrow that might have come to my heart', he reported that his intelligence indicated that the ships of Brittany had been hauled out of the water as they had no intention of returning to sea that year. Howard himself appears to have got the fleet at last into Southampton Water by 1 June in time to meet the king, who, orally, cancelled the expedition against Brittany.

Having read of the problems which Howard experienced leaving Plymouth Sound, it may be appropriate to move ahead three-quarters of a century to the most famous departure from that haven in adverse conditions. When the Armada was reported as being off the Lizard, another Howard, Lord Charles of Effingham, was Lord Admiral and found himself in similar straits in Plymouth Sound, except that he had the incomparable, bowls-playing Francis Drake as his naval advisor, and Drake, by example and determination to warp rather than whine, hauled the English fleet out of the Sound in a timely enough fashion to gain the weather gage of the enemy by the following dawn.

Yet the strainable west-south-west winds, cursed by Howard, could prove difficult enough even for a skilled seaman like Drake. His great voyage of circumnavigation began with his departure from

Plymouth's defences were for a long time neglected until Elizabeth charged Drake with the task and a local levy was raised to pay for them. This plan, showing the fields of fire of defending batteries and forts, was drawn by Sir Richard Grenville. (National Archives, Kew)

Plymouth on 15 November 1577 only for a gale off the Lizard to drive his squadron to seek shelter in Falmouth, where, to save *Pelican* from being driven ashore, Drake had to order her main mast be cut down. Similar drastic action in *Marigold* did not prevent her grounding. The sore-damaged fleet had to limp back to Plymouth for repairs and did not finally get away until 13 December. Such events illustrate the paucity of sheltered harbours along England's western peninsula.

As a major forward operating base, Plymouth needed sure defences. In this it had, unlike Portsmouth, the advantage of a great champion in the person of Sir Francis Drake, who was appointed in 1590, when invasion scares were rife, in command of the defence of the town. The task, as so often with the spendthrift economics of the government, involved barrel-scraping. Drake managed to gather some armed vessels and a few potential fireships to use against an anchored enemy, and to place a small garrison on St Nicholas's Island (now Drake's Island) at the northern end of the Sound. A few pieces of artillery were borrowed to place on the Hoe and in the old castle but, when he stood back and looked at what he had achieved, Drake saw that it was not good. He therefore petitioned the Privy Council for funds to improve on the makeshift and to build a proper fort on the Hoe where, curiously, Henry had not placed one in his great building programme of 1538–45. Drake's argument was that:

> The fort being once erected, the town and the whole country should be more resolute and safe, which would be a great encouragement to the realm, and the enemy, knowing the artillery to be out of danger, would with less boldness enterprise that way. Now the harbour lying without any defence to make long resistance ... so that if the enemy had made his approach ... he had assuredly taken the town without resistance and carried away their ordnance.[36]

A year after receiving Drake's submission the Privy Council appointed a commission to examine the need to fortify Plymouth. The resultant report proposed that £5,000 be spent on walling the town and

building a fort on the Hoe. The council thought the cost too high and organised modifications to the plan which, unsurprisingly, in the end cost more.

Another year was to pass before, in May 1592, Elizabeth, noting that the port was one to which her navy had frequently to resort, and that it was not well defended from the sea against 'outward enemies in these dangerous times', required it to be made defensible by enclosure with a ditch, wall and bulwarks. Ever mindful of her subjects' love, the queen ordered that this work should not be paid for by the towns-people but by levying a tax of 18d on every hogshead barrel (fifty-four gallons) of pilchards transported by foreigners and 12d for every similar hogshead exported by Englishmen, with the tax remaining in force until the job was completed and paid for.[37] Once again the contrast with her father and his massive, rapid and expensive fortifications of the whole south coast is made obvious. The work at Plymouth was eventually completed in 1596 after the government had been forced to draft in an additional labour force of 500 men.

The East Coast

The English military required havens along the east coast for one main purpose only – to provision by sea ships and soldiers moving against Scotland. Because this was an occasional activity, no permanent ports or structures were required other than strong castles to defend the northern river crossings along the coastal road. Thus Newcastle, the Humber and Berwick all had a part to play, most especially when the state of the roads made it easier and more reliable to move an army by sea than over land or to divide the deployed forces between the two, although the availability of shipping could be a problem – as it proved in the 1544 campaign, when the coast towns had to be trawled for suitable vessels in which to embark the army.

Dublin

Probably the least-favoured and least-supported Tudor seamen were those who formed the small squadron that was based in Dublin. Their task, to keep the Scots galleys from reinforcing Irish rebels, was neither easy nor rewarding; their achievements are as yet not fully recorded.

Calais

Apart from Dublin, England's only other port away from the mainland was Calais, which the Tudors held for only the first half of their dynasty, although they captured and occupied Boulogne from 1544 to 1550. Calais was the route into the continent for English wool and the disembarkation point for armies invading France. Yet it was seldom used as a port in which to base a small fleet, although the harbour and its shallow waters offshore were capacious enough to provide for a squadron of rowboats or galleasses. The town itself was the centre of the English pale, which ran eighteen miles along the Channel coast and up to nine miles inland. Well fortified, with a good coastal defence in Fort Risbank, it was to greet Henry when he arrived both at the head of an army, in 1513 and 1544, and as a prestigious and peaceful monarch in 1520 on his way to the Field of the Cloth of Gold. On each of these occasions, as with the army landings in 1522 and 1523, the town's port would have been filled with transport vessels, vict-uallers and their escorts, warships, ferries and despatch boats. Yet although Calais was always considered to be a part of England, never 'abroad', its seaborne defences did not measure up to its being considered 'one of the most principal treasures belonging to this realm' and necessary for the defence of the country and the control of the Narrow Seas.[38] If it had been, Calais and Dover would have formed a northern Scylla and Charybdis between whose powerful defences, fixed and floating, none could pass without permission. This was the view of Lord Russell, who, writing to the Privy Council as the army was disembarking in 1544, thought the town ideal for supplying the fleet with bread and beer, especially as locally it was being offered at 16s per tunne whereas the beer being embarked at Sandwich was costing 20s per tunne.[39]

The speed of the inevitable French assault in 1558 left Mary scrambling to assemble her relief fleet on the English side of the Channel, and by the time that was ready to depart, it was too late to provide assistance to the already defeated garrison, who could have been supported had the ships been based there during the crisis.

With Calais lost, its greatest contribution to the English cause was when it provided a temporary anchorage for the Spanish Armada in 1588; until then the fleet had been immune from gunfire, and Calais's shallow roads offered the English an ideal opportunity to attack it with fireships.

Overseas

Away from the Channel, ideas of overseas bases were slow to take shape but the concept of controlling key waterways was being developed.

The South-West Passage

Although the English had entered the Pacific through a south-west passage, the intellectual goal remained the shivering chimera proposed by proponents of both a north-east and a north-west passage to Cathay. However, although the idea of holding ports and forts abroad ahead of opening such routes was occasionally raised, it did not translate itself into action. Hakluyt recommended that the English should seize the Straits of Magellan, as they were 'the gate of entry into the treasure of both the East and the West Indies. And whoever is Lord of this Straight may account himself Lord also of the West Indies.'[40] Hakluyt did not justify that last claim, and his plan had other shortcomings: he advocated that the fort he proposed should be manned by *cimmarones*, the escaped Negro slaves of the Caribbean, men brought up in the equatorial region, whom he would see settled in the icy south overseen by a few English captains and a good navy. Understanding of the queen's mind as well as any courtier, he suggested that it be seized by pirates, who could then be disowned should such a disavowal prove politic. Once seized, the settlement could then be reinforced by condemned English men and women, who could seek 'hope of amendment' in thus serving their nation. This is one of the first suggestions for penal colonies on record.[41]

Although a few Englishmen, slaves and felons would have been thankful that this idea was not taken up, the Spaniards, having been goaded by Drake to make such a move, established a fort in the straits in 1584 with some 350 settlers. The result was as one might have anticipated; by 1587, when Cavendish passed through unimpeded, only twenty of them were alive, and two years later Chidley found just one survivor. The eventual British response to controlling the Atlantic entrance to the straits was the settlement on the Falkland Islands, but to a certain extent the other door was left open and the Juan Fernandez Islands, of Robinson Crusoe fame, were not claimed by the

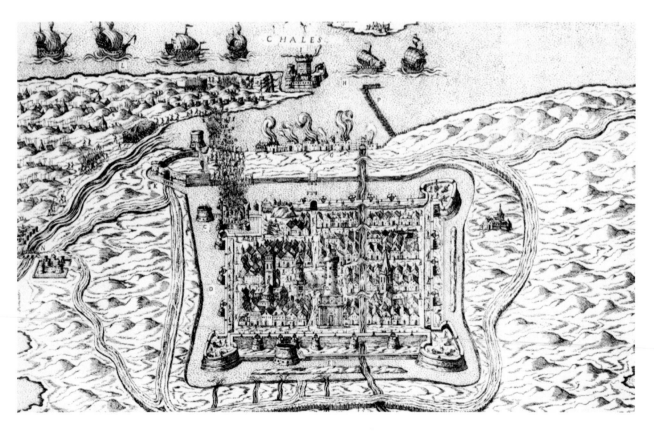

The successful French assault on Calais in 1558 was the result of an English failure to provide naval support in time. Before its capture, it had provided the English with a convenient and heavily defended port through which they could trade and land soldiers for campaigns in Northern Europe, but it was never a naval base.

crown. If they had been, the battle of Coronel in 1915 might have had a different outcome.

The Azores

In 1581 England almost gained her first foreign naval base. The year before, King Henry of Portugal had died childless and, before his own right to that throne could be challenged, Philip of Spain had the Duke of Alba march across the border to claim the nation for Spain. There was some resistance centred on the prior Dom Antonio, an illegitimate nephew of King Henry, but this faded away and Dom Antonio fled to France and then England, where he lobbied hard for support to reclaim the kingdom. He held one trump card. Terceira in the Azores had held out against the Spanish takeover and might have been used as a base to launch an uprising into Portugal. It was a strategy in which Dom Antonio hoped to interest the English, and with good cause.

Once the West and East Indies trade had been established, both inward and outward fleets and single ships headed for one central Atlantic hub to replenish before continuing with their voyage. This hub was the Azores, claimed by the Portuguese in 1439. Now that it was in Spanish hands, wealth beyond imagining was passing through its waters. The predator nations, England and France, were not unaware of the geo-political importance of the islands and cast covetous eyes upon them, for, with a base in Terceira, they could fall almost at will upon approaching treasure fleets, the distribution of wealth from which Dom Antonio promised to share generously.

Dom Antonio, seeing that his need and English greed could be served by the one objective, lobbied hard, reasoning, logically, that Terceira might be taken by forces under his flag but including a fleet commanded by Drake acting independently from the English crown, thereby avoiding a severing of diplomatic relations between England and Spain.

The idea was considered in April 1581 at the highest level, with Walsingham and Leicester providing the political input while Drake and Hawkins considered the naval requirement. This was put at eight ships, six pinnaces and 1,000 men, with the fleet to include the usual mix of royal and private ships. With the force levels agreed, the meeting turned to the costs, and these eventually proved too high for the venture. This being so, Burghley became anxious about the political repercussions and the scheme folded – fortunately, in the light of what happened next.

In the spring of 1582 a French force commanded by Philip Strozzi and including some English vessels sailed with the intention of landing on Terceira, the one island in the Azores that had declared for Dom Antonio. In response, King Philip despatched a fleet commanded by Don Alvaro de Bazan to prevent the landing. The fleets met in two

A map of the Spanish fort on the Straits of Magellan established in 1584. When Cavendish visited it in 1587 it was in such a poor state that he rechristened it Port Famine.

battles off the island. The first encounter was indecisive, but in the second, on 26 July, off Punta Delgada, the French were routed, and a year later Bazán returned and carried out a most impressive amphibious assault on Terceira in which his galleys, working inshore, were able to provide supporting fire to the landing force. The battle of Punta Delgada had repercussions wider than the fate of the Azores and the Portuguese throne, however. It convinced the Spanish, especially the Admiral Santa Cruz, who had poured scorn on the fact that the small English contingent present at Punta Delgada had chosen to flee rather than fight, of their superiority at sea, and consequently, when it came to planning the Armada campaign, Santa Cruz believed that the English fleet would fade away before the might of Spain.

That encounter was six years into the future, and by that time Santa Cruz was dead, but it is not possible to argue with great conviction that, had Walsingham and Drake been given their way, success would have crowned their efforts. The decisive Spanish thrust at the islands was more powerful than any force which the English fleet proposed could have repelled. Not for the last time, what appeared to be courtly caution and queenly parsimony saved the sailors from over-stretching their eager but meagre resources.

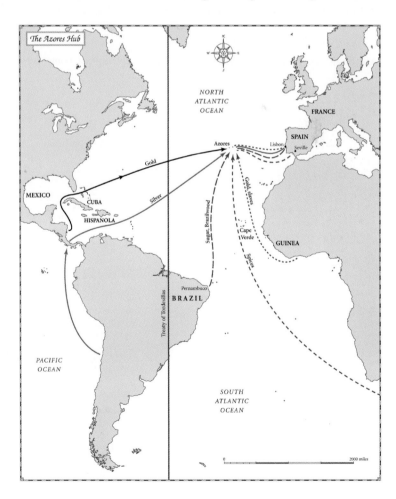

As long as the major trade routes led from the Iberian peninsula to the East and West Indies the Azores would be the focus point for all merchant shipping on these voyages as well as those wishing to attack these richly laden vessels The importance of control of this critical sea area is evident from this map

De Kraeck van Ste Tso mo

6

Chapter Ten

Plunder, Piracy and Professionalism

MISTRESS PAGE. *For sure unless he know some strain in me that I know not myself, he would never have boarded me in this fury.*
MISTRESS FORD. *Boarding call you it? I'll be sure to keep him above deck.*
MISTRESS PAGE. *So will I. If he come under my hatches, I'll never to sea again.*
Shakespeare, The Merry Wives of Windsor

It was an age of state-sponsored plunder. Henry Tudor plundered his peers; Henry VIII plundered his priests, and, with the cupboard then bare, Elizabeth won great acclaim for plundering foreigners as part of state policy. The latter made economic sense. In the absence of a bond market and with no monopoly over a valuable source of wealth such as gold, silver or spices, the government had to substitute plunder for debt if it was to pay for its wars. Yet war also removed markets, and merchants had either to let their vessels rot at empty wharfs or arm suitable ships to seize the goods they lacked on the open-waters market. Spain itself had few goods that the English merchants desired, but it was the entrepôt for what they richly prized; gold, silver, spices, jewels, sugar and ivory. Pre-war traders had to sail there with generally low-value bulk items such as grain and woollen goods for sale and purchase at a high price at markets where they themselves could never strike favourable bargains. In the open ocean, or in distant ports, they could obtain the same goods merely for the price of some powder and shot and the loss of some seamen, all of which came cheap. The profit soared beyond the dreams of avarice and led to the development of London as the world's emporium once the trade was, once more, legitimised. Yet for many merchants the difference between trade and plunder was simply the issue of whether or not the goods had been paid for; if they were seized from a potentially hostile or competitive power holding to a different religious creed, then the action could be claimed to have served God, government and greed alike. Thus the state wealth of Tudor England was

founded on a 'plundocracy', to which the navy was the major contributor for the last sixty years.

This age of avarice thus engendered a century of endemic piracy with the crown, at the start, concerned with the pursuit of pirates and, at the end, with their support. This meant that many mariners were both poachers and game-keepers, and frequently both at the same time. Often a career move, as in the case of Frobisher and Drake, led to the legitimisation of their activities, and often advancement, as in the case of Howard of Effingham and Thomas Seymour, created opportunities to make illegal activities untouchable. Yet whether or not the ship being intercepted belonged to a merchant or a pirate, its pursuit and capture led to the training of English seamen in the art of fighting at sea. Learned fighting instructions could develop the concept of war at sea being an extension of land warfare, with fleets drawn up into van, main and wings and closing to fight a soldiers' battle afloat, but this was not the school to which England's naval men were sent.

The 'trickle-down' effect of plunder: Henry VIII's dissolution of the monasteries put a lot of money into the Treasury through sales of property like the great estate of Buckland Abbey, near Plymouth. It was purchased by Richard Grenville, who eventually sold it to Francis Drake, demonstrating the enormous returns to be gained from piracy or privateering.

They learned their trade in battles of no renown, in conflicts of dubious legitimacy, in unrecorded clashes often devoid of chivalry. They were sea wolves, not sea knights, and they learned to fight dirty. This was what the English did best, and they did it frequently and with relish, winning through against great odds, because for many of them life itself was not much to lose. Piracy trained the English well. When it came to the greatest fight of all, those used to plying the long West and East Indies bus routes could not be expected to master the sea-wise fighters of southern England.

Protection

There were annual voyages that warranted protection. The wine trade from Gascony was one where a convoy system had long been in place, while the Icelandic fishing fleet was often 'wafted', or convoyed, home. Yet venturing up the Channel, or even across it at its narrowest point, could be perilous for any who tried to run its length alone. The wool merchants certainly found it so and approached Henry VIII in 1511 to voice their complaints about the depredations of the Scottish pirate Sir Andrew Barton, who was seizing their goods as they sailed towards Flanders. Barton, it would appear, justified his actions because he held a letter of reprisal, but as this was for goods seized from his father by the Portuguese its validity is highly questionable. The merchants' grievance was overheard by the attainted Earl of Surrey, who, undoubtedly seeing here an opportunity to be restored to his dukedom of Norfolk, volunteered his two sons, Edward the younger and Thomas, to 'waft' the wool fleet and, if possible, seek out and destroy Barton's fleet of two ships. The brothers made contact with Barton in foggy weather off the Downs and, while Edward pursued and captured the escorting pinnace, *Jennet Pirwyn*, Thomas Howard fought a hard fight with Barton's *Lion* which ended when Barton was killed by an arrow. Both ships were taken into their Thames, and, in a rare act of clemency, the king granted the surviving crew a safe passage home provided that they eschewed all future piratical activity. The ships themselves were enrolled into the king's own fleet, an action that led to much protest from James IV. Thus the Howard brothers gained their first experience as Henry's sea commanders in the fight against piracy that was to be pursued, with more or less effort, throughout his reign. In 1511 the future naval Clerk Controller, John Hopton, was ordered to sea to pursue pirates, and their prosecution remained a primary concern of the king, sometimes through preventive action, sometimes, when it suited, by proclamation.

Henry remained concerned about piracy. In 1527 he ordered Arthur Plantagenet, then Viscount Lisle, to 'make inquisition concerning and punishing all treasons, murder, piracies etc. committed at sea within the jurisdiction of the Admiralty',[1] for it would seem that during this period English sailors were, unusually, more sinned against than sinning. In April 1528, William Gonson, on patrol and escorting duties in the Channel, reported daily encounters with French and Dutch ships of war 'seeking prizes',[2] including three Dutch ships intent on seizing the wheat-laden ships Gonson was escorting from Boulogne to London. The fact that it was worth risking life for a hold of grain speaks eloquently about the times and about how endemic piracy was.

So in 1536, when the Holy Roman Emperor, Charles V, clashed

For much of the sixteenth century a state of near anarchy existed on the high seas. When possible English merchants sought protection for their vessels from friendly warships but only the main convoys, to Bordeaux for wine, and to Iceland for fish, were provided with escorts as a matter of course. This detail from a contemporary map shows a large warship protecting the coastal trade in Weymouth Bay. (British Library)

with the French king, Henry, wanting to ensure his own neutrality, issued a proclamation directing his subjects 'on pain of the king's high displeasure and indignation and forfeiture of all their goods and also imprisonment of their bodies not to take advantage of the belligerents by seizing their goods'.[3] This was no idle measure for purposes of presentation. As Henry had found with the Barton case, unchecked piracy could affect state relations, and it continued so to do throughout the century, with English, Dutch, Spanish and French governments all accusing the others of failing to control, or even of encouraging, their pirates.

Low-level piracy was an ever-present activity within the Channel, where, with a good lookout and a favourable wind, a pirate could sail after breakfast, seize a passing ship and return in time for supper. In a subsistence economy he would not have cared too much what cargo had been captured, for everything could either be eaten or sold to improve the brutish conditions of the sea peasantry. Having seized the goods, the pirate had to decide what to do with the captured vessel and her crew. The presence of the former might cause awkward questions to be asked locally; the survival of the latter might cause even more embarrassing depositions to be made in court. Many a fine vessel would have been scuttled, many an innocent mariner drowned, unless of course they were marketable with few questions being asked. However, low-level pirates when caught faced the ultimate penalty. On 27 February 1535 the Admiralty Court passed a sentence of death on six of them,[4] but there were many more willing to take their place.

Perennial pirate activity made the Channel the most lawless place in Europe, and few could sail it with equanimity. In times of war it was even riskier, as pirates were handed written authority from the state which they could use to intercept all but their own countrymen. The result was that governments were constantly protesting about state-sponsored theft, in most cases both hypocritically and to no avail. In England the pursuit of such pickings reached a stage whereby the Cinque Ports themselves supported other nations' pirates. The vice-admiral, Fitzwilliam, wrote to Cromwell in February 1537 that he had heard that certain Flemish pirates were lying in the Camber and

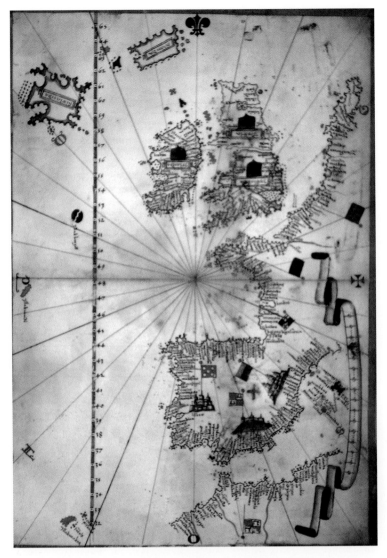

For petty piracy few waters were more dangerous than those of the coast between Harwich and the Firth of Forth. The permanently strained relationship between England and Scotland meant that for most years pirates could justify their actions as being in pursuit of national policy. The political fact that Scotland and England were two separate and opposing kingdoms influenced the creator of this map, who shows the two nations divided by a wide channel.
(Royal Naval Museum, Portsmouth)

robbing English vessels while being victualled by merchants in Rye.[5] Fitzwilliam's letter, copied to the Warden of the Cinque Ports, would have been an interesting read for that gentleman, who would have been faced with some embarrassing explaining. On a practical side Fitzwilliam dispatched the hard-working *Minion* to join Willoughby and Kirke in 'wafting' into the Thames any English ships lying at the Camber.

As the danger increased the king found it necessary to appoint Sir John Dudley as vice-admiral to patrol the Channel with four ships in order to prevent French and Flemish ships from seizing English vessels in total disregard of England's neutrality. Henry was, however, still determined at this stage not to give cause for offence himself, and instructed Dudley in March 1537 to:

preserve discipline among the young men and not allow attempts for covetousness or any breach of treaties. He shall endeavour to prevent unlawful taking of prizes and do his best to compel restitution or apprehended offenders, taking the ship to one of the king's ports until he know further the King's pleasure and having an inventory made of all things in her signed by the captain and master, and setting the prize at liberty. He must, however, use foresight and avoid danger, not to cast himself into the hand of enemies.[6]

One cannot imagine a Drake taking much notice of the last part of those instructions, but Henry had it far easier than did Elizabeth when she was faced with the need for accurate inventories, for the gold and jewellery of New Spain was not yet being transported to Europe. For the most part English naval vessels on interdiction duties would find bulk items of small value within the holds of those that they stopped and searched. Henry, for example, in his orders quoted above, had been most keen that Dudley should recover a ship of his laden with brazil wood which the 'Admiral of Sluys' had seized after she left Southampton. A few days later, Dudley, being alerted by the presumably repentant mayor of Rye of a robbery off the coast, sailed and, finding the suspect pirate anchored in the Downs, anchored close by and began parleying. His report brings the event to life:

Seeing what a great brag they set upon it, for they made their drumsalt to strike alarm, and every man settled them to fight, the Sweepstake then being four miles behind us, but Lyon was to come to an anchor within a little of the other ship, [I] caused his master gunner to lose a piece of ordnance by the Admiral's ship, not touching him by a good space but he sent one to my ship and mocked not with me, for he break down a great piece of the deck of my ship and hurt one of my gunners. I then trifled no more but laid her aboard and after a short fight she surrendered.[7]

The other ship fought until she saw that her admiral had surrendered and then slipped her anchor and sailed off, pursued by *Lyon* and *Sweepstake*. The 'Admiral of Sluys' was anything but defiant. He claimed the shipment of brazil wood had been seized by another pirate, also known as the admiral of Sluys, and that his men had fought against his orders. In a later report he also claimed that he and his men had turned to piracy because his owner, the master of Camfyer, 'sent out so many ships without wages that they must be robbers'.[8] There then came a piece of Gallic charm in that, as Dudley reported, 'he does not deny that he has borrowed now and then a piece of wine of Englishmen and sometimes a barrel or two of herrings but it was with their good wills'. The shocked admiral informed him that this was just not on: 'I told him that this was not the fashion of gentlemen and Englishmen would be severely punished for taking anything of the Emperor's subjects' – just a few lines that show that for all the feuding, slaughter, robbery and guile opponents could still treat each other with gentlemanly respect. It was a style that Drake was to make a fashion and that became yet another naval tradition. We see it manifest here for the first time in Dudley's dealings with his captive.

This was not the end of the matter, for the Privy Council required the Mayor of Southampton to make a report of the 'depredations of

Flemings' affecting his shipping. The mayor responded with a lengthy account beginning with the activities of the 'Admiral of Campvere' who had seized Gascon wine from a ship off the Isle of Wight and then taken ships laden with herring and clothing.[9] Three features stand out in this lengthy list of seizures: firstly, how close to the English coast many of them took place, for example within the Solent; secondly, what inexpensive and everyday items the pirates seized; and thirdly, how carefully every item was accounted for; for example when the 'Admiral of Sluys' boarded the ship belonging to John Baddill of Hythe, he removed:

> Three barrels of beer, price 7s 6d., a last of fresh herring £4, an anchor and cable 40s., five bows and four sheafs of arrows 16s 8d., nine frieze mantles 30s., two cloaks 10s., 20 jerkins, petticoats and slops, and 20 shirts 40s., two violet coats 10s. ... a coat of 2s 4d., and money 2s 8d., four frocks 10s., also victuals 26s 8d.[10]

That short list gives us some idea of the basic living standard enjoyed by most English and Flemish seafarers who were prepared both to risk so much on passage and to seize so little by way of reward. Below the grandeur of the court subsistence was the harsh way of life for most. Forty years later the cargo available for interdiction had increased in value over a thousand-fold, and the area where it was to be taken had moved from the coastal waters of the Channel to the open Atlantic. It was in its search for and the taking of this new wealth from both Indies that the English navy developed its professionalism. Piracy was clearly in the infant navy's genes. Yet at the same time the nation had to occupy itself with endeavouring to keep its own moat free of felons.

In July 1537 Sir John Dudley was ordered back to sea to patrol between the Downs and the Scillies and into the Severn estuary with 'a good eye to the succour of English merchants', apprehending, if Dudley had the advantage of strength, any French or imperial vessels suspected of 'spoiling' English shipping and punishing them as pirates.[11]

It began dully. On 1 August Dudley reported that he and Sir George Carew had seen not one man-of war of any nation.[12] A fortnight later he reported to Cromwell that he and Carew were 'the heaviest of men that ever bare lives to have done so little service in so long space'.[13] He did, however, add the cautionary note that he had informed the king that George Carew's ship was taking in so much water that the master was unwilling to continue sailing in her with winter coming on. A few days later they captured two Breton pirates who were waiting off Portsmouth for two other ships to sail from there with one of the few valuable cargoes to be at sea, £3,000 of tin.[14] Instead of bringing his prizes to the Thames, as he had stated he was doing, it appears that Dudley sailed westward again, for on 28 August Cromwell was informed by Sir William Godolphin that the vice-admiral had taken four Frenchmen after a spirited fight at Mount's Bay in Cornwall, an act which brought a swift protest from the French ambassador, Castillon.[15] This was somewhat disingenuous, for the French were in marauding mood. Early the next year four French ships drove a laden 'argosy' sailing from Southampton aground just below the unmanned fortifications of Portsmouth, boarded her and sailed her away.[16] Henry, however, at this stage was determined to indicate to his potential European adversaries that he was sending his navy to sea only in response to complaints of piracy from his merchants. Indeed,

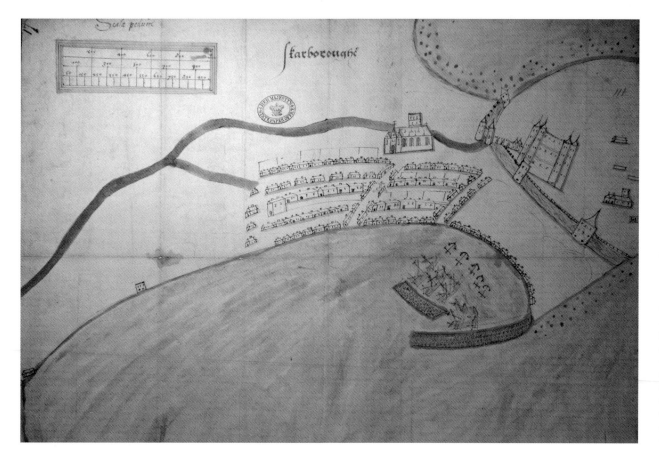

The waters off Scarborough were a favourite haunt for Scottish pirates who soon learned that the town's defences were seldom manned and, even when they were, had limited supplies of ammunition and few experienced gunners. The citizenry appealed to Henry VIII for assistance but were told to rely on self help or pay the Crown dearly for support. This contemporary map shows that the town had little to rely on for defence beyond the medieval castle on the bluff above the town. (National Archives, Kew)

Henry had even handed the pirate 'Admiral of Sluys' over to imperial jurisdiction.[17] We can assume that the miscreant was treated lightly.

The royal clamp-down on piracy continued year upon year. In 1539 Henry ordered the arrest of all ships, English or otherwise, who were operating without a royal licence.[18] Later that year Fitzwilliam, the Lord Admiral, now the Earl of Southampton, boarded and seized the ship of a Spaniard lying off Newport, Isle of Wight, that he suspected of illegal trading and seized its money and goods. In his report to Cromwell on the matter he also expressed his belief that there was much 'deceitful packaging' of dutiable goods often practised to the king's loss.[19]

The English did not have it all their own way: even in the North Sea coastal traffic required escorting when the troubles were at their greatest. During the free-for-all that existed in 1544 and 1545 the Privy Council ordered that ten ships laden with wool were to be 'wafted' from Boston, through Yarmouth Roads and Orford Ness and 'through the Sands' to the Downs, an inshore passage that should have been normally free of risk while the English fleet was at sea.[20] But these were not normal times: Henry was trying to bully the Scots into agreeing to the marriage of Prince Edward to the young Scottish princess Mary Stuart, and his 'rough wooing' included an amphibious assault on the Firth of Forth which did not impress the relatives of the potential bride, who responded in kind.

In November 1544 the Mayor and Alderman of Hull complained that the state had been very 'slack in furnishing ships of war for their defence', and that they had had to man three themselves, paying for them out of their citizens' pockets. Two of these had been driven home by the Scots fleet while the third was sheltering at Dover, leaving just *Trinity* of a hundred tonnes and a thirty-tonne bark to defend their shipping. The worthies of Hull, it can be supposed, were writing in support of their friend at Scarborough, who, having been taken to task for not providing vessels for the defence of their traffic, had written to Shrewsbury that they had only 'four small crayer under 50 tons, good to pass by the coast, but not meet for war but to wait on greater ships', and that these ship had a dearth of ordnance. However, if they were given guns and ammunition and an impressment order they would be prepared to send them to sea as warships.[21] A few days later the burgesses of Whitby, fearful as to which way the wind was blowing, wrote a letter to explain that they could not furnish ships for war because all theirs had been sold, 'owing to the decay of the harbour'. However, of course, if the means could be found to 'amend' the harbour then no finer haven existed between the Humber and the Forth in which warship could ride: a gallant attempt to reap local benefits from the international crisis.[22]

The Channel was constantly in need of sweeping against pirates. In 1576 Henry Palmer was told to clean it of those who 'infested the narrow seas' and preyed on honest merchants. The following year both licences to plunder and orders against sea-rovers were issued, raising the question of who was authorised to do what unto whom. In the same year, Elizabeth cancelled a two-page letter authorising Sir William Morgan to sail on a voyage of discovery with a two-line codicil stating, 'instead of this make a permission to take pirates, according to her majesty's warrant', which gives us an idea of where her priorities lay.

The need to 'waft' even coastal convoys continued throughout the century. For example, in October 1591 two masters of Trinity House were instructed to inspect the wine fleet and order any strengthening measures they thought necessary, including impressing two war-like merchantmen lying in Thames which they were to fit out as escorting warships. In 1596 the burgesses of Newcastle were again being criticised for losing ships to Dunkirkers and were told to furnish their ships with 'iron ordnance, powder and some calivers or muskets'.[23] Yet the emphasis had changed. The second half of the century saw the English far more interested in plunder than in protection.

Plunder

Plunder and piracy: it is as difficult to compartmentalise these activities as it is to assign titles to their perpetrators: rover, pirate, freebooter, corsair, buccaneer (for the term 'privateer' and the conditions for operating as one had yet to evolve). Nevertheless, whatever their title, and claim of legitimacy, the best generic term for these activities is 'maritime armed robbery'. There was a legal nicety. The Admiralty Court could issue a 'letter of reprisal' which enabled a merchant who had been robbed by foreign subjects and not received redress to seize goods, of a value equivalent to his loss, belonging to fellow nationals of the offender. This was a specific, targeted, legal and internationally recognised peace-time device. In time of war a sovereign could issue a general proclamation authorising seamen to seize enemy shipping. Neither method was adhered to, as the authority for action was used as a starting line, not a limiting one; legitimacy was based on the size of the booty and the person whose fingers were allowed in the pie. Having introduced these caveats, it must be said that a system of restitution could and did work without resort to 'letters of reprisal'. In July 1546 the owners of the *Katheryn of Bristol*, while sailing from Neath to La Rochelle, fell in with a Breton ship whose master owed them £100. Seemingly amicable discussions led to both ships sailing to St David's, where 'without compulsion, the Breton delivered him 11 tun of wine, price £22, and 9 ton of salt, price £6, as parcel of the said £100'.[24]

More often than not, however, the state protected that which its citizens had procured, however it was obtained. In early 1529 Margaret of Savoy, the Emperor's Regent in the Netherlands, wrote to Henry about an unfortunate Spanish ship-owner, Jehan Dacorde, who had been forced to shelter his fleet from the weather in the Camber, near Rye, only to have two of his ships sunk by Frenchmen and a further four driven ashore and plundered by them. To further his woes the grounded vessels were stripped of their rigging and ordnance by the English. His call on the Privy Council for restitution having fallen on deaf ears, he was asking the regent for letters of marque, which she was loath to issue without informing Henry first so that compensation could be awarded by her ally.[25] It probably wasn't.

Letters of reprisal served, however, one excellent purpose at the outbreak of hostilities: they released the sea dogs of war to chase and snarl at enemy shipping in advance of the mobilisation of the Navy Royal, with its victualling needs and limited numbers of hulls. In effect those who took them up acted as an advance party of maritime mercenaries but one who, cleverly, paid for themselves and made no demands on the state coffers. It also meant that not only was the fight taken to the enemy coast but also the Navy Royal could be kept together to defend the home shores.

If the Tudors had to act under a semblance of legality in times of peace, conflict created an open season. By 1543, with an isolated England under threat from a continental alliance, Henry invited his pirates to strike the first blow, and in December 1544 he issued a declaration which gave 'full power and licence to all singular, his subjects of all sorts, degrees and conditions, that they and every of them, and, at their liberty , without incurring any loss, danger, forfeiture, or penalty ... prepare and equip to the sea such and so many ships and vessels furnished for war', in return for which they were to 'enjoy to his and their proper use, profit and commodity, all and singular such ships, vessels, munition, merchandise, ware, victuals and goods of what nature and quality soever it be'.[26]

Moreover the king called upon the 'officers of port towns to help that this liberty may have substantial effect; and forbidding the taking of mariners, munition or tackle from such as so equip themselves'. Given the enthusiasm with which those so licensed pursued their opportunities and the way they handled those whom they captured, this proclamation of legal maritime banditry takes its place with all state-licensed thuggery, be its perpetrators wearing brown or black shirts or seamen's jerkins.

The free-for-all at sea that the issue of letters of reprisals created during the otherwise phoney war against the mainland Europeans in 1544 and 1545 caused continuous tension between Henry and the emperor, with both parties justifying their own subjects' behaviour at sea while condemning similar activities by the others. In January 1545 English warships took thirty Flemish ships laden with salt and brought them into the Thames.[27] However, on St David's Day that year there came a tectonic shift in the scale of plunder available at sea. On that day Robert Reneger, using an inapplicable letter of marque granted in 1543 and a dreamed-up story of deprivation, seized the *San Salvador* on passage from Hispaniola to Seville. The gold bullion part of her cargo alone was estimated at £4,300 (£1.3 million in modern terms). Faced with this new source of income and ambassadorial protests, the king acted swiftly. The bullion was sent to the Tower for safe keeping and dust-settling storage while, the officially disowned Reneger and four of his ships, *Trinity Reneger*, *James Reneger*, *Gallion Reneger* and a French prize, *Marlion*, joined the Lord Admiral at Portsmouth to meet the French invasion fleet in July. One can assume that his support was neither unexpected nor embarrassing and, this being the case, that Reneger had been acting at the least as an auxiliary to the Navy Royal. Van der Delft, the imperial ambassador in London, reported to Charles V that he had been welcomed 'civilly rather than cordially' by the Privy Council when he went to raise the unresolved matter of Spanish goods being seized by Reneger; in his description, Reneger, 'having outraged all treaties and rights ... instead of being punished like a pirate, was treated like a hero'.[28] The wise Van der Delft saw through the English game, which was, as he reported, to 'seize every-

thing they meet at sea as French' and then refer claimants to the Admiralty. To support their position the English mariners were, so Van der Delft alleged, falsifying bills of lading and selling the goods at 'wretched prices', presumably in order to get a quick sale, thereby making recovery all the more difficult. Of course, the Privy Council counter-claimed, citing wrong rendered unto English merchants by the emperor's subjects and commands. It was classic international intransigence, with neither side willing to stop its privations first, thus condemning many merchants and ships' crews to a miserable existence, but, luckily, out of view of those at court, whose main concern continued to be the balance of gain. Charles V was not fooled either, succinctly telling both Chapuys and Van der Delft that they should inform the Privy Council that the emperor could not accept excuses for English attacks on his neutral ships because 'Netherlands merchants can easily be distinguished' and Henry was 'so well obeyed' that he could ensure compliance with his own letters of marque.[29] The king was, certainly, prepared to be even-handed. In 1546 he issued a letter to all magistrates ordering them to arrest all ships of Cork arriving in England unless restitution was paid to the Portuguese merchant Peter Alves, who had been seized along with his ship, *Sancta Maria de Sae*, and landed in Wales while the ship and its cargo of salt, oil and vinegar were taken to Cork, 'whose inhabitants, favouring the pirates, bought the ship and goods'.[30]

That order can almost be seen as the end of the pretence of legality

Trading hulks were the most common and easiest merchant ships to capture while on passage through the Channel. Their cargoes tended to be basic commodities but, added to the marketable value of this, came the opportunity for ransoming hostages and selling on the ship itself. Some thirty Flemish hulks like these were captured in January 1545 alone.

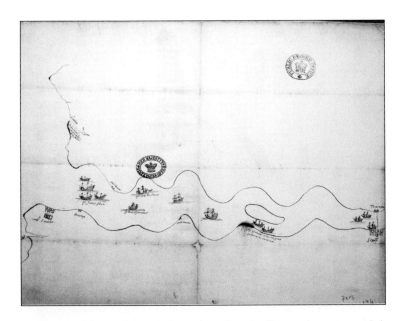

The mouth of the Guadalquiver, downstream from Seville, was the most crowded anchorage in Europe, and the richest. Outgoing convoys would assemble here while those returning heavy laden would have to anchor to wait for the tide to carry them up to the city. The gently sloping beaches also provided ample space for ships to be careened and made seaworthy for their next voyage. This English document from the State Papers is thought to date from 1604, but in detailing where the galleons lie and the 'bank with treasure', it suggests an ongoing official interest in the capture of Spanish bullion. (National Archives, Kew)

at sea, for where Reneger led the rest followed, establishing rapidly the concept that officers in the sovereign's service were as much entitled to break the law at sea to their master's advantage as well as anyone else. Thus Thomas Wyndham, a naval man, went on a plundering voyage a few years after Reneger's return in *Mawdelyn Russell*, owned by the Lord Privy Seal, John Russell, Earl of Bedford, who had himself been the Lord Admiral from 1540 to 1542. In July 1545 Antonio Derretarbio, the Portuguese master of *Sant Pedro*, forwarded a petition protesting that he and his companion, Fransisco de Ugarte in *Santa Maria*, on passage with a cargo of salt from France, had been intercepted by two of the king's ships and, despite their protestations of neutrality, been escorted into Dover, where they were flung into jail and so badly treated that de Ugarte had died. What is more, their cargo had been unloaded and sold along with many items from their impounded ship. In a modest claim Derretarbio simply requested payment for his freight and costs for his thirty days' forced stay at Dover.[31] It should come as no surprise that the person behind this shameful seizure was Thomas Seymour, who two years later was to be promoted to Lord High Admiral, an advancement that was due more to his sister's willingness to be bedded by Henry than to his own professional skill and integrity. By Edward's reign, Seymour, thanks to his sister's marriage, the king's uncle and a member of the Protectorate, was encouraging pirates to use the waters around his lands in the Isles of Scilly as a safe haven from which to plunder English merchants.

The remaining sixty years of the Tudor fighting navy were dominated by such state-sponsored plunder. And England's neighbours soon realised this. In April 1546 Lisle wrote to Paget, 'every Spaniard,

Portugal, or Fleming that comes from the south is robbed by our adventurers ...'.[32] Mary, who was far more astute than is generally believed, issued her own letters of reprisal for the war against France in June 1557. Having been informed 'that diverse of her subjects inhabiting the coasts, using traffic by sea and others desire to equip ships at their charge for the annoyance of the French', she licensed all subjects without penalty and without putting up any bonds '... to prepare as many ships against her enemies as they think convenient'. What is more, they were to be allowed to keep both the vessels they captured and their cargo and munitions without making an account to the court.[33] This was the true spirit of free enterprise, and when the officials at Rye tried to impose 'sundry exactions' on ships to their 'great hindrance', Mary gave them a blast, claiming that by their actions they were making the coast 'worse defended, the enemy encouraged and their majesties worse served'.[34]

Elizabeth was never too fussy about whom her seamen attacked, although she did issue, in March 1586, a reminder to the vice-admirals in the counties that reprisals should be taken only against Spanish and Portuguese vessels. Her main concern was that the treasury should get its cut from the activities of her pirates, so she was constantly proclaiming, as in 1563 and 1591, that whoever broke bulk of any prize, before lawful title had been ruled upon by the Court of Admiralty, would be imprisoned and the prize forfeit.[35] This order was based on a long-established understanding that goods that were lying loose on deck could be seized by the boarding party but those which lay secured below had to be inventoried and accounted for. Elizabeth's threat seems not to have been heeded, for that December the queen ordered all those who had received any 'foreign coin, bullion of gold or silver, jewels, pearls, tones, musk, wrought or raw silk, cochnilia, indigo, or other merchandise' within ten days to present evidence of purchase along with the price paid and the name of the seller. Any persons failing to do so were threatened with being treated as felons and abettors of pirates. Mary had not been so protective of her rights but was concerned with protecting her subjects. In July 1553 she ordered William Tyrell as her vice-admiral to take *Jennet* and *Greyhound* to sea, both to seek out what the French were up to on the other side of the Channel and to provide protection to the queen's subjects from 'pirates and rovers upon the seas'.[36] The following year, the Venetian ambassador, Soranzo, reported that Queen Mary allowed 100,000 ducats a year 'for the cost of ten armed ships which from year to year are kept at sea for the protection of merchandise against corsairs'.[37]

Yet buccaneering was potentially too great a source of income to the state for its perpetrators to be handled harshly. Small-scale or, of course, foreign piracy was another matter, and those unlucky to be caught did often hang for their offences: Drake was knighted.

In Elizabeth's time, even minor offenders could gain the queen's sympathy right up to her closing days. In 1603 the Portsmouth pirate William Piers attacked the Venetian ship *Veniera* and seized some 100,000 ducats of goods, making good his escape mainly because lawful English merchants refused to help in the pursuit. When the newly-appointed Venetian ambassador, Giovanni Scaramelli, delivered a letter of protest from the Serene Republic to the queen in February 1603, she assured him that she would do all that lay in her power to settle the matter. Yet when Scaramelli returned for a second audience, Elizabeth informed him that they should just talk about pleasant matters which did not include Piers and piracy. She could scarcely do otherwise, for at the same time her own councillors were plotting piratical raids against Venetian shipping. Scaramelli had to await the arrival of James on the throne and Piers's betrayal by a companion to gain the satisfaction of seeing the pirate in jail under threat of execution. However, he was released under the traditional pardons granted to mark the coronation, although James's agent had declared, when soliciting the support of the Venetian ambassador for his king's accession to the English throne, 'when it come to my master's turn he will put an end to this great buccaneering'.[38]

Pirates who were apprehended in anti-piracy sweeps were dealt with severely unless they had contacts, influence or usable skills. Thus in 1540, when Henry despatched a large fleet in response to an invasion scare, six Portuguese pirates were caught and executed, while Lord Russell informed the Privy Council in August 1545 that a Scot who had taken two Spanish ships laden with wine and woad and had cast all the men overboard had been imprisoned by the authorities at Brest for drowning the men.[39]

Such action was of little avail; the plunder continued on such a scale that in 1577 the brilliant polymath John Dee, in his treatise in support of the permanent establishment of a Petty Navy Royal, included in his argument the views of merchants as to:

> How great value to them, and consequently to the public weal of this Kingdom, such a security were? (a) Whereby, both outward and homeward, continually their merchant like ships, many or few, great or small, may in our sea and somewhat further, pass quietly unspilled, unspoiled, and untaken by pirates or others in time of peace, (b) What abundance of money is lost by insurance given or taken, would by this means also, be greatly out of danger?[40]

Dee also saw that piracy itself provided a good training for a fighting career at sea and suggested that the establishment of a Navy Royal of some seventy-six ships would encourage pirates to cease swashbuckling and join a legitimate arm of their trade. Dee was thus proposing a formalising of the arrangement by which the queen benefited from the roving nursery that had made good seamen of Frobisher and Drake.

If the failure of a government to abide by its own rule of law defines a rogue state, then, in regard to piracy, Elizabeth and her court epitomised such a nation. Five facts support this position: the administrative ones that divided spoil among sovereign, Lord Admiral and the pirate and also appointed the Admiralty Court and Lord Admiral

For nearly four centuries Execution Dock at Wapping was where captured pirates sentenced to death were hanged or, in the worst case, hung in chains to be drowned by the incoming tide. (National Maritime Museum neg 6588)

to adjudicate in questions of legitimacy in which they stood to benefit; the inclusion of naval vessels on, and state investment in, piratical voyages; the welcoming, flattering and protection of successful pirates at court; and, finally, the appointment of such pirates to positions within the Navy Royal. Reneger joined Lisle against the French in 1545; Mary appointed a pirate, Peter Killigrew, to command one of her own warships in 1557; and Elizabeth made her most successful corsairs admirals. The two best-known commoners of her reign, Sir Francis Drake and Sir Walter Ralegh, were both pirates, as was Martin Frobisher.

The division of piratical spoil was something that Elizabeth monitored closely; after all, plunder was providing her state with a very important part of her income, and one that avoided over-taxing her subjects, which was an important factor for a queen who prided herself on the love in which she was held. When it was properly administered she received one-half of the profits from letters of

Galleys were a surprisingly common sight off the English coast in the sixteenth century. Trading galleys could fall easy prey to assault so they needed every man onboard to be proficient in the use of small arms to repel pirates from boarding. In the Venetian case rules stipulated the arms required to be carried by each merchant and gave clear instructions as to how they were to be stowed for easy access. (British Library)

reprisal, the Lord Admiral one-tenth, and the captain, his crew and the investor the remainder. Over the years this provided, as is shown in the table on p. 195, a significant topping-up of her treasury and one which she was loath to forfeit to mollify any ambassador or foreign potentate, however righteous their indignation. And they did often have due cause for indignation.

Not that the queen needed intermediaries when circumstances conspired in her favour. In November 1568 four Genoese ships, fleeing from Huguenot pirates sought shelter in West Country ports. When their cargo was examined it was found to be gold bullion being ferried to the Netherlands to pay the Duke of Alba's troops. Safe passage was requested of the queen and might have been granted had not bad news of Hawkins's defeat at San Juan de Ulua reached England at the same time opening a debate about 'compensation'. On this pretext Alba's gold, valued at £30 million, was locked away in the security of the Tower, where possession was to prove an important part of the law.

Of course, such windfalls could not be relied upon, and the queen's corsairs had to go and pluck such riches from the sea. The most successful of these was Francis Drake.

Drake had served his apprenticeship in coastal trade, honed his professional skills as a slaver; made his fortune as a pirate and earned his fame as a warrior. He thus combined a career representing every facet of Tudor maritime activity, with the state a partner in each of the last three. The nascent slave trade was very uncertain, requiring the Spanish in the West Indies to acquiesce in the illegal importation of slaves transported in English hulls, and it has to be assumed that this, combined with his narrow escape from San Juan de Ulua, with its miserable return journey and the ensuing accusations that he had abandoned Hawkins in his distress, convinced Drake that there was a more certain way to make his fortune at sea. And this was piracy – pure piracy, for the government issued no letters of reprisal to legitimise his early voyages, which thus lie outside the scope of this work. However, when Drake returned to Plymouth in August 1573 with a small fortune, worth some £6 million in modern terms, the Privy Council sat up and took notice, and so when he proposed his next great venture, to enter the Pacific and prey upon the vessels that crawled slowly from the mining ports to Panama, there can be no doubt that the queen and her ministers were prepared to invest in the enterprise, Elizabeth probably being the major sponsor and in any case expecting the major share of the profit. The voyage, which became the famous circumnavigation, thus also represented the first major example of state-sponsored piracy.

However, before that time, Drake's earlier return with plundered wealth from Philip's New Spain was in danger of embarrassing the queen, who was moving towards patching up her quarrels with Philip, something she achieved with the Convention of Bristol in 1574. During this period Drake was sent across the Irish Sea to lend support to the bedlam that was unfolding in Ireland as Essex tried to subdue Antrim. This deployment kept Drake hidden to avoid awkward questions while using his skills to keep the Scots at bay. He returned to prepare for the voyage that would make him both immortal and rich, for, whatever secondary aims are attributed to the first circumnavigation of the globe by an Englishman, there can be no doubt that above anything else this was to be a plundering expedition, with the large,

So confident were the Spanish of their total ownership of the Pacific coast of South America, to the exclusion of any interlopers, that Drake's small but heavily armed Golden Hind *was able to seize with little effort other than a show of aggression much larger vessels. The taking of* Cacafuego *made his voyage – all he then had to do was throw off any pursuers and complete the very long voyage home through uncharted oceans.*

rich cargo ships of the Pacific Ocean his principal target.

A more detailed description of Drake's circumnavigation is recounted elsewhere, but if plunder was its aim then he was not disappointed. This was fox-in-the-henhouse stuff, for no Spanish master, sailing his lightly-armed vessel gently up the placid coast of Peru, would have suspected that any other sail that he sighted was not in the service of the same sovereign. It is true that there had been a panic when Drake's one-time companion, John Oxenham, slipping across the isthmus of Panama, had looted much treasure in his few small boats. But Oxenham had been captured, tortured and executed; the threat, as far as the locals could tell, was over. Drake, and later Cavendish, informed them that it was not.

The reward for the pirate and his queen was enormous. Drake took a share of £10,000 for himself from the loot unloaded from *Golden Hind* and paid off his crew with a further £25,000. Any discussion as to whether or not his voyage had been sanctioned by the crown, and had in effect been a naval commerce raid, can be resolved by glancing at the order written in the queen's hand to Edmund Tremayne, clerk to the Privy Council, stating that he should 'assist Francis Drake in sending up certain bullions brought into the realm by him, but to leave so much of it in Drake's hands as shall amount to the sum of £10,000, the leaving of which sum in his hands is to be kept most secret'.[41]

The 'certain bullions' amounted to £160,000 for the queen (the equivalent of one year's income from all other sources) and a return of £47 in the pound for the other shareholders. Perhaps *Golden Hind* should have been again renamed as *Golden Egg* or *Golden Fleece*. Certainly the queen's goose kept laying. In 1587, returning from the successful but financially neutral Cadiz raid, Drake detoured to the Azores and captured the fabulously wealthy Portuguese carrack *San Felipe*. After a lengthy and detailed mouth-watering inventory was made, the sum realised, apart from the ship and her fittings, was £112,000, of which Her Majesty took £50,000 and Drake £20,000. These royal returns might pale into insignificance when set alongside

Golden Hind *was admired by her foes as representing the acme of small ocean-going vessels. Not only did she sail well but she was sturdy, as her grounding and successful refloating demonstrated; nevertheless, she could carry a weight of ordnance far heavier than other ships of similar size. Although no plans survive of the ship, this modern reconstruction is based on existing written records.* (Veres László)

the £3.3 million that Philip of Spain had received from the Americas between 1570 and 1580, but if the rewards were significantly different so were the outgoings. Philip's treasure ships failed to prevent his several bankruptcies; Elizabeth's pirates kept her state afloat, and a large number remained active throughout the latter part of her reign; according to one estimate, between 1589 and 1591 an average of over 230 ships were actively engaged in 'privateering' on any day of the year, while in the last thirteen years of Elizabeth's reign there were probably never less than a hundred English ships at sea with letters of reprisal.

Keeping the myth of piracy as a plague rather than a state-sponsored blessing was achievable through the transparent expedient of having the Lord Admiral issue letters of reprisal and pocket 10 per cent of the profits. In addition, Howard of Effingham had his own pirate fleet, as did several of those close to the throne, including the queen's favourites. Obviously it was important that the due process of law was observed to allow redress of grievances, but this could be catered for by having the Admiralty judge, Sir Julius Caesar, an appointee and payee of the Lord Admiral.

The system served the state so well that Elizabeth's other famous pirate, Walter Ralegh, was able to make his money in comfort, content to despatch others to make that part of his fortune that he could not gain from flattering the queen. To achieve this he put together a formi-

dable fleet, the pride of which was *Ark Ralegh*, a 500-tonne heavily armed warship built in 1586, while he part-owned, hired or invested in other piratical ventures from which he gained much reward. When the queen favoured Ralegh with the gift of the land of the traitor Babington and appointed him captain of the guard responsible for her safety, he, now wealthy almost beyond his extravagant dreams of avarice, responded by selling her, cheaply, *Ark Ralegh*, which, re-christened *Ark Royal*, became the most modern vessel in her fleet, more than capable of serving as Effingham's flagship in the fight against the Armada. Thus the first warship to bear one of the Royal Navy's most illustrious warship names began life as a pirate ship and was presented to the crown by a pirate. There are few clearer examples of the symbiotic relationship between crown and corsair.

While Drake, Ralegh and Frobisher voyaged through life from modest beginnings towards their anticipated fortune, they were in company with one who, although he occasionally outshone them, was taking passage in the opposite direction. George, Third Earl of Cumberland, had been born into wealth but with a love of gambling. He sent his men to sea to feed his habit and, at the end of a highly successful piratical career which included the seizure of the greatest of them all, *Madre de Dios*, he died penniless, his fortune dissipated in gambling and other reckless pastimes. Yet his was a bright and burning comet.

Cumberland, like of many of the queen's corsair commanders, began his sea career by investing in pure piracy. However, in 1588 he was appointed in command of the Navy Royal ship *Bonaventure*, where his ability and position made one of the signatories on the important resolution drawn up by Effingham on 11 August to call off the pursuit of the Armada. The following year Elizabeth entrusted him with *Golden Lion*, which he had to fit out and provision at his own expense, for a spoiling expedition to the Spanish coast. This yielded little profit, but one year later Cumberland took two French ships which belonged to the Catholic League and could therefore be considered fair, if not legal, game and emptied eleven Baltic merchant vessels

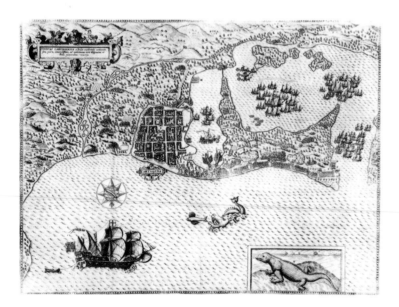

By taking Cartagena in February 1586 Drake demonstrated that, at his best, he was a superb commander of amphibious operations. Both the squadron and the land forces, under Carleill, acted speedily and boldly, taking a town which, although not well fortified, had manpower enough to repel the attackers. However, Drake lacked sufficient forces to hold the town for any length of time and, after a disappointing return from pillage and extortion, his land and sea commanders advised withdrawal.

This Visscher engraving of Golden Lion shows the fine lines of one of Hawkins' conversions to race-built galleon. She served as Lord Thomas Howard's flagship during the Armada campaign when, with the Spanish close to the Isle of Wight, he had to use his boats, like the one shown in the picture, to tow him towards the enemy when the wind died. To emphasise the royal involvement with privateering, the following year the queen lent the ship to the Earl of Cumberland for his privately-funded expedition to the coast of Spain.

of their cargo, which, he claimed, belonged to a Lisbon merchant and thus also was above-board booty. Cumberland's greatest success was to be in 1592, when a squadron of his own ships sailed to the Azores in company with a royal fleet, commanded by Sir John Borough, with the aim of intercepting ships returning to Spain or Portugal. This operation was supported by another flotilla, under Sir Martin Frobisher, operating off the coast of Spain and thus discouraging any Spanish fleet from departing to provide support to the carracks sailing towards the Azores. That task cannot have been to Frobisher's liking; grudge-bearing as he was, he would have seen his force as doing much work but with little chance of reward in the way of prizes. Off Spain all they managed to capture was a large Biscayan loaded with ironmongery. Richer pickings by far waited off the Azores.

As was often the case, the first attempts at plunder were not successful: one carrack out of a group of four was intercepted but anchored close inshore and was set on fire by her crew when they abandoned her. Nevertheless, rough interrogation of two of the crew elicited the information that several ships from Goa were shortly due to rendezvous at Flores.

When one of these, the Portuguese carrack *Madre de Dios*, appeared on the horizon the royal-corsair public-private-public partnership could not have believed its luck. She was enormous and, although, like a baited bear, too strong for any one of her assailants, she fell to the pack.

The close co-operation between corsair and queen was well illus-

trated when Sir John Borough in Ralegh's *Roebuck* and the vice-admiral, Sir Robert Cross, in the navy's *Foresight*, the first of Hawkins's race-built galleons, came alongside together after the queen's ship *Dainty*, having made the initial attack, had to pull back to nurse her wounds. It was a long fight, and at one stage it did look as if *Madre de Dios* would shake off her assailants, for *Roebuck* was pierced below the water-line by a shot from a cannon perrier and began to flood uncontrollably. Borough was forced to withdraw to effect repairs, and *Foresight* disentangled herself at the same time. Much chagrined, the English watched their quarry sail on towards the safety of Flores. This was too much for Cross, and he persuaded his reluctant crew to try again. In a desperate measure he placed his ship across the bows of the Portuguese and then fought her unaided for three hours before help in the shape of two of Cumberland's ships arrived to storm on board and capture the vessel, leading to accusations that the pirate allowed the navy to do the hard work and then nipped in to lay claim to the prize when she could no longer defend herself. The carnage was terrible. The decks of *Madre de Dios* were covered with the dead, dying and hideously mutilated. Immediately he saw this, the vice-admiral ordered his own surgeons on board to do what they could. Then, slithering around on the blood-soaked decks, he took a look at his prize.

Soon pirates and naval seamen were everywhere, and it would be foolish to expect that either thought about much else but personal gain. There was sufficient nutmeg, ginger, cinnamon and cloves to give

191

Many large carracks carried in their holds greater wealth than non-trading nations created in one year. Capturing one gave the attacking commanders and their backers riches beyond their wildest dreams. The shares handed down to the common seamen were far less generous. This picture depicts Sir James Lancaster's squadron capturing a carrack laden with calico off the eastern coast of India during the first voyage organised by the East India Company in 1602. The English vessels are Red Dragon *(Cumberland's old* The Scourge of Malice*),* Hector, Ascension *and* Susan. *This was also the first voyage where we have evidence of lemon juice being used as an antiscorbutic. Lancaster himself is one of a handful of Tudor seamen who deserve greater recognition for their exploits and involvement in the move from plunder to legitimate trade.* (Royal Naval Museum, Portsmouth)

each one of them a jolly red nose for a jolly long time. The cargo included 500 tons of spice, 8,500cwt of pepper, 900cwt of cloves, 700cwt of cinnamon, 500cwt of cochineal, 59cwt of both mace and nutmeg, fifteen tons of ebony and two great crosses, along with copious jewels, pearls, silks, ivory, tapestries, silver and gold.[42] This cornucopia was probably worth about £75 million in today's currency at the moment of capture; pillaging by the pirates diminished this to a declared total of £45 million, which was further reduced when, with her arrival in Dartmouth, traders descended on the vessel with ready money to purchase whatever they could. The scale of removal prior to arriving back in England can be gauged by the fact that this 1,600-tonne ship was reported as drawing thirty-one feet on departure from Cochin but only twenty-six feet on her arrival at Dartmouth.

The government moved rapidly to regain control. Ralegh, in disgrace in the Tower for marrying Bess Throckmorton without the queen's permission, was released and, under escort, told to go to Dartmouth and sort things out. Robert Cecil had already been despatched to take an inventory and audit. On their journey west they passed many a traveller returning to Exeter, wafted along in a haze of perfume. Cecil impounded what he could, threw unhelpful innkeepers in jail, and ordered all mail bags to be searched, in the process of which gold amulets and bejewelled cutlery were recovered. Once the scale of the pilfering was obvious a proclamation was issued, charging all who had taken or received goods from the carrack from the moment of capture to declare these to their local magistrate on pain of both forfeiture and loss of their share of the benefits arising.[43] Those through whom mail and packages were transported were likewise told to detain anything they thought might be linked to the carrack.

The precision of Cecil and the popularity of Ralegh did little either to halt the pilfering of goods or to encourage their return. The total sum to share out among the investors, less some jewels, was put at £141,200, plus the ship herself. When it came to the legal distribution Ralegh was made to pay for his misdemeanours; having invested £34,000, he was reimbursed with £36,000. The same amount was granted to Cumberland for his initial investment of £19,000. The London merchants with £12,000 doubled their input, while Elizabeth's two ships and £1,800 earned her half of the declared proceeds, some £80,000. Some, however, did not live to enjoy their share: in March 1594 Sir John Borough was killed in a duel. Cumberland, as might be expected, blew his handsomely, although a part went on the building at Deptford of the 900-tonne *Scourge of Malice*, its name infused with threat, 'the best ship built by any subject'.[44]

The seizure of the great carrack was a highlight in a continuing commerce war, the aim of which was to bankrupt Spain by challenging her at sea, where her resources were at their most valuable and vulnerable. All who pursued this aim, whether corsairs or naval commanders, were instigating state policy, and it therefore mattered not whether they were naval officers or embarked in the queen's ships. For example, in the late summer of 1592 Thomas White in *Amity* brought two Spanish prizes into the Thames, a Biscayan and a flyboat, which he had engaged off the coast of Barbary that July. For five hours, at never more than a cable's length distant, the foes exchanged fire and manoeuvred for advantage. Thirty-two rounds of great shot are said to have struck *Amity* along with at least 500 rounds of musket fire (although how this figure was arrived at would be hard to guess). In return *Amity's* gunners claimed that the scuppers of the enemy ran red until, at last, an honourable surrender was negotiated and the English boarded to strike their opponents' sails because the latter had sworn never to strike to an Englishman. On board were found 1,400 chest of quicksilver and a hundred tunnes of 'excellent' wine, amounting to an estimated loss to the King of Spain of £707,000.[45] Even if both the bounty and its value are exaggerated, the strategic, and financial, wisdom of augmenting the navy with pirates and reprisalists is obvious.

The concern remained that many light fingers could remove small but valuable goods from prizes. In December 1591 and again in August 1594 proclamations were issued against those who secretly bought or took away goods from prizes before they were accounted for and authorised for removal.[46] The proclamation refers to this habit as a frequent abuse, which, given the circumstances, can hardly be surprising; one full pocket of jewels would provide a poor seaman with enough wealth to live comfortably for the rest of his life. The penalties ordered were, therefore, harsh. Anyone who boarded a prize without permission and who bought, bartered, bargained or begged goods was to forfeit the goods and, along with the seller, to be thrown in jail where they were to remain until the Privy Council ordered their release. This was the equivalent of an indeterminate sentence, for if there was no one to remind the council or plead a case, a prisoner could languish inside for a long time. Furthermore, to prevent and discourage such incidents, customs officers were commanded to board

any prize and remain on board until the cargo had been mustered and its distribution arranged.

The Cadiz voyage of 1596 caused similar orders to be issued, but this time an additional clause had to be entered, for it had been noted that certain ships were following the fleet, not to do service but to make private gains by buying up spoils from the seamen and soldiers while at sea.[47] The officers of the towns where such goods might be landed for sale were warned to keep an eye open for such suspect items.

However unfair the distribution, and it reflects an accepted norm, the important factor is how much the crown benefited from such enterprises. It may seem strange that an account of the Navy Royal should dwell long on what were smash-and-grab raids, but those are what the English did and did well. David Loades makes a similar point: 'Strictly speaking, privateering is not naval history, but it would give a distorted picture of the sea war against Spain to omit all reference to it. As we have seen the Queen herself was a privateer, having authorized and participated in a number of expeditions which, without her sanction, would have been simply piratical.'[48]

Of course, there is a legal distinction between actions taken against an enemy once war has been declared and those initiated during a period of tension against neutral shipping. Drake's actions in the Pacific were the direct forebear of Admiral Anson's circumnavigation between 1740 and 1744, which was 'made' – forget the horrendous loss of life – by his capture of the silver-laden Spanish galleon *Nostra Signora de Cabadonga*. The exploits of commerce raiders of the twentieth-century world wars, involving both warships and armed merchant vessels, are their direct descendants.

Most studies of the Tudor navy concentrate on the events surrounding the defeat of the Spanish Armada, but this was short-lived, atypical not only of that century, but of all the centuries of naval warfare that followed. What trained the navy, instilled spirit into generations of fighting seamen and taught commanders the ways of leadership were fights such as that with *Madre de Dios* and the many single-ship engagements of no renown. The importance of the rovers

The wealth of Spain came from the mines of South America and required two lengthy sea voyages separated by an overland crossing before they were safe in the royal coffers. Both on land and sea the gold and silver offered opportunities for the bold to intercept and seize. As the century progressed, however, the Spanish adopted better convoy protection methods, newer and faster hulls to outsail their predators, and cleverer intelligence and counter-intelligence, so that many English voyages ended in frustration. Images like this inflated the sense of Spanish America being the treasure house of the world.

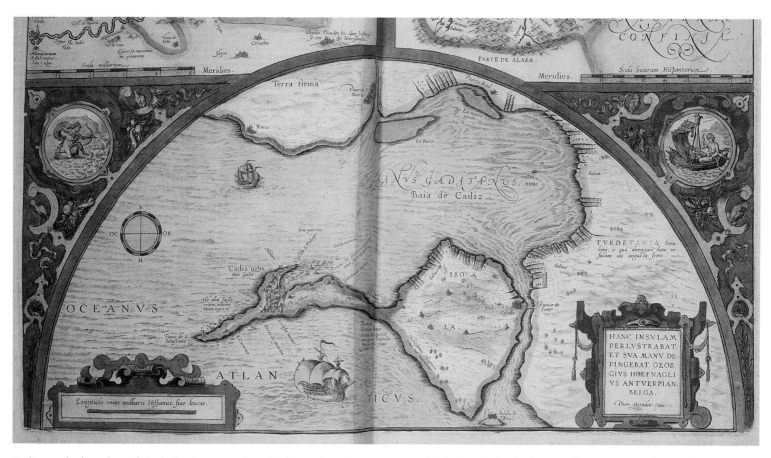

Cadiz was the focus for raids by both privateers and royal-led fleets. Its wide entrance proved little obstacle for the determined mariner and its local galley squadron proved incapable of driving off ships commanded by determined captains who had the sea room (even inside the harbour) to manoeuvre against the threat.
(Royal Naval Museum, Portsmouth)

in the latter part of the century was realised by, among others, Alexander McKee, the discoverer of the wreck of *Mary Rose*, who entitled his book about Drake's circumnavigation *The Queen's Corsair*. Susan Roland's more recent *The Pirate Queen* concentrates on the symbiotic relationship between Elizabeth and her pirate adventurers. Each needed the other, but the greatest want was that of the queen, as Roland makes clear in her accurately entitled chapter 'The Quest for Cash'. 'Plunder' might not be a pleasant term, but it would be incorrect and idle to deny that this was an important and successful part of English state policy for most of Elizabeth's reign. She may have felt that she had little choice: her father had sold much of the monastic lands that financed his ventures, and with high inflation and little economic growth in the years since his death few other options were available to her to fund the protection of her realm against a mighty empire. Piracy was a simple, productive and powerful source of cash with the added benefit that it did not entail parliamentary approval for an unpopular increase in taxes at a time when failing harvests were regularly causing poverty and hardship. Foreign booty enabled the queen to increase her naval budget from an average of £25,000 per year between 1566 and 1585 to £87,000 per year between 1585 and 1603, when the country was at war with Spain.[49] This excludes her investment in specific operations such as the Cadiz raid of 1596, but she always anticipated a positive return from such joint ventures.

Elizabeth's parsimony is legendary, and the navy – both its ships and its men – felt her meanness. The 'ordinary' budget of the navy was reduced from £13,000 at the start of her reign to £6,000 by 1564, but against this have to be set the arrangements that she made with John Hawkins to run a tighter, more efficient and less corrupt administration. Even in the years of greatest danger the 'ordinary' budget moved between £5,000 and £12,000 a year, far below that necessary to keep a fleet operational, especially at a time of rapidly-rising inflation. This is not a dated phenomenon: several times in recent years the quaysides of naval dockyards have been crowded with warships confined to harbour as a rise in the price of fuel or other financial crisis has restricted their deployment. At least with wind being a free motive force the Tudor navy did not have to take the price of oil into consideration.

In fact, given that in the years of the Spanish war Elizabeth expended £4 million on her land army with little return, the £1.5 million she spent on the navy was money well spent. Only her father, through the capture of Thérouanne, Tournai and Boulogne, was able to claim some return from his overseas land campaigns. Elizabeth could not, but her pirates could and did. The table opposite shows how expenditure on the navy varied during her reign.

As the war petered to its eventual close the incidence of piracy seemed to increase, as did the involvement of government officials at the highest level: Sir Robert Cecil, inheriting his father's position as the queen's secretary but not his elder's honesty, had a 'nice' arrangement with Lord Howard that involved victualling and manning the latter's private vessel *Truelove* at the queen's expense while it sailed on a lucrative piracy voyage.[50] If such behaviour resulted in cases being brought to the attention of the High Court of Admiralty, pressure could always be brought upon the presiding judge, the quaintly-named Sir Julius Caesar, to ensure that the outcome involved state officials in no embarrassment. In the end the war made the Admiralty rich in goods and poor in reputation, and it became notorious as the nation's most corrupt branch of both law and administration. This was the inevitable outcome of a war waged for profit; those who controlled its pursuit became the champions of pillage. The trend continued for centuries: in 1744 Anson, who lost all but one of his ships and most of his men, received one of the most effusive welcomes given to a sailor by a grateful nation, for seizing just one very richly stowed merchant ship.

As Elizabeth's war against Spain dragged towards its conclusion it could be seen that the narrow aim of a keeping England independent of Spanish and Catholic interests had been far exceeded. Spain was finished. Exhausted by defeats in the Netherlands on land and against the English at sea, it lacked the reforming will to move from its mercantilist chains into the post-war world. Its defeat cleared the way for the next struggle for global hegemony: England versus the Dutch and then the French. Andrews has estimated that the English captured over 1,000 Spanish vessels during the war leading to the Casa de Contratación's warning in 1608 that, whereas in 1580 Spain had 1,000 sea-going vessels and Portugal some 400 together with 1,500 caravels, the nations now had hardly enough to continue with their overseas trade.[51] The action of the plunderers, state or private, did not win the war but it ensured that only one nation would emerge with an enhanced future.

Ashore in England it did more than contribute to the state's coffers: not only did it make a few merchants and courtiers extraordinarily well off, but it enthused them to invest their profits in the joint stock companies on which Britain's overseas trade would be founded. Even those who did not gain financially were paid in pride, for the sea dogs' exploits created a national spirit. In small hamlets and havens throughout the country, local men were returning from voyages with their own shares from the plunder, and even if these pickings were small the tales they told would have been tall. They inculcated a feeling in the ports, villages and market towns that this was a war in which they were all participating and in which they could share some of the rewards. At a time when the wool trade had collapsed, and both population and poverty were growing, it gave pride when there could well have been discontentment.

Ideas of Commonwealth

Away from the plunder route, the Tudors did seek new directions to increase their trade. Their problem was that two of their primary interests, the north-west and north-east passages, led down cul-de-sacs of ice while the third, the route from Guinea to New Spain, involved taking a cargo of slaves to a destination where they were considered illegal traders. The exploits of Chancellor and Willoughby, Davis and Frobisher lie outside the scope of this book apart from the fact that their voyages established the tradition of exploration and hydrography which the Royal Navy carried on with success and aplomb in succeeding centuries. Of Hawkins's early voyages the same exclusion applies. Only his 1567 slaving voyage is relevant because he sailed with ships hired from the queen and flying her standard, which meant that when the voyage ended in the ignominious defeat at San Juan de Ulua his sovereign was implicated. Two other positives emerged from that disaster. Firstly, it gave Francis Drake a chance to show his incredible leadership and seamanship skills when he shepherded his small overcrowded *Judith* safely home nursing an implacable hatred of perfidious Spain. Secondly, it gave the more mature Hawkins occasion to reflect on the shortcomings of Her Majesty's ships and to seize the opportunity, when it arose, to build hulls better suited to future battles.

Elizabeth's great favourites, Leicester, Essex and Ralegh, compensated for their good looks by shortcomings in the management

Examples of Naval Expenditure

Dates	Average annual income	Naval expenditure per annum	Naval expenditure as % of whole	State's return from selected plunder operations
1558–65		£143,000		Nil
1566–70	£157,000	£27,500	18	
1571–5	£179,000	£26,500	15	
1576–80	£142,000	£26,200	18	1580, Drake, £50,000
				1585, *Santa Maria*, £10,000
				1587, *San Felipe*, £35,000
				1588, Cavendish, £30,000
1591–5	£335,000	£63,000	24	1592, *Madre de Dios*, £80,000
1596–1600	£442,000	£127,300	29	
2009	£14,080 billion (GDP)	£10 billion	0.8	Nil

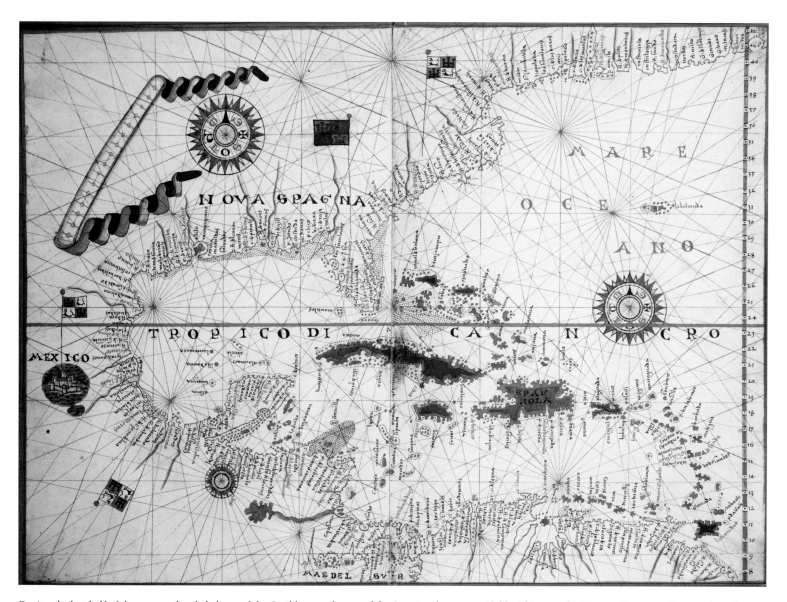

During the last half of the century detailed charts of the Caribbean and coast of the Americas became available. This one of 1572 provides many direction lines for passage planning and shows the position of the seldom visited Bermudas with some accuracy. (National Maritime Museum F1755)

department, but whereas the first two confined their failures to Ireland and the Netherlands the greater-visioned Ralegh managed to expand his disasters to two further continents. His charm, his silver tongue and golden prose have given his reputation that which his achievements alone could scarcely deserve. With him as the champion of English colonisation there could be only one outcome, and this, disaster, was duly delivered.

Plunder apart, this was an age of failure by the English to achieve great things overseas. Trade had been initiated along the Guinea coast, but this was abandoned, as was a precarious foothold in Virginia, while a similar idea in Newfoundland also came to nothing. In the icy wastes of northern America Frobisher's settlement had failed, and he had brought back from their ships laden with black rocks more use for aggregate than for yielding gold.

Domestic trade was suffering with the loss of the Antwerp cloth trade and the lack of alternative markets. The nation seemed doomed at

one stage to be 'ever like sheep to haunt one trade', in the words of Richard Eden in his work of 1555, *The Discovery of the New World or West Indies*. That trade and naval influence went hand in hand was also appreciated by many. Hakluyt, in his *Discourse of Western Planting*, published in 1584, emphasised that a settlement in Virginia would not only dominate the Newfoundland fisheries but be well placed to intercept the treasure fleets sailing from the Gulf of Mexico. In addition, most perceptively, he thought that the colonies would not only be able to grow foodstuffs that would be lacking in England during a continental war but would provide the fleet with strategic goods such as pitch, tar and masts. For this he saw that the navy had a role in patrolling and supporting fortified settlements founded in safe havens and good harbours. His vision incorporated a blue-water fleet, the advantages of which lay, as Ralegh pointed out in typically stirring words, in the fact that 'he who commandeth the sea, commandeth the trade and he who was lord of trade of the world is lord of the wealth of the world'.

As these new market opportunities were investigated, so they produced an effect on how the navy at war might operate. Any ship wishing to return safe from a voyage to the Levant needed to be stout and well armed, as must have been the aptly named *Tiger*, whose eastern trip brought forth one of Shakespeare's most famous lines:

Her husband to Aleppo's gone, master of the *Tiger*.

These ships were easy to take up from trade in time of crisis, with no need for either additions to their upper works or the provision of arms, so, like the warships of the privateers, they could be mustered ready to serve and with a crew experienced in fighting at sea. With such ships available – and the Thames would often have several hundred lying in it reaches – the nation could afford to keep the Navy Royal small, especially once senior navy men, like Hawkins and the Howards, came to own similar vessels which they felt obliged to provide when necessity demanded. This may have had an opposite effect in those ports away from London, where the bounteous arm of Admiralty was not so apparent. The excuses made by towns not to provide ships to defend against the Spanish Armada read like a contemporary version of the parable of the reluctant wedding guests. Southampton pleaded that poverty prevented it from providing two ships and a pinnace; East Bergholt, cleverly, blamed the prohibition on the export of Suffolk cloth for its lack of resources; others stated that they could meet charges but only if their neighbouring towns were made to join in as well.[52] This was not the response to a call to arms that would later be seen with the Dunkirk 'Little Ships' of 1940; it was evidence of a nation not at ease with itself. Disguised by the imports of rich plunder, the state of those who relied on the traditional exports of wool and cloth had been forgotten. Their responses show they had been hurt and hurt hard. Yet back in London the merchants and naval commanders saw and responded to a common cause by deploying together in public-private partnerships.

It was this urgent need to find new markets for cloth that had prompted the initiative to seek a north-east passage to Cathay, and this had the added advantage that the people of these colder climes *en route* might welcome good English cloth to keep them warm.

Merchants also began to sail beyond Biscay and the Straits of Gibraltar to try their luck on the coast of Guinea, from which the dominant European power in the region, Portugal, banned them. In fact, the first voyage, led by Thomas Wyndham with a fleet of three ships, *Lion* and two royal vessels, *Primrose and Moon*, in 1553, was possible only because of the defection of two experienced but dissatisfied Portuguese pilots, Antonio Ane Pinteado and Francisco Rodriguez. Pinteado was appointed second-in-command, but this did

The settlement of Sao Jorge da Mina was the first European colony in sub-Saharan Africa, established on the Guinea coast by the Portuguese in 1482 to tap the gold trade. In 1554 John Lok made a highly successful trading voyage to Guinea returning with both gold and ivory. However, it was to become the centre of the trade in 'black gold' – slaves – and ten years later this led John Hawkins into the region to usurp the Portuguese monopoly on this profitable trade in human beings.

197

not mean that he was listened to: ignoring his advice, the already failed merchants dwelt over-long in the Bay of Benin, and consequently, of the 140 who had originally sailed, only forty, not include either Wyndham and Pinteado, returned home in the two king's ships, having abandoned *Lion* for lack of a crew.

Disregarding that failure, other voyages were soon underway, with those of 1554 and 1556 returning with rich cargoes of gold, ivory and pepper. This encouraged further state participation, and two royal ships were included in the four vessels that were provided for the 1558 voyage. This was yet another disaster: just two ships returned with only twelve men fit to man them both. Somehow, the navy was not deterred, and in 1561 four royal ships were committed to yet another voyage to Guinea, including the hardest-working royal vessel in time of peace,́ *Minion*, best known for being one of the ships that John Hawkins had with him in the debacle at San Juan de Ulua in 1568. In the unsuccessful 1561 voyage *Minion* was battered twice by severe storms, but this did not prevent her despatch again in 1564. This time she staggered home with wealth in her hold, but was the sole survivor, having seen her escort, a ship owned by the Navy Board member Benjamin Gonson, blown up and her other consort captured by the Portuguese. The English tried again but by 1565 had to admit that Guinea trading voyages were not worth the risk, nor had reward enough to pay for their losses. So they turned to slavery instead, using, by consent, the same royal hulls to ship their human cargo at great

potential profit to both merchant and queen.[53] Thus the state continued to use its lesser or elder vessels to trade for the monies needed to pay for the whole fleet's upkeep. This was admirable and became distorted only when the prospect of bullion clouded judgement and the state's senior maritime servants' eyes became focused not on trade but on plunder.

The link between plunder and trade continued even when legitimate trading organisation such as the 'Company of London Merchants Trading to the East Indies' was formed, for not only was a member of its committee, George Clifford, Earl of Cumberland, the nation's most high-profile surviving pirate, but the ship which led the company's first expedition east, although renamed *Red Dragon*, was none other than Cumberland's well-armed pirate ship, *Scourge of Malice*, which had been launched by the queen! That her weaponry was not there just for defence must be obvious.

The Americas

When it comes to noting the legacy of any organisation, what it did not do is as important as what it achieved, and in one major area of future development the Navy Royal played no role at all – colonisation. Here the English were not just backward: they were inefficient and ill-suited to the task. The comparison with Spanish achievements on the west coast of the Americas alone is cause for the Anglophile to blush.

McDermott sums up the English colonising failure succinctly: 'Unlike Frobisher's prospective colonial experiment eight years before, the Roanoke project had been viable. It failed, perhaps, not so much upon a point of supplies, or even the poor choice of site; but because the necessary mind-set that allowed Europeans to exist far from their native lands for years at a time had yet to be acquired by Englishmen.'[54]

A part of this failure must be put down to the non-involvement of naval forces. Drake made a typical robust contribution by destroying the offensively positioned Spanish settlement of St Augustine, in Florida, on 27 May 1585, from where an attack could have been launched at Roanoke with the destructive finality with which the French settlers in Florida had been slaughtered in 1565. However, on arrival at Roanoke he came, he saw, he evacuated. But at least his actions caused the colonists to abandon the colony; the next time, the nation would abandon the colonists to their mysterious and total eradication. The only way this tentative toe-hold could have survived was for it to have had a squadron of its own ships and a guaranteed supply train. State parsimony gave it neither, and it died.

The English chosen settlement was neither north nor south and suffered because of this. North, and a catch of furs would have provided income and encouraged others to sail west; south, and sugar or specie would have made merchants salivate. The crop most suitable

George Clifford, 3rd Earl of Cumberland . 1588

George Clifford, 3rd Earl of Cumberland, managed to acquire and dissipate several fortunes during a career as a highly successful privateer and a very unsuccessful gambler. His greatest prize was Madre de Dios, *captured off the Azores in 1592 and for which his personal return, the queen having made sure she was well compensated, was about £4 million in today's values. Cumberland also succeeded in taking Santa Cruz, which had defeated Drake, although he gained little wealth from so doing. He was one of the founding members of the East India Company, thus marking the change from a century of piracy to one of trade. (Wikimedia)*

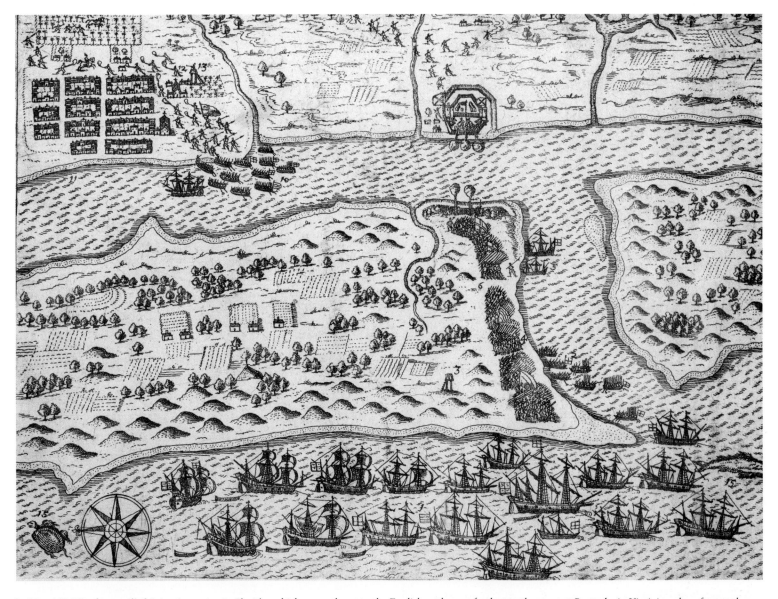

In May 1586 Drake attacked Saint Augustine in Florida, which was a threat to the English settlement further up the coast at Roanoke in Virginia only, a few weeks later, to help with the abandonment of that precarious outpost. (National Maritime Museum PX7331)

for Virginia was tobacco, for which both the ground and the market had to be cultivated. Even then, the Virginian tobacco plant was inferior to that being grown in New Spain. With no gold to appeal to the mercantilists and no spices or furs to encourage the merchants, the settlers had nothing to offer that would ensure that they would not be forgotten.

Supporters of the Tudors' age of glory generally denigrate the successes of the next dynasty, the Stuarts, but it was in their time that the settlements in America became established. The Tudor colonial

legacy is zero, and their exploratory legacy registers but little more. Tudor trade shows few new markets and little expansion from traditional exports. What the Tudors did create was a fighting navy, which learned its trade as pirates and plunderers and won because it could fight with greater experience – and more dirtily – than any opposition. Yet when it failed, it was most often because the strategic and commercial aims of expeditions clashed. Ultimately, when the lessons of successful trading and colonisation were learned, the English had a navy capable of defending traders, explorers and colonists.

Chapter Eleven

The Fighting Fleet

Near to the coast I have descried, my Lord,

As I was busy in my watchful charge,

The proud armada ...

Which, at the first far off when I did ken,

Seemed as it were a grove of withered pines,

But drawing near, their glorious bright aspect,

Their streaming ensigns wrought of coloured silk,

Like to a meadow full of sundry flowers,

adorns the naked bosom of the earth.

Majestical the order of their course,

Figuring the horned circle of the moon.

Shakespeare, Edward III

Shakespeare's description of the famous crescent formation of the Armada, albeit using the metaphor for an earlier conflict, is one of his few references to the fighting navy in his plays, although many plots involve shipwreck and piracy. In one of his few other references to England's seas, John of Gaunt, in his famous speech in *Richard II*, talks of the Channel as England's defensive moat while failing to give credit to its guardians. Taking that analogy one step further, if one regards Tudor England as a citadel, then those guardians had three main tasks: to repulse any assault; to protect supplies; and to sally forth to attack and defeat the enemy. This they achieved, and in doing so they learned much and matured more.

From the accession of Henry Tudor to the death of Elizabeth, England was at war for some forty-eight years. If one adds to that the 'cold war' years of 1567 to 1580 and the almost continuous need for anti-piracy operations, then Tudor naval vessels were on operational deployments for over a hundred years non-stop. Furthermore, many naval commanders from Edward Howard, Lisle, Reneger and Killigrew to Frobisher, Drake, Hawkins and Monson gained exceptionally useful 'peace-time' training from acting either against or as pirates. Thus, although the English had less experience in set-piece naval warfare than other European nations, her commanders became

more battle-hardened and capable of fighting as independent captains than did their opponents. Added to that is the fact that in this century the navy moved away from the medieval concept, being used primarily to ferry the army abroad and to fight occasional coastal battles at close quarters, to become a fleet that could act independently far from home and use its own gunners to engage at range. This development, supported by better victualling and sea-keeping qualities, meant that by the end of Elizabeth's reign the navy had changed from being an adjunct to state policy to the prime method of its enforcement. In achieving this dominant position the navy had to learn to fight as a fleet, to deploy to distant waters, to overcome the fear of galleys and to learn how best to use longer-range and more powerful weaponry.

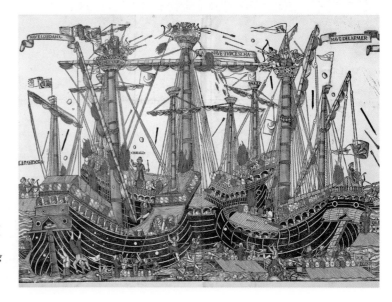

The battle of Zonchio, fought between the Venetians and the Ottomans, in 1499 is often quoted as the first recorded use of heavy guns in ships, yet as this picture shows it was dominated by the kind of traditional close-quarters combat that fighting at sea had always involved. Each of the ships shown was carrying about 2000 sailors and soldiers and, while anti-boarding netting is discouraging physical assault, a veritable rain of arrows, musketry and incendiary devices are being cast from the fighting tops onto the foe beneath. There is no evidence of artillery being used at such short range and it was fire that proved to be the most devastating weapon, destroying three of the ships. (British Museum)

European Developments

As England's naval commanders and theorists developed their ideas as how best to employ their weapons to command the sea around them, other northern navies were also disputing the control of the seas. In what could probably be considered the first modern naval campaign in that its aims were purely maritime, Denmark and Sweden fought seven major naval engagements between 1563 and 1570, as Sweden sought to confirm its independence. These were fleet battles, with the Danes still relying on the old tried and tested tactics of boarding and entering while the Swedes preferred to stand off, using their modern guns to batter their enemies. We know little about these wars but they did demonstrate that weight of armament could outweigh the presence of troops as a decisive factor in ship-to-ship fights. What is more, a tactical plan and a system of command and control seem to have been exercised, such as would not become apparent in the English navy before the Dutch wars of the seventeenth century.

In 1582 a naval battle was fought in the open waters off Punta Delgada in the Azores for the control of those Portuguese islands, whose mother nation had recently been seized by Philip of Spain. It was a crucial fight, for command of the Azores allowed a power to either choke or facilitate the passage of both specie and spices through this mid-ocean hub. In 1582 the French had tried to gain control and were decisively defeated by the Spanish commanded by Alvaro de Bazan, Marquis of Santa Cruz. The battle hinged on a mêlée fought around the Spanish galleon *San Mateo*, which was attacked by seven French ships including that of their admiral, Philip Strozzi. Realising the pivotal nature of this fight, Santa Cruz weighed in. Strozzi's ship was boarded, and when the French admiral fell mortally wounded, the rest of his ships either surrendered or fled. The few English ships which had hovered around the engagement also fled, perhaps influencing Santa Cruz's view as to how successful a large armada launched

against England might be. His views and confidence were boosted the following year when he consolidated the Spanish hold over the Azores by leading a great fleet of galleys, which disgorged their troops directly on to the beaches of still-defiant Terceira and overwhelmed the inhabitants after a fierce artillery and musket exchange.

Punta Delgada had been a battle begun by ships fitted with heavy guns firing at range, but ended by boarding and fighting with swords and muskets. Thus towards the end of the century boarding remained the way that the Spanish, influenced by their experience with galleys, considered such engagements should be decided. They also felt this strongly during the Armada campaign. From the Escorial palace, Philip directed his commanders to overcome the English supremacy in gunnery by getting alongside – a close encounter that the English successfully avoided. Yet whether the 'Lutheran Hens' chickened out of hand-to-hand combat, as the Spanish soldiers believed, or had developed a superior method of fighting remains a debatable point. What is certain is that in 1582 the Spanish had demonstrated a mastery of both open seas naval warfare and amphibious operations; it was a professionalism that the English sometimes matched but never surpassed.

In the Mediterranean an entirely different form of naval warfare, fought between great squadrons of galleys, was to reach its climax when a Christian force commanded by Don John of Austria crushed the Turkish fleet at the battle of Lepanto. By this time galleys had been equipped with heavy, centrally mounted forward-facing guns capable of sinking ships; on either side of these, between two and four lesser guns added their weight of shot to make these ships powerful adversaries not just against their own kind but also against sailing ships. For many years sailing ships lacked equivalent forward-facing guns with which to handle these opponents, and the galleys, whose greater manoeuvrability in light airs and confined seas gave them dominance in inshore waters. Although masters of the non-tidal Mediterranean, galleys were not

In light winds a squadron of galleys aimed to surround a slow-moving vessel under sail, like a wolf pack. To capture all the action an artist might have to reduce the range between the combatants but in this Breughel engraving, which shows one carrack being boarded from a galley, the fight would be appear to be reaching its bloody close-quartered climax. (Scala Archives)

A naval battle from the Warwick Roll (of about 1485) shows the typical sea warfare of the pre-artillery age. A barrage of anti-personnel weapons – longbows, crossbows, spears and darts (even a rock thrown from the fighting top) – precedes what would become a boarding action. (British Library)

considered suitable warships to deploy in the rougher northern waters, where the battle against tidal streams, currents and weather could exhaust their oarsmen and swamp their craft with their low freeboard.

Nevertheless, the occasional deployment of these craft into the Channel and western approaches concerned the English for most of the century and influenced both the design of certain classes of ship to counter them and the deployment of warships to oppose them.

The English Way

Henry VII's two great ships, *Regent* and *Sovereign*, were designed and armed to fight at close quarters using hundreds of small-calibre guns mounted high up on their castles, where they just waited for the range to close. This concept of boarding was spelled out in Thomas Audley's fighting instructions of 1530, which included the famous advice:

> In case you board your enemy enter not till you see the smoke gone and then shoot off all your pieces, your port-pieces, the pieces of

hail-shot, crossbow shot, to beat his cage deck, and if you see his deck well ridden then enter with your best men, but first win his tops in any wise possible. In case you see rescue, scuttle the enemy ship but first take the captain with certain of the best with him, the rest be committed to the sea, for else they will turn upon you to your confusion.[1]

The Problem with Boarding

There were several problems with boarding apart from the seamanship necessary to close with a ship that did not wish to join company. Firstly, in closing to grappling range a ship exposed itself to all the close-range weaponry that its enemy could throw at it. This was not just gunfire. In the taking of the carrack *Santa Anna* Cavendish's crew were repulsed by well-hidden men with:

> lances, javelins, rapiers, and targets, and an innumerable sort of great stones, which they threw overboard upon our heads being so many of them, they put us off their ship again, with the loss of two of our men which were slain ... We new trimmed our sails, and gave them a fresh encounter with our great ordnance and also with our small shot, raking them through and through, to the killing and maiming of many men.[2]

This stand-off activity, after many hours, achieved the aim and, incidentally, but not critically, placed the *Santa Anna* in danger of sinking so that she surrendered. It should also be noted that the range at which Cavendish was engaging with his heavy guns was sufficiently close to be also within small-arms range.

Against the anti-boarding weapons of lances, bill hooks and other pole weapons, the sailor had to leap across the gap between two ships with only a sword in hand. He might also have found himself trying to clear the anti-boarding rigging stretched across the waist, which was one reason why an entry via the bow or stern came to be preferred. All the time he would also be subject to assault from the fighting-tops of many vessels.

The attacking ship's master would also have had his concerns. A forceful alongside without benefit of fenders could create severe damage not only to masts, yards and rigging but to the ship's side itself. Then there was the danger that a grappled vessel would not be able to free herself from engulfing fire or explosion, as happened to *Regent* after *Cordelière* caught fire in 1513.

Boarding another warship also required the presence of a well-trained soldiery. Once England, with its small population, had decided that her fleet had to be able to act independently of her army, which might be engaged in concurrent land operations, the number of soldiers available for the 'army of the sea' reduced significantly. This meant that boarding with overwhelming superiority was often not an option; commanders were thus forced to fire their heavy guns for longer and more destructively at a range outside that necessary for boarding.

A further difficulty arose if either help arrived for the boarded vessel or her assailant was driven off by weather or enemy fire, leaving a boarding party behind. In the first instance Audley's instructions were brutally effective: throw the captured crew overboard. Monson experienced all these problems and more in his corsairing days before he was eventually captured on the deck of a prize. Abandoned overnight in one prize, he fought on, although the enemy placed charges on the deck below and blew up the flat he was defending. On another occasion, Cumberland released six out of a dozen prizes he had taken, only for them to return to attack the ship which Monson had taken. He hurled himself awkwardly into his boat lying on the other side and so escaped capture; his lasting limp became a constant reminder of this adventure.

For all the above reasons, either softening up the opposition or, best of all, achieving a surrender prior to boarding had advantages. Yet gaining access to the enemy through either an opposed or a negotiated boarding remained the aim. For there was never a ship so humble that it was not carrying something of benefit to the acquisitive English seamen, who could not appropriate such goods, or a ransomable crew, from a sunk or sinking ship. Battering was thus not an alternative to but a precursor of boarding.

We have no evidence as to when this concept might have changed, but when the first opportunity to board since 1513 came about, in 1545 during the French wars, the English declined so to do. However, as the century progressed, various ways to engage an enemy at sea were tried, a development somewhat obscured by the dominance that the unique and unrepresentative Armada campaign has had over the thinking of naval historians. Many see that campaign as demonstrating a move from ship-boarding to ship-sinking tactics brought about by the change of the armament suite from short-range to long-range guns. This view is expressed succinctly by Mattingley, in his description of Hawkins's race-built galleons:

> The man-killing guns were reduced in number, the ship-killing guns were increased. Iron guns gave way to brass, and culverins and demi-culverins, long guns throwing an eighteen or nineteen pound shot with relatively high muzzle velocity and fair accuracy at ranges upward of a thousand yards, more and more replaced the stubbly barrelled smashers like the demi-cannon, a thirty pounder with a short uncertain range.[3]

This is incorrect. As the century progressed man-killing did not wane nor ship-sinking increase. Light shot fired at long range arrives at its target, if by chance it is accurate enough, all passion spent; heavy shot pummelled in body-blows makes itself felt deep down and dangerous. It is a boxing-match: arm's-length punches score points but win no knock-outs: they require solar-plexus punches and powerful hooks. If the English were fitting their fighting fleet to sink ships then the record shows them to have been unable to deliver those necessary body-blows. And yet they triumphed, and the wars of the century show how they responded to the challenge so to do.

Detail from a contemporary map showing anti-boarding netting rigged over the low and vulnerable waist of the ship. Such netting continued to feature on most warships all the way to the end of the century and well into the seventeenth when it was used as an anti-piracy measure by merchant ships. (British Library)

In the Armada campaign only one ship was sunk through receiving a ship-killing battering, and it is difficult to name another in the century sunk through the effects of long-range assault. In engagements after the Armada campaign, when Spanish ships could be considered to be well armed, the story remained the same. The *Revenge* famously endured a day and a night in close contact, with heavily armed galleons firing into her from ahead and astern as well as on both beams, and yet it was a storm, a few days later, that drove her ashore; she didn't even sink in the gale. What is more, it was the fact that 'forty of our poor hundred were slain, and half of the rest of us maim'd for life, In the crash of the cannonade ...'[4] that led to her surrender, not the fact that the ship was sinking. The truth remains that ships surrendered more frequently than they were sunk, and they struck their colours not because they were in a sinking condition but because they had too few men left to continue the fight. Heavy armament killed men more easily at range, and with less risk to one's own, than did close-encounters fighting, but – and this is a similarity with land battles – victory came with the possession of the field and with an enemy dead, dying and destroyed. Heavier weaponry was just a more efficacious way of achieving this aim. There is also a practical view that supports this contention. The English, from mid-century onwards, lusted after prizes, whether taken through piracy or more legitimate means. The key to a successful pirate attack was a quick approach, preferably on an unsuspecting vessel, a sharp volley, a rapid boarding and a seizure of the target intact. Drake's capture of the *Cacafuego* in the Pacific is the classic example, and his taking of *Rosario* shows a different method of achieving the same aim. The antithesis is the burning of *Las Cinque Llagas* in 1593 through too hot an assault and the failure to capture a rich carrack off St Michael in the Azores in 1597 because of an over-eager approach. The experienced English way was to close and close fast to seize and slay, but in major fleet engagements, when the aim was to defend the realm, discretion proved the better part of valour.

FIGHTING THE FRENCH, 1509–1550

The Fight with Sir Andrew Barton, 1511

The fight between the Howard brothers and Sir Andrew Barton in 1511, covered in Chapter 10, became the subject of a long and jolly ballad, the first of several to feature the Howards. It had been a swift action, but one achieved through the traditional method of grappling, boarding and killing men at close quarters, which both future admirals would have been brought up to consider was correct at sea. In their lifetimes this medieval concept was to change, but not before Edward Howard had lost his life boarding the enemy.

The Fleet Deploys, 1512

Edward Howard's success against Barton was rewarded by his being appointed the first sea-going fighting Lord Admiral for many a long year. Henry VIII's plan for invading France was well advanced, and he needed a fleet commander for two tasks: the traditional one of convoying the army overseas; and for blockading the French fleet in Brest and thus guaranteeing Henry and his army an unopposed crossing to Calais.

The war began with an English fleet escorting a force of some 12,000 men, destined for Gascony, past Brest, before they turned to take control of the Channel by seeking out and destroying the French fleet and its allied merchant shipping. Although the idea of a fleet mobilisation was new, the reaction was good. On 25 January 1512 Parliament agreed that war should be made on the French king; by 29 February orders had been issued for 'setting forth of the King's army of the sea', which included the following (and they were to change little over the century):

1. Indentures and instructions to be devised for the admiral and treasure won (half the prizes were to be reserved for the king).
2. The appointment of a substantial person in every ship to oversee the king's victuals and control expenditure by a rate delivered to him.
3. The indenture of the captain of every ship with the king.
4. Mariners coming to Greenwich to be assigned what ships they should go in; bursars to note their day of entry and to provide pay and victuals until they set forth.
5. The number and portage of the ships to be determined, and the number of dead shares and their allocation to the crews.
6. The ascertaining of the number of guns of every sort and the

England's early Tudor naval operations focused on Brittany and the area around Ushant they called 'The Trade': initially, with Henry VII endeavouring to preserve Breton independence from France; and then Henry VIII determined to bottle the French fleet up in Brest to allow him to control the Channel crossings. In Elizabeth's reign the Spanish erected a fort to control the exit from Brest which led to the land assault in which Frobisher was fatally wounded. (Map by Peter Wilkinson)

amount of shot and powder necessary, and also the number of bows, arrows, bowstrings, 'man pikes' and bills; 'a substantial man may be appointed in every ship to have charge of them'.

There were also injunctions to forbid gambling and swearing and to hold a daily service; this moral and spiritual guidance was repeated in every subsequent fleet deployment.[5]

The arrangements for the ships was supervised by Edward Howard, who authorised payments to be made for ordnance and other necessary equipment, but it was not until 7 April that he was formally appointed as admiral of a fleet of eighteen ships and '3000 men harnessed and arrayed for the war ... Of which 3,000, 18 shall be Captains, 1750 shall be soldiers, 1237 shall be mariners and gunners'.[6] The ratio of soldiers to sailors is significant, as it indicates that the concept of a naval battle being won through boarding and hand-to-hand fighting still held good. Howard's experience that year would begin the modification of this principle; for comparison, *Revenge* sailed to meet the Armada in 1588 with 126 soldiers, 270 mariners and thirty-four gunners embarked.

The admiral made three forays to the French coast that year. Having completed his escorting duties and made sure that 'no French ship dare leave port',[7] he returned to Southampton to replenish and

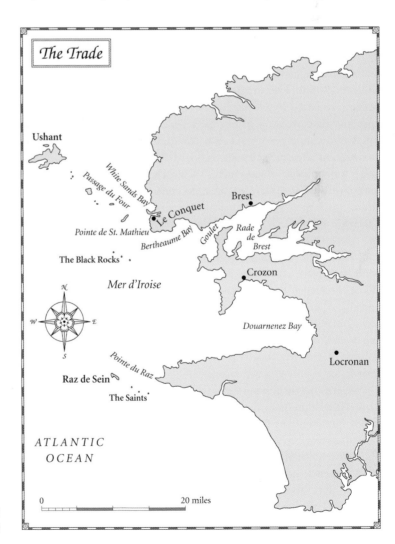

debrief the king, before sailing to assault the Breton towns of Crozon and Le Conquet. Then, on his third voyage, having by now embarrassed the French admiral sufficiently to get him to put to sea, he got the chance for a fight.

The Last Battle of the Old Age – Pointe de St Matthieu, 1512

Howard sailed back to the Trade (Ushant) in August with a fleet that had been increased to twenty-five ships. His swift turn-around meant that the combined French and Breton fleet was caught unawares anchored in Bertheaume Bay, off Brest, where the officers were providing onboard entertainment for local dignitaries and their families to celebrate the feast of St Lawrence, a very popular saint in Brittany.

The sudden arrival of the English caused consternation, with most of the French fleet slipping their anchors and scuttling back towards Brest. Yet before they reached safety, a most significant, although short, engagement took place between the two flagships, Edward Howard's *Mary Rose* and René de Clermont's *Grand Louise*. The latter, in his written report, stated that he was dismasted by Howard and lost some 300 seamen. If this were true, and there was every reason for the retreating admiral to exaggerate the event (which was not reported by Howard), then it would have been the first occasion in history on which ships fitted with gunports engaged each other and did so at range without endeavouring to board. This short and insignificant engagement was thus the harbinger of many more sea fights to come, which would reach their climax almost 300 years later at Trafalgar in 1805.

Meanwhile, an engagement that represented equally the end of the old school of ship fighting was taking place elsewhere and upwind of Howard. While the French fleet fled, the Breton commander and local hero Hervé de Portzmoguer, despite having many families on board for the feast, cut his cables and turned to face the foe. It was around his flagship *Cordelière* that the battle was concentrated.

Several English ships had tried to grapple *Cordelière* before the elderly *Regent* secured alongside her, enabling the crews to fight a fierce battle at close quarters, with many of the weapons that would be at home in a land battle. After many hours of close-quarters fighting, and just as the English were about to board, *Cordelière* caught fire. The flames spread rapidly, aided by the fact that men could not be spared to fight the fire.

Grand Louise, *the French flagship of René de Clermont in 1512, fled from Edward Howard's attack off Brest but claimed she had been dismasted by Mary Rose. This contemporary picture shows that she was fitted with gunports but circular ones which must have been more difficult to secure than the square English ones.*
(Mary Rose Trust)

Fire was the most potent weapon any ship possessed but, if uncontrolled, it could devastate friend and foe alike – *the* Regent *blew up in 1512 while entangled with the Breton flagship* Cordelière, *which may have been set alight by her own crew to prevent her falling into English hands.*
(Mary Rose Trust)

Eventually it reached the powder kegs, blowing both ships to smithereens and killing at least 1,500 people, including the women and children whom Portzmoguer had not had time to land. Among *Regent*'s dead were her captain, Henry's jousting companion and Howard's brother-in-law, Sir Thomas Knyvet, and Sir John Carew, one of that West Country family whose sons were to fall frequently in their sovereign's service.

Pointe de St Matthieu thus witnessed both an old-fashioned, grapple-and-board battle and a more modern gun fight. Although the honours were just about even, this was the result of an accident, and without it the French would have been decidedly bested by the English. Although that boarding had cost the king over 500 of his men, he remained in control of the Channel, for, as Edward Howard reported to Wolsey, the nation's fishermen were fishing uninterrupted in home waters, while he did not expect any French man-of-war over sixty or eighty tonnes to be at sea north of Brest that winter. Howard was also confident that were 'my bark [*Lizard*] and the new bark that Sir Stephen Bull is in with one good ship to lie ... in the Camber [Rye], and another in the Wight, that there shall stir not a Frenchman but he shall drink to his oysters ... for there is nothing to be feared from great ships which dare not keep the Narrow Seas these winter nights, without harbours.'[8] In Howard's brave words we see the doctrine so vital to England's interests of commanding the Channel whatever the weather and time of year. Howard stated that he 'dare lay my life' on his opinion: the next year he was required to do just that.

Bertheaume and White Sands Bays, 1513

Over the winter, Howard's main concern was the urgent need for victuals and clothing for the sailors kept at sea, without which they could not 'abide' and would 'sicken every day'.[9] As ever, he was concerned with the well-being of those under his command, a trait not invariably apparent in Wolsey, Henry or many of their other commanders. As is so often in the correspondence of the time, the writer highlights a concern that must have been as apparent to the opposition. In this case, Howard emphasises the shortcomings to French strategy of their not having a Channel naval port: it was a defect that was to be rectified by the new king, Francis II, when he ordered the building of Le Havre for this purpose.

While the English decided on a repeat performance the following year, the French resolved to do something to change the outcome, and that involved galleys. Henry, although convinced of the strength of his 10,000-man navy, knew that with both France and Scotland likely to be united against him aided, possibly, by Denmark, he needed support especially around Ushant, where he knew the French fleet strengthened by the galley squadron to be a formidable adversary. He wrote therefore to Ferdinand requesting that his father-in-law supply additional warships.[10] However, in full knowledge of how the King of Aragon had treated the English army the year before, he could not have been too confident of a timely response; in this he was right and the Spanish store ships that did arrive in Southampton many months late were more of a nuisance than a useful addition, for, unbeknown to Henry and the emperor, Ferdinand was arranging a peace treaty with the French behind their backs.

Galleys were not ideal weapons of war for northern waters. Rough seas, strong currents and tidal streams all mitigated against the advantageous use of these vessels with their low freeboard and muscle-power propulsion. Yet, when used defensively in sheltered coastal waters, they could play a significant role, and, for this reason Louis ordered a squadron, under the command of the experienced Prégent de Bidoux, to sail from the Mediterranean and join up with his fleet at Brest.

Henry, through the sophisticated intelligence system that covered all of Europe at the time, must have been aware of Louis's decision. He was already, according to Lorenzo Pasqualigo, a Venetian, 'building a new ship or carrack of 4,000 butts, with three decks. Its name is 'Regent' the same as the ship which was burnt ... This ship will carry 2,000 men and 200 pieces of ordnance, so that it will be the largest and most powerful ship that ever put to sea.'[11]

But Badoer, the Venetian ambassador, also reported that Henry 'would have given a thousand ducats a month each for four light galleys and two bastard galleys'.[12]

Edward Howard, sailing from the Thames in the spring of 1513, would have been aware of the galley threat to his force, but he does not seem to have been over troubled by it, as he explained to the king:

> Sir, as for the galleys, we make great way with them ... if there come any other by day or by night, the boats and small vessels and rowbarges and row-galleys shall lay them sharply aboard, and rather than they should escape us, I have assigned William Harper, the *Thomas of Hull*, my bark, Sir William Trevynan's bark and two or three small ships ... though they should run them aground for to make them sink. And, Sir, if they come amongst us, they shall not escape clean with good.[13]

As previously, the administrative arrangements were planned in meticulous detail, with every ship and its captain, master and crew numbers listed along with the costs of support.[14] Among the new names appearing this year was *Maria de Loreta*, a 1,500-tonne merchant ship seized by the navy after her owner sold her to France rather than England, who had requested to purchase her. When Howard arrived off Brest he found the enemy fleet safe within their haven, where contrary winds prevented him getting out and common sense prevailed on them to stay put. Prégent was however not there. Foiled by bad weather from carrying out a raid on the West Country, he had put into St Malo, from where, having been informed of Howard's arrival, he sailed and descended on the unsuspecting English at anchor in

Bertheaume Bay provides a sheltered anchorage on the seaward side of Brest Roads. It was here that the French and Breton fleets, with many visitors from shore, were celebrating Saint Lawrence's day in 1512, when they were surprised by the arrival of Edward Howard's fleet. The following year the English in turn were surprised while anchored here by the French galleys. (Author)

White Sands Bay, Brittany. When the French galleys retired into this bay, having inflicted damage on Edward Howard's fleet off Brest in 1513, the English admiral launched a boat attack on them, only to lose his life in the repulsed assault. (Author)

Bertheaume Bay. In his first attack he sank one transport and badly holed Sir Stephen Bull's command, *Less Barke*. Having thus announced his arrival he retreated, around the headland, into White Sands Bay, where he moored his galleys stern to the shore, their guns facing out to sea, and with the additional protection of two fortified headlands. From here, where he was able to replenish and exercise his men, he posed an ever-present threat to the English, and any supporting victuallers that needed to sail by, while being virtually impregnable himself. Howard had to test that invincibility: either that or retreat ignominiously to Plymouth and incur the king's displeasure. After a land assault was repulsed, the admiral loaded some boats with soldiers and trusty friends and rowed into the attack. He himself, with a few others, actually managed to scramble on board the French admiral's galley, only to be flung overboard on the pikes of the defenders. The remaining craft, having taken casualties at range, rowed back. The next day, leaderless and dispirited, the English sailed back to the West Country, where Edward's elder brother, Thomas, was appointed admiral in his stead.

As an operational navy the English had the stuffing knocked out of them by the nature of their defeat at White Sands Bay. From then on, for some seventy years, the fear of galleys was to dominate English naval thinking, until John Hawkins provided the design solution with his race-built galleons.

Skirmishes, 1514–1544

In his much longer period in command of the navy following his brother's death, Thomas Howard showed himself to be a far more cautious commander, preferring to establish the enemy's disposition and intention through intelligence rather than seeking out and destroying them himself. He did, however, sail *Mary Rose* north so he could join his father on land to defeat the Scots at Flodden Field, a result that at last restored the elderly Earl of Surrey to his Norfolk dukedom, with Thomas taking the Surrey title as a courtesy. That apart, the years after 1514 saw no major battles at sea, although a number of skirmishes and anti-piracy patrols kept the navy active even in periods of peace, while the short French war of 1522–4 saw little naval activity apart from raids. This was to change after 1534, when Henry felt that the 'great matter' of his divorce from Katherine was worth a separation from Rome, and England, distancing herself from Europe, brought war closer to her shores. From then on the state had to think defensively.

Henry's Last Scottish War, 1543–1547

In April 1539 fear of invasion was kindled by reports of fifty great ships of war lying off Texel. Preparations were made to defend Kent when this fleet anchored off North Foreland, but it soon slipped away down Channel on an entirely different mission. However, the next few years saw a change in English defence policy, from one based on offence to one of defence, the surviving evidence of which is the chain of coastal forts stretching from the Thames to Wales. The next enemy, however, was to be the Scots, whom Henry, ever subtle, tried to bully into agreeing a marriage between his son Edward and their young princess, Mary Stuart.

In August 1543 Lord Admiral Lisle reported to the king that Sir Richard Mawnsfeld and his company had met up with sixteen French ships on passage to Scotland and had a great fight, but were unable to inflict much damage as the French kept 'so good order'. However, *Sacre of Dieppe* had been twice boarded by *Minion* and *Primrose* but escaped, as 'did all but one hoy'. On arriving in Edinburgh, Henry was informed, the French boasted that they had slain the captains (Baldwin and Willoughby) and many men, proving that one small French ship could out fight two of the English king's best. However, to soothe the king's temper, Henry was told that the French had taken only one prisoner, a poor bricklayer, and that although they boasted of a victory 'he had never seen a ship so more beaten that the *Sacre*'.[15] On such engagements are the timbers of a fine naval tradition laid.

By 1544 the Scots had become masters of the North Sea. Late in the year they seized *Anthony of Newcastle*, an eighty-tonne vessel, as

well as many smaller craft. At the time when that incident was reported by the Earl of Shrewsbury,[16] land commander in the north, they had only six or seven sail at sea but were expected to be joined by a squadron of ten or twelve more commanded by John Barton, the bearer of a family name that would have been familiar to Henry and Norfolk from their early anti-piracy adventures. On the same day (3 November) as Shrewsbury was writing to the king, the President of the Council of the North, Philip Lentall, wrote to the Lord President, to inform him that the Scots had taken six ships in the past week between Flamborough Head and Whitby. To add insult to injury they had then anchored within gunshot range of Flamborough Head and allowed the garrison (of two gunners) to fire four times over their heads, after which engagement the English had run out of powder![17]

Lentall's pen, with its courteous request for more shot and powder, must have greatly toned down its owner's ignominious rage. On 6 November the Privy Council informed Shrewsbury that the king was sorry that 'his loving subjects had suffered loss by the Scots', but marvelled that Newcastle and the other ports had not manned any vessels in their own defence. Moreover, because the king was not prepared to spare any ships, Shrewsbury was invited to encourage self-help. This was what was being done in the West Country, where between twelve and sixteen ships were being kept on patrol for just £10,000, while Rye was benefiting by keeping three ships of its own at sea. A similar private convoy system was protecting the East Anglian herring fishermen. The letter ended with the less than subtle threat that because it 'were over burdensome that the King should set ships to defend all parts of the realm, and keep the Narrow Seas withal. They of Newcastle are the more bounden to show themselves loving subjects in this as they are not charged with subsidies and 15ths as others are.'[18] One can presume that the Geordies took the hint.

The Scots continued to 'hover upon the coasts'. Yet if the navy was not able or willing to challenge them, then there were private adventurers willing to try. On the last day of March 1546 John Dymock wrote to the Lord President, Paget, recommending that a letter of marque be issued to a likely lad who had served the emperor at sea and had a ship of fifty tonnes and a crew of '40 tall men' which

Broughty Castle on the Tay was captured by the English in 1547 in an amphibious assault. It was held until 1550.

he was prepared to fit out against the French and Scots if he was granted leave to sell the goods he captured in England.[19]

It is difficult to draw tactical conclusions from a naval war in which both sides appeared willing and content to keep their distance. The one strategic lesson was that a fleet in being remains a threat to any enemy operating away from its home waters, and much more so when it retains its total integrity and does not lose or damage ships in engagements that of themselves will not affect the outcome of the war. Galleys remained a threat, with Leo Strozzi demonstrating the power of their ordnance by sinking one ship and battering St Andrews Castle into submission in July 1547 during an unchallenged deployment into waters far north for his vessels; he returned just before an English naval force commanded by Lord Clinton sailed up the coast accompanying Somerset's land forces. Naval amphibious forces proved their worth by taking the isle of Inchcolm and Broughty Crag but also demonstrated that, once ashore, they needed reliable re-supply if they were to hold out. The lack of this led to the abandonment of Inchcolm, with Broughty holding out in a parlous state.

A NEW ENEMY

Between the Treaty of Boulogne with France in 1550 and the open war with Spain that began in 1585 the seas were seldom quiet. Mary's French war, in which Calais was lost, was just a part of a general skirmishing state of hostility that existed when vessels of the European nations fell out with each other at sea. Adding to this mistrust was the continuing activity of pirates, which made the second half of the century a time of perpetual strife. Part of the reason was that the sea had no boundaries comparable with the established frontiers on land, the crossing of which indicated a hostile act. Ships' captains could chance their arm without heed to diplomatic niceties and, with bravado and luck, get away with it. Yet an idea of a closed sea existed not only along the Channel coast but further afield, with the Portuguese claiming rights over the waters of western Africa and the Spanish, by virtue of the Treaty of Tordesillas, insisting on their trading monopoly in the New World. Both rights were challenged by the English, but with mixed results.

The Guinea Fights, 1557

In late January 1557 William Towerson, in the 120-tonne *Tiger* and with the sixty-tonne *Hart* in company, had joined up with two French ships to seek for slaves in Guinea, a cargo to which the Portuguese claimed sole rights, which they maintained a squadron to enforce. Discovered *in flagrante* by a five-ship flotilla, Towerson's squadron prepared to fight by working to gain the weather gage, with the intention of closing their opponents and boarding them. Not only were the Portuguese having none of this but their lighter carvels were armed with powerful-enough guns to incline their opponents to keep their distance, while their own ships handled well enough to dance out of such danger. To enforce their advantage the Portuguese also sailed in line ahead, each of their ships being able to bring her broadside to bear as she drew level with the ship opposite. It was a meeting of two methods: Towerson's traditional close-and-board and the Portuguese

Jesus of Lubeck was a large, ungainly and unweatherly merchant vessel bought for Henry VIII by Thomas Seymour and of little use as a royal warship. Her claim to infamy rests with her career as a slaver hired out by Elizabeth to John Hawkins who had to abandon her during the treacherous Spanish attack at San Juan de Ulua in 1568. (Drawing by Peter Kirsch based on the Anthony Anthony Roll)

gun-ship battle. There is no doubt as to which was the superior.[20]

San Juan de Ulua, 1568

John Hawkins's early slave-trading ventures lie outside the scope of the book, but it is worth noting that in 1567 he sailed on the final one of these voyages with a flotilla of six vessels including two royal ships on lease, the elderly 700-tonne great carrack *Jesus of Lubeck*, purchased by Henry in 1544, and the newer, but allegedly unlucky, 100-tonne *Minion*. Hawkins also claimed the right to fly the royal standard to indicate that this was a voyage sponsored by Her Majesty among others.[21]

Even prior to his departure Hawkins had had a stand-off with the Spanish while still at anchor in Plymouth, when seven Netherlands-bound vessels had entered that port in a belligerent manner and neither dipped their ensigns nor fired a salute. Custom of the sea demanded a response, and Hawkins, suspecting treachery, had opened fire. The confrontation ended with no damage to either side but with a clear indication that although England and Spain were not at war, neither were they at peace. Sailing to the Americas, Hawkins knew that he was entering an area where any interloper was treated by the Spanish as hostile. His aggressive sales techniques in those waters would ensure that should he meet up with a comparable force he could not expect the outcome to be as un-bruising as it had been in Plymouth Sound.

For most of the voyage Hawkins kept clear of enemy shipping, but when hurricane winds forced him to take shelter in San Juan de Ulua, the day before a Spanish fleet arrived, he knew he was going to have to fight for his life. His first astute move had been to moor the four English ships, together with their prize and one French ship that had joined him, at the seaward end of the low reef that forms the breakwater to the harbour. He had also, as an aggressive defensive measure, taken over the island's gun batteries.

His wisdom in so doing was proved the next day when the fleet bringing the new Viceroy of New Spain, Don Martin Enriquez, arrived and found the English commanding the port. This was a situation totally offensive to the new viceroy, who considered righting the affront to be an excellent way to demonstrate his resolve as he took up his new post. He therefore replaced the truce agreed with treachery, planning to seize the unsuspecting English ships via a hulk which was all that lay between the two fleets.

The watchful English spotted the soldiers being brought on board the wooden hulk and opened fire. The Spanish responded by attacking and taking the shoreside batteries and turning their guns on the English, who were now desperately hauling themselves out into the harbour, where they might get underway. At first Hawkins's gunners gained the upper hand, firing at point-blank range into the Spanish *Almirante*, which caught fire when her magazine exploded, and the *Capitana*, whose upper works crumbled under the rapid and repetitive fire. In the ship-on-ship action the English dominance was absolute. The tide turned when the Spanish shore batteries opened fire. At first their guns proved too light to cause much damage to the hulls of their enemy, who were gradually opening the range, but then the Spaniards changed their target to the masts and their ammunition to chain shot. *Jesus*'s weather-weakened foremast fell first, while her much-pierced main was too far gone to bear the strain of a sail – *Jesus of Lubeck* was going nowhere. What is more, as she was an old-design ship her main armament consisted of her stern-chasers and broadside guns. The latter, especially, had done great service, but the batteries lay on the island ahead, a direction in which none of *Jesus*'s main armament could be brought to bear. Meanwhile, other guns had holed the little *Angel* below the water-line and she sank while still at her moorings. Drake, as always swift to respond to any threat of danger, had managed to take his undamaged *Judith* clear of the action, where he was later joined by *Minion*, the only other survivor of the battle, who had managed to extract herself from the harbour with the survivors from the sunken ships. That night Drake abandoned his cousin and his consort to make a solo voyage home.

Leaving aside the hatred of the Spanish which their betrayal had kindled unquenchably in Drake's breast, it is difficult to see whether any lessons were learned directly from this, the greatest defeat inflicted on English naval units during the century. Yet when Hawkins designed his race-built galleons, they were lighter and more heavily armed than *Jesus* and thus easier to handle in confined waters. They also had forward-facing guns placed right forward below the beak-head. Many have attributed the introduction of the latter to the desire to engage the galleys better, but these were more a fear than a threat in the northern waters that were still the main patrol area of the navy. As Hawkins sketched out his magnificent design was it the batteries of San Juan de Ulua rather than the basilisks of Leo Strozzi that he had in mind?

Spanish Ships of War at Sea

The lengthy war with Spain that occupied the latter part of Elizabeth's reign had an equally lengthy prelude, in which both piratical skirmishes and fleet deployments played a part. In much the same way as in Henry VIII's reign, a papal bull, this time *Regans in excelsis*, which denounced Elizabeth as a heretic, declared open season on the English. However, what was different from 1570 onwards was that the queen had Englishmen prepared to build and finance their own vessels to act as both a proxy and an auxiliary navy for the mutual benefit of state and trade. This generally involved bedevilling Spain, and eventually their deprivations forced the Spanish king to make an offensive response.

The First Battle of the Atlantic

The nature of the sea war with Spain would be very familiar to students of the Atlantic conflicts of the twentieth century. Convoys, wolf-packs and countermeasures, as well as the threat of invasion, all feature in what was to be a struggle for mastery of both the Narrow Seas and the wider ocean. Like its more recent successors it was a long campaign, of which one year can serve as an example.

The Fight of *Content*, 1591

In June 1591 a squadron of three English privateers owned by the pirate governor of the Isle of Wight, Sir George Carey, later Lord Hunsdown, was surprised by a superior Spanish force of six off Cuba. In the fight that followed Carey's own ship *Content* fought with several of the enemy at a time, including a galley which gave her 'five cast pieces out of her prow' but the crew were dissuaded from boarding through being 'galled' by musketry and by having a ball of fire thrown into them. The fierce fight lasted from seven in the morning until eleven at night, at which time a favourable wind allowed the English to draw away. *Content*'s own armament consisted just of a minion, a saker, a falcon and two port bases but these, together with their muskets, kept three ships of between 600 and 700 tonnes and two galleys clear of her. In return Carey estimated that 'The armadas shot their great ordnance continually at her, not so few as 500 times. And the sides, hull, and mast of the *Content* were sowed thick with musket bullets.'[22]

Two observations may be drawn from this eye-witness account. Firstly, the rate of fire of both Spanish and English ships was higher than one round per gun per hour, and secondly, even heavy weaponry had limited ship-killing ability. As ever had been and for a long time would be, it was killing people that counted. Heavy ordnance just made that killing more effective. Until the advent of the iron-hulled ship and the plunging and explosive shell it was almost impossible to sink a wooden warship by gunfire alone. Fire and explosion were the great ship-sinkers in time of conflict, and this fact was known and acted upon throughout the century, with warships being equipped with the ordnance necessary to start fires in their opponents' vessels. The problem with wildfire is that it was, as the name suggests, uncontrollable, so its use had to be circumspect: throwing it into a ship with which one had become grappled or entangled might send both vessels up in flames.

In June 1594, finding his boarding party unable to progress because of stout resistance from the crew of the Portuguese carrack that he had boarded, *La Cinque Llagas*, Captain Downton in *Sampson* set fire to a mat on the carrack's beak-head. The flames rapidly spread to her bowsprit and topsail and then engulfed the vessel. *Sampson* herself had a lucky escape, as Downton reported: 'We desired to be off from her, but had little hope to obtain our desire; nevertheless we plied water very much to keep our ship well. By God's providence only, by

This detail from a sixteenth-century map of the Cadiz area shows the ideal scenario for a galley attack on a sailing ship: numerous galleys surround their victim, approaching from angles that make counter-fire difficult. However, in this very area the Centurion *fought off the concerted attack of five galleys.* (Royal Naval Museum, Portsmouth)

the burning asunder of our spiritsail-yard with ropes and sail, and the ropes about the spirit-sail of the carrack, whereby we were fast intangled, we fell apart.'[23] Incidentally, Downton also reported that two of his ships had 'plied' the carrack 'with their great ordnance' from evening until midnight, when they boarded: another lengthy engagement with little obvious damage being inflicted.

Centurion's Battle with the Galleys, 1591

It was not only Hawkins's race-built galleons that were to gain the measure of the galleys. Rather surprisingly, some armed merchant vessels also seem to have managed to drive such predators away. On Easter Sunday 1591, *Centurion*, described as 'a very tall ship of burden but yet weakly manned',[24] with her crew of just forty-eight, was attacked while becalmed in the Straits of Gibraltar by five Spanish galleys, each of whom was manned by five to six hundred men. Two of these grappled her on either side while their admiral secured himself astern, from where his shot badly damaged *Centurion's*, main mast, mizzen and stern and ripped apart her sails.

The fight lasted for five and a half hours, during which time the ship's crew had not only to repel boarders but to throw overboard wildfire which was hurled on board on five occasions. Finally, when her ammunition was expended and four of her men killed and many more injured, the Spanish retired, leaving their prize bloodied but unbowed and with such a reputation that six galleys closing the next day left her alone. Not so *Dolphin*, which had sailed in company but was not attacked until the fight with *Centurion* was over. She was set ablaze, and when the flames reached her magazine she blew up with total loss of life.

The Little *Revenge*, 1591

Defeated although they may have been in the coastal seas, the Spanish

were no easy foe out in the broad Atlantic, as another Howard, Lord Thomas, came to realise very quickly in 1591. The strategy that led to his encounter with the Spanish fleet was due to Hawkins's visionary but impractical proposal to deploy to the Azores in some strength.

The position of the Azores as a hub in the Iberian maritime organisation had long been recognised. The fleets from both the Caribbean and West Indies converged here on their outward and inbound voyages for much-needed mid-ocean replenishment, as did the great carracks heading from the East Indies to Lisbon laden down with spices and other oriental produce. This concentration of wealthy cargoes in one small sea area attracted pirates and privateers, and several fortunes were made in these waters.

Hawkins, however, felt that the Azores hub offered the opportunity to combine national strategy with the opportunity for personal gain, a heady mix for a public-private partnership, especially given the queen's well-known reluctance to commit either funds or fleets to foreign adventures. Hawkins set out to prove that his new design of ship had the improved sea-staying qualities that would enable the fleet to keep station away from home waters for a lengthy period of time. As a result he championed a plan to keep two squadrons each of six ships at sea, one off the Azores and one cruising the coast of Iberia, relieved on station so that a constant pressure was exerted on the Spanish trade routes.

In response to Hawkins's ideas, Cumberland cruised the Azores in 1589 with his own pirate ships but had a miserable patrol, which failed to intercept both the *flota* from New Spain and the East Indies carracks, and eventually his one rich prize with its cargo of hides, sugar and cochineal became a total wreck in Mount's Bay. Frobisher, acting as long-stop off Portugal, had better luck and his voyage was 'made' but not spectacularly. Fear of the English had, in fact, led Philip to delaying the treasure fleet's departure until the following year – a fact of which, given that state secrets leaked as badly as did *Revenge*, Hawkins was fully aware.

A hands-on man, Hawkins got to sea himself the following year. For seven months he cruised, first off Spain and then, relieving Frobisher, off the Azores. To no avail. Equally aware of English plans, Phillip had ordered the delayed *flota* to make a winter passage, knowing that the English would not be lying in wait in such inclement weather. Having pulled off this coup the Spanish followed up by sailing their swift *gallizabras* to Portugal before Frobisher arrived on the Azores station. Triumphant, but still cautious, Philip then suspended further sailings until 1591. Hawkins now saw an opportunity for his own more seaworthy ships to intercept two years' worth of treasure off the Azores.

Yet the fleet which, after much discussion over both constitution and command, did sail was far smaller than the opportunity demanded. Leaving aside parsimony, there were probably two reasons for this. Firstly, the new strategy envisaged the navy remaining on station for a long period of time, with new vessels being sent out periodically to relieve them, and secondly, the English were in denial about the floating countermeasures that Spain had built well and in record time.

Through a mix of post-Armada euphoria, exaggerated claims and the desire not to admit how unsuccessful Drake's follow-up attack had been, the English had underestimated Philip of Spain's resilience and his determination to defeat the annoying and embarrassing island of heretics, a task that he realised had to be achieved first of all at sea. The king was as lucky as Elizabeth had been with Hawkins: he found in Alonso de Bazan, brother of the famous Santa Cruz, a man who like Hawkins had both great sea experience and a mind suited to shipbuilding and strategy. So in 1589 the fight back began, with Spain's northern shipyards building, as an adaptation of the English galleon, twelve large vessels which were named after the Apostles. Nine more fighting vessels were built at Lisbon, and with his own ship-building capacity now at full stretch Philip hired twelve large Ragusan ships to join his fleet. The Spanish had also examined new ideas for ship design to suit their need to protect the Atlantic passage of their treasure. Instead of just concentrating on more powerful escorts, they produced the *gallizabra*, a small, fast, heavily-armed treasure ship capable of independent passage because it could outsail any opposition. For the first time in the maritime conflict the actuality of power projection at sea moved in favour of Spain.

Command of the English fleet in 1591 was given to Lord Thomas Howard, whose uncle was Lord Admiral, with Richard Grenville as Vice-Admiral, possibly on the suggestion of Ralegh, who was disappointed at not being allowed to sail himself. The flagship was *Defiance*, Grenville sailed in *Revenge*, and they were accompanied by the 600-tonne *Elizabeth Bonaventure* and 550-tonne *Nonpareil* (formerly *Philip* and *Mary*) along with the 200-tonne *Crane* and two smaller ships of under a hundred tonnes, *Charles* (owned by the Lord Admiral) and *Moon*. In accordance with the strategic plan, *Moon* and *Nonpareil* returned home in July, to be replaced by the better armed and heavier *Golden Lion* and *Foresight*, but the paper plan of despatching a continuous flow of relief shipping proved difficult to implement in practice because back in England port after port

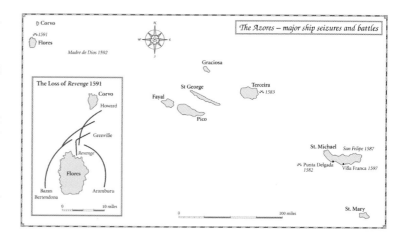

The waters around the Azores held the key to the trade war between England and Spain for both inward and homebound convoys needed to sail through these seas. The English were never powerful enough to dominate the islands and too often were too poorly served by intelligence (both information and brains) to seize the opportunities that were presented. (Map by Peter Wilkinson)

responded to the Privy Council's request for shipping with excuses. This was perturbing, for the first intelligence of a Spanish counter-offensive was being digested. However, renewed efforts meant that, as well as the royal ships *Lion* and *Foresight*, six armed merchantmen were found to be available for an Azores voyage. Bad weather delayed their departure, and by the time they got away, on 17 August, it was too late for them to give Howard's squadron any practical support. Having taken passage, as instructed, via the coast of Portugal, the fighting merchantmen were only a week out in the Atlantic when Howard most needed them. Howard did, however, receive an intelligence update from Burghley delivered by a pinnace in early July that gave him some inkling of the Spanish ships of war at sea.

However, forewarned was not forearmed for Howard, who could either remain on station with the ships he had or retire in the face of an unconfirmed threat, thereby throwing away any prospect of capturing or disrupting the treasure fleet. There can be no doubt, if he had waivered, of what the views of his second-in-command would have been. Yet it would not only have been the intelligence received that was been preying on the admiral's mind, for, after an unusual period of healthy living, the inevitable consequences of a long period at sea began to be apparent as ship after ship reported a rapid rise in sickness. Howard was forced to lead his ships into a bay in Flores, where the sick could be landed, and the ships scrubbed out and ballasted with clean stone to take the place of the noxious stew that was swilling in their holds. The reduction in the numbers of fit seamen also led to Howard taking the drastic measure of sinking Sir George Carey's *Content* and transferring her crew to other vessels.

By contrast, Don Alonso de Bazan would have felt comfortable as he sailed with his force towards Terceira and his rendezvous with the treasure fleet off the Azores, the scene, along with Lepanto, of his elder brother's greatest triumphs. He now had the opportunity to place his own name alongside that of his sibling in his nation's maritime pantheon. Even more anxious for success was Bazan's vice-admiral, Martin de Bertendona, afloat in the 876-tonne *San Bernabe*. He had commanded the Levant squadron in the Armada campaign and was thus seeking revenge in more than one way. A comparison of the strength of the two sides indicates that Bertendona would be granted no better opportunity.

The moment the powerful Spanish fleet set sail, the English were turned from predators to prey, unaware of the force that was slowly advancing towards them from the east. And as that force approached the Azores it was gathering further intelligence to enable it to make its battle plan.

Bazan called first at Terceira, where he was informed that the English were lying off the western isle of Flores, but, eager as he was, to sail on, strong westerlies kept him on the eastern edge of the archipelago. He was also told that there were only twenty-two ships in the English fleet, of which just six were the queen's fighting galleons. Given the odds, his challenge was no longer to win a victory at sea, but to surround and totally annihilate the enemy: Howard's disposition would make the task easier. A day out from Flores, and with local pilots joining his ship to update him, Bazan called a council of war to plan the action. The English, so he was informed, were in a bay on the north-west side of Flores concentrating on maintenance of both ships and men.

Bazan ordered an encircling operation. He would lead one group around from the south-west, while the Castillian squadron, under Marcos de Aramburu, would approach on the other side and close the channel between Flores and Corvo. Surprise would be achieved, not only because both groups would be hidden behind the island's high hills until the last moment, but also because they would time their synchronised arrival for dawn, when the morning breeze would also be in their favour.

As the jaws began to close on the unsuspecting English they were thrown two small life-lines. The Earl of Cumberland, cruising off the coast of Portugal, had been aware of the Spanish fleet's departure and had despatched Captain Middleton in *Moonshine* to warn Howard. This was, in Tennyson's words, the 'pinnace like a fluttering bird' that arrived at the English anchorage on 30 August, overtaking the Spanish with just hours to spare. The second piece of luck was that Bazan's dawn attack was delayed by a few hours because he had slowed so not to leave astern a damaged Santander galleon.

Surprised and alarmed, Howard had no time to discuss tactics; in danger of being sealed into the bay, he had no option but to order his fleet to weigh as fast as possible, in some cases by cutting their cables. Even so it was a close-run thing. Using similar tactics to those employed by Howard of Effingham to get his fleet out of Plymouth and to windward of the Armada in 1588, Thomas Howard led his fleet safely through the closing jaws, although the ships did have to fire their broadside weapons to discourage the Spanish from closing too rapidly. They all got through, save two – *Revenge* and the victualler *George Noble*, which for all that is known may have been engaged in the same rescue work as Grenville, who seemed determined to ferry his sick from the shore before sailing. By the time this was completed, the pincers were effectively closed.

There was still a chance of escape. If *Revenge* had unfurled her main sail then her superior sailing abilities might well have helped her escape, but to follow this course would have seemed, to Grenville, to

The aptly-named island of Flores in the Azores offered both water and sustenance to those who had spent long months at sea. It was Thomas Howard's decision to take his fleet here for recuperation that was to lead to the loss of Revenge *in 1591.*
(Portuguese Tourist Board)

213

be running away. With his main sail furled, the traditional state for it to be in when going into battle, he could indicate that he scorned his opponents and was willing to give battle. So, rather than leap away between the enemy and the island, he chose to force his way between the Spanish jaws, just as Howard had but, of course, by now with much less sea room in between. He almost made it, and it would be wrong to believe that he did not intend to break out; it was just that 'the greatness of his mind' – as Ralegh kindly described his belligerent bone-headedness – deterred him from doing so in a way that might have inferred cowardice.

Revenge, the third of the race-built galleons built under John Hawkins's guidance, was laid down in 1575. Of 450 tonnes, she was ninety-two feet long with a beam of thirty-two feet (almost the ideal 3:1 ratio), and had a draught, when laden, of fifteen feet. Although no contemporary drawings of her exist, it is known that she had four masts and carried an armament of forty-six great guns on two decks. She served, with distinction, as Drake's flagship during the Armada campaign and again in his less glorious descent on Spain the year after. Yet she was considered unlucky, and with due cause, for it is recorded that she ran aground six times and sprang such bad leaks on three occasions that she almost foundered. In the 1589 expedition Drake only just managed to get her home before her pumps were defeated by the leaks. On another occasion she was overturned on the shore and had to be righted and pumped out before she could be refloated and repaired. Yet such misfortune merely seems to indicate how robust Hawkins's design was. Her accident-prone fourteen-year career also indicates that she spent a great deal of her life at sea: for, launched in 1577, she was built in time to take part in the busiest prolonged period of naval activity in the Tudor century.

Having exchanged fire with Howard, the great galleons of Spain turned together to await the little *Revenge*, which approached *gallardeano*, all of a swagger, or in today's language, full of machismo and cahones. Grenville sailed determinedly towards them and broke through the line of Castilian ships, beyond which he could see Howard watching and waiting. However, even having demonstrated his prowess, he did not order the main sail to be unfurled, and was thus overhauled by the great galleon *San Felipe*, which took the wind from his sails.

The *San Felipe* grappled *Revenge* and threw a small boarding party on board. However, Grenville's gunners had been holding fire for just such a moment and now, with the ships lying side by side, they opened up with their devastating broadside, which stove in *San Felipe*'s side and blew her away from *Revenge*. A close encounter such as this suited the English gunners. Hawkins had designed his race-built galleons to lie low in the water, which meant that their two rows of guns could inflict damage on an enemy very close to the latter's water-line while shot from the higher-built Spanish galleons would pass either harmlessly overhead or through the sails, rigging and masts – which, although it could severely curtail movement, would not affect the ship's fighting integrity. The gunners in *Revenge* seem to have manned the starboard guns while leaving the port unattended, for as was usual in these ships, there were not enough of them to stand to on both sides.

Even as the distance between the ships increased, *Revenge*'s musketeers and murderers were still able to fire upon the Apostle's exposed personnel. Too damaged to play a further active role in the fight, *San Felipe*, by remaining up wind, prevented *Revenge* from getting underway again: from this moment the English galleon was dead in the water, although very much alive above it.

As *San Felipe* fell away Bertendona brought *San Bernabe* crashing into *Revenge*'s unguarded port side and threw on board grapnels secured by lengths of chain, as had happened in the disastrous fight between *Regent* and *Cordelière* in 1513. With their starboard side secure, *Revenge*'s gunners dashed across the decks and opened up on their assailant with their lighter upper tier of guns, causing great damage to her masts and rigging and discouraging any concerted attempt to board. At about this moment the faithful *George Noble* hailed *Revenge* to offer assistance, only for Grenville to tell her to save herself – the fewer men, the greater the share of glory. The fact that she did get clear does indicate that there was still sea room available, if only Grenville could have cut himself free of *San Bernabe*'s iron embrace, a move that Bertendona was determined to prevent. At the same time, the fierceness of the English resistance was preventing any significant number of the enemy crew from boarding their own ship.

Night brought no respite to either side, for *Revenge* could still sting. In the dusk *San Cristobel* rammed her stern and sent a large number of boarders across, who drove the small group of defenders forward until the latter managed, by a concentration of small arms fire

Revenge was judged to be an unlucky ship, although Drake favoured her; yet her recovery from several groundings and floodings demonstrate that Hawkins built her well and she was to withstand a terrible pounding from the Spanish fleet before going down in one of the severest storms ever to have struck the Azores. (Veres László)

damaged her so badly that she sank shortly afterwards, as did, in the early morning light, *La Serena*.

That dawn revealed the beleaguered ship to be a mastless hulk, her upper works shot away, slowly settling in the water but still armed and dangerous. Less stout vessels would have sunk. *Revenge*'s frequent groundings had shown her to be well built; now she was demonstrating her physical strength in a manner that would fill her builders and designers with pride.

However, few of her already much-reduced crew were capable of fighting, for many were dead and many were injured and could fight no more. Surrender seemed the only logical option, but not to the mortally wounded Grenville. 'Sink me the ship, master gunner', does seem to be a succinct summary of his desire, and he was not alone in feeling that it was 'better to fall into the hands of God, than into the hands of Spain'. However, Captain Langhorn and the master felt that honour would not be added to by suicide and negotiated a surrender with terms that included the immediate release of prisoners once the fleet had returned to Spain. Given the treatment that was usually the fate of captured English sailors, including flaying, burning, long and solitary incarceration and galley service, the deal was as exceptional as the action itself. Bertendona, his honour satisfied, and aware of the chivalry with which that other great English corsair, Drake, had treated his Spanish captives, asked only that the gentlemen on board pay a ransom fitting to their circumstances; the crew would be sent home immediately. Even these terms did not satisfy Grenville or his master gunner, who had to be restrained to prevent his blowing up the ship until a boat arrived to take them over to Bazan's *San Pablo*. There, after three days of care and courtesy, Sir Richard Grenville died and was buried at sea with full military honours.

But *Revenge* was not so named for nothing. A great storm was to deny the Spanish their prize, for she was cast away under the cliffs of Terceira, where, a local resident, recounted that she:

> ... brake in a hundred pieces and sunk to the ground, having in her 70 men, Galicians, Biscayans and others, with some of the captive Englishmen, whereof but one was saved that got up upon the cliffs alive, and had his body and head all wounded, and he being on shore brought us the news, desiring to be shriven, and thereupon he died.[25]

It was a bad night to be at sea. In one of the fiercest storms to have been experienced in these waters, Bazan lost up to fifteen of his fleet, while the much-anticipated treasure fleet lost as many as seventy vessels. J H van Linschoten mentions that twelve ships were driven aground on Terceira and that for twenty days after the week-long storm subsided bodies were being washed ashore. Other islands claimed at least eleven more wrecks.[26]

When these losses are examined the battle of the Azores can be seen to have been not an English defeat but a naval victory, for although Howard's departure and the loss of *Revenge* mean it cannot claim to be a triumph, the record clearly shows who the victor was, especially if it is acknowledged that the Spanish fleet was in these waters to counter the English presence and thus laid itself open to both the violence of the storm and the enemy. There was also a more significant outcome, in that the English policy of patrolling off the Azores and Iberia often caused the treasure fleets to be delayed in sailing, with

A rather Edwardian rendition of 'The last fight of the Revenge*'. Although the headstrong Grenville is rightly blamed for sailing* Revenge *into a fight she could not win and from which she could have escaped, out of such heroics the navy built an unsinkable tradition that was proudly upheld centuries later, during the Second World War, by* Glowworm, Jervis Bay *and* Li Wo, *whose captains all received well deserved Victoria Crosses for attacking a far superior enemy.*

and a determined charge, to drive the *Cristobel*'s men back to their own ship and their doom, for *Revenge*'s gunners had manned the stern-chasers and, sending a salvo of shot into her bow, already damaged in the collision, drove her off in a sinking condition.

Then *Ascuncion* made her attempt, but it was the same story: a tide of boarders was driven back by shot and steel, pikes and port pieces. *Ascuncion*'s discomfort was added to when a seamanship error caused *La Serena*, the flagship of the hulks and therefore a ship that should probably not have been involved, to hole her as her captain also tried to get alongside *Revenge*. When he did grapple and board, it was only for his boarding party to be repulsed in their turn. With small arms ammunition running low, *Revenge* still had loaded major armament that had not been brought into action. Now, seeing the damaged *Ascuncion* secured up forward, the *Revenge*'s gunners, running beneath the mêlée on the upper decks, fired their ship's bow-chasers into the Spaniard. The force of the blast not only drove her away but

215

occasionally a whole year passing without their arrival in Spain. This disruption caused soldiers to mutiny and the state to become bankrupt, consequences achieved by a small nation with a powerful navy.

The Man-Killing, Ship-Sinking Argument

Many years later Nelson won his great sea battles without having to sink an enemy ship. In the battle of the Nile it was most noticeable that French ships surrendered when their casualties made it impossible for them to fight on, while, at range, it was the loss of rigging and masts that was far more devastating than the staving-in of their sides.[27] Few of the Armada ships lost rigging or were dismasted. What Tudor naval engagements demonstrate is not a fleet that was fighting in a new way but a fleet whose immaturity as a fighting force meant that it could not maximise the opportunities with which it was presented. Not that this mattered. Faced with a fighting bull loose in their front yard, few would challenge the beast close up, but rather would, keeping out of harm's way, encourage it to wander off elsewhere and might even have the patience to persuade it to depart, even were it to chew a little foliage, as the French did on the Isle of Wight in 1545. This is what Howard's strategic surety, not his commanders' tactical competence, enabled the English to do in 1588 and thus avoided turning the passage of a self-defeating foe into an engagement from which the Spanish might have gained some credit and comfort.

The First Modern Battle – The Isle of Pines, 1596

The beginning of the end of Tudor England occurred in 1595 when two elderly seamen were inveigled and flattered enough to believe that their powers had not diminished below those sufficient to deal the Spanish in the West Indies a destructive blow. Yet by this date the elder John Hawkins was in his mid-sixties, and Francis Drake a weary fifty-four. Nevertheless the foolishness of old age and the desire not to 'rust unburnished but to shine in use', plus the lure of gold, had both men take their creaking and cantankerous bones on board a queen's ship for the last time as they sailed out of Plymouth on their journey to eternity. Their fate and that of the enterprise is described later, but it is

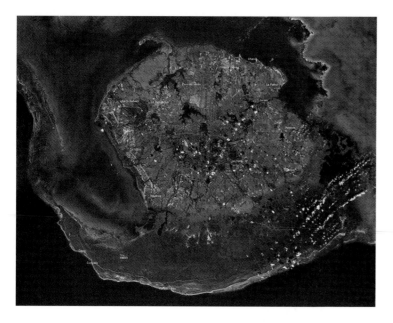

how the deployment ended that is more significant for the development of naval warfare.

It could have gone badly wrong for the same reason as did Thomas Howard's confrontation with the Spaniards in 1591. Yet again, a Spanish fleet, this time under the command of Avellanda, was despatched to intercept an unsuspecting English force, about whose aims it was to gain frequent intelligence. The English were further disadvantaged in that by the time the two fleets came in sight of each other, on 1 March, both English admirals were dead and the remains of the squadron were being commanded by Thomas Baskerville, a land general who had no experience of sea warfare.

Off the Isle of Pines in southern Cuba, Baskerville despatched three pinnaces to investigate a bay for a suitable anchorage where the fleet could take on water and repair leaks that had sprung in a great storm a few days earlier. Luckily, his ships had not entered the bay before the Spanish were sighted heading towards them.

The Spanish had already skirmished with a small, detached element of Baskerville's fleet commanded by William Winter in *Foresight*, who had abandoned the main body some days earlier. It had been an inconsequential engagement, with Winter refusing to come 'board to board' as he did not have 'authority to lay any ship aboard whereby he might endanger this her majesty's'.[28]

Baskerville was made of sterner stuff. Instead of endeavouring to escape, he first turned to recover his pinnaces, and then arranged his

Baskerville, seeking to water off the Isle of Pines in southern Cuba was lucky to have sighted the approaching Spanish fleet before his fleet came to anchor. As it was this inexperienced general, with a fleet that had lost both its admirals, Drake and Hawkins, successfully fought off his attackers in what was the first action of the age of sail fought by ships in line ahead. (Satellite image from Wikimedia)

naval ships in line ahead to engage the pursuing Spaniards, while his merchant ships stood off awaiting the opportunity to join in. He had initially held the weather gage but, realising that this would have driven him dangerously close inshore, he yielded that initiative to the enemy, who outnumbered the English by twenty to fourteen. The fight lasted for much of the day, with Baskerville avoiding being boarded as well as altering course to ensure that he would be able to outsail the Spanish if it came to a race to round Cape Corrientes, which led into the Straits of Florida, the route home.

Both fleets formed two squadrons and came to close quarters, with the English, led by Vice-Admiral Traughton in *Bonaventure*, holding fire until, within maximum effective range, they discharged both their heavy ordnance and their musketry at the foe. Ship after ship passed down the Spanish line thundering out its broadside weaponry as the English came within range. They fired accurately, swiftly and to such effect that they drove off the Spanish vice-admiral's squadron, one ship of which caught fire and blew up. For the Spanish, Baskerville's tactics were 'altogether strange', and, with the odds now decisively in favour of the English, Avellanda was content to keep the weather gage and to follow out of range. When one English merchant ship fell astern, Avellenda closed in, but when both *Bonaventure* and *Defiance* dropped back he thought better of it, especially as Baskerville showed himself ready to continue the fight. The English then resumed their passage after an engagement in which they had fought off and significantly damaged a superior enemy while suffering only minimal casualties themselves, although one ship, *Help*, was captured in a separate encounter. The Spanish excused their failure by stating lamely that they had hoped to catch the English at anchor and had then found their own ships too badly fouled by weed to offer a speedy enough pursuit.

Until the emergence of a permanent fleet the Navy Royal's main purpose was to ferry the army across the Channel, as in this engraving of Henry VIII laying siege to Boulogne in 1544.

Little is recorded of the battle of the Isle of Pines, which is a pity because it marked a successful end to a disastrous episode in English naval history, and the beginning of a new way of fighting, for this battle had far more in common with the fleet engagements of the Dutch Wars of the following century than with the unmanaged mêlées of the Armada campaigns. If one is looking for a date when the navy came of age, then St David's Day 1596 is a far better choice than that of 1545 selected by Corbett. And it was in a battle led by a general, not an admiral, but so were to be those key encounters of the Dutch wars.

DEFENDING THE MOAT – THE ARMADA CAMPAIGNS

The Battle of the Solent, 1545

Both the French and Spanish sailed armadas against England. None achieved success, and only one, the earliest and largest, got English soil on its soldiers' boots. That French assault was also the one with the clearest and most limited, although still questionable, strategic aim. In 1544 the English had taken Boulogne and were just succeeding in holding on to it through re-provisioning its besieged garrison by sea. Francis proposed to cut off that sea support. Close inshore he knew the answer. He had commissioned four new galleys at the dedicated facilities at Rouen and had ordered a further twenty-five to sail round from the Mediterranean under the command of the experienced Italian

217

Leo Strozzi. When the galleys arrived in May 1545, the captains also included another highly-regarded commander, Antoine Escalin, Baron de la Garde. This obvious emphasis on galleys was sensible, given that Francis's aim seems to have been to repulse the English in the shallow waters off Boulogne and attack them in the sheltered waters of the Solent, which was the second element in his plan. If he could destroy the English fleet where it lay and capture Portsmouth, he would gain both military advantage and a most powerful bargaining chip.

To support the galley force Admiral Claude D'Annebault assembled at Le Havre, Honfleur, Harfleur and adjacent harbours a fleet of between 120 and 300 vessels, the estimate varying much depending on the sizes of vessel included. He gathered this force very swiftly and efficiently, so much so that he was ready to get to sea well ahead of the French army assembling to assault Boulogne. Instead of holding the navy in port, inevitably a wrong decision in an age when the availability and edibility of victuals deteriorated rapidly, Francis ordered D'Annebault to sea with Portsmouth his objective. There was another reason to get the ships out. D'Annebault may have been fast but Dudley, newly restored to sea and elevated to the title of Lord Lisle, had been faster and by June had 160 ships operational in his fleet.

In mid-June Lisle despatched a force to enter the Seine and disrupt French naval preparations. As the ships approached, the fickle summer breeze died and left his force becalmed and at the mercy of the galleys which rowed out to meet him. Disaster was averted when a strong wind forced the galleys to return to harbour, but this also drove the English off the coast and back to Portsmouth. A few days later they returned with thirty fireships escorted by Sir John Berkeley in *Less Bark*. This attack too was thwarted when the potential fireships, all impressed merchantmen, took advantage of a fresh gale to try to escape their fate.

Although the English attacks failed, the French preparations descended into farce. Francis had built himself a flagship in 1521, the modestly named *Grand François*. This 1,500-tonne prestige vessel was fitted with a tennis court and a windmill, but her crew of 2,000 never had an opportunity to enjoy her charms afloat because she was unseaworthy. So for the 1545 campaign the flagship nominated was the 800-tonne *Caraquon*, and it was on board her, on 6 July, that Francis entertained his commanders before they set sail. Perhaps the chefs in the galley overdid the flambé, for shortly after the king departed, the flagship burst into flames. Abandoning ship in an orderly fashion, most of the crew were saved, along with the wages, which were transferred to the next ship in size, *Maitresse*. Her departure was marred by her running aground as she left harbour, and she was forced to return to Le Havre on 18 July, the day before what might have been a decisive battle.

The English, meanwhile, had, prior to their return to Portsmouth, sailed west and encountered some twenty-one enemy galleys off Alderney, where an engagement of several hours resulted in both sides claiming more success than can be substantiated by fact. The timing of the skirmish does, however, create an interesting question, for it seems to have taken place at the time when the French were ready to sail. Had they done so and made straight for Portsmouth they might have

taken possession of the Solent, leaving Lisle embarrassingly having to fight his way in. The other possibility is that these were galleys on their way to join the main fleet, and that intelligence had given Lisle an opportunity to attack these lethal weapons ahead of their joining the main French fleet. Be that as it may, Lisle's fleet was providing Portsmouth with protective wooden walls by 13 July, well ahead of the French arrival.

Five days later Henry, who had come to Portsmouth with both his Privy Council and his army, summoned his naval commanders to dinner on board Lisle's flagship, *Henry Grace à Dieu*, to discuss the tactics he wished to see employed: there is no reason to suppose that, with the king present, Lisle would be granted, as he himself sycophantically acknowledged, much independence. Tradition has it that during this meeting rumours of the French arrival were reported. Henry, who was no sailor, rapidly excused himself and was rowed ashore while the other commanders returned to brief their crews.

The French came to anchor in St Helen's Roads, from where they landed troops on the beaches of the Isle of Wight. Although this might seem tactically strange, Du Bellay suggested that a show of strength on the island, including the firing of the countryside and the killing of his people, would so insult Henry that he would be honour bound on seeing 'the wasting and burning of his realm' to sail over, in which case the French could swiftly re-embark and assault the then less well-defended Portsmouth. If that was the intention they had misjudged their monarch, for Henry would have been content for the isle to have been ravaged rather than risk his kingdom.

That afternoon the galleys rowed toward Lisle's fleet to get a closer view and report back. They were driven away by the English rowbarges but returned the next morning, their actions being described by Du Bellay, a French eye-witness:

> ... the weather favoured our attempt, beyond our wishes; for it proving, in the morning, a perfect calm, our galleys had all the advantages of working, which they could desire, to the great damage of the English, who, for want of wind, not being able to stir, lay exposed to our cannon. And being so much higher and bulkier than our galleys, hardly a shot missed them; while they, with the help of their oars, shifted at pleasure, and thereby avoided the danger of the enemy's artillery.[29]

Henry, watching from the shoreline, must have been afeared; in such conditions as these his great friend Edward Howard had lost ships off Brest in 1513. Yet no losses occurred here. The galley squadron, with elite commanders and in perfect weather, withdrew after several hours when a breeze got up, having inflicted no notable damage. Maybe Lisle was able to use ships' boats to pull the larger vessels stern-to so that guns could be brought to bear on the lighter attacking craft; maybe the few rowboats and galleasses that the English possessed were threat enough to keep Strozzi at bay.

By mid-afternoon Lisle was underway and heading towards the French. As the English fleet caught up with, and prepared to pass, the retiring French galleys, *Mary Rose* made a major alteration to port, heeled over and, unable to stem the flow of water through her low and

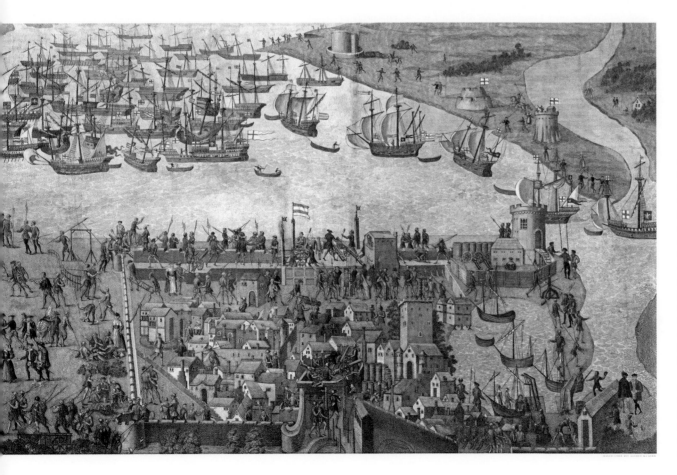

Although this contemporary engraving of the 1545 battle of the Solent was drawn to reflect the close relationship between Henry VIII and his Master of Horse, Sir Thomas Browne (in the foreground), it does show with clarity the events surrounding the loss of Mary Rose, whose masts are just visible off Southsea Castle and the deployment up-threat of the French galleys whose commanders would have enjoyed exploiting the protected waters off Spithead.

219

open starboard gunports, heeled over and sank, leaving just her masts exposed and only thirty men to be rescued out of over 500 on board. Neither Sir George Carew nor Roger Grenville, father of the more famous Richard and apparently the ship's captain, survived to explain just how the accident happened. Although it is clear that the open gunports were the catalyst, without a board of enquiry the detailed causes of her capsize remain the subject of much debate.[30]

On board *Great Harry* Lisle would also have been concerned with the reasons why *Mary Rose* had foundered, yet he was a seasoned warrior and used to witnessing loss. Tactically the sinking of *Mary Rose* was of little immediate consequence for an admiral approaching within gun range of an enemy fleet at anchor, over which he possessed the advantage of manoeuvrability, fresh crews and home waters. The English were within minutes of putting into practice the instructions laid down in Audley's fighting instructions of 1530. Had they done so, they would have stood every chance of achieving a favourable result, and, with the king a spectator, it would have been for Lisle a performance to equal the jousts. Yet he turned away and forsook the opportunity to become England's first great fighting admiral, and to place the name of the Solent alongside that of the Armada and Trafalgar.

Why was this decision taken? Fear or whim provides no satisfactory explanation for his retirement. With naval signalling in its infancy, if the English captains had been instructed to attack the French some of them would, in all likelihood, have done so. Perhaps Lisle had thought that his approach would scare the French away; possibly the shore-based Commander-in-Chief, appalled by witnessing the sinking of *Mary Rose* and, of course, not knowing the reason for her loss, had made a clear signal from Southsea Castle for the rest of his ships to disengage.

There is another and more likely possibility. In both the 1545 and 1588 campaigns important meetings took place before the fleets met: the first between Henry and Lisle and the other commanders, the second between Howard and Drake. Without being privy to their eve-of-battle plans, we can only surmise why events took the course that they did. In the battle of the Solent, the inability to be the fly on the cabin bulkhead is more than just frustrating, for without any indication of the battle plan, we are left with the strange fact that the two largest sailing fleets ever assembled came within range of each other, with no elements preventing their contact, and traded insults rather than iron shot. The most likely reason must be that Henry was determined not to risk his ships and thus pass the advantage to the French, who were, it was obvious, not going to achieve much where they lay. If so, then Lisle was the first of many admirals who, avoiding impetuosity, thought it wiser to keep his fleet in being as an ever-present threat. This was not the path to glory but it was both sensible and successful.

In fact the French anchorage indicated a tactical naivety in the inexperienced D'Annebault, whose knowledge of amphibious operations was even less than his experience of sea command. The French were endeavouring to land and support an army from an unprotected anchorage without achieving control of the water around. What is more, the ideal vessels for landing operations were galleys, the very craft needed to threaten an approaching enemy force. Both

D'Annebault and Lisle knew that the position was unsustainable. In a letter to the king on 21 July, Lisle stated that he had just experienced a short sharp gale and realised that the French would be able to ride out such a storm comfortably unless the English harassed them, in which case they would have to 'loose anchor and abide us under small sails; and once loosed they could not with that strainable wind fetch the Wight again and would have much ado to escape a danger called the Owers',[31] a tactic that Drake would wish to repeat in similar circumstances in 1588. Yet, like Drake, Lisle did not utilise this piece of local knowledge. Neither did he try to bring it about by the use of fireships, which would achieve devastating results in similar circumstances in 1588 – another example of how fleet fighting thought progressed over the next forty years. Instead, he waited patiently for the French to suffer reverses on the Isle of Wight and for the perennial problem of the lack of victuals to drive D'Annebault from the coast and back to Le Havre, which indeed happened after a swift and equally unsuccessful landing at Seaford in Sussex and a disembarkation of troops. Lisle then had a few days' grace to put in place arrangements for raising *Mary Rose*, an evolution in which sound theory foundered through the inexperience of the Venetian team contracted to carry out the task.[32]

Lisle then sailed for another action in the Channel, one so desultory that it reinforces the impression that both nations' kings and admirals believed that as long as their fleets stayed afloat no advantage would pass to the enemy. Like Jellicoe at Jutland, over 350 years later, Lisle was the one man capable of losing the war in an afternoon. He chose not to take on the risk, and Henry's fleet and throne survived. The next occasion on which the realm was threatened, Elizabeth was on that throne, and the navy that sailed to meet the challenge had much changed. Nevertheless, Lord Admiral Charles Howard's tactics in 1588 would much resemble those of Lisle in 1545.

The Spanish Threat

Whereas the Henrician navy could manage, with some difficulty, to blockade Brest and threaten Le Havre, Elizabeth's fleet could sail further and with more force. Thus as Le Tréport was to the fleet in Henry's time, so Cadiz was to that of Elizabeth, demonstrating quite clearly the improvement in power, operational range and ambition in the developing navy. Planned in the light of clear intelligence that the Spanish intended to launch an enterprise against England, Drake's raid on Cadiz is one of the earliest examples of a nation getting its retaliation in first. It is also a clear indication that the fleet was coming of age and becoming capable of imposing the strategic aim of making the state's frontier the high-water mark of its enemy's coast.

Philip's decision to mount the 'enterprise against England' also made strategic sense. He needed to ferry troops, supplies and pay to his forces fighting in the Netherlands and required the silver that was meant to be crossing the Atlantic to achieve this. The English were preventing him from achieving this, both in the Channel and off the Azores. Philip could thus either divide his fleet to fight a naval war on two fronts or unite it with his superior army to crush with overwhelming force, the (conveniently heretic) dragon in its lair. Drake's raid on the Indies in 1586 made the decision to mount the operation inevitable, while the execution of Mary Queen of Scots hastened the

Sea walls were built around most of the Cadiz peninsula in response to the English assault of 1596. However, the artillery behind the low battlements was of little threat to those wishing to attack shipping anchored out in the capacious harbour. (Author)

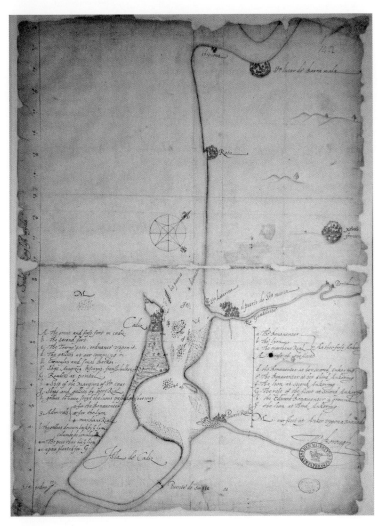

This sketch map of the Cadiz operations is signed by Borough and enclosed with his official report of the action. (National Archives, Kew)

date. The English knew that it was coming and also realised that they had to do their utmost to delay and disrupt the great Armada, a policy which Drake was the obvious choice to deliver. The way in which he did this marks the highlight of his career and the best feat of English naval arms in the whole century.

Cadiz, 1587

Cadiz is remembered both for Drake's successful prosecution of the Spanish inside the harbour and for his unsuccessful prosecution of his vice-admiral, William Borough, outside. It thus shows him both at his devastating best as a fighting leader and at his excruciating worst as a force commander.

The operation went well from the first. Drake received his orders on 15 March 1587, and they were, for a public-private partnership enterprise, simple. He was to 'impeach the provisions of Spain' being sent to the armada being prepared in Lisbon; he was to 'distress the ships within the havens themselves'; and, this done, and as a sop to the accompanying merchant adventurers, he was to take any wealthy prize that might heave into view. Finally, common sense required him to engage the Spanish fleet if it had already put to sea.[33]

Drake sailed on 2 April. The Privy Council, certain that he had cleared the coast by the 9th, sent Elizabeth's usual message recalling him, by the hand of one of Hawkins's nephews who was sure to understand, with a nod and a wink, that delivery was not what was expected. Thus Elizabeth, as with Mary Stuart's death, could claim for her diplomatic audience that her commander had acted against her wishes, while acknowledging, privately, that he had achieved all that she had asked.

Drake's fleet consisted of four royal ships: *Elizabeth Bonaventure* (his flagship), *Golden Lion* (Vice-Admiral Borough), *Dreadnought* (Rear-Admiral Fenner) and *Rainbow* (Captain Henry Bellingham) and two pinnaces. Twelve merchant ships had signed for the voyage while Drake and Lord Admiral Howard supplied five more. The merchant owners were grocers, fishmongers, drapers, men whom had suffered an economic downturn as a result of the falling away of trade with Spain. It was as if Messrs Fortnum and Mason, John Lewis and Morrison, faced with falling profits, had decided to seize oil-tankers on the high seas.

The fleet of twenty-four, only a little dispersed by storms, made a swift passage down the coast of Spain, arriving on 19 April off the well-protected port of Cadiz, where intelligence gleaned on the voyage that indicated a large group of armada ships and supplies lay at anchor. Stopping neither to consult nor to brief, Drake sailed into the open-mouthed, capacious bay of the outer harbour, much to the surprise of the Spanish ahead of him and many of the fleet behind him; luckily the latter followed, while many of the former fled.

Not so the local galley squadron, who rowed out to meet the intruder. It should have been no contest. Conventional wisdom, which Borough held dear, would have expected Drake to be sunk. Instead he engaged and, by expert ship-handling in the less than confined waters of the outer harbour, drove the galleys away, sinking one in the process. Skulking behind protective shoals, the galleys took no further part in the contest, leaving Drake, anchored beyond the range of the shore batteries, a free and destructive hand. First to fall was a weighty

Genoese galleon, which, after a fierce exchange of fire, sank at her moorings, leaving the English to pass the night away torching all the other vessels in the outer harbour.

Dawn saw Drake leading a fleet of pinnaces into the inner harbour, where the destruction continued with a large galleon, owned by Santa Cruz, being the star victim. While he was thus engaged, Borough had himself rowed over to *Bonaventure* to enquire as to what was going on. After the two admirals eventually met up Borough, unsatisfied with his admiral's actions, withdrew *Golden Lion*, which had received a shot below the water-line, to a safer anchorage. Drake was furious, and his temper was not eased when Borough questioned his next decision, on leaving Cadiz, which had been to land and seize the forts at Sagres, the spiritual home of Henry the Navigator, so that the English could stay on the coast to carry out another of their aims, to disrupt coastal shipping. Borough was arrested and relieved of his command

Drake was in his element. He added to his torching of thirty-five ships and their stores in Cadiz with the capture of ships laden with barrel-staves heading for Lisbon, and with the destruction of the tunny fishing fleet whose catch would have been placed in those barrels. When he sailed for Lisbon, the wily old sea dog Santa Cruz ignored the challenge to come out and fight. In view of Drake's failure to force the passage of the Tagus in support of Norris in 1589, his decision to lie off Lisbon rather than enter the river at a time when everything was going his way was a small sign of things to come.

The spat with Borough now reached boiling point when the crew of *Golden Lion*, in which the vice-admiral was confined, detached themselves and made an independent passage back to England. Drake tried Borough, *in absentia*, with mutiny and desertion and, without any evidence, had him found guilty and sentenced to death. Then, with no hope of action off Lisbon, he took his fleet to the Azores, where he fulfilled the third aim of his voyage when he fell in with and captured the great Portuguese argosy *San Felipe*. She was the greatest prize seized in his life-time. Weighed down with spices and other Eastern exotics, her cargo was estimated to be worth £120,000 (£11 million in modern currency).[34] The voyage was 'made', and monarch and merchant could be content. Drake was not. He returned determined that Borough should be punished. The friends of the vice-admiral, an excellent seaman and Clerk of Ships, were equally determined he would not. In the end both men received subtler punishments. Borough was placed in command of a galley in the Thames when the great Armada came, rather than a commanding a galleon as his experience and seniority deserved; Drake, who might have expected to lead the fleet out of Plymouth, sailed as vice-admiral under Lord Charles Howard. Given the character flaws exposed by the Burrough affair, this was a wise decision by the Privy Council: the fate of Drake's later expeditions confirmed the view that he was a gifted corsair but not a good commander-in-chief.

The Spanish Armada, 1588

The belief that the despatch of Philip of Spain's armadas against England was driven by religious fervour is simplistic. European

The route of the Armada around the British Isles. (Map by Peter Wilkinson)

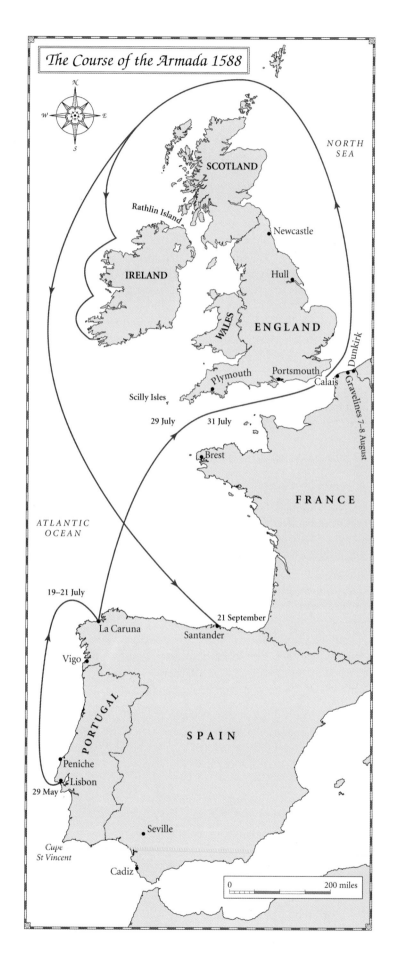

The Course of the Armada 1588

nations, of both shared and opposing religions, clashed whenever it was advantageous for one or both so to do. From his small den, the spider of the Escorial had seen his web stretching to encompass all the known world. Yet the English fly had the temerity to prance upon his threads and seize his succour before it came within his grasp. Unmolested, that same fly even caused mayhem at the very entrance to his lair. If these deprivations were allowed to continue the web would weaken and the spider starve. Religious reform was the excuse, not the aim, but it did provide the fervour to motivate many an otherwise reluctant marine crusader. This included the most reluctant of all, Medina Sidonia, who, like D'Annebault before him, was inexperienced and had to resort to exhortation as a vain substitute for sound strategic planning and the issue of rational fighting instructions plans, stating that 'The saints of heaven will go in company with us, and especially the holy patrons of Spain and, indeed, those of England, who are persecuted by the heretics and cry aloud to God for vengeance, will come out to join and help us.'[35] Sidonia knew what the odds were and that many would be sailing not 'in confident hope of a miracle' but in courageous acceptance of a martyrdom. Love might conquer all; faith would fall before fusillades.

Drake had gained favour and renown for his famous raid on Cadiz the year before. Yet even he, never too bashful to be boastful, admitted that he had only singed the King of Spain's beard – embarrassing, but superficial, harm. Henry Jackman, the Member of Parliament for Calne in Wiltshire, provided the comparison with the Armada battle when he said that in the latter, 'the teeth and jaws of our mightiest and most malicious enemy [have] been broken', a most apt and fortuitous metaphor.[36]

Yet although the damage that Drake inflicted in 1587 did not significantly affect the Armada's composition or logistical support, the national pride and confidence that his voyage engendered in England and its disheartening of the opposition in Spain cannot be underestimated. If the Armada correspondences of England and Spain are compared there can be little doubt as to which side was, in modern parlance, 'up for it' and saying 'bring it on'. The question for the English was where to pitch up for the fight.

Like Philip, Elizabeth had her own ideas on strategy, voicing an opinion that her fleet needed to be divided into roughly similar strength eastern and western squadrons. Through the treachery of Sir James Croft, Philip was soon aware of this plan, writing to Sidonia:

> The success of this enterprise depends on your going to the heart of the matter; and even if Drake should have sailed for these waters with a fleet, intending to create a diversion and so embarrass you, as is reported from England, yet you should not turn back, but continue on your course, not seeking out the enemy even if he should remain here. If, however, he should pursue and overtake you, you may attack him, as you should also do if you meet Drake with his fleet at the entrance to the Channel; because if the enemy's forces are so divided, it would be well to defeat him by stages and thus prevent those forces from uniting.
>
> If you do not encounter the enemy until you reach Margate, and should find there his Admiral of England with his fleet alone – or even if he should have united with Drake's fleet, yours will

still be superior to both in quality, and also in the cause you are defending, which is God's ... you may give battle, trying to gain the wind, and all possible advantage from the enemy; and trusting to the Lord to give you victory[37]

– which shows an impotent mix of strategic gobbledegook with spiritual naivety – poor Sidonia to have to serve such a master. Elizabeth's idea was also suspect, but in England subordinates could beg to differ and lobby for change.

Drake, heady with his exploits, wanted to sail yet again for the Spanish coast but had been forbidden by Elizabeth so to do, a policy which she reinforced by refusing to mobilise the fleet she had paid off. Her favourite corsair may have been furious, but Elizabeth was acting on good intelligence that supported her notorious parsimony rather than letting pecuniary matters dominate policy. She knew that Drake had gained her a year and that it was best to husband scarce resources until they were most needed. To keep the fleet in readiness cost her £5,000; she did not consider this money to be well spent when winter gales protected England's coast better than any storm-tossed ships, which, safe and maintained in port, would be in better shape for the summer season. Elizabeth knew that Drake could be relied upon to sail from Plymouth should the need arise and that Sir Henry Palmer's squadron in the Downs would make short work of Parma should he be mad enough to try and cross the Channel in flat-bottomed boats. The queen wintered in contentment.

The English hibernation lasted until January, its end symbolised by the appointment, on 31 December 1587, of Lord High Admiral Howard of Effingham as commander-in-chief. Drake was then confirmed as commander of the independent western squadron on 2 January. Again, this was an intelligence-led decision, for Burghley had been informed that Philip had ordered his fleet to be assembled at Lisbon by mid-February, hinting at an April sailing date. Its concentration in one port was meat for the hungry Drake, who was given authority to lead a raid on the Spanish ports only for it to be withdrawn before he could get to sea. Further, and probably planted, intelligence indicated that Philip had decided to call the whole thing off, possibly because of the death of Santa Cruz, the fleet commander. This fooled only the one person who mattered, Elizabeth. Drake was confined to the Cattewater.

His enforced inactivity brought spleen to his pen, and he bombarded the Privy Council with notes, one stating, 'As God in his goodness hath put my hand to the plough, so in his mercy it will never suffer me to turn back from the truth', which was, as he saw it, that with fifty ships he could cause more damage off the coast of Spain than with twice that number in the Channel. His frustration gave rise to one of the best summaries of naval strategy ever penned. Writing to the queen on behalf of those 'poor subjects, who for the defence of Your Majesty, our religion and our native country, have resolutely vowed the hazard of our live', he went on to say, 'the advantage of time and place in all martial actions is half a victory, which being lost is irrecoverable.'[38] Hawkins agreed. He was already voicing the idea of a permanent patrol off the coast of Spain, which would be attempted three years later. With the indecision of order and counter-order frustrating the fleet, Howard demonstrated his wisdom by casting his vote

Philip of Spain left his land and sea commander little opportunity to use their initiative as circumstances changed. He expressly ordered his 1588 armada, along with its invasion force, to land on this beach at Margate, which would have meant a lengthy voyage for Parma's unseaworthy craft had they even been available for the Channel crossing. (Author)

... if there may be such a stay or stop made by any means of this fleet of Spain, so that they may not come through the seas as conquerors ... then shall the Prince of Parma have such a check thereby as were meet ... Good my lords, I beseech you to consider deeply [the division of the fleet] for it importeth but the loss of all.

Thomas Fenner shared the general frustration, writing to Walsingham, 'I would to God we had been now upon that coast; the impediment would have been great upon their army gathering together ... We rest here a great number of valiant men, and to great charge upon my gracious mistress, and a great grief of mind to spend Her Majesty's treasure and do nothing upon the enemy.'[39]

When a comparison is made between the letters written by the commanders on each side a striking difference is revealed. The English want God to look kindly on their best-laid plans; the Spanish want him to make up for their deficiencies. The English champ at the bit; the Spanish accept the inevitable. The English are thrilled by their ships and their men; the Spanish are indifferent. Examination of the correspondence alone would give a researcher, ignorant of the outcome, a very good idea as to who was going to be victorious.

On 31 May Howard was ordered west, leaving a small number of vessels behind to augment Lord Henry Seymour's squadron patrolling off Dunkirk to intercept Parma. Among those left behind were the two-year-old race-built galleons *Vanguard* and *Rainbow*: should Parma sail, Howard felt that he should at least be challenged by vessels suitable for the status of his nephew Seymour to command. He sailed, fully aware that the Privy Council had been won over by Drake's forward strategy of taking the fleet back to Spain, and, although he remained commander-in-chief, he needed to listen to his subordinate's advice. It could have led to a stormy relationship, but when Howard entered Plymouth, with all the pomp of a Lord Admiral, Drake sailed out with sixty ships bedecked in their finery, their decks manned with cheering sailors whose drums and trumpets added to the welcoming cacophony, convincing the Lord Admiral that his vice-admiral bore no grudge.

United, the fleet was intended to sail with little delay to Spain. The wind frustrated that aim, and the ships remained tossing at the anchors within Plymouth Sound. Elizabeth was still reluctant to allow Howard to sail south, fearing that he might miss the Armada on its northward journey. Howard, sarcastically, wrote to the council that he was 'glad there be such at Court as are able to judge what is fitter for us to do than we here'. Naval historians have generally sided with Howard. It is true that, confined to Plymouth, he missed a chance to attack eighteen vessels, storm-scattered remnants of the Armada's first approach, which had hove to off the Scillies waiting for an improvement of the weather. Not only that, but the small West Country town was fast running short of victuals and the crews were going hungry. Just in time, orders came for sailing, and on 4 July the fleet weighed with Corunna its objective, the port in which Sidonia's forces were regrouping.

Even before the ships turned south to pass Ushant a wind from that direction stayed them in their tracks for another week. It was not until 21 July that they arrived within reach of Corunna, only to be becalmed and then driven back by further southerly winds. By this

for Drake, with a humility seldom voiced by the English nobility except when trying to avoid the scaffold. 'I confess', he wrote, 'my error ... I did and will yield ever unto them of greater experience.' He continued, 'The opinion of Sir Francis Drake, Mr Hawkins, Mr Frobisher and others that be men of greatest judgement and experience, as also my own ... is that the surest way to meet with the Spanish fleet is upon their own coast or in any harbour of their own, and there defeat them.' Howard's great skill in suborning his own ego to nurse those of others is nowhere better shown than here with his willingness to accept advice and ask for instruction. Medina Sidonia had some of the same attributes but was encased in a system that made of them weaknesses, not strengths.

Frustrating as this order/counter-order may have been, its benign consequence was that the English kept themselves well watered and fed. The Spanish soldiers and sailors suffering similar delays were confined to their ships with provisions running low before their anchors were weighed from the mud of Spain.

Drake, convinced that he had the best strategic overview, set down in a letter to the council how he saw things should happen. Rightly, he saw that the greater threat to the English nation was that posed by Parma's army awaiting transportation from the Netherlands to the Bay of Margate. Although, wisely, he did not say so, his seaman's opinion of England's land forces was probably not great, and, faced with Spanish professionals led by the greatest warrior of the day, he would probably have had his concerns justified. Loved by the queen, Leicester (the son of Henry's admiral, Lord Lisle) was a loser as a land commander, even escorting Elizabeth to quite the wrong location, Tilbury, for her finest set-piece speech of scorn and defiance. Drake wanted to avoid the risk of a disastrous land campaign by preventing the junction of Parma and his escorting Armada, and to maximise his chance of success he wished to achieve this by destroying the Armada as far west as was possible. For this to happen he needed a combined fleet. Imploringly, he wrote:

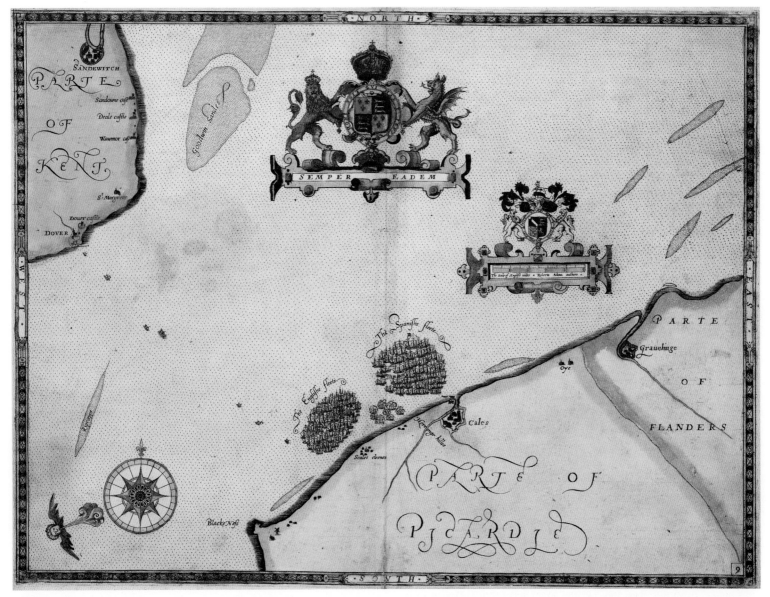

Based on information supplied by Lord Howard, Robert Adams made a series of engravings in 1590 to show the course of the Spanish Armada. In this one he shows the climactic event, the launch of the English fireships off Calais. (National Maritime Museum F8047)

time even Drake was nervous, fearing that the Armada might have sailed past them. Back in Plymouth they found their armed merchant ships much damaged by the gales and in need of urgent repairs. So, despite their professional opinion, Elizabeth was proved right, her doubts more valid than her admirals' desires.

There was one other cause for concern which was left unsaid: the quality and expertise of the opposing commanders. Leaving aside the inexperienced Howard and Medina Sidonia, the contest would have been between Drake, Frobisher and Hawkins on one side, and Recalde, Oquendo and Bertendona on the other. The English were renowned skirmishers and risk-takers, but none had fought in anything resembling a fleet engagement, and neither did they possess the sea-going galleasses which the Spanish had in squadron strength. On the other hand, Don Juan Martinez de Recalde, at sixty-two, had fought at sea in most known oceans and seas. He also had a clear understanding of the tactical setting, stating with obvious irony:

O, when we meet the English, God will arrange matters so that we can grapple and board them, either by sending some unexpected weather or, more likely, depriving the English of their wits. If we can come to close quarters, Spanish valour and Spanish steel, together with the great number of soldiers embarked, will make our victory certain. Yet, unless God help us by a miracle the English, whose ships are faster and handier than ours, with many more long-range guns, and who are aware of these advantages as well as we are, will not close with us, but stand off and destroy us with their culverins, without our being able to do them serious hurt.[40]

'We sail', Recalde concluded with the famous phrase, 'in confident hope of a miracle', although he was too old a salt to believe that concept.

Miguel de Oquendo had won glory at Terceira by coming through fire and flame to the rescue of Santa Cruz, who was in danger of being overpowered by the French flagship. Like him, Don Martin de Bertendona, in *Regazona*, was also brave and was one of the commanders who sought to bring the English to close quarters during the passage up the Channel, although the ships of his Levant squadron were, as has been remarked, not designed for northern waters.

The Spaniards were open-seas sailors. What they were not used to was ship-handling in confined waters such as the Channel and, more crucially, in shoaly waters, as off Calais and Gravelines. Monson summed up their shortcomings in his tracts stating that the Spanish were 'Providently cautious ... because their breeding has not been to sail amongst sands, or in seas so narrow ... that wind which is secure upon one shore is death upon another and tides that sometimes are advantageous to them, at other times may prove dangerous.'[41] In other words, at the time when the English were expanding their navigational skills and studying new books on the subject of ocean voyaging, the Iberians, who had led the way across the seas, had in so doing lost the art of pilotage. Monson warned that the English must not suffer the same fate, calling for the employment of '... expert and skilful pilots that make the Narrow Seas their daily trade and practice'.

Add to that loss of skill the tight formation in which Sidonia confined his fleet, and the Spanish could not have been confronted in a less advantageous location than that in which they eventually met up with the English. In open waters, where they had sea room, they might well have been able to give a better account of themselves and broken through the English fleet, gaining either a clear run up the Channel or, arriving at an unguarded Plymouth, the chance to seize the harbour and land their troops, thus dividing both the English sea and land forces into those needed in the west and those gathering to oppose Parma. Given Philip's adamantine orders, this was an unlikely scenario, but the English were not to know that. The mariners of England might have wanted to meet the foe further south but Elizabeth was proved right in her desire to keep them on a tight leash. In the first days of close contact the English inflicted little damage on their enemy; if a meeting further west had taken place with similar results the battle might well have been lost before the Channel was gained.

On 31 July, the first day of the engagement, off Devon, *San Salvador*, for reasons that remain mysterious, blew up and drifted out of line. Recalde, in *Santa Ana*, unable himself to reach the damaged vessel ahead of the approaching enemy, summoned assistance. In the manoeuvres that followed Pedro de Valdes rammed *Santa Catalina*, sheering off the bowsprit of his own *Rosario* as a result. The additional strain on his forestay led to its snapping and the fore mast itself crashing down and entangling the main mast as it fell. The ship fell astern, and, after attempting to take her in tow, Sidonia abandoned her to her fate as night fell.

That night Drake was appointed to lead the English fleet, fallen in astern of the Armada. With lantern lit he did so, until the nagging concern that *Rosario* might be a prize worth his taking got the better of his fleet duty. Then, light extinguished, he turned back to demand Valdes's surrender at dawn. Having been informed just who his challenger was, the Spaniard willingly capitulated and joined Drake in *Revenge* at the start of three years' pleasant captivity until his family handed over a ransom of £3,000 to get him home. *Rosario*, towed into Torbay, yielded a much greater reward. His prize secured, Drake

rejoined the fleet, which, in the absence of his guiding light, had almost become a part of the Armada itself and had had to extricate itself from an embarrassing and threatening situation.

Howard was angry but not furious; he would succumb to similar temptation when *San Lorenzo*, the largest of the galleasses, drifted rudderless on to the sands, also as a result of a collision in the confusion off Calais. Had Drake been a Spaniard he would probably have swung for his behaviour, for Sidonia brooked no disobedience, but the downside of such control was, of course, the stifling of initiative, which began at the top with the landlocked Philip demanding adhesion to a fatally flawed plan. The English, from Elizabeth down, seem to have acted as the very antithesis, adhering to no plan in particular and thus gaining strength through flexibility.

As it was, superb Spanish seamanship and fleet discipline allowed Medina Sidonia a safe and timely passage through his fleet's watery valley of the shadow of death, but when they arrived at the end the ships had nowhere to go and no contingency plan. Philip did not deal in alternatives. The Armada would arrive, Parma would sail out, and together they would cross to the North Foreland. The king does not seem to have told Sidonia what to do in the event of his being stood up. Calais and the fireships were the result; the battle of Gravelines, the outcome; the cost, the nightmare passage home. Medina Sidonia, having thrust his scratched arm through the tight coarse sleeve of the Channel, found not Parma's welcoming hand to grasp but the cold closed fist of the cliffs of Calais. Here he needed the support of the one class of ship he had not brought with him – galleys. He had sailed with just four, which had all been dispersed in the great storm in Biscay, never to rejoin. For inland waters, Sidonia was left with a squadron of pinnaces too lightly armed to strike fear into either the English fleet off shore or the Dutch 'sea-beggars' that it was assumed were waiting to descend on Parma's ill-equipped and undefended punts. Yet Dunkirk lay just twenty-five miles up coast from Calais, just the sort of distance that could be patrolled and controlled by a squadron of galleys supported by galleasses. The provision of just four galleys illustrates Philip's strategical illiteracy. Time and again he told his commanders to rendezvous off Margate, failing to appreciate the fact – and unprepared to be briefed – that the invasion's slim chance of success had to be based on Parma's flimsy boats being escorted from the moment they left Dunkirk. Galleys could even have been built by Parma in the Dunkirk shipyards and would have provided one final and valuable service to the armada by pushing the fireships clear of the fleet. In the event the fireships themselves spluttered out harmlessly ashore, but it was the fear they engendered that was their most powerful attribute. The cables would not have been cut if galleys had been available to reassure the nervous and calm the panic.

For a week the English had pounded away at the Spanish fleet but to little avail. Their one tactic seemed to be to avoid a close-quarters encounter, either ship-on-ship, or as part of a general action. Only Frobisher seemed to have tried to bring on such a fight, but then he had also withdrawn before committing himself.

As with Lisle's failure to attack the French in 1545, we do not know the final orders that Howard gave to his captains prior to warping out of Plymouth on 30 July. While aware that the confident hope of prize money featured as prominently in the English minds as

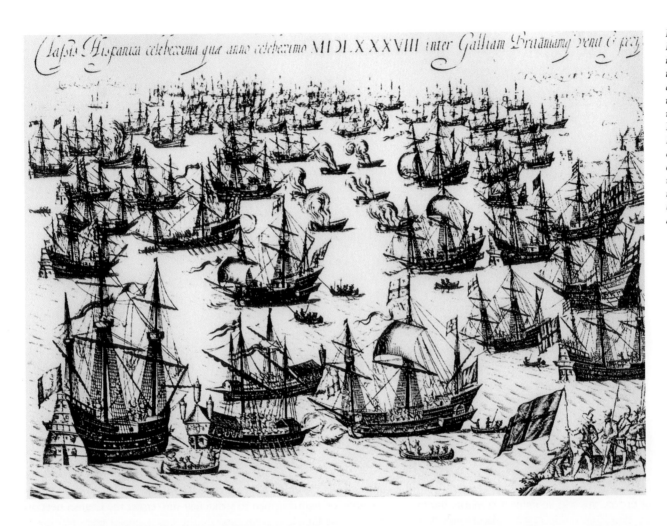

Claſsis Hiſpanica celeberrima qua anno celeberrimo MIDLXXXVIII inter Galliam Britanniamq́ venit & fecit

It was not just the English who had an interest in the fate of the Armada, but its defeat was celebrated with almost as much relief in the Netherlands. This Dutch engraving combines various episodes, but like most representations includes in the background the fireship attack.

that of a miracle did in the Spanish fleet, we are therefore presented with a question on tactics that may be a reflection of either ship design and equipment or the obeying of fighting instructions. Howard appears to have resolved that none were to attempt boarding, earning the English the sobriquet of 'Lutheran hens' from the frustrated Calderon, who also thought that the queen had ordered that, 'on pain of death, no ship of hers was to come to close quarters with any of ours'.

Howard and Drake were both on board new galleons which they knew could close to musket-ball range only to glide away again. Yet for the most part, until Gravelines they chose to stand off and expend their ammunition to little purpose. If the strategic plan was to keep their fleet in being, this made sense of the circumstances and the challenge, which was, at the last, to prevent Spanish soldiers from landing on English soil, and as long as Howard had supremacy at sea this could be done. If this was the overarching aim, then it explains the fact that the English, apart from the hot-headed Frobisher, never put themselves in harm's way, and that even those most desirous of glory or gold did not even bump against a tempting prize that was not already unfit to fight. Then, when the Armada was driven out of Calais Roads, all hope of linking up with Parma gone, the reins came off and Howard's bears were unleashed for what was to be the only major battle of the campaign.

Gravelines opened as a mêlée. The Spanish were disordered, while the English were disorganised, for the ability to command and control

a fleet in battle by signal was a development for the future; this one was a free-for-all.

Having suffered the fiasco of the night before, Sidonia did his best to re-establish the Armada's tight formation. Ordering a northward course to clear the shallows, he despatched his pinnaces to round up his scattered remnants and then, when content with the depth of water under his hull and to windward, he turned, cornered, to face his foe. It was Drake who led the attack, supported by the Fenner family in *Nonpareil*, *Swiftsure* and *Aid*. Now the English ships were prepared to venture closer to *San Martin*, which by most accounts received a great weight of shot although still able to return fire. Drake passed on, earning from Frobisher, who was leading his squadron into attack astern of him, the epithets of 'coward' and 'traitor' – a Yorkshireman voicing his county's opinion of effeminate, wealthy southerners.

Under intense pressure, Spanish discipline and seamanship held fast. Within a short space of time the beleaguered Sidonia was joined by Recalde, Bertendona, Oquendo and a significant portion of their squadrons. By the time the eastern English squadron, led by Seymour and Winter, arrived, it was faced not by a confused group of vessels but by two squadrons, each of sixteen warships, forming a screen around their commander-in-chief. It was bravely done but too late. Here, in the tight bottom of the North Sea, there was no longer sea room for the Spaniards to use to advantage. Many of their ships were already shot-shattered so that any further damage would be devas-

An anonymous near-contemporary oil painting of the English fireship attack on the Spanish off Calais. In the foreground an English galleon bears down on a galleasse, while to the left another English ship is in rather closer combat with a big Spanish ship than was the norm during the whole campaign. (National Maritime Museum BHC0263)

229

tating. Pinned in, they fought on, not just in the face of their adversaries of the past week, who were themselves approaching exhaustion, but under assault from the fresh eastern squadron.

San Felipe, her rudder shot away, and *San Mateo* were soon in difficulties and drifted into two other ships on their wing. Sidonia, as so often, rescued them, but this time it could only be temporarily. Both ships drifted away to the shores off Ostend, where those whom the seas did not drown were despatched by the Dutch unless they could be ransomed. Back at sea, Captain Robert Crosse, in the elderly galleon *Hope*, achieved the only success due to gunfire alone when he sank the 650-tonne Biscayan galleon *Mario Juan*. For many others the damage inflicted, both human and material, was beyond control, but its effect had not yet become totally destructive. Had the weather been less kind, even those still seaworthy might have fallen to the English, but just as many were being pushed into the shallows, the wind changed and they managed to clear both the shoals and the English and head north on a course which Howard and his vice-admirals felt content to let them pursue unhindered. The threat was over.

Given that the Spanish encountered the English in their home waters and passed through relatively unscathed, it would seem to be the tactics of the latter, who failed to disrupt, damage or destroy the Armada's formation, that need critical examination.

Much of the Armada debate has centred on the concept that the English won because they had changed their tactics from one of boarding to one of standing off – that is, from man-killing to ship-killing. However, the evidence indicates that success was achieved despite rather than because of this decision. It is also wrong to think that a major change in fighting policy had taken place. Visscher's engraving of *White Bear* at the time of the Armada shows shear hooks at the end of the yards on both her fore and main masts. In this respect she is identical to the great carracks drawn in 1546 by Anthony Anthony. This hints that what happened in the Channel in 1588 was a strategic decision for a specific set of circumstances, not a change in naval warfare. If it were the latter it was an aberration, an aberration so wrong-minded that it would run quite contradictory to the second most famous signal of England's greatest admiral: engage the enemy more closely. That, and that alone, was how enemy ships were destroyed at sea. Yet wars rather than battles, as Howard demonstrated in 1588, could be won employing different tactics drawn up for the occasion.

For, given the fact that boarding was the English experience, born of the need to capture prizes rather than sink them, it seems strange that not one opposed boarding took place in the week-long struggle. Admittedly, the Armada's formation was designed to deter close interference, but we also have Recalde's view, reported above, that engaging at close quarters was the only way to enable the miracle to happen: the adoption of tactics that countered their own strength was not going to help the cause, although, of course, the English did not wish for such entanglements. Thus the idea that the English were content to stand off and fire at a safe range gained favour, but what did this achieve? Mainly, a vast expenditure of ammunition that could have caused great embarrassment had Parma chosen to sail the invasion fleet out from Dunkirk. Enfolded inside the great Iberian hulks with a carapace of galleons, able to withstand the reduced weight of

shot that the English had left, a safe crossing just might have been possible. The hulls of the Spanish ships did receive a great deal of shot, but that was where they were best equipped to absorb it. The presence of heavy ordnance on board the English ships did not replace the need to batter at close range and then board to achieve a devastating decisive victory, but at this stage of their development, it would appear that either English commanders thought that it had or, more acceptably, national strategy precluded such tactics. In the Dutch wars that followed in the next century, the lethal combination of battering and boarding was, at last, unleashed by a navy maturing and aware of its strength. But then that war was against a strong opposition who wished to stay and fight but did not intend to invade.

Faced with an enemy that was reluctant to fight, Howard, while constantly aware of the impact of wind and tide on both true and relative positions, was in the fortunate position of selecting how and when he might wish to engage. From astern the hulls of the Spanish ships would have presented a small target at which to aim, but their sail area would have been much greater. Early on in the running fight, Howard realised how easy a prey a dismasted ship could be when *Rosario* was captured without a fight; surely, the idea of firing into the enemy's rigging to achieve similar isolation and capitulation must have occurred to him and his commanders? It does not seem to have been tried. Instead sporadic firing at range against thick hulls from which the shot might just bounce off, appears to have been the only tactic employed. The most vulnerable part of any vessel's hull was her rudder, which was exposed to those astern, and Hawkins's new galleons had bow-chasers which could be employed to pound away at their opponents' stern especially as the Armada's slow speed of advance gave the English gunners a relatively stable platform from which to aim and fire. They did not do this and thus missed another opportunity for destroying the enemy, whose fate was decided by the wind and not weaponry.

Yet neither was the statement true that the English victory was due to the fact that 'God blew his wind and they were scattered'. By the time the wind blew, although defeat was not inevitable for the Spanish, victory, in the sense of a linking up with Parma's land army and a successful passage across the Channel, was highly unlikely. Indeed, this Spanish Armada was doomed before it sailed because Philip, trying to reconcile his land commander's plan with his admiral's vision, had successfully incorporated the flaws in both while failing to introduce improvements. There was only one part of England, or Wales, where a fleet sailing from Spain could be landed, replenished and defended, and that was the West Country. Falmouth, for example, could have been seized for long enough to see whether a Catholic uprising might occur. Any movement further east, with the English fleet in being, guaranteed only failure and the drowning of many of the soldiers who were to be ferried from Flanders, even if they had managed to escape the clutches of the Dutch sea-beggars. Medina Sidonia, inexperienced as he may have been personally, had the means to damage the English fleet. It is an error to think that he was not well supported by professional fighting commanders, each of whom if so ordered could have closed and fought hard against the shepherding foe. Instead, Sidonia allowed the strait-jacket that the little tailor in the Escorial had issued him with to forbid the three actions that might have given him a

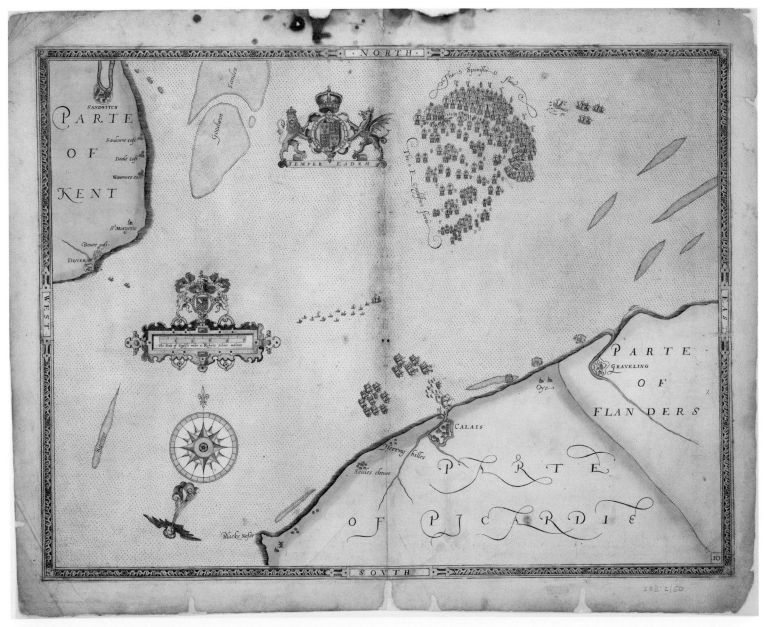

The tenth in the Adams series shows the aftermath of the fireship attack, with the Armada sailing northward pursued by elements of the English fleet. Meanwhile, Howard's boats attack the stranded galleasse San Lorenzo *off Calais.* (National Maritime Museum F8048)

chance of success: a landing at Falmouth, an assault on the English fleet within Plymouth Sound and a general free-for-all in the western Channel. Once he had failed to initiate all of these, the safe arrival of the great majority of his fleet off Calais was of as little significance as its hasty and disorganised departure from that anchorage under the threat of fireships that all ran aground and burned out harmlessly. The wind that followed added the final insult, but the injury had been done many months previously.

In the end the bill for such an enterprise was not considered as great as later students were to make out. Of the 130 ships that sailed from Spain some fifty-four returned, and the losses among the warships reflected more on their original seaworthiness than on the damage that was inflicted by English shot or Atlantic storms (see the table below).

Spanish Armada Warship Losses, 1588

Squadron	Sailed	Lost	Reached Spain
Andalusian	10	2	8
Biscayan	10	4	6
Guipucoan	10	3	7
Levant	10	9	1
Total	40	18	22

Worse was to happen in the years that followed. The armadas of 1596 and 1597, better planned and more secretive, were both scattered by weather. The one Spanish success, when a fleet of thirty-five ships succeeded in landing 4,500 troops inappropriately and untimely at Kinsale in 1601, also came to nothing, with Leveson blockading the harbour and Mountjoy investing the force by land. They surrendered in January 1602.

Vroom's gritty picture of the Cadiz fight of 1596 shows the English and their Dutch allies handling both Spanish galleons and galleys. Once again the ranges are shortened to create the scene but the record confirms that the galleys fled. (Bridgeman Art Library)

Worse was also to happen to the English. The fame and failure of Philip's enterprise of England has hidden the fact that the English riposte, Drake's assault on Lisbon in 1589, was also a fiasco.

The Parliament of 1593 opened with a splendid oration by the speaker, Sir John Puckering. In it he pointed out that, far from learning his lesson from defeat, the King of Spain was 'more furiously enraged than ever before', and that 'Finding that in the last fight by sea his ships were disadvantaged by the breadth of their building and high carriage of their ports and ordnances, he hath now lately both changed the form of his shipping and built new, after the mould and manner of the English navy.'[42] Although these new-built ships were never to challenge in the Channel, England's mariners ignored the warning to their frustration and cost.

What the Armada did achieve is best summarised in the last paragraph of Garrett Mattingley's masterful *The Defeat of the Spanish Armada*:

> Meanwhile, as the episode of the Armada receded into the past it influenced history in another way. Its story, magnified and distorted by a golden mist, became a heroic apologue of the defence of freedom against tyranny, an external myth of the victory of the weak over the strong, of the triumph of David over Goliath. It raised men's hearts in dark hour, and led them to say to one another: 'What we have done once, we can do again.' In so far as it did this the legend of the defeat of the Spanish Armada became as important as the actual event – perhaps more important.

The most important strategic lesson that the English learned was that, narrow as it was, the Channel was the ditch the nation had to die for. It was many centuries before armadas on the scale of those sixteenth-century ones were seen again in the Channel. Both Napoleon and Hitler planned but never launched them. In fact the next one ferried an English army from Dunkirk to Kent in 1940, while in 1944 that army, replenished, restored and reinforced, returned to France. History will be the better if that marked the end of such armadas.

Counter-Armada Tactics

In the defeat of the Spanish Armada much has been made of the role of gunnery and the concept of engaging at range. The argument for the development of a fighting navy in this book has much emphasised the experience and determination of English crews, schooled in plunder, to grapple and board an opponent. Yet in the two major armada campaigns of 1545 and 1588 such tactics were not employed, which defeats the whole argument – or does it?

What the English were quite prepared to do was to shepherd their enemies on to the shoals, allowing the sands to inflict the damage, with less collateral effect, than close-quarters fighting would impart. They would have known that the Spanish masters were essentially ferry men; sailing to and from set ports in set seasons on set routes with only an ocean between them. They were not used to manoeuvring in confined waters.

One has to be careful with the simple similes. The confrontation along the length of the Channel in 1588 resembled neither wolves snapping at the heels of a flock of sheep nor sheepdogs rounding up the same, for, rather like fierce geese, the Spanish could at all times stretch out their necks and spit to effect. What the English did, and did well, was to escort those alien geese off their own property while at the same annoying them sufficiently to prevent their grazing. Replenishment at sea could not be undertaken while underway, for it required either a boat transfer between victualler and warship or a gentle coming-together of two ships with the minimum of headway. So although the Armada's victualling train lay inside the protective crescent of the fighting fleet it was unable to deliver its life-saving stores to those ships as long as the English were in attendance. By the time Sidonia had brought the grand fleet to anchor in Calais Roads the need for replenishment was paramount, and a quiet night and, probably, an uninterrupted day would have been necessary to carry out the operation. This they were denied; they sailed out famished towards a horizon over which lay starvation and disease. How desperate their situation was can be gauged by the fact that the English in the coastal waters of their own nation died in droves as well, and for the same two reasons.

The Spanish returned home, but the failure of the English to sink and destroy their great ships meant that, as far as Philip was concerned, they were bloodied but unbowed. Twice more he would risk his fleet in these northern waters; twice more they would be scattered without even coming in to contact with the foe. The next occasion on which the fleets met in strength was to be in the waters of the Azores, where Santa Cruz had won magnificently against the French in 1582, but before that famous battle single or limited ship engagements were being fought at regular intervals.

The Defeat of the Galleys

To be fair to Thomas Howard, when he was appointed Lord Admiral in 1513, in place of his brother, Edward, he inherited a very dispirited force, who had fled from Brest following their admiral's death. The new admiral summarised their concerns in letters to both the king and Wolsey, telling the latter that 'Never man saw men in greater fear than all the masters and mariners be of the galleys ...'.[43] It was a fear that the cautious Howard was to share.

To a large extent the ongoing fear of the galleys was irrational. The French never stationed sufficient of them in the Channel to challenge the English at sea, and as long as the latter reigned off shore, the galley's advantage in coastal waters could be overcome. Nevertheless, as an operational navy, the English had had the stuffing knocked out of them by the nature of their defeat at White Sands Bay. From then on, for some seventy years, the fear of galleys remained a constant concern of the English fighting admirals, although this was, for most of the century, to be a perceived rather than a present danger. The French did, however, bring a significant galley squadron with them for the invasion attempt of 1545, when it was very active during the battle of the Solent.

The Birth of the Broadside?

When Admiral D'Annebault brought his fleet back to sea having failed in that invasion attempt of 1545, he met the English in a desultory action in calm waters, the main exchange taking place on 15 August when an expenditure of some 300 cannonballs by each side resulted in a few broken oars in Admiral Tyrell's galleasse, *Grand Mistress*. Not

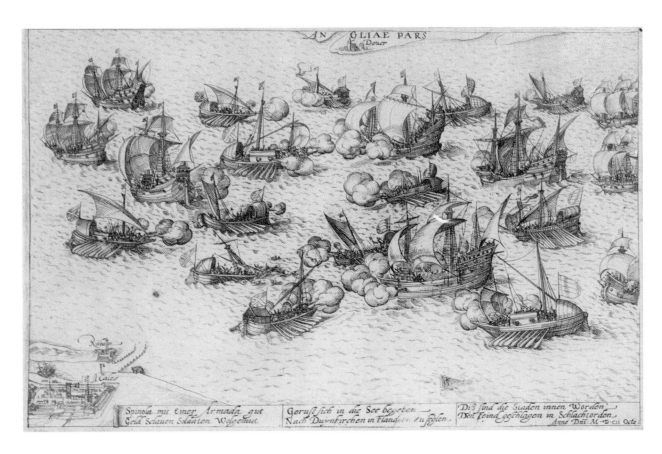

On 23 October 1602 Sir Robert Mansell finally rid the English fleet of any fear of galleys when he destroyed all but one of Spinola's vessels between Dover and Calais. Note the fine drawing of the French port in the bottom left hand corner. (National Maritime Museum PU5023)

withstanding the light damage, this fight off Shoreham was not without significance, principally because Lisle's letter to the king praised the ability of his oared vessels to 'handle the galleys as well with their sides as with their prows'.[44]

In these few words some naval historians have identified the beginnings of the naval broadside, even though the firing vessels were so shaken by the force of the discharge of their own weapons that they needed extensive repairs. Corbett, who makes reference to this damage, goes on to assert, however, that the year 1545 'best marks the birth of English naval power'. This is too strong a view, for the engagement marks, if anything, the turn of the tide of an old concept of naval warfare, for the main protagonists had been oared vessels, whose appearance in these waters was peculiar and whose days in most seas were numbered. More importantly, the occasion marks, along with the battle of the Solent a few days earlier, the introduction of a major strategic concept, the fleet in being.

That war drew to a close in 1546 with a number of skirmishes involving galleys. A significant engagement took place on 18 May when the French galley *Blanchard* was captured along with her Portuguese pilot, Fernando Oliviera, who volunteered to instruct Henry's shipwrights in the art of galley construction. The arrival of *Blanchard* in London was cheered by large crowds, emphasising the importance that was placed on beating these ships.

As might be expected, much action took place close to besieged Boulogne, even while peace negotiations were taking place. For example, on 20 May the Earl of Hertford reported that a French foist had seized three supply boats near the harbour mouth but had in turn been intercepted by four of the new shallops (presumably the

rowbarges) and forced to give up two of her prizes. That afternoon the main English fleet arrived and was challenged by ten galleys making 'a jolly brag' towards them. However, the sight of six English warships approaching frightened the galleys into shallow water, where they were shot at but received no damage. The next day the English tried to intercept the French galleys which were engaged in troop ferrying. *Grand Mistress* and *Anne Gallant*, both 450-tonne well-armed ships, and *Salamander* and *Greyhound*, two lighter galleasses, supported by six of the rowbarges, closed in but were driven off by the galleys, which overtook the laggardly rowbarges in the calm. The English then came about and in turn drove the galleys back, capturing one of them.[45] The capture greatly hurt the French admiral, who, thinking he was involved in a peace process, protested to Lisle that his commanders afloat had thought that the English were closing them 'to be merry togethers', and that this was also the reason why they had not fired back during the English attack the day before. He then asked for his galley back.[46]

The Battle of the Channel Islands, 1548

The war with Scotland that Edward had inherited had led to a French galley fleet sailing to Scotland. Once it had returned to France, its commander, Leo Strozzi, was ordered to take his squadron to attack the Channel Islands, where Sark had already been seized. He sailed in early August with twelve galleys and a similar number of transports carrying 2,000 troops. William Winter, alerted by the earlier incursion, was waiting off the islands and intercepted Strozzi. In a major change of fortune the French were driven off, with much damage being inflicted on the galleys, one of which was captured. This battle of no renown marks a turning point and one achieved by the old-style ships. It also marks the start of a series of successful engagements conducted by William Winter, a salt horse of exceptional talent at sea and unfortunate activity ashore, where he was locked up in the Tower for several years for his involvement in Wyatt's rebellion of 1554; he was released by Mary in 1557 to get back to the navy, where his true talents lay as both a commander and an administrator.

Throughout the century the English had built, hired or commandeered oared vessels. Few of those constructed in English yards were galleys, and those that were did not meet up with an equivalent enemy force to dispute mastery of the Narrow Seas. Instead, the English removed their fear of galleys by confronting them with sailing ships better equipped to handle them at range because they were fitted with powerful forward- and after-facing guns and heavy guns on the broadside. Once these galleons were operational the days of the galley were numbered. Given that relationship between galley and galleon, the conventional wisdom has been to credit John Hawkins, the mastermind behind galleon development, with designing his ships with that confrontation in mind. Before acceding to this it must be borne in mind that Hawkins was a trans-Atlantic commander who had never had to fight galleys. His vision encompassed the galley-free open ocean, and he would have to be credited with the prescience to anticipate the fights within the confines of Cadiz harbour. Furthermore, the record of Hawkins's fighting predecessors, such as Lisle and Winter, showed that galleys could be well beaten with the ships that they had manned. The galleon won not because it was designed so to do but because it was the ultimate fighting ship of its age whatever the challenge.

In Cadiz in both 1587 and 1596 English galleons bested Spanish galleys and destroyed the ships which they were protecting. As a counter-attack against Drake's fleet off Lisbon in 1589 showed, even when conditions were right for them, the galleys could not be confident of victory.

While, on that occasion, the English were concentrating on the re-embarkation of Norris's soldiers, a squadron of twenty-one galleys sailed out of St Julian's, on the seaward side of the Tagus estuary. Their limited objective consisted of three small ships, including William Hawkins's 120-tonne bark, *William*, which had become detached and becalmed away from the fleet. Each ship fought back, although *William* was set alight and abandoned. Then *Dreadnought* was seen being pulled towards the fray by her three boats. The galleys fled. They had had an English fleet anchored in full view of their base for weeks, and this was their sole attempt to attack. Far from the English being afraid of the galleys, the fear had been passed over to the enemy.

Nevertheless, the Spanish continued to deploy galleys northwards to where they felt that conditions were appropriate. This meant the shallow waters off the Netherlands, where a squadron of six vessels, commanded by Frederico Spinola, arrived in 1599. Although they were despatched to challenge Dutch flyboats, their proximity to the English coast could not be ignored, and Elizabeth had four galleys of 100 tonnes built in the Thames to counter the threat. The opposing galleys never met. Instead, in 1602, an English fleet commanded by Sir Richard Leveson, supported by William Monson, met Spinola much further south, where the Genoese admiral, bringing further reinforcements to Flanders, had been diverted to protect a 1,700-tonne richly laden carrack, *San Valentino*, lying in the shelter of Cezimbra near the mouth of the Tagus. Unperturbed by their presence, Monson, in

Galleys were most useful for amphibious operations as can be seen in the drawing showing an abortive French raid on Brighton during the reign of Henry VIII. Note the warning beacon mounted so that it could be lowered to refuel while ablaze.
(British Library)

Garland, anchored within range and proceeded to give them a pasting with his heavy weaponry. The result was a total victory for the English, with Monson negotiating, at leisure, the surrender of the carrack's treasure worth £44,000.

The bloodied Spinola sailed on, but his movements were now well known, and he was intercepted off Dover by Sir Robert Mansell. Outgunned, all the galleys were destroyed apart from Spinola's own, which limped into Calais. With that defeat the fear of the galleys, which had lasted since 1513, was finally laid to rest and the English navy was ready to move to the next stage of its development to become a tactically controlled fighting fleet ready to wage war against other ships of the line.

RAIDS AND AMPHIBIOUS ASSAULTS

Raiding, 1512–1550

Every Tudor warship was capable of putting men ashore to attack coastal defences or settlements. Indeed, a seaman in the sovereign's service was more likely to come in contact with the enemy on shore than at sea. At the start of the century ships sent landing parties ashore on raids with limited aims and for short periods, often just to gather provisions or water. As the century moved on, and soldiers started to be embarked specifically to fight ashore, the scope increased to include large-scale amphibious operations. These were always the hardest branch of warfare to co-ordinate; on many occasions ambition exceeded capability, and most of the failures of the fleet involved such amphibious activity. This increase in scope and ambition may be put down to the influence of Drake, who had shown that a fleet well handled, especially if arriving unexpectedly, could inflict damage, sap morale and sail away well laden, without incurring great losses of its own.

It seems paradoxical that, in an age when so much warfare concerned quarrels among kings or nobles as to which was the mightier, it was considered legitimate to inflict devastating damage on innocent, uninvolved and un-consulted civilians. For this, the navy was ideally suited, being able to move faster and to arrive with less warning than an army trudging along poor roads. The naval commanders did not miss the opportunities presented. France, Scotland and Spain were all to suffer from such raids, while later in the century the Atlantic islands and the Indies were similarly assaulted. Of course, on many occasions, such as the Cadiz expeditions, the aim was primarily military, but even during these operations civilians suffered much from, what is now euphemistically referred to as collateral damage.

Thus in his plans to blockade the French fleet at Brest Sir Edward Howard included operations to raze the local villages and the towns of Crozon and Le Conquet, the latter a particular English favourite for spoiling. It was to be burned again in 1557 when Admiral Clinton, unable to assault the strong walls of Brest with 3,000 men, attacked the smaller town as a consolation prize.

Thomas Howard followed where his brother led, sending naval forces to raze villages off Cherbourg while he himself led a very strange and successful raid against well-walled Morlaix in 1522, when he should have been escorting Charles V from Southampton to Spain, having been appointed an admiral in the imperial navy solely for this

Although the walls of Morlaix were imposing, Thomas Howard took the town in 1522 with a lightly armed assault by boat. Contemporary gossip and tradition hints at treachery. (Author)

Morlaix was a wealthy town with many grand merchant houses. One of the few to survive the English attack was this one, used by Anne, Duchess of Brittany and queen of France, during her visits. (Author)

mission.[47] Along the Channel coast, Le Tréport was burned at least three times in the century, with the raid by Fitzwilliam in 1523 being noteworthy mainly because this unnecessary, and diversionary, spoliation enabled the Duke of Albany to sail unhindered by the occupied English fleet to Scotland, a passage that Fitzwilliam was at sea to prevent. One hopes that his share of the fish seized, the only booty, made his failure more tolerable. In September 1545, with the French fleet back in port, Lisle landed over 6,000 men at Memovale, three miles west of Tréport, drove off the defenders and set light to the town, its abbey and three nearby villages, re-embarking with just the loss of three men, two of whom had been reckless.[48]

The assault of civilian targets continued. In the 1544 Scottish war a lengthy newsletter to Lord Russell stated that while the army retired by land the 'ships upon the sea were not idle, and left neither ship, crayer nor boat belonging to any village, town, creek or haven, on either side of the Firth, between Stirling and the mouth of the river, unburnt, or brought away; which containeth in length 50 miles'.[49]

They also burned a number of towns and villages as well as, more legitimately, razing Inchgarvie Castle and seizing ships from the harbour at Leith, which they ballasted with '80,000 cannon shot of iron' that they found in the town, although that figure may be exaggerated.

What such violence against civilians achieved, apart from increasing their hatred of the enemy and replenishing the ships offshore, is hard to tell, but a hint that it provided a propaganda opportunity is given by a letter from Hertford to the king, also written during the 1544 raids against Scotland, informing Henry that he thought 'the King's device very good, that when raid and burning are made, bills should be set on the church door or other notable place, purporting, "they might thank their Cardinal therefore"': the Scottish Cardinal Beaton being one of the many whose implacable opposition to the marriage of Edward to Mary Stuart Henry was trying to change through his 'rough wooing'.

It was in supporting incursions into Scotland that joint, as opposed to amphibious, operations demonstrated their worth through the navy nurturing and reinforcing land forces moving along fixed routes close to the sea. Somerset, marching north from Berwick in late August 1547, was shadowed offshore by Lord Clinton with a fleet of sixty-five ships including victuallers whose naval bombardment of the Scottish flank helped in the decisive defeat of the Scots at Pinkie Cleugh. Ten years later similar support was to be provided when John Malen, cruising the Narrow Seas in 1557, witnessed the clash between the Count of Egmont and the French forces marching to seize Dunkirk, and brought his ten ships close inshore to bombard the French lines until they broke. Sadly, Malen's habit of making inshore passages ended four years later with his loss, along with all his ship's company, when he drove *Greyhound* on to a sand bank off Rye.

Ireland, 1573–1602

As the century progressed so the concept of amphibious operations rather than unplanned assaults gained credibility. There is no evidence to support the view that reports of Drake's success in the West Indies influenced this development, but he did play a significant part in the one truly amphibious operation of the protracted Irish campaigns, the notorious assault on Rathlin Island, which gave him his first experience of working closely with the queen's men – in this case, Walter Devereux, the First Earl of Essex, who had been sent in August 1573 to pacify and colonise Ulster, a task that was beyond the comprehension and the capability of the force allocated to him, as it was for his son after him.

One of the irritations that Essex faced was the influence and incursion of the Scots, who claimed settlers' rights over a swathe of northern Ulster, where they were supported and re-supplied by boats from Scotland that used windswept Rathlin Island, north-east of Antrim, as a staging post. In times of trouble, they also used the island as a shelter for their women and children, who took refuge in its apparently impregnable castle. Essex believed that to seize the castle and intercept Scottish galley traffic would not only hinder the Scots' logistic lines but also imprison their families and so deflate their morale. To accomplish this he recruited Drake and some ships that the latter had found serviceable in the Indies.

By May 1575 a squadron was formed from Drake's ships and, in July, they sailed from Carrickfergus to escort a landing force of 300 footsoldiers and eighty horsemen, under the command of John Norris, to Rathlin Island. One of the darkest episodes in English–Irish history was about to unfold. Sugden hints that Drake, who took no part in the land operations, might have wanted to have starved the inhabitants into surrender, [50] but Essex's dramatic and draconian plan led to some 400 defenceless people being slaughtered. One wonders whether the humane Drake ever referred to the events in the many days he and John Norris spent together on subsequent expeditions.

The navy under William Winter played an important role in achieving the surrender of the Spanish forces trapped in Smerwick fort in 1580. In this picture Marlyon, Revenge *and* Tiger *are named. They are anchored so that they can bring their bow or stern chasers, their heaviest armament, to bear, while at the same time presenting the minimum target for the defenders – who were all slaughtered after they surrendered.* (National Archives, Kew)

With Rathlin seized, an English garrison was placed in the castle, but it was removed when the commitment to supporting it by sea was not forthcoming. This was a lesson that was slow to be learned, for as Drake might have inferred from his prayer, in amphibious matters it is not the assault but the holding on until it is secure that yieldeth the true glory.

Drake had, of course, gained his experience in attacking settlements in the New World for personal gain, and when he became the leading exponent of similar, state-sponsored operations, it was the desire for private gain as well as public benefit that was to prove to be the poison in the potentially powerful alliance of naval and civilian ships that had to be brought together to finance these expensive expeditions.

The Spanish in Ireland

Ireland was, of course, regarded as a friendly and welcoming territory upon which the Spanish could land forces to challenge the English. Yet when they did, concerted and combined operations sealed in their unfortunate soldiers close to their point of disembarkation, ensuring, in the ferocity which marked the fighting in Ireland, that they would never see Spain again.

Smerwick, 1580

A force of 400 Spanish and Italian papal mercenaries was landed at Smerwick in September 1580 by Don Juan Martinez de Recalde, who had taken advantage of a temporary withdrawal of the English naval patrols off that coast. Ill equipped for Irish guerrilla warfare or weather, they took refuge, with 200 native sympathisers, in the local castle, whose siting on a peninsula eased their entrapment by Lord Grey's land army. Their fate was sealed when Admiral Winter returned to bombard them with his stern-chasers, from a sea from which they could no longer expect relief. After their unconditional surrender they were promptly massacred, their execution being supervised by Walter Ralegh.

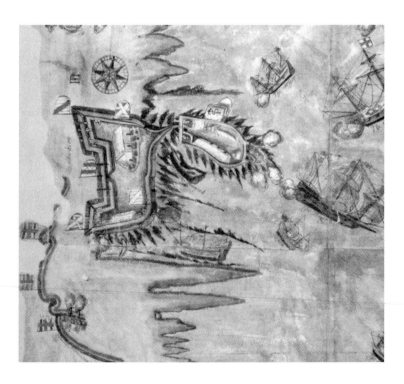

Castlehaven, 1602

Spanish persistence was seldom rewarded. In 1601 the Spanish landed another force at Kinsale, where it was promptly surrounded, abandoned, cut off and then surrendered when the exhausted relief force was defeated in sight of the besieged. The navy, under Leveson, landed reinforcements at Kinsale but then sailed to nearby Castlehaven harbour, where another smaller Spanish force, under Pedro de Zubiaur, had brought the remnants of his fleet to land more troops. By the time he arrived the Spanish had placed batteries to defend the harbour mouth, and it was through their fire that Leveson, in *Warspite*, led his fleet to attack the ships beyond. It was a notable victory. The Spanish flagship was driven on to the rocks, two more ships were driven ashore, another two were beached by the crews, and the remaining one was sunk. After the engagement, in which *Warspite* was shot through a hundred times, the English were becalmed for two days in the harbour within range of the Spanish guns. Eventually, and successfully, Leveson had them all warped out. It had been a triumph of command.

Naval operations off Ireland are usually regarded as a side show, but they produced one clear statement of naval strategy that was to hold good for centuries. In contrast to the response received by Essex in 1575, Mountjoy, the Irish land commander in 1601, was denied a standing naval patrol in his waters. Instead the Privy Council adopted the naval lobby's view, voiced by Leveson, that 'It is much more honourable for the queen and safe for the State to maintain a fleet upon the coast of Spain than to stand upon the defensive at home.'[51] By this time experience had shown this to be so, but it had been a hard-won fight.

MAJOR ELIZABETHAN AMPHIBIOUS OPERATIONS

With the production of more seaworthy ships, both naval and merchant, and the growing value of attainable plunder, later Elizabethan naval deployments moved from unplanned raids to joint force and joint-stock amphibious operations. The results, however, seldom matched the expectation, as the table below shows.

From the table it is very evident that the desire for gain, either to replenish the state coffers or to enrich the private investor, was not compatible with military success. One can add to this the disastrous effect of placing command in the hands of a popinjay like Essex, especially on a voyage where his arch-rival for Her Majesty's favour, Ralegh, was also sailing, thus allowing their rivalry to work its insidious effects.

Elizabethan Amphibious Operations

	1585-6	1587	1589	1595-6	1596	1597	1601
Destination	West Indies	Cadiz	Spain	West Indies	Cadiz	Azores	West Indies
Aim (see below)	A	B	C	D	E	F	G
Commander(s)	Drake	Drake	Drake	Drake, Hawkins	Charles Howard, Ralegh, Essex	Essex, Ralegh	Cumberland
Ships							
Royal		6		6	19		
Private		10		21			
Merchant/pirate		7			11		18
Victuallers					74		
Dutch					18+6		
Total							
Success or failure	Failure	Success	Failure	Failure	Success	Failure	Failure

Aims:

A
- To release English ships from Spanish ports
- To intercept the home-bound *flota*
- To attack both Canaries and Cape Verde Islands
- To attack Santa Domingo, Cartegena
- To visit and replenish English colonists at Roanoke

B To disrupt the preparations for the Spanish Armada

C
- To destroy Spanish shipping returned from Armada
- To place Dom Antonio on throne in Lisbon
- To seize an island in the Azores
- To capture treasure ships

D
- To take a rich carrack at San Juan de Puerto Rico
- To seize Panama

E To attack the Spanish in Cadiz

F
- To destroy the Spanish fleet at Ferrol.
- To capture the treasure fleet off the Azores.
- To establish a base in the Azores

G
- (not strictly a naval operation but included for comparison)
- To impoverish the King of Spain by seizing his ships
- To take San Juan de Puerto Rico

Note: The Cadiz raid in 1587 was not an amphibious operation but is placed here for comparison.

1585

Drake began the first of his official amphibious operations against Spain with the one simple aim of securing the release of English merchant ships impounded in Spanish ports. What he did after that the queen was content to leave to his initiative, as long as they both agreed that he could be 'disavowed' rather than she disconcerted. It was obvious, however, that Elizabeth wished her investment of £10,000 and two royal ships, *Elizabeth Bonaventure* and *Aid*, to produce a handsome return, and this would be forthcoming only from the seizure of the treasure fleet, which would also have the commendable result of denying Philip much-needed specie. Indeed, the Spanish were of the view that 'the principal purpose of this corsair is to prevent your Majesty and private persons from receiving revenue'. If that had been adhered to the voyage might have achieved its aim.

The one authorised aim was soon achieved. Drake, sailing on 14 September, landed off Bayona and, with his presence and that of twelve companies of soldiers (2,300 men) under the command of Christopher Carleill, threatening the town and nearby Vigo, the merchant ships were released, and the fleet allowed to water and replenish. Yet the achievement of the aim denied the English a chance to achieve the secondary purpose, for the Mexican *flota* had arrived safely in San Lúcar, at the mouth of the Guadalquivir, in late September, followed by that from Tierra Firme shortly afterwards, while Drake did not sail from Spain until early October. There followed a razing and ransoming for little gain that began with Carleill capturing and torching Santiago in the Cape Verde Islands, and then the taking and holding, for what would be a most disappointing ransom, of the town of Santo Domingo in Hispaniola. However disappointing the yield, the assault on Santo Domingo was brilliantly executed, combining all the elements essential for success. The first of these was surprise: by the time the citizens learned of the strange fleet in the offing, Carleill had carried out an unopposed landing on a secure beach ten miles from the city. His troops

One of a series of watercolour enclosures that seem to relate to correspondence about the Drake and Norris 1589 operations in northern Spain. This one shows Corunna, where the English forces took and burnt the lower town (on the narrow isthmus), but failed in their assault on the upper town. Local legend attributes the failure to an amazon called Maria Pita who reportedly killed the English standard-bearer. Needless to say, it is not mentioned in any report from Drake and Norris. (National Archives, Kew)

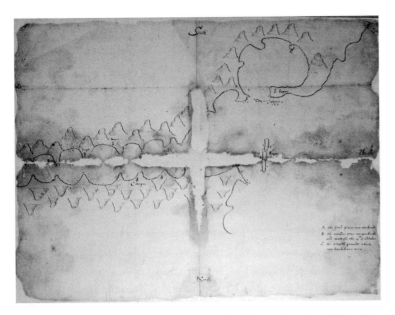

A map enclosed in a letter from the fleet to Walsingham in October 1585, with a rough sketch of the ria of Vigo and the bay of Bayona, showing the places where the English landed the troops and watered their ships. (National Archives, Kew)

arrived just after Drake, and with the aid of a captured pilot, had brought the fleet close to the harbour, where he diverted the local resources to his colleagues' benefit. Faced with the twin attack, resistance crumbled, and the inhabitants fled to begin days of miserable negotiations for the return of their sacked town, which they achieved eventually for a sum well below that which Drake had originally estimated it was worth. With those few crumbs in his pocket Drake re-embarked his troops and sailed almost due south to the pre-warned but tremulous city of Cartegena.

It was another brilliantly executed assault. Drake sailed rapidly into the harbour while Carleill landed to assault a well-defended trench and wall that barred his approach. At least it would have done, had not the general discovered that the defences could be skirted by keeping to the shore-line. This done, and with Frobisher destroying the last fort that held out, the citizens fled and the negotiations began. The result was the same as at Santo Domingo: insufficient loot to kindle further interest in continuing the operation.

With the inevitable decision to sail away, via the nascent and precarious English settlement in Roanoke, the expedition threw away one of its secondary aims, which had been to take and hold Panama. In so doing it probably spared many their lives, for the English lacked the ability to secure, with any hope of permanency, bases overseas, even just across the Channel. Frustrated, and with its backers out of pocket, the expedition arrived home having demonstrated that the tactical skills for successful amphibious operations existed in the state armoury but were useless without a firm and single strategic aim.

Drake took little away from his raid on Santiago in the Cape Verde Islands in 1585 apart from fever which killed over 300 of his crew and weakened many more. However, the picture does show the English tactic of landing troops away from the fleet so that they could carry out an assault on a town's inland walls while the fleet battered them from seaward. (British Museum)

1589

Drake's descent on Cadiz in 1587, described earlier, was not an amphibious operation, but its singularity of purpose provided its potency. In the year of 1589 the English showed that they had learned nothing from either Drake's success at Cadiz or his failure during his previous Indies voyage.

This inability to grasp the success of singular aims encompassed even Drake himself, for it was he and Sir John Norris who proposed an expedition to destroy the Spanish ships as they lay in a state of disrepair in Spanish ports after their horrific circumnavigation of the British Isles. So far so good, but then they proposed also to take the pretender Dom Antonio with them and place him on the Portuguese throne before seizing a base in the Azores.

The queen and Burghley were wiser, yet again. For them the aim had to be the defence of the realm, and if this could be achieved by the total destruction of the Spanish naval threat in its ports, then that alone made the voyage worthwhile, and all other considerations would be secondary. This clear, and sensible, priority was expressed in her orders issued to Drake and Norris in February, only for them to ignore both her instructions and their limitations: too few professional soldiers, too many amateur volunteers; too little investment, too great anticipation of return; too few victuals, too many mouths to feed; too large a force for anti-armada attacks, too few to take Lisbon.

Drake demonstrated his dislike of his orders when, instead of working his way along the northern Spanish coast, destroying shipping as he went, he landed at the empty harbour of Corunna rather than at the bustling Santander where a fleet lay unmanned and undefended. Here, as in 1586 in the Indies, a successful landing, with all enemy forces defeated, petered out when it was found that the troops had insufficient artillery to take the upper town, which should never have been an objective in any case. The force, reduced by the desertion of the Dutch and diseased through excessive drinking, then sailed on to Lisbon, where the precarious balance between success and failure in

amphibious operations was upset in favour of the latter.

Norris, along with the popinjay Essex, who was absent without leave, landed in boat-swamping seas off Peniche, a massive forty-five miles away from Lisbon. Drake, for a reason that has never been satisfactorily explained, did not try to force his way past the forts at the mouth of the Tagus to give support to the army before Lisbon but waited, ineffectually and unsupportively, off Cascaes, where the receipt of a strongly worded letter from the queen left him in no doubt as to her opinion of his conduct so far: she considered it to be treacherous. Restoration to favour would require a bold and successful conclusion to the troubled expedition. This Drake intended to achieve with a smaller group sailing on to the Azores, but foul weather caused this one hope of salvation to be abandoned. Much reduced by disease and desertion, the dispirited force made a disjointed journey back to England. The Azores had to wait for another few years before they, yet again, became an objective following an unsuccessful amphibious assault on Spain. In the meantime, as a result of Drake's personal decision to ignore his primary aim, the Spanish were able to have at least sixty of the ships that had returned from the Armada campaign back at sea by the end of 1589 as well as beginning, in Santander, the building of vessels fit to compete with English galleons.

The Final Voyage, 1595

It might be thought that the experience gained between 1585 and 1589 would be reflected in the production of sounder plan for future amphibious operations. It was not to be. Similar delays, disagreements, divisions and diversions to those that had dogged earlier expeditions meant that the Indies voyage of 1595 ended in failure, compounded by the deaths of the joint leaders, Hawkins and Drake. The voyage, originally planned around a dubious plan to seize Panama, was problematical from the beginning, although even the

The beautiful fort at Belem on the Tagus guarded the seaward approach to Lisbon. At this point the river is wide and it remains a mystery why Drake did not try forcing a passage past the defences in support of Norris's march on Lisbon in 1589. The presence of his fleet off the city could have turned embarrassing failure into total success. (Portuguese Tourist Board)

cautious Elizabeth was prepared to back it heavily. However, she changed her mind after delays in departure convinced her, as she told the expedition leaders, that the Spanish 'have sufficient warning to provide for your descent'. In view of further intelligence indicating that the Spaniards intended to mount another armada, she demanded that the voyage be limited to six months and must include an outward detour to destroy shipping lying in Spanish ports.[52] A further amendment was made when reports of a richly-laden galleon lying rudderless in San Juan de Puerto Rico reached the expedition leaders. This was a chance to 'make' the voyage, and if it had been seized and acted upon with alacrity it might have been carried off with aplomb. It started well, for just twelve days after receiving this information, on 28 August, the fleet got underway, but on 15 September a Spanish force of five frigates sailed from Seville to retrieve the treasure. A race was on, but only the Spaniards knew that they were taking part.

Drake and Hawkins, partly because of the poor victualling arrangements that the former had made, diverted into Grand Canary, where they arrived on 26 September for a fruitless two-day scuffle. They departed on the day the pursuing Spanish Admiral, Pedro Tello, arrived to find that the English had gone but, carelessly, had left behind the intelligence that they were sailing for San Juan. A warning was despatched, arriving at San Juan a week before the English hove into view. The English were then to compound their error by failing to sail to intercept Pedro Tello immediately they became aware of his presence off Guadeloupe, thus enabling him to arrive ahead of them at San Juan and add to the defences, with both his ships and his men, who assisted the workforce engaged in strengthening the shore fortifications.

Drake and Hawkins thus arrived off a town that, probably for the first time in this region, waited for them with some degree of confidence. As they anchored, John Hawkins, a man whose breadth of vision had invigorated the English navy both at sea and on land, died. Nevertheless, the English attack went ahead and was repulsed, as Pedro Tello and the town governor proved themselves capable of countering all of Drake's stratagems. With nothing to show for their efforts, the English reverted to the original plan and sailed away in a desultory fashion, via several small and insignificant towns, towards Panama, whose poor defences were improved in the three weeks' grace which Drake's detours had granted them.

When the English arrived on 27 December they repeated the errors of the Lisbon expedition. Baskerville was landed with too few men, too far from his objective and in a season when mass movement along the tracks was difficult. He then, after two days' yomping, had to try and overcome a superior force that was well dug in across a pass. He tried, was repulsed and retreated. Drake's death a few days later, on 23 January 1596, was a sombre and fitting conclusion to an expedition which, ideally, should not have taken place, and once launched should have been conducted with speed. The sole saving grace was that Baskerville, now in command, handled his ships so well that, off the Isle of Pines south of Cuba, they fought their way past the fleet of eight galleons and thirteen armed merchantmen commanded by Bernardino Delgadillo de Avellaneda, which had sailed from Seville on 3 November with orders to intercept and destroy Drake's force.

The sorry ends of both Drake's and Hawkins's careers highlight the question of the purpose of the Tudor navy. While its primary role

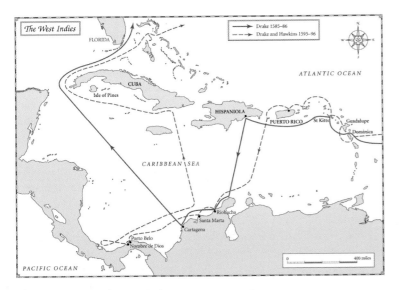

Drake's voyages to the West Indies. (Map by Peter Wilkinson)

had to be to protect the shores of England against invasion, which might require it both to blockade enemy ports and destroy enemy shipping, should the latter subordinate aim have included the search for booty? Certainly the admirals, whether shore-based or afloat, would have supported this idea, as would, on most occasions, a cash-strapped sovereign. Yet, time and again, conflicting concerns prevented the interception of rich cargoes at sea. Even the Puerto Rico galleon could more easily have been taken by a swift group of privateers than by a more cumbersome fleet of naval vessels with several aims and severe restraints. However, someone had to pay, and if the state could or would not, few of its seamen would risk much without the chimera of riches.

Hawkins had tried to reconcile the conflicting interests by formulating a strategy that would combine his own interests and those of the state. His efforts ended in the loss of *Revenge* in 1591. After Hawkins's own death, the end of the century saw his ideas put into disjointed practices that included one spectacular amphibious success and one failure, both involving the same personalities, Essex and Ralegh.

Cadiz, 1596

The fears of a new armada that had led to Elizabeth putting a time limit on Drake's Panama expedition had not died down by the time Baskerville arrived home. In response an Anglo-Dutch force was assembled to descend on the Spanish ports. Critically, as far as planning was concerned the queen paid the expense, and although sixty-eight merchant ships sailed with Lord Admiral Howard they had been 'taken up from trade', giving their owners no incentive for gain except the safe return of their vessels. This simplified the aim to the singular one of burning the King of Spain's ships of war:

> ... in his havens before they should come forth to the seas, and therewith also destroying his magazines of victuals and his munitions for the arming of his navy, to provide that neither the rebels in Ireland should be aided and strengthened, nor yet the king be able, of a long time, to and have any great navy in readiness to offend us.[53]

The one point that this clear instruction made obvious was that, for the aim to be achieved, it had to be an amphibious operation. It is noteworthy also that the order is for total destruction rather than booty; the fear of indiscipline through looting and drunkenness seems to have been addressed.

The fleet assembled at Dover in April, and on 1 June it sailed south for a destination that Howard, determined to retain his command over the volatile Essex and Ralegh, kept to himself until their arrival off Cadiz, his chosen destination. Surprise was maintained by keeping well out to sea and using scouting pinnaces to spy out the coast, so that, although the inhabitants had a night's warning, it was insufficient for them to rally their defences.

Fire from Fort San Felipe and its squadron of galleys was treated contemptuously as the English sailed into the outer harbour, driving the Spanish towards the inner harbour and causing them to snarl up as they were forced into the narrow entrance. At this stage the English anchored overnight; the next day the commanders jostled for position to lead the assault on the four Spanish galleons that lay across the entrance to the inner harbour, inside which lay a great fleet of merchant ships laden with supplies destined for the New World. Ralegh knew where honour dictated his target should lie, for one of the galleons was *San Felipe*, which had taken *Revenge* in 1591. He steered *Warspite* straight for her, and a fierce close-quarters battle ensued in which Ralegh himself was severely injured. He had the satisfaction, however, of watching both *San Felipe* and *San Tomas* blow up and their crew, horribly scorched, leap into the water, where vengeful Dutchmen in boats slaughtered them. 'If any man desire to see hell it was there most lively figured' was Ralegh's description of what he had witnessed. John Donne, another eye-witness, saw it as a poetic paradox:

> Out of a fired ship, which, by no way
> But drowning, could be rescued from the flame,
> Some men leap'd forth, and ever as they came
> Neere the foes ships, did by their shot decay;
> So all were lost which in the ship were found;
> They in the sea being burnt, they in the burnt ship drown'd'

The other two galleons, *San Mateo* and *San Andreas*, were captured to become part of the English fleet, and many other vessels were set alight.

Earlier, Essex had made a common error in an amphibious assault when he tried to land through surf, but Ralegh intervened to save the day, and Cadiz fell shortly afterwards. Its fall diverted attention away from the wealthy merchant fleet in the inner harbour, whose owners sent to the English a deputation offering to pay a ransom for the security of their goods. Accepting this would have been quite contrary to the English orders, but it was tempting. However, before they could yield to avarice the Spanish authorities set the whole fleet alight. Millions of ducats went up in smoke, scores of traders were bankrupted, and as a result trade with South America ceased for one whole year. Thus the Spanish inflicted upon themselves a wound far greater than the English would have done. Elizabeth, who well understood the value of that pyre, was most unimpressed that it had not been seized before the flames took hold, even though her own orders proposed destruction. She would not have placed much worth on the most valu-

In this busy picture of 1596 the English fleet streams into Cadiz harbour while landing parties are being put ashore both to east and west of the town, which then only occupied a small part of the peninsula. The galleys are shown retreating towards Gibraltar. (National Maritime Museum PW4432)

able and enduring prize brought back to England; Essex removed the Bishop of Faro's library and gave the books to his friend Thomas Bodley, who used them as the basis of his new library in Oxford.

Essex had been a lone voice arguing that the English should retain Cadiz as a forward-operating base. Everyone else was for home. Whether the city could have been held over time is doubtful, and many years later, Gibraltar was to prove to be the more strategic base. However, the concept was one of the few of this worthless man's ideas that made some sense. His inability to think straight was soon to be shown shortly afterwards in the Island Voyage to the Azores.

The Island Voyage, 1597

One of Howard's greatest attributes as a commander was that he was able to control and calm the sensitivities and egos of such men as Essex and Ralegh. The importance of this attribute was ignored in 1597 when the two bristling competitive fighting cocks, each more interested in their own honour and rivalry than in the success of their

mission, were appointed as admiral and vice-admiral of the Azores deployment – the Island Voyage – without a wiser, more experienced head to bang theirs together.

The initial problem was, however, one of contradictory aims rather than divided command. Like Drake and Hawkins's voyage of 1595, this one was being planned while the threat of a new armada was foremost in the queen's mind. She thus wanted her admirals to launch an attack on Ferrol first to ensure that no armada could sail before the fleet returned from the Azores. To this end a large number of troops were made available for amphibious assaults on the Spanish ports. Essex, taking advantage of delays caused by bad weather, landed most of these before finally sailing from England, using the excuse that intelligence indicated that an armada could not sail before the next year. His selected rendezvous was off the Azores, where, with the reduced troop numbers, the only possible aim that could be achieved was the seizure of the treasure fleet.

Instead of planning the necessary ambuscade, Essex sailed hither and thither, failing to keep a rendezvous with Ralegh and exploding in fury when the latter, using his initiative, landed and took Fayal. Thomas Howard, the rear-admiral, patched up the quarrel, but the anger had inflamed Essex's brain, for instead of moving west to intercept the treasure fleet, he took his force east to St Michael, thus allowing the *flota* to anchor safely under the guns of Angra in Terceira. Frustrated, Essex now ordered an attack on St Michael, hoping to achieve at least the expedition's third aim of establishing a base in the Azores. Ralegh was ordered to make a demonstration before the town, while Essex landed at Villa Franca and mounted an assault from the rear. Ralegh demonstrated. He demonstrated all day. It was to no avail. Essex failed to show up, having found the land around Villa Franca too pleasant to walk away from. The last chance of salvaging something from the expedition came when a large and richly laden Portuguese carrack, mistaking Ralegh's fleet for the Spanish one, chose to sail into the bay where the English were anchored. Sadly, an over-eager Dutchman gave the game away, allowing the prey to escape.

The Island Voyage had been a complete disaster. It was almost made worse by the fact that, contrary to Essex's view, the Spanish had sailed for England while he was in the Azores. This armada had a better aim than its 1588 predecessor. The commander, Don Martin, was ordered to collect a squadron of galleys on passing Blavet in Brittany, capture Falmouth, sail to the Scillies to await Essex's fleet, and on its defeat return to Falmouth, from which the troops would march into England. This was eminently achievable, especially in the absence of the opposing fleet. Ralegh and Essex got home just in time to organise the turn-around of their ships but they were not required. The late October gales scattered the Spaniards before they rounded Ushant.

Ralegh escaped censure. Essex received his reward in that Charles Howard, the Lord Admiral and Thomas Howard's brother, was elevated to the earldom of Nottingham, which gave him precedence over the younger man. The citation also mentioned Howard's good services at Cadiz, a triumph that Essex had considered was primarily of his making. He had a sulk.

The Island Voyage illustrated more than most others the foolishness of command being given to those whose primary aim was competitive self-aggrandisement rather than service. It also showed that the command of the seas had become too professional a pursuit to be entrusted to amateurs. The century had begun with none of the sovereign's servants experienced in sea command. By its half-way point both plunder and anti-piracy patrols had produced men to whom command could be entrusted and respect paid. By its end only those who had spent many years at sea could hope to confound the professionals of other nations. Strangely, one of the best admirals of the next century would be James Stuart, a man who would one day be king. He achieved his authority and success through professional knowledge and fearless leadership, qualities that made him an heir of the commoner Drake, not the noble Essex.

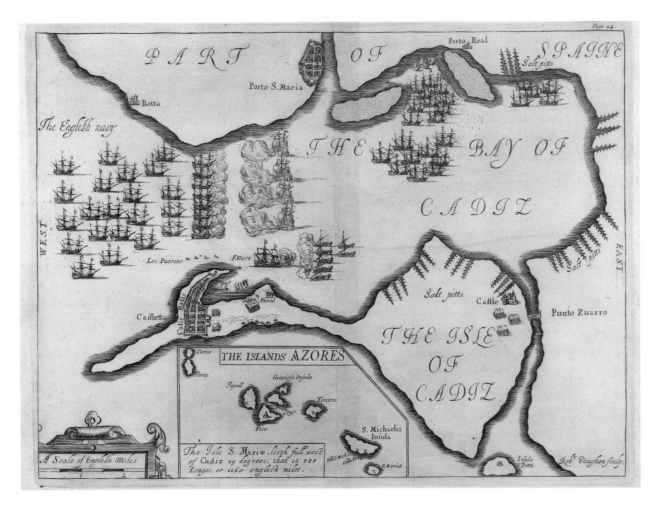

In this picture, once thought to represent Drake's raid of 1587 rather than Howard's of 1596, the Spanish defence of the inner harbour by its four large 'Apostle' galleons is clearly shown. They were soon overpowered by the belligerent Ralegh in Warspite *with two,* St Philip *and* St Thomas, *blowing up while* St Andrew *and* St Matthew *were taken back to England. The inset illustrates the follow-up Azores operation. (National Maritime Museum PW4433)*

The seizure of San Juan de Puerto Rico, 1598

To mount three major naval expeditions in as many years would have strained the resources of a nation with greater wealth than England. That another deployment took place straight away reflects the peculiarly English condition of having both a navy and an almost identical fleet of pirates and armed merchantmen. This voyage was undertaken only with the latter ships and was led by that great pirate, the Earl of Cumberland, who possessed in his flagship the 600-tonne *Scourge of Malice*, the heaviest armed ship for her tonnage afloat, fitted as she was with three demi-cannon, sixteen culverins, twelve demi-culverins and eight sakers, over sixty-three tons of ordnance in all.

Cumberland showed his originality of mind when, instead of lying in wait for richly-laden spice or treasure ships, he decided to sail to Lisbon and capture the outward-going flotilla with its less romantic but solid cargo of wages and supplies. On 6 March 1597 the earl led his force of eighteen ships south. With a single aim, 'to destroy shipping and so impoverish the King of Spain', a single commander and a simple partnership, success beckoned. Then, in a storm, the flagship's main mast was sprung, and Cumberland took shelter at Peniche to effect repairs. Although he ordered the rest of the fleet to remain over the horizon, the forest of masts was sighted and Lisbon alerted. The convoy stayed in harbour.

Showing that not too much had been learned from Drake, the foiled earl sailed for the Canaries, where, with drunken crews and no gains, the captains agreed to sail on to Puerto Rico to attempt San Juan, which Drake had failed to capture. The question remains, why? It had been proved that towns 'afforded little of wealth to be taken because riches of value will either be buried or secretly conveyed away', while townsfolk were prepared to let their property burn rather than pay an extortionate ransom.

The one plus for the English was Cumberland's leadership. Landing 1,000 men five leagues from the town, he found that they were separated from their objective by a narrow causeway which could be crossed only three abreast, while at the far end a raised drawbridge created a further obstacle. With his soldiers forced to take a difficult detour under fire, Cumberland returned on board, only to emerge two hours later with Plan B. The troops were re-landed beyond the creek entrance and their flank protected by a ship, which was sacrificed on the shoals while the rest of the ships fired at the town. It fell without a fight, with only the castle at the end of the peninsula offering any enduring resistance; it surrendered after an eleven-day siege.

The English remained in San Juan undisturbed by the Spanish until mid-August, by which time over 400 of them had died from illness. They returned out of pocket, a final demonstration that the successful conclusion of amphibious operations demanded a maturity of preparation and execution which the English navy and army did not yet possess.

To counter the use of Portsmouth as an operational base, Francis I of France founded Havre de Grace or Franciscopolis, soon known simply as Le Havre, at the mouth of the Seine and almost opposite Portsmouth. It was an object of English intelligence efforts from the outset, and eventually in 1563 it was briefly occupied by the English in support of French Huguenots. This drawing shows the French siege that was to recapture the town. (National Archives, Kew)

Maritime Intelligence

In an age when the view from the crow's nest on a clear day defined all that was known, it was important to use every possible means to keep the admiral informed of enemy activity and the disposition of his fleet. Thomas Howard, Earl of Surrey, was, as befitted his character, a great user of spies and reconnaissance, often using the information that he gleaned as a reason for inactivity. When both Calais and Boulogne were in English hands, spying on the French was much easier than when their main fleet was in the harbour at Brest. One of the best examples of the work of an 'espial' was sent to Henry VIII by Lord Poynings while he was at Boulogne. The 'espial' had travelled to Rouen, Le Havre and St Valers. At the former he found three galleys with just the pilots and 'slaves' on board and with all their artillery lying at the dock side. Downstream, at Le Havre, were a hundred ships of war and a further 200 victuallers, and on the dock side here were 200 bronze an iron guns, forty of which he described a 'great pieces of brass'. Other munitions were stacked up alongside, while gossip suggested that twenty-two galleys from Marseilles were expected daily. The report continued with similar detail. It would certainly have been sufficient for the Privy Council to consider how best to deploy the navy and to make a calculated guess as to when the French might get to sea in strength.[54]

It was, of course, a two-way process. Hertford, during the rough wooing of Scotland in 1544, reported to the king in March that the French were boasting that they always knew where the king's ships lay and could thus pass them at night without danger.[55]

A year later William Damesell uncovered a sabotage plan at the emperor's court, where he had learned that a Frenchman, banished from his country for manslaughter, was proposing to earn forgiveness by sailing in company with a convoy of ships bound for England laden with gunpowder, into which he would lob, while at sea, 'certain fireworks to destroy the ships'.[56]

The greatest gamble on correct intelligence came with the short campaign of July 1545 to oppose the French armada which sailed on

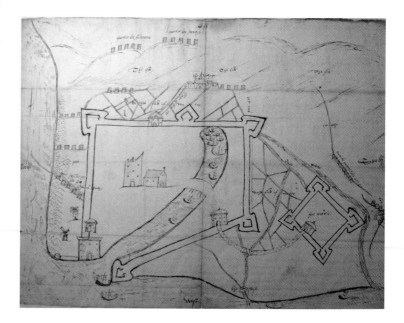

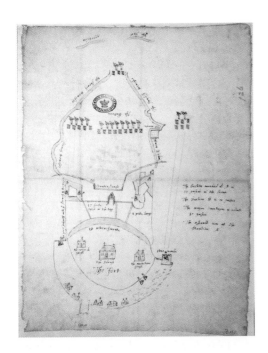

This sketch of the Spanish fort on the peninsula overlooking the Goulet, the narrow approach to the harbour off Brest, shows the defences against which Frobisher led the attack and lost his life. Well considered strategic thinking would have led the Spanish to have seized control of this critical site, if only temporarily, before launching armadas against England.
(National Archives, Kew)

dered, to which the response was that it would be better to reduce the pension and let the English keep Boulogne.

Lack of clear intelligence ahead of the arrival of the 1588 Spanish armada had meant that the English naval commanders had endeavoured to sail too early to counter the threat with a significant chance of success. As it was, it was the arrival of *Golden Hind*, bearing Captain Fleming's sighting report, a few hours before the invasion fleet sailed by that ensured that the English were able to work their way out of Plymouth Sound just in time. If that intelligence had not been received and if – a big if – the Spanish had been sufficiently flexible to divert into the Sound, the English fleet could have been destroyed as it lay at anchor. Intelligence, whatever, the gap between receipt and reaction, was always timely.

The most famous piece of intelligence was carried in 'a pinnace like a fluttering bird' that was despatched by the Earl of Cumberland, cruising off the Portuguese coast, to warn Lord Thomas Howard in the Azores of the imminent arrival of the Spanish war fleet in strength. The alarm was raised with just sufficient time for the English to weigh anchor and avoid being trapped in a bay in Flores. All, that is, apart from the rash Sir Richard Grenville, who decided to stay and fight thus losing *Revenge* and gaining renown.

Summary

With naval success came the realisation that the England could fight better, more cheaply and more effectively afloat than it could on land, where her lack of a standing, professional, army led to little gain and great loss. However, several lessons had to be learned and major adjustments made before the nation was able to maximise the potential of a fighting navy. The first was that sea command could not be considered the preserve of the nobility, whose supposedly inbred flare for campaigns ashore could not be transferred successfully to conflicts afloat. The second was that such an investment and commitment could not be delivered with a part-time, un-administered amateur force. With these issues addressed, progress was made so that by the close of Elizabeth's reign, the English had a navy that could command her coastal waters and challenge all comers in bluer seas. This position was achieved by building the right type of warships, retaining them at the required strength, improving their weapon fit and, by and large, keeping their crews fed, watered and paid. Thus a force that fought its first engagement as a land army at sea off Ushant in 1512 fought its last serious encounter as a naval fleet in 1596, employing tactics that would hold good for centuries to come. Along the way, it had driven the galley threat from the seas it sailed in, and paid for its keep by bankrupting a rival nation. It was truly a proud and powerful wooden wall.

13 July. By 15 July Henry himself had arrived at Portsmouth, where his army had been ordered to assemble on Southsea Common. This was an enormously risky decision. An army moved at around twelve miles a day, and Portsmouth lies seventy miles from London. With the English fleet anchored in the Solent, D'Annebault could have made an unchallenged, undetected and unreported passage up the Channel and put a substantial army ashore in Kent, where, even if they had not marched the short distance to the capital, they could have reduced the countryside to ruin. Henry, however, appears to have known Francis's mind. In Hall's chronicles, published in 1548, it is stated that 'The king then lay [at Portsmouth], for he had knowledge by his spies, that the French army intended to land in the Isle of Wight, wherefore he repaired to that coast, to see his realm defended.'

Certainly the Spanish knew that the French plan was 'to send 300 ships, 25 galleys and 5 galleasses, with 10,000 men to establish a fort on the coast of the island of England [Isle of Wight] and then land their men near Boulogne, close the harbour with wooden boom, and make a fort on the beach like that which the English demolished'.[57] Personal approaches were also being undertaken, with the same letter recording that the Admiral of France had recently sent his secretary to the 'Admiral of England' suggesting an increased pension (the French payment agreed on to end earlier hostilities) if Boulogne was surren-

Castle in the Downes

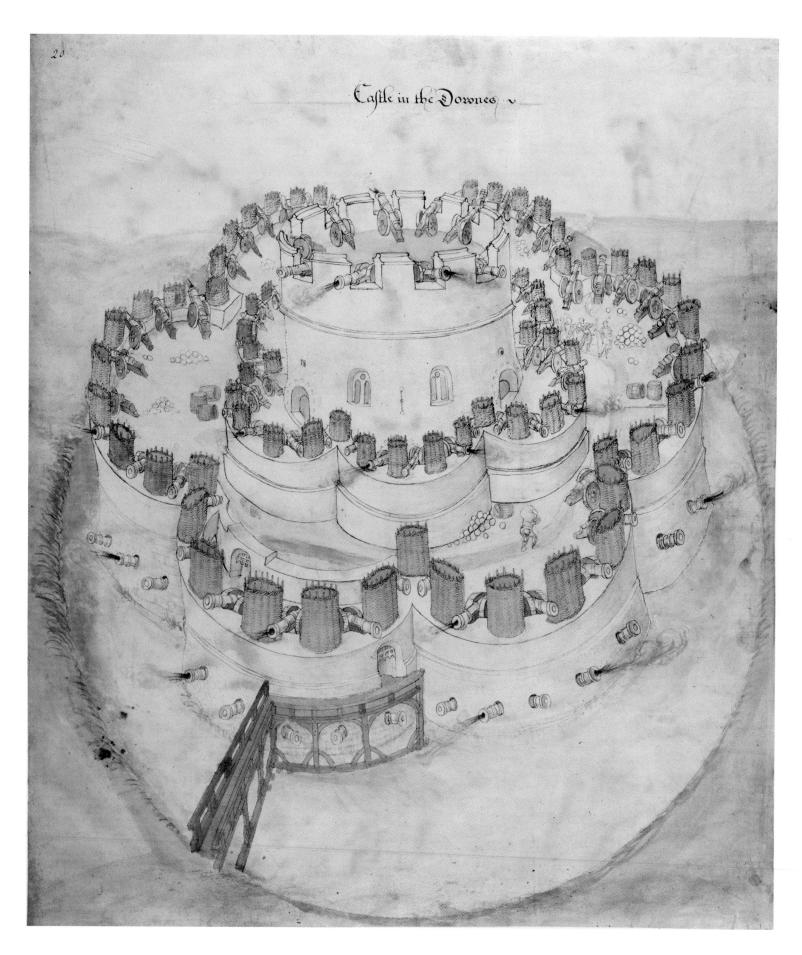

Chapter Twelve

Shore Support

'I have taken a plank and rope and nail, without the King his leave,
After the custom of Portesmouth, but I will not suffer a thief.
Nay, never lift up thy hand at me – there's no clean hands in the trade.
Steal in measure,' quo' Brygandyne. 'There's measure in all things made!'
Rudyard Kipling, 'King Harry and the Shipwrights, 1487', in Rewards and Fairies

The claim that the Tudors founded the English navy rests not only with their creation of a permanent, specialist fleet of royal warships but also with their provision, to support them, of dockyards and a shore administration. Establishing the latter was a gradual process, in terms of appointments, range of responsibilities and efficacy, while the former began with the change from the purchase and adaptation of merchant ships to the ordering of purpose-built vessels during the reign of Henry VII, along with the building of a dry-dock in which they could be refitted. This process was continued by his heirs, with the supporting infrastructure support mostly based at Portsmouth and in Kent.

Maintenance

The creation of a standing navy was only in part predicated on the existence of a fleet, for it was the continual maintenance of that fleet, so that it was available to slip to sea at short notice, that made the arrangement cost-effective. Henry Tudor's great contribution to the creation of a standing navy was to have a dry dock constructed at Portsmouth into which his ships could go for refit and repair. He had no wish to see his investment rot away at moorings in the Hamble, and frequent dockings were the way to avoid this, as well as an opportunity for modernising his ships. His spendthrift son also realised this and made sure that those vessels in which he had invested his money were manned by ship-keepers both in the winter and during the longer periods of months or years when they were laid up in special ponds or

A sixteenth-century drawing of 'A castle in the Downs' (Deal) equipped for battle. It shows the use of sand-filled wicker baskets designed to add protection for the gunners both from direct gunfire but also ricochets and shards flying off the stonework. (British Library)

moorings so that they could be maintained on a regular basis and brought back out of reserve when required.

The condition of the laid-up ships and the time needed to put them to sea were, not unnaturally, a cause of concern not only for the crown but for foreign ambassadors as well. Chapuys, the long-standing imperial ambassador to the court, was one of those keeping an eye on things. In December 1533 he informed his master, Charles V, 'The King's Council have lately called those who have the management of the King's ships, commanding them to get them ready, and desiring to know if the whole could be in readiness by May 1; but they have given them to understand it was impossible to do so within 12 to 13 months.'[1]

This alarming news, Chapuys continued, had resulted in work being ordered to bring the coastal defences up to standard, and also in Cromwell and the king making overtures to Lübeck, a city-state renowned for the size and quality of its ships. In 1536 Chapuys reported that Henry's major warships were in such a poor state of repair that it would require eighteen months' work to make them seaworthy. This view seems to have been reached also by Thomas Cromwell, who in the same year wrote a justification of the work that he had done since he became Chief Minister. This included the statement that he had 'new made the *Mary Rose*, the *Peter Pomegranate*, the *Lyon* [*Lion*], the *Katheryn Galley*, the *Bark*, the *Minion*, the *Sweepstake* and purchased sufficient wood for the new making of *Henry Grace à Dieu* and *Great Galley*'.[2] This overhauling and continued maintenance meant that as the nation moved slowly towards yet another pointless war the fleet should have been ready to get to sea at short notice. However, a report on the size and state of the fleet in the Thames in January of 1539 stated that *Mary Rose*, *Peter Pomegranate* and *Minion*, which were 'new made, standing in their docks, mast ready but not raised up, cannot be ready to sail under three months time', though *Primrose* and *Sweepstake* could be sailed within twenty days and *Great Galley*, *Less Bark*, *Jennet* and *Lion* could get underway in thirty days. There was, however, a problem with both manpower – over 500 shipwrights, caulkers and mariners were needed if they were all to get ready together – and storage for cordage, which might have to be placed in a private warehouse at Deptford. One of the practical suggestions made in the report was for *Less Bark* to sail to Portsmouth with masts and spars but to go via Brittany to collect a cargo of salt, the sale of which would help offset the cost of mobilisation.[3] The note also highlighted the problems of overwintering ships in the Thames, which could cost over £1,000 per year while at the same time risking ice damage. The writer suggested either keeping them elsewhere or building more docking facilities in the river. Such pressures on the administrators had to lead to more shore support.

In times of peace the smaller vessels in the king's fleet proved far more useful than the great ships moored in the Thames. Two of them, *Minion* and *Mary Guildford*, were in constant use conveying goods for use either in the shipbuilding programme or for transporting goods to the king's liking, such as wine, or disliking, such as Anne of Cleves.

Portsmouth

There is much to suggest that Henry Tudor intended shifting the focus for maintaining the royal ships from the Thames to Hampshire. If so, however, the plan was short-lived. Once Henry VIII had settled into kingship, the fleet's shore support once again became centred to the east of London, while Brygandyne, the Clerk of Ships, had his baili-wick eventually limited to Portsmouth.

Robert Brygandyne, whose name must be associated with Portsmouth's brief, early rise to prominence, was one of those important people in history about whom we know little apart from their achievements. He lived at Smallhythe on the banks of the River Rother, close by the shipyard where *Regent* was built, and the evidence indicates that *Mary Fortune* was built, literally, in his back yard. In 1495 he moved to Portsmouth to supervise the building of the 'dry dock' in which both *Regent* and *Sovereign* would be refitted. It is often claimed that this was the world's first dry dock, but it did not have a movable caisson to allow ships to enter and leave at any state of tide. Instead, it was closed off with two laterally displaced gates, between which tons of infill had to be placed; to keep the dock dry many days therefore had to be spent digging it out for each undocking.[4] This arrangement made it indistinguishable from several similar structures apart from its large size.

Whatever its primacy, the creation of England's first permanent dry dock at Portsmouth was a significant milestone along the way to maintaining a fleet in good repair and improving the longevity and usefulness of royal ships. Indeed, the dock's first two customers, *Revenge* and *Sovereign*, were transformed from medieval clinker to carvel-sided vessels here. Although Robert Brygandyne project-managed the complicated building programme, the dock was designed by Sir Reginald Bray, Treasurer of War, more famous as the architect of St George's Chapel at Windsor, yet another indicator of the great importance Henry Tudor placed on the creation of this facility. The Portsmouth dry dock may

Portsmouth's narrow entrance provided excellent protection for a fleet and a capacious inner harbour in which ships could be laid up in reserve; its defensive assets were far superior to those available at Cadiz for the Spanish fleet, where a wide harbour entrance invited assault. (Author)

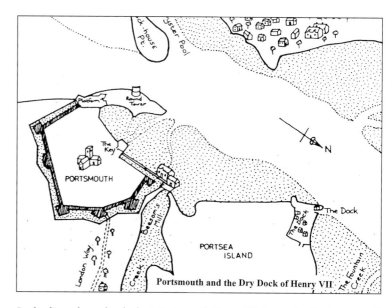

By funding a large dry dock at Portsmouth Henry VII began the development of the town both as an operational and a maintenance base for the Royal Navy. (Mary Rose Trust)

have been a more mundane and less enduring building than the chapel, but in its dimensions it was a similar-sized enterprise. It took forty-six weeks to build, including a break between November and February when winter made work impossible.

Its gates were massive. As many as 113 loads of timber were hauled to Portsmouth to build them from 4,524 feet of planks. The sides of the dock were also built from timber, and much iron work was required to hold the structure firm. Although the gates were designed to hold back the tide, with their timbers being well caulked, they appear not to have had the snug fit associated with later gates, including the familiar ones that form the locks on canals. Extra labour had therefore to be spent on infilling and tamping down the gap between the gates to prevent the ingress of the tides, which was too great a leak to be handled by the 'Ingeyn to draw water owte of the

After the launch of Mary Rose *in Portsmouth Henry VIII moved his shipbuilding operations back to the Thames until the 120-ton galleasse* Jennet, *shown here, was laid down at Portsmouth in 1536.* (British Library)

seid dokke' and the human chain of buckets. Over 600 tons of rocks, rubble and clay, much of it brought over from the Isle of Wight, were required to keep the dock dry, and wheelwrights in Havant were called upon to provide carts for hauling this enormous load to the dock head.

That the dock was intended to be watertight without the infill can only be surmised, but the belief is supported by the titanic effort required to fill in the gap between the gates after a ship had entered and to clear it out before she could be refloated. Ten weeks were spent on the initial laying of the 'great Roke Stone & Gravell'. Then, when he was ready to receive *Sovereign*, Brygandyne had to employ 160 extra men, besides her ship's company, to labour day and night to dock her. Getting her out was even more costly. Twenty workmen worked day and night between the tides for four weeks to dig out the fill. The operation cost £8 4s 10d in wages and £4 3s 4d in victuals; given that the task was carried out during the month of January, each workman must have felt he deserved every penny that he received.[5]

Yet Henry Tudor must have been convinced that he was spending his money wisely. *Sovereign* emerged, after an eight-month refit, to be hired out to James Ffynch, a merchant, for a voyage to the Levant. *Regent* spent a much shorter time in dock because she was required to sail to support a war against the Scots. Thus both the king's purse and

his position were enhanced and protected by the work in the dock. Alongside this busy refitting dock, slipways were created on which *Sweepstake*, *Mary Rose* and *Peter Pomegranate* were built: dry docks are not ideal places for a new build because they necessitate the use of cranage to hoist and lower timbers and shores and the constant clambering up and down by the workforce.

After Henry Tudor had built and ordered his new ships from Portsmouth no further vessels were laid down here until *Jennet* in 1536. Even then her construction was delayed when plague, which had been severe inside the city walls, spread to the shipyard, where the workmen lived in crowded conditions. They downed tools, and it was decided to discharged them until winter, when the plague would have worked itself out.[6]

So although the development of Portsmouth was an important part of Henry Tudor's naval plans, it was not considered to be so by his successors. Nevertheless, refitting, overwintering and maintenance kept a reasonable number of people employed there, some 798 men during Henry VIII's first French war.[7] These included a hundred gunners, a hundred brewers, millers and horse keepers, seventy coopers, forty lightermen and a hundred ship-keepers. A hint that the pay of these men may have been appropriated by the light-fingered comes in a letter from the Bishop of Winchester, Richard Fox, who was in charge of logistics in Hampshire, to the national logistics supremo, Thomas Wolsey. On 10 May 1514 Fox wrote that he hoped Wolsey would 'remember the bill concerning the keepers of the king's brew house and gunners of the tower and the blockhouse of Portsmouth, who had no wages for a long season'. On 12 June he reminded Wolsey of this failure and added the threat that 'the gunners and keepers of the brew houses at Portsmouth will depart unless a warrant is sent for their payment'.

Brygandyne himself was also subject to tardy recompense and had to write to Richard Palshide at Southampton customs, from whose dues the naval shipbuilding programme at Portsmouth was funded, on 9 June 1511 to beseech him, in somewhat ingratiating tones, to settle his invoices. At the bottom of this letter John Dawtrey, the head of customs in Southampton, minuted: 'Master Brygandyne, the indenture you write for is in my coffer of iron at London, where no man can see it till my coming thither by no means, but I shall be always ready to follow and to fulfill your desire therein as for it is all one to me,'[8] an early version of the 'cheque in the post' ploy, for three weeks later payment appears to have been made.

The brief ascendancy of Portsmouth ended with the appointment, in 1512, of John Hopton as Clerk Controller with responsibilities for the storehouses in Kent. His salary of £33 6s 8d per year was roughly twice that being paid to Brygandyne, whose role in the years up to his retirement in 1523 became less important and whose successor, Jermyn, was little more than the custodian of the dry dock.

This does not mean that investment ceased. In 1530 Portsmouth dockyard saw another expansion, with nine additional acres being purchased from eleven landowners for £9. The perimeter was then enclosed with quickset hedging and thorn bushes, through which several gates were interspersed, the whole as usual being accounted for in precise detail.[9] Inside the boundary much work continued, with a new dock for 'the grounding of the *Mary Rose*, the *Peter Pomegranate* and the *John Baptist*' being cut as well as a storehouse, called the 'Long House', being built and winding gear positioned for hauling other ships on to the shore. A flood into the dry dock where *Great Harry* was undergoing refit necessitated employing more labour, while others were provided further up the Solent at Burseldon to dock *Gabriel*. The reference to 'new' docking and to manning capstans at 'each tide' would suggest that despite the permanent dock that had been built here in Henry Tudor's time, docks were still being dug out as temporary features whenever a demand arose. This document also indicates that, apart from maintenance, the annual costs involved in keeping the fleet in ordinary were high. The *Great Harry* employed seventy-five ship-keepers, each of the remainder of the fleet not many less: at salaries of 10s 4d per month, this amounted to a sizable call on the king's resources and shows, as well as any other statistic, that Henry was determined to keep faith with his standing navy.

Portsmouth had one further fall in its fortunes when, in 1550, the Privy Council ordered all ships laid up in that harbour to be brought around to the Medway, by which time the Tudor navy's shore support was based at three Kent storehouses and shipyards (Chatham, Woolwich and Deptford) and Portsmouth, all of which had lodgings available to members of the Navy Board during official visits.

The Kent Yards

Deptford had been a royal ship-building centre for at least a century before 1487 when Henry Tudor paid £5 for the hire of a storehouse there. On taking up his appointment in 1512, John Hopton, was charged with the care of newly created storehouse at both Deptford and Erith. The latter was built in a four-acre orchard hired for £32 from a Robert Page which, presumably, ran down to the water's edge where the ships were drawn up for it later had to be abandoned when it was found to be regularly flooded by high tides. While Erith decayed, Woolwich, where Henry's great ship, *Henry Grace à Dieu*, was built in 1514, became a prominent centre for naval activity, and a rope yard was built there in 1574. In 1578 John Hawkins was paid £150 to construct a set of movable gates at Deptford which would allow ships to enter and depart at any state of the tide, and it is this innovation, more than Brygandyne's dock at Portsmouth, that can claim to be the forerunner of the modern dry dock.

If Woolwich was to be Henry's favoured shipyard, the evidence shows that the attention that his father paid to Portsmouth ill-prepared Henry to restart production at the former site. When *Henry Grace à Dieu* was ordered, over 250 craftsmen had to be recruited from elsewhere to build the great ship. Most of the nation's ports made a contribution, with workers being drawn from, *inter alia*, Plymouth, Smallhythe, Poole, Ipswich, Dartmouth, Southampton and even Hull, York and Beverley. They were paid for their travel, fed well and housed in dormitories, sometimes three to a bed. The dockyard at Woolwich was built up from ground already owned by the state, and parcels of adjacent property rented either annually or bought from the owner. Thus Sir Edward Boughton used to receive £6 13s 4d per year for a two-acre site in which lay two docks, but in 1546 this site was purchased outright.

One of the problems faced by ships moored over winter in the Thames was damage caused by ice floes. *Sovereign*, for example, while she lay at Erith had to have a wooden barrier erected upstream of her to divert dangerously large jagged piece of ice ramming against her hull. Perhaps this was one of the reasons why, in 1517, John Hopton was required to build a 'pond' at Deptford of sufficient size to hold the king's five great ships, *Mary Rose*, *Peter Pomegranate*, *Great Galley*, *Great Bark* and *Less Bark*. This was no mean structure, being timber-clad and fitted with great gates at the river end, the management of which was entrusted to the 'keeper of the plug'.

With the creation of the pond at Deptford and the continuation of shipbuilding both here and at Woolwich, Kent's dominance was assured. A snapshot of relative importance can be seen in the expenditure during the war of 1544, in which Deptford cost £18,824, Woolwich £3,439 and Portsmouth only £1,211; very few dockyard staff were retained at Portsmouth, compared with the eighty or so shipwrights and caulkers on the books at Deptford. In the period from September 1548 to October 1551, £30,300 was spent at Deptford, £6,600 at Gillingham, £2,054 at Woolwich and only £1,157 at Portsmouth. The picture did alter. In *A Book of Sea Causes*, a stock-taking report produced by the Admiralty Board for Elizabeth on her succession, at a time when the country was concluding a war with France, 195 shipwrights, artificers and labourers were shown as being employed at Deptford, 175 at Woolwich and a further 154 at

Drake's Golden Hind *was the first English ship to be preserved for public display. She was kept in a dry dock at Deptford until Stuart neglect led to her rotting away. Today a replica is open to the public in similar circumstances at St Mary Overie Dock near London Bridge.* (Author)

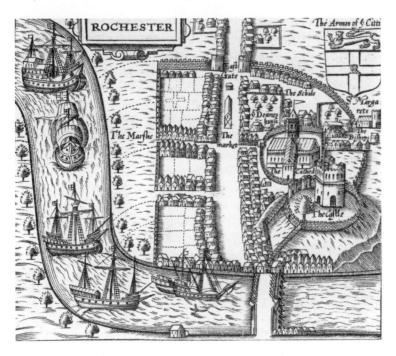

As this sixteenth-century engraving shows, the bridge at Rochester marked the limit of navigation on the River Medway for naval vessels. Below the bridge lay ample room for a fleet to be moored in safety provided the seaward defences were well maintained.

Portsmouth, showing that hostilities did lead to a transfer of resources to the forward-operating base.

In 1581 Deptford became the first dockyard with a visitor attraction when *Golden Hind* was placed here, in a dock built for the purpose, to show off the vessel in which Drake had completed his circumnavigation, and that vessel drew the crowds from the day Elizabeth came down to knight her favourite corsair until Stuart neglect led to her being broken up during the reign of Charles II. The cost for the 'house' and museum for *Golden Hind* was estimated to be £220 – the cost of those for *Mary Rose*, to be completed in 2012, is £30 million! At the same time the riverside wharfage at Deptford was increased by some 600 feet, indicating the number of vessels that needed to be tied up there.

The Thames-side dockyards were also blessed with the presence of the two most brilliant families of shipwrights, the Petts and the Bakers. John Pett had worked on *Regent* in her 1599 rebuild, while Peter Pett's career began with Edward VI and lasted until his own death in 1589. The even more skilled and influential Matthew Baker, also following in his father's footsteps, not only designed significant ships, but formalised and set down instructions for his trade, thus turning an arcane and dark art into a scientific concept open to all. Until Baker's time every ship that was built took its form from the vision of its own master shipwright, who would be present at the site. After Baker, a design could be drawn up and specifications sent to numerous shipwrights, who could then work to the pattern. This was a breakthrough of enormous significance because it led to the creation of uniform classes of ship whose building and fitting-out requirements would be known to the administration and whose handling characteristics would become common knowledge among masters and commanders. At last, a fleet that could respond as one could put to sea.

The Medway

In the year of Henry VIII's death, 1547, a payment of 13s 4d was made for the hire of a storehouse at Gillingham, from which small beginning grew the mighty naval yard of Chatham. Over the next few years several ships were laid up near Rochester, an arrangement which was formalised in June 1550 when the Privy Council declared this to be the place where all ships that were paid off had to be brought. The Medway, it was felt, with its slow-running water, good tidal range, sheltered moorings and hazard-free channel, was an excellent place to position ships under care and maintenance. In addition, the tidally exposed mudflats allowed their hulls to be inspected regularly and preserved. So that August, William Winter, the Surveyor of the Navy, travelled to Portsmouth to bring all the decommissioned ships laid up there round to the Medway. Although other Thames-side locations were used in the years that followed, by 1564 nearly the whole fleet of some twenty-three vessels could be seen on the flats below Rochester Bridge.

The provision of shoreside support for this reserve fleet was slow, and it was not until 1570 that, with the building of a mast pond at Chatham, the dockyard really became established. Money was also spent that year on furnishing a house for the use of the Lord Admiral and Navy Board, and in the following year the building of a forge and other dockyard appurtenances shows that a nascent yard was being formed, although it was not until the reign of James I that Chatham was to have its first dry dock, an indication of how well the drying mud flats served for graving the ships. Chatham's growing importance can also be seen from a one-year snapshot: in 1584 the 'ordinary' costs here amounted to the significant sum of £3,680 while those at Deptford were a minute £205, Portsmouth's a minuscule £30 and Woolwich's an infinitesimal £18. In the last decade of the century a great three-storey storehouse was built at Chatham, only for it to burn down in 1593 at a cost of £2,341.

Stealing in Measure

Any work commissioned by the Exchequer created the opportunity for making money over and above the costs submitted. That these chances were seized should come as no surprise in an age when wealth-creation was sufficient justification for underhand behaviour. Nor, at the lower end, where subsistence wages were being paid, should it be at all surprising that workers relieved their employer of mundane but useful articles. A free spar of wood carried home from the dockyard burned just as brightly, and boiled as many pots, as one that was paid for with a few spare coins. Further up the food chain, literally, a side of beef might easily slide off a wagon as it passed by a victualler's house. The grandeur of John Dawtrey's house in Southampton reflects the fact that as, Collector of Customs, paymaster for the Portsmouth-built ships at the beginning of the sixteenth century and victualling commissioner for Hampshire, responsible for provisioning the fleet under the first two Howards, he was in a position to make a lot of money.

The dismissal of William Commersall as Clerk of Ships in 1495 and the appointment of Robert Brygandyne to succeed him hint that Henry Tudor was aware that all was not well, for such positions were usually allocated for life. The overbalancing of perks into greed, as hinted in Kipling's poem, may well have been the cause. Certainly, the story he tells has some links with reality, for *Mary of the Tower* was stripped bare by the workforce on the Hamble in 1485.

Yet an investigation of Brygandyne's accounts could indicate that he behaved in a similar fashion. *Sweepstake* and *Mary Fortune* had sailed for Scotland in May and June 1497 and returned to the Thames and Winchelsea respectively by the late autumn. They were then subject to inventory; Brygandyne explained with regard to *Sweepstake*:

> There is spent perished broken lost and wasted to and for the defence and safe keeping of the said ship as well being in the King's wars in his noble army upon the sea in the coasts of Scotland against his ancient enemies and rebels the Scots as resting in sundry havens and places within this realm these parcels of stuff tackle apparell and other aillamentes of war here after ensuing within the time of this account.[10]

After such a short deployment it might be expected that the list of lost and worn-out items would be short. Nevertheless, Brygandyne's inventory for both vessels is charged with the word 'feeble', and this dismissive word appears against all but thirty-four of the eighty-five items in the *Sweepstake*'s inventory. The latter includes the masts and yards, anchors and iron work, with nearly every piece of cordage condemned as 'feeble'. The ship and her boat had also lost several oars.

Now, when *Regent* entered Portsmouth in 1495 it seemed unre-

Robert Brygandyne learned his shipbuilding skills at the small village of Smallhythe, near Tenterden in Kent, where he lived in this house. In Tudor times most backyards leading down to the River Rother were shipyards. Today it is possible to leap across the small stream that remains winding its way to the sea many miles away. (Author)

markable that Brygandyne should write a long list of items headed 'Also there is perused worn, rotten, broken, wasted, spent, lost and consumed and by long continuance enfeebled these parcels of stuff tackle and apparrell ...'; after all, the ship, built in 1488, was going into dry dock to be refitted. But the new-built *Sweepstake* and *Mary Fortune*? We have no record of the fate of the enfeebled items nor of how or when they were replaced, but shipwrights had a reputation for managing their ships for their own benefit, although Robert Brygandyne, as Kipling's poem indicated, was above all such dealings.

We have no record of what armament these galleasses carried – they were all probably handguns of some description – but we do know what other ordnance stores were provided, expended and returned by both smaller ships and these are shown in the table opposite.

This represents a considerable loss from ships acting as independent units. A large amount of gunpowder consumed ashore was explained away by gunners claiming 400lb from broken barrels by way of duty payment, while the remaining army 'ravenously dispoiled' many items during the short battle at Halidon Hill. But how to explain the losses, and very similar ones at that, on board two small vessels whose armament stores were solely for their own use? Perhaps there was a sea fight about which we know nothing, but neither vessel appears to have suffered damage or required repairs, besides which, an engagement in which all one's gunpowder was expended would have left one open to capture by an enemy in close contact. If there was no fight, and such expenditure cannot be explained away by exercise practice, the possibility remains that the ships returned having used a reasonable amount of stores, only for the accountants ashore to 'miscalculate' that which was being returned. By comparison the issues and returns of the 1595 Indies expedition show a much more understandable level of expenditure from a fleet that saw a great deal more action.[11]

Expenditure of Armament Stores, *Sweepstake* and *Mary Fortune*, 1497

	Provided		Expended		Remaining	
	Sweepstake	*Mary Fortune*	*Sweepstake*	*Mary Fortune*	*Sweepstake*	*Mary Fortune*
Bows	30	30	24	14	6	16
Bowstrings	36	48	36	36	0	12
Arrows	40	60 sheaves	30	30	15	30
Bills	25	25	17	13	8	12
Gunpowder	60	60 barrels	60	60	0	0
Lead shot	6	6cwt	6	6	6	0
Iron dice shot	46	46lb	46	46	0	0
Spears	15	21	11	9	4	12
Tampions	300	300	300	300	0	0

Tudor naval administrators produced incredibly detailed inventories and invoices whenever they built or laid up a ship, deployed a fleet, itemised loot or paid their seamen. A glance indicates that every nail or length of cordage was carefully recorded and every man's entitlement duly listed. And yet ... ! Somehow it seems just too exact and one is left with a suspicion that these long lists may be neither wholly accurate nor totally honest, concealing in their openness underhand dealings.

The graft that may have existed among naval shipbuilders in Henry Tudor's reign has already been mentioned. In the succeeding reign the 'custom' continued. A complaint voiced on behalf of the prior of Christ Church, Canterbury, in 1509, to Brygandyne states not only that the timber felled on his lands at Orpington, 'for the making of the King's ships', includes 'much young wood' but that 'the fellers have undermeasured by many tons' what they removed.

An incomplete document of 1522 tabulating the amount of timber felled in Cattall and Cheshunt woods for the king's and the cardinal's buildings states, '1,432 cartloads of oak tops and underwood have been embezzled and wasted'. There is no reason to suppose that similar malpractice was not taking place with the timber for the king's ships. Yet it must also be supposed that individuals such as the Clerk of Ships, Brygandyne, were as straight as the times, the tradition and their position allowed.

This was not the view of an unknown suppliant who wrote to Thomas Cromwell in 1535, stating that for the want of an auditor empowered to call the king's 'paymasters and clerks of the king's buildings, ships, and artillery to account, many of these officers have made no account for seven or eight years, and many things for the King's advantage have been forgotten past examination'. The plaintiff cites examples and then states that although his superior has purchased two benefices through his fraud, he, the whistle-blower, is being thrust out so that:

> he for his diligence is now in election to be made a bishop; and I, for my true service for twenty years, to be made a beggar. So that

> when the works [at Thornbury] break up he may go to his diocese with a cross and a mitre *in pontificalibus* a-preaching; and I into my country, with a staff and a wallet, ragged and jaffed, *in paupertabilus*, a-begging

– an example to others to live at ease and keep their own counsel.[12] It can be hoped that Cromwell looked kindly on the writer and rewarded him for the spirit of his composition, whatever else his case deserved.

The decision to keep the fleet in being meant a perpetual need for funding even when ships were not required for royal purposes. Thus the Treasurer of the Chamber's accounts for 1530 show many examples of naval maintenance expenditure including:

> carriage to the waterside 2s. To nine men of Hamble working the pumps 3 days and nights, at 6d. a man, day and night. Victuals to 200 men of the country to man the capstans, and wind up the ship into her dock. 10s. reward to the patron of the *Palamonta* for 40 Ragusans, with their boats helping to tow the ship up into dock.[13]

The same set of documents, while listing wages for ship repairs and the mending of the storehouses, including thatching the Long House at Portsmouth, lists the ongoing costs of retaining ship-keepers on laid-up vessels. For example, the four ship-keepers on board *Trinity Ditton* were paid 10s 4d each per month for four months.

Expensive it might be, but the continual programme of maintenance continued. In April 1541 the French ambassador, Morillac, reported to Francis I that the king's ships were being caulked and repaired every two years, which was much needed, but that it would be St John's tide (27 December) before they were finished unless more workmen were employed.

The state of the navy was investigated and inventories made on frequent occasions, but primarily at the end of a campaign and on the succession of a sovereign. This meant that during a protracted period of peace in a long reign the opportunity to exceed the 'custom of Portsmouth' was a clear and present one. Ironically it was to be John Hawkins, who made his fortune, and almost lost his freedom, in that most deprecated of occupations, slave-trading, who added lustre to his

ANNº DÑI 1581.

ÆTATIS SVÆ 44.

John Hawkins was one of the few Elizabethan seadogs who made a notable transition from merchant-pirate to administrator and it was the fleet that he created that proved itself ready and able to defeat the Spanish Armada. An anonymous oil painting made about 1581. (National Maritime Museum BHC2755)

name in that most admirable task, as a rooter-out of corruption. Yet it is for the years that he spent as an insignificant and not too successful slaver (1562–8), culminating in the disastrous fight with the Spaniards at San Juan de Ulua, that he remains best known, rather than for the far longer and much more significant time he spent from 1578, when he became treasurer of the navy, until in 1595 death released him from that job which he performed so admirably but had grown to hate. For it was in this period that Hawkins became associated with two major developments which remoulded warships and reformed administration. The development of the race-built galleon has been covered earlier; the impact it had on the final defeat of the galleys cannot be over-emphasised, but neither can Hawkins's bureaucratic reforms, which until the end of Elizabeth's reign prevented naval administration from becoming too cosy a family sinecure.

John Hawkins's appointment to a place on the Navy Board was

based on his claim that he could save the state money and yet still deliver a better fleet. This improvement was not going to be achieved by more competent administration alone; from the start Hawkins made clear that excessive expenditure indicated corrupt practice or, more euphemistically, unjustified profits, for no one at this time felt it was inappropriate for government officials to benefit from their position if the opportunity arose and, indeed, their payment by the state was predicated on them gaining lucrative rewards from other sources linked to their position. Hawkins's reforms were thus aimed not so much at rooting out fraud as at the regularisation of reward and the governing of greed.

Hawkins charged the Navy Board, and in particular the brothers Sir William and George Winter, who held the posts of Surveyor, Master of Naval Ordnance and Clerk of Ships, of making unreasonable profits. If he were appointed treasurer, Hawkins stated, he would

Elizabeth's long serving Secretary of State, William Burghley, Lord Cecil, worked tirelessly for peace and to avoid English isolation but was pragmatist enough to realise that, if matters came to blows, the navy would need sufficient men and materials to defend the realm. If he could not achieve peaceful co-existence he made sure that war would end with only one outcome. (Wikimedia)

reduce the 'ordinary' costs for keeping the fleet from £6,000 to £4,000 and still produce better results, while the 'extraordinary' costs of rebuilding and refitting were also far more expensive than they should have been. The incisive thrust came with his claim about overcharging and malpractice, which was based on an examination of the books. For example, while some £9,000 had been charged to the crown for timber since 1570, only half of this had been provided for the queen's ships; the rest had gone for private use.

Hawkins's agreement as treasurer of the navy was that he would be paid £5,714 to spend on the 'ordinary' budget with, needless to say, any accrued savings being his to keep. The 'extraordinary' budget would vary year on year, but in his attempt to control and forecast what this might be Hawkins saw a need for a planned maintenance regime whereby the twenty-four ships that made up the queen's navy would each be routinely overhauled and refitted at least every three years depending on their size. Linked to this was a further contract with the master shipwrights, Pett and Baker, who were also suspected of making excess profits, that regularised their payments for repairs to £1,000 per year, while Hawkins was authorised to oversee and approve their work. By regularising the work undertaken in the naval yards Hawkins was able to reduce the opportunities for corruption; the inevitable consequence was that those who no longer stood to gain so much found reasons to criticise their critic. As these included not only his fellow members on the Navy Board but also the shipwrights, Hawkins found himself friendless in his professional business.

The shipwrights soon found fault in the way Hawkins administered their pay, accusing him of retaining some of it for himself, which he undoubtedly did, although he justifyied it quite openly as a form of bank charges linked to regular payments. Others also found opportunities to criticise the new treasurer, causing him to write to Burghley:

the adversaries of the work have continually opposed themselves against me and the service so far as they durst be seen in it. So that among a number of trifling crossings and slanders, the very walls of the realm have been brought in question; and their slander hath gone very far and general to the encouragement of the enemies of god and our country, only to be avenged of me and this service, which doth discover the corruption and ignorance of the time past.14

Faced with the mounting criticism of the treasurer, the queen ordered five members of the Privy Council, including the Lord High Admiral, supported by four members of the Navy Board, including Hawkins, and the two master shipwrights, Pett and Baker, to 'inquire of abuses hereto committed and to set down remedies for preventing the same'.15

The commissioners appear to have been both fast and thorough, inspecting in January 1584 twenty-two ships of the fleet and finding them to be in a 'serviceable state for any sudden service'. What deficiencies that were noticed they attributed to faults dating from before Hawkins's appointment, and most of these were probably due to malpractice by Matthew Baker. Fortified by the findings, Hawkins now proposed to unite the 'ordinary' and 'extraordinary' expenditure into one budget of £5,714, which was formalised in a new agreement with the Privy Council drawn up in 1584.16

If Hawkins thought that he had both cleared his name and frustrated his enemies he was wrong. William Winter was scathing in his criticism, describing Hawkins's new arrangement, in a letter to Burghley, as 'but cunning and crafty to maintain his pride and ambition, and for the better filling of his purse and to keep back from discovery the faults that are left in her majesty's ships'. Burghley, probably the wisest and most worldly of Elizabeth's inner circle, saw exactly where Winter was coming from and for the moment ignored his vituperative comments. Yet if Burghley could ignore official complaints by those in authority, he gave in to an anonymous criticism of Hawkins in 1586 about the state of the ships and Hawkins's own malpractice. The treasurer was accused not only of overcharging the queen for repairs to her vessels newly returned from the West Indies but also of buying timber with the queen's money only to use it to repair his own ships.

Burghley invited a colleague to draw up formally the charges that were being insinuated against Hawkins. They had a familiar ring for anyone acquainted with naval malpractice. There were six main ones which, although they could be levelled at other members of the Navy Board, were listed mainly to unhinge Hawkins. They can be summarised as follows:

1. Buying in bulk and selling to the crown or others at a high price;
2. Owning his own ships as well as managing Her Majesty's – a clear conflict of interest;
3. Being in partnership with naval contractors;
4. Selling his own goods to the navy – another conflict of interest;

5. Setting his own price for goods and then approving payment himself;
6. Imposing a price below the market level for goods in short supply;
7. Failure to keep proper records.

Any one of these could be seen as offering an opportunity for corrupt practice, and combined they represented a licence for money-making malfeasance on an enormous scale. The writer of the report also included, for good measure, another criticism so heinous that it had to be reported orally to Burghley, who, as he had asked for it, was now not in a position to ignore what was in fact mere innuendo. More substance could be drawn from the shipwright's report which Pett and Baker handed to Burghley in October 1587. This cleverly exonerated them of any poor workmanship but hinted that the fleet was not all that it should be given the attention and money that Hawkins claimed to have spent on it.

The treasurer responded by defending his stewardship, but he clearly had had enough and requested that his contract be cancelled and that he be allowed to return to sea to wage war against the Spanish. This request was ignored. Instead, Burghley ordered yet another report on the condition of the navy, this one headed by Hawkins's erstwhile enemy Winter. The treasurer was exonerated, for the report concluded that he had carefully performed his duties in such a way that there could be no cause for complaint.

The criticism however continued, but the vindication was clarion-clear and was given in the most critical of circumstances by the man with most to lose should the fleet prove defective – Charles Howard, the Lord Admiral. Joining the fleet ahead of the arrival of the Spanish Armada, the admiral inspected each vessel thoroughly, getting into every nook and cranny in which it was possible for him to insert himself. He was delighted by what he saw, finding neither leaks nor rotten timbers and expressing himself willing to cross the Atlantic in any one of the ships. Later, when *Elizabeth Bonaventure* went aground off Flushing, Howard went aboard her and was greatly impressed that in the period that she was firmly aground, 'there never came a

A modern reconstruction of the White Bear, *a race-built galleon of the type that was the great Elizabethan contribution to naval architecture. Both the overall concept, and the longevity of many of the ships built to this pattern, reflect great credit on the administration of John Hawkins.* (Veres László)

As shown in these details from the 'Embarkation of Henry VIII' engraving, the harbour entrance at Dover underwent a series of alterations and improvements in the sixteenth century, including the building of two defensive towers at the end of the entrance walls. The style of design can be seen today in the contemporary Round Tower at Portsmouth. They pre-date Henry's great programme of coastal fortification, which left Dover largely untouched.

spoonful of water into her well ... except a ship be made of iron, it were to be thought impossible to do as she has done'. At this time *Elizabeth Bonaventure* had been in the queen's service for twenty years; she was not broken up until 1611. Such seaworthiness and longevity were not a product of malpractice.

In the end the readiness of the fleet to sail out, meet and manage the Spanish Armada was vindication enough for John Hawkins's business practices. Shortly before the great confrontation he wrote, although sick and sore at ease himself, to Burghley: 'This shall be a thing most manifest to your Lordship and the whole world, that the navy is in good and strong estate.' Howard could say a thankful 'Amen' to that and was prepared, such was his belief in Hawkins, that the return to harbour of the badly leaking *Hope* was a matter of little consequence.

After Hawkins, there was a long period with no one worthy to pick up his mantle. The ships deteriorated and the 'steal in measure' principle was disregarded; sawn timber charged to the crown was used for private furnishing and supplies for the fleet were ill measured and not properly accounted, a situation made more possible by the absence of a Paymaster of the Navy for several years and the fact that the accounts could not be signed off without the counter-signatures of two members of the Navy Board who benefited from malfeasance. The stage was being prepared for the arrival of Samuel Pepys, the 'Saviour of the Navy'. Sadly, it was the elderly Nottingham, who as Lord Howard of Effingham had been the saviour of the navy in 1588, who

created the family-supported sinecures and evildoing that would need the honest genius of Pepys to repair.

The dysfunctional state of administration and the state of disrepair of the fleet nearly brought about at least two maritime disasters. On the 1596 Cadiz expedition the six-year-old *Merhonour* nearly sank from a leak, while one year later Essex reported that his 620-tonne *Due Repulse*, new-built in 1595, had to have eighty tonnes of water pumped out of her daily while 'Her main and fore masts cracked, and most of her beams broken and rent, besides the opening of all her seams.'[17]

Surprisingly after such an inauspicious start to her career, *Due Repulse* was to serve in the navy until 1645, a longer career than those of many better-built warships. She may have been an exception to the general malaise that was evident as Elizabeth's long reign drew to an end. Nine vessels were condemned almost immediately James came to the throne, and by 1618 only seventeen galleons, one pinnace, one ketch and one discovery vessel were left from her great fleet.

Protecting the Fleet

Although it was during the following century that the nadir of English sea preparedness was highlighted by De Ruyter's descent on the Medway, in an age when intelligence was never totally reliable, the unexpected arrival of a foreign fleet bent on mischief could never be precluded. The English played this famously to advantage, twice at Cadiz and in the West Indies, but were not immune to similar mischief themselves. The need for defences for vessels at anchor or laid up was therefore a most necessary consideration, as was the provision of strong points to repel or discourage amphibious assault.

The big drive for coastal defences came when Henry realised that his policies had left him friendless in Europe. In November 1533, the year of the king's official marriage to Anne Boleyn and five years before the papal bull of deprivation called for open season against England, the ever-observant Chapuys reported back to Charles V that the Duke of Norfolk had 'sent orders to various places to make blockhouses and fortresses in defence against sudden invasion'.[18] However, it was an invasion scare in 1539 that provided the spur to make a concrete response to abstract concerns, for it made Henry commission coastal surveys to highlight the weaknesses in England's defences. There were many, and the reported deficiencies led to the state undertaking the biggest defensive building programme in the Channel since the Romans had constructed the forts of the Saxon shore, and the most expensive until Palmerston's follies were erected in the nineteenth century in response to another invasion scare. And it was expensive. It has been calculated that between 1539 and 1547 Henry spent 29 per cent of his ordinary budget on fortifications which stretched from Harwich to St David's.[19] If the rebuild at Berwick is included in the account, £208,636 was spent in fortifying the English shore during these years – a truly staggering amount. The forts were a magnificent achievement: ironically, the king who demolished more great buildings than any other monarch ended his reign with a major and enduring building programme, and although none of the forts so constructed could compare with the glory of, for example, Fountains Abbey, they were built with skill and flare and to a practical design over which the king himself had great influence.

The need for coastal fortifications coincided with an appreciation that the effect of modern artillery on traditional castles was likely to be devastating and the cost of reinforcing against such ordnance prohibitive. At Tournai, during his three-year tenure from 1515 to 1518, Henry had walls built twenty-two feet thick at prodigious cost. Such expenses the treasury could seldom afford and thus endeavoured to avoid paying for, as happened at Dover, Berwick and Portsmouth, where unpaid and disgruntled builders were forever threatening to walk out. With such a background, the chances of providing a chain of traditionally constructed forts delivered on time and within budget seemed slim.

The solution began with the king's master gunner, William Hart, who back in 1522 had surveyed the nation's northern fortifications. On his return he proposed lowering the high walls of the traditional

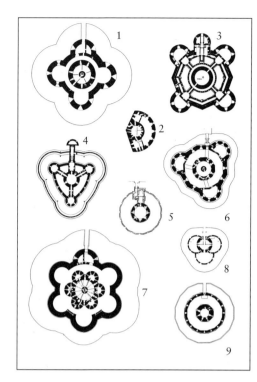

It might be fanciful to consider that the designs of Henry VIII's coastal fortifications were based on the Tudor Rose but the resemblance is most obvious from these drawings. To a common scale, they are: 1 Walmer; 2 Portland; 3 Camber; 4 Sandgate; 5 Pendennis; 6 Hurst; 7 Deal; 8 St Mawes; 9 Calshot. (English Heritage)

medieval castle and using the rubble and tamped-down earth to infill and strengthen what would now be gun bastions. He also saw a need for flanking fire to add to the defence along walls and moats. From this concept, Henry himself, assisted by ideas that were being developed in Italy, seems to have sketched out the plans for his first batch of forts, which were completed in an amazingly short time. Between mid-1539 and the end of 1540 work began on over thirty fortifications, of which ten qualified by size to be considered as castles.

To say that the design of these forts was based on the Tudor Rose would be whimsical but not inaccurate; architects do have such flights of practical fancy. The majority of forts were formed from a series of concentric circles, with the outer wall being formed from semi-circular towers that lie petal-like in plan. The walls themselves were low-lying and thick, scarcely visible to an opponent at sea or landing on a beach, but giving the defenders much protection and an all-round field of fire both at range and close in. What is more, this was achieved at a much reduced cost than hitherto, for the low walls, packed with earth, required fewer skilled stonemasons to construct and required them to be on site for less time. Nevertheless, for today's visitor the skilled workmanship displayed in rounded stone, bevelled edges and well-drained roofs and walks belies the fact that they were constructed in record time, showing that even vandals can build well.

The first group of forts were built at one-mile intervals between Sandown, Deal and Walmer in Kent to defend both the coast and the anchorage at the Downs, although the fleet would have had to take advantage of the deep water close inshore to come under the protection of their guns. This two-mile stretch of shingle, lying close to the Continent, would have been an ideal site for any invasion from eastern France or Flanders. Its steep beach could be used for landing at any state of the tide, with covering fire being provided by ships either lying close in or, in the case of galleys, actually beached themselves. The rising beach also provided cover for troops scrambling ashore, and once a beach-head was secured the way inland lay across flat field and not up the steep white cliffs for which this coast is famed. It was at Deal that the 'Bastard of Fauconberg' had landed in 1471 in support of his cousin Warwick and where the pretender Perkin Warbeck put 300 of his supporters ashore in 1495 to challenge Henry Tudor, and so it is no wonder that Henry began his shore defence programme here. Their presence may have influenced Philip of Spain's decision to ignore Deal and select Margate as the invasion beach for the 1588 Armada, which would have involved a longer and trickier passage around North Foreland for Parma's light craft.

Henry bypassed Dover in his major building programme,

Deal Castle today probably represents the most complete and least altered of Henry's medium size fortifications and it still dominates the anchorage of The Downs. (Author)

constructing the next forts in the chain at Sandgate and Camber to cover the shallow waters either side of Romney Marsh. Westward of them a long stretch of coastline was left undefended until Portsmouth, later the most fortified port in the world, which lay protected behind forts that guarded both the eastern and western entrance to the Solent. Weymouth, Dartmouth and Falmouth were all similarly defended, while beyond the latter a few minor gun emplacements were erected. Thus Henry provided for the defence not only of the likeliest invasion beach in the east, Deal, but also of the most probable port of entry in the west, Falmouth, and added security to his key operating base in between, Portsmouth. The fact that, when the time came, neither of England's enemies selected the most obvious sites to land indicates either that the forts achieved their aim or that her foes had not done their homework.

However, once built, the forts were often left uncared for, until someone drew attention to their state of disrepair. Thus in 1570 steps were taken 'to increase the means of defence at Sandwich and the three castles between that place and Dover and Dover Castle itself'. Other sites lay undisturbed for far longer.

Like so many similar fortification chains, they did not get an opportunity to show their worth against the opponents they were designed to defy. The guns of Southsea Castle are pictured in the Cowdray print as firing at the French in 1545 but, given how far away the enemy fleet was anchored, this would have been an ineffectual volley. The Downs forts got involved in the Civil War and Deal Castle itself was bombed by the Germans in the Second World War, but only Elizabeth's Upnor was ever called upon to defend the fleet. Now, almost five centuries later, the surviving forts, mostly under the care of

Upnor Castle was built in a few years to protect Elizabeth's fleet moored in the Medway. When the Dutch attacked in the following century the castle gunners acquitted themselves well but the Tudor-era defences – not greatly enhanced in the interim – proved totally inadequate. A number of capital ships were sunk or burnt, and the fleet flagship was carried off to the Netherlands in triumph; it was the greatest humiliation in the history of the Royal Navy. (English Heritage)

English Heritage, are a joy to wander around and a marvel of military design to wonder at.[20]

The Medway moorings' most infamous event came in 1667 when the Dutch descended on the river and variously burned and captured the poorly defended fleet. Yet the possibility of such an attack and the vulnerability of the site were well recognised in Elizabeth's time, especially because the ships moored here had had their armaments unloaded, their rigging landed and their crew reduced to a few shipkeepers. Neither had the anchorage existed when Henry built his great coastal fortifications, and 50 of his five Thames-side blockhouses, only one guarded this area and that was at Sheerness. So Elizabeth, therefore, ordered a castle to be built at Upnor to defend the anchorage in 1559, the first year of her reign. The structure that arose combined great beauty with operational functionality. It began with a low waterbastion, behind which rose a residential block, the roof of which also served as a gun emplacement, as did two flanking towers.

The speed of construction, as with Henry's forts, was impressive, but not as far as the queen was concerned, for in 1561 Elizabeth, very much of the opinion that two years were more than adequate to finish the work, was demanding a progress report from the Lord Admiral, despite which the task was not completed until 1564. At the same time defences were created down river, with William Winter surveying the lower reaches of the Medway and proposing a fort at Swaleness, opposite Queenborough. In addition the passage via St Mary's Creek which would allow Upnor to be outflanked was closed by a series of wooden piles, while Sir John Hawkins introduced a sea patrol off Sheerness to examine any vessels heading for the Medway.

Hawkins, in conjunction with William Bourne, the master gunner at Upnor, was also responsible for the building of a chain across the river, designed to prevent any enemy ship from passing beyond the castle. This was completed in October 1585 with one end fixed and the other passed over two great pulleys, enabling the chain to be lowered and raised as required; when it was raised, its great weight was supported beneath five barges.

In response to criticism by Lord Admiral Howard in 1596, further work was carried out at Upnor between 1599 and 1601, including the construction of a wooden palisade in front of the bastion to protect

the walls from assault by both enemy and debris, while a landward ditch enclosed the whole structure. The bastion and other buildings were also reinforced and improved, and in 1603 another survey praised both the structure and its ordnance, which by then consisted of a demi-cannon, seven culverins, five demi-culverins, a minion, a falcon, a saker and four fowlers. Later surveys were to indicate several areas of disrepair, but when the great attack came in 1667 the garrison acquitted itself well, although the chain was broken, allowing the Dutch to rampage successfully upstream.

Beacons

Beacons were fitted and refurbished along the coast, ready to be fired as both a warning and a summons to arms on the approach of any sizeable enemy fleet which might threaten invasion. The legacy of this chain of flaming signals remains in the numerous 'beacon hills' shown on Ordnance Survey maps. The system was vital to ensure that the disparate groups that needed to come together when no standing army was in existence could do so in a timely fashion. What was not needed was a false or premature alarm. Thus in 1544 the Privy Council ordered Lord St John to order two beacons to be set

> together from the Downs to the Isle of Wight, in such places as shall be thought meet, and watchmen appointed to them with orders to fire the one if they see at least 10 sail of enemies. The country shall not move upon sight of one fire in one place, but when two fires are made they shall repair to the coasts; and the watchmen shall not fire both beacons unless they see the enemies land.[21]

This plan was reinforced by Henry's order in 1545 that 'Men shall not rise to defend the coast except that they see two fires to be borne at once and that the watch man set his beacons on fire except it be well known that there be ten French sail on the coast.'[22]

The system could be abused in a most unexpected way. In July 1586, with invasion fever fermenting, Richard Noyse, Charles Robert, Zachary Mansell and a few others were charged at Southampton of conspiracy to fire the beacons around the town so that, in the subsequent confusion, they could enter the empty houses and rob them.[23] As always the cost of defence was a concern. In the face of representation that beacon watching should be discontinued, the Privy Council agreed that it would like to stand the watchers down but dared not to do so because of intelligence reports of an approaching Spanish assault. However, the council was prepared to reduce the cost by having the positions manned by only three or four vigilant staff 'when there are land winds blowing and at spring tides'.[24] Beacon manning was, however, recognised as a superfluous winter activity. In 1591 the duty was discontinued on 26 December, but the following year relief from this tedium was advanced to 23 October.

However, the need to set up beacons carried with it a cost that some local communities felt had to be claimed back. The accounts of Dover from 1526 list 'fagots to make a fire at Bredon stone to warn Thomas Arbour when the French ships of war were in the Narrow Seas, one penny'. This can be compared with, in the same accounts, the sum of 16s 1d for a supper, wine, ale and beer at the mayor's election, which gives some idea as to the order of priorities even in a front-line town like Dover.

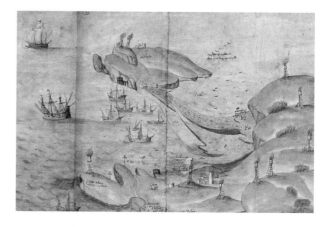

Beacons, such as these ones shown around Portland, provided the swiftest way of passing information about an enemy approach or landing. In times of tension they were manned continually with a respite during the winter. The drawing shown here was completed at Greenwich after Thomas Cromwell ordered maps to be drawn to show the complete coastal defences of the realm. (British Library)

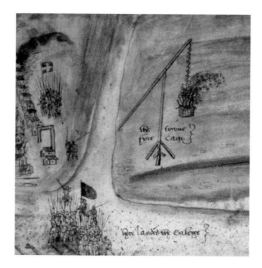

This beacon at Brighton was pivoted so that the brazier could be lowered and rekindled swiftly thus ensuring the warning of danger would not be ignored. (British Library)

The Move to Management

With the retirement of Robert Brygandyne in 1523 and John Hopton's death in 1524, the first moves to create a proper naval administration were introduced. The most noticeable features were to be its leanness as an administrative body and the longevity of both the establishment and the holders of office. One reason for this was that, unusually for Tudor appointments, the men selected came to their office not through favouritism or fawning but through the relevant experience that they had gained and the skills that they could offer. This was so from the start. Brygandyne and John Hopton both had commanded at sea. Hopton's successors, for his office was split, were Thomas Spert, Clerk Controller, who had been master of both *Mary Rose* and *Henry Grace à Dieu*, and William Gonson, Keeper of Storehouses, a merchant and entrepreneur with many business interests. Their growing responsibilities were reflected in the fact that they both received more than had been paid to Hopton, with Gonson's growing dominance soon to be reflected in the increase in his pay to twice that of Spert.

Death, or the shadow of death, continued to be the catalyst for change, and in the 1540s it was apparently the lessening of Henry's own faculties that acted as a spur for reform. His last Lord Admiral, Viscount Lisle, John Dudley that was, was a fighting and a thinking admiral who could see that the support that he had needed while afloat could be improved. The deaths of others helped him to bring this about. Spert, who died in 1541, had been succeeded by the ineffectual John Osborne, who himself died in 1545. William Gonson, an able, busy man, committed suicide in 1544, while the country was at war with France, and his inexperienced son Benjamin was appointed a 'treasurer of sea causes'. The arrangements give every sign of creaking, as did Henry's own bones, and one cannot imagine him devoting his time to working out a better system for administering the navy while his mind was otherwise occupied.

On the other hand, one can almost visualise Lisle deciding that something must be done and sketching out his ideas on paper. Reform began with a 'memo' which listed seven offices of admiralty. These were the existing three:

Clerk Controller
Clerk of Ships
Keeper of Storehouses

to which were added:

Lieutenant (Vice-Admiral)
Treasurer
Surveyor and Rigger
Master of Naval Ordnance

From March 1545 the gathering of these seven office holders was entitled 'the King's Majesty's Council for his Marine Causes', and it remained in a recognisable form (more commonly referred to as the 'Navy Board') through centuries of general upheaval and reform. Death, this time, gave the organisation a shaky start; the death of John Winter, the first treasurer, at the end of 1545 caused some uncertainty as to who should hold what office, but in 1546 official confirmation was made of the appointments as shown in the table below.

The Members of the 'Council for Marine Causes' in 1546

Post	Holder	Remuneration per annum including clerks and boat hire
Lieutenant (chairman)	Sir Thomas Clere	£275
Treasurer	Robert Legge	£220
Surveyor and Rigger	Benjamin Gonson	£145
Controller	William Broke	£155
Master of Naval Ordnance	Sir William Woodhouse	£238
Clerk of Ships	Richard Howlett	£133 6s 8d
Keeper of Storehouses	William Holstock	£133 6s 8d

Of these, Clere, Broke and Gonson and Woodhouse had all exercised

sea command, while Legge was heavily involved with fisheries. It was a board whose experience was obvious, and although nepotism was, and would continue to be, evident, it was of a benign kind, with relatives being given preferment only if they knew the business. Rudimentary it may have been, but it was well in advance of the *ad hoc* arrangements in existence among the other European powers, and when England was preparing for and engaged in war it gave her the edge over her opponents. Unlike the equivalent bodies elsewhere, the English Navy Board was never filled with those whose noble birth was considered reason enough for them to gain a seat. Yet the creation of such powerful posts, often with the holders linked through marriage, did have its downside – a lack of accountability in an age of avarice.

The members of the new-formed Navy Board was also assisted by the fact that in Lisle they had a Lord Admiral who not only was interested in their business but had held great positions of power until, as a Privy Councillor, he allowed first his rivalry with the Seymours and then his opposition to Mary's accession to lessen his interest in maritime administration. His less ambitious successor as Lord Admiral, Lord Clinton, however, during his thirty years in office, did involve himself closely with the board. The other enduring feature of the board was its civilian nature: its members were answerable to an administrator rather than an admiral, a system that would at a future date result in the creation of both a First Lord of the Admiralty (a political post) and a First Sea Lord (a naval professional) working together to deliver government policy.

That first major change to the arrangements established by Lisle arose when suspicion of inefficiency in money matters led to the Navy Board being placed under the supervision of the Lord Treasurer, the Marquess of Winchester, with the Treasurer of the Navy acting as his deputy on the board. From this emerged the adoption, in 1557, of an annual budget of £14,000 to cover 'ordinary' expenses, thus guaranteeing the maintenance of the fleet. Although this grant was always under pressure, and the means by which it was managed varied, the arrangement, which lasted until the 1590s, was a benign one which guaranteed the core needs, leaving debate only over the extraordinary expenses that arose during crisis or war. In another ironic reflection of the age, the Marquess of Winchester borrowed the state's money for his own use and encouraged his tellers to do likewise. In 1571 these officials defaulted, creating a £44,000 debt for the crown. Winchester followed the approved scandal-avoidance measure by dying in 1572, with debts, including those from 'borrowed' money, totalling £46,000. Even Burghley's assumption of personal responsibility for treasury matters neither restored confidence nor prevented further scandal. The shipwrights merely followed their masters' example, and when Charles Howard, in the latter years of his term as Lord High Admiral, showed himself to be consumed with greed, those in naval service did not have to look too far for a crook to copy.

The obvious function missing from the Navy Board, the vital one of victualling, was not included until 1550, when Edward Baeshe was appointed the Surveyor of Victuals, a post that he would hold until his death in 1587.

With the death of Legge in 1548, and the promotion of Benjamin Gonson as his successor, the board was to gain some of its most significant appointees, for in Gonson's place arrived William Winter, whose brother George was to become Clerk of Ships in 1560. The major change occurred when Gonson died in 1577 and his son-in-law, the great John Hawkins, at last moved on to the board in a position he had been hankering after for many years. For a brief period nepotism worked well, enabling men of talent and experience to work together, secured by bonds of marriage as well as self-interest.

Hawkins, whose creation of the race-built galleon was arguably the most significant change to ship design in the century, was, ironically, also responsible for one of the most contentious arrangements that were to be introduced in naval administration. In 1575 he organised for himself a contract whereby, for a fixed sum, he would maintain twenty-five of the queen's ships. A similar contract was put in place for the shipwrights Pett and Baker to ground and grave the ships. The result was faction: sides were taken mainly with the aim of passing expensive work on to the other contractor, and there were arguments as to whether or not certain work could be undertaken within the agreed budget without shortcuts or skimping. There was good cause to suspect the underhand. If plunder was permitted at sea, then its cousin, corruption, could be expected to be admitted on shore. Matters came to a head during Hawkins's tenure, but there had been ample precedent.

In an age that allowed men for the first time to read the Bible in English, the spirit that motivated many meant that King David's treatment of Naboth and Uriah the Hittite was looked upon more as an exemplar than as a warning, while Solomon was admired less for his wisdom than for his wealth. Given a society where an official position of state opened the opportunity for men of little means to obtain great wealth, it is not surprising that such sinecures allowed corruption to feature as a constant motif in the administration, fitting-out and provisioning of the Navy Royal.

It would be good for Lord Howard of Effingham's reputation to conclude the century with a positive, but the story ends with the perquisites of power tainting his reputation. The corrosive corruption that this created is best summed up by Andrews:

> By the end of the war the Howard regime in the admiralty had already undermined that sense of unity and devotion that had shone through in the hour of crisis; the pernicious influence of the Howards was a manifestation of the disease inherent in the system of patronage, a manifestation worse than most because the opportunities for private gain at the public expense were greater here than elsewhere and because the normal restraints of law and morality were more easily overborne where the proper business of all concerned was robbery with violence.[25]

Not only did Howard appoint his relatives to positions of gain, but he smiled benignly as stores were purchased at too great a cost and disposed at when still serviceable, and posts of responsibility sold to the highest bidder. In just two pages of his magisterial book *The Safeguard of the Sea*, Rodger records corruption so widespread and sickening that the stench still turns the stomach. Most pernicious of all is the way in which the Howard clan came to regard the monies in the seaman's charitable Chatham Chest as their own piggy-bank, obstructing claimants and borrowing from it for their own purposes.

Corruption is an insidious illness in any corporate body, requiring close examination if the symptoms are to be detected and the co-operation of some insiders if the true extent of its spread is to be identified. If all live content and benefit from it, its tumour may be considered benign for a long time and the disease may thrive undetected and untreated. For this reason its prevalence in the Tudor navy is often hinted at but seldom displayed. One reason is that officers of state were expected to benefit in kind from holding an office that dealt with supplies for the building and support of the Navy Royal; it was the degree to which they did so that could cause occasional consternation.

The Chatham Chest

Although the Bible had been translated into English, the idea that pure religion might be based on a charitable response to the cries of the poor, widowed and the fatherless in their affliction was not absorbed by England's ruling class. The Tudors had a robust approach to the concept of unemployment or sickness benefit and little sympathy with disability pay. Parishes could and did show compassion to their own, but were prepared to use dogs and cudgels to drive the indigent beyond their bounds.[26] Discharged seamen, especially the old and lame, limping along lanes a long way from home, could anticipate such treatment. Like the soldiers returning from the wars, they might have expected better, not bitter, treatment: they expected mostly in vain.

Injured seamen did from time to time get compensation for their hurt. The payments made by John Dawtrey in 1512 included 'The King's reward to 60 seamen hurt in his service ... £20.'[27] Included in the lengthy accounts for the war at sea a year later is the note: 'Walter Loveday, captain of *Anne Gallant* ... to give to each of his soldiers 2 s. because they lost their victuals by the sinking of the said ship in Plymouth Haven when she was grounded in order to amend such hurts as she took on the rock in Brittany.'[28] At the same time a John Soome, petty officer in *Lizard*, who was 'sore hurt in the King's service in Brittany', was awarded 20s. As *Lizard* was Edward Howard's bark the injuries could have been received in the assault on the galleys.[29]

After Thomas Howard's raid on Brittany in 1522, the king was petitioned to provide support for John Moysse, who was injured at Morlaix while helping to lay a gunpowder charge and was present when it exploded, not having done such work before. As a result he was reported as being sore, burned and blinded and having 'a poor old wife dependent on him who is unable to work for her living'.[30]

If one-off payments like this required the approval of the king it would appear that caring for those injured on duty, or the dependents of those killed, was not considered an important state responsibility, and that there was no moral contract to be kept. The dissolution of the monasteries, and the hospitals that they administered, removed one source of care for the wounded mariner; the closure of the Maison Dieu, which provided both medical care and support to the traveller, a sort of Tudor YMCA, removed another.

If an injured or indigent seaman had little hope of relief, a widow or a destitute wife was even less likely to draw forth pity. Although *Emmanuel* and *Julian*, held in Spain in 1586, were merchant ships, the response to the crews' wives pleas of penury would have been the same even if they were navy men. In this case, the ships' owners pleaded their own strained circumstances as an excuse for not providing relief,

Following their departure from the pillaging of Morlaix in 1522 the drunken English soldiery fell asleep at this fountain where they were discovered and slaughtered by the French. Up to 500 may have died here at the Fontaine des Anglais but Thomas Howard makes no mention of the incident in his report as the victims were all common men. One of the wounded from this expedition is known to have petitioned the king for relief, but the singularity of this entreaty underlines the general lack of disability provision. (Author)

provided an allowance equal to six months' pay for widows of those seamen who had died in the recent campaigns. The money raised for relief was provided by a contribution of thirty shillings from members of the Privy Council, twenty shillings from knights and five shillings from burgesses, while a committee was named to authorise payment to the needy whom Hawkins singled out for relief.

Together with the Chatham Chest, Hawkins also created a hospital at Chatham, which received a royal charter in 1594 as the Hospital of Sir John Hawkins. It was tasked with providing relief for ten or more poor mariners and shipwrights. For a man in the making of whose millions many seamen had died, it was a poor enough salver of conscience, yet in an age notable for its callousness to the poor, Hawkins's two initiatives for the relief of suffering shine out more strongly than any of his coastal beacons.

Whether Howard's complaints about the treatment of his sick sailors played on Elizabeth's conscience we do not know: what is known is that between 1591 and 1593 the problem of managing an indigent population, including elderly and wounded veterans, was addressed by both Parliament and the crown but, as ever, it was compromised by a meanness of spirit.

In November 1591 a proclamation was issued against vagrant soldiers, who, of course, included sailors.[34] This was predicated on the belief that a great number of them were wandering through the country claiming to have served abroad when, in fact, many had either never left these shores or had run away. Any such vagrant who could not show his 'passport' of dismissal from military service was to be punished most severely as a felon 'that hath run away and left the service traitorously'. The proclamation went on to deal briefly with care before returning to its main purpose:

> The Treasurer of Wars will make payment of sums of money to those who lawfully return to conduct them to the places where they were levied. Furthermore for the repressing of the great number of mighty and able vagrants now wandering abroad under pretence of begging as soldiers, by whom open robberies are committed, the Lieutenants of every county ... are charged to appoint Provost Marshals for the apprehension of such offenders and to commit them to prison thereupon to be executed.[35]

The conduct payment authorised in the proclamation was set at 5s, in exchange for which the recipient had to surrender his 'passport' for a new one that gave sufficient time for the bearer to reach his home area. Before departing it was required that he be warned against lingering in a roguish manner, for if he failed to complete the journey in the time allocated he could be seized and punished as a vagabond. Thus did the state try to avoid responsibility for rising inflation, reduction in job opportunities and the discharge of servicemen. The parishes to whom these out-of-work veterans were returning could, of course, avoid hand-outs by questioning the authenticity of their claims – a practice which the state too could employ to save money.

In April 1593 a commission was appointed to examine the claims of veterans to have been hurt in the Armada campaign and the conflicts in France and the Low Countries.[36] This amounted to an interrogation so that precise dates and locations where individuals claimed that they had been injured could be checked with those who

while the City of London did not help, considering the destitute wives to be the merchants' responsibility.[31] Just a few lines in the record cast a penetrating light on a world where to be poor and unprotected brought forth scorn not pity.

When the threat of invasion by the Spanish Armada had passed, apart from a few shadowing pinnaces, the majority of the English fleet headed for Harwich, Margate and Dover with the intention of re-supplying their ships with both munitions and victuals. While gunpowder and shot were no longer vital, food and drink were urgently required, for the fleet was now suffering from a major outbreak of disease, with men dying in their scores. On 22 August Howard wrote to the Privy Council: 'The infection is grown so great that those that come in fresh are soonest infected, they sicken one day and die the next.'[32]

Neither could Hawkins, the treasurer, ease the problem by discharging the crews because there was no money available to pay their wages. Indeed, the government felt that it could withhold such pay, allowing the deaths to reduce the wage bill. In probably one of the most callous of notes, Burghley wrote to Hawkins, 'I marvel that where so many are dead on the seas the pay is not dead with them.'[33] The concept of paying the money to the mourning widows or other dependents seemed alien to the Lord Treasurer, who had grown enormously wealthy himself in the queen's service without experiencing the rigour of defending the realm in person.

The deaths, suffering and impecunious state of the sailors who had driven the Spanish Armada from the shores preyed on Hawkins's conscience. In 1592 he persuaded both Howard and Drake to join him in establishing the 'Chatham Chest', a large safe box into which funds levied on seamen's wages would be placed to provide relief to those who had been incapacitated through naval service. The demands on the chest were so high that in 1593 Parliament had to pass a relief act to provide additional assistance for destitute mariners. This followed an act of unusual generosity on the part of the queen herself, who

had been their commanders at the time. It was intended to limit the call on charitable funds agreed a few days later in the House of Lords, whereby relief was to be provided for the injured by the following contributions: 'Every Archbishop, Marquis, Earl and Viscount ... 40s., every Bishop 30s., and every Baron 20s.' The almoner, the Bishop of Worcester, was appointed to collect the money from the bishops, while Lord Norris was to pass the plate among his fellow Lords Temporal. To emphasise the voluntary nature of this payment, a clause was inserted to state that the sums were given willingly; however, those who had failed to attend the Parliament were made to pay double. As the membership of the Commons during this parliament included both Sir Francis Drake and Sir Walter Ralegh it can be assumed that their lordships' benison met with approval. By June the Sheriffs and Justices of the Peace throughout the land were invited to appoint officers to administer the funds so raised.[37] In August, when Hawkins was commanded to ship 700 men back from France, the orders were very precise as to how each man's name and destination were to be recorded, and they emphasised the need for the proper 'passports' to be issued.[38] The state had no wish to fund more than could prove they were entitled to assistance, however grievous their circumstance or legitimate their claim: charity but of the sea-cold sort.

The Admiralty Court

One area where self-interest rather than charity ruled over maritime affairs was in the administration of justice. An Admiralty Court had been long in existence and had taken up residence in Southwark in 1410. As the navy grew, so did the power and sphere of interest of this court which was ordered to keep regular records in 1524; a few years later, the renaming of the organisation as the High Court of Admiralty signified its close ties with the new post of Lord High Admiral. The justices of the court could therefore have their freedom to act with commendable judicial independence severely curtailed. This mattered much, for the court was required to exercise jurisdiction over, *inter alia*, collisions at sea; spoil and piracy; shipwreck; letters of reprisal; salvage; impressing of seamen; infringement of royal trading monopolies; examination of ships and witnesses; contempt of the admiral; perquisite; maritime torts and the management of harbours, rivers, pilots, and mariners. Two linked key factors were common to most of the issues in this long list: firstly, they nearly all involved the payment or receipt of money in some form and, secondly, wherever they did the Lord High Admiral stood to benefit from a favourable ruling. This meant that the long-serving, quaintly-named judge of the court, Sir Julius Caesar, was stabbed more often in the back by his friends than was his original namesake.

In 1575 an agreement was reached between the Lord Chief Justice and the High Court of Admiralty defining their legal boundaries, and thus financial benefits, but this failed to receive parliamentary ratification. As a result furious turf wars took place, with writs being issued and rulings being challenged. Eventually, in 1585, the Admiralty judge, Dr David Lewes, successfully defended the range of his judicial authority before the Privy Council, but this did not bring to an end the challenges to various rulings of the court. It is not surprising, therefore, that in the same year, Elizabeth, taking advantage of a temporary vacancy in the post of Lord High Admiral, took the opportunity to grant the Admiralty Court permission to sit with undiminished authority during the interregnum. From that date the connection between court and admiral was severed and judicial independence became possible, but it was not plain sailing – too much financial gain was at stake.

The government was also required to rule on international law, which affected the legitimacy and scope of its naval operations overseas. The first great claim to sovereignty over the seas came with the Treaty of Tordesillas, which, following a bull issued by Pope Alexander VI in 1494, drew a line from north to south through the Atlantic and granted to Spain the trading rights to the west and to Portugal those to the east. This ruling was felt by other nations to be one more honoured in the breach than the observance, but government support was needed to avoid charges of piracy, or worse, being brought against those who challenged the duopoly. In 1580, following Drake's successful plundering circumnavigation, Elizabeth ruled that the freedom of the seas was common to all and that no claims could be made to ownership of the ocean. By 1602 she had refined her judgement, in a disagreement over Danish northern fishing rights, by proclaiming that the 'Law of Nations alloweth of fishing in the sea everywhere', although she reinforced the idea of territorial waters by stating that states could exercise jurisdiction over their coastal waters. Such a framework was sufficient for trade and its rougher companion, plunder, to operate with national legality, and also for foreign vessels that were too close inshore to be seized and their catch or cargo confiscated.

Intelligence

Throughout the century information leaked, and occasionally flowed, from the courts of all European powers, none of whom seemed able to caulk their porous seams. Ambassadors earned their keep, or ironically – since many of them had to support themselves from their own resources – justified their personal expenditure by keeping their superiors well informed of both events and rumour and just occasionally mistaking one for the other. The Venetians were brilliant and verbose, but the imperial, Spanish and French ambassadors to the Tudor court were adept at sniffing out unconsidered trifles. The English also were competent at overt intelligence-gathering. On the covert side they also had excellent informants. Thomas Howard, Earl of Surrey, as befitted a scheming courtier, was adept at seeking out intelligence, often as an alternative to more positive activity. Lisle, however, sought information for advantage. In 1546 he examined mariners captured by Hertford to ascertain tidal information about Etaples, which was attracting the English as a possible port from which to provision the recently captured but now threatened Boulogne. The admiral was able to surmise that:

> Their depositions agree that at spring tide more than four fathoms of water flow as high as the quay of the town and at neap tides 3 ½ fathoms, and that there is never less than four fathoms upon the bar at full sea, also that the channel is almost an arrow shot over. The haven is subject to all winds blowing strainably at N.W. and W.N.W., but that might be remedied by a mole or pier. At full sea there is more water at Estaples than at Dieppe. If these sayings are true there is no haven like it on this side the mouth of the Seine;

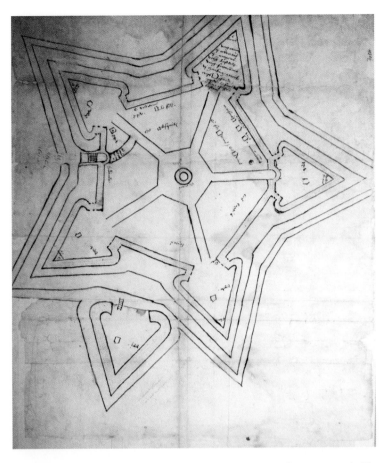

An English drawing of the outlying Fort de Chatillon at Boulogne was probably made as part of the 1544 campaign to capture the town. If so, it is a good example of technical intelligence-gathering. (National Archives, Kew)

and, seeing how it dominates all Boulogne, so that without it the enemy could neither victual Andres, Hardelowe, nor the new fort, nor any garrisons on this side Montreuil, nor keep an army in the field without aid of the Emperor's countries, the writer wish it was the King's.[39]

Lisle went on to suggest that if the war continued, the town should be taken by a force of 3,000 footmen and 500 horsemen and garrisoned with troops from elsewhere at less expense.

This letter is quoted at length because it shows more clearly than most other correspondence a strategic option based on gathered intelligence that in its lucidity and reasoning would be a credit to future centuries with their much more sophisticated intelligence-gathering resources. Indeed the description of the harbour at Etaples would grace any modern pilot. In 1914 Lisle's vision came true when this sleepy fishing port on the River Canche became a British base and departure point for reinforcements going to the front. It gained notoriety in 1917 when the harsh conditions in its camps resulted in a mutiny.

It was in the murkier water of espionage, double agents, and counter-intelligence, during the reign of Elizabeth, that the English were to become recognised as masters because they possessed a strange genius in the person of Secretary Walsingham.

Walsingham's greatest triumph was, of course, the affair of Mary Queen of Scots, which lies outside this account. What the navy needed

from him and his agents was information as to an enemy's strengths, weaknesses and sailing intentions. This was critical, not only because fleets could pass in the night or out of sight, but most importantly because a fleet that sailed too early could run out of supplies just when it needed to engage and remain in contact with an enemy.

The murky stream began, however, with Hawkins and Burghley. After the former's defeat at San Juan de Ulua, he set about trying to obtain the release of thirty of his men who were incarcerated in Seville. The first attempt involved promising de Spes, the Spanish ambassador, that if the Englishmen were freed, Hawkins would abandon plans for revenge attacks on Spanish shipping and ports. Unfortunately, the ambassador did not believe him, and Hawkins was drawn into a world of treachery and espionage from which he emerged with his reputation besmirched. If one tries to untangle the convoluted plots, it appears that in 1571 Hawkins offered to provide ships to serve with Spain against England while, simultaneously keeping Burghley informed of his every move, claiming that by his machinations he expected that:

1. The practices of the enemies will be daily more and more discovered;
2. There will be credit gotten for good sums of money;
3. The money shall be employed to their own detriment.[40]

In the end, eighteen prisoners were released in September 1571, but it is debatable whether or not Hawkins's proposed treachery influenced this decision. By the end of that year, with no intelligence coup to report, the career of John Hawkins, secret agent, was over and he was able to move on to becoming John Hawkins, Navy Board member, a role that suited him and his country better.

While Hawkins and Burghley had been amateurs, the great Elizabethan spy master, Walsingham, was highly professional. Occasional correspondence, with the risk of interception and capture of the informer, worried Walsingham, who needed to be surer of his sources in the time of the invasion threats from 1585 onwards. Thus, as the storm threatened, he came up with a plan entitled 'A Plot for Intelligence out of Spain', which listed the ways by which he could improve the reliable flow of intelligence. These included:

1. Sir Edward Stafford [ambassador in Paris and a Spanish double agent] to draw what he can from the Venetian ambassador.
2. To procure some correspondence with the French king's ambassador to Spain.
3. To take order with some at Rouen to have frequent news from such as arrive out of Spain at Nantes, Le Havre and Dieppe.
4. To make choice of two especial persons, French, Flemings or Italians to go along the coast of pain to see what preparations are a making there. To furnish them with letters of credit.
5. To have intelligence at the Court of Spain, one of Finale [northwest Italy], one of Genoa.
6. To have intelligence at Brussels and Leiden.
7. To employ Lord Dunsany [living in Ireland].[41]

Walsingham was also able to raise official funds to support this scheme but, like the ambassadors, he also had to reach into his own pocket. He had several notable coups, the foremost of which was to have made a contact within the household of the Marquis of Santa

Cruz, the Armada's commander-in-chief, although the latter's death prior to the fleet sailing somewhat negated this achievement. Nevertheless, mainly through a network established by Anthony Standen, a friend of the Duke of Tuscany's ambassador in Madrid, Walsingham was fed not just titbits but whole dishes, which included information on the ships, especially the feared galleys, being provided to Philip, and also on the damage to both property and morale inflicted by Drake's raid on Cadiz. He was able to pass the information that he had gleaned on the size of the Spanish sea and land forces to England's commanders so that they could make an informed guess as to where and in what strength the enemy would land and then make defensive provision, but the key question remained, when would they sail? On this one issue there were many false alarms, each of which engendered some degree of mobilisation, and each of which involved some degree of cost, to the ire of the parsimonious queen. It was important to the state that such false intelligence did not result in the navy being stood down at just the wrong moment. The responsibility resting on Walsingham and his agents was immense. He even had to judge whether or not the intelligence provided by friends in high places was true or not. In March 1588 Howard, anchored in the Downs, wrote to him stating that the Spanish would sail with the 'light moon' on the 20th of that month with 210 ships and 36,000 men, numbers sufficiently close to the 130 ships and 30,693 men that Medina Sidonia had available to lend the report credibility. Howard was convinced and, in a side-swipe at Walsingham's methods and influence, wrote in the report, 'I fear me ere it would be long before her majesty will be sorry that she has believed some as much as she has done, but it will be very late.'[42]

The queen was still hoping for peace, and was loath to mobilise and offer Spain an excuse for aggression. A frustrated Walsingham thus had to act as a punch-ball between her and her admirals; the pummelling made him ill but protected Howard. In the end, the bruising was worth it, for in April 1588 Walsingham forecast that the Armada would sail in May; it slipped down the Tagus on the 29th of that month.

However, even the best of spies are not necessarily accurate weather forecasters, and the Spanish, beset by storms, had to take refuge in Corunna, eventually arriving off the Lizard on 29 July when, despite all the intelligence-gathering, they came within an ace of catching the English unawares in Plymouth Sound. Part, just a part, of this final unawareness of impending danger may be attributed to Walsingham, who wrote on 19 July, 'For the navy of Spain, we have lately received news that by reason of their great want, as well of mariners as of necessary provisions, but especially through the infection fallen among their men, they are forced to return and have dispersed themselves',[43] which was accurate in its causes but wrong in the effect. A bold descent into Plymouth could have changed the outcome; Walsingham, wearing himself out in the service of an ungrateful queen, deserves better comment on his moment of triumph. Along with his knowledge of the Spanish forces and plans, he knew well the character of both Medina Sidonia and his master in the Escorial, neither of whom were impetuous or improvisers. Knowing the man and knowing the plan, Walsingham also knew that as long as the English fleet were restrained in exercising those very attributes themselves they would prevail. Keeping Howard in harbour was prob-

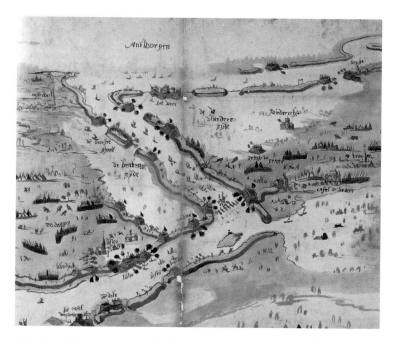

This pictorial map was sent to Walsingham in March 1585 by an English spy in the Netherlands. It shows Parma's operations around Antwerp, including the famous bridge of boats, which was about to be attacked by Gianibelli's 'Hellburners'. The use of such sources allowed Walsingham to predict with reasonable accuracy the sailing of the Armada. (National Archives, Kew)

ably, in fact, his greatest contribution to the campaign.

But, as with Henry in 1545 and the French descent on the Solent, Elizabeth had a good idea as to where the Spanish might come ashore. The land commanders were warned:

> After our hearty commendations to your Good Lordship where her majestie hath received certayn advertysments of the discovery of ye spanish fleett upon ye coast of fraunce, amoungst which ther are a good nomber of Gallyes, and it is supposed they will direct thear cours into ye narrow seas. Wee do pray your Lordship that you will tak order with all expidition, that ye forces of ye hors and foote of that countye of Kent under your liutenancye may be assembled and quartered at Margett, and at Sandwich that they may be thear in a redines to be addressed to such place as shalbe meetest to withstand ye enemye so praying your Lordship to take present order accordingly wee bydd your Lordship very hartely farwell from ye Court at Nonsuch ye 28 of August 1588.[44]

Such information could have been achieved only from spies risking a great deal to discover and report their findings. So, at a time when those caught spying were subject to the thumbscrew and the rack, it is cheering to record the fate of one, Nicholas Ousley, who having bribed his way out of a Spanish jail, was rewarded for 'sending good intelligence' by being granted 'a lease of St. Helen's in London'.

Walsingham fully deserves a place among those illustrious names more often associated with the development and triumphs of the English navy, so it would be appropriate for his contribution to be highlighted by one of them. Drake, one rarely given over to praise the exploits of others, graciously acknowledged the spy master's contribution, writing to him, 'I will not flatter you, but you have fought more with your pen than many have in our English navy fought with their enemies, and but that your place and most necessary attendance about her majesty cannot be spared, your valour and desserts in such place opposite the enemy had showed itself.'[45]

A Philosophy for Sea Causes

In the 1470s Sir John Fortescue wrote, in *The Governance of England*, 'it shall be necessary that the king have always some fleet upon the sea, for the repressing of rovers, saving of our merchants, our fishers, and the dwellers upon our coats; and that the king keep always some great and mighty vessels, for the breaking of an army when any shall be made against him upon the sea'. However, the development of a royal navy, from the hiring of merchant ships, through their purchase and conversion into warships to the building of a fleet, was undertaken without any blueprint that laid down what the size of this fleet should be and what types of ships should make up its numbers. This state of affairs lasted until Elizabeth's accession, when a detailed audit of the state of the navy, known as 'A Book for Sea Causes', included the recommendation that the future fleet should comprise '24 ships of 200 tons and upwards, four Barks of 60 – 80 tons, and two Pinnaces of 40 tons – a total of 30. Of the ships, four are to be of 600 tons or more, four of 500, four of 400, six of 300 and six of 200'.[46] This was the ideal size for the new type of galleon then emerging.

Some years later, the polymath Dr John Dee, in *The Perfecte Arte of Navigation,* put the case for a Petty Navy Royal of '... three score tall ships, or more, but in no cases fewer; and they to be very well appointed, thoroughly manned, and sufficiently victualled'.[47] This number, "to beck and check' all those 'frequenting our seas', was not selected at random. Dee saw such vessels as being needed to discourage invasion; protect merchant shipping, and thus reduce assurance costs; train pilots and navigators; apprehend the 'abominable thieves that steal our corn and victuals'; provide 'expert and hardy crews for war; 'displease and pinch the petty foreign offender at sea'; provide gainful employment for reformed pirates; act as a deterrent against those who would 'be so stout, rude and dishonourably injurious' to English merchant shipping; and protect English fishing grounds and boats; and all for profit. Dee's persuasive argument was that such investment would pay for itself:

> So that this Petty Navy Royal is thought to be the only Master Key wherewith to open all the locks that keep out or hinder this comparable British Empire from enjoying by many reasons, such a yearly Revenue of Treasure, both to the Supreme Head and the subjects thereof – as no plat of ground or sea in the whole world else, being of no greater quantity – can with more right, greater honour, with so great ease and so little charges, so near at hand, in so short time, and in so little danger, any kind of way, yield the like to either King or other potentate and absolute Governor

John Dee, a Welsh polymath, provided the philosophical reasoning to support both a great fleet and to deploy vessels in search of a north-west passage to China and mineral wealth in unclaimed lands. (Wikimedia)

thereof whatsoever. Beside, the Peaceable Enjoyment to enjoy all the same, for ever; year, yearly and yearly, by our wisdom and valiantness duly used, all manner of our commodities to arise greater and greater; a well in wealth and strength as of foreign love and fear, where it is most requisite to be ... so that not one such foreign enemy would adventure, first to break out into any notable disorder against us.

Dee, for all his lyrical Welsh verbosity, was both prescient and right. Prophesying the creation of a British Empire he saw that, for such an organisation to survive and thrive, it would need the protection of the Navy Royal. Yet his vision was too pure for the age, full as it was of rose-pink positives. Dee became an advisor to the few expeditions that set out to find either the north-west or the north-east passage, but the size and number of ships involved betray the English lack of willingness to invest in going where no one had been before. It was so much easier to plunder the ships of Spain than to establish new routes and realms. England's search in the sixteenth century for new markets is a tale of limited investment, unlimited personal endurance and ultimate failure.

Hakluyt

If any child wished to read a single book of historic derring-do, then Richard Hakluyt's *The Principal Navigations, Voyages, Traffiques and Discoveries of the English Nation* (1589) is the epic that they should be given. Far easier to read and more down-to-earth than the contemporary heroic poem by Camoens, *The Lusiads,* which dealt with the story of how the Portuguese had 'tracked the oceans none had sailed before', Hakluyt's book aimed to encourage his fellow countrymen to follow the path of those who had led the way. In recounting the successes and failures of English seafarers, Hakluyt was not uncritical, stating in his introduction, 'I heard both in speech and read in books other nations miraculously extolled for their discoveries and notable enterprises by sea, but the English of all others for their sluggish security, and continual neglect of the like attempts especially in so long and happy a time of peace, either ignominiously reported, or exceedingly condemned.' However, he was too good a patriot not to try and claim some parity for his fellow countrymen, writing in his preface to his second edition of 1598:

> Be it granted that the renowned Portugal Vasco da Gama traversed the main ocean southward of Africa. Did not Richard Chancellor and his mates perform the like, northward of Europe? Suppose that Columbus that noble and high-spirited Genoese escried unknown lands to the westward of Europe and Asia: did not the valiant English knight Sir Hugh Willoughby; did not the famous pilots Stephen Burrough, Arthur Pet, and Charles Jackman accost Novaya Zemyla to the north of Europe and Asia?

– to which the obvious, and devastating, retort has to be, 'Who? Where? And for what?'

Yet Hakluyt continued: 'Howbeit you will say perhaps, not with the like golden success, not with such deductions of colonies, nor attaining of conquest. True it is, that our success hath not been correspondent unto theirs: yet the difficulty and danger of searching was no whit less.'

From such a position arose the ability to make of Scott's failure to be first to the South Pole and his death on the return journey a triumph of English endeavour. Such a spirit could constantly turn defeat into victory, turn Dunkirk into D-Day and rescue soldiers from the beaches of Crete although it was death so to do.

Hakluyt's aim was to encourage overseas expansion either by transporting several thousand willing citizens to the 'great and ample country of Virginia', with its 'rich and abundant silver mines' (he did lie when his proposals made it necessary) or by finding a market 'for our woollen cloth'.

Of course, for either of these aims to be achieved, both settlers and merchants would need the support of the Navy Royal. Equally importantly, the emerging navy would also provide the ships and crews to map the coast and chart the depths to make such voyages safe. Hakluyt, as England's first geographer, laid the foundation on which the hydrographic structure of the Navy Royal would be built.

Fighting Instructions

Another branch of naval philosophy in which those in England safe abed could indulge was the laying down of rules telling the admirals how to fight. There is little indication that Edward Howard had intended explicit rules as to how he intended to engage the French in 1512 and 1513 but his brother, the autocratic Thomas, produced instructions for his captains prior to the fleet's departure in 1521. As might be expected, given his personality, these were strong in the requirement for respect and enforcing the sanction of death.[48] Among his nine commandments, for he was just modest enough not to write ten, were:

1. No ship, except those appointed, to give chase ... on pain of death.
2. Every master to keep his lead and sound out any danger, according to the old customs.
3. No one to enter port without authority.
4. Before sunset every ship to come under the lee of the Admiral to know what course to keep.
5. Every ship had to have a quartermaster and boatswain.
6. When they land soldiers, the crew and gunners to defend the boat must not leave it on pain of death.

Codification of the various laws and traditions began by borrowing from abroad, mainly from the work of Alonso de Chaves, a servant of Charles V, who wrote a treatise that set out to show that, despite all the uncertainties pertaining at sea, he who had a plan was best placed to be victorious. Chaves championed the idea of ships fighting in formation and seizing the weather gage from which to descend on the enemy, on whom, when in range, they should 'commence to play their most powerful artillery, taking care that the first shots hit, insamuch as

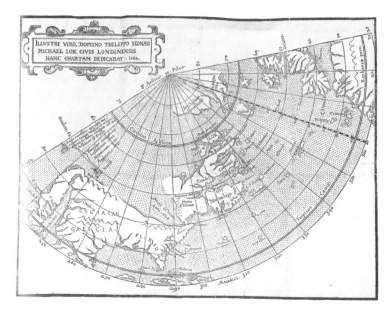

Michael Lok's map for Hakluyt shows a clear route through open Arctic seas. The chimera of a north-west passage was supported by maps drawn without much hydrographical intelligence but liberally relying on imagination. (Author)

they are the largest they strike dread and terror in to the enemy; for seeing how great the hurt they suffer, they think how much greater it will be at close range'. Although this missed the fact that longer-range artillery necessarily had the smaller calibre and arrived with the least velocity, nevertheless it championed the idea of constant fire, which, at closer range, would include smoke, flame and din to add to the shock and awe of the shot itself.

Henry's desire to produce such orders for his sea commanders led to Thomas Audley's 'Booke of Orders for the Warre both by Sea and Land' being commissioned by the king and published in 1530. The sovereign's failure to connect with the problems facing his commanders can be seen from the fact that Audley was a landlubber, a courtier, who rose to be Lord Chancellor while never getting his feet wet. His work reflects his inexperience but, in the management of a fleet, as opposed to its fighting, he laid down a requirement which, if he had observed it, would have saved Drake from getting into trouble at Cadiz in 1587

> The admiral shall not take in hand any exploit to land or enter into any enemy harbour with the king's ships unless he call a council and makes the captains privy to his device and the best masters in the fleet or pilots, known to be skillful men on that coast or place where he intendeth to do his exploits, and by good advice. Otherwise the fault ought to be laid on the admiral if anything should happen but well ... And if he did an exploit without assent of the captains and it proved well, the king ought to put him out of his room for purposing a matter of such chance out of his brain, whereby the whole fleet might fall into the hands of the enemy to the destruction of the king's people.[49]

When Drake accused Borough of failing to support him when he entered Cadiz in 1587, his vice-admiral countered by stating that the admiral had not consulted his captains as required by Audley's instructions.

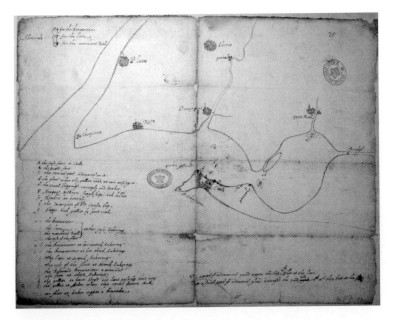

A plan of the 1587 Cadiz operation where friction between Drake and his second in command could have been avoided if more formal instructions had been available. (National Archives, Kew)

In early August 1545 Lord Admiral Lisle, endeavouring to engage the French invasion fleet, produced two sets of instructions which reflected his own sea experience as well as the ideas of Alonso de Chaves. Lisle desired each of his ships to be given sea-room by keeping at least half a cable (one hundred yards) apart and then selecting and closing each their own target, except that honour dictated that the enemy flagship be reserved for the admiral. To achieve this Lisle ordered a fleet disposition of twenty-four ships in his vanguard, forty in his main body and forty galleasses stationed on the wings to enfold the enemy and support the main fleet, especially to 'beat off the galleys from the great ships'. Most importantly for future naval thinking, Lisle desired his van to 'pass through' the enemy fleet, thus introducing the idea of 'breaking the line', which was to be an ambition of most commanders in future fleet engagements in the eighteenth and nine-teenth century.[50] Strangely, these orders were issued not for the battle of the Solent on 19 July, but for any chance encounter in the weeks that followed. Perhaps Lisle realised that the lack of a plan on the first occasion led to the lack of achievement.

After Lisle, there is a long silence in the production of fighting instructions. Frustratingly, we are not privy to the orders drawn up by Charles Howard in Plymouth Sound prior to sailing to meet the Armada. It is evident that he must have discussed a plan of sorts, not only with Drake, but also with all his captains, for the English fleet acted as one in both its shadowing and its attack on the Spanish. None followed their piratical instincts and closed and boarded an opponent except, like Drake, before negotiating a surrender, nor, after Howard himself had

been carried away by the hint of booty, did any copy his bad example.

A hint of what Howard intended may be found in the lengthy orders issued by Ralegh for his disastrous final voyage to Guiana in 1617. He had spent the previous twelve years in prison, during which time naval strategy and tactics would not have been the subject dearest to his heart. He probably drew his ideas from others, especially the views of those who had so well governed the great fleets of 1588. From their experience he emphasised a key rule that 'No man shall board his enemy's ship without order, because the loss of a ship to us is of more importance to us than the loss of ten ships to the enemy.'[51]

If evidence of a command similar to that short and sensible sentence by Ralegh could be found emanating from the pen of Howard in 1588, then the thinking behind the tactics that his fleet employed in the Channel would become clear. Although it was a policy that many shore-side critics would find to be honoured more in the breach than in the observance, the dull concept of keeping a fleet in being, rather than going for risky glory, was to serve Britain well for centuries to come.

Between Howard's success and Ralegh's failure came the disas-trous Indies voyage of Drake and Hawkins in 1595–6. On the return leg the dispirited fleet, now commanded by the army general Baskerville, was intercepted by a Spanish fleet under an experienced naval commander. There should have been only one outcome in the waters off Cuba. Instead, as was reported, Baskerville formed his ships in to two divisions, each in line ahead, and:

> was the foremost and so held his place until, by order of fight, other ships were to have their turn according to his former direc-tions, who wisely and politically had so ordered his vanguard and rearward; and as the manner of it was altogether strange to the Spaniards, so might they have been without hope of victory, if their general had been a man of judgement in sea fights.

Thus a century which began with the theorist Chaves stating that 'some may say that at sea it is not possible to order ships and tactics in this way, nor arrange before hand so nicely for coming to the attack ... and thus there is no need to develop an order of battle since order cannot be kept' ended with a demonstration by the English which vindicated the Spaniard's idea that '... he who has taken up the best formation and order will be victor'.

Yet this dominating position was achieved only because by the end of the sixteenth century England also had an administration capable of planning, funding, building, manning, victualling, maintaining and supporting a naval force that would keep her shores free from invasion and her sea-goers safe from assault. In addition, her harbours had been made easier to enter through buoyage and sea-marks, and her latest ships were capable of seeking out new ports for trade. That this posi-tive state was not exploited to the full owes more to the morals of those administrators than to any failings in the design. The corrosion of corruption rotted the timbers of her ships as quickly and effectively as any marine *teredo*.

271

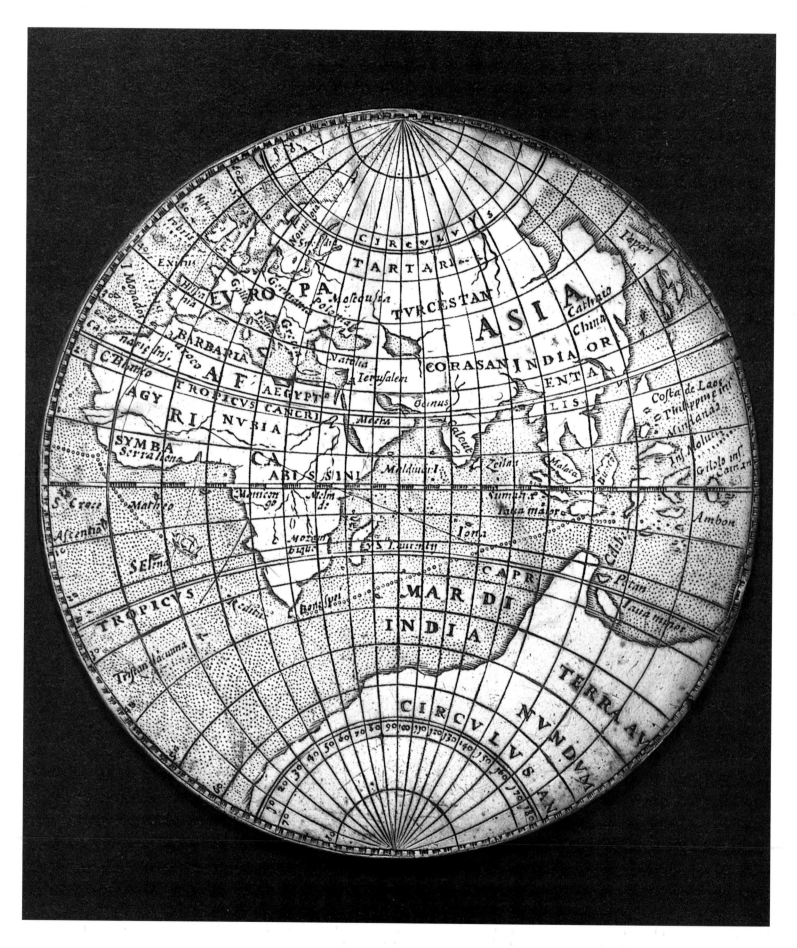

Chapter Thirteen

The Legacy

*'You would not have me go down in history as the 1st Sea Lord of the day
who made so bad a struggle that our rulers gave up the heritage of Command
of the Sea which we have held for over 300 years'*
Admiral Beatty to his wife, 23 January 1931[1]

When Elizabeth, stubborn and upright to the end, finally succumbed to the inevitability of death, an age ended, as much because of what had been as because of what was to come. The perceived failures of the Stuart regime made many look back to an age when all seemed right with the world. Two larger-than-life monarchs, Henry and Elizabeth, achieved an apotheosis that neither truly deserved, but which was their reward for their supposed support of triumphant Protestantism and defence of the 'demi-paradise' which England, for the vast number of its citizens, was not. Indeed, much that needed to change under the Tudors did not, and religious persecution and political intolerance, which every monarch practised, remained as a poisoned chalice for their successors to collect and drink. Neither did they achieve a land at peace with itself: Ireland, Scotland, the North, Kent, East Anglia and the West Country, the religious and the poor had all had their protests and been condemned without concession. Trade had remained static, while prices had soared, and only plunder increased. The new merchant trading companies were formed at the end of the age, not the beginning. Royal societies, royal collections, commonwealths, were all Stuart contributions to the state. Donne and Shakespeare, late arrivals, blossomed as the Tudor leaves fell, and fruited under the new regime.

Yet Shakespeare became the Tudor propagandist by giving his medieval monarchs and courtiers identifiable Tudor attributes; and he also glorified the little realm, set in a silver sea, that was bold enough

Michael Mecator's medal struck to celebrate Drake's circumnavigation symbolises the fact that England's maritime reputation was not built initially on the achievements of the navy, but on the exploits of enterprising, piratical individuals. When the navy co-opted these talents, it set itself on the road to greatness. (National Maritime Museum E2316-1)

to defy the world. However, the creation of that myth had started earlier. Thomas Cromwell had contributed to it in the Act of Restraint of Appeals in 1533, which stated:

> ... it is manifestly declared and expressed that this realm of England is an empire, and hath been accepted in the world, governed by one supreme head and king having the dignity and royal estate of imperial crown of the same, unto whom a body politic, compact of all sorts and degrees of people, divided in terms and by names of spirituality and temporality, be bounden and ought to bear, next to God, a natural and humble obedience.

Such inventive nonsense continued to be written to support all dubious legislation, and yet the language can be seen reflected in many of Shakespeare's most grandiloquent utterances about kingly authority. In many ways state and stage fed each other's fantasies. Later generations looking back on the Tudors accepted the fiction and made of it a fact.

But it was not all fantasy. If it had been it would have failed. There, on the rude rough sea that surrounded this little empire, a fleet was created that would allow the realm, whatever its flaws, to flourish. This was where the Tudor genius and its legacy lay: unconcerned by faction, a force was created which, rather than defend a faith, defended a nation.

Yet its true worth was seldom acknowledged. If the faith that Drake fought for held faith with him, and he were able to sit around a table with his sea dogs in some celestial cabin, and look down on the nation that he defended and saved, he might reflect wryly that subsequent generations have paid far more attention to the conflicts of conscience that, in the end, left England 'Catholic' and the affairs of bed chambers that gave star status to the insipid and irrelevant wives of Henry and the foppish useless favourites of Elizabeth. He might feel, rightly aggrieved, that the deeds his crews wrought warrant little more than a paragraph or two in general histories rather than being confined mostly to specialist works aimed at anoraks rather than academics.

Yet his fate, and that of his fellows, was to be confined to myth: to 'Drake's Drum' and 'The Little Revenge'. Even the almost contemporaneous Shakespeare ignored the Navy Royal. Although many of his works have sea scenes they deal mainly with pirates and merchants, for the bard would have heard the latter tell tales of the former, both in the taverns that surrounded the Globe and on board ships berthed in the Thames. Thus, although it is possible to cut and paste a naval deployment from Shakespeare's works, the Navy Royal has no role in his plays. Spenser, the writer of the age's epic, *The Faerie Queene*, made it a pastoral poem, giving just five lines to a maritime simile. Only Donne, sailing as a volunteer with Essex to both Cadiz and the Azores, left some little record of life on board a naval ship.

Drake, however, could not claim that he was a part of a fully mature and professional fleet. The joint-stock ventures on which he mostly sailed had not the professional strength that they needed to face their greatest challenge in the next century. The ships required to be improved, the officers and men needed better training and fighting instructions and communications, command and control had to be clarified.

In the civil war that was to split the navy, the Commonwealth genius Blake was told that his orders were 'to pursue, seize, scatter, fight with and destroy'.[2] That Lord Charles Howard had no such precise and clinical orders when he sailed to meet the Armada is obvious from the result of the physical encounter. Blake, Rupert, James Stuart and Monck would have smashed into them and filled the seas with masts and spars. In 1652 the Commonwealth stated 'that the safest and surest defence of this Kingdom is our Navy, and that we can never be hurt by land by a foreign Enemy, unless we are first beaten at sea'.[3] That this was true then was due to the fact that an English fleet, one hundred years earlier, had demonstrated it so to be, and in a way that ensured that, whatever the vicissitudes of state, the navy would always be ready to defend that kingdom.

References

Chapter One
Background: Father to the Man
1 *L&P*, I/I, 1005.
2 NRS, 1993.
3 *LPV*, 1554.
4 *L&P*, XIX/I, 817.
5 See Skidmore, *Edward VI*.
6 Quoted in Sugden, *Sir Francis Drake*.
7 See Skidmore, *Edward VI*.
8 Quoted in Wilson, *Sir Francis Walsingham*.
9 Ibid.

Chapter Two
Ship Types
1 See Hutchinson, *Medieval Ships and Shipping*.
2 The print is commonly referred to as the 'Cowdray print'.
3 Quoted in McKee, *King Henry VIII's Mary Rose*.
4 *L&P*, XX/I, 1235.
5 *L&P*, XX/II, 136.
6 See Hakluyt, *The Principal Navigations*.
7 Quoted in Sugden, *Sir Francis Drake*.
8 *L&P*, I/I, 1475 and 1522 and CSPV, 1509–19.
9 CSPV, V, 703.
10 *L&P*, II/I, 1113.
11 CSPV, II, 1041.
12 CSPV, IV, 722.
13 See Guilmartin, *Gunpowder and Galleys*.
14 For a vivid description of life on board a war galley see Bradford, *The Great Siege*.
15 See *L&P*, III, 384–637, a fascinating story involving the king, Wolsey and Thomas Howard, as well as the Venetian ambassador and galley captains.
16 *L&P*, XIX/II, 752.
17 *L&P*, XIX/II, 812.
18 Quoted in Barker, *Fernando Oliviera*.
19 *L&P*, XXI/I, 700.
20 See Harrison, *The Elizabethan Journals*.
21 Based on Nelson, *The Tudor Navy*.
22 Quoted in Rowse, *Sir Richard Grenville*.
23 *L&P*, XIX/II, 617.
24 See Oppenheim, *Naval Accounts and Inventories*.
25 See Childs, *The Warship Mary Rose*.

Chapter Three
Building the Fleet
1 CSPE, CCLXXXVI.
2 See Hutchinson, *Medieval Ships and Shipping*.
3 See Oppenheim, *Naval Accounts and Inventories*.
4 Ibid.
5 *L&P*, V, 220.
6 *L&P*, IX, 1025.
7 *L&P*, XII/II, 794.
8 *L&P*, II/I, 1086.
9 *L&P*, XII/I, 843.
10 See *AMR* and Childs, *The Warship Mary Rose*.
11 *AMR*, I.
12 *L&P*, VIII, 586.
13 *L&P*, IX, 60.
14 *L&P*, Appendix, 1415.
15 See Oppenheim, *Naval Accounts and Inventories*.
16 *L&P*, I/I, 2968. This included 4,700 tenpenny nails, 3,900 eightpenny, fivepenny and threepenny nails and lists of hawsers, beer for workmen and the amount of rosin and pitch to be used in waterproofing.
17 *L&P*, II/I, 1113. This is another indication that *Mary Rose* was not named after Henry's sister: he was unlikely to name two vessels after her, however much of a favourite she was. His own daughter, Mary, was not born until after the launch described.
18 *L&P*, XIV/I, 144.
19 *L&P*, I/I, 1727, 1728.
20 *L&P*, I/I, 1661.
21 *L&P*, V, 220.
22 *L&P*, XIX/II, 630.
23 After Henry's divorce from Katherine of Aragon she was renamed just *Peter*, strengthening the custom of using saints' names.
24 Vaux, *The World Encompassed by Sir Francis Drake*.
25 Quoted in Rodger, *The Safeguard of the Sea*.
26 Boxer, *The Tragic Story of the Sea*.
27 See Oppenheim, *Naval Accounts and Inventories*.
28 *L&P*, I/I, 1748.
29 Sadly, no masts were recovered from *Mary Rose*.

30 L&P, XI, 240.
31 Quoted in Loades, *The Tudor Navy*.
32 See Knighton and Loades, *The Anthony Roll*.
33 Oppenheim, *A History of the Administration of the Royal Navy*.
34 Quoted in Rodger, *The Safeguard of the Sea*.
35 Boxer, *The Tragic History of the Sea*.
36 Oppenheim, *Naval Accounts and Inventories*.
37 *L&P*, XIV/II, 129.
38 *L&P*, XIV/II, 781.
39 *L&P*, XIX/II, 617.
40 Monson, *Naval Tracts*.

Chapter Four
Arming the Fleet
1 See Corbett, *Drake and the Tudor Navy*.
2 See Oppenheim, *Naval Accounts and Inventories*.
3 Laughton 'Early Tudor Ship-Guns'.
4 See *L&P*, I/I, 324, 325, 355, which discusses costs, the provision of metal, the desire of the gun-founders to remain in Flanders and the determination to prevent the Scottish king from securing a similar service.
5 Quoted in Oppenheim, *A History of the Administration of the Royal Navy*.
6 British Library, Harley MS 309, folios i–xi. See Corbett, *Fighting Instructions 1530–1816*.
7 Bourne, *The Arte of Shooting in Great Ordnance*.
8 Pelegrin Venier to his brothers, CSPV, II, 629.
9 *L&P*, XX/I, 1023.
10 Hakluyt, *The Principal Navigations*.
11 LMR, 7.
12 Corbett, *Drake and the Tudor Navy*.
13 See Guilmartin, *Gunpowder and Galleys*.
14 Harrison, *The Elizabethan Journals*.
15 *L&P*, I/I, 209.
16 *L&P*, I/I, 287.
17 *L&P*, V, 664.
18 *L&P*, XX/I, 987.
19 Nelson, *The Tudor Navy*.
20 British Library, Royal MSS, Axxxi.
21 As with William Winter's bombardment at Smerwick in 1580.
22 Strachan, 'Sampson's Fight with Maltese Galleys, 1628'.

23 See Childs, *The Warship Mary Rose.*
24 See Nuttall, *New Light on Drake.*
25 Oppenheim, *Naval Accounts and Inventories.*
26 Edward Howard, commenting on how his fleet performed in a race in 1513, remarked that both *Christ* and *Katherine Fortileza* were top-heavy because of too much weaponry fitted high up.
27 Bethune, *The Observations of Sir Richard Hawkins.*
28 *LMR*, 13.
29 Nuttall, *New Light on Drake.*
30 Strachan, 'Sampson's fight with Maltese Galleys, 1628'.
31 Monson, *Naval Tracts.*
32 Bourne, *The Art of Shooting.*
33 Corbett, *Drake and the Tudor Navy.*
34 See www.alderneywreck.com.
35 Kemp, *The Campaign of the Spanish Armada.*
36 Laughton, *State Papers Relating to the Defeat of the Spanish Armada.*
37 See Guilmartin, *Gunpowder and Galleys.*
38 Quoted in Hart-Davis, *Armada.*
39 Rodger, 'The Development of Broadside Gunnery'.
40 Quoted in Clowes, *The Royal Navy: A History*, Vol I.
41 *AMR*, III.
42 Monson, *Naval Tracts.*
43 Taylor, 'Carrack into Galleon'.
44 Hume, Calendar of State Papers, Spanish, Vol IV, Elizabeth, 1587–1603, London, 1892.
45 'A Booke of Orders for the Warre both by Sea and Land', 1530, British Library, Harley MS 309. See Corbett, *Fighting Instructions 1530–1816.*
46 Bourne, *The Art of Shooting.*
47 Corbett, *Drake and the Tudor Navy.*
48 Andrews, *The Last Voyage.*
49 In Monson, *Naval Tracts.*
50 Guilmartin, *Gunpowder and Galleys.*
51 See Rodger, *The Safeguard of the Sea.*
52 *CSPV*, II, 78.
53 *CSPV*, II, 102.
54 *CSPV*, II, 522, 524.
55 *L&P*, I, I, 1007.
56 *LMR*, 30.
57 *L&P*, XVIII/II, 129.
58 *L&P*, IV/II, 4998.
59 Quoted in Harrison, *The Elizabethan Journals.*

60 Quoted in Cruickshank, *Henry VIII and the Invasion of France.*
61 Hakluyt, *The Principal Navigations.*

Chapter Five
Feeding the Fleet
1 *L&P*, XIX/I, 543.
2 *L&P*, I/I, 124.
3 *L&P*, I/I, 1524.
4 See Trow-Smith, *A History of British Livestock Husbandry to 1700.*
5 *L&P*, I/II, 2833.
6 See Weir, *Henry VIII, King and Court*, xv.
7 *L&P*, I/I, 1080.
8 *L&P*, 27, 71.
9 See Harrison, *The Elizabethan Journals.*
10 *L&P*, I/I, 1132.
11 *AMR*, IV, 606–7.
12 *LMR*, 12.
13 *LMR*, 14.
14 *LMR*, 15.
15 Lord Thomas Howard to Privy Council, *LMR*, 30.
16 *AMR*, IV, 408–15.
17 *L&P*, I/II, 1913.
18 *L&P*, I/II, 1944.
19 *LMR*, 30.
20 *CSPE*, CLXXXVI, 1.
21 *LMR*, 48.
22 *L&P*, I/I, 1316.
23 *L&P*, I/I, 1844.
24 *L&P*, XX/II, 265.
25 *L&P*, XX/II, 184.
26 *L&P*, XX/II, 185.
27 *L&P*, XX/II, 5.
28 *L&P*, XX/II, 4.
29 *L&P*, XX/II, 387.
30 Quoted in Loades, *The Tudor Navy.*
31 Quoted in Oppenheim, *A History of the Administration of the Royal Navy.*
32 *CSPE*, CXCIX, 27/28.
33 Letter to the queen, 13 April 1588, quoted in Laughton, *State Papers Relating to the Defeat of the Spanish Armada.*
34 Ibid.
35 *CSPE*, CCVIII, 78.
36 Laughton, *State Papers Relating to the Defeat of the Spanish Armada.*
37 *CSPE*, CCXIV, 43.
38 *CSPE*, CCXIV, 53.
39 *CSPE*, CCXV, 55.
40 *CSPE*, CCXXXVIII, 164.
41 Quoted in Laughton, *State Papers Relating to the Defeat of the Spanish Armada.*

42 Fernández-Armesto, *The Spanish Armada.*
43 Laughton, *State Papers Relating to the Defeat of the Spanish Armada.*, vol II, 138–9, 141.
44 Ibid.
45 Ibid.
46 See Hanson, *The Confident Hope of a Miracle.*
47 *LMR*, 30.
48 *LMR*, 30.
49 *L&P*, I/II, 1864.
50 See Laughton, *State Papers Relating to the Defeat of the Spanish Armada.*
51 *L&P*, I/I, 2305.
52 *L&P*, IX, 377.
53 *LMR*, 57.
54 *LMR*, 53.
55 *L&P*, IV/II, 2746.
56 *L&P*, IV/II, 3610.
57 Now restored and open to the public.
58 *L&P*, I/I, 1453.
59 *L&P*, I/I, 1661.
60 *L&P*, I/II, 1913.
61 *L&P*, IV/III, 6138.
62 *L&P*, XX/II, 303.

Chapter Six
Command and Control and the Company
1 *L&P*, II/I, 1113.
2 *L&P*, XX/I, 1235.
3 *L&P*, XX/I, 1237.
4 *L&P*, XX/II, 26.
5 *L&P*, XX/II, 39.
6 *L&P*, XX/II, 62.
7 *L&P*, XX/II, 108.
8 *L&P*, XX/II, 391.
9 *L&P*, XX/II, 264.
10 Quoted in Glasgow, *The Royal Navy in Philip and Mary's War, 1557–58.*
11 *APC*, 6: 639.
12 *CSPM*, 599/600.
13 See Clowes, *The Royal Navy: A History* Vol I.
14 *CSPM*, 730.
15 *CSPE*, CCXXIV, 53.
16 See Laughton, *State Papers Relating to the Defeat of the Spanish Armada.*
17 *LMR*, 29.
18 *Henry VIII*, Act I, Scene 1.
19 *LMR*, 54.
20 *L&P*, XI, 385.
21 Lambert, *Admirals.*
22 Quoted in Skidmore, *Edward VI.*

23 *L&P*, XIX/II, 501.
24 *L&P*, XIX/II, 549.
25 *L&P*, XIX/II, 562.
26 *L&P*, XIX/II, 563.
27 *L&P*, XIX/II, 580.
28 *L&P*, XIX/II, 588.
29 *L&P*, XIX/II, 597.
30 *L&P*, XIX/II, 600, 601, 617.
31 *L&P*, I/I, 244.
32 *L&P*, I/I, 1453.
33 Published by the NRS as *The Naval Tracts of Sir William Monson*, 1902–14.
34 See bibliography. John Sugden's *Sir Francis Drake* is a thoroughly excellent biography.
35 *L&P*, I/I, 1660.
36 *L&P*, IX, 60.
37 *L&P*, XXI/I, 498.
38 Quoted in Andrews, *Trade, Plunder and Settlement*.
39 Morrison, *The Elizabethan Journals*.
40 *L&P*, XIX/I, 531.
41 *CSPE*, CCVIII, 46.
42 *L&P*, XIV/I, 711, 712.
43 See Lacey, *Sir Walter Ralegh*
44 *CSPE*, CCLXXXIII, 1.
45 See Hakluyt, *The Principal Navigations*.
46 See Nuttall, *New Light on Drake*.
47 Quoted in Rowse, *Sir Richard Grenville*.

Chapter Seven
A Sailor's Life
1 *LMR*, 4.
2 See Smith, *A Seaman's Grammar*.
3 Ibid.
4 *L&P*, I/II, 2763.
5 See Andrews, *The Last Voyage*.
6 See *AMR*, IV.
7 Ibid.
8 Quoted in McDermott, *Martin Frobisher*.
9 Ibid.
10 *AMR*, IV.
11 *L&P*, XX/II, 3.
12 *L&P*, XX/II, 238.
13 *L&P*, XX/II, 346.
14 *L&P*, XX/II, 368.
15 *L&P*, XX/II, 405.
16 *L&P*, XX/II, 513.
17 *L&P*, XX/II, 513.
18 See Laughton, *State Papers Relating to the Defeat of the Spanish Armada*.
19 Quoted in Oppenheim, *A History of the Administration of the Royal Navy*.
20 Monson, *Naval Tracts*.
21 Hakluyt, *The Principal Navigations*.

22 Ibid.
23 Smith, *A Seaman's Grammar*.
24 *AMR*, IV.
25 'Surgeons of the Mary Rose'.
26 Andrews, *The Last Voyage*.
27 Quoted in Cruickshank, *Henry VIII and the Invasion of France*.
28 Stirland, *Raising the Dead*.
29 Hakluyt, *The Principal Navigations*.
30 Smith, *A Seaman's Grammar*.
31 *AMR*, IV.
32 See, for example, the orders of Sir Edward Howard, *L&P*, I/I, 1133.
33 Hakluyt, *The Principal Navigations*.
34 *AMR*, IV gives a detailed account of musical instruments current at the time.
35 See Palmer, *The Oxford Book of Sea Songs* and Firth, *Naval Songs and Ballads*.
36 'A Booke of Orders for the Warre both by Sea and Land', British Library, Harley MS 309, folio 42. See Corbett, *Fighting Instructions 1530–1816*.
37 Hakluyt, *The Principal Navigations*.
38 See Kelsey, *Sir John Hawkins*.
39 See Nuttall, *New Light on Drake*.
40 Ibid.
41 Sadly, only a little of this survives, as British Library, Sloane MS 61.

Chapter Eight
Pilotage, Navigation and Seamanship
1 NRS, 1929.
2 *L&P*, I/I, 1732 and 1739.
3 *L&P*, XX/I, 1255.
4 See Taylor, *A Regiment for the Sea and Other Writings*.
5 However, John Smith in *A Seaman's Grammar* considered the log line and seaman's glass 'so uncertain, it is not worth the labour to try it'.
6 *L&P*, IV/II, 2751.
7 Bethune, *The Observations of Sir Richard Hawkins*.
8 *LMR*, 38.
9 Now in the library of the Royal Geographical Society, London.
10 *The Art of Navigation* in England.
11 Hakluyt, *The Principal Navigations*.
12 See Williamson, *The Cabot Voyages*, and Firstbrook, *The Voyage of the Matthew*.
13 See Andrews, *Trade, Plunder and Settlement*.
14 See Taylor, *A Regiment for the Sea and Other Writings*.

15 Smith, *A Seaman's Grammar*.
16 See Nuttall, *New Light on Drake*.
17 The 'Straits of Salted Fish', otherwise the Straits of Anian, so called because of the great fisheries on the Newfoundland coast, Letter from the Licentiate Velverde to Philip II, quoted in Nuttall, *New Light on Drake*.
18 This also gives us a clear idea of Spanish bureaucracy. Faced with a plundering pirate loose upon their coasts, the local authorities spent much time and ink trying to sort out the problem of da Silva's four missing shirts.
19 See Bawlf, *The Secret Voyage of Sir Francis Drake*, and Wilson, *The World Encompassed*.
20 Quoted in Wallis, 'The Cartography of Drake's Voyage'.
21 Hakluyt, *The Principal Navigations*.
22 *LMR*, 13.
23 *LMR*, 47.
24 *LMR*, 23.
25 *LMR*, 47.
26 *L&P*, XIX/II, 601.
27 *L&P*, XIX/II, 597.
28 Unwin, *The Defeat of John Hawkins*.
29 As recorded by *Mayflower* in 1620 and her replica in 1957. See Philbrick, *Mayflower: A Story of Courage*.
30 After Nelson, *The Tudor Navy*.
31 Studied in detail in Guilmartin, *Gunpowder and Galleys*.
32 Willis, *Fighting at Sea in the Eighteenth Century*.

Chapter Nine
Havens and Harbours
1 See Loades, *The Tudor Navy*.
2 *LMR*, 38.
3 *L&P*, Appendix II, 1726.
4 *L&P*, XXI/I, 682.
5 *L&P*, XXI/I, 682.
6 Pritchard, *Deal*.
7 *LMR*, 47.
8 *L&P*, XIV/I, 714.
9 *L&P*, VII, 66.
10 *L&P*, XII/I, 92.
11 Quoted in Leach, *Dover Harbour, Royal Gateway*.
12 *CSPE*, CLXXV, 40/41.
13 *CSPE*, CCVIII, 85.
14 *L&P*, XXI, I, 702.
15 *APC*, 1595–6.
16 See Oppenheim, *Maritime History to 1688*.

17 *CSPE*, CCLVI, 82. For a detailed account, see Hyde and Harrington, 'Faversham's Role in the Armada and Counter-Armada'.
18 *LMR*, 4.
19 *L&P*, I/I, 2574.
20 *L&P*, I/I, 2785.
21 *L&P*, XIV/I, 573.
22 *L&P*, XIX/I, 659.
23 *L&P*, XIX/I, 718.
24 *L&P*, XIX/I, 719.
25 Skidmore, *Edward VI*.
26 *CSPM*, 674.
27 *CSPE*, CLXXXIV, 49 and CLXXXX, 15.
28 *CSPE*, CCV, 59.
29 *LMR*, 52.
30 *LMR*, 21.
31 *L&P*, I/II, 1869.
32 *LMR*, 21.
33 *LMR*, 22.
34 *LMR*, 25.
35 *L&P*, I/I, 1675.
36 Drake and Blitheman to the Privy Council, 3 May 1590, quoted in Sugden, *Sir Francis Drake*.
37 *CSPE*, CCXLII, 31.
38 *L&P*, XXVII, 63.
39 *L&P*, XIX/I, 724.
40 Hakluyt, *The Principal Navigations*.
41 Taylor, *The Original Writings of the Two Richard Hakluyts*.

Chapter Ten
Plunder, Piracy and Professionalism
1 *L&P*, IV/II, 3747.
2 *L&P*, IV/II, 4143.
3 Marsden, *Documents Relating to Law and Custom of the Sea*.
4 *L&P*, VIII, 281.
5 *L&P*, XII/I, 528.
6 *L&P*, XII/I, 601.
7 *L&P*, XII/I, 656.
8 *L&P*, XII/I, 663.
9 *L&P*, XII/I, 718.
10 *L&P*, XII/I, 718.
11 *L&P*, XII/II, 393.
12 *L&P*, XII/II, 416.
13 *L&P*, XII/II, 535.
14 *L&P*, XII/II, 563.
15 *L&P*, XII/II, 670.
16 *L&P*, XIII/I, 485.
17 *L&P*, XIII/I, 191.
18 *L&P*, XIV/I, 141.
19 *L&P*, XIV/I, 573.

20 *L&P*, XIX/I, 237.
21 *L&P*, XIX/II, 620.
22 *L&P*, XIX/II, 621.
23 Harrison, *The Elizabethan Journals*.
24 *L&P*, XXI, I, 1879.
25 *L&P*, IV, III, 5134.
26 *L&P*, XIX, II, 766.
27 *CSPV*, 325.
28 *L&P*, XX/I, 922.
29 *L&P*, XX/I, 1004.
30 *L&P*, Appendix II, 1882.
31 *L&P*, Appendix II, 1704.
32 *L&P*, XXI, 563.
33 *CSPM*, 615.
34 *CSPM*, 632.
35 See Harrison, *The Elizabethan Journals*.
36 *APC*, 4:17–18.
37 *CSPV*, 1554.
38 See De Lisle, *After Elizabeth*.
39 *L&P*, XX/II, 190.
40 Quoted in Ronald, *The Pirate Queen*.
41 *CSPE*, 1580, 30.
42 List taken from Lacey, *Sir Walter Ralegh*.
43 Proclamation 311, in Humphrey Dyson, 'A Book Containing All Such Proclamations as were Published During the Reign of the Late Queen Elizabeth', 1618, British Library.
44 See Harrison, *The Elizabethan Journals*.
45 Ibid.
46 Proclamations 302 and 326, in Dyson, 'A Book Containing All Such Proclamations'.
47 *APC*, 26:120.
48 Loades, *The Tudor Navy*.
49 See Wheeler, *The Making of a World Power*.
50 See Andrews, *Elizabethan Privateering*.
51 Ibid.
52 *CSPE*, CCVIII-97/102.
53 Thus Hawkins's first slaving voyage included the royal ships *Jesus of Lubeck*, *Solomon*, *Tiger* and *Swallow*.
54 McDermott, *Martin Frobisher*.

Chapter Eleven
The Fighting Fleet
1 'A Booke of Orders for the Warre both by Sea and Land', British Library, Harley MS 309, folio 42. For an extract see Corbett, *Fighting Instructions, 1530–1816*.
2 See Hakluyt, *The Principal Navigations*.
3 Mattingley, *The Defeat of the Spanish Armada*.
4 A Tennyson, 'The Revenge: A Ballad of the Fleet'.

5 *L&P*, I/I, 1661.
6 Spont, *Letters and Papers*.
7 *L&P*, I/I, 1216.
8 *L&P*, I/I, 1480.
9 See Spont, *Letters and Papers*.
10 *L&P*, I/I, 1657, 1659.
11 *CSPV*, 217.
12 *CSPV*, 218.
13 *LMR*, 16.
14 *L&P*, I/I, 1661.
15 *L&P*, XVIII, 867.
16 *L&P*, XIX/II, 540.
17 *L&P*, XIX/II, 539.
18 *L&P*, XIX/II, 560.
19 *L&P*, XXI/I, 496.
20 For a detailed account and the lessons to be drawn from the fight, see Guilmartin, *Gunpowder and Galleys*.
21 Rayner Unwin's most readable *The Defeat of John Hawkins* remains the best account of this significant episode.
22 Hakluyt, *The Principal Navigations*.
23 Ibid.
24 Harrison, *The Elizabethan Journals*.
25 The eye-witness, the Dutchman van Linschoten, is quoted in Rowse, *Sir Richard Grenville*.
26 The Fight and Cyclone at the Azores', quoted in Rowse, *Sir Richard Grenville*.
27 See Lavery, *Nelson and the Nile*.
28 From Mainwaring's narrative in Andrews, *The Last Voyage*.
29 Quoted in McKee, *King Henry's VIII's Mary Rose*.
30 See Childs, *The Warship Mary Rose*.
31 *L&P*, XX/I, 1237.
32 See Childs, *The Warship Mary Rose*.
33 See Sugden, *Sir Francis Drake*.
34 She was carrying the cargo from two ships, *San Lorenzo* having had to unload hers after springing a leak. Although she was larger than Drake's three attacking ships combined, they managed to get alongside under her guns.
35 O Herrera et al, *La armada invencible*, Valladolid, 1929.
36 Harrison, *The Elizabethan Journals*.
37 Quoted in Kemp, *The Campaign of the Spanish Armada*.
38 Laughton, *State Papers Relating to the Defeat of the Spanish Armada*.
39 Ibid.
40 Mattingley, *The Defeat of the Spanish Armada*.

41 Monson, *The Naval Tracts.*
42 Harrison, *The Elizabethan Journals.*
43 *LMR*, 18.
44 Quoted in Corbett, *Drake and the Tudor Navy.*
45 *L&P*, XXI/I, 874.
46 *L&P*, XXI/I, 890.
47 See Childs, *The Warship Mary Rose.*
48 *L&P*, XIX/I, 533.
49 *L&P*, XIX/I, 231.
50 Sugden, *Sir Francis Drake.*
51 Corbett, *Successors to Drake.*
52 See Andrews, *The Last Voyage.*
53 Quoted in Loades, *The Tudor Navy.*
54 *L&P*, XX/I, 925.
55 *L&P*, XIX/I, 228.
56 *L&P*, XX/I, 428.
57 *L&P*, XXI, 682.

Chapter Twelve
Shore Support
1 *L&P*, VI, 1510.
2 *L&P*, XIV/II, 1231.
3 *L&P*, XIV/I, 143.
4 See Oppenheim, *Naval Accounts and Inventories.*
5 Ibid.
6 *L&P*, XII/II, 794.
7 See Spont, *Letters and Papers.*
8 *LMR*, 2.
9 *L&P*, IV/III, 6138.
10 See Oppenheim, *Naval Accounts and Inventories*
11 See Andrews, *The Last Voyage.*
12 *L&P*, IX, 1083.
13 *L&P*, V, 685.
14 Public Record Office, Kew, SP, 12/170/57, folios 86–7; quoted in Kelsey, *Sir John Hawkins.*
15 Public Record Office, SP, 12/165/50, September 1583, folios 168–9.
16 See Kelsey, *Sir John Hawkins.*
17 Quoted in Rodger, *The Safeguard of the Sea.*
18 *L&P*, VI, 1460.
19 Rodger, *The Safeguard of the Sea.*
20 For further details see Merriman, 'Realm and Castle, Henry VIII as European Builder'.
21 *L&P*, XIX/II, 496.
22 *L&P*, XX, 672.
23 *CSPE*, CXCL, 1586. During the 200th anniversary celebrations of the battle of Trafalgar police in Portsmouth noted a sharp rise in burglaries as the inheritors of Richard Noyse, knowing that crowds would be gathering on the seafront at Southsea to watch the ships and fireworks, took advantage to break into the empty houses and flats of the spectators.
24 See Harrison, *The Elizabethan Journals.*
25 Andrews, *Elizabethan Privateering.*
26 See Duffy, *The Voices of Morbath.*
27 *L&P*, I/I, 1414.
28 *L&P*, I/I, 2305.
29 *L&P*, I/I, 2305.
30 *L&P*, Appendix 1, 364.
31 *CSPE*, CLXXXVII, 58/63.
32 *CSPE*, LXXI, 12/215/40.
33 *CSPE*, CXIII, 12/212/66.
34 Proclamation 300. See Harrison, *The Elizabethan Journals.*
35 Ibid.
36 *APC*, 24:159.
37 *APC*, 24:296.
38 *CSPE*, LXXXVI, 245.
39 *CSPE*, XXI/I, 693.
40 Quoted in Hutchinson, *Elizabeth's Spy Master.*
41 Ibid.
42 Ibid.
43 Ibid.
44 Gristwood, *Elizabeth and Leicester.*
45 Hutchinson, *Elizabeth's Spy Master.*
46 See Loades, *The Tudor Navy.*
47 Quoted in detail in Ronald, *The Pirate Queen.*
48 *CSPE*, III/II, 2296.
49 Published in Corbett, *Fighting Instructions, 1530–1816.*
50 Ibid.
51 Ibid.

Chapter Thirteen
The Legacy
1 Quoted in Lambert, *Admirals*, a work which gives a very thoughtful review of the role of Howard of Effingham in creating a model navy.
2 E T Page, *Robert Blake: Admiral and General at Sea*, London, 1900.
3 C Spencer, *Rupert of the Rhine*, Weidenfeld & Nicolson, 2007.

Bibliography

The principal sources for anyone wishing to study the events of Henry VIII's reign are the State Paper (SP) series, easily accessible at the National Archives, Kew, and gradually making their way on to the internet. These are:

Letters and Papers Illustrative of the Reigns of Richard III and Henry VII
Letters and Papers, Foreign and Domestic, of the Reign of Henry VIII, 1509–47
Calendar of State Papers, Domestic
Calendar of State Papers, Spanish
Calendar of State Papers, Venetian

Extracts from these, and other sources, have been carefully gleaned, by editors for both the Navy Records Society and the Hakluyt Society, to create separate publications related to particular wars or voyages. Brought together, and with excellent introductions, they give the reader a feel for the excitement, effort, administration, loss and occasional blunder that were a part of every campaign.

The recently published *Archaeology of the Mary Rose*, in five volumes, is an encyclopaedic and very readable description of all that was found on board the ship and the hull in which the finds lay, and is a 'must' for any student wishing to research the vessel itself in any detail and the world in which she floated.

Abbreviations

AMR	*Archaeology of the Mary Rose*
APC	*Acts of the Privy Council*
CSPE	*Calendar of State Papers, Domestic, Elizabeth*
CSPM	*Calendar of State Papers, Domestic, Mary*
CSPV	*Calendar of State Papers, Venetian*
EHR	*English Historical Review*
HT	*History Today*
LMR	*Letters from the Mary Rose*
L&P	*Letters and Papers, Foreign and Domestic, of the Reign of Henry VIII*
MM	*Mariner's Mirror*
NRS	Navy Records Society

Books

Andrews, K R, *Elizabethan Privateering*, Cambridge University Press, 1964

Andrews, K R, *The Last Voyage of Drake and Hawkins*, Cambridge University Press, 1972

Andrews, K R, *Trade, Plunder and Settlement*, Cambridge University Press, 1984

Bawlf, S, *The Secret Voyage of Sir Francis Drake*, Walker & Co, 2003

Barker, R A, *Fernando Oliviera: The English Episode 1546–47*,

Academia de Marinha, Lisbon, 1992

Bethune, C R D (ed), *The Observations of Sir Richard Hawkins*, Hakluyt Society, 1847; ed J A Williamson, London, 1933

Bindoff, S T, *Tudor England*, Penguin, 1950

Bourne, W, *The Art of Shooting in Great Ordnance*, London, 1587

Bourne, W, *A Regiment for the Sea*, London, 1577

Boxer, C R (ed), *The Tragic Story of the Sea*, Hakluyt Society, 1959

Bradford, E, *The Great Ship*, Hamish Hamilton, 1986

Bradford, E, *The Great Siege*, Hodder & Stoughton, 1961

Brenon, G, and Statham, E P, *The House of Howard*, Hutchinson, 1907

Brewer, J S, Gairdner, J, and Brodie, R H (eds), *Calendar of Letters and Papers, Foreign and Domestic, of the Reign of Henry VIII, 1509–47*, London, 1862–1932

Brown, R, et al (eds), *Calendar of State Papers*, Venetian, London, 1864–1940, 38 vols

Butler, N, *Dialogical Discourses*, NRS, 1929

Byrne, M StC (ed), *The Lisle Letters*, Secker & Warburg, 1983

Campbell, J, *History and Lives of the British Admirals*, London, 1813

Childs, D J, *The Warship Mary Rose*, Chatham, 2007

Clowes, W L, *The Royal Navy: A History from the Earliest Times to the Present Day*, vol I, London, 1897

Collado, L, *Pratica manuale di artiglieria*, Venice, 1641

Corbett, J S, *Drake and the Tudor Navy*, Longmans, 1917

Corbett, J S (ed), *Fighting Instructions 1530–1816*, NRS, vol 29, 1905

Corbett, J S (ed), *Papers Relating to the Navy during the Spanish War, 1585–7*, NRS, Vol 11, 1905

Corbett, J S, *Successors to Drake*, London, 1900

Cornou, J, *L'Héroique Combat de la Cordelière 1512*, Sked, 1998

Cruickshank, C, *Henry VIII and the Invasion of France*, Alan Sutton, 1990

Dasent, J R (ed), *Acts of the Privy Council*, London, 1890–1907

Dash, M, *Batavia's Graveyard*, Weidenfeld & Nicolson, 2002

Davies, J, *The King's Ships*, Partizan, 2005

Davies, N, *The Isles: A History*, Macmillan, 1999

Dee, John, *The Perfecte Arte of Navigation*, London, 1577

De Lisle, L, *After Elizabeth*, Harper Collins, 2004

Duffy, E, *The Voices of Morbath*, Yale University Press, 2001

Eldred, W, *The Gunners Glasse*, London, 1646

Elton, G R, *England under the Tudors*, Methuen, 1955

Fernández-Armesto, F, *The Spanish Armada: The Experience of War in 1588*, Oxford University Press, 1988

Firth, E H (ed), *Naval Songs and Ballads*, NRS, 1907

Firstbrook, P, *The Voyage of the Matthew*, BBC, 1997

Friel, Ian, *The Good Ship*, British Museum Press, 1995

Gairdner, J, et al (eds), *Letters and Papers Illustrative of the Reigns of Richard III and Henry VII*, London, 1862–1910

Gardiner, J (ed), *Before the Mast: Life and Death Aboard the Mary Rose*, AMR, vol IV, Mary Rose Trust, 2005

Griffiths, R A, and Thomas, R S, *The Making of the Tudor Dynasty*,

Alan Sutton, 1985

Gristwood, S, *Elizabeth and Leicester*, Bantam, 2007

Guilmartin, John, *Galleons and Galleys*, Cassell, 2002

Guilmartin, John, *Gunpowder and Galleys*, Conway, 2003

Hakluyt, R, *The Principal Navigations, Voyages, Traffiques and Discoveries of the English Nation*, London, 1589

Hall, E, *Hall's Chronicle: The Union of the Two Noble and Illustrious Families of York and Lancaster*, London, 1542

Hall, E, *The Triumphant Reign of King Henry the Eighth*, London, 1547

Hanson, N, *The Confident Hope of a Miracle*, Doubleday, 2003

Hardy, R, *Longbow*, Mary Rose Trust, 1976

Harrison, G B, *The Elizabethan Journals*, Anchor, 1965

Hart-Davis, D, *Armada*, Bantam, 1988

Hildred, A (ed), *Weapons of Warre: The Armaments of the Mary Rose*, AMR, vol III, Mary Rose Trust, 2009

Horsley, John, *Tools of the Maritime Trade*, David & Charles, 1978

Hume, M A S (ed), *Calendar of Letters & State Papers Relating to English Affairs Preserved Principally in the Archives of Simancas*, London, 1892–9 [*Calendar of State Papers, Spanish*]

Hutchinson, G, *Medieval Ships and Shipping*, Leicester University Press, 1994

Hutchinson, R, *The Last Days of Henry VIII*, Weidenfeld & Nicolson, 2005

Hutchinson, R, *Thomas Cromwell*, Weidenfeld & Nicolson, 2007

Hutchinson, R, *Elizabeth's Spy Master*, Weidenfeld & Nicolson, 2007

Jones, M, *For Future Generations*, AMR, vol V, Mary Rose Trust, 2003

Kelsey, H, *Sir John Hawkins*, Yale University Press, 2003

Kemp, P, *The Campaign of the Spanish Armada*, Phaidon, 1988

Knighton, C S, and Loades, D, *Letters from the Mary Rose*, Sutton, 2002

Knighton C S, and Loades, D M, *The Anthony Roll*, NRS, 2000

Lacey, R, *Sir Walter Ralegh*, Weidenfeld and Nicolson, 1973

Lambert, A, *Admirals*, Faber and Faber, 2008

Laughton, J K (ed), *State Papers Relating to the Defeat of the Spanish Armada*, NRS, vols 1–2, 1894

Lavery, B, *Building the Wooden Walls*, Conway, 1991

Lavery, B, *Nelson and the Nile*, Chatham, 1998

Leach, D, *Dover Harbour, Royal Gateway*, Riverdale, 2005

Leland, J, *Leland's Itinerary of England and Wales in about 1535–1543*, London, 1710–12; London, 1906–10, reprinted 1964

Liaster, T, and Renshaw, J, *Conservation Chemistry: An Introduction*, Royal Society of Chemistry, 2004

Loades, D, *England's Maritime Empire*, Longmans, 2000

Loades, D, *The Tudor Navy*, Scolar, 1992

Lucar, C, *Three Bookes of Colloquies Concerning the Arte of Shooting in Great and Small Pieces of Artillerie ...*, trans. N Tartaglia, London, 1588

Marsden, P (ed), *Sealed by Time*, AMR, vol I, Mary Rose Trust, 2003

Marsden, P (ed), *Your Noble Shippe: Anatomy of a Tudor Warship*, AMR, vol II, Mary Rose Trust, 2008

Marsden, R G (ed), *Documents Relating to Law and Custom of the Sea*, Hakluyt Society, vol 49, 1915

Mattingley, G, *The Defeat of the Spanish Armada*, Jonathan Cape, 1959

Mattingley, G, *Renaissance Diplomacy*, Cape, 1955

McDermott, J, *Martin Frobisher*, Yale University Press, 2001

McKee, A, *From Merciless Invaders*, Souvenir Press, 1963

McKee, A, *King Henry VIII's Mary Rose*, Souvenir, 1973

McKee, A, *How we Found the Mary Rose*, Souvenir, 1982

Monson, Sir William, *The Naval Tracts of Sir William Monson*, ed M Oppenheim, NRS, vols 22, 23, 43, 45, 47, 1902–14

Mudie, C, *Sailing Ships*, Adlard Coles Nautical, 2000

Nelson, A, *The Tudor Navy 1485–1603*, Conway, 2001

Nuttall, Z, *New Light on Drake*, Hakluyt Society, series II, vol 34, 1914

Oppenheim, M, *A History of the Administration of the Royal Navy*, London, 1896

Oppenheim, M, *Maritime History to 1688*, Victoria County History of Kent, vol II, London, 1926.

Oppenheim, M (ed), *Naval Accounts and Inventories of the Reign of Henry VII*, NRS, vol 8, 1896

Palmer, R (ed), *The Oxford Book of Sea Songs*, Oxford University Press, 1986

Parry, J H, *The Age of Reconnaissance*, Weidenfield & Nicolson, 1973

Patterson, B, *A Military Heritage*, Fort Cumberland & Portsmouth Military Society, 1984

Perry, M, *Sisters to the King*, André Deutsch, 1998

Philbrick, N, *Mayflower: A Story of Courage*, Viking, 2006

Platt, C, *Medieval Southampton*, Routledge & Kegan Paul, 1973

Plowden, A, *Lady Jane Grey*, Sutton, 2003

Plowden, A, *Elizabeth I*, Sutton, 2004

Pritchard, S, *Deal*, London, 1864

Ridley, J, *Henry Eighth*, Constable, 1984

Robinson, J M, *The Dukes of Norfolk*, Oxford University Press, 1982

Rodger, N A M, *The Safeguard of the Sea*, Harper Collins, 1997

Ronald, S, *The Pirate Queen*, Sutton, 2007

Rowse, A L, *Sir Richard Grenville of the Revenge*, Jonathan Cape, 1937

Rule, M, *The Mary Rose: The Excavation and Raising of Henry VIII's Flagship*, Conway, 1982

Sim, A, *Food and Feast in Tudor England*, Sutton, 1997

Skidmore, C, *Edward VI, the Lost King of England*, Weidenfeld & Nicolson, 2007

Smith, Captain John, *A Seaman's Grammar*, London, 1627; ed K Goell, Michael Joseph, 1970

Spont, A, *Letters and Papers Relating to the War with France 1512–1513*, NRS, 1897

Stirland, A J, *Raising the Dead*, Wiley, 2000

Sugden, J, *Sir Francis Drake*, Pimlico, 2006

Taylor, E G R, *The Haven Finding Art*, London, 1971

Taylor, E G R (ed), *The Original Writings of the Two Richard Hakluyts*, 2 vols, Hakluyt Society, London, 1935

Taylor, E G R (ed), *A Regiment for the Sea and Other Writings on Navigation by William Bourne*, Hakluyt Society, vol 121, 1963

Trow-Smith, R, *A History of British Livestock Husbandry to 1700*, Routledge & Kegan Paul, 1957

Twiss, Sir Travers (ed), *The Black Book of Admiralty*, Rolls Series, 1871–6

Unwin, R, *The Defeat of John Hawkins*, Allen & Unwin, 1960

Vaux, W S W (ed), *The World Encompassed by Sir Francis Drake*, Hakluyt Society, 1854

Waters, D W, *The Art of Navigation in England in Elizabethan and Early Stuart Times*, Hollis and Carter, 1958

Weir, A, *Henry VIII: King and Court*, Jonathan Cape, 2001

Wenham, R B (ed), *The Expedition of Sir John Norris and Sir Francis Drake to Spain and Portugal*, NRS 127, 1988

Wheeler, J S, *The Making of a World Power*, Sutton, 1999

Williamson, J A, *The Cabot Voyages and Bristol Discovery under Henry VII*, Hakluyt Society, Vol 120, 1962

Wilson, D, *Sir Francis Walsingham*, Constable, 2007.

Wilson, D, *The World Encompassed*, Hamish Hamilton, 1977

Willis, S, *Fighting at Sea in the Eighteenth Century*, Boydell, 2008

Wilson, D, *Sir Francis Walsingham*, Constable, 2007

Witherby, C T, *The Battle of Bonchurch*, published privately, 1962

Wood, R, *The Wooden Bowl*, Stobart Davies, 2005

For youngsters:

Norris, S, *Run Away to Danger*, National Maritime Museum, 2005

Essays and Articles

Adair, E R, 'English Galleys in the Sixteeth Century', *EHR*, vol 35, 1920

Anderson, R C, 'Henry VIII's Great Galley', *MM*, vol 6, 1920

Bennell, J E G, 'English Oared Vessels of the Sixteenth Century' (2 parts), *MM*, vol 60, 1974

Boulind, R, 'Drake's Navigational Skills', *MM*, 54, 1968

Braddock, N, 'Victualling Rates for Henry VIII's Fleet', unpublished essay, Mary Rose Trust, 1994

Carr-Laughton, L G, 'The Square-Tuck Stern and Gun Deck', *MM*, vol 40, 1961

Corbett, J, 'The Lord Admiral's Whistle', *MM*, vol 3, 1912

DeVries, K, 'The Effectiveness of Fifteenth-Century Shipboard Artillery', *MM*, vol 84, 1998

Dobbs, C T C, and Bridge, M, 'Preliminary Results from Dendrochronological Studies on the Mary Rose', *Proceedings of the Eighth International Symposium on Boat and Ship Archaeology*, Gdansk, 2000

Eley, P, 'Portsmouth Breweries 1492–1847', *Portsmouth Papers*, vol 51, 1988

Fox R, and Barton, K, 'The Fourteenth Century Dock in Oyster Street', *Post-Medieval Archaeology*, vol 20, 1986

Glasgow, T, 'The Royal Navy in Philip and Mary's War, 1557–58', *MM*, vol 53, 1967

Glasgow, T, 'The Navy in the First Elizabethan Undeclared War', 1559–60', *MM*, vol 54, 1968

Gunn, S, 'The Duke of Suffolk's March on Paris in 1523', *EHR*, vol 101, 1986

Gunn, S, 'Tournaments and early Tudor Chivalry', *HT*, vol 41, June 1991

Hall, N, 'Building and Firing a Replica Mary Rose Port Piece', *Royal Armouries Yearbook*, vol 3, 1998

Hall, N, 'Casting and Firing a Mary Rose Culverin', *Royal Armouries Yearbook*, vol 6, 2001

Howard, G F, 'Gun Port Lids', *MM*, vol 67, 1981

Hyde, P, and Harrington, D, 'Faversham's Role in the Armada and Counter-Armada', *Archaeologica Cantiansis*, vol 122, 2002

Jones, M, et al, 'Sulfur Accumulations in the Timbers of Henry VIII's Warship Mary Rose', *Proceedings of the National Academy of Sciences of the United States*, vol 102, 2005

Kybett, S M, 'Henry VIII – A Malnourished King?', *HT*, vol 39, September 1989

Laughton, L G C, 'Early Tudor Ship-Guns', ed M Lewis, *MM*, vol 46, 1960

Lawson, W, 'The Boatswain's Call: Its Role in the European Maritime Tradition', *Second Conference of the ICTM Study Group on Music Archaeology*, Vol I, Royal Swedish Academy of Music, 1986

McKee, A, 'Henry VIII as Military Commander', *HT*, vol 41, June 1991

Merriman, M, 'Realm and Castle: Henry VIII as European Builder', *HT*, vol 41, June 1991

Parker, G, 'The Dreadnought Revolution of Tudor England', *MM*, vol 82, 1996

Quinn, D B, 'Artists and Illustrators in the Early Mapping of North America', *MM*, vol 72, 1986

Richardson, G, 'Good Friends and Brothers? Francis I and Henry VIII', *HT*, vol 44, September 1994

Rodger, N A M, 'The Development of Broadside Gunnery, 1450–1650', *MM*, vol 82, 1996

Scammell, G V, 'European Seamanship in the Great Age of Discovery', *MM*, vol 68, 1982

Strachan, M, 'Sampson's Fight with Maltese Galleys, 1628', *MM*, vol 55, 1969

Taylor, A, 'Carrack into Galleon', *MM*, vol 36, 1955

Vaughan, H S, 'Figure-Heads and Beak-Heads of the Ships of Henry VIII', *MM*, vol 42, 1914

Wallis, H, 'The Cartography of Drake's Voyage', in N J W Thrower (ed), *Sir Francis Drake and the Famous Voyage, 1577–1580*, University of California Press, 1988

Watt, J, 'Surgeons of the Mary Rose', *MM*, vol 69, 1983

Appendix 1

Chronology

MONARCH
Lord Admiral

RICHARD III
1483
25 July **John Howard, First Duke of Norfolk**

1485
1 August Henry Tudor sails from Harfleur for Milford Haven
22 August Henry defeats Richard III at Bosworth Field and becomes Henry VII

HENRY VII
21 September **John de Vere, Thirteenth Earl of Oxford**

1487
June Lambert Simnel lands from Ireland and is defeated

1489
February Treaty of Dordrecht guarantees Brittany's independence: English forces sent to duchy

1491
December Anne of Brittany marries Charles VIII of France

1492
2 August Columbus sails from Palos to cross the Atlantic
October English force lands at Calais to fight French
English ships, under Sir Edward Poynings, assist in seizure of Sluys
November War ended by Treaty of Etaples
12 November Columbus lands on Watling Island, Bahamas, West Indies

1495
July Perkin Warbeck's failed invasion lands at Deal

1496
England joins 'Holy League' against France
Scots raid north country in support of Warbeck
Dry dock built at Portsmouth

1497
English raids on Scotland
May John Cabot sails from Bristol in *Matthew* to cross Atlantic
June Cabot lands in Newfoundland
English navy sails for Scotland
Cornish rising defeated
August Cabot returns to England
September Truce of Ayton with Scotland
Warbeck lands in Cornwall
October Warbeck defeated

1498
May Cabot sails with six ships to cross Atlantic and disappears

1502
Peace between England and Scotland

1503
August James IV of Scotland marries Princess Margaret of England

1509
22 April Henry VII dies

HENRY VIII
1511
August Howard brothers defeat Scottish pirate, Sir Andrew Barton
November England joins 'Holy League' against France

1512
June Dorset's army landed at Fuentarabia to fight in Navarre
10 August Battle of Pointe de St Matthieu; *Cordelière* and *Regent* blow up

1513
17 March **Sir Edward Howard**
English fleet sails from Thames to blockade Brest
April French galleys attack English fleet
25 April Sir Edward Howard killed attacking French galleys, Whitesands Bay, English retire to Plymouth
4 May **Lord Thomas Howard, Earl of Surrey**
June Henry VIII leads army into France
August Battle of the Spurs
Capture of Therouanne and Tournai
Scotland declares war on England
9 September Battle of Flodden Edge: Scots routed, James IV killed, a Howard triumph

1514
Trinity House created
April French galleys burn Brighton
May Sir John Wallop raids Breton coast
June Truce with French; Princess Mary betrothed to Louis XII
September Mary escorted to France for marriage to Louis

1517
June Ship pond constructed at Deptford

1518
Treaty of London with France

1520
31 May Henry embarks at Dover for Field of Cloth of Gold meeting with Francis

1521
May Secret treaty of Bruges between England and Empire against France

1522
May–June Emperor Charles V visits England
June England declares war on France
13 June English raid Cherbourg
1 July Surrey leads assault on Morlaix
English raids on Brittany

1523
August Fitzwilliam on patrol in Channel, attacks Le Tréport: French fleet evades patrols and lands Albany to Scotland
September Suffolk leads short invasion of France

1525
January *Katherine Galley* captured by French
August Treaty of More brings peace with France
25 July **Henry Fitzroy, First Duke of Richmond**

1526
January Peace with Scotland

1528
January England declares war on Empire

1529
Peace with Empire

1532

Scottish ships attack English shipping in North Sea

1536

16 August **William Fitzwilliam, First Earl of Southampton**

1539

December Fitzwilliam escorts Anne of Cleves from Calais to Deal

1540

28 July **Lord John Russell, First Earl of Bedford**

1542

October England declares war on Scotland; Norfolk makes desultory raid on Scotland
25 November Scots defeated at Solway Moss
14 December James V dies; succeeded by infant Mary
December **Edward Seymour, First Earl of Hertford**

1543

26 January **John Dudley, Viscount Lisle**
July English defeat French squadron off Forth

1544

May English land at Leith and capture Edinburgh
14 September English capture Boulogne
December Privateering war against France and Scotland

1545

Navy Board established
1 March Reneger seizes *San Salvador* off Cape St Vincent
3 July French land 3,000 troops in Scotland
19 July *Mary Rose* lost in otherwise incident-free battle of the Solent
15 August English and French fleets minor engagement off Shoreham
2 September Lisle raids Le Tréport

1546

18 May *Galley Blanchard* captured from French
7 June England and France at peace

1547

28 January Henry VIII dies

EDWARD VI

`17 February **Thomas Lord Seymour**
7 March Scottish ships *Lion*, *Lioness* and *Marie-Galante* seized off Yarmouth
29 May Rebel Scottish Protestants seize St Andrews Castle; Cardinal Beaton assassinated
September English invade Scotland and defeat Scots at Pinkie supported by naval bombardment; English garrison Inchcolm, Innckeith and Broughty Castle

1548

January French ships resupply Scotland
February English garrison Dumfries
April English garrison Haddington
22 June French land 6,000 troops at Leith
August Mary Queen of Scots marries King of France

1549

July French seize Sark
August France declares war on England; Boulogne besieged; Haddington evacuated
English defeat French galleys off Guernsey
28 October **John Dudley, Viscount Lisle, First Earl of Warwick**

1550

February Broughty Castle evacuated
March Peace with France; withdrawal from Boulogne
14 May **Edward Fiennes, Lord Clinton, First Earl of Lincoln**

1553

May Willoughby and Chancellor sail for north-east passage
July Death of Edward VI: Northumberland fails to place Lady Jane Grey on throne; navy declares for Mary

MARY

1554

January Wyatt's rebellion
Chancellor returns from Moscow
20 March **William Howard, First Lord Howard of Effingham**
25 July Mary marries Philip of Spain

1555

Mary creates Muscovy Company – Sebastian Cabot, first governor
Chancellor sails for Russia

1556

Chancellor perishes

1557

April Thomas Stafford lands from France and seizes Scarborough Castle
June England declares war on France; Cherbourg raided
12 August Sir John Clere drowned landing on Orkney

1558

1 January French take Calais
10 February **Lord Clinton, First Earl of Lincoln (1572)**
Borough sails to visit Casa de Contratación
13 July English bombard French army at Gravelines
31 July English burn Le Conquet
17 November Death of Mary

ELIZABETH

1559

2 April Peace of Câteau-Cambrésis with France
May Protestant rebellion breaks out in Scotland
10 July Francis II becomes King of France: Scotland and France united
August French force lands at Leith
December Sir William Winter ordered to intercept French ships on course for Scotland

1560

January French fleet on passage to Scotland driven back by gales; Winter blockades Forth
April French army besieged in Leith
Clinton patrols western approaches
6 July Treaty of Edinburgh leads to French withdrawal from Scotland
December Death of Francis II dissolves Franco-Scottish union

1561

Elizabeth invests in Hawkins's second slaving voyage

1562

October French Huguenots gift Le Havre to England in return for support in religious war

1563

28 July English garrison in Le Havre surrenders

28 September English and French fleets clash off La Rochelle

1568
17 September John Hawkins's squadron attacked in San Juan de Ulua; loss of *Jesus of Lubeck*
November Ships carrying gold to pay Alba's army in Netherlands take refuge in Plymouth and have money removed to London

1569
November Revolt of northern earls

1570
Papal bull against Elizabeth: fleet mobilised

1572
22 July Drake attacks Nombre de Dios

1577
15 November Drake sails on circumnavigation

1578
July Drake executes Doughty for treachery at St Julian's, Patagonia

1579
28 February Drake captures *Nuestra Señora del la Concepción* [*Cacafuego*]

1580
31 January Henry of Portugal dies and Philip of Spain occupies Portugal
26 September Drake returns from circumnavigation
9 November Spanish troops surrender at Smerwick

1581
Levant Company formed

1582
26 July Santa Cruz defeats Franco-Portuguese naval force in Azores
23 September Fenton in fight with Spanish ships off Brazil

1583
Humphrey Gilbert sails on unsuccessful voyage to establish English colony in America
July Spanish take Terceira in Azores, ending Portuguese resistance in islands

1585
8 July **Charles Howard, Second Lord Howard of Effingham**
Drake sacks Santiago and Cartagena
Richard Grenville lands English colonists in Virginia
Cavendish sails on circumnavigation

1586
1 January Drake seizes Santo Domingo
10 February Drake seizes Cartagena
Drake evacuates English colony at Roanoke

1587
17 April Drake attacks Cadiz and 'singes King of Spain's beard'
June Drake captures *Sao Phelipe* off Azores
4 November Cavendish captures *Santa Anna* off lower California
Ostend, with English garrison, captured by Spanish
Second attempt to settle in Virginia

1588
18 May Armada sails
19 July Armada sighted off Lizard
20 July English fleet meets Armada off Plymouth
27 July Armada anchors off Calais; English launch fireships
29 July Armada dispersed at battle of Gravelines

1589
24 April Drake and Norris land at Corunna
16 May English launch assault on Lisbon
October Spanish fortify Blavet

1590
John White finds no settlers alive at Roanoke

1591
1 September *Revenge* captured and lost off Flores in the Azores
Centurion defeats five Spanish galleys

1592
3 August *Madre de Deus*, the richest ship yet captured, taken off Azores and brought to Dartmouth

1594
June *Dainty*, captained by Richard Hawkins, captured in south Pacific

November English troops take Spanish fort at Brest; Frobisher fatally wounded

1595
24 July Spanish galleys raid Penzance
28 August Drake and Hawkins sail for West Indies; Baskerville is land commander
12 November Drake and Hawkins repulsed at San Juan, Hawkins dies
31 December Baskerville's attack on Panama repulsed

1596
28 January Drake dies off Porto Bello
1 March English under Baskerville drive off Spanish fleet off Isle of Pines, Cuba
21 June Anglo-Dutch naval force, under Howard, Essex and Ralegh, seizes Cadiz
October Spanish armada dispersed by gales off Cape Finisterre

1597
17 August Essex leads naval force on 'Island Voyage' to Azores
22 October Spanish Armada scattered in western approaches

1598
6 June Cumberland captures San Juan de Puerto Rico

1599
September Spinola's galleys stationed in Netherlands

1601
January Essex's rebellion and execution
23 September Spanish troops land at Kinsale
6 December Leveson destroys Spanish fleet at Castlehaven

1602
2 January Spanish troops at Kinsale surrender
3 June Leveson and Monson seize *Sao Valentinho* in Cezimbra Roads
23 September Spinola's galleys defeated in Straits of Dover

1603
24 March Death of Elizabeth

Appendix 2 The Ships of the Tudor Navy[a]

Date built, purchased or captured if known; otherwise first listing	Name	Type[b]	Tonnes	Guns	Battle honours * = flagship	Last recorded	Remarks: fate, where known
HENRY VII							
1473 purchased	Grace Dieu	Carrack				1486	
1478 purchased	Carycon	Carrack				1496	Renamed Mary of the Tower
1478 purchased	Trinity	Carrack				1503	
1478 purchased	Fawcon	Carrack				1485	
1470 purchased	Garse	Carrack				1485	
1483 purchased	Bark of Hampton	Carrack			Brest 1512–13	1509	
1485 purchased	Nicholas	Ship			Brest 1512–13	1485	
1485 purchased	Governor	Carrack				1488	
1487 purchased	Mary and John (i)	Carvel	180			1522	
1488 built Rother	Regent	Carrack	1,000	225	Scottish war 1497, Brest 1512–13	1513	Destroyed in fight with Cordelière
1488 built	Sovereign (i)	Carrack	800	141	Brest 1512–13	1521	Condemned
1488 Scottish prize	Michael	Ship				1513	
1490 Scottish prize	Margaret (i)	Ship				1508	
1497 built Rother	Mary Fortune	Galleasse	80		Scottish war 1497, Brest 1512–13, Solent 1545	1527	Renamed Swallow 1512
1497 built Portsmouth	Sweepstake (i)	Galleasse	80		Scottish war 1497, Brest 1512–13	1527	May be Katherine Pomegranate
HENRY VIII							
1509 built Portsmouth	Mary Rose	Carrack	500	60	Brest 1512–13, Scotland 1514	1545	Capsized in battle of Solent 1545, raised 1982
1509 built Portsmouth	Peter Pomegranate	Carrack	450	60	Brest 1512–13, Scotland 1514, Solent 1545	1552	Condemned
1511 Scottish prize	Jennet or Jennet Prywin	Ship	70		Brest 1512–13, Solent 1545	1514	Captured from Scottish pirate Andrew Barton; originally named Andrew Barton
1511 Scottish prize	Lion (i)	Ship	120	36		1513	Captured from Scottish pirate Andrew Barton. Sold
1512 built	Anne Gallant (i)	Ship	140		Brest 1512–13	1518	Wrecked
1512 purchased	Christ	Ship	300		Brest 1512–13	1515	Captured by Turks
1512 purchased	Dragon (i)	Ship	100			1514	
1512 built	Henry Galley	Galley	80			1513	Lost at Sea
1512 Genoese prize	Maria de Larreto	Carrack	800		Brest 1512–13	1514	Returned to Genoa
1512 purchased Genoa	Katherine Fortileza	Carrack	550		Brest 1512–13	1521	Condemned

Date built, purchased or captured if known; otherwise first listing	Name	Type[b]	Tonnes	Guns	Battle honours * = flagship	Last recorded	Remarks: fate, where known
1512 purchased Genoa	*Gabriel Royal*	Ship	700		Brest 1512–13	1526	
1512 purchased	*John Baptist*	Ship	400	22	Brest 1512–13	1534	Wrecked
1512 purchased	*Mary George*	Ship	250		Brest 1512–13	1526	
1512 purchased	*Mary James* (i)	Ship	240		Brest 1512–13	1529	
1512 purchased	*Lizard*	Ship	120		Brest 1512–13	1522	
1512 purchased	*Great Nicholas*	Ship	400		Brest 1512–13	1522	
1512 built	*Great Bark*	Ship	250		Brest 1512–13	1531	Sold
1512	*Barbara of Greenwich*	Ship	140		Brest 1512–13	1514	
1512	*Rose Galley*	Galley	80			1521	
1512	*Katheryn Galley*	Bark	80			1524	Captured by French 1524
1512	*Less Bark*	Ship	180	109	Scotland 1514	1552	
1513	*Black Bark*		70			1514	
1513 purchased	*Great Barbara*	Carrack	400		Brest 1512–13	1524	
1513 purchased	*Henry Hampton*	Ship	120		Brest 1512–13	1521	
1513	*Mary Imperial*	Ship	100			1525	
1514 built	*Henry Grace à Dieu*	Carrack	1,500	100	Scotland 1514, Solent 1545	1553	Also known as *Great Harry*, renamed *Edward* on accession of Edward VI; burnt accidentally in Thames
1514 purchased Lübeck	*Great Elizabeth*	Carrack	900	97		1514	Wrecked off Calais escorting Mary to France
1517 built Greenwich	*Great Galley*	Galleasse	800		Scotland 1514, Solent 1545	1562	
1517 purchased	*Mary Gloria*	Ship	300			1522	
1519 built	*Katherine Bark*	Ship	100			1525	
1519	*Trinity Henry* (i)	Ship	80				
1522 French prize	*Bark of Morlaix*	Ship	60			1530	
1522 French prize	*Bark of Boulogne*	Ship	80			1525	
1522	*Great Zabra*	Pinnace	50			1525	
1522	*Less Zabra*	Pinnace	40			1525	
1522	*Magdeline*	Ship	120			1525	
1522 captured	*Mary Grace* (i)	Hoy	90			1528	
1522	*Mary and John* (ii)	Galleon				1530	
1523 captured	*John of Greenwich*	Ship	50			1555	
1523 built	*Primrose* (i)	Ship	160			1549	
1524 built	*Minion* (i)	Ship	100		Solent 1545	1539	Given to Thomas Seymour, 1549

Date built, purchased or captured if known; otherwise first listing	Name	Type[b]	Tonnes	Guns	Battle honours * = flagship	Last recorded	Remarks: fate, where known
1524 built	Mary Guildford	Ship	160				Sold
1530 built	Trinity Henry (ii)	Ship	250	64		1558	
1535 built	Sweepstake (ii)	Ship	300	84	Solent 1545	1559	
1535 built	Mary Willoughby	Ship	140	23		1573	Captured by Scots 1536, recaptured 1547
1536 built	Lion (ii)	Galleasse	140	50		1552	
1539 purchased	Matthew	Ship	600	131	Solent 1545	1558	
1539 built Portsmouth	Jennet	Galleasse	180	41	Solent 1545	1580	Converted to galleon 1558
1542 built	Dragon (ii)	Galleasse	140	45	Solent 1545	1552	
1543 built	Galley Subtile	Galley	200	31	Solent 1545	1560	Condemned
1543 built	Pauncy	Ship	450	97		1558	Condemned
1543 built	New Bark	Galleasse	200	53		1565	Converted to galleon 1558
1543 French prize	Artigo	Ship	140			1547	Sold
1544 purchased Hamburg	Jesus of Lubeck	Carrack	700	70	Solent 1545	1568	Captured by Spanish at San Juan de Ulua
1544 purchased Hamburg	Marryan	Ship	500	63		1551	Sold for £400
1544 purchased Hamburg	Struce	Ship	450	39		1552	Sold for £200
1544 purchased Hamburg	Mary Hambro	Ship	400	70	Solent 1545	1558	Sold for £20
1544	Great Pinnace	Pinnace	80	17		1545	
1544	Less Pinnace	Pinnace	40	17	Solent 1545	1549	
1544 built	Falcon	Pinnace	83	26	Solent 1545	1578	
1544 built	Swallow (ii)	Galleasse	200	26	Solent 1545, Armada 1588	1603	Converted to galleon 1558
1544 Scottish prize	Unicorn (i)	Galleasse	240	50	Solent 1545	1552	Sold for £10
1545 Scottish prize	Salamander	Galleasse	300	49	Solent 1545	1559	Condemned
1545 purchased Danzig	Christopher of Bream	Ship	400	53		1556	Sold
1545 captured	Mary Thomas	Ship	10			1546	
1545 captured	Mary James (ii)	Ship	120		Solent 1545	1546	
1545 captured	Mary Odierne	Ship	70			1545	
1545 captured	Trinity (ii)	Ship	80			1545	
1545 captured	Sacrett	Ship	160			1559	Condemned
1545 built	Roo	Pinnace	80	20	Solent 1545	1547	Captured by French
1545 French prize	Marlion	Pinnace	40	12	Solent 1545	1549	
1545 built	Saker	Pinnace	50	20	Solent 1545	1565	

Date built, purchased or captured if known; otherwise first listing	Name	Type[b]	Tonnes	Guns	Battle honours * = flagship	Last recorded	Remarks: fate, where known
1545 built	Hind	Pinnace	80	28	Solent 1545	1557	Sold for £8
1545 built	Brigantine (i)	Pinnace	40	21		1552	Captured by French
1545 built	Hare	Pinnace	15	10		1573	Sold
1545 built	Mermaid	Galley	200			1563	
1545 built	Grand Mistress	Galleasse	450	28	Solent 1545	1552	
1545 built	Anne Gallant (ii)	Galleasse	450	50	Solent 1545	1559	
1545 built	Greyhound (i)	Galleasse	200	45	Solent 1545	1562	Converted to galleon 1558, wrecked 1562
1545 built	Hope Bark	Bark	80	5		1548	
1546 purchased	George	Galleasse	80	28		1558	
1546 built	Hart	Galleasse	300	56		1568	
1546 built	Antelope	Galleasse	30	44	Armada 1588	1649	Burnt by Parliament
1546 built	Tiger (i)	Galleasse	160	43		1605	Converted to galleon 1570
1546 built	Bull	Galleasse	160	26	Armada 1588, West Indies 1595	1589	Converted to galleon 1570, renamed Adventure 1594
1546 purchased	Phoenix	Pinnace	40	37		1573	Sold
1546	Trego Reneger	Pinnace	20			1549	
1546 built	Double Rose	Rowbarge	20	9		1557	
1546 built	Flower de Luce	Rowbarge	20	9		1562	Captured by French
1546 built	Sun (i)	Rowbarge	20	8		1565	
1546 built	Portcullis	Rowbarge	20	7		1563	Condemned
1546 built	Harp	Rowbarge	20	7		1548	Sold for £165 4s. 0d.
1546 built	Cloud in the Sun	Rowbarge	20	9		1548	Sold for £165 4s. 0d
1546 built	Rose in the Sun	Rowbarge	20	10		1552	Condemned
1546 built	Hawthorne	Rowbarge	20	7		1548	Sold for £165 4s. 0d.
1546 built	Three Ostrich Feathers	Rowbarge	20	7		1548	Sold for £165 4s. 0d.
1546 built	Falcon in the Fetterlock	Rowbarge	20	11		1549	Sold for £165 4s. 0d.
1546 built	Maidenhead	Rowbarge	20	7		1552	Condemned
1546 built	Roseslip	Rowbarge	20	8		1552	Condemned
1546 built	Gillyflower	Rowbarge	20	7		1552	Condemned

Edward VI

1548	Black Pinnace	Pinnace	80	17		1548	
1548	Spanish Shallop	Pinnace	20	7		1548	
1549 French prize	Great Bark Aiger	Ship	300			1549	

Date built, purchased or captured if known; otherwise first listing	Name	Type[b]	Tonnes	Guns	Battle honours * = flagship	Last recorded	Remarks: fate, where known
1549 French prize	Black Galley	Galley	200			1549	Recaptured by French
1549	Swift	Pinnace	60			1558	
1549	Moon (i)	Pinnace	60	12		1553	Lost off Guinea
1549	Seven Stars (i)	Pinnace	60			1558	
1549	Mary Norwell	Ship	80			1549	
1549 captured	John	Ship				1549	
1549 captured	Lion (iii)	Ship				1549	Lost off Harwich
1549	Margaret (ii)	Ship	60			1549	
1549 captured	Nicholas (ii)	Ship				1549	
1549 Scottish prize	Katherine	Ship	100			1549	
1550	Small Swallow	Pinnace	30			1549	
1550	Bark of Bullen (ii)	Bark	60			1553	Given away
1550	Jer Falcon	Ship	120			1558	Condemned
1551	Edward Bonaventure	Ship	160			1556	Sailed with Chancellor and Willoughby to Russia 1553. Wrecked off Aberdeen

Mary

1554 built	Philip and Mary	Galleon	550	50	Armada 1588 Azores 1591, Cadiz 1596, Lisbon 1589,	1645	Renamed Nonpareil 1584; sold
1556 built	Mary Rose (ii)	Galleon	600	39	Armada 1588, Cadiz 1596	1618	Condemned
1557 built	Golden Lion	Galleon	600	50	Cadiz 1587, Armada 1588*, Cadiz 1596, Azores 1591	1698	Lord Thomas Howard's western squadron flagship 1588. Sold

Elizabeth

1558 French prize	Sprite	Ship	30			1559	
1558 purchased	Minion (ii)	Ship	300		San Juan de Ulua 1569	1570	Sold
1559 built	Elizabeth Jonas	Galleon	740	56	Armada 1588	1618	Condemned
1559 built Deptford	Hope (i)	Galleon	416	33	Armada 1588, West Indies 1595	1645	Broken up
1560 built	Bark of Bullen (iii)	Bark	50			1578	Sold
1560 purchased	Primrose (ii)	Ship	800	43		1575	Sold
1560 purchased	Victory (i)	Ship	530	55	Armada 1588*	1608	Hawkins's flagship 1588. Broken up.
1560 French prize	Mary Grace (ii)	Victualler	100			1562	
1560 French prize	Speedwell (i)	Galley				1580	Broken up
1560 French prize	Trywright	Galley				1579	Broken up

Date built, purchased or captured if known; otherwise first listing	Name	Type[b]	Tonnes	Guns	Battle honours * = flagship	Last recorded	Remarks: fate, where known
1561 built	*Triumph* (i)	Galleon	740	60	Armada 1588*	1618	Frobisher's flagship 1588. Condemned
1562 built Deptford	*Aid*	Ship	240	25	Armada 1588, Lisbon 1589	1599	Broken up
1562 gifted by French	*Ellynore*	Galley	180		Armada 1588	1600	Sometimes *Bonavolio*, the disgraced William Borough's command in Thames 1588
1562 built	*Post*	Brigantine				1556	
1562 built	*Makeshift* (i)	Brigantine				1564	
1562 built	*Search*	Brigantine				1564	Sold
1563 built	*White Bear*	Galleon	730	50	Armada 1588	1629	Sold
1563 built	*Guide*	Brigantine				1563	
1564	*George Hoy* (i)	Hoy	50			1585	
1562 French prize	*Serpent*	Pinnace					
1567 purchased	*Elizabeth Bonaventure*	Galleon	600	47	Cadiz 1587, Armada 1588, West Indies 1595, Azores 1591	1611	Broken up
1570 built	*Foresight*	Galleon	295	30	Armada 1588, West Indies 1595, Lisbon 1589, Azores 1591	1611	Broken up
1573 built Deptford	*Dreadnought*	Galleon	360	40	Cadiz 1587, Armada 1588, Cadiz 1596	1648	Broken up
1573 built Deptford	*Swiftsure* (i)	Pinnace	350	40	Armada 1588, Lisbon 1589	1624	Lost off Flushing
1573 built	*Swallow* (iii)	Pinnace	40	8	Armada 1588	1603	Condemned
1573 built Deptford	*Achates*	Ship	100	20	Armada 1588	1605	Sold
1573 built Deptford	*Handmaid*	Ship	90			1600	
1577	*Elizabeth* (i)	Pinnace	40	16			
1577 built	*Revenge*	Galleon	450	46	Armada 1588*, Azores 1591*, Lisbon 1589	1591	Drake's flagship 1588. Foundered after battle of Azores 1591
1577 built Deptford	*Scout*	Bark	140	20	Armada 1588	1604	Condemned
1578	*Dennis*	Explorer				1578	Lost in Arctic
1579 built	*Merlin*	Pinnace	50	10	Armada 1588	1607	
1583	*Delight*	Explorer	120			1583	Wrecked
1583	*Desire* (i)	Explorer					
1583 built	*Brigantine* (ii)	Ship	90		Armada 1588		
1585	*Talbot*	Ship					
1585	*Greyhound* (ii)	Ship					

Date built, purchased or captured if known; otherwise first listing	Name	Type[b]	Tonnes	Guns	Battle honours * = flagship	Last recorded	Remarks: fate, where known
1585 built	Pegasus	Ship				1599	Lost at sea
1585 built	Cygnet	Pink	30	3	Cadiz 1587, Armada 1588	1603	Condemned
1586 built Deptford	Rainbow	Galleon	384	60	Cadiz 1587, Armada 1588*, Cadiz 1596	1680	Flagship of Admiral Henry Seymour's eastern squadron 1588. Sunk as breakwater at Sheerness
1586 built Woolwich	Vanguard	Bark	449	60	Armada 1588*, Cadiz 1596	1667	Flagship of Vice-Admiral Winter's eastern squadron 1588. Sunk as breakwater, raised and sold
1586 built Deptford	Tramontana	Galley	132	21	Armada 1588, Cadiz 1596	1618	Broken up
1586 built Chatham	Seven Stars (ii)	Pinnace	140	5			First naval vessel built at Chatham
1586 built Woolwich	Charles (i)	Pinnace	70	16	Armada 1588, Cadiz 1596	1616	
1586 built Deptford	Moon (ii)	Pinnace	59	9	Armada 1588, Cadiz 1596, Azores 1591	1626	Condemned
1586 built Woolwich	Advice	Pinnace	42	9	Armada 1588	1617	Sold
1586 built Chatham	Sun (ii)	Pinnace	39	9	Armada 1588		
1586 built Limehouse	Makeshift (ii)	Pinnace	49	9		1591	Lost at sea
1586 built Limehouse	Spy (i)	Pinnace	42	9	Cadiz 1587, Armada 1588	1613	
1586 built	Trust	Pinnace				1586	
1587 built Deptford	Ark Royal	Galleon	550	55	Armada 1588*, Cadiz 1596	1636	Built by Ralegh as Ark Ralegh. Lord Howard's flagship 1588. Wrecked off Tilbury
1587 built	Popinjay	Galleon				1601	Condemned
1588 Spanish prize	Rosario	Carrack	1,150	46		1622	Broken up
1588 purchased	George Hoy (ii)	Hoy	100		Armada 1588		
1588	Larke	Pinnace	50				
1588	Defence	Ship	160		West Indies 1595	1599	
1588	Violet	Ship	220				
1589 purchased	Dainty		200			1594	Captured in South Pacific by Spanish when Sir Richard Hawkins in command
1590 built Deptford	Defiance	Galleon	440	45	Azores 1591	1650	Sold
1590 built Deptford	Garland	Galleon	532	50	West Indies 1595	1618	
1590 built	Answer	Galleon	220	21		1629	Sold

Date built, purchased or captured if known; otherwise first listing	Name	Type[b]	Tonnes	Guns	Battle honours * = flagship	Last recorded	Remarks: fate, where known
1590 built	*Advantage*	Galleon	170	18		1613	Burnt
1590 built	*Crane*	Galleon	200	24	Cadiz 1596, Azores 1591	1629	Sold
1590 built	*Quittance*	Galleon	215	25	Cadiz 1596	1618	Condemned
1590 captured	*Black Dog*	Ship	120			1590	
1590 built Woolwich	*Mer Honeur*	Galleon	690	41	Cadiz 1596*	1650	Lord Thomas Howard's flagship 1596. Sold
1590	*Lion's Whelp* (i)	Pinnace				1591	Lost at sea
1591 built	*Primrose Hoy*	Hoy	80			1618	Condemned
1591 French prize	*French Frigate*	Pinnace	15	2		1618	Condemned
1592	*Flight*					1592	
1592 built Deptford	*Mercury*	Galley	80	6		1611	Sold
1592 purchased	*Eagle*	Hulk	895			1683	Sold
1592	*Flirt*	Ship				1592	
1593 built Bristol	*Hawk*	Discovery	100			1593	
1594	*Minnikin*	Ship				1595	
1594 built Deptford	*Adventure*	Galleon	275	26		1645	Broken up
1595 built Deptford	*Due Repulse*	Galleon	620	50	Cadiz 1596*	1645	Earl of Essex's flagship 1596
1595	*Francis*	Discovery				1595	Captured by Spanish
1596	*Warspite*	Galleon	520	35	Cadiz 1596*	1645	Sir Walter Ralegh's flagship 1596. Sold
1596 Spanish prize	*St Andrew*	Galleon	900	50		1604	Captured Cadiz 1596. Given away
1596 Spanish prize	*St Matthew*	Galleon	1,000	50		1604	Captured Cadiz 1596. Given away
1597	*Splendid*	Ship				1597	
1599	*Daisy*	Pink		4		1599	
1599 built	*Bear* (i)			2		1599	
1600	*Discovery*	Discovery				1620	
1601 purchased	*Lion's Whelp* (ii)	Ketch	90	11		1625	Given away
1601 built Deptford	*La Superlativa*	Galley	100	7		1618	Condemned
1601 built Woolwich	*La Advantagia*	Galley	100	7		1618	Condemned
1602 built Deptford	*La Volatilla*	Galley	100	7		1618	Condemned
1602 built Limehouse	*La Gallarita*	Galley	100	7		1618	Condemned

a. Based on the exemplary research of Arthur Nelson in *The Tudor Navy*.
b. Pinks and Hoys were small victualling supply ships; a brigantine was a small two-masted vessel generally used around the coast, similar to a ketch.

Appendix 3
A Ship's Company

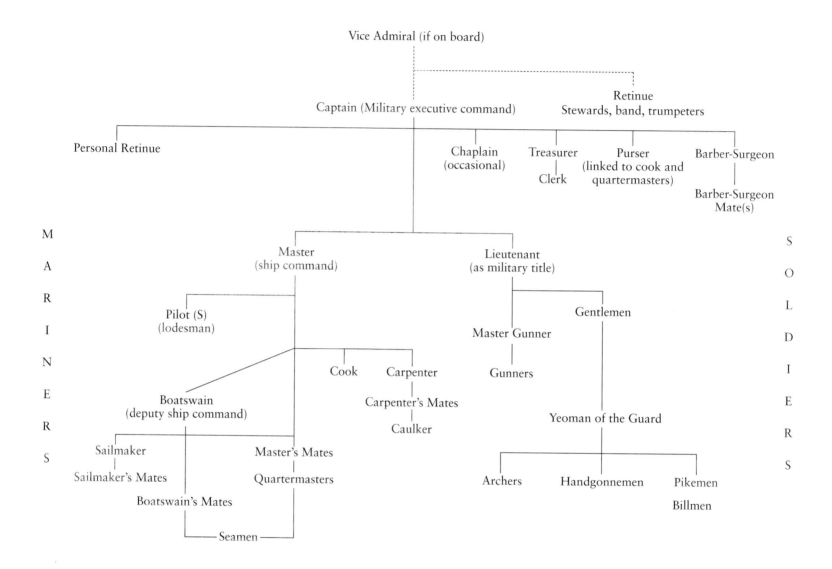

Appendix 4

Gun Drills for Breech-Loading and Muzzle-Loading Guns

There is no record of gunnery drill orders for the firing of naval weaponry, but a system must have existed to ensure the safe and efficacious use of ordnance. Drill A is based on the research work of Nicholas Hall of the Royal Armouries and Alexzandra Hildred of the Mary Rose Trust.[i]

A. Breech loader, e.g. port piece

Elevate gun by lowering back of sledge on to ground, remove elevating post, check barrel-retaining ropes
Remove forelock, wedge and chamber
Place chamber to rear of gun (left)
Clean chamber
Load with cartridge, wadding
Ram
Insert tampion and hammer flush with chamber mouth
Lay down chamber, insert handspikes
Load projectile into breech end of barrel and hold
Lay chamber in sledge, remove handspikes
Use handspikes to drive chamber forward; insert forelock and wedge
Drive home chamber by striking wedge
Check alignment and fit of chamber to barrel
Place elevating post in socket
Depress the gun by raising the trail
Lay for line
Elevate or depress as required and position retaining peg at position requested by gun captain sighting
Check recoil ropes and barrel-retaining ropes
GIVE FIRE

Knock out forelock and remove wedge
Insert handspikes and remove chamber
Elevate and remove post
Upend chamber and sponge
Examine for any residue
Clear vent
The gun crew required to carry out this drill was a minimum of six.

B. Muzzle loader, e.g. culverin

Put back your Peece
Order your Peece to load
Search your Peece
Spunge your Peece
Fill your Ladle
Put in your Powder
Empty your Ladle
Put up your Powder
Thrust home your wad
Regard your shot
Put home your shot gently
Thrust home your last wad with three strokes
Gage your Peece
GIVE FIRE

[i] A Hall, in Hildred, *Weapons of Warre: The Armaments of the Mary Rose.*

Appendix 5

Keeping it in the Family: The Tudor and Howard Lord High Admirals

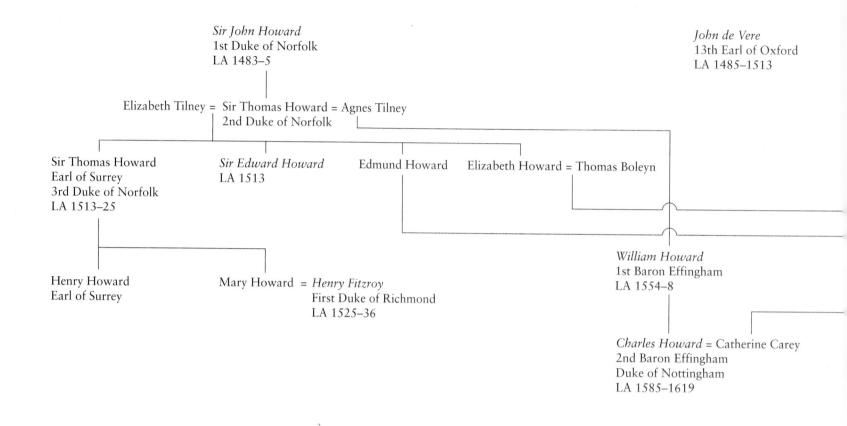

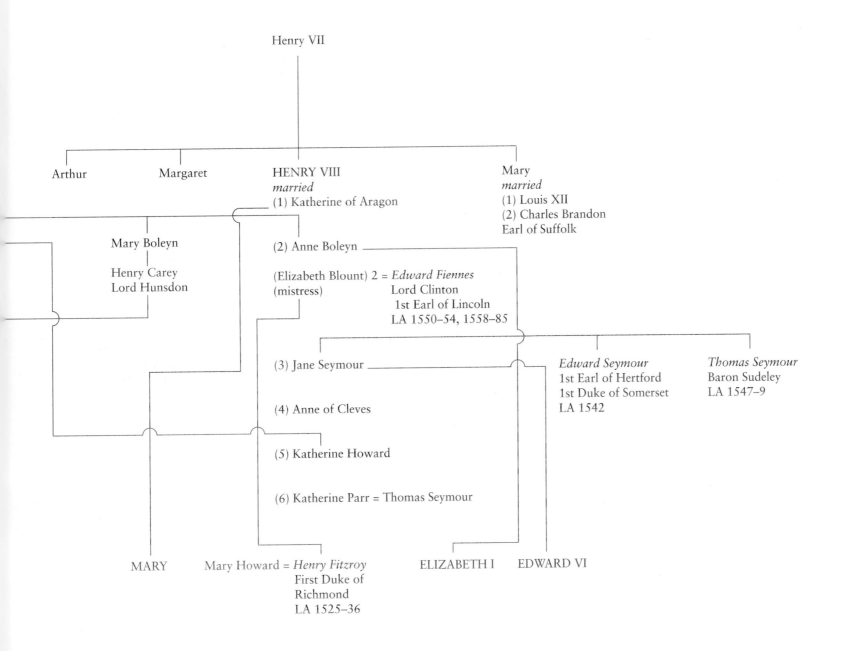

Henry VII

Arthur   Margaret   HENRY VIII
                      married
                      (1) Katherine of Aragon

Mary
married
(1) Louis XII
(2) Charles Brandon
Earl of Suffolk

Mary Boleyn

Henry Carey
Lord Hunsdon

(2) Anne Boleyn

(Elizabeth Blount) 2 = *Edward Fiennes*
(mistress)   Lord Clinton
                          1st Earl of Lincoln
                          LA 1550–54, 1558–85

(3) Jane Seymour

Edward Seymour
1st Earl of Hertford
1st Duke of Somerset
LA 1542

Thomas Seymour
Baron Sudeley
LA 1547–9

(4) Anne of Cleves

(5) Katherine Howard

(6) Katherine Parr = Thomas Seymour

MARY   Mary Howard = *Henry Fitzroy*
                      First Duke of
                      Richmond
                      LA 1525–36

ELIZABETH I   EDWARD VI

Lord Admirals Appointed from Outside the Houses of Tudor and Howard
John de Vere was the son of the 12th Earl of Oxford and Elizabeth Howard, first cousin to the 1st Duke of Norfolk
William FitzWilliam, 1st Earl of Southampton, 1536–40, was half-brother of Sir Anthony Browne, Master of King's Horse
John Lord Russell, 1st Earl of Bedford, 1540–42
John Dudley, Lord Lisle, 1st Earl of Warwick, Duke of Northumberland 1543–7, 1549, was son of Henry VII, tax gatherer
and Speaker of the House of Commons, and father of Elizabeth's favourite, Earl of Leicester

LA = Lord Admiral

Appendix 6

Officials of the Navy Royal

Lord Admiral

1483 John Howard, First Duke of Norfolk
1485 John de Vere, Thirteenth Earl of Oxford
1513, March Sir Edward Howard
1513, May Lord Thomas Howard, Earl of Surrey, Third Duke of Norfolk
1525 Henry Fitzroy, First Duke of Richmond
1536 William Fitzwilliam, First Duke of Southampton
1540 John Lord Russell, First Earl of Bedford
1542 Edward Seymour, First Earl of Hertford
1543 John Dudley, Viscount Lisle, First Earl of Warwick
1547 Thomas Lord Seymour
1549 Lord Lisle, First Earl of Warwick
1550 Edward Fiennes, Lord Clinton, First Earl of Lincoln
1554 William Howard, First Lord Howard of Effingham
1558 Lord Clinton
1585 Charles Howard, Second Lord Howard of Effingham, First Earl of Nottingham

Clerk of Ships

1485 Thomas Roger
1488 William Commersall
1495 Robert Brygandyne
1523 Thomas Jermyn
1538 Edmund More

Clerk Controller

1512 John Hopton
1524 Thomas Sperte
1540 John Osborne
1545 William Broke

Keeper of Storehouses

1524 William Gonson
1545 Richard Howlett
1548 William Holstock

Officers of the Navy from 1546

Lieutenant (Vice-Admiral)

1546 Sir Thomas Clere
1552–65 Sir William Woodhouse (office discontinued on death of Woodhouse)

Treasurer

1546 Robert Legge
1549 Benjamin Gonson
1578 Sir John Hawkins
1595 Roger Longford
1598–1604 Fulke Greville, First Lord Broke

Surveyor and Rigger

1546 Benjamin Gonson
1549 Sir William Winter
1589 Sir Henry Palmer
1598–1611 Sir John Trevor

Master of Naval Ordnance

1546 Sir William Woodhouse
1552–3 Sir Thomas Wyndham
1557 William Winter (already Surveyor – discontinued 1589)

Controller

1546 William Broke
1561 William Holstock
1589 William Borough
1598–1611 Sir Henry Palmer

Clerk of Ships

1546 Richard Howlett
1560 George Winter
1588 Benjamin Gonson jnr
1600 Peter Buck

Surveyor of Victuals

1550 Edward Baeshe
1587 James Quarles
1595 Marmaduke Darrell

Appendix 7

Visiting the Tudor Navy

Although only one original ship from our Tudor past remains, sufficient replicas and buildings on shore exist to excite the imagination and provide the student or enthusiast of any age with a feel for what life must have been like for the sixteenth-century seafarer.

Ships
Mary Rose
HM Naval Base, Portsmouth, Hants: www.maryrose.org; telephone 02392 750521
The raising of *Mary Rose* in 1982 was watched on television by millions of people world-wide. The recovery of the ship's starboard side and its restoration made available for viewing the only remnant we have of a Tudor ship, but of equal importance are the thousands of artefacts that were recovered at the same time. The display of these, in the museum at Portsmouth, really does give the visitor a wonderful opportunity to see how the Tudor seamen lived. From cannon to combs and cooking, all is displayed, making a visit a truly memorable experience. The quality of visit will be further enhanced when, thanks to a grant from the National Lottery, a new museum opens in 2012.
Golden Hind
Brixham harbour, Brixham, Devon: www.goldenhind.co.uk; telephone 01803 856223
Open daily from March to the end of October, *Golden Hind* provides a wonderful opportunity to wander around a replica of the ship in which Francis Drake sailed around the world. A great deal of attention is paid to delighting the younger visitor, and the programme does often involve pirates; not historically accurate but great fun.
Golden Hinde
St Mary Overie Dock, Cathedral Street, Southwick, London: www.goldenhinde.org; telephone 020 7403 0123
Skilled costumed interpreters work hard to bring Drake's flagship to life, and a hands-on approach is encouraged. The site is also close to the reconstruction of Shakespeare's Globe Theatre and other historic parts of the Thames waterfront, making it well worth while to spend a day in the area.

Matthew

Great Western Dockyard, Gas Ferry Road, Bristol: www.matthew.co.uk; telephone 0117 927 6868

This reconstruction of the ship in which John Cabot sailed to Newfoundland not only is berthed close to her original dock but lies alongside the SS *Great Britain*, thus increasing the value of a visit. The opportunity to experience what life must have been like for those pioneer explorers is not one that should be missed by anyone interested in the age of discovery.

The Alderney Wreck

Alderney Museum, The Old School House, High Street, St Anne's, Alderney: www.alderneywreck.com

Discovered in 1997, this is the most exciting find since *Mary Rose* was raised. The ship, as yet unnamed, sank in 1592 and thus represents, small as she is, the final chapter in Tudor naval history. Careful and well-argued research has produced a most excellent website, giving each artefact has a significance well beyond its immediate provenance.

Fortifications

English Heritage: www.english-heritage.org.uk

Most of Henry VIII's surviving coastal fortifications, along with Elizabeth's castle at Upnor near Chatham, are in the custodial care of English Heritage, although some, such as Southsea Castle, are cared for by local authorities. Their state of repair, and later modifications, make them a varied bunch, but, as they range from the Thames to Falmouth, there is always one within reach of the visitor to the south coast. The following are just a selection, moving from the Thames down the Channel in a clockwise direction:

Tilbury Fort: There is no evidence in this later structure of the site where Elizabeth made her rallying speech to her troops during the Armada campaign.

Upnor Castle: A most beautiful small castle and one of the few to have seen action, during the Dutch attack on the Medway in 1667, the nadir of British naval power.

Deal and Walmer castles: Deal Castle is one of the best preserved and most comprehensible of these fortifications; nearby is Walmer Castle, which has been much altered to fulfil its position as the official residence of the Lord Warden of the Cinque Ports.

Hurst Castle: The castle here was probably a manned military fortification for longer than the others and so has been extensively added to and modified. Nevertheless, a walk along the shingle spit (or a ferry ride from Lymington) is well rewarded both by the position of this isolated windswept fort and it contents.

Yarmouth Castle: Built on the Isle of Wight, opposite Hurst, this is another gem of a castle, well worth a ferry ride from Lymington.

Portland Castle: From here one can look down on the waters where Frobisher challenged the Spaniards to close and engage during the Armada campaign. It later was fought over during the Civil War. Its interior has, however, been much altered.

Pendennis and St Mawes castles: On either side of the entrance to Falmouth harbour, these twin castles have a history of activity that stretches up to the present. St Mawes is probably the best preserved of Henry's forts and is an architectural gem. Pendennis, much larger, has also had many more alterations.

Other Fortifications

Southsea Castle

Clarence Esplanade, Southsea: www.southseacastle.co.uk; telephone 02392 827261

Another castle that saw action during the repulse of the French in 1545, during which action *Mary Rose* sank, her foundering witnessed by Henry from the castle.

Portsmouth, Round and Square towers and walls

Tudor Portsmouth lies hidden away, but a walk along the sea-front from Southsea Castle to the Camber takes in England's most historic anchorage and is always full of interest.

Houses

National Trust: www.nationaltrust.org.uk; telephone 0844 800 1895

Although early English houses are a feature of the National Trust's property portfolio, those with a maritime link are few. The best to visit are:

Buckland Abbey, Devon: Home of both Sir Richard Grenville and then Sir Francis Drake, the artefacts include Drake's drum and many other links to Drake's occupancy.

Compton Castle, Devon: The family home of the Gilberts and a fine example of a fortified manor house.

Smallhythe Place, Tenterden, Kent: A half-timbered house built in the sixteenth century when the village was a bustling shipbuilding site. Nearby is the house that was owned by Brygandyne, project manager of the building of *Mary Rose* (at Portsmouth) and *Mary Fortune*, which, along with *Regent*, was built at Tenterden.

Tudor Merchant's House, Tenby, Pembrokeshire: A fine three-storey house furnished to show how a Tudor merchant lived.

Other Properties

Tudor Merchant's House, Southampton Bugle Street, Southampton: www.southampton.gov.uk/leisure/heritage; telephone 023 8065 5904

Tudor Southampton, lying close to the city's medieval walls, is a hidden gem just a short walk from the bustling shopping centre. John Dawtrey's house is the major attraction and is being magnificently restored thanks to a grant from the National Lottery. The wealth of those who were involved in providing logistic support to the navy is made no more obvious than within the walls of this great building.

Sea Captain's House, Barbican, Plymouth 33 New Street, Barbican: www.plymouth.gov.uk; telephone 01752 304774

At no other site in the country can one feel that one is walking on the cobbles and floorboards that were trodden by Hawkins and Drake. Nearby are the Mayflower steps where the Pilgrim Fathers embarked for the final time before setting out for America.

National Maritime Museum

Greenwich, London: www.nmm.ac.uk; telephone 020 8858 4422

The museum has a fine display of Tudor navigational instruments, charts and globes as well as a wonderful collection of contemporary drawings and paintings, most of which are not on display but the ever-helpful custodians are swift to respond to any request. At the time of writing there is a permanent exhibition on the subject of 'Tudor Exploration'.

Index

Page numbers in *italics* refer to illustrations

A

Act of Maintenance of the Navy (1540), 12
'Admiral' of Sluys, 183
Admiralty Board, 263
Admiralty, Court of, 182, 185, 195, 188, 266
Americas, settlements, 198
amphibious operations, 140, 142, 152, 239
Anian, Straits of, 153, 155
Anne of Cleves, 107
Anthony Anthony and Anthony Rolls, 20, 32, 39, 42, 48, 74
Antonio, Dom, 179, 241
archery, bows and arrows, 79–81, 89
Armada, Spanish, 74, 91–4, 120, 164, 165, 176, 224, 234
arquebus, muskets, 81
astronomical observations, 140, 142, 151, 152
Audley, Sir Thomas, Lord Audley, 60, 75, 131
avarice, 181
Avellanda, Bernardino, 243
Azores:
    Fayal, 245
    Flores, 212
    Island Voyage (1597), 244
    strategic importance, 79, 211
    Terceira, 213

B

Badoer, Andrea, 207
Baeshe, Edward, 86, 90
Baker, Matthew, shipwright, 35, 253
ballast, 49, 128
Barber Surgeons, 123
barrels, *86*, 89
Barton, Sir Andrew, 182, 204
Baskerville, Sir Thomas, 30, 78, 216
battles:
    Azores (Flores) (1591), 212
    Gravelines (1588), 227
    Isle of Pines (1596), 216
    Lepanto (1571), 202
    Pinkie Cleugh (1547), *108*
    Pointe de Ste. Matthieu (1512), 206
    Punta Delgada (1582), 202
    Terceira (1582), 202, 213
    The Solent (1545), 71, 217

White Sands Bay (1513), 30, 207
Zonchio (1499), 69, *201*
Bazan, Don Alvaro de, Marquis de Santa Cruz, 91, 179, 202
Bazan, Alonso de, 212
beacons, 262
beer and brewing, 95, 96
Bellay, Martin du, 21
Bergenhier, Jacques, 60
Berkeley, Sir John, 60
Bertendona, Martin de, 212, 226
Berthaume Bay, 206
Bidoux, Prégent de, 26, 207
Blavet, 245
Blount, Elizabeth, 108
boarding, opposed, 66, 132, 203, 205, 230
boats, 28, 29
boatswains, 121
boatswains' calls, 121, *164*
Book of Sea Causes, 135
booty, 132, 184, 194
Bordeaux, 13
Boulogne, *15*, 110
Bourne, William, 70, 74, 150, 153
Borough, Sir John, 191
Borough, Stephen, 144, 150
Borough, Sir William, 150, 221
Boulogne, 110, *267*
Brandon, Charles, Viscount Lisle, Duke of Suffolk, 14, 175
Bray, Sir Reginald, 36
Brest, 'The Trade', *17*, 97, 103, 205, *206*
Bridport, 40, 47
Brighton, 30, *236*
Bristol, 40
Brittany, 40
broadsides, 76, 235
Browne, Sir Anthony, 14, 173
Brygandyne, Robert, Clerk of the Ships, 36, 38, 39, 46, 53, 252
Bull, Sir Stephen, 207
Burghley, William Cecil, Lord, 41, 85, 87, *257*, 258, 263

C

Cabot, John, 146, 147
Cabot, Sebastian 129, 130
Cadiz, 236, *244*, *245*
    expeditions to (1587), 221; (1596), 243
Caesar, Sir Julius, Admiralty Court Judge, 16

Calais, 14, 33
    loss of, 104, 170, 172, 226
Camber, The, 172, 182, 185
Cape Horn, 154
Cape of Good Hope, 155
Cape Verde Islands, 153, 241
capture, of seamen, 117
careening, 54
Carew, Sir George, 101, 121, 184
Carew, Sir Peter, 102
Carey, Sir George, Lord Hunsdown, 210
Carleill, Christopher, 240
carpenter, ship's, 122
Cartagena, 190
carvel building, 36
Casa de la Contratación, 143, 144, 195
Castillon, French Ambassador, 37, 40, 184
Castlehaven, 239
Cathay, 14, 147, 148, 197
Cattewater, 175, 223
caulking, 53
Cavendish, Thomas, 156, 178, 203
Cecil, Robert, 192, 195
Celebes, The, 155
Cezimbra, 237
chain mail, *82*
Channel, The English, 162, 170, 214, 223
Channel Islands, 235
Chapuys, Eustace, 26, 249
Charles V, Holy Roman Emperor, 25, 26, 101, 186
charts, 150
Chatham, 167, 253
Chatham Chest, 265
Cinque Ports, 171
Clere, Sir Thomas, 90, 102
Clermont, René de, 206
clinker building, 36
Clinton, Edward Fiennes, 1st Earl of Lincoln, 49, 103, *104*, 108, 237, 238
clothing of crew, 120
coastal defences, 169, 260
    castles and forts:
    Deal, 261
    Dover, *259*
    Flamborough Head, 208
    Hurst, 173
    Plymouth, 177
    Scarborough, 242
    Southsea, 177

Upnor, 261
Walmer, 261
combs, 127
convoys, 182, 185, 205
cooking, 129, 130
Corunna, 93, 95, 225, *240*
Council for Marine Causes, 90, 263
Cowdray, engraving, 60, 163, *173*, *219*
Cromwell, Thomas, 37, 39, 171, 249, 255
Cross, Sir Robert, 191
Crozon, 237
Cumberland, George Clifford, Earl of, 73, 114, 190, *198*, 204, 246

D

daggers, 82
damage control, 132
D'Annebault, Claude, 218, 220
Darcy, Lord, 14, 86
Dartmouth, 148, 173, 175, 192
Dawtry, John, 86, 89, 97, 176
deadeyes, *47*
Dee, John, 144, 188, 269
Delft, van de, 27
Deptford, 139, 167, 252
desertion, 98
Devereux, Robert, 2nd Earl of Essex, 238
Devereux, Walter, 1st Earl of Essex, *105*, 244, 245
discipline, 131, 132
disease and sickness, 94, 125, 126
Donne, John, 52, 243
Dorset, Earl of, 14, 86
Dover, 170
Downs, The, 169, 183
Drake, Edmund, 15, 167
Drake, John, 117
Drake, Sir Francis, 22, *113*
    Armada campaign, 92, 95, 223
    circumnavigation, 17, 41, 54, 143, 151 *et seq*
    death, 242
    expeditions (1587), 95; (1589), 105, 241; (1595), 22, 24, 97, 242
    in Ireland, 24
dry docks, 250, 251
Dudley, John, Viscount Lisle, Duke of Northumberland, 63, 110, 125, 169, 208
    attempted coup, 103
    piracy patrols, 183, 184
    victualling concerns, 90

E

East India Company, 198

Echingham, Sir Edward, 90
Edward VI:
    death of Seymour, 110
    interest in navigation, 102
    view of England, 16
    visits Portsmouth, 173
Elizabeth I, *100, 105*
    Armada campaign, 223
    caution, 104
    commander-in-chief, as, 104, 241, 268
    parsimony, 188, 194
    ship building, 33
England:
    living conditions in, 15, 94, 99, 115
    population, 16
    seafaring, 11
    state of nation, 14
Enriquez, Don Martin, 161
Erasmus, view of the English, 15
Etaples, 110

F

Falmouth, 177
Ferdinand, King of Aragon, 207
Fighting Instructions, 270, 271
fire fighting, 132
fireships, 82, 83, 93
FitzRoy, Henry, Duke of Richmond, 106
FitzWilliam, Sir William, Earl of Southampton, 37, *105*, 106, 107, 159, 170
flags and bunting, 48
Flanders, 62
Fletcher, Francis, 41, *155*
Fontaines des Anglais, *265*
Fortescue, Sir John, 62
Framlingham, 103
Frobisher, Sir Martin, 124, 144, 148, 149

G

gambling, 130
Gascony, 16
Gilbert, Sir Humphrey, 147, 148, 156, 162
Gillingham, 167, 170
Goodwins, The, 169
Gonson, Benjamin, 263
Gonson, William, 90, 107, 263
Greenwich, 167
Grenville, Sir Richard, 30, 212
Guinea:
    fight, 208
    voyages, 198
gunfounding, 58, 62
gun chambers, *59*, 67
gun drills, 60, 76

gun ports, 51, 64
gun range, 77, 78
gun shot, *64*
guns: characteristics:
    rate of fire, 73
    ship fits, 61–71
    types:
        basilisks, 58
        bombards, 64
        breech-loading, *59*
        bronze, *58*, 61
        cannon, 61
        cannon perrier, 64
        cast iron, 63
        culverins, 61, *62*
        demi-culverins, 61, 63, *67*
        falcons, 64
        murderers, 58
        muzzle-loading, 62
        port pieces, 58, *60*
        sakers, 61, 63
        serpentines, 58
        slings, *59*
        stern chasers, 42
        swivel, 67
        wrought iron, 58
gunners, 73–5
gunpowder, 72
guns, man-killing/ship-sinking, 216
gunsmiths, 63

H

Hakluyt, Richard, 60, 147, 156
Hamble River 249, 255
Hawkins, Sir John, *15, 256*
    design of galleons, 28
    shipbuilding reforms, 256–9, 264
    St Juan de Ulua, 209
Hawkins, Sir Richard, 67, 142
hawsers, 47
health, of seamen, 90, 93–4, 123–9
Henry V, 36
Henry VII, 14, 16, *16*, 20, 21, 31, 36, 37, 53, 61, 104, 167, 172, 249, 250–1, 252, 254
Henry VIII:
    as commander-in-chief, 101, 102
    coastal defences, 251–3
    Portsmouth, 102
    shipbuilding, 38, 207
    ship launching, 38, 207
    wars against France, 206
Hopton, John, 182
Hore, Richard, 147
hour glass, 141

Howard of Effingham, Charles, 1st Earl of
Nottingham:
    Armada campaign, 223 *et seq*
    avarice, 181, 264
    care of men, 94, 109, 116
    leadership, 109
Howard of Effingham, William, 91, 109
Howard, Sir Edward:
    actions off Brittany, 30, 206, 207
    death, 207
    fights Andrew Barton, 31, 182
    sailing race, 158
    victualling concerns, 8
Howard, Lord Thomas, Earl of Surrey, 3rd
Duke of Norfolk:
    fights Andrew Barton, 31, 182
    personality, 106, 246
    relationship with Wolsey, 106
    victualling concerns, 88
Howard, Lord Thomas, 1st Earl of Suffolk,
22, 212, 245
Hull, Kingston upon, 185

I

Iceland, 87
impressments, 116, 117
incenderies, 69
intelligence, 246, 266
Ireland, 238
Isle of Pines, 161

J

James IV, 38
James VI, 17, 33
Johnson, Henry, 63
Jones, Dr Mark, 35

K

Katherine of Aragon, Queen, 25
Killigrew, Peter, 188
Kings Lynn, 47, 48
Kinsale, 234
Knyvet, Sir Thomas, 90, 112, 206

L

Lancaster, Sir James, 24, 60, 83, 115, *192*
latitude, 151
Le Conquet, 237
Le Havre, 246
letters of marquee, reprisal, 185
Leveson, Sir Richard, 104, 114, 234, 237
linstocks, 59, 125
Lisbon, 30, 73
Locronan, 40

longitude, 153

M

maintenance, of ships, 32, 249
Malen, John, 238
Malines, 58
manning, of ships, 74, 205
Mansell, Sir Robert, 237
Mary I:
    as commander-in-chief, 103
    encouragement of learning, 144
    loss of Calais, 104
    naval budget, 103
    shipbuilding, 33
Margate, 85, 94, 158
master gunners, 73, 74
McKee, Alexander, 35, 194
Medina Sidonia, Duke of, 75, 105, 226, 231
Medway, 167, 173, 253
Mercator, Ferdinand, 148, 155
Monson, Sir William, 55, 78, 114, 203, 226,
237
Morlaix, 237
music, musical instruments, 130, 131

N

naval expenses, 195
Navigation Acts, 12
navigation, instruments, 152, 153
navigation theory, 144, 154
Navy Board, 90, 253
Navy Royal, 19, 33
Newfoundland, 87, 156
Newcastle upon Tyne, 13
Norfolk *see* Howard
Norris, Sir John, 30, 105, 124, 238
North-West Passage, the, 148, 154

O

Oliviera, Fernando, 26
Oquendo, Miguel de, 226
Ordinary, ships in, 252, 254, 257, 258
ordnance *see* guns
Owen, brothers, gun founders, 62
Oxenham, John, 189

P

Palmer, Henry, 185
Parma, Alexander Farnese, Duke of, 71, 105,
224, 226
Parr, Katherine, 110
pay, 75, 97, 99
Petty Navy Royal, 144, 188
Philip II, of Spain, 16, 95, 103, 173, 190,

212, 220, 223
Piers, William, 187
pilotage:
    charts, *10*, 138
    compasses, 138, 140
    lead and line, 142
    log and line, 141
    passage planning, 137, 159
    passage speed, 159
    tides, 138
pilots:
    John Bartelot, 143
    Nuno da Silva, 143, 153
    John Wodlas, 169, 172
pirates, piracy, 182, 188
Plantagenet, Arthur, Viscount Lisle, 39, 112,
162
plunder, 181, 185
Plymouth, Plymouth Sound, 92, 156, 175, 224
Poole, *153*, 174
Poppenreuter, Hans, 58
Portsmouth, 90, 96, 126, 137, 139, 172,
250, 251
Portzmoguer, Hervé de, 112
Privy Council, 72, 89, 90, 94, 103, 111, 125,
140, 169, 172, 173, 177, 185, 212, 221,
222, 246, 258
prizes, prize money, 55, 187, 193, 204, 222,
237

Q

Quarles, James, 92, 96
quartermasters, 121

R

Rainsborrow, Captain William, 65
Ralegh, Sir Walter, 112, 148, 190, 192, 196,
243
Rathlin Island, 238
Recalde, Juan Martinez, 225
religion, 133–6
Reneger, Robert, 186
religion, 133, 135
Roanoke, 198
Rogers, Thomas,
rope walks, 47
Rother, river, 38
Rule, Dr Margaret, 35
Russell, Lord John, 1st Earl of Bedford, 14,
107, 187
Rut, John, 147
'rutter', 138
Rye, 182, 183, 187, 208

S

Saint Helen's, 219
San Juan de Puerto Rico, 24, 242, 246
San Lucar de Barrameda, 240
Sandwich, 96
Santander, 93
Scaramelli, Giovanni, 187
Scotland, 16, 208
seamanship, 158
seamen:
    conditions of service, 115, 117
    clothing, 120
    personal hygiene, 127, 128
    skeletons, 125
Seymour, Edward, 1st Earl of Hertford, Duke of Somerset, 14, 63, 107, 110
Seymour, Sir Henry, 224
Seymour, Jane, 110
Seymour, Sir Thomas, 16, 30, 110, 111, 161, 187
Shakespeare, William, 122, 147, 169, 197, 201
shear hooks, 66
shipbuilding:
    anchors, 55
    bulkheads, 51
    carvel method, 36
    castles, 44, 52
    clinker method, 36
    decks:
        main, 51
        orlop, 50
        upper, 53
    fighting top, 69
    frame, 43
    hatches, 50
    hold, 45
    keel, 41
    keelson, 41
    masts, 45
    planking, 43, 44
    pumps, 50
    rigging, 46
    rudder, 42
    sails, sail cloth, 40, 48
    stem, 42
    stern, 42
    wales, 44
    whipstaff, 43
    yards, 46
shipkeepers, 98
ship's bell, 142
ship handling, 158, 162
ship losses: English; Spanish Armada, 231

ship names, 40
ship purchases, 55
ship types:
    carrack, 20
    frigate, 24
    galleasse, 21, 77
    galleon, 28, 66–8
    galley, 25–8, 26, 77, 234, 235
    gallizabra, 212
    pinnace, 22
    rowbarge, 27, 32
    victuallers, 90
ship worm, 53
ships' boats, 28
ships
    English:
    (see Appendix 2 for full list)
    Advantage, 28, 48
    Aid, 227
    Alderney wreck, 68
    Amity, 193
    Anne Gallant, 22, 26, 235
    Antelope, 22
    Anthony Craddock, 40
    Ark Royal (*Ark Ralegh*), 28, 29, 48, 190
    Black Pinnace, 23
    Bull, 22, 28
    Centurion, 211
    Christ, 32
    Content, 210
    Dainty, 67
    Dreadnought, 41, 221, 236
    Elizabeth Bonaventure, 24, 28, 221, 240
    Elizabeth Jonas, 41, 94
    Falcon, 148
    Foresight, 28, 191
    Foyst, 26
    Gabriel Royal, 41
    Gallion Reneger, 186
    Galley Blanchard, 26
    Galley Subtil, 26, 27
    George Noble, 213
    Gillyflower, 28
    Golden Hind (formerly *Pelican*), 24, 35–41, 52, 67
    Golden Hind (pinnace), 247
    Golden Lion, 33, 221
    Grace Dieu, 36
    Grand Mistress, 235
    Great Bark, 32, 104
    Great Elizabeth, 55, 69
    Great Harry, see Henry Grace à Dieu
    Great Nicholas, 32, 55
    Greyhound, 22, 23, 71, 235

Hart, 22
Help, 217
Henry Grace à Dieu, Great Harry, 32, 39
Hope, 117
James Reneger, 186
Jesus of Lubeck, 41, 83, 161
John Baptist, 32
Judith, 83
Katherine Fortileza, 32, 44, 55, 58, 69, 159
Less Galley, 60
Lyon, 183
Maidenhead, 28
Maria de Larreto, 32
Marie Orford, 44
Marigold, 162
Mary Craddock, 40
Mary Guildford, 147
Mary Rose (1509–45), 32, 35, 37, 43, 48, 51, 61, 73, 74, 98, 101, 158, 185, 186, 279
Mary Rose (ii), 33
Mary Sampson, 64, 69
Matthew, 35, 36
Mawdelyn Russell, 187
Mayflower, 35
Minion, 83, 208
Moon, 198
Moonshine, 213
Nonpareil, Nonsuch, 33, 227
Pauncy, 104
Peter Pomegranate, 31
Philip and Mary, 33
Rainbow, 28, 221
Red Dragon, 198
Regent, 31, 36, 58, 61, 81, 206
Repulse, 104
Revenge, 12, 28, 117, 211, 214
Roebuck, 191
Rose in Sun, 27
Roseslip, 28
Royal Prince, 68
Salamader, 22, 235
Samson, discovery vessel, 147
Scourge of Malice, 193
Scout, 67
Solomon, 123
Sovereign, 12, 31, 36, 37, 58, 61, 67
Sovereign of the Seas, 68
Speedwell, 55, 161
Sun, 24
Squirrel, 162
Sweepstake, 31, 37, 183
Swiftsure, 227

Tiger, 22, 28, 29
Trinity Henry, 41
Trinity Reneger, 186
Trinity Sovereign, 98
Triumph, 48
Trywright, 55, 161
Unicorn, 22, 23
Vanguard, 28, 171, 224
Victory, 79, 119
Warrior, 51, 119
Warspite, 28, 68
White Bear, 41, 65, 230
William, 236
French and Breton:
Caraquon, 218
Cordelière, 81, 206
Ferroniere, 26
Galley Blanchard, 26, 235
Grace á Dieu, 83
Grand François, 218
Grand Louise, 206
La Maitresse, 218
Marlion, 186
Sacre de Dieppe, 208
Scottish:
Andrew Barton, Jenny Pirwyn, 31, 55
Lion, 31
Margaret, 31, 38
Michael, 38
Spanish and Portuguese:
Ascuncion, 215
Cacafuego, 189
La Cinque Llagas, 210
La Serena, 215
Madre de Dios, 20, 190
Rosario, 226
San Andres, 55, 243
San Bernabe, 212
San Cristobel, 214
San Lorenzo, 226
San Mateo, 55, 230, 243
San Martin, 75

San Felipe (Sp), 230; (Port), 214
San Salvador, 226
San Tomas, 243
San Valentino, 237
Sant Pedro, 187
Santa Anna, 203
Santa Maria, 30
Santo Alberto, 54
Sao Thomé, 42
shipwrights:
    Baker, Matthew, 35, 253
    Pett, Peter, 103, 253
shot, 69–72
Sidney, Sir Philip, 94
Smallhythe, 38, 172, 250
Smerwick, 30, 238
Smith, John, 70, 150
Solent, The, 20, 60, 71, 107, 111, 163, 172–5, 184, 217–20
Southampton, 88, 175, 176, 183, 184, 205
'Spears', The King's, 112
Spert, Sir Thomas, 140, 262
Spice Islands, 155
Spinola, Frederico, 236, 237
station keeping, 164
Straits of Anian, 148, 155
Straits of Magellan, 127, 178, *179*
Strozzi, Leo, 209, 219, 236
Strozzi, Philip, 179, 202
swords, 82

T

tactics, 132, *202, 203, 204, 211*
Tagus, river, 236
Tamar, river, 175
Thames, river, 167
Thérouanne, siege of, 194
tides and tidal streams, 138
Tilbury, 105
timber, 39, 63
time keeping, 141
tobacco, 157

Tordesillas, Treaty of, 146
Tournai, 107, 194, 260
Towerson, William, 162
Tréport, Le, 125, 237
Trinity House, 50, 139, 140, 144
Tyrell, Captain William, 22, 187

V

Van de Delft, 186
Venice, Venetians, 13, 25,
victuals, victualling:
    accounts, 86
    allowances, 87
    barrels, foists, 89
    calorific value, 88
    diet, 87
    organisation, 86
    provision of, 86
    purchase, 86
    shortage, 89, 92, 94
Vigo, 240
Virginia, 28, 30, 157

W

Walsingham, Sir Francis, 17, 63, 73, 94, 179, 266–8
watertight integrity, 43, 44, 50, 161
weather gage, 162
White, Thomas, 193
wildfire, 81
wind and weather, 148, 159, 161, 170, 175, 215
wine trade, 13, 184
Winchester, Marquess of, 90, 92, 103
Winter, Sir William, 28, 63, 73, 87, 161, 236, 253
Wolsey, Thomas, 85, 88, 89
Woodhouse, Sir William, 90, 104
wool trade, 13, 157
Woolwich, 28, 36, 252
Wyndham, Sir Thomas, 187, 198